Environmental Contracts

Comparative Approaches to Regulatory Innovation in the United States and Europe

Comparative Environmental Law & Policy Series

VOLUME 1

Editors

Eric W. Orts
Professor of Legal Studies and Director, Environmental Management Program
The Wharton School, University of Pennsylvania

Kurt Deketelaere
Professor of Law and Director, Institute for Environmental and Energy Law
University of Leuven

Editorial Board

Professor Ben Boer, *University of Sydney*
Professor Michael Faure, *University of Maastricht*
Professor Alberto José Blanco-Uribe Quintero, *Central University of Venezuela*
Professor Richard Macrory, *University College London*
Professor Ari Ekroos, *Helsinki University of Technology*
Professor Jerzy Sommer, *Polish Academy of Sciences*
Professor Willemien du Plessis, *Potchefstroom University*
Professor Richard Revesz, *New York University*
Professor Daniel Esty, *Yale University*
Professor René Seerden, *University of Maastricht*
Professor Cary Coglianese, *Harvard University*

The aim of the Editors and the Editorial Board of this series is to publish works of excellent quality that focus on the comparative study of environmental law and policy of countries or groups of countries.

Through the comparative study of environmental law and policy, the Editors and the Editorial Board hope:
- to contribute to the improvement of the quality of environmental law and policy in general and environmental quality in particular;
- to increase the access to environmental information and environmental justice for students, academics, non-governmental organizations, government institutions, and business;
- to facilitate cooperation between academic and non-academic communities in the field of environmental law and policy throughout the world.

The titles published in this series are listed at the back of this volume.

Environmental Contracts

Comparative Approaches to Regulatory Innovation in the United States and Europe

Edited by

Eric W. Orts
and
Kurt Deketelaere

KLUWER LAW INTERNATIONAL
London / The Hague / Boston

Published by
Kluwer Law International Ltd
Sterling House
66 Wilton Road
London SW1V 1DE
United Kingdom

Kluwer Law International incorporates
the publishing programmes of
Graham & Trotman Ltd,
Kluwer Law & Taxation Publishers
and Martinus Nijhoff Publishers

Sold and distributed in
the USA and Canada by
Kluwer Law International
675 Massachusetts Avenue
Cambridge MA 02139
USA

In all other countries, sold and distributed by
Kluwer Law International
PO Box 322
3300 AH Dordrecht
The Netherlands

ISBN 90-411-9821-0
© Kluwer Law International 2001
First published 2001

Library of Congress Cataloging-in-Publication Data

Environmental contracts : comparative approaches to regulatory innovation in the United States and Europe / edited by Kurt Deketelaere and Eric W. Orts.
    p. cm. -- (Comparative environmental law & policy series; v. 1)
    Includes index.
    ISBN 9041198210 (hardbound : alk. paper)
    1. Environmental law--United States. 2. Environmental law--Europe. I. Deketelaere, K. (Kurt) II. Orts, Eric W. III. Series.

K3585 .E577 2000
344.4'046—dc21   00-060039

Printed and bound in Great Britain by Antony Rowe Limited

TABLE OF CONTENTS

PART III   THE LAW AND ECONOMICS OF
ENVIRONMENTAL CONTRACTS
AND REGULATION

PART IV   A COMPARATIVE CASE STUDY:
ELECTRICITY AND CONTRACTS

List of Contributors

Jonathan Z. Cannon is a former general counsel to the U.S. Environmental Protection Agency and currently is the Director of the Environmental Program and a professor at the University of Virginia Law School.

Christopher F. Clark is a project manager of the energy division with Environmental Futures, Inc. in Boston Massachusetts.

Cary Coglianese is an associate professor at the John F. Kennedy School of Government, Harvard University.

Na Li Dawson is a Ph.D. candidate and research assistant in the Department of Economics at the University of Connecticut.

Kurt Deketelaere is the Director of the Institute for Environmental and Energy Law and a professor in the Faculty of Law, Katholieke Universiteit Leuven.

Magali A. Delmas is an assistant professor at the Bren School of Environmental Science and Management, University of California, Santa Barbara.

Daniel C. Esty is the Director of the Yale Center for Environmental Law and Policy, Associate Dean of the Yale School of Forestry and Environmental Studies, and a professor at Yale Law School.

Michael Faure is professor of comparative and international environmental law and academic director of METRO, the institute for transnational legal research of the law faculty of Maastricht University.

Donald Geffen, Ph.D., is a Research Associate at the Strategic Management Research Center of the Carlson School of Management at the University of Minnesota and an independent consultant.

Lekha Gopalakrishnan, Ph.D., is a J.D. candidate (2000) at the University of Texas Law School.

Geoffrey C. Hazard, Jr. is Director Emeritus of the American Law Institute and Trustee Professor of Law at the University of Pennsylvania Law School.

Dennis D. Hirsch is an associate professor and Director of the Environmental Law Concentration at Capital University Law School.

vii

Jason Scott Johnston is Coordinator of the Program on Law and the Environment and a professor at the University of Pennsylvania Law School.

Yong Kang is a Ph.D. candidate in Public Policy and Management Department in the Wharton School of the University of Pennsylvania.

Matthew J. Kotchen is a Ph.D. candidate in the Department of Economics and School of Natural Resources and Environment at the University of Michigan.

Howard C. Kunreuther is Co-Director of Risk Management and Decision Processes Center and Cecilia Yen Koo Professor of Decision Sciences and Public Policy and Management at the Wharton School of the University of Pennsylvania.

Thomas P. Lyon is an associate professor at the Kelly School of Business, Indiana University at Bloomington.

Alfred A. Marcus is Chair of the Strategic Management and Organization Department and a professor of management at the University of Minnesota.

John W. Maxwell is an assistant professor at the Kelly School of Business, Indiana University at Bloomington.

Michael R. Moore is an associate professor in the School of Natural Resources and Environment at the University of Michigan.

Patrick J. McNulty is a senior fellow in the Risk Management and Decision Processes Center of the Wharton School of the University of Pennsylvania.

Felix Oberholzer-Gee is an assistant professor in the Public Policy and Management Department at the Wharton School of the University of Pennsylvania.

Eric W. Orts is Director of the Environmental Management Program and professor in the Legal Studies Department at the Wharton School of the University of Pennsylvania.

Kathleen Segerson is a professor in the Economics Department of the University of Connecticut.

René Seerden is an associate professor in comparative administrative and environmental law in the Faculty of Law of the University of Maastricht.

Ken Sexton is the Bond Professor of Environmental Health and Director of the Center for Environment and Health Policy at the School of Public Health, University of Minnesota.

David B. Spence is an assistant professor, Legal Environment of Business, Graduate School of Business, University of Texas.

Geert Van Calster, Ph.D., is a senior research fellow in the Institute of Environmental and Energy Law, Faculty of Law, Katholieke Universiteit Leuven, and a member of the Brussels Bar.

Ann Terlaak is a Ph.D. candidate at the Bren School of Environmental Science and Management, University of California, Santa Barbara.

Hans H.B. Vedder is a research fellow in the Center for Environmental Law, Faculty of Law, University of Amsterdam.

Acknowledgments

The editors would like to thank a number of people without whom this book and the academic conference on which it was based would not have been possible. First, we were assisted by three academic co-coordinators of the conference. Geoffrey Hazard of the University of Pennsylvania Law School gets credit for suggesting "environmental contracts" as an organizing idea for the conference. As discussed in our Introduction, this idea has the virtue of combining the comparative perspectives of both the two different legal systems of the United States and Europe on environmental regulation and the two different disciplines of law and economics. Jason Johnston, also of the University of Pennsylvania Law School, organized the primary panel addressing the latter, cutting-edge topic of the law and economics of environmental contracts. And last only in alphabetical order, Howard Kunreuther of the Wharton School of the University of Pennsylvania provided invaluable insights from his experience in the running of conferences in his role as a Co-Director of the Risk Management and Decision Processes Center.

For financial support, we thank the German Marshall Fund, which provided a generous grant specifically for a conference on environmental contracts that emphasized a US–European comparative perspective. In addition, the Ius Commune Research School funded travel to the conference for some of the European participants. The Ford Motor Company Fund supported the conference through a multi-year grant to the Wharton Environmental Management Program. Financial support was also provided from a number of sources within the University of Pennsylvania. The Dean's Office of the Wharton School provided both funding and public recognition by designating the effort an impact conference. The Legal Studies Department and the Risk Management and Decision Sciences Center also provided resources, as did the University of Pennsylvania Law School.

Administrative and editorial assistance was provided by a small army working at the Wharton School. We thank two Penn law students, Lauren Hanrahan and Raha Ramezani, for expert editing (especially of formatting and endnotes); three Penn undergraduate students, Tiffany Fujioka, Denise Shumway, and Emma Walker, for editing and word processing; a temporary word processor, Jonathan Cole, for intensive and expert work; a temporary editor, Myra Lotto, for help in writing the English language correctly; and the best business administrator and administrative assistant at the Wharton School, respectively, the omnicompetent Tamara English and Andrea King.

Finally, we thank the European Union Affairs Research Program within the Fulbright Scholar Program for providing one of us (Orts) to visit the other (Deketelaere) for a semester that included a fateful lunch that inspired us to start this project.

Eric W. Orts, *Philadelphia*
Kurt Deketelaere, *Leuven*

Preface

Much has been written over the last few years about regulatory reform in the environmental realm. One of the most important themes to emerge from the debate over the direction of the "next generation" of environmental law and policy centers on the opportunities for gains in both the efficiency and effectiveness of environmental programs through the use of contracts. In this volume, Eric W. Orts and Kurt Deketelaere have drawn together some of the top academic talent from across the world to address the question of how environmental contracts and other collaborative approaches to pollution control might enhance regulatory results.

While some environmental advocates have pejoratively dismissed "voluntary" programs as unreliable and unworkable, there is a growing body of scholarship that seeks to develop the concept of "command and covenant" approaches to regulation.[1] The theoretical logic behind expanded use of enforceable regulatory contracts is powerful. First, contracts provide an important mechanism for flexibility in the face of sometimes calcified and bureaucratic systems of environmental protection. Second, environmental contracts can be constructed to create incentives for polluters to control emissions and types of environmental harm that currently fall outside the regulatory ambit. Even more importantly, contractual relationships may induce industry to bring forth information about where environmental harms are and how they might be addressed that would otherwise not be available in the regulatory process.

In addition to the incentives created for careful analysis and risk reduction on the part of regulated industries, environmental contracts can lower the costs of controlling pollution in ways that benefit not only the industries involved but society more generally. One of the common conclusions from the spate of recent regulatory reform studies, including my own "Next Generation Project," is that efficiency matters. Indeed, ongoing public support for environmental protection depends substantially on whether people perceive themselves to be receiving good value for the money invested. Environmental contracting, by permitting parties to work around inefficient regulatory rules and mechanisms, potentially ensures that superior environmental results will be achieved at lower costs.

---

[1] See E.D. Elliott, "Toward Ecological Law and Policy" in M.R. Chertow and D.C. Esty (eds), *Thinking Ecologically: The Next Generation of Environmental Policy* (Yale University Press, 1997), p. 183.

As the nature of the environmental challenge evolves away from an emphasis on big smokestack industries towards more diffuse sources of pollution that demand more deft regulatory strategies, contracts provide an important opportunity to tailor environmental programs to particularized circumstances. The facts that contract systems promote innovation and induce parties to look beyond the existing set of observed harms, established technologies, and known policy options add to their attraction.

This book provides not only an introduction to the underlying theory of environmental contracts but also reviews in some detail the existing state of the art in practice. Understanding how environmental covenants have worked in the Netherlands and how collaborative regulatory efforts have been implemented throughout Europe provides an important foundation for exploring the role of environmental contracting in regulatory reform more broadly. This volume also reviews the pilot projects employing various contract mechanisms that have been launched in the United States, including the Environmental Protection Agency's Project XL and the efforts in some states, such as Minnesota, to use contracts to make their environmental regulatory systems more flexible and effective.

There are, unquestionably, limitations to contracting as an approach to environmental problems, and this book does not ignore these challenges. Several chapters focus on the difficulty of undertaking case-by-case negotiations when there are a large number of firms involved in an environmental issue. Other authors highlight the complex political economy of environmental regulation as a difficulty that must be overcome for contracts to become a mainstream regulatory tool. Whether the transaction costs of negotiated regulatory approaches can be justified is another important question that is taken up.

The search for future environmental programs that produce better results at lower costs than those of today requires exploration and testing of a range of potential reforms. Environmental contracts remain among the set of policy options that offer significant promise. This volume helps move forward the thinking about the role of contractual arrangements in the environmental domain. Anyone interested in environmental protection—including regulators, business people, environmental group officials, and academics—will find this volume to be invaluable.

Daniel C. Esty
Yale University

1. Introduction: Environmental Contracts and Regulatory Innovation

Eric W. Orts and Kurt Deketelaere

To many, the word coercion implies arbitrary decisions of distant and irresponsible bureaucrats; but this is not a necessary part of its meaning. The only kind of coercion I recommend is mutual coercion mutually agreed upon by the majority of people affected.[1]

Garrett Hardin's recommendation of "mutual coercion mutually agreed upon" might be read as a general admonition to democratic legislatures concerned with regulating environmental problems. Environmental problems generally create "a tragedy of the commons," and the usual manner of regulation is to pass statutes or delegate authority to administrative agencies to enact and enforce rules. Looking more closely at Hardin's words, however, reveals that even in the late 1960s, before the first Earth Day and the dawn of extensive environmental regulation in both the United States and Europe, Hardin was not sanguine about administrative regulation.[2]

In the last several decades, command-and-control methods of regulation have achieved some success, especially as compared with the disasters in other parts of the world without strong environmental law such as in China and Russia.[3] But command-and-control has also been roundly criticized

---

[1] G. Hardin, "The Tragedy of the Commons" (1968) 162 *Science* 1243, 1247.

[2] In both the US and Europe, major environmental legislation at the national level was enacted in the early 1970s. See S.P. Johnson and G. Corcelle, *The Environmental Policy of the European Communities* (Graham & Trotman, London, 1989), pp. 1–2; F.P. Grad, "Foreword: A Symposium on the United States Supreme Court's 'Environmental Term' (1991–1992)" (1993) 43 Wash U J Urb & Contemp L 3, 4. See also D. Burtraw and P.R. Portney, "Environmental Policy in the United States" in D. Helm (ed.), *Economic Policy Towards the Environment* (Blackwell, Oxford, 1991), p. 289 (describing earlier significant environmental regulation as mostly at the state or local level).

[3] For an up-beat though flawed account of the success of environmental law, see G. Easterbrook, *A Moment on the Earth: The Coming Age of Environmental Optimism* (Penguin Viking, New York, 1996). For a critique of Easterbrook's science by the members of the Environmental Defense Fund, see M. Oppenheimer, D.S. Wilcove and M.J. Bean, "A Moment

1

for its ineffectiveness and inefficiency relative to alternatives.[4] As a result, academic environmental law has been characterized by a succession of various proposals for law reform.[5]

1 THE EVOLUTION OF ENVIRONMENTAL LAW

First and perhaps most conspicuously, traditional command-and-control—whether in the form of highly detailed legislative statutes or administrative regulations—has been the subject of reform proposals that recommend market-based regulation.[6] These alternative approaches come in several varieties.[7] Some propose market-based methods, such as tradable permits or emission charges, to improve the efficiency of traditional regulation. Others urge a redefinition or improved specification of property rights to "internalize" the costs that Hardin was one of the first to see are imposed on the natural environment as "externalities."[8] Yet another approach recommends that the government establish labeling schemes or use other mechanisms to harness economic market forces, such as deposit-and-refund regulations or government subsidies for the development of environmentally beneficial technologies.

A second group of reform proposals focus on mandatory or voluntary environmental management and auditing processes as a form of self-regulation or indirect "reflexive" regulation.[9] A third and related area of inquiry considers

---

of Truth: Correcting the Scientific Errors in Gregg Easterbrook's *A Moment on the Earth*" (1995) 25 Envtl L 1293. For a readable and informed account of the environmental problems of China and Russia, see M. Hertsgaard, *Earth Odyssey: Around the World in Search of our Environmental Future* (Broadway Books, New York, 1998), pp. 1–6, 119–143, 156–188, 221–259.

[4] See B.A. Ackerman and R.B. Stewart, "Reforming Environmental Law" (1985) 37 Stan L Rev 1333; R.W. Hahn and R.N. Stavins, "Incentive-Based Environmental Regulation: A New Era for an Old Idea?" (1991) 18 Ecology L Q 1 (1991); J.E. Krier, "The Pollution Problem and Legal Institutions: A Conceptual Overview" (1971) 18 UCLA L Rev 429; T.H. Tietenberg, "Economic Instruments for Environmental Regulation" in *Economic Policy Towards the Environment*, supra note 2, pp. 86, 95–97, table 4.1. For one of the best attempts to defend command-and-control regulation against its critics, see H. Latin, "Ideal Versus Real Regulatory Efficiency: Implementation of Uniform Standards and 'Fine-Tuning' Regulatory Reforms" (1985) 37 Stan L Rev 1267.

[5] Given its normative content, much of academic law in the US may be characterized as proposals for law reform. For a critical description of this tendency, see P.W. Kahn, *The Cultural Study of Law: Reconstructing Legal Scholarship* (University of Chicago Press, 1999), pp. 19–22, 40.

[6] See, e.g., sources cited supra note 4.

[7] For an overview of different kinds of market-based regulation, see R. Stavins, "Market-Based Environmental Policies" in P.R. Portney and R.N. Stavins (eds), *Public Policies for Environmental Protection* (World Resources for the Future, Washington, 2nd edn, forthcoming 2000); E.W. Orts, "Reflexive Environmental Law" (1995) 89 Nw U L Rev 1227, 1241-52. See also K. Deketelaere, "New Environmental Policy Instruments in Belgium" in J. Golub (ed.), *New Instruments for Environmental Policy in the EU* (Routledge, New York, 1998).

[8] For a good introduction to economic concepts relating to environmental regulation, see D. Helm and D. Pearce, "Economic Policy Towards the Environment: An Overview" in *Economic Policy Toward the Environment*, supra note 2, at 1.

[9] Leading examples include International Standard Organization's environmental management and quality standards (known as ISO 14000) and the European Union's Eco-Management and

how mandatory or voluntary disclosure of accurate information about environmental performance may strengthen incentives through both economic markets and private litigation, such as claims for "toxic torts."[10]

These various recommendations for market-based, reflexive, or informational regulatory reform share a common skepticism of centralized administrative environmental law.[11] In this respect, they are in keeping with challenges to conventional models of administrative government in political science and economics. Public choice theory and economic analysis emphasize the dangers of "rent-seeking" and other self-serving practices of government officials.[12] The advent of the related field of positive political theory also concentrates on the interests that bureaucrats, politicians, and even judges may have in seeking their own ends rather than those of the public.[13] These new disciplines add analytical vigor and sometimes empirical substance to Hardin's worry about "arbitrary decisions of distant and irresponsible bureaucrats."[14]

Reform proposals that entail lessened reliance on central governmental authority find themselves in some tension with another very influential direction of reform: comprehensive comparative risk regulation. This approach, which is based on the science of comparative risk assessment, emphasizes the irrationality of the potpourri of law that affects risk and recommends its rationalization. An expert administrative "super-agency" is

---

Audit Scheme. See N. Gunningham, "Environmental Management Systems and Community Participation" (1998) 16 J Envtl L 319; N. Roht-Arriaza, "Shifting the Point of Regulation" (1995) 22 Ecology LQ 479 (1995); Orts, supra note 7.

[10] See P.R. Kleindorfer and E.W. Orts, "Informational Regulation of Environmental Risks" (1998) 18 *Risk Analysis* 155; C.R. Sunstein, "Informational Regulation and Informational Standing" (1999) 137 U Pa L Rev 613.

[11] A fourth discernible trend in recent years in the US is the increasing use of criminal law as an instrument of environmental policy. See, e.g., M.A. Cohen, "Environmental Crime and Punishment: Legal/Economic Theory and Empirical Evidence on Enforcement of Federal Environmental Statutes" (1992) 82 J Crim L & Criminology 1054; R.J. Lazarus, "Meeting the Demands of Integration in the Evolution of Environmental Law: Reforming Environmental Criminal Law" (1995) 83 Geo LJ 2407. This trend may be interpreted as either an attempt to increase economic incentives for compliance or a reaction against assessing at least some kinds of environmental harms in terms of economic calculations. This direction of legal reform is difficult to classify because it can support a strong traditional view of command-and-control regulation as well as alternative approaches.

[12] For an introduction to public choice theory as it relates to law, see D.A. Farber and P.P. Frickey, *Law and Public Choice: A Critical Introduction* (University of Chicago Press, 1991); J.L. Mashaw, *Greed, Chaos, and Governance: Using Public Choice to Improve Public Law* (Yale University Press, 1999). For a criticism of public choice theory in law, see also R.H. Pildes and E.S. Anderson, "Slinging Arrows at Democracy: Social Choice Theory, Value Pluralism, and Democratic Politics" (1990) 90 Colum L Rev 2121.

[13] On positive political theory and law, see D.A. Farber and P.P. Frickey, "Foreword: Positive Political Theory and Public Law" (1992) 80 Geo L J 457. For two recent applications of positive political theory to judging, see R.L. Revesz, "Environmental Regulation, Ideology, and the D.C. Circuit" (1997) 83 Va L Rev 1717; F.B. Cross and E.H. Tiller, "Judicial Partisanship and Obedience to Legal Doctrine: Whistleblowing on the Federal Courts of Appeals" (1998) 107 Yale L J 2155. For a strongly worded rebuke of both articles by an American federal judge, see H.T. Edwards, "Collegiality and Decision Making on the D.C. Circuit" (1998) 84 Va L Rev 1335.

[14] See supra text accompanying note 1.

usually recommended, and the best known proponent of this view in the United States is probably Stephen Breyer, a former Harvard Law School professor who now sits as an Associate Justice on the US Supreme Court.[15] But the scientific tools of risk assessment and analysis may be employed by decision makers at any level, from government representatives negotiating international treaties to individual business firms assessing their own comparative risks of operation.[16] One proposal for reform along these lines in the United States would mandate a comprehensive comparative risk analysis for any new federal statute or regulation.[17] A more moderate version of this reform would require a comparative risk analysis of any new regulation and its public disclosure, though without dictating a particular regulatory result. As of this writing, a bill along the lines of this more moderate approach has been introduced with bipartisan support in the US Congress.[18] In general terms, the methodology of comparative risk regulation is to analyze the trade-offs of different environmental risks and the regulatory costs of reducing them, usually as measured in terms of effects on human health (e.g., the number of deaths caused by different environmental risks on average annually) per regulatory dollar or euro expended.[19]

This book explores the potential of another alternative form of environmental regulation that may include elements of these various proposals for command-and-control, market-based, reflexive, informational, or risk-based regulatory reform. However, we believe that it is useful to consider this

---

[15] See S. Breyer, *Breaking the Vicious Circle: Toward Effective Risk Regulation* (Harvard University Press, 1993). See also B.C. Mank, "Protecting the Environment for Future Generations: A Proposal for a 'Republican' Superagency" (1996) 5 NYU Envtl L J 444. For a "softer" version that concedes the "limits of equity and public acceptance" of comparative risk regulation, see F.B. Cross, "The Public Role in Risk Control" (1994) 24 Envtl L 887, 958. For criticism of comprehensive comparative risk regulation, see C. Gillette and J. Krier, "Risk, Courts, and Agencies" (1990) 138 U Pa L Rev 1027; L. Heinzerling, "Reductionist Regulatory Reform" (1997) 8 Ford Envtl L J 459; D. Hornstein, "Reclaiming Environmental Law: A Normative Critique of Comparative Risk Analysis" (1992) 92 Colum L Rev 562.

[16] See J.D. Graham and J.B. Weiner, "Confronting Risk Tradeoffs" in J.D. Graham and J.B. Weiner (eds), *Risk versus Risk: Tradeoffs in Protecting Health and the Environment* (Harvard University Press, 1995), pp. 1, 4. See also J.D. Graham and J.K. Hartwell (eds), *The Greening of Industry: A Risk Management Approach* (Harvard University Press, 1997).

[17] See Risk Assessment and Cost-Benefit Act of 1995, H.R. 1022. This bill, which was part of the Republican-sponsored "Contract with America," passed the House of Representatives, but was not taken up in the Senate. Compromise proposals also failed. See C.R. Sunstein, "Congress, Constitutional Moments, and the Cost-Benefit State" (1996) 48 Stan L Rev 247, 269–271, 274–281. For a more recent argument in favor of a comprehensive risk assessment regulation, see W.K. Viscusi, "Regulating the Regulators" (1996) 63 U Chi L Rev 1423.

[18] See Regulatory Improvement Act of 2000, H.R. 331; Regulatory Improvement Act of 1999, S. 746. See also D.P. Clarke and K.E. Kunzer, "A New Right to Know" (1999) 16 Envtl Forum 22 (describing the legislation and arguing in favor of it). For a view arguing that the bill would harm environmental and other risk regulation, see D.C. Vladeck, "The Regulatory Degradation Act" (1999) 16 Envtl Forum 26.

[19] See, e.g., Viscusi, supra note 17, at 1460 (noting that "risk–risk analysis and its variants that consider the mortality consequences of regulatory expenditures are probably the most visible policy assessment techniques of this type"). For criticism of the undue influence on scholarship and politics of one estimate of costs of lives saved under various regulations, see L. Heinzerling, "Regulatory Costs of Mythic Proportions" (1998) 107 Yale L J 1981.

alternative approach to environmental law reform as distinct, namely, what we will call "environmental contracts."

2 THE EUROPEAN ORIGIN AND PRACTICE OF ENVIRONMENTAL CONTRACTING

An approach that relies on regulatory contracts in environmental law is not new. As a number of the chapters in this book describe, environmental "agreements" or "covenants" have been used for several decades in many European countries.[20] Leading countries in the use of environmental agreements include Belgium (especially Flanders), France, Germany, and the Netherlands.[21]

Environmental agreements were first used in France and Germany in the early 1970s.[22] In France, a significant legal practice of different kinds of environmental agreements developed.[23] *Contrats de branche* were agreements between the national government and various business sectors for subsidies. These agreements, however, soon ran afoul of the emerging internal market regulations of the European Community. *Programmes de branche* and *programmes d'entreprise* replaced the agreements that contemplated subsidies. These *programmes* were agreements made between the government and an industrial group (*de branche*) or a specific firm (*d'entreprise*). They were often legally enforceable. In the 1980s, the French national government entered some broad agreements with other public entities designed to achieve several environmental objectives (*contrats de plan*). But this period of regulatory experimentation came to end in 1985 when a case settled in the *Conseil d'Etat* determined that the use of contractual techniques

---

[20] See especially the chapters in Part II of this book by Van Calster and Deketelaere, Faure, Seerden, and Vedder. For earlier discussions of this phenomenon in European environmental law, see E. Rehbinder, "Ecological Contracts: Agreements Between Polluters and Local Communities" in G. Teubner, L. Farmer, and D. Murphy (eds), *Environmental Law and Ecological Responsibility: The Concept and Practice of Ecological Self-Organization* (John Wiley & Sons, Chichester, 1994), p. 147; Ida Koppen, "Ecological Covenants: Regulatory Informality in Dutch Waste Reduction Policy" in *Environmental Law and Ecological Responsibility*, supra, p. 185.

[21] See, e.g., Communication from the Commission to the Council and European Parliament on Environmental Agreements, COM(96)561 final, annex, pp. 23–25, 27–28. In the Netherlands, for example, more than 100 environmental agreements are negotiated under the amended National Environmental Policy Plan, which covers thousands of companies that are responsible for 90 percent of the country's industrial pollution. Ibid., at 27–28. See also H. van Zijst, "A Change in Culture" (1993) 10 Envtl Forum 12 (describing the Dutch "covenanting" system). For a summary of recent literature on the use of environmental agreements of various kinds in nine European countries and rough empirical estimates of their number and legal characteristics (e.g., enforceable or entirely voluntary), see Environmental Law Network International (ed.), *Environmental Agreements: The Role and Effects of Environmental Agreements in Environmental Policies* (Cameron May, 1998), pp. 32–68 (describing environmental agreements in Belgium, Denmark, France, Germany, Italy, the Netherlands, Poland, and the United Kingdom).

[22] See *Environmental Agreements*, supra note 21, at 40, 45.

[23] Ibid., at 40–44.

instead of ordinary regulatory methods was illegal if legislation provided for ordinary means of regulation (e.g., through command-and-control). Nevertheless, voluntary agreements to perform above and beyond legal requirements reappeared in France in the 1990s (*accordes-cadres* and *engagements voluntaires*). The interesting phenomenon of the "river contract," in which various interests come together to make agreements concerning water pollution and other matters concerning the use of a shared river, appears also to be originally a French invention.[24] In Germany, environmental agreements have also become very popular. However, virtually all of almost 90 agreements that have been identified in Germany are voluntary agreements (*freiwillige Vereinbarungen*) or so-called "self-commitments" (*Selbstverpflichtungen*) that are not legally enforceable.[25] Nevertheless, these agreements made between business and government may substitute for otherwise applicable regulations (*normersetzende/normvertretend Absprachen*) or actually replace procedural requirements or alter previous regulatory decisions (*normvollziehende Absprachen*). Thus they have a real effect on the practice of environmental law in Germany. In addition, it is important to note that German environmental agreements are usually negotiated without the involvement of third parties such as environmental or consumer groups.[26]

It is no accident that the European commentators chosen to write chapters for this book are from the Netherlands and Flemish Belgium where, as Michael Faure observes in his chapter, environmental contracts have become "relatively popular." These Dutch-speaking parts of Europe have had extensive experience with environmental agreements. Successful experiments with the Dutch approach to "cooperative" or "collaborative" regulation began in the early 1980s under the catch phrase of *verinnerlijking* (internalization). In addition to the formulation of a series of ambitious National Environmental Policy Plans, the Netherlands committed itself to an approach that involved the formation of "new partnerships" both within government (integrating national, regional, and municipal levels) and between government and business.[27] Negotiations within these groups led to the emergence of environmental covenants (*milieuconvenanten*), most of which had the status of legally enforceable civil contracts.[28] Leading

---

[24] River contracts have also begun recently to be used in Belgium, especially in the French-speaking Wallonia region. Ibid., at 36. For an interesting overview presenting mixed results about the "river contract" for the Upper Meuse initiated in 1991, see D. Missone, "The River Contract of the Upper Meuse" in *Environmental Agreements*, supra note 21, at 225.

[25] See *Environmental Agreements*, supra note 21, at 45–47.

[26] Ibid., at 48.

[27] For an overview of the approach to environmental law and policy developed in the Netherlands, see P.E. de Jongh and S. Captain, *Our Common Journey: A Pioneering Approach to Cooperative Environmental Management* (Zed, London, 1999); M.A. Hajer, "*Verinnerlijking*: The Limits to a Positive Management Approach" in *Environmental Law and Ecological Responsibility*, supra note 20, p. 167. See also sources cited supra notes 20 and 21.

[28] See *Environmental Agreements*, supra note 21, at 56–57; R. Seerden and M. Heldeweg, "Public Environmental Law in the Netherlands" in R. Seerden and M. Heldeweg (eds), *Comparative Environmental Law in Europe: An Introduction to Public Environmental Law in the EU Member States* (METRO, Antwerp, 1996), pp. 269, 290–291 (describing environmental

examples include the following: regional agreements for land use and environmental protection made among different government levels (*Ruimtelijke Ordening en Milieubeheer*), a successful Hydrocarbons 2000 Agreement between the national government and industry groups signed in 1989 (which resulted in a 50 percent reduction of emissions ahead of schedule in the mid-1990s), a Covenant to Combat SO_2 and NO_x Pollution between the national government and the Dutch Electricity Generating Board in 1990, a Primary Metals Covenant on pollution emissions negotiated in 1992, and a Chemical Sector Covenant entered in 1993.[29] Nonprofit environmental groups were initially skeptical, but for the most part even they have admitted that the use of these covenants have achieved significant environmental success. For example, the Dutch nonprofit organization, the Society for Nature and Environment (*Stichting Natuur en Milieu*), endorsed the Covenant to Combat SO_2 and NO_x Pollution in 1995, expressed optimism for the Primary Metals Covenant in 1997 (after criticizing it for failing to meet interim goals in 1994), and estimated that the Chemical Sector Covenant had achieved the greatest relative success of the various agreements in 1996.[30]

In his chapter in this book, René Seerden reviews the legal structure of environmental agreements in the Netherlands and focuses in particular on the recent Agreement on Packaging and Packaging Waste in 1997. This Dutch agreement is of special interest because it was entered pursuant both to the European Union's Directive on Packaging and Packaging Waste of 1994 and subsequent enabling legislation adopted at the national level in the Netherlands. Seerden also usefully delineates three types of environmental agreements in the Netherlands: (1) those between the central government and industrial groups or associations of businesses, (2) those between the central government and lower level regional and local governments, and (3) those between government authorities and individual companies. This distinction is helpful when considering experiments with environmental contracts in other places, including the United States.

Given its extensive experience with environmental contracts as an instrument of regulatory policy, the Netherlands provides an important comparative case study. Perhaps more importantly, the Netherlands has recently adopted a set of guidelines for the negotiation of environmental agreements, which were formulated through discussions with relevant stakeholder interests in 1995.[31] In his chapter, Seerden describes these guidelines or "Instructions for Agreements" (*Aanwijzingen voor convenanten*) in detail. They are worth comparative consideration in other countries in Europe and

---

agreements in the Netherlands as "legally binding"). For further discussion, see also the chapters in this book by Seerden, Vedder, and Hirsch.

[29]   See de Jongh and Captain, supra note 27, at 149–166.

[30]   Ibid., at 156, 163–164, 166.

[31]   See *Environmental Agreements*, supra note 21, at 57. See also de Jongh and Captain, supra note 27, at 160 (setting forth basic "ground rules of covenants" that have been adopted for the use of all regulatory contracts in the Netherlands, as well as for environmental agreements in the European Union).

elsewhere (including the United States) where experiments with environmental contracts are beginning. Dennis Hirsch also discusses the Dutch approach in his chapter to gain a comparative perspective on developments in US law.

Similarly, and not incidentally, the Dutch-speaking Flemish region of Belgium has also adopted a legal decree on environmental covenants in 1994.[32] Unlike the Dutch guidelines, the Flemish decree is intended to be legally enforceable, as described in Michael Faure's chapter in this book. (The Flemish decree is also reproduced as an annex to his chapter.) Interestingly, the decree resulted from a recommendation of an Inter-university Commission on the Reform of Environmental Law composed of academics.

Initial experience with agreements negotiated under the Flemish decree is discussed here in the chapters by Faure and by Geert Van Calster and Kurt Deketelaere. Faure gives some general legal and economic arguments in favor of the approach. For example, given a need for some form of environmental regulation, negotiated contracts that are tailored to specific situations hold out the prospect of solutions that "mimic" the market. At the same time, there are corresponding dangers. Administrative capture, for example, may become easier in negotiated agreements. The Flemish decree attempts to avoid some of these pitfalls. For example, negotiated regulations must not violate other preexisting regulations. Transparency is encouraged by requirements of public notice and public consultation.

In their chapter, Van Calster and Deketelaere note that the Flemish decree has resulted in a number of agreements, but all of them so far are in the waste sector. They suggest that Europe may follow the Flemish approach: to recognize the benefits of environmental agreements but also to remain cautious of their dangers. (Their chapter also reproduces in an annex a list compiled by the European Commission of various environmental agreements used at the national level.) In any event, Flemish Belgium, as well as the Netherlands, promises to provide an interesting case study in environmental agreements at the national and regional level, though in a different and much more divisive federal context.[33]

The experience of environmental contracts in Dutch-speaking parts of Europe is also important because of the influence their citizens may have on environmental policy in the European Community. European-level interest in integrated environmental policy, including environmental agreements, was spearheaded by Dutch leaders of the European Commission's Directorate

---

[32] See *Environmental Agreements,* supra note 21, at 33. See also the chapter in this book by Van Calster and Deketelaere.

[33] For an introduction to environmental law in Belgium, a small but interesting federal state within an increasingly federal Europe, see K. Deketelaere, "Public Law in Belgium in General and in the Flemish Region in Particular" in *Comparative Environmental Law in Europe,* supra note 28, at 33; E.W. Orts, "An American Perspective on Belgian and British Environmental Law within Europe" in K. Deketelaere and M. Faure (eds), *Environmental Law in Belgium and the United Kingdom: A Comparative Analysis* (Intersentia, Antwerp, 1999).

General for the Environment (DG XI).[34] Laurens-Jan Brinkhorst and his deputy Robert Donkers pushed forward the EC's Fifth Environmental Action Program called "Towards Sustainability," which included the themes of informational disclosure and integrated policy planning familiar in the Netherlands. Another Dutch citizen, Marius Enthoven, was appointed to head DG XI in 1994, and the evolution of environmental policy continued in a similar direction. The importance of the Fifth Action Program on the law of environmental agreements at the European Union level is further discussed in the chapter in this book by Van Calster and Deketelaere, though the authors conclude that "the jury is still out" as to whether the EU remains "truly committed to moving in this direction" in the future.

Recently, the European Union as a whole has formally embraced the use of environmental agreements, at least in principle. The European Commission specifically endorsed this method of regulation in its Communication on Environmental Agreements in 1996, which recognizes the "main advantages" of environmental agreements to include: promoting "a pro-active attitude on the part of industry," providing "cost-effective, tailor-made solutions" to particular environmental problems, and allowing for "a quicker and smoother achievement of objectives" than alternative regulatory approaches.[35] Van Calster and Deketelaere's chapter discusses this Communication in critical detail and puts it in perspective by giving a background account of an important seminar organized by the Union of Industrial and Employers' Confederations of Europe. In this seminar, the head of DG XI, Commissioner Bjerregaard, expressed skepticism about using environmental agreements at the European level. Van Calster and Deketelaere conclude in their study here that it is not clear that the Commission "really believes" that environmental agreements will become "a major tool of policy in the EU."

Nevertheless, the European Council has similarly embraced environmental agreements, at least by formal resolution.[36] Again, however, when one looks to actual practice, attitudes seem to change. Environmental agreements have been employed at the EC level beginning in 1997 with an agreement negotiated with industry associations to achieve goals of "eco-efficiency" by reducing the energy use of televisions, VCRs, and washing machines by 20 percent.[37] Van Calster and Deketelaere examine in detail the environmental agreement negotiated with car manufacturers for CO_2 emissions meant to begin European compliance with the Kyoto Protocol on Climate Change. They conclude that even though an agreement between the European Automobile Manufacturers Association and the Commission was eventually reached in 1998, and then endorsed by the European Council, it is doubtful that the process of using an environmental agreement contributed significantly to the outcome. Van Calster and Deketelaere

---

[34] See de Jongh and Captain, supra note 27, at 206–210.
[35] Communication on Environmental Agreements, supra note 21, at 3.
[36] Council Resolution on Environmental Agreements, 1997 OJ (C 321) 6.
[37] See de Jongh and Captain, supra note 27, at 211.

compare this EC agreement with the approach used to negotiate environmental standards for automobile and fuel emission standards in the Auto Oil Program, which resulted in European legislation adopted by the Council in 1997. They conclude that the Auto Oil Program's regulatory negotiation (or what American lawyers would call "reg neg") was at least as good and probably better in terms of substantive results than the EC environmental agreement for CO_2 automobile emissions. On the basis of their comparative study and given that the Commission has announced plans for an Auto Oil II Program for tougher emissions standards, Van Calster and Deketelaere argue that the "reg neg" approach of the Auto Oil Program may well be superior to both traditional regulation and voluntary environmental agreements, though they emphasize that the devil is in the details. In other words, the particular regulatory method best suited for a particular environmental problem depends on the details of the problem, including its geographical scope, the number of actors who contribute to the problem, and other factors. At most, however, Van Calster and Deketelaere find the Council's attitude toward environmental agreements "lukewarm," which is at least better than the "hostile" view of the less powerful but arguably more democratic European Parliament.

In addition, Van Calster and Deketelaere point out that whatever European Community institutions may say about the desirability of environmental agreements, such agreements face significant legal barriers in European Community law. Along with the chapter by Hans Vedder, they show that European law regarding the free movement of goods, competition law, and state aid set significant limitations on the scope of environmental agreements. Familiarity with the "constitutional law of Europe" is therefore required to avoid the risk of having an environmental agreement set aside by the European Court of Justice as a violation of EC Treaty provisions. As Hans Vedder's chapter explains, EC law is complicated in this respect. Environmental agreements must not only pass muster under the EC Treaty's prohibition on interstate restrictions on the free movement of goods (analogous to the dormant Commerce Clause in the US), but must also satisfy review under the EC Treaty's stricter competition rules (roughly analogous to US antitrust law). Vedder's chapter argues for a "seamless web" approach that would apply a uniform standard to the review of environmental agreements under these two bodies of EC Law but such a "seamless web" approach has not yet been adopted. As a result, EC competition law has not yet explicitly recognized environmental considerations as an exception.

The Dutch tank storage case decided by the European Court of Justice provides a good illustration. In this case, as Vedder describes it, the Court struck down fixed surcharges under an environmental agreement as a violation of EC competition law. As Vedder also discusses, the Commission's and Court's views in this area may be evolving, as indicated by some non-public "comfort letters" issued more recently by the Commission and a recent decision by the Court of Justice that allows "social considerations" to provide a possible exception in competition law. At least, the law in this field is uncertain, and "group exemptions" for environmental agreements are still forbidden.

At the level of the nation-state, environmental agreements are sometimes regarded more favorably. Vedder gives the example of the FKS plastic pipe recycling case decided in the Netherlands. Not surprisingly, the Dutch competition authority found a fixed surcharge applied to contractors for recycling costs to be permitted under Dutch competition law. Unlike the European Court of Justice, the Dutch case recognized environmental considerations explicitly as an allowable basis for an exception.

More generally, the conflict in Europe that can arise between environmental agreements and the EC Treaty highlights the general policy conflict that can pit environmental values against the economic values of free trade. As Vedder recognizes, this conflict has not yet arisen in the United States, but if experiments with environmental contracts continue in the US then experience in Europe may foreshadow legal developments in Commerce Clause and antitrust jurisprudence.[38] Developments in the European Union regarding emerging conflicts between economic trade and environmental principles may also provide a microcosm of the same conflict on the international level addressed primarily, for the moment at least, by the World Trade Organization.[39]

3 EXPERIMENTS WITH ENVIRONMENTAL CONTRACTS IN THE UNITED STATES

What, then, does European experience have to contribute to the increasing interest shown in the United States for voluntary environmental agreements, bargaining approaches to regulation, and perhaps even enforceable environmental contracts? Other chapters in this book begin to shed light on this question with accounts of recent experiments in environmental law in the US.

Experience in this area begins with voluntary programs encouraged by the Environmental Protection Agency (EPA) in the late 1980s and early 1990s. Perhaps the best known voluntary program of this kind was the 33/50 Program, which loosely resembled the Dutch Hydrocarbon 2000 Agreement, though the US program was probably not as successful.[40] The EPA invited more than 8000 companies to participate in this voluntary program to reduce industrial emissions, but only about 1300 agreed.

---

[38] For a recent study along these lines, see D. Geradin, *Trade and the Environment: A Comparative Study of EC and US Law* (Cambridge University Press, 1997).

[39] See, e.g., D. Esty, *Greening the GATT: Trade, Environment, and the Future* (Institute for Int'l Economics, Washington, 1994).

[40] See de Jongh and Captain, supra note 27, at 230–231 (comparing the 33/50 Program with the Dutch Hydrocarbon 2000 agreement). For assessments of the 33/50 Program from an economic perspective, see S. Arora and T.N. Cason, "An Experiment in Voluntary Environmental Regulation: Participation in EPA's 33/50 Program" (1995) 28 J Envtl Econ and Mgmt 271; M. Khanna and L.A. Damon, "EPA's Voluntary 33/50 Program: Impact on Toxic Releases and Economic Performance of Firms" (1999) 37 J Envtl Econ and Mgmt 1. For an overview of various voluntary environmental programs in the US, see also Orts, supra note 7, at 1284–1287.

Participating companies pledged to reduce their emissions of 17 named chemicals by 33 percent by 1992 and 50 percent by 1995 (with 1988 serving as the base year). Environmental groups criticized the program, though most companies that participated met the voluntary targets established. Green Lights was another EPA-sponsored voluntary program that encouraged energy efficient lighting, and Energy Star was a voluntary labeling program designed to encourage the development of energy-saving computer equipment. The chapter in this book by Alfred Marcus, Don Geffen, and Ken Sexton reviews the experience in the US with these kinds of voluntary programs for "pollution prevention." All of the early voluntary programs, however, were exactly that: strictly voluntary. There were no binding legal obligations, contractual or otherwise.

Regulatory negotiations or "reg negs" were another experiment that began in the 1980s.[41] The approach was codified in 1990 in the Negotiated Rulemaking Act.[42] About a dozen of these negotiated regulations have now been conducted by the EPA. Because they result in legally enforceable regulations, reg negs are probably a better starting point than purely voluntary programs for considering the origins of the idea of environmental contracting in the US. A number of the chapters here discuss the US experience with reg negs as one example, among others, of environmental contracting.

For Jon Cannon, who draws on his experience as a former general counsel for the EPA, negotiated regulations are a type of "bargaining" and, like any contractual negotiation, the success of regulatory bargaining depends on what each side brings to the negotiating table. In his chapter, Cannon describes the current zest for bargaining at the EPA as a result predominantly of political factors. The EPA has a strong environmentalist culture, but it also must engage in a complex political and legal "dance" with the President and Congress, on one hand, and the federal courts who decide cases brought by both business interests and nonprofit environmentalists on the other. The EPA has a desire to control the regulatory agenda itself—and in this respect it provides a strong counterexample to the relatively weak European Environmental Agency in the EU[43]—and its regulatory bargaining initiatives can be understood in terms of the EPA's agenda. Project XL, discussed in detail further below, is one example. Another important regulatory initiative in the 1990s, which Cannon describes as "reinvention at the core," appears in the EPA's efforts to use a bargaining approach to revise its tropospheric ozone pollution standards. In 1995, the EPA convened the Ozone Transport Assessment Group (OTAG) with 37 eastern states and the District of Columbia. Beginning in 1997 with the recommendations formulated by OTAG, the EPA attacked the ozone pollution problem through

---

[41] See, e.g., P. Harter, "Negotiating Regulations: A Cure for Malaise?" (1982) Geo L J 1.
[42] 5 U.S.C. §§ 561–570 (1994).
[43] In Europe, the primary authorities for the enforcement of environmental law remain at the national and, increasingly, the regional level. Because the European Environmental Agency (EEA) is designed primarily to gather and disseminate information rather than to enforce EC environmental law, it is likely to continue to resemble the EPA only in its English acronym. See Orts, supra note 7, at 1314.

issuing strict new ambient air standards for ozone, recommending an adjustment of the legal standards of implementation, and requiring 22 eastern states to revise their air pollution standards accordingly. Cannon describes the bargaining that the EPA conducted with Congress and the President's representatives, as well as the eventual litigation of the substantive standards and procedures of the reform effort in the federal courts.[44] In comparison with Van Calster and Deketelaere's discussion of environmental law in Europe, Cannon offers a similar account of political considerations, including the usual trade-offs between environmental protection and economic costs, though translated into the different federal legal structure and context of the United States.

In his chapter, Cannon also offers some more theoretical considerations about the nature of using "bargaining" or negotiation in the regulatory process. Given that administrative agencies seek to advance their own interests through a bargaining process, and even though an agency may honestly see its interest as in the "public interest," the question inevitably arises about the political "legitimacy" of this administrative use of power. Bargaining for innovative solutions to regulatory problems implies a more active role for an administrative agency such as the EPA. If the results of innovative regulatory bargaining are in fact superior in both enhancing regulatory effectiveness and reducing economic costs of the regulation, then may the use of administrative power to reach such positive results also be deemed "legitimate" from the point of view of democratic theory? As Cannon points out, commentators differ in answering this question. Strict adherents to traditional "rule of law" principles believe that the loose use of administrative power through innovative regulatory bargaining threatens to undermine democratic government. Administrative agencies, they argue, should focus on law enforcement and leave lawmaking to Congress, the President, and the states. Others respond that such views of democratic legitimacy are outdated in a world of administrative bureaucracy and complex regulatory problems. In this modern world, the "rule of law" virtues are overestimated. One might say, following this argument, that the proof is in the pudding of regulatory innovation: better regulation achieved through proper bargaining and consultation will tend to result in more popular regulations. What could be more democratic?

Without necessarily resolving this larger theoretical issue, Cannon's chapter ends with an implicit warning that the two theoretical conceptions of democratic legitimacy are not strictly separated in practice. An administrative agency that adopts a more innovative "bargaining" style of regulation may risk losing the "sharp edge" of a reputation for "credible enforcement" that takes the rule of law especially seriously.

Geoffrey Hazard and Eric Orts discuss environmental contracting in more general terms as well. They claim that bargaining in the form of what they call "environmental contracts" occurs in the everyday practice of environmental law in the US. They describe the current system as "a shifting

---

[44] See *American Trucking Associations v. EPA*, 175 F.3d 1027 (D.C. Cir.), modified on rehearing, 195 F.3d 4 (1999), cert. granted, 147 L. Ed. 2d 231 (2000); *State of Michigan v. EPA*, 2000 U.S. App. LEXIS 3209 (D.C. Cir. 2000).

inventory of piecemeal contractual negotiations in the context of adversarial rulemaking and enforcement." In this sense, the litigation-loving US system of environmental law may be even more "contractual" in its actual operation than in European law and elsewhere. For the most part, the enforcement of US environmental law and issuing permits under it are accomplished through negotiation and settlement, in other words, by contract. Regulation-by-litigation characterizes much of the environmental law of administrative agencies. Therefore, recent innovations such as negotiated rulemaking, Project XL, and the Common Sense Initiative, all of which seek overtly to negotiate agreements about regulation among interested parties, represent only slight departures from the usual course of business, not radical changes.

For Hazard and Orts, the conceptual distinction between "regulation" and "contracts" is not always clear in practice, and the line between "government as sovereign" and "government as contracting party" similarly raises difficult questions. Because government itself is often justified in terms of political theories of social contract, it is difficult to argue that contractual negotiation in the process of making regulations is necessarily illegitimate. Environmental contracting may instead be viewed as a "hybrid" that combines some of the best (and worst) aspects of private and public law. Legal support for a contractual approach may also be found in the US Constitution, for example, in the Contracts Clause. In one recent case, the US Supreme Court upheld a claim under a regulatory agreement against the government's argument that it had a sovereign right to renege.[45] If this rule were generalized, regulated entities may have a greater tendency to trust that the government would not change its mind after a regulatory agreement (or the next election) and become more willing to invest the time and effort needed to negotiate regulatory contracts.

In more general theoretical terms, Hazard and Orts argue that environmental contracts may provide a practical method to practice "deliberative democracy" and square the circle of "will" and "reason" necessary for democratic legitimacy. They claim also that environmental contracting may provide an especially practical means for addressing international environmental problems, which are characterized by an absence of effective government authority. For example, the international formation of quasi-autonomous nongovernmental organizations or "quangos" by international agreements may help to overcome "the multi-jurisdictional problem" posed by many environmental issues.

Cary Coglianese, in his contribution to this book, takes up a theoretical challenge to regulatory strategies of environmental contracting or what he calls attempts to regulate through "consensus." The ideals of "teamwork, community, and harmony" implied by the idea of consensus are "attractive," argues Coglianese, but following them broadly would result in "a significant shift in prevailing modes of governmental decision-making

---

[45] *United States v. Winstar*, 518 U.S. 839 (1996).

in the United States." He argues that the empirical evidence of regulatory experiments such as Project XL and the Common Sense Initiative do not make the case for such reform. Drawing on previous research, he also argues that negotiated regulations such as those encouraged under the Negotiated Rulemaking Act do not support the argument for environmental contracting.[46] Collaborative approaches to regulation risk "decentering the state" as the accountable authority in environmental law and, as a consequence, also tend to shift the focus of regulation away from the public interest and toward the various particular (often private) interests that negotiate and bargain over regulations.

Coglianese emphasizes that he is not arguing against increasing the amount of public deliberation in regulation and legislation through "feedback" mechanisms (such as the required notice and comment provisions of the Administrative Procedure Act) or processes to encourage public "input" (such as through roundtable discussions or information gathering). Instead, his target is "consensus," which he describes as a "collective" regulatory process that aims "to establish agreement among all the participants, with the expectation that the government will use the agreement as the basis for its policy decision." Consensus, in other words, captures many of the proposals for regulatory innovation examined by other authors in this book under the general heading of "contracts" or "agreements."

In his chapter, Coglianese usefully outlines some of the promised benefits of regulatory reform based on environmental contracts: reduced conflict, increased compliance, improved policy, and expanded participation. He finds none of these advantages to be persuasive. Conflict and litigation remain pervasive in the US, whether or not consensus-based methods are employed. Increased compliance from "buy in" of participants (especially business) is empirically unproven. Improved policy results and expanded participation may be achieved as well or better by other regulatory processes. Moreover, Coglianese identifies six "pathologies" of regulation by consensus: (1) a bias toward tractability and reaching some agreement as opposed to a focus on the public interest as the highest priority; (2) imprecision of resulting regulations driven by the need to find language to encompass compromises; (3) a tendency to find agreement on "the lowest common denominator" of a problem; (4) increased time and expense or, as the economists writing in this book would say, increased transaction costs; (5) unrealistic expectations among the parties; and (6) the creation of "new sources of conflict" when traditional antagonists such as business people and environmentalists try, paradoxically and often unsuccessfully, to find common ground. Illustrations of these pathologies of consensus include the following. Despite much public bluster and expense, the Clinton Administration's Common Sense Initiative from 1994 to 1998 to "reinvent regulation" for six different industrial sectors failed to result in meaningful regulatory changes. The Enterprise for the Environment initiative begun in 1996 that sought agreement based on the dialog among various interests

---

[46] See also C. Coglianese, "Assessing Consensus: The Promise and Performance of Negotiated Rulemaking" (1997) 46 Duke L J 1355.

produced only broad statements of abstract "vision" and "platitudes." Talks in the International Standards Organization for environmental management standards (ISO 14 000) resulted in agreement only to "least common denominator" provisions, notably excluding third-party verification of reports and public rights to information. And the EPA's Project XL led mostly to disappointed expectations, high transaction costs, and lingering questions about whether business and government resources devoted to this regulatory initiative could be justified in comparison with other pressing needs.

Two other chapters in the book focus specifically on Project XL. Dennis Hirsch presents an overview and background of Project XL. He explains how it grew out of general dissatisfaction with the inefficiency and inflexibility of command-and-control regulation in the US. As originally conceived within the EPA in 1995, Project XL focused on four main components: (1) regulatory flexibility to be given by the EPA (and perhaps state agencies as well), (2) a plan by the regulated entity to achieve "superior environmental performance" by taking a new approach, (3) "stakeholder involvement" in the process of negotiating a Project XL agreement, and (4) a "site specific" focus to allow the EPA and participating state environmental agencies to tailor regulations to specific conditions. The EPA contemplated four different types of "sites" for Project XL: business or industrial facilities, business or industrial sectors, government agencies, and communities. Project XL agreements are proposed by one of these "sites," selected by the EPA for participation, negotiated, and then formalized in a Final Project Agreement (FPA). The FPA looks a lot like a contract, but with one key difference. In comparison, for example, with environmental agreements negotiated under the Flemish decree in Belgium, FPAs are not legally enforceable as a contract. Instead, the EPA may adopt a special regulation through the ordinary administrative processes (including requirements of public notice and comment) to adopt an FPA formally. Although the EPA says that Project XL negotiations must be open to all "stakeholders," third parties such as national or local nonprofit environmental groups are rarely signatories to an FPA.

Hirsch provides details in the form of two case studies of Project XL. First, he examines what seems to be a successful example of a regulatory trade-off based on specific local conditions of a Merck & Co. Project XL for a manufacturing facility near the Shenandoah National Park in Virginia. In general terms, the EPA and state agencies agreed to allow Merck's facility to increase emissions of volatile organic compounds (VOCs) in return for reductions beyond regulatory requirements of SO_2 and NO_x. Because specific meteorological conditions meant that the larger emissions in VOCs did not result in more ozone pollution in the area, and because lower emissions of SO_2 and NO_x produced less acid rain and ozone pollution (with benefits especially for the nearby national park), this Project XL provided a "win-win" situation for everyone. In his chapter, Jon Cannon also provides an account of this Merck Project XL and gives more details about the pollutants involved and the Clean Air Act regulatory changes required. Cannon agrees with Hirsch in concluding that the Merck Project XL resulted in the "cleaner, cheaper, smarter" regulatory bargain, providing at least one possible counterexample to skeptics of Project XL.

The Weyerhauser Project XL on the Flint River in Georgia is another example discussed by Hirsch. In this case, the EPA and state agencies agreed to reduce regulatory inspections and streamline reporting requirements in return for a promise from Weyerhauser to adopt an ISO 14 000 compliant environmental management system and to experiment with "a holistic, multi-media approach to pollution reduction." The company hopes that significant pollution reduction will result, and the EPA seems to be treating it as a test case or real-life laboratory experiment.

Hirsch's chapter then provides an overview of similar developments in the Netherlands and compares them to Project XL. In particular, the use of environmental agreements in the Netherlands tends to differ from Project XL in the following characteristics: a tendency in the Netherlands to focus on large "sectors" rather than specific "facilities," a tendency in the Netherlands to focus on agreements to achieve new standards or goals rather than to bargain for regulatory "flexibility" or exceptions, the enforceability of Dutch environmental agreements as civil contracts in comparison to the FPAs of Project XL, and the relative lack of participation of nonprofit environmental organizations in the Netherlands in actual negotiations of environmental agreements. Hirsch explains the relative success of environmental agreements in the Netherlands as compared to the US experiment with Project XL by reference to the huge difference between the two countries in terms of size, heterogeneity, and perhaps the unique "polder" experience of a small and densely populated nation-state that has been dependent for centuries on the cooperative maintenance of a large system of dikes to keep out the sea.

Despite heavy criticism from various quarters, perhaps most especially environmentalists, Hirsch argues that Project XL stands as a successful regulatory experiment in the US that should continue. He extends an argument that he makes elsewhere that the EPA has the legal authority to pursue Project XL though a number of channels, including enforcement discretion, flexible interpretation of legal requirements, the authority to waive statutory requirements, and the method of site-specific rulemaking.[47] But he also argues for legislation to strengthen Project XL by expanding the EPA's authority "to replace binding regulatory requirements with site-specific agreements." Hirsch's chapter reviews the history of proposed federal legislation along these lines, including the most recent Second Generation Environmental Improvement Act that was introduced with bipartisan support in the House of Representatives in late 1999.[48]

In the second chapter in the book to focus specifically on Project XL, Alfred Marcus, Don Geffen, and Ken Sexton offer a decidedly less optimistic estimation based on their personal study of (and involvement in) the 3M project in Hutchinson, Minnesota. "Caring committed people with different beliefs and opinions worked diligently and in good faith over a two-period," they report, "to forge a cooperative, mutually agreeable pilot

---

[47] D. Hirsch, "Bill and Al's XL-ent Adventure: An Analysis of the EPA's Legal Authority to Implement the Clinton Administration's Project XL" [1998] U Ill L Rev 129.
[48] Second Generation of Environmental Improvement Act of 1999, H.R. 3448.

project that would result in a series of 'win-win' outcomes." But their hopes were dashed when the project ended in a "stalemate."

Like Hirsch and others, Marcus, Geffen, and Sexton find the origins of Project XL in the general dissatisfaction with command-and-control regulation, especially among business interests and within the EPA. Some nonprofit environmental organizations, such as the Environmental Defense Fund (EDF), also began to believe that command-and-control regulation needed reform. Business interests began to exhibit at least some movement toward "corporate environmentalism" and "self-regulation." Disasters such as Bhopal and the Exxon Valdez touched even some of the coldest financial hearts in the business world. Collaboration between businesses and nonprofit environmental organizations became more common. Even McDonald's collaborated with EDF in a highly publicized project to reduce waste.[49] The chemical industry formed a self-regulatory group called "Responsible Care." The idea of "sustainable development" gained currency.

The Clinton Administration's proposal for Project XL seemed to fit perfectly with this restlessness with the current system of environmental protection and a general desire to do better. But the 3M case indicates some significant problems in practice. First, the requirement for an XL facility to show "superior environmental performance" can be troublesome. A problem at the 3M plant in Minnesota was how to explain to the EPA and environmentalists that overall growth of a facility resulting in increased production meant "superior environmental performance" when the overall emissions of VOCs would increase (even though they were decreasing substantially as a percentage of production). Other problems concerned duration of an agreement and how it would be enforced in case of violation.

The collapse of the 3M Project XL weakened the momentum of the initiative substantially. Other businesses watching from the sidelines concluded that the effort was not worth the risk of public failure. The number of proposed projects dwindled below the EPA's expectations.

At the same time, some of the best lessons are learned through failed experiments, and the 3M case may help to prove the rule. As Marcus, Geffen, and Sexton show, both the EPA and business community learned from the experience. One concrete result was the EPA's publication in 1997 of a notice providing a definition of "superior environmental performance."[50] Less progress seems to have been made, at least from a business point of view, in terms of recognizing excellent past environmental performance when setting "baselines" for the measurement of future performance. The chapter concludes that Project XL's future success will depend on several complex factors, including whether the parties to an agreement can build the necessary trust and whether generally favorable political conditions exist relating to the perception of a regulatory reform effort (i.e., seeing Project XL as a genuine, broad-based reform effort rather than as a political ploy to reduce

---

[49] See "McDonald's Corporation 1992: Operations, Flexibility and the Environment" in F.L. Reinhardt and R.H.K. Vietor (eds), *Business Management and the Natural Environment* (South Western College Publishing, 1996), p. 3–84. (reprinting Harvard Business School case).

[50] 62 Fed. Reg. 19872 (1997).

the influence of the EPA). In this sense, Marcus, Geffen, and Sexton echo Jon Cannon's perception of the heavily political nature of environmental law and proposals for its reform. A reform agenda that attempts to experiment with various different regulatory innovations (and not only Project XL), including a system to oversee and measure resulting performance, may help to transform political arguments about environmental law reform into technical ones.

4 ENVIRONMENTAL CONTRACTS FROM AN ECONOMIC PERSPECTIVE

Economic measurements, of course, are one essential component for any reform effort in environmental law to succeed. Reducing the economic cost of achieving particular environmental benefits is now virtually universally recognized (at least among legal academics in the US) as one of the primary goals for reform. In this respect, the jurisprudential movement of law and economics, which has a strong following in the United States and is beginning also to grow in Europe has had an important influence on the academic study of environmental law.[51]

In his chapter, Jason Johnston leads a series of separate considerations of environmental contracts from an economic as well as legal perspective. First, his chapter expands the list of the kinds of environmental contracts in the United States that should be considered. In accord with other contributors, Johnston counts Project XL as the recent initiative in regulatory reform that "goes the furthest in replacing the default command-and-control regime of limits on emissions to specific media with more flexible, site-specific regulation." In addition to the examples of Project XL discussed above, he adds the Intel Project XL negotiated for its facility in Chandler, Arizona. This case seems to provide a middle range outcome between the apparently unmitigated success of the Merck Project XL in Virginia and the relative failure of the 3M Project XL in Minnesota. The Intel Project XL seems to be seen as a success from the point of view of the company and local community groups in Arizona, but it has been criticized by national environmental groups, such as the Natural Resources Defense Council, which had been excluded

---

[51] For the most influential work in this respect, see R. Posner, *The Economic Analysis of Law* (5th edn, Panel Publishers, New York, 1997). Although slow to cross the Atlantic, the influence of law and economics is growing in Europe. See, e.g., R. Posner, "The Future of Law and Economics in Europe" (1997) 17 Int'l Rev L and Econ 3. For examples of this trend in research, see M. Faure, J. Finsinger, and J. Siegers (eds), *Regulation of the Professions: A Law and Economics Approach to the Regulation of Attorneys and Physicians in the U.S., Belgium, the Netherlands, Germany, and the U.K.* (Paul & Co., 1993); C. Berstrom, P. Hogfeldt, J.R. Macey, and P. Samuelsson, "The Regulation of Corporate Acquisitions: A Law and Economics Analysis of European Proposals for Reform" [1995] Colum Bus L Rev 495; U. Mattei and R. Pardolesi, "Law and Economics in Civil Law Countries: A Comparative Approach" (1991) 11 Int'l Rev L and Econ 265.

from the process. For Johnston, then, Project XL provides an example of one interesting outcome that may be predicted for the general use of environmental contracts: the relative decrease in the influence of national environmental and industry groups (who are most effective in lobbying at the national level) and the corresponding increase in the influence of local organizations, including local environmental and community groups, local business interests, and state regional and municipal governments.

Perhaps more important than Project XL, however, are other somewhat less ambitious environmental contracts that are being adopted in greater numbers in other areas. For example, Johnston identifies habitat conservation plans (HCPs) negotiated with local landowners and regional governments by the US Department of Interior under the Endangered Species Act (ESA) as a major type of environmental contract. HCPs began to be negotiated in the early 1980s, but their numbers began to increase significantly after the Clinton Administration resolved to make the ESA more "user friendly" in 1994. In an HCP, the government promises that further habitat mitigation efforts will not be required for a landowner in the future, in return for the landowner's promise to undertake concrete mitigation or restoration of habitat as a condition for development. HCPs are authorized under Section 10(a) of the ESA adopted in 1982.[52] The popularity of HCPs increased dramatically when the Clinton Administration began to vigorously enforce the ESA prohibition of "incidental takings" of endangered and threatened species by eliminating their habitat. By late 1999, more than 250 HCPs had been agreed and 200 more were in the process of being negotiated. About half of these HCPs contain "No Surprises" clauses that assure the private party that the government will not change its regulatory position for a specific term in the future.

Johnston also identifies brownfields redevelopment agreements under Superfund clean-up regulations and wetland mitigation agreements as two other environmental contracts involving real estate. Brownfields agreements respond to two well-known problems with US Superfund law: (1) they imposed very stringent technical clean-up requirements that were irrationally expensive in proportion to the resulting environmental benefits, and (2) they imposed liability on current landowners who had nothing to do with the original contamination of the soil or groundwater. In 1995, the EPA announced a plan that allowed for the government to negotiate prospective-purchaser agreements (PPAs) with new purchasers of contaminated land. Under a PPA, a prospective purchaser agrees to a specified level of clean-up of the property, and in return the government (usually both the EPA and corresponding state agencies) promises not to bring civil enforcement actions in the future. The agreements are expected to bring local

---

[52] 18 U.S.C. § 1539(a)(1)(b) (1999). An HCP was also central in the legislative resolution of the dispute between environmentalists and the Pacific Lumber Co. concerning the preservation of the old-growth redwood Headwaters Forest in the state of Washington. See 16 U.S.C. § 471j (1999).

economic benefits, such as redevelopment of urban areas. They are also intended to be legally enforceable contracts.

Similarly, wetlands mitigation agreements are well-established in law and practice under Section 404 of the Clean Water Act.[53] An in-kind exchange of wetlands-for-wetlands is one sort of agreement that is contemplated, but Johnston's chapter discusses also the increasing use of "in-lieu mitigation" agreements, which allow a developer and the government to agree on a fee paid to an independent administrator to acquire or otherwise preserve wetlands elsewhere to offset the developer's destruction of wetlands. These agreements are not explicitly authorized by statute or regulation, but arise through the discretion of permits negotiated with local groups by the Army Corps of Engineers (which has a primary role in wetlands regulation in the US). The fee administrators in these agreements are often local environmental organizations, such as local chapters of the National Audubon Society or the Nature Conservancy.

Having identified these kinds of environmental contracts, Johnston's chapter then offers an original interpretation of them from a law and economics point of view. Beginning with the view of private contracts that emphasizes a "default rule paradigm," Johnston adapts this concept to the context of environmental law, in which the "default rule" is described as "status quo environmental regulation." "What distinguishes environmental contracts from private contracts," Johnston argues, "is that one of the parties to the environmental contract—the environmental regulator—is also responsible for implementing the default outcome, the status quo regime." Whether these contracts will improve on the default regime therefore depends on a number of factors, including the incentives of the regulators, the information available to the parties, and the extent to which everyone affected by the externalities of a particular problem are included in the negotiation of a contractual solution.

Johnston draws several important conclusions from his analysis. First, his model of strategic environmental regulation is essentially "political" in terms of establishing the background of "credible" enforcement. This supports or at least parallels observations made in other chapters. In addition, Johnston draws an interesting comparison between the US and Europe on this political dimension. In the US, with its "executive democracy," the most important political dynamic for federal environmental policy revolves around the elections of the President and Congress, a political context that can change relatively easily and dramatically in terms of whether Democrats or Republicans control one branch of government or the other or both. In Europe, at least at the nation-state level, the prevailing form of "parliamentary democracy" avoids this political unpredictability to some degree. In any event, whatever the form of government, political change will alter the status quo default rule of environmental regulation, which directly affects the incentives of both governments and private parties to agree to environmental contracts. Thus the temporal dimension of political change is

---

[53]   33 U.S.C. § 1344 (1999).

especially important when considering the normative desirability of environmental contracts. As Johnston observes, environmental contracts bind the regulator as well as the private parties to the contract, which may affect incentives positively or negatively depending on various factors, including the future career plans of government regulators and the perceived benefits and costs to the parties of traditional regulation compared with innovative environmental contracts. An additional complication of the temporal dimension concerns the issue of one generation of regulators making "deals" that will bind future generations.

As mentioned above, another interesting result of Johnston's analysis is that environmental contracts will tend to lessen the influence of national nonprofit environmental organizations, such as the Sierra Club or National Resource Defense Council, and increase the clout of local groups. This analysis may help to explain the antipathy that many environmental organizations display about experiments in environmental contracting. However, the same is true for business interests. Large national business associations will tend to lose influence, and local businesses will tend to gain power under environmental contracts. Whether this sort of shift in influence is normatively good or bad from the perspective of environmental protection and economic efficiency is an open question. On one hand, large organizations may have advantages of economies of scale in conducting scientific research about environmental problems. On the other hand, environmental contracts seem to shift the focus of analysis from, again in Johnston's words, "remedial process inputs" to "concrete environmental outputs." This approach makes cross-media trade-offs easier than under traditional regulatory approaches in which responsibility for different pollution media is usually delegated to different enforcement offices. One key element in determining the best course for regulation is to examine the role of information about particular environmental problems and how it is produced and disseminated. At least some kinds of these problems demand the addition of "carrots as well as sticks to the regulatory toolkit," and environmental contracts provide one method of providing such positive incentives.

The chapter by David Spence and Lekha Gopalakrishnan also addresses the political economy of environmental contracts. Given regulatory experiments such as Project XL and regulatory negotiations, Spence and Gopalakrishnan ask why the EPA has not been able more easily or effectively to draw larger lessons from these collaborative efforts for more general innovations in environmental regulation. Their conclusion, in economic terms, is that even though collaborative efforts reflect the potential for "positive sum" gains for environmental regulation, particular interests or "stakeholders" in the regulatory process nevertheless view the regulatory bargaining as "zero sum" and therefore tend to "veto" reform proposals.

The chapter begins its analysis with useful distinctions between regulatory "relief" and "reform" and between "substantive" and "procedural" efficiency in regulation. In the US in recent years, both Democratic and Republican administrations have focused relatively consistently on "regulatory reform," which Spence and Gopalakrishnan define as trying to figure out "how best to achieve a given standard" of environmental protection at the least cost. The economic critique of the lack of "substantive efficiency" of command-and-control regulation is well-known. The EPA's joint study with Amoco of the company's benzene emissions at its Yorktown, Virginia refinery remains one of the most striking examples: regulatory flexibility could have yielded $25 million in savings for the company and at the same time reduced benzene emissions five-fold. Such studies argue strongly in favor of regulatory reform. But "procedural efficiency," which refers primarily to the elements of the regulatory process meant to reduce the risks of administrative capture, is also very important. As Spence and Gopalakrishnan argue, the worry about capture of the administrative process is high on the agenda of many national environmental groups and other pro-environmental interests.

With these conceptual clarifications in mind, Spence and Gopalakrishnan then advance the basic neoclassical economic idea of "Pareto optimality," which assumes that if some people can be made better off by a change in the status quo and if nobody would be made worse off, then the change is economically rational or "Pareto superior." They introduce a standard economic model of an Edgeworth Box to study the bargaining process for environmental regulation. Considering Project XL and reg negs as examples of bargaining that can produce Pareto superior results, they ask why some interests, notably large nongovernmental environmental groups, tend to resist these reforms. Through an economic analysis, they conclude the basic problem is one of perspective about the ends and means of bargaining. Business interests see the obvious Pareto improvements offered by reform and become frustrated at environmentalists' failure to recognize the obvious "positive sum" gains. However, environmentalists worry instead about the possibility of "zero sum" losses that may result from an erosion of their bargaining position. They focus on the "end" of overall pollution reduction and environmental protection, and from this perspective Pareto improvements are not necessarily sufficient. In fact, inefficient regulation may perversely lead environmentalists to veto Pareto optimal reforms because they can—or believe that they can—extract greater concessions from business because of the high costs to business of inefficient regulations. Strategic bargaining of this kind, then, may explain both the impatience that some business interests have shown with reform proposals, especially after debacles such as the 3M Project XL negotiation, and the wariness that environmental interests have exhibited toward collaborative reform. Again, the most fundamental explanation is a general disagreement about the political ends of regulatory reform, which can then lead to strategic rather than good faith negotiations about the most efficient regulatory means to this end. In this respect, though by a somewhat different route, Spence and Gopalakrishnan confirm Johnston's argument that national environmental organizations are reluctant to support environmental contracts.

Spence and Gopalakrishnan conclude that some regulatory inefficiency will inevitably continue because it at least in part reflects deep political disagreements. At the same time, the chapter offers strong arguments against some other objections to collaborative environmental reform efforts. For example, they argue that the "rule of law" or legitimacy argument against reform does not withstand close analysis, because at least in the cases of Project XL and reg negs the EPA retains the authority to disassociate itself from the regulatory bargain. They also suggest that the "Trojan horse" argument raised by some environmentalist opponents to collaborative law reform transmogrifies into a "red herring" when various monitoring devices are considered as solutions, including EPA oversight and the mandatory release of various kinds of reports and information. Thus Spence and Gopalakrishnan's chapter also holds out the possibility for some degree of progress in environmental regulation if collaborative efforts can be built on trust and verification.

The next three chapters discuss the phenomenon of what economists call "environmental voluntary agreements" (EVAs) from different theoretical perspectives. EVAs are seen as bargains or contracts made between regulated entities and the government as a substitute for more direct command-and-control regulation. The problem for economists is to explain why and when EVAs happen.

John Maxwell and Thomas Lyon first present an explanation for the advent of EVAs in the 1990s in the US by drawing on the institutional economic theory associated with the Nobel prize winner, Douglass North.[54] From an institutional perspective, they identify four major groups that are "both affected by environmental policy *and* have the ability to bring about changes in the policy." They are the regulated entities, the EPA (and corresponding state agencies), national nonprofit environmental organizations, and the Congress. Maxwell and Lyon conclude that the regulated entities and the EPA have the most to gain from EVAs, and by adopting them they are able to "wrestle power from national environmental groups and the Congress."

Institutional change at this level does not come about easily, however, and Maxwell and Lyon recognize that inertia favors the status quo of command-and-control regulation. They claim that four "shocks" occurred to encourage the rise of EVAs in the US: (1) increasing complexity of environmental law as the corpus of statutes, regulations, and cases expands,[55] (2) technological innovation and scientific progress, (3) regulatory budget cuts, and (4) increasing use and effect of citizen lawsuits. These four "shocks" took place roughly simultaneously in the US in the 1980s, and the EVAs negotiated by industry and the EPA was one response. If this institutional analysis is correct, then one might predict that the use of EVAs may decline in the future if, for example, regulatory budgets are restored or enhanced (through, for example, a strongly pro-environmental President and Congress) and citizen suits were curtailed (for example, through Supreme Court decisions on standing).[56]

---

[54] See D. North, *Institutions, Institutional Change and Economic Performance* (Cambridge University Press, 1990); D. North, *Structure and Change in Economic History* (W.W. Norton & Company, New York, 1982).

[55] This phenomenon may also be described as "proliferation of law" or "juridification." See Orts, supra note 7, at 1239–1241.

[56] The US Supreme Court has decided several environmental cases that create hurdles for citizen lawsuits under the doctrine of standing. For discussion of these cases and their impact, see J.D. Echeverria and J.T. Zeidler, "Barely Standing" (1999) 16 Envtl Forum 21; C.R. Sunstein, "What's Standing After *Lujan*?: Of Citizen Suits, 'Injuries,' and Article III" (1992) 91 Mich L Rev 163. One closely watched recent case, however, upheld a citizen lawsuit under the Clean Water Act. *Friends of the Earth v. Laidlaw Environmental Services, Inc.*, 120 S. Ct. 693 (2000).

The chapter by Magali Delmas and Ann Terlaak gives a comparative economic perspective on EVAs in Europe, where over 300 agreements have been negotiated in the 1990s. Delmas and Terlaak offer a competing explanation for EVAs drawing on two streams of economic theory: (1) the "new institutional economics" that emphasizes the "dynamic capability" for learning exhibited by successful business firms and the interests that these firms have to innovate and create knowledge or new "competencies"[57] and (2) the "transaction costs economics" associated with, for example, Oliver Williamson, which in the regulatory context focuses on the costs of negotiating agreements.[58]

Delmas and Terlaak see EVAs as "hybrid governance" structures that tend to be less stable than command-and-control regulation (and in this respect they support the argument of Maxwell and Lyon). Delmas and Terlaak suggest that EVAs will be more or less common depending on two major factors: (1) whether they present firms with the opportunity to innovate and enhance their technical knowledge, and (2) the transaction costs of the EVA arrangement. The transaction costs of EVAs are affected most by the availability of monitoring mechanisms, the credibility of the regulatory authority, and the protection of property rights. Monitoring, for example, raises the important problem of "free riding" by firms that do not "buy in" to the EVA. Other commentators have also noted the importance of regulatory credibility. Like Johnston, for example, Delmas and Terlaak argue that uncertainty about future regulatory regimes will tend to increase the costs for firms contemplating an environmental contract or EVA. A credible threat of command-and-control regulation if an EVA is not agreed, however, will increase the costs of not coming to an agreement.

Delmas and Terlaak's chapter then draws on examples from both Europe and the US to consider how particular EVAs can be classified in terms of innovation potential and transaction costs. The Dutch Environmental Agreement in the Chemical Industry, as noted above, is a success story in the field. It scores highly on both dimensions, providing industry the valuable opportunity to exchange valuable information about innovation and also having low transaction costs due to annual monitoring and reporting as well as internal and external sanctions. The French End-of-Life Vehicle Agreement represents, according to Delmas and Terlaak, an example of high innovation potential (given the opportunity to share technical information about recycling, shredding, dismantling, etc.) but also high transaction costs (lacking any threat of internal or external sanctions against those

---

[57] Delmas and Terlaak explain that the "dynamic capabilities approach" draws on theories of evolutionary economics, a resource-based theories of the firm, and knowledge-based theories of the firm. See, e.g., R. R. Nelson and S. G. Winter, *An Evolutionary Theory of Economic Change* (Harvard University Press, Cambridge, 1982); M. Peteraf, "The Cornerstones of Competitive Advantage: A Resource-Based View" (1993) 14 Strategic Mgmt J 179; B. Kogut and U. Zander, "Knowledge of the Firm and the Evolutionary Theory of Mulitnational Corporations" (1993) 25 J Int'l Bus Studies 625.

[58] See O. Williamson, *The Economic Institutions of Capitalism: Firms, Markets, Relational Contracting* (Free Press, New York, 1985); O. Williamson, *The Mechanisms of Governance* (Oxford University Press, 1996).

who do not participate). The EPA's Design for the Environmental project falls also in the middle with both significant opportunities for firms to share information and learn, but no "stick" to discourage free riders. A third category involves low innovation potential but also low transaction costs. In this uninspiring category, Delmas and Terlaak put the German Declaration on Global Warming Prevention, which is easily joined (because virtually costless) but not very effective (because most of the innovation has been gained or would have been gained anyway).

Delmas and Terlaak's chapter concludes with a more optimistic assessment than Maxwell and Lyon give of the future of EVAs, at least in Europe. But Delmas and Terlaak suggest that EVAs should offer the incentive of innovation and shared knowledge to business participants and, perhaps more importantly, should provide both internal monitoring to prevent free riders and the threat of external regulation if an EVA is not successful in dealing with a particular problem or encouraging enough participation. Otherwise, the success of EVAs will be limited.

The third chapter to consider the economics of EVAs by Kathleen Segerson and Na Li Dawson also recognizes the importance of transaction costs and the potential for free riding. In the category of EVAs, Segerson and Dawson include business-led voluntary initiatives (e.g., the chemical industry's Responsible Care program), negotiated agreements between regulated entities and the government (e.g., Project XL or European environmental contracts), and voluntary programs urged by environmental agencies but without direct regulatory consequences (e.g., the 33/50 Program). The extent of participation in any of these kinds of EVAs depends, from Segerson and Dawson's economic perspective, on two factors: (1) market-driven incentives (such as "green demand" from the firm's consumers, suppliers, or customers and general reputation benefits) and (2) the responses of firms to government inducements, which can sometimes be positive (e.g., subsidies or tax breaks) but are usually negative (e.g., the threat of more expensive and onerous command-and-control regulation). Transaction costs will also be included in a particular firm's calculations of the costs and benefits of participating in a voluntary program.

Segerson and Dawson agree with other contributors that a key element in this calculation will be the costs of free riding. In any EVA, some firms will be tempted to gain the benefits (including freedom from an alternative command-and-control regulation) without participating in and bearing the costs of the EVA. Segerson and Dawson investigate this problem through an economic analysis that draws on previous economic treatments of voluntary agreements[59] as well as the economic literature on international

---

[59]   See, e.g., C. Carraro and F. Lévêque, "Introduction: The Rationale and Potential of Voluntary Approaches" in C. Carraro and F. Lévêque (eds), *Voluntary Approaches to Environmental Policy* (Kluwer Academic Publishers, Dordrecht, 1999), p. 1; K. Segerson and N. Li, "Voluntary Approaches to Environmental Protection" in H. Folmer and T. Teitenberg (eds), The International Yearbook of Envtl and Resource Econ 1999/2000 (Edward Elgar, Cheltenham, 1999), p. 273; K. Segerson and T. Miceli, "Voluntary Environmental Agreements: Good or Bad News for Environmental Quality?" (1998) 36 J Envtl Econ & Mgmt 109.

environmental agreements.[60] Their analysis yields two counterintuitive results with respect to the effect of free riders on EVAs. First, contrary to the assumptions of some other contributors in this book, they find that the relative costs of free riding do not necessary increase with the number of firms involved in a voluntary agreement. Instead, the key economic question is the extent to which an EVA offers economic gains to the participating firms compared with the default command-and-control regime. To this extent, firms will rationally participate in EVAs even with the risk of free riders. Second, and again contrary to conventional wisdom, Segerson and Dawson's analysis concludes that this result will not necessarily alter in situations when mostly large firms are involved. According to their analysis, the effect of increasing industry size will reflect the relative cost inelasticities for voluntary as compared with mandatory regimes regardless of the costs of free riders.

The difference between large and small firms is also considered in the last chapter in the part of the book on economic perspectives by Howard Kunreuther, Patrick McNulty, and Yong Kang. This chapter focuses on third-party inspections as an alternative to command-and-control regimes. Its primary topic is the new requirement for risk management plans (RMPs) under Section 112(r) of the Clean Air Act Amendments of 1990.[61] But the chapter also identifies a number of examples of using third-party inspections as a regulatory alternative, often coupled with another kind of contract not yet considered here, namely, the private insurance contract. These examples include a third-party inspection regime established in the state of Massachusetts for the regulation of underground storage tanks, a recent voluntary compliance program entered by the EPA and the National Pork Producers Council under the Clean Water Act that includes provisions to train independent inspectors, and the case of third-party inspection and mandatory insurance under state law for steam boilers dating back to the 1860s.

The economic problem, according to Kunreuther, McNulty, and Kang, is the classic one of a tendency for human beings to underestimate the risks of high-consequence, low-probability events. For example, the risk of a "worst case" chemical accident, such as the one that occurred in Bhopal in 1984, tends to be systematically discounted in the real world for a number of reasons. First, it is technically difficult to compute the costs and benefits of high consequence but low probability events. Second, business firms tend to make decisions on short time horizons and therefore short change long-term risks. Third, firms and especially small firms have limited assets compared to the possibility of catastrophic risk. Insolvency, bankruptcy, and limited liability thus limit the rational consideration of these risks. Fourth, human beings have a proven psychological or cognitive inability to consider differences of very low probabilities rationally. For example, one study demonstrated that most people cannot meaningful distinguish

---

[60] See, e.g., S. Barrett, "Self-enforcing International Economic Agreements" (1994) 46 Oxford Econ Papers 5; C. Carraro and D. Siniscalco, "International Environmental Agrements, Incentives and Political Economy" (1998) 42 Eur Econ Rev 3.

[61] 42 U.S.C. § 7412(r) (1999).

among catastrophic risks of one in 100,000, one in a million, and one in ten million. Fifth, the externalities of some large catastrophic risks (such as the financial risk to other private property owners living in the vicinity of a plant) are not included in a firm's calculations. Regulation of some form is therefore usually necessary in these situations.

Sheer numbers of regulated entities, however, may make command-and-control infeasible or at least prohibitively expensive. Kunreuther, McNulty, and Kang observe, for example, that the EPA's Region III covers Pennsylvania, New Jersey, Delaware, Maryland, Virginia, West Virginia, and the District of Columbia with 5,000 chemical facilities regulated under the Clean Air Act, but Region III has only three auditors to inspect these facilities. Third-party inspection therefore offers the prospect of saving costs not only for business firms (who may get added flexibility) but also regulators.

The chapter reports on a pilot study for third-party inspection of RMPs under the Clean Air Act in the state of Delaware with a generally favorable conclusion. Small firms, however, may present a particularly difficult problem because they will usually have lower thresholds for risk prevention. Inspection requirements coupled with insurance contracts may provide a solution. In addition, the chapter emphasizes that key ingredients in a successful third-party inspection approach include optimally calibrating the default governmental fine for failing to comply and properly protecting the auditors themselves with respect to potential legal liability.

5   A COMPARATIVE CASE STUDY: "GREEN" ELECTRICITY CONSUMER CONTRACTS

The last part of the book shifts attention to a different kind of environmental contracting, namely, the everyday contracts between a business and its individual consumers that have "green" or "environmentally friendly" features. Some of the more general economic discussions, such as the chapter by Segerson and Li, recognize that consumer demand for such "green" products and services may play an important role in environmental voluntary agreements that involve business-to-business alliances or business-to-government programs. But business-to-consumer contracts may also be considered yet another type of environmental contracts.

The two chapters included here on environmental contracts with consumers empirically examine two programs involving the production and sale of "green electricity." Consistent with the comparative approach of this book, one of the chapters examines a program in the US (Detroit) and the other a program in Europe (Zurich).

The chapter by Matthew Kotchen, Michael Moore, and Christopher Clark puts individual contracts for green electricity in theoretical context. These contracts fit with the so-called "third wave" in environmental regulation of informational disclosure strategies.[62] In "green electricity" programs, utilities

---

[62]   T. Tietenberg, "Disclosure Strategies for Pollution Control" (1998) 11 Envtl and Resource Econ 587. See also supra note 10 and accompanying text.

provide an environmentally beneficial product and disclose details about it to consumers through marketing and advertising. The movement toward deregulation of electricity in the US may thus result in competition not only on price but also the environmental characteristics of the product. Already, 42 utilities in 15 states offer "green electricity" programs, and these numbers will very likely increase as deregulation continues. Kotchen, Moore, and Clark recognize that these kinds of consumer environmental contracts for electricity cannot supersede the need for regulation of pollution for electric power production, but they argue convincingly that consumer environmental contracts can complement regulation and help to achieve social environmental objectives.

Green electricity programs come in two basic varieties: capacity-based and energy-based. Capacity-based programs allow for the purchase of electricity generated from "sustainable" or renewable resources (usually solar energy). Energy-based programs give consumers the option to purchase a particular percentage or "block" of their electric power from renewable resources.[63]

Kotchen, Moore, and Clark study the motivations of consumers who participate in Detroit Edison's SolarCurrents green electricity program. Consumers may elect to purchase 100-watt blocks of solar energy each month and must sign a two-year contract to enroll in the program. Because consumers must pay a premium, their participation cannot be explained purely in terms of financial interest. A broader conception of utility or human behavior is required, and Kotchen, Moore, and Clark survey a number of possible explanations, including the altruistic motivation to contribute to the public good of a healthier environment and underlying pro-environmental value orientations. Their survey shows that the most popular reason that consumers give for participating in SolarCurrents was a personal value orientation of "biocentrism." These consumers purchased solar electricity because they believed that doing so would reduce air pollution and "improve the health of natural ecosystems." The survey also finds that Detroit consumers valued the perceived regional benefit that using solar energy would provide for residents of southeastern Michigan more than the potential to "slow the rate of global warming." Placing last in the reasons given were feelings of "warm-glow altruism," i.e., a desire to participate in the green electricity program "regardless of its environmental effects."

Felix Oberholzer-Gee, in his chapter studying the green electricity program of the Zurich Electric Power Company, finds a strikingly different result. Also using a survey (though with different questions), Oberholzer-Gee finds that the strongest reason given by Swiss residents participating in

---

[63] In Pennsylvania, for example, Green Mountain Energy is one alternative available to consumers. A choice is offered of three choices in decreasing order of environmental ratings and expense: "Nature's Choice" (100 percent renewable energy with an independent "Green-e" certification), "Enviro Blend" (50 percent renewable energy and 50 percent from natural gas or water power), or "Eco-Smart" (99 percent from natural gas or water power). A web-based "eco-calculator" allows consumers to compare how much of a premium they would pay for each alternative comparison with monthly estimates from their current electricity supplier. See <http://greenmountain.com/electricity/products/compare_pa.asp>, 1 March 2000.

a solar power purchasing program that charged six times as much for solar energy as for "regular" electricity was warm-glow altruism, which he defines as the positive feelings that one may have in contributing to a cause perceived to be for a "public good" without any assurance that the contribution will result in the consequences hoped for or provide some other personal benefit.

As Oberholzer-Gee points out, green electricity programs provide a couple of excellent characteristics from the social scientific perspective of studying consumer environmental behavior. First, the issue of quality of a product does not matter. Unlike organic apples, for example, which a consumer may select because of perceived "healthy" quality or taste rather than environmental considerations (i.e., no pesticides used to grow them), electricity produced by solar energy has a uniform quality (i.e., the environmentally friendly nature of production appears to be the only significant variable). Second, reputational effects of altruistic behavior are minimized in the case of choosing an electricity provider. For other kinds of pro-environmental behavior, such as participating in a voluntary neighborhood recycling program, one may worry more about one's reputation in deciding to participate (or not) rather than any intrinsic motivation to contribute to an environmental good. Because one's mail, including utility bills, is usually private, the problem of reputational bias in studying the phenomenon of green electricity participation is reduced. In the design of his survey questionnaire, Oberholzer-Gee controlled reputational bias as well as social desirability bias (i.e., the tendency for people to report an exaggerated concern with issues deemed to be socially desirable in order to present themselves in the best light).

The conclusion of the Zurich study is that feelings of warm-glow altruism as well as direct concern for altruistic effects matter most for Swiss citizens in the green electricity program. If true, then some interesting implications for the promotion of green energy programs may follow. As Oberholzer-Gee observes, Zurich Power spent heavily on advertising the positive environmental effects of solar energy. If consumers are motivated as much by an expectation of feelings of warm-glow altruism as by a more hard-nosed consequentialist belief in the likelihood of altruistic results, then perhaps environmental marketing strategies should promote the "personalities and lifestyle" of those who participate in the program, though the risk is also that environmental "fashions" of this sort can easily come and go.

6   THE STRUCTURE OF THE BOOK

The chapters in this book are organized loosely in the order above. However, because the balance of the chapters are written by Americans (with the only excuse that the conference from which this book arose was in Philadelphia), it begins with a discussion of the experience with the nascent use of environmental contracts in the United States in Part I. Readers who wish to begin with an understanding of the experience in Europe may therefore wish to start with Part II, which includes chapters on environmental agreements used in the European Community and its Member States. In general, however, the book is meant to be used comparatively for readers in both the United States and Europe—and elsewhere as well. Part III collects the chapters that are most relevant for readers with an interest in economic perspectives on environmental contracts. Part IV includes two comparative empirical studies of consumer uses of environmental contracts.

7 LESSONS LEARNED AND FUTURE RESEARCH

The discussion in this introduction can only scratch the surface of the rich details and varying insights provided in the chapters of this book, and it cannot be read as a substitute for them. Our purpose in collecting some of the main ideas here is not only to give readers a taste of each chapter—with the hope of enticing the reader to read and digest them more thoroughly—but also with an aim to give our own perspective of directions that these contributions give for future research in the area of environmental contracts.

First, we believe that this collection illustrates the value of comparative discussions of environmental regulation in the United States and Europe. Even though the legal systems and cultures are very different, they are also similar in their generally "western" orientation compared with many other parts of the world. The US and European systems of law therefore stand to gain significantly in drawing comparative lessons from each other, a task that can only be useful if both Americans and Europeans learn more about each other's legal and social systems. Environmental regulation, which addresses problems that are increasingly transcontinental in scope, is one important set of topics that can benefit from comparative study.

Specifically with respect to environmental contracts, European practice appears to be in many respects ahead of the US. At one time, the US appeared to Europe as unquestionably in the vanguard of environmental protection. In the early 1980s, for example, some policy makers in the Netherlands—now considered by many observers as one of the most advanced countries in terms of its environmental regulation—saw the United States as "ahead of us in their environmental policies," and they "borrowed many ideas" from the US that influenced the Dutch approach.[64] With respect to environmental contracts, however, Europe may well have gained the lead in terms of experience. As the chapters in Part II demonstrate, European environmental agreements have become relatively common as an instrument of regulation (or an alternative to regulation that may otherwise be imposed). As the US continues various kinds of experiments with environmental contracting—such as Project XL, the Common Sense

---

[64] See de Jongh and Captain, supra note 27, at 27–28 (recognizing "environmental impact assessments" as a particularly influential idea).

Initiative, habitat conservation plans, interstate pollution reduction agreements, and other "partnerships" between government and business—
the European experience is important to consider. For example, perhaps the
Common Sense Initiative would have proven more successful had the
lessons of negotiating European environmental agreements been better
learned in the US—and maybe future efforts along similar lines will be
rewarded for the same reason.

At the same time, Europeans may learn much from continuing American
experience, especially as European environmental law begins to move in a
"federal" direction in terms of the increasing influence of the legal institutions of the European Union and the potential conflicts that Member States
are likely to have with this new federal power. The jurisprudential development of the concept of "subsidiarity," for example, may benefit from comparison with American constitutional principles of federalism, and vice
versa. Another relative advantage of some American academics in comparison with their European counterparts appears in the economic study of
regulation. Most of the chapters in Part III testify to the strong influence of
law and economics in the US. Whatever one may think of the relative merits
of this approach as a matter of jurisprudence, it is very difficult to argue
that comparative economic costs of different kinds of regulatory strategies
should not matter in a world of scarce resources—whether scarce resources
are conceived as an economic problem, an environmental problem, or,
perhaps most accurately, both. On the level of practice as well, the EPA's
programs under the headings of "partners for the environment" and "innovative partnerships for environmental compliance" merit close attention in
Europe, perhaps especially with respect to areas in which the US seems to
maintain an advantage, such as in administrative enforcement and information technology.[65]

More generally speaking, environmental law reform in both the US
and Europe has recently emphasized a broad concern with increasing the "flexibility" of regulation in order to reduce its economic costs,
increase its variability, and enhance innovation in solving problems.[66]

---

[65] According to the EPA, "nearly 7,000 businesses, trade associations, citizens groups, state
and local governments, and universities" participated in "EPA partnership programs" in 1998.
These include three programs in agriculture, one to improve indoor air quality, one to promote
water conservation, eight to promote energy efficiency and address global climate change,
three to promote pollution prevention technology, two to reduce waste, and three to promote
regulatory innovation (including Project XL). US EPA, Office for Reinvention, Partners for
the Environment (July 1998). Partners were set to increase to 13,000 in 40 different programs
in 2000. <www.epa.gov/partners/partnerships.html>, 3 March 2000. In compliance and
enforcement, the EPA has coordinated nine groups in the agriculture, automotive, chemicals,
paints, printing, printed wiring boards, metal finishing, and local government areas, all of
which have websites. US EPA, Office of Enforcement and Compliance Assistance, EPA
Compliance Assistance Centers (Fall 1998). For an argument that reform of US environmental
law should maintain its traditional emphasis on strong public and citizen enforcement,
see C. Rechtschaffen, "Deterrence vs. Cooperation and the Evolving Theory of Environmental
Enforcement" (1998) 71 S Cal L Rev 1181.

[66] See EPA, Reinventing Environmental Protection: 1998 Annual Report (1999), pp. 38–52
(emphasizing recent "more tailored, flexible approaches" to regulation); K. Deketelaere and H.
Somsen, "Conference Report: Flexible Environmental Regulation in the European Union"
(1998) 8 Eur Env L Rev 356 (reflecting on similar commitments in Europe).

Environmental contracts may be seen as one type of regulatory instrument that may be employed in different ways and at different levels as part of this general trend toward finding efficient and effective alternatives for particular kinds of environmental problems. As understanding grows of both the science of environmental problems and the strengths and weaknesses of different regulatory approaches, society may become more adept at designing environmental regulation to fit the problem—rather than forcing environmental problems that notoriously defy political and legal boundaries into preconceived regulatory boxes. Comparative continental experiences are likely to be mutually informative and helpful in this ongoing process of scientific and regulatory learning.[67]

One further substantive area of research suggested by the contributions in this book relates to nonprofit environmental organizations. Increasing experimentation with partnerships, voluntary agreements, and environmental contracts, as well as new information technology, will strongly influence the future role of nonprofit environmental organizations. From different perspectives within economics, the chapters in Part III agree that environmental contracts in general tend to decrease the relative influence of national nonprofit environmental organizations in favor of more local and community-based groups. This important conclusion merits further research both in theory and empirical research. One possible interpretation is that as environmental law grows to include other approaches in addition to traditional command-and-control regulation, the role of environmental groups will (or normatively should) also change. Economies of scale in research may favor the production of new scientific and social knowledge in nationally or internationally centralized organizations. A role for traditional large-scale regulatory lobbying will no doubt also remain, but criticism of centralized command-and-control regulation may partially undermine the argument for making large-scale lobbying and litigation the major or only reform strategy for an environmental organization. At least, the emerging importance of local environmental contracting—whether in the context of a Project XL facility proposal, an urban brownfield redevelopment, or a habitat conservation plan—suggests the need for vigorous development and involvement of local environmental and community organizations. Although this development may reduce the relative influence of large national environmental organizations, it may also present a possible opportunity to these organization to reorganize themselves to focus on growth at the grassroots, such as in local chapters. From an environmentalist perspective, this development may be positive in encouraging more people to become active in projects that encourage the appreciation of

---

[67] For a series of perspectives on the role of learning in environmental law, see D. Farber, "Environmental Protection as a Learning Experience" (1994) 27 Loyola LA L Rev 791; C.M. Rose, "Environmental Lessons" (1994) 27 Loyola LA L Rev 1023; R.H. Rosenberg, "Evolving Consensus: The Dynamic Future of Environmental Law and Policy" (1994) 27 Loyola LA L Rev 1049.

a sense of "place" within the natural environment.[68] Moreover, some of the
most intransigent kinds of environmental problems may demand a more
local approach. Without local participation of community groups and local
citizens, for example, it is difficult to see how problems such as nonpoint
source water pollution can be addressed.[69] Comparative lessons from experience both in the US, such as with the recent "riverkeeper" movement,[70]
and in Europe, such as with the idea of "river contracts," may provide the
raw material for the development of effective "watershed partnerships" in
the future.[71] In addition, the increasing use of habitat conservation plans
may indicate that local environmental contracts may be particularly appropriate for what has been called "ecosystem management."[72]

By no means have the chapters here exhausted the topic of environmental
contracts. Further comparative work between the US and Europe on a number of levels and with respect to a number of subjects is justified. The economic arguments about the comparative virtues (or vices) of environmental
contracts compared with other forms of regulation (or no regulation)
will also continue. We also believe that the chapters here collectively indicate that the regulatory innovation of environmental contracts deserves a
broader study in other places in the world and possible application to international environmental problems. Japan, for example, has had considerable
experience in the use of environmental agreements.[73] Broader comparative
studies are warranted in the future. On the international level, one of us has
already argued in a chapter of this book (by Hazard and Orts) that environmental contracts may provide particular benefits in the context of global

---

[68]   For an interesting reflection on the importance of a sense of "place" in the environment,
which leads to a sense of "bioregions" rather than politically defined states and nations, see
G. Snyder, *The Practice of the Wild* (North Point Press, San Francisco, 1990), pp. 25–44. See also
E.T. Freyfogle, *Bounded People, Boundless Lands: Envisioning a New Land Ethic* (Island Press,
Washington, 1998).
[69]   For an argument along these lines, see J. Schilling, "Localities as Special Forces" (1999) 16
Envtl Forum 30.
[70]   For an account of the relatively litigious "riverkeeper" movement in the US, which began
with a nonprofit group organized to police the Hudson River and now counts more than 20
different "keeper" groups for rivers, bays, and sounds, see J. Cronin and R.F. Kennedy, Jr., *The
Riverkeepers* (Simon & Schuster, New York, 1999).
[71]   A large number of citizens groups have been organized around watersheds in the US, and
the EPA promotes this activity through "Adopt a Watershed." See <www.epa.gov/adopt>,
3 March 2000. For a comprehensive account of US environmental law regarding watersheds,
see R.W. Adler, "Addressing Barriers to Watershed Protection" (1995) 25 Envtl L 973.
[72]   See J.O. Melious and R.D. Thornton, "Contractual Ecosystem Management under the
Endangered Species Act: Can Federal Agencies Make Enforceable Commitments?" (1999) 26
Ecology L Q 489. For general discussions of ecosystem management strategies for biodiversity
preservation, see T.P. Duane, "Community Participation in Ecosystem Management" (1997) 24
Ecology L Q 771; O.A. Houck, "On the Law of Biodiversity and Ecosystem Management"
(1997) 81 Minn L Rev 869; B.C. Karkkainen, "Biodiversity and Land" (1997) 83 Cornell L Rev 1.
For details on habitat conservation plans, see J.B. Ruhl, "How To Kill Endangered Species,
Legally: The Nuts and Bolts of Endangered Species Act 'HCP' Permits for Real Estate
Development" (1999) 5 Envtl L 345; S-L. Hsu, "The Potential and the Pitfalls of Habitat
Conservation Plans under the Endangered Species Act" (1999) 29 Envtl L Rep 10592. For HCP
case studies, see <www.ncedr.org/casestudies/hcp.html>, 5 March 2000.
[73]   See Rehbinder, supra note 20, at 151 (collecting sources).

environmental problems. (See also the discussion of international environmental agreements in the chapter by Segerson and Li.) Further research is also merited in this direction. For example, how might an approach using environmental contracts address such difficult problems as global climate change or the loss of biodiversity?

Finally, we think that the connections of environmental contracts to conceptions of democratic politics deserve future attention. Environmental contracting may help to provide one regulatory path toward what the French philosopher, Luc Ferry, calls a "democratic ecology."[74] Processes of deliberation and communication in policy making, though no doubt having costs and pitfalls as well, hold out at least the possibility of resolving some of the very tough problems that require balancing the interests of humanity with the closely related though not always identical interests of the natural environment.

At the Wharton impact conference in Philadelphia at which the chapters collected here were first presented, discussed, and debated, we invoked a quotation from another French philosopher on environmental issues. This passage serves as well for a conclusion of this introduction and a plea for future research in the same spirit. In a book appropriately called *The Natural Contract*, Michael Serres writes,

Solitude slides so quickly toward inventive delirium and error that the site of knowledge production is never a relation between an individual and his object, but rather one between a growing body of researchers checking on one another and a carved out specialty, defined and accepted by them.[75]

We hope that this book will contribute to this ongoing process with respect to the topic of environmental contracts and regulatory innovation.

---

[74] L. Ferry, *The New Ecological Order* (C. Volk, trans.) (University of Chicago, 1995), pp. 127–146.
[75] M. Serres, *The Natural Contract* (E. MacArthur and W. Paulson, trans.) (University of Michigan, 1995), pp. 20–21.

Part I
Environmental Contracts and Regulatory Innovation in the United States

2. Bargaining, Politics, and Law in Environmental Regulation

*Jon Cannon**

1 INTRODUCTION

Collaboration is in fashion at the US EPA. "Cooperation," "partnerships," "negotiation," and "collaborative efforts" have become watchwords for the EPA's reinvention of its regulatory programs.[1] These approaches all involve interest bargaining among the Agency and those who affect or who are affected by its decisions, and I will refer to them generally as "bargaining" or "bargaining approaches."

There has always been bargaining in the implementation of the federal environmental regulatory program, but it is now more pervasive, open, and respectable than ever. Bargaining approaches, it is argued, can lead to more sensible, less burdensome, and perhaps even environmentally more beneficial results, while dispelling the curse of adversarialism that hangs over the regulatory order. Not accidentally, this new emphasis on negotiation and accommodation accompanies the political devaluation of "command-and-control"

*My thanks to Elizabeth McGill, Richard Merrill, Daniel Esty, Jody Freeman, Bradley Karkkainen, E. Donald Elliott, Alan Eckert, and Richard Ossias for their very helpful comments on earlier drafts of this paper. My thanks also for the indefatigable research assistance of Meredith Miller and Caleb Jaffe.

[1] See, e.g., C. Browner, "Environmental Regulatory Reform" (1997) 15 Pace Envtl L Rev 45, 52–53 (embracing "partnership" approaches to achieve "more flexible, common sense, innovative and less burdensome" solutions to environmental problems); President's Council on Sustainable Development, *Sustainable America* (U.S. Government Printing Office, Washington, D.C., 1996), p. 7 (advancing as the Council's "most important finding[,]... the potential power of and growing desire for decision processes that promote direct and meaningful interaction involving people in decisions that affect them"); Enterprise for the Environment, *The Environmental Protection System in Transition: Toward a More Desirable Future* (CSIS Press, Washington, D.C., 1998), pp. 4, 49–50 (former EPA Administrator Ruckelshaus as project chairman) (recommending "collaborative problem solving and integrated policymaking by all branches and levels of government" and the creation of decision processes that meaningfully involve affected stakeholders and engage all citizens in protecting the environment); National Academy of Public Administration, *Resolving the Paradox of Environmental Protection: An Agenda for Congress, EPA, and the States* (Washington, D.C., 1997), pp. 20–25 [hereinafter NAPA].

regulation, which characterizes many of the statutory requirements that the EPA is charged to administer.[2]

Fruitful bargaining in environmental regulation (and perhaps in any regulation) may depend on the ability of an agency to press the bounds of its statutory authority. This is particularly so under the detailed command-and-control provisions of many environmental statutes. The EPA's ability to find flexibility in such tight legal structures creates assets in the hands of the Agency in negotiations with industry and environmental groups as well as its political overseers. The EPA can use these assets to reach bargains with those outside the agency that promote the Agency's environmental mission, reduce the costs or intrusiveness of environmental requirements, and increase acceptance of the Agency's programs. For reasons that I will discuss, the EPA has more of these assets than it has had in the past and therefore greater ability and inclination to undertake serious bargaining.

From sharply different perspectives, some critics celebrate regulatory reinvention,[3] others mourn it,[4] and still others are waiting to decide.[5] All seem focused, at least ultimately, on a normative assessment of what's happening. What I offer in this chapter are some descriptive claims about what is happening at the EPA, why it is happening now, and the limits on those phenomena. I rely on the bargaining construct—viewing the EPA as an interested party operating with a political framework—to help explain a set of agency actions. I describe changes in the political climate that, ironically, have freed the Agency to make more extensive use of bargaining; explore the Agency's use of its enhanced bargaining power; and attempt to define the effective limits of that power. I also evaluate concerns that might be raised about the legitimacy of the EPA's actions—an issue implicit in the tension between an agency's use of regulatory flexibility and traditional rule of law principles;[6] and I find traditional rule of law principles alone to be unpersuasive on this issue. Finally, I offer some observations on the immediate future of environmental law reform.

2   BARGAINING AT THE EPA

My analysis groups together a range of cooperative, collaborative, and other negotiating modes as interest bargaining,[7] although the dynamics of

---

[2] See, e.g., K. Werhan, "Delegalizing Administrative Law" (1996) 1996 U Ill L Rev 423, 424. Rena Steinzor defines "command and control rules" as those that "impose detailed, legally enforceable limits, conditions, and affirmative requirements on industrial operations, generally controlling sources that generate pollution on an individual basis. For example, air emissions of pollutants from each regulated source are limited to specified amounts, with the regulated entity further required to install a technology to meet those limitations and to monitor its emissions continuously." "Reinventing Environmental Regulation" (1998) 22 Harv Envtl L Rev 103, 104.

[3] See J. Freeman, "Collaborative Governance in the Administrative State" (1997) 45 UCLA L Rev 1.

[4] See Werhan, supra note 2.

[5] See D. Farber, "Taking Slippage Seriously" (1999) 23 Harv Envtl L Rev 297, 315–20.

[6] For a discussion of this tension, see M. Seidenfeld, "Bending the Rules: Flexible Regulation and Constraints on Agency Discretion" (1999) 51 Admin L Rev 429, 436 and n. 24.

[7] See G. Winter, "Bartering Rationality in Regulation" (1985) 19 L & Soc'y Rev 219.

bargaining may differ significantly among these modes. This broad reliance on interest bargaining as a tool for interpreting agency behavior might be subject to question. For example, Jody Freeman has disputed the adequacy of "interest representation theory" or "the vocabulary of pluralism" fully to explain what happens in successful collaborative efforts.[8] In exploring the potential of "collaborative governance," she observes that by sharing information, developing trust and adopting a problem solving orientation, parties can achieve creative solutions that were not previously considered.[9] Freeman focuses on processes in which parties have reconceptualized a problem or reinterpreted their own interests to reach a resolution. But even these processes, as she notes, also "involve bargaining and the pursuit of self-interest."[10] Collaborative undertakings "do not somehow free participants of the interests which they bring to the table."[11] Or as Susan Rose-Ackerman has put it, a "regulatory negotiation is not analogous to a therapy session or a friendly, disinterested discussion of policy options. ... [P]arties are bargaining under conditions in which their interests are, in part, opposed."[12]

I have chosen to use the lens of interest bargaining because of its descriptive power across a variety of negotiating contexts. It seems particularly helpful in interpreting the related phenomena that are this chapter's main subject: the EPA's current emphasis on stakeholder outreach, consultation, and negotiation; its appetite—in some venues—for adventurous interpretations of its statutes; and its resistance to amendments to its statutory authorities, even where the proffered amendments would reduce the legal risks in the Agency's chosen course of action.

In its bargaining mode, the Agency makes offers of certain treatment under its regulatory scheme in return for undertakings by others, and it does so in a way designed to maximize interests that are, at least in part, opposed to the interests of others in the negotiation. This behavior departs overtly from a traditional view of agency decisionmaking, in which, from a stance of neutrality, the agency makes decisions based on the information before it, its statutory mandate, and (to the extent it has discretion) its expert view of where lies the public interest.[13] The Agency instead is "understood less as an authoritative decisionmaker and more as one among many participants in the formulation and implementation of public policy."[14] More specifically, by placing itself in a bargaining relationship, the Agency signals that it may have something to gain from the interchange and has therefore put its distinct interests at issue.

---

[8] Freeman, supra note 3, at 5.
[9] Ibid., at 18–33. See also E. Weber, *Pluralism by the Rules: Conflict and Cooperation in Environmental Regulation* (Georgetown University Press, 1998), p. 11.
[10] Freeman, supra note 3, at 71–72.
[11] NAPA, supra note 1, at 112.
[12] S. Rose-Ackerman, "Consensus vs. Incentives: A Skeptical Look at Regulatory Negotiation" (1994) 43 Duke L J 1206, 1209–10.
[13] Rational choice theorists might argue that the Agency is, in fact, always acting in its own interest.
[14] Werhan, supra note 2, at 424.

The interests of the Agency, in its bargaining mode, are often at stake in complex ways. Negotiations may be carried out not just with parties immediately involved; typically, in fact, the EPA is also bargaining, implicitly or explicitly, with its political overseers in the White House and in Congress, with the states (its co-implementers), and with various constituencies outside of government.

Agency bargaining in its regulatory programs is not new.[15] Dan Farber recently concluded that bargaining among government agencies, environmentalists and regulated entities has been pervasive in environmental regulation and has inevitably involved "slippage"—divergence from strict adherence to statutory mandates or "compliance."[16] At the same time, he acknowledges that the Clinton Administration has shown a particular appetite for "renegotiating regulatory standards"[17] and engaging in "affirmative slippage"—varying from existing standards in ways designed to produce environmental benefits.[18] The remainder of this paper examines why this is so and what it may mean for the legitimacy and future direction of environmental programs.

3   THE AGENCY'S INTERESTS

If interest bargaining is key to understanding the Agency's behavior, it becomes important to understand what the Agency's interests are. Although the Agency's interests are many (and capable of diverse characterizations), two seem dominant in the Agency's regulatory role. Both are "policy-maximizing" interests.[19]

The first is the Agency's interest in making (and being seen as responsible for making) environmental gains. It is no accident that all EPA Administrators but one in both Republican and Democratic Administrations have identified themselves or invited themselves to be identified with a pro-environmentalist agenda—from Bill Ruckelshaus, "Mr. Clean," forward.

---

[15]   For the historic role of bargaining in regulatory programs, see Winter, supra note 7 at 230–232.

[16]   Farber, supra note 5, at 315.

[17]   Ibid., at 307.

[18]   Ibid., at 318.

[19]   The early literature suggested budget maximization as the key interest of agency officials. See W. Niskanen, *Bureaucracy and Representative Government* (Aldine-Atherton, Chicago, 1971). More recent accounts, in focusing on the policy-making process, have "depict[ed] agencies as 'policy maximizers' rather than 'resource maximizers.'" D. Spence, "Administrative Law and Agency Policy-Making: Rethinking the Positive Theory of Political Control" (1997) 14 Yale J on Reg. 407, 415. I focus on "policy maximizing" interests here. But these interests are not unrelated to budgetary considerations. The Agency's commitment to its environmental mission may drive its interest in adequate funding as well as "good" policymaking. See K. Shepsle and M. Bonchek, *Analyzing Politics: Rationality, Behavior, and Institutions* (W.W. Norton and Co., New York, 1997), pp. 347–348. Also, the Agency's success in maintaining control of its regulatory agenda may consist in part in avoiding vindictive budgetary cuts.

The one exception is Ann Burford, who was perceived to have an anti-environmentalist bias and who was forced to leave the Agency.[20] (I am distinguishing the orientation of EPA Administrators from the perceived orientation of their administrations; Burford aside, the policy preferences of EPA Administrators in Republican administrations have been "consistently to the left of the President's.")[21] The public expects that the Agency's leadership will be identified with its mission, and has reacted poorly when that seemed not to be the case.

The relatively pro-environment leanings of the Agency's leadership are supported by—perhaps, in part, driven by—the shared values of the EPA staff. Most EPA employees are attracted by the Agency's mission and are sympathetic to it;[22] thus, an environmental ethic is part of the culture of the Agency.

The second dominant interest qualifies, and contains, the first. This is the Agency's interest in not being overruled by its overseers in the White House, in Congress, or in the courts. I will characterize it generally as the EPA's interest in maintaining control of its agenda—of protecting its prerogatives on issues within its purview.

This interest in keeping control drives the EPA in two related ways. First, it pushes the Agency to consult widely with constituent groups and to make deals that meet or assuage the concerns of those groups. The EPA does this in order to maximize satisfaction or at least minimize discontent among constituent groups, and the public more broadly, in order to prevent that discontent from triggering overruling actions by the White House and Congress. Second, the EPA's interest in keeping control, combined with Congress' and the White House's interests in political oversight (i.e., their competing control interests), drives the Agency In a complex dance with the its two political overseers. On issues likely to attract attention from Congress or the White House, the EPA must assess whether it might be vulnerable to reversal or having its authority curtailed and, where it is vulnerable, it must decide whether to adjust its behavior to avoid or minimize the risk.[23]

The EPA's third institutional overseer, the federal judiciary, also impacts its behavior, although not always in ways one might expect. In recent years, a third to a half of the Agency's significant national rules have been challenged in court.[24] A significant portion of these challenges have been

---

[20] See, e.g., Seidenfeld, supra note 6, at 475 and nn. 188–190; Spence, supra note 19, at 431.

[21] Spence, supra note 19, at 431.

[22] See ibid., at 424 and sources cited therein.

[23] In commenting on regulatory reforms he undertook as EPA Administrator in response to mounting political criticism in the late 1970s, Douglas Costle stated that "the agency 'wanted to be out in front in this situation in order to control its own destiny.'" R. Harris and S. Milkis, *The Politics of Regulatory Change: A Tale of Two Agencies* (Oxford University Press, 1989), pp. 250–251.

[24] See C. Coglianese, "Assessing Consensus: The Promise and Performance of Negotiated Rulemaking" (1997) 46 Duke L J 1255, 1299-1300 (finding that for the 1989–1991 time period, about 35 percent of significant nationally applicable rules under the Clean Air Act and the Resource Conservation and Recovery Act were challenged); Memorandum from M. Goo, Attorney, Office of General Counsel, EPA, to J. Cannon, General Counsel, EPA 4 (23 April 1996) (finding that 47 percent of significant nationally applicable rules promulgated by EPA between November 1993 and November 1995 were challenged in court).

settled; in the cases that have gone to decision in the U.S. Court of Appeals for the D.C. Circuit, where many of its rules are reviewed, the Agency typically has received fully favorable decisions in only about half, although affirmance rates have varied.[25] Nevertheless, on issues with high political visibility, the prospect (or even the high probability) of an adverse judicial ruling may have less effect on Agency decisionmaking than signals from the White House or Congress. First, the ability of the White House or Congress to inflict harm on the Agency is likely to be greater than that of the courts. The courts cannot fire or humiliate the Agency's leadership, curtail its authorities, or cut its budget.[26] Second, the Agency may be able to postpone or avoid judicial review. Even if review cannot ultimately be put off, by the time the courts have opined, the bargain that the EPA has struck (or the offer it has extended) may be so widely relied upon, congressional override of an adverse court ruling might be quite likely. This is not to minimize the importance of judicial review;[27] it is simply to note what is already widely understood—that there are circumstances in which the Agency will pursue options with relatively high risk of judicial reversal for reasons that are perfectly consistent with its interests.

4   POLITICAL CONTEXT

Politics bears significantly on the Agency's ability to engage in regulatory bargaining as well as on the directions taken by the Agency in its negotiations. Each negotiation has its own political mini-environment, but features of the macro-environment are also important to understanding the Agency's behavior.

4.1   A Very Short Political History of the EPA through 1994

The EPA is almost thirty. The major regulatory statutes under which it operates were enacted in the first ten years of its existence, although they have continued to be debated and revised.[28] Almost from the outset, EPA's administration of these statutes was the subject of competition between the

---

[25]   See "Materials prepared for J. Cannon, General Counsel, EPA, for speech to District of Columbia Bar Association" (February 1997) fig. 3 (on file with author); Coglianese, supra note 24, at 1309 n. 249 (D.C. Circuit entirely affirmed 51 percent of EPA rulemaking cases adjudicated between 1979 and 1990).

[26]   See, e.g., M. McCubbins, et al., "Administrative Procedures as Instruments of Judicial Control" (1987) 3 J L Econ and Org 243, 249–50.

[27]   For further discussion of the indirect as well as direct constraints on Agency bargaining stemming from judicial review, see infra text accompanying notes 154–176.

[28]   See R. Percival, et al., Environmental Regulation: Law, Science and Policy (2nd edn, Little, Brown & Co., Boston, 1996), pp. 106–108 (providing a statutory chronology).

White House and Congress for control of the environmental agenda.[29] Generally, the White House's Office of Management and Budget, which is charged with oversight of federal agencies' regulatory activity, has been preoccupied with preventing dominance of Agency policymaking by environmentalists and EPA's staff sympathetic to their point of view. Dominant forces in past Congresses have suspected the Agency's capture by economic interests, and have fought to limit OMB influence over the Agency's policy.[30]

One strategy used by Congress in this battle has been successive tightenings of EPA statutes, with provisions for citizen enforcement, in an effort to ensure that the laws would be implemented and enforced precisely as Congress intended. Reauthorizations of major environmental laws from 1977 to 1990, as Richard Lazarus has observed, "all exhibit the same trend. Each eliminated substantial EPA discretion, imposed more deadlines, and included more prescription."[31] This trend culminated with the passage in 1990 of the 700-page Clean Air Act Amendments, which stand as an imposing monument to the regulatory state—"one of the most complex pieces of regulatory legislation … ever adopted, and one of the most impenetrable."[32] The fundamental purpose of all these reauthorizations was "to minimize the possibility of bureaucratic neglect and compromise and of agency capture by regulated industry."[33]

In addition to increasingly prescriptive statutory mandates, the Agency's history has also been marked by intense oversight by both its political principals, Congress and the White House. "Beating up on EPA" is a tradition on the Hill.[34] The Agency is within the jurisdiction of some ninety congressional committees and subcommittees.[35] Agency officials appear in hearings before those committees and subcommittees dozens of times during each Congress, in addition to responding to extensive requests for documents, submitting congressionally mandated reports, and attending informal meetings with members or congressional staff.[36] The hearings have often been used to subdue and correct Agency officials. Until the transfer of power to a new Republican majority in 1994, "[v]eteran subcommittee leaders tended to view [environmental laws] as *their* laws, and were not shy about explaining to administrators what they meant."[37]

---

[29]   See R. Lazarus, "The Tragedy of Distrust in the Implementation of Federal Environmental Law" (1991) 54 J L and Contemp Probs 311, 348 [hereinafter Lazarus, "Tragedy"].

[30]   See ibid., at 337.

[31]   Ibid., at 340–341. See also Steinzor, supra note 2, at 106.

[32]   H. Nickel, "Now the Race to Regulate" [January–February 1991] Envtl F 18–22.

[33]   Lazarus, "Tragedy" supra note 29, at 320.

[34]   J. Mashaw, *Greed, Chaos and Governance: Using Public Choice to Improve Public Law* (Yale University Press, 1997) p. 184.

[35]   See S. Rep. No. 101-262, at 27 (1990).

[36]   See R. Lazarus, "The Neglected Question of Congressional Oversight of EPA: Quis Custodiet Ipsos Custodes (Who Shall Watch the Watchers Themselves)?" (1991) 54 J L and Contemp Probs 203, 212.

[37]   R.S. Melnick, "Strange Bedfellows Make Normal Politics" (1999) 9 Duke Envtl L and Pol'y F 75, 85.

White House oversight has focused on ensuring that the Agency policy reflects adequate attention to efficiency, cost-effectiveness, and ease of implementation. Often in the first two decades of the environmental era, the EPA struggled with the White House to realize its environmental mission. This struggle was typically less observable than oversight hearings on the Hill, whose purposes could include public chastisement, but it was none-theless vigorous. Although the influence of Congress and the White House can be overstated,[38] their involvement in the Agency's business has been pervasive and intense, and for most of the Agency's history, it has come from competing points of view.

Historically, this intense oversight, coming as it has from all sides, encouraged caution by the Agency in interpreting its statutory authorities. In addition to positioning the Agency to defend challenges in court (often brought by environmental groups), strict adherence to statutory directives could protect the Agency against attacks from the Hill that it was violating its duty to follow the law, as Congress wrote it. It could also provide the Agency a credible defense against charges that its actions lacked common sense and a platform for resisting efforts by the White House to weaken its environmental programs: "The law gives us no choice." For these reasons, allegiance to the "rule of law"—at least at the policy level—served the Agency during much of its history and became a significant part of the cul-ture of the Agency. This inhibited the EPA's appetite for regulatory bargain-ing with either industry or environmental groups, where bargaining could be characterized as exceeding the Agency's authorities. Increased statutory prescriptiveness, sometimes withering oversight, and controversy tended to force the Agency into a defensive posture, discouraging flexibility and inno-vation in its regulatory programs.[39] This occurred despite recognition by the Agency's leadership of the desirability of collaborative approaches and alternatives to command-and-control regulation.[40]

A fitting coda to this era of EPA history, as well as perhaps a foreshadow-ing of things to come, was the Amoco Yorktown project. In 1989, Amoco invited the EPA to visit the company's Yorktown, Virginia refinery to wit-ness how poorly the Agency's regulations were working in practice.[41] Project investigators found that the EPA's single-media regulations were less cost-effective than a plant-wide, multi-media approach that would allow the facility to reallocate requirements to achieve the same overall level of environmental protection.[42] In following EPA's regulations, Amoco was reducing airborne hydrocarbon emissions by 7,300 tons per year, at a

---

[38] See Spence, supra note 19, at 421.
[39] See Lazarus, "Tragedy" supra note 29, at 359.
[40] See Weber, supra note 9, at 59–60.
[41] See P. Howard, *The Death of Common Sense: How Law is Suffocating America* (Random House, New York, 1994), p. 7.
[42] See B. Mank, "The Environmental Protection Agency's Project XL and Other Regulatory Reform Initiatives: The Need for Legislation Authorization" (1998) 25 Ecology L Q 1, 12; R. Stewart, "Environmental Quality as a National Good in a Federal State" (1997) 1997 U Chi Legal F 199, 223.

cost of $2,400 per ton.[43] A more flexible approach would have allowed Amoco to reduce hydrocarbon emissions and hazardous waste by 7,500 tons per year, at $500 per ton.[44] The project came to a close amid concerns that the EPA did "not have the statutory flexibility to support alternatives developed through the assessment,"[45] and the recommendations of the report for innovative regulatory approaches were never implemented. But the unrealized Yorktown venture represented an opportunity that the Agency, in a changed political environment, could seize to its advantage.

4.2 Upheavals, 1994 to the Present

The political forces that have defined the EPA's operating environment were radically realigned in 1994. The process of realignment actually began in 1992, when the first Democratic Administration in over a decade came into power with a Vice President who was an avowed environmentalist. Although committed to environmental quality, the new Administration was also sensitive to growing criticisms of government bureaucracies (including, perhaps especially, the EPA) as inefficient, burdensome, and unresponsive. The National Performance Review, begun soon after the new Administration took office, under the Vice President's direction, was designed to address those concerns, and it featured a push for administrative reforms of regulation. Despite these and other efforts by the Administration to capitalize on reform sentiments, the Republicans captured both the Senate and the House of Representatives in 1994.

The new Republican majority came armed with the Contract with America, which contained provisions aimed at improving the efficiency and cost-effectiveness of regulations and protecting property rights and the procedural rights of regulated entities.[46] It was construed by environmental groups, EPA, and the Administration as a frontal assault on the existing environmental regulatory regime. At its core, the challenge went to the standards by which decisions are to be made under these laws and the level of environmental protection afforded; its aim was to make economic cost-benefit justification a touchstone of EPA decision-making, moderating standards that make human health and environmental concerns controlling.[47]

---

[43]   See National Academy of Public Administration, Setting Priorities, Getting Results: A New Direction for EPA (Washington, D.C., 1993), p. 98.

[44]   See ibid.

[45]   Ibid., see Stewart, supra note 42, at 223.

[46]   See H.R. 9, 104th Cong. (1995) (particularly Titles I–IV, passed by House of Representatives).

[47]   See H.R. 9 § 422 (requiring EPA to certify that incremental benefits of new EPA rules "will be likely to justify the rules" incremental costs and that other approaches would be either less cost-effective or would provide less flexibility; providing that these new decisional criteria would "supersede the decision criteria for rulemaking otherwise applicable under the statute pursuant to which the rule is promulgated"); H.R. 9 § 441 (providing for judicial review to assure Agency compliance with these requirements).

In the end, this attempt at broad scale revision of the environmental laws collapsed. Landy and Dell have ascribed the failure of regulatory reform legislation to Presidential politics and in particular to Senator Dole's desire to win the Republican presidential nomination against conservative rivals.[48] But the underlying circumstance of its failure was overwhelming public support of strong federal environmental controls.[49] Fueled in part by the EPA's and the White House's characterization of the Contract's environmental provisions as "rollback" of environmental protections, public sentiment against the reforms persuaded the Republican majority to abandon the cause.[50] The consensus support for strong environmental controls that had underwritten two decades of growth in the federal regulatory apparatus held, at least for the time being.

Nevertheless, there remained, underneath the general support for environmental standards, a strong countercurrent of public resentment at the intrusiveness, rigidity, and costliness of the implementing machinery— resentment perceived by the White House as well by Congress. That countercurrent may simply represent what Lazarus has diagnosed as the public's schizophrenia in regard to environmental programs—widely shared aspirations for environmental quality coupled with resistance to implementing programs, particularly those that impose perceptible costs.[51] In any event, it represents a continuing exposure to the EPA's programs, particularly the more prescriptive and costly ones, such as the Clean Air Act.[52] Having abandoned its frontal assault, Congress has chipped away at

---

[48]   M. Landy and K. Dell, "The Failure of Risk Reform Legislation in the 104th Congress" (1998) 9 Duke Envtl L and Pol'y F 113, 121–123; see also J. Graham, "Legislative Approaches to Achieving More Protection Against Risk at Less Cost" (1997) 1997 U Chi Legal F 13, 57.

[49]   See Landy and Dell, supra note 48, at 125 nn. 62–64; R. Percival, "Regulatory Evolution and the Future of Environmental Policy" (1997) 1997 U Chi Legal F 159, 167–171.

[50]   See J. Cushman, Jr. "GOP Backing Off From Tough Stand Over Environment"; [26 January 1996] N.Y. Times A-1; P. Roberts, "A Green Coup?" [20 November 1995] New Republic 25. For the views of key congressional staff on the regulatory reform debate, see K. McSlarrow, "Senate Perspectives on Regulatory Reform Legislation" (1996) 48 Admin L Rev 328; N. Kenkeremath, "Legislative Efforts Concerning Risk Assessment and Cost-Benefit Analysis for New Regulations" (1996) 48 Admin L Rev 321, 325–326.

The 104th Congress did produce a series of less intrusive "regulatory reform" measures, including the Unfunded Mandates Reform Act of 1995, Pub. L. No. 104-4, 109 Stat. 48, the Paperwork Reduction Act of 1995, Pub. L. No. 104-13, 109 Stat. 163, and The Small Business Regulatory Enforcement Fairness Act of 1996, Pub. L. No. 104-121, 110 Stat. 857. The implementation of these statutes is discussed in M. Romine, "Politics, the Environment, and Regulatory Reform at the Environmental Protection Agency" (1999) 6 Envtl Lawyer 1. Also, as the 1996 congressional elections approached, Congress enacted two pieces of bipartisan environmental legislation that included both reform features and increased environmental safeguards—the Safe Drinking Water Act Amendments of 1996, Pub. L. No. 104-182, 110 Stat. 1613, and the Food Quality Protection Act of 1996, Pub. L. No. 104-170, 110 Stat. 1489.

[51]   See Lazarus, "Tragedy" supra note 29, at 314.

[52]   For example, the Agency expressly declined to implement the Employee Trip Reduction requirement of the 1990 Clean Air Act Amendments in order avoid threatened revisions of the Act by Congress. This strategic retreat is credited with holding off significant revisions of the Act. See C. Oren, "Getting Commuters Out of their Cars: What Went Wrong?" (1998) 17 Stan Envtl L J 141, 145; Farber, supra note 5, at 301–303 (discussing "negative slippage" in the form of non-implementation of mandates that would have politically unacceptable consequences).

specific requirements in appropriations riders and attachments to other leg-islation and is generally seen as poised to do more, if it can without serious political cost.

Ironic as it may seem, the Republican Congress with its reform agenda has, in a sense, liberated the EPA. Although it must be concerned that Congress may curtail its authorities, the Agency's successful showdown with Congress in 1995–1996 has made Congress reluctant to make signifi-cant changes in environmental statutes without the EPA's concurrence (lest it be accused again of rollback). At the same time, the Republican majority's indifference (if not hostility to) to the EPA's statutory mandates creates assets in the hands of the Agency. These assets are in the form of increased latitude to relax or modify specific regulatory requirements, which the Agency can offer in return for support of its pursuit of larger environmental goals. The Agency has used these assets in its collaborative reinvention pro-grams, discussed below, which are designed at least in part to insulate the Agency from further congressional interference as well as to honor White House reinvention commitments and diffuse criticism of its programs gen-erally; but the Agency has also used these new assets to advantage in important settings outside of "reinvention." By finding flexibility where its statutes have previously been interpreted to provide none, and where before the political climate in any event would not have tolerated flexibility, the Agency can not only protect itself from Congressional intrusions but can also aggressively bargain with others to advance its environmental agenda.

It is this intriguing irony of the present situation that I will explore in the two examples that follow. They both involve trading off technology-based pollution control requirements against undertakings designed to achieve enhanced environmental quality. Technology-based requirements typically require emissions controls for particular pieces of equipment or opera-ting units at a facility based on the expected performance of pollution control equipment; these requirements are classic "command-and-control" regulation.

5   TWO CASES

5.1   Project XL

The EPA's flagship reinvention initiative was Project XL (for "Excellence in Leadership"), which was unveiled in the first part of 1995 along with a number of other initiatives.[53] The project invited industries and communities to come forward with projects that could achieve "superior environmental results" and reduce burdens on regulated entities if the EPA would relax or waive specific regulatory requirements.[54] The project was

---

[53]   See Regulatory Reinvention (XL) Projects, 60 Fed. Reg. 27,282 (1995) (announcing "Solicita-tion of Proposals and Request for Comment").
[54]   Ibid., at 27,287.

announced by President Clinton himself, who mentioned "throw[ing] out the EPA rulebook" in pursuit of common sense solutions to environmental problems.[55] The Agency's statutes have no general variance authority,[56] and many commentators have argued the lack of legal authority for the XL program.[57]

The Agency's official position has been that it can carry out XL within the scope of its existing authorities.[58] In the widely quoted assessment of an anonymous EPA staffer, however—and you can see why anonymity would be preferred here—"If it isn't illegal, it isn't XL."[59] Although that sound-bite is itself a caricature, in a number of XL projects the Agency has stretched the limits of its authority, as one of the first successful XL projects—Merck's Stonewall facility—demonstrates.

Merck's Stonewall plant is a pharmaceutical facility near Elkton, Virginia, not far from the Shenandoah National Park.[60] The company proposed voluntarily to convert Stonewall's steam-generating powerhouse from coal to natural gas.[61] The area around Stonewall meets the air quality standards for all "criteria pollutants" (CO, ozone, particulates (PM10), lead, SO_2, NO_x) and is thus designated an attainment area. Under the Clean Air Act, the boiler conversion, as a "major modification," was subject to Prevention of Significant Deterioration (PSD) review,[62] with its associated requirement of Best Available Control Technology (BACT), and New Source Performance Standards (NSPS).[63]

The conversion would "result in an up-front estimated reduction of over 900 [tons per year] of actual criteria air pollutants, primarily SO_2 and NO_x emissions."[64] The company offered to undertake this conversion, with its attendant environmental benefits, in return for increased operating flexibility, including the freedom to make unilateral changes in operations that would otherwise be subject to further PSD permitting and technology-based pollution control requirements. The company was particularly interested

---

[55] "Remarks on Regulatory Reform in Arlington, Va." (26 March 1995) 31 Weekly Comp Pres Doc 426.

[56] But see D. Hirsch, "Bill and Al's XL-ent Adventure: An Analysis of the EPA's Legal Authority to Implement the Clinton Administration's Project XL" (1998) U Ill L Rev 129, 164–172 (arguing for use of an "implied waiver" theory for Project XL).

[57] See Mank, supra note 42; R. Steinzor, "Regulatory Reinvention and Project XL: Does the Emperor Have Any Clothes?" (1996) 26 Envtl L Rep 10,527 [hereinafter Steinzor, "Emperor's Clothes"]; Hirsch, supra note 56.

[58] See "Status of Recommendations Made by the National Academy of Public Administration on Reforming the Environmental Protection Agency: Hearings Before a Subcomm. of the Senate Comm on Appropriations," 104th Cong. 113 (1996) (statement of F. Hansen, Deputy Administrator, EPA).

[59] Steinzor, "Emperor's Clothes" supra note 57, at 10,527 (citing "What's Up with Project XL: Project XL Update" (11 March 1996)).

[60] See Project XL Site-Specific Rule-Making for Merck & Co., Inc. Stonewall Plant, 62 Fed. Reg. 15,304, 15,305 (1997) (notice of proposed rule-making) [hereinafter Merck Proposed Rule].

[61] See ibid., at 15,306.

[62] 42 U.S.C. § 7475.

[63] 42 U.S.C. § 7411.

[64] Merck Proposed Rule, supra note 60, at 15,306.

in avoiding BACT and NSPS requirements for future modifications or new installations at the plant.[65]

After months of negotiations involving the EPA, the Department of Interior (representing the interests of the Park), the Virginia Department of Environmental Quality, and community representatives, a bargain was struck in a Final Project Agreement.[66] The agreement is codified in a "site specific rule" for the Merck plant and a PSD permit which has been issued by the Virginia Department of Environmental Quality in accordance with the rule.[67]

In return for agreeing to install the new boiler and to reduce its overall emissions below its historic emission levels, the facility is granted the ability to balance emissions increases and decreases among various criteria pollutants—SO_2, ozone (volatile organic carbons (VOCs) as indicator pollutant), NO_x, CO and PM10—without triggering further PSD review. After installation of the new boiler, total emissions of these pollutants will be capped at 1200 tons per year (TPY), 300 TPY below the levels reflecting the Stonewall plant's recent actual emissions.[68] The facility will also be subject to separate pollutant-specific caps ("subcaps") for NO_x, SO_2 and PM10 emissions; these "subcaps will keep SO_2 and NO_x emissions below recent actual emission levels and PM10 emissions will not significantly increase above the recent actual emissions level."[69] There are no subcaps, however, for CO or VOC emissions.

Thus, if Merck significantly reduces its emissions of NO_x, SO_2 or PM10, it will be able to significantly increase its emissions of CO or VOCs within the total emissions cap; in fact, significant future increases in VOC emissions due to production changes are contemplated by the agreement with Merck. These increases will not be subject to further PSD review, as they would be under otherwise applicable regulations.[70] They will also not be subject to the requirements of BACT that apply to sources subject to PSD review, as those requirements have been traditionally understood.[71] For future new installations or process changes involving significant increases in VOCs (or CO), BACT in the peculiar circumstances of the Merck facility will demand only "good environmental engineering practice."[72]

---

[65] Telephone interview with M. Kiss, Department of Environmental Quality, Commonwealth of Virginia (August 1999). Flexibility may be particularly important in the pharmaceutical industry that requires the ability to make rapid and frequent process changes (in order to change product lines). See Hirsch, supra note 56, at 144.

[66] Merck & Co., Inc. Stonewall Plant, Project XL Final Project Agreement, Executive Summary, 16 January 1997, <http://www.epa.gov/ProjectXL/merck/011697.htm>, last updated 9 December 1999.

[67] Project XL Site-Specific Rulemaking for Merck & Co., Inc. Stonewall Plant, 62 Fed. Reg. 52,622 (1997) (announcing concise statement of basis and purpose "Final Rule") [hereinafter Merck Final Rule].

[68] Ibid., at 52,626.

[69] Ibid., at 52,624.

[70] "The statutory PSD requirements for the VOC and CO emission increases that are possible under the total emissions cap will be satisfied pursuant to this site-specific rule and the PSD permit." Ibid.

[71] See 42 U.S.C. § 7475(a)(4).

[72] Merck Final Rule, supra note 67, at 52,639.

The site-specific rule also creates for Merck's facility "alternative means of compliance" with the New Source Performance Standards that are currently or potentially applicable to new or modified sources within the facility.[73] Alternative compliance allows the facility to comply with the NSPS for volatile organic storage vessels (Subpart Kb) or other NSPS that become applicable in the future "by reducing its site-wide emissions caps."[74] Thus, Merck will be able to comply with NSPS that become applicable to sources within the Stonewall plant by obtaining offsetting emissions elsewhere in the plant or simply by drawing down on its emissions reserves under the site-wide cap. For volatile organic storage vessels, this option is unconditional; for other types of sources, the EPA retains the ability, under the site-specific rule, to require compliance with the NSPS if "necessary for achieving the objectives of the regulation."[75]

In its proposal for the site-specific rule, the EPA "acknowledge[d] that the BACT provisions, as well as other provisions, of the proposed rule and the draft permit, are in some ways in conflict with existing Agency guidance and interpretations of the Act."[76] A brief examination of the Agency's established interpretations of BACT and NSPS requirements reveals the extent to which this is true, and raises in obvious ways the issue of whether the Merck rule accords with the statute. For major new stationary sources and major modifications of stationary sources in attainment areas, the Clean Air Act and EPA rules require application of "the best available control technology for each [regulated] pollutant."[77] Best available control technology is defined by statute as "the maximum degree of reduction of each [regulated] pollutant ... emitted from or which results from any major emitting facility, which the permitting authority, on a case-by case basis, ... determines is achievable for such facility through application of production processes and available methods, systems, and techniques ... for control of each such pollutant."[78] BACT must also be no less stringent than any NSPS applicable to the source.

In its PSD regulations, the EPA states that BACT applies to "each pollutant" that will be emitted in significant amounts (new source) or in significantly increased amounts (modified source).[79] It also states that BACT applies to the "unit" which is responsible for the increased emissions.[80] The permitting authority is to select the pollution control option that offers "the lowest emissions level" for that "unit"—unless the applicant can show that

---

[73] Ibid., at 52,625.
[74] Ibid., Merck Proposed Rule, supra note 60, at 15,314.
[75] Ibid., at 52,641. See 60 C.F.R. § 60.1(d)(3).
[76] Merck Proposed Rule, supra note 60, at 15,312.
[77] 42 U.S.C. §§ 7475, 7479. See 40 C.F.R. § 52.21(j)(2)–(3).
[78] 42 U.S.C. § 7479 (3).
[79] 40 C.F.R. § 52.21(j)(2)–(3).
[80] 40 C.F.R. § 52.21(j)(3). See EPA, *Draft New Source Review Workshop Manual: Prevention of Significant Deterioration and Nonattainment Area Permitting* (EPA, Office of Air Quality Planning and Standards, TTN-Web, Washington, D.C., October 1990), p. B4 [hereinafter 1990 Draft Manual] ("The BACT requirement applies to each individual new or modified affected emissions unit and pollutant emitting activity at which a net emissions increase would occur").

economic costs, adverse environmental impacts from the pollution controls or energy impacts warrant a less stringent option.[81]

In determining to equate BACT with "good environmental engineering practice" for the Merck facility, the EPA noted "the significant environmental benefits from the [voluntary] powerhouse conversion and site-wide emissions caps."[82] These benefits include the gross emissions caps and the subcaps on specific pollutants other than CO and VOCs. Thus, as regards future significant emissions increases from units emitting VOCs, the Agency justifies good environmental engineering as BACT by reference to controls that may apply to other pollutants or to other units elsewhere in the plant. The question is whether this justification meets the statutory definition of BACT for "each" pollutant and "each" source covered by the requirement.

"Good environmental engineering practice" is not defined in the site-specific rule or in the PSD permit. The permit offers a list of examples of good environmental engineering practice for the batch pharmaceutical industry but the list by its terms is not limiting.[83] The determination of what may amount to "good environmental engineering practice" will be made by Merck in its implementation of the PSD permit, not by a permitting official as in the case of traditional PSD review. Thus, in striking a bargain that everyone might agree is more sensible for Merck and better for the environment, the EPA has retained BACT only in vestigial form, having largely dealt away the substance.

Similar questions are raised by EPA's interpretation of technology-based NSPS requirements. The EPA has promulgated New Source Performance Standards for categories of sources; these standards apply uniformly within each category or subcategory for which they have been set. NSPS apply to at least two types of sources at the Merck plant and apply potentially to others that may be built or modified at the facility.[84]

Under the statute, NSPS apply to "new stationary sources," which are sources for which construction or modification has commenced after a certain date; they are "a standard for emissions of air pollutants which reflects the degree of emission limitation achievable through the application of the best system of emission reduction which ... the Administrator determines has been adequately demonstrated."[85] As in the case of BACT, EPA regulations have interpreted NSPS to require reductions by the particular piece of equipment (the "affected facility") whose construction or modification triggers the application of the standard.[86] This interpretation was mandated by the D.C. Circuit Court of Appeals in *Asarco, Inc. v. EPA*,[87] which rejected the

---

[81] 1990 Draft Manual, supra note 80, at B25–B28.
[82] Merck Proposed Rule, supra note 60, at 15,311.
[83] See Prevention of Significant Deterioration Permit and Stationary Source Permit to Modify and Operate the Merck Stonewall Plant, § 1.3.2.c (10 February 1998).
[84] Merck Proposed Rule, supra note 60, at 15,314.
[85] 42 U.S.C. § 7411(a)(1).
[86] See, e.g., 40 C.F.R. § 60.40b(a).
[87] 578 F.2d 319 (1978).

Agency's efforts to "bubble" between new and existing units ("facilities" in the court's nomenclature) in determining the applicability of NSPS. Under the EPA rule that was before the court in that case, NSPS would not have applied where emissions increases from modified units were offset by decreases at other units in a plant.[88] The court held that such netting of emissions between new and existing units could not be reconciled with the language and intent of the NSPS provisions.[89]

In the Merck rule, by allowing alternative compliance with NSPS by reductions at sources other than those specified in the standards (i.e., at "existing" as well as "new" sources), the Agency has pushed past the interpretation of the statute in *Asarco*. The Agency has also taken the further step of allowing NSPS to be met by reductions in pollutants other than those specified in the standards (e.g., reductions in SO_2 to compensate for increases in VOC emissions that might be the subject of an NSPS). The Agency does not explain how the applications in Merck can be reconciled with the statutory provisions for limitations on emissions of air pollutants specified in "standards of performance" for "new sources." It simply states that the Agency's "decision to make [them] available at this facility is linked to the full set of the facility's obligations in this project."[90]

The point here is not whether the Agency would or would not be sustained in judicial review on these points. The issues will likely never to be litigated, at least directly, because the periods for review of the site specific rule and the PSD permit have expired, and no review has been sought. The point is the extent to which, in a bold reinterpretation of its authorities, the Agency has pushed beyond the politically conditioned restraint of the past in order to reach a "cleaner, cheaper, smarter" bargain.

Here, as in Project XL generally, the EPA has used the slack created by strong deregulatory currents on Capitol Hill and elsewhere to strategic advantage. It has traded politically devalued prescriptive requirements (technology-based requirements for BACT and NSPS) and procedural hurdles (separate PSD permits for significant new installations and significant modifications) to achieve commitments to overall superior environmental performance. Other XL projects are similar in these respects; a number entail "bubbling," as in the case of Merck, offering increased flexibility in return for plantwide environmental performance commitments.[91] Through these bargaining ventures, the Agency has managed so far to take the reform initiative away from Congress, blunting efforts for potentially wider

---

[88]   See ibid., at 328.

[89]   See ibid., at 329.

[90]   Merck Proposed Rule, supra note 60, at 15,315.

It can be argued that *Asarco* should be revisited in light of the Court's subsequent holding in *Chevron U.S.A. v. Natural Resources Defense Council, Inc.*, 467 U.S. 837 (1984), which allowed "bubbling" by EPA in determining the applicability of PSD review as it defined anew the discretion of administrative agencies to interpret ambiguous statutory provisions.

[91]   See Notice of Availability of the Imation Project XL Proposed Final Project Agreement: Imation Corp., Camarillo, Cal. Plant, 64 Fed. Reg. 37,785 (1999); Project XL Site-Specific Rulemaking for Andersen Corporation's Facility in Bayport, Minn., 64 Fed. Reg. 19,097 (1999); Weyerhaeuser Project XL Final Project Agreement, 62 Fed. Reg. 4760 (1997).

or deeper statutory reforms, while at the same time advancing its environmental mission (or at least being seen as still faithful to it).

Congressional hearings on Project XL reflected the questions that commentators have raised about EPA's legal authority to carry out XL. But the focus of those hearings was not on whether the Agency should discontinue XL because of a lack of authority, but on whether Project XL should be codified as a formal variance procedure.[92] Senator Bond, who chairs the Senate appropriation subcommittee for the EPA, was particularly concerned that the Agency be able to respond creatively to "a situation like the Amoco-Yorktown project," which he understood to have failed because of lack of legal authority.[93] Initially at least, the Agency resisted Congress' overtures to legislate Project XL.[94] Later the Administration offered its support for a bill introduced by Senator Lieberman that would allow EPA's consideration of petitions for "innovative environmental strategy agreements" under carefully defined circumstances.[95] Without strong support from any quarter, the legislation died at the end of the 105th Congress and has not been reintroduced.[96]

The Agency's reluctant support for legislative change—even change that is designed to authorize a program the Agency has already initiated—is predictable in light of its interest in keeping control of the environmental agenda. In amending the Agency's statutes Congress may alter provisions in a way that the EPA does not favor. The Agency might also resist such a change, or be only nominally supportive, because enactment would confer a political advantage on Congress and would detract from the Agency's ascendant role in the realm of environmental policy. As it is now, the Agency has considerable latitude to create and dispense flexibility. A statutory variance provision, which would define the circumstances under which variances might be granted, would change the default rules under which bargaining now occurs and could limit the options that might otherwise be available in the current reinvention climate.

(*cont.*)

Increased use of plantwide bubbles has been advocated as a means to reduce risk in a more cost-effective way. See Stewart, supra note 42, at 223–225; E.D. Elliott and G. Charnley "Toward Bigger Bubbles" (Winter 1998) Forum for Applied Research and Public Policy 48. But see Steinzor, "Emperor's Clothes" supra note 57.

[92] "Status of Recommendations Made by the National Academy of Public Administration on Reforming the Environmental Protection Agency: Hearing Before a Subcomm. of the Senate Comm. on Appropriations," 104th Cong. 113–115 (1996) (questions by Sen. Bond).

[93] Ibid., at 114–115.

[94] Ibid., at 113–115 (testimony by F. Hansen, Deputy Administrator, EPA). See also "Regulatory Review: Hearings Before the Subcomm. on Financial and Management Accountability of the Senate Comm. on Governmental Affairs" (1996) (statement of C. Gray).

[95] S. 1348, 105th Cong. (1997); see Letter from Carol M. Browner, Administrator, U.S. Environmental Protection Agency, to Senator Joseph I. Lieberman (29 October 1997); Statement of Kathleen A. McGinty, Chair, White House Council on Environmental Quality (30 October 1997).

[96] But see H.R. 3448, 106th Cong. (1999) (bill to improve management of environmental information and provide for "innovative strategy agreements").

5.2 Ozone

While advanced as a major policy initiative, the implementation of Project XL project has been largely confined to site-specific deals. The Agency has been at pains to isolate those deals from its mainstream statutory interpretations and applications, in order to avoid unintended consequences for its core programs, while acknowledging that lessons learned from XL projects might in the future become the basis for broader changes.[97] However, outside of Project XL, the EPA has used the same technique of trading off devalued prescriptive requirements in an effort to facilitate acceptance and implementation of its broader environmental goals. An example of this is the Agency's strategy to address the seemingly intractable eastern ozone problem. The creation of the strategy, which included bargaining by the Agency with the White House and Congress, with the states in the region, and with various constituent groups, illustrates a use of interpretational flexibility similar to that evident in Project XL.

High levels of tropospheric (ground level) ozone in summer months persist in California and in a wide area in the eastern US. Past efforts to reduce those levels have focused on reducing ozone-causing emissions from local sources in areas with unhealthy levels of ozone; these efforts have not had great success, particularly in the eastern US where high ozone levels in the northeast may result, not just from local emissions, but also from emissions of ozone precursors in the south and the midwest. In 1995, the Agency fostered a collaborative effort by state environmental program directors from 37 eastern states and the District of Columbia to study the regional ozone transport problem.[98] The Ozone Transport Assessment Group (OTAG) conducted modeling to determine the effect of emissions from upwind states on downwind states in the northeast and mid-Atlantic. The group also made recommendations, agreed to by most but not all of the participating states, on measures to address the transport problem. These recommendations were general, however, and the difficulty of the process leading to them indicated that a consensus solution between upwind and downwind states on the level of ozone reductions and the allocation of ozone reduction requirements would be unlikely.[99]

In 1997, after it received the OTAG's report and recommendations, the EPA launched a three-part regulatory strategy to attack the ozone problem. Within the space of fifteen months, it: revised the national ambient air quality standard (NAAQS) for ozone, making the standard more stringent;[100] negotiated a plan for implementing the new standard with

---

[97] See Merck Proposed Rule, supra note 60, at 52,622.
[98] See Ozone Transport Assessment Group, *Executive Report* (NTIS, Washington, D.C., 1997) [hereinafter OTAG Report].
[99] See ibid., at 51–59. Five states voted against sending the OTAG Report's recommendations to EPA; others agreed but with caveats. See Ozone Transport Assessment Group, Issue/Notes (19 June 1997).
[100] National Ambient Air Quality Standards for Ozone, 62 Fed. Reg. 38,856 (1997) [hereinafter Ozone Standards]. Agency review of possible revisions to the ozone NAAQS had been underway for some time prior to the convening of OTAG; the issue of the NAAQS revisions was not

OMB;[101] and issued a call to 22 states east of the Mississippi for regional reductions in ozone-causing nitrogen oxide emissions under their State Implementation Plans (SIPs) (NO$_x$ SIP call).[102]

That strategy has been partially disrupted, at least momentarily, by the recent D.C. Circuit Court of Appeals decision in *American Trucking Associations v. EPA,*[103] in which the court remanded EPA's revised ozone NAAQS as violative of the non-delegation doctrine; in a separate action, *State of Michigan v. EPA* the D.C. Circuit has largely affirmed the NO$_x$ SIP call.[104] In its "blockbuster" ruling in *American Trucking,*[105] the court concluded that the Agency had not articulated an "intelligible principle" to constrain its discretion in choosing a standard and that therefore the revised ozone NAAQS reflected an unconstitutional delegation of authority by Congress. (The court reached the same result for the Agency's new NAAQS for particulates, which had been issued simultaneously with the ozone NAAQS.) The court's initial opinion also seemed to conclude that, even if the EPA were able to promulgate a revised ozone NAAQS that identified an "intelligible principle" acceptable to the court, the EPA would not be able to enforce the new standard. A second opinion on rehearing has softened that conclusion, but leaves considerable doubt over whether and on what terms a revised standard might be implemented. The Supreme Court has granted a review. I will leave analysis of the D.C. Circuit's decisions and their implications to other commentators. My focus here is the formulation of the Agency's ozone strategy and the interplay of political forces and legal accommodations that shaped it.

The revised NAAQS for ozone was issued in July 1997. The revised standard was more stringent than the pre-existing standard and was predicted to more than double the number of areas that do not meet the ozone NAAQS.[106] Simultaneously with the issuance of the new ozone NAAQS,

---

addressed in OTAG's recommendations for measures to reduce ozone transport. However, the Agency's decision to revise the NAAQS, along with the other elements discussed here, became an integral part of the of the strategy to address the eastern ozone problem.

[101] Implementation of Revised Air Quality Standards for Ozone and Particulate Matter, 62 Fed. Reg. 38,421 (1997) (taking the form of a memorandum from W.J. Clinton, President of the United States, to C.M. Browner, Administrator of the Environmental Protection Agency) [hereinafter NAAQS Implementation Plan].

[102] Finding of Significant Contribution and Rulemaking for Certain States in the Ozone Transport Group Region for Purposes of Reducing Regional Transport of Ozone, 63 Fed. Reg. 57,356 (1998) [hereinafter NO$_x$ SIP Call].

[103] 175 F.3d 1027, 1057 (D.C. Cir. 1999), modified on rehearing, 195 F.3d 4 (1999), cert. granted, 68 U.S.L.W. 3724 (22 May 2000), 68 U.S.L.W. 3739 (30 May 2000).

[104] No. 98-1497, 2000 WL 180650 (D.C. Cir. 3 March 2000). The NO$_x$ SIP call was based both on the ozone NAAQS that was in effect prior to the 1997 revisions and on the revised ozone NAAQS. After the court's decision in *American Trucking Ass'n,* EPA moved in *State of Michigan v. EPA* to stay consideration of the NO$_x$ SIP call issues involving the revised ozone standard, and the court granted the motion. Thus, the court's ruling in *State of Michigan v. EPA* only addresses issues involving the pre-existing standard. EPA has separately issued NO$_x$ emission reduction orders to powerplants and other facilities within the region under Section 126 of the Clean Air Act. See S. Twomey, "EPA Orders Plants to Cut Nitrogen Oxide Emissions" [18 December 1999] Washington Post A6.

[105] R. Lazarus, "National Air Standard Ruling a Blockbuster" (July–August 1999) Envtl F 8.

[106] See 28 Env't Rep (BNA) No. 10, at 430 (4 July 1997).

the President issued a NAAQS implementation plan directing the Agency to extend the statutory time frames for applying local planning requirements in areas not meeting the revised standard and to minimize or eliminate the local controls that would otherwise be required by statute for these areas.[107]

The purpose of the plan was to shore up support for the new ambient air quality standard—to assure the public that the new standard would be implemented in a way that would minimize compliance costs in areas that would now be in violation of the NAAQS; to address criticism that the new standard was too expensive and would discourage development in these areas; and to reduce the danger of action by Congress overruling the new standard, as some in Congress were considering.[108] The plan was also meant to assuage White House concerns about strengthening the standard. As indicated by the timing of its issuance, the implementation plan was negotiated through an OMB process and issued as a condition of White House approval of the NAAQS. When the President announced his decision to support the new NAAQS, he stressed "the flexibility [provided by the plan] in how these standards are implemented."[109]

In addition to blunting opposition to the revised NAAQS, the plan also was intended to accommodate and gather support for the Agency's emerging regional approach to ozone reductions and to provide incentives for states to respond positively to the soon-to-be-issued call for regional controls. That call went out in 27 October 1998, in the form of an EPA directive to 22 states and the District of Columbia that they adopt measures to reduce emissions of NO_x, a by-product of combustion and one of the chief precursors of ozone.[110] This regional "NO_x SIP call" required reductions by upwind as well as downwind states, in recognition of the regional nature of the ozone pollution problem.[111]

The NAAQS implementation plan helped make both the revised NAAQS and the regional NO_x reduction strategy politically feasible. It did so by offering regulatory relief to states that were likely to have new non-attainment areas under the stricter standard. If they participated in the regional reduction plan, requirements for local controls in those areas, including stringent requirements for new and modified major sources, would be reduced or eliminated.[112]

When an air quality standard has been adopted or revised, the Clean Air Act requires all areas within each state to be classified as attainment, non-attainment, or unclassifiable based on the monitoring data available.[113] When an area is designated nonattainment under Part D of Title I of the Act, special planning and control requirements go into effect. The state must

---

[107] NAAQS Implementation Plan, supra note 101, at 38,421.
[108] See 28 Env't Rep (BNA) No. 11, at 464 (11 July 1997).
[109] See 28 Env't Rep (BNA) No. 3, at 398 (27 June 1997).
[110] See NO_x SIP Call, supra note 102, at 57,356.
[111] See ibid., at 57,359. SIP refers to "state implementation plans" required under the Federal Clean Air Act.
[112] See NAAQS Implementation Plan, supra note 101, at 38,425–38,426.
[113] See 42 U.S.C. § 7407(d).

commit to implement control measures necessary to attain the standard. In addition to this general requirement, the Act requires a number of specific measures in non-attainment areas. These include the requirement that new or modified sources in the area comply with the lowest achievable emissions rate (or LAER).[114] LAER is defined as "the most stringent emission limitation which is achieved in practice" by the type of facility in question.[115] Unlike BACT, which applies to new or modified sources in attainment areas, LAER applies to sources in non-attainment areas. Also unlike BACT, the statute's definition of LAER does not provide for consideration of "energy, environmental and economic impacts and other costs" that are typically the basis for reducing the level of control required. Historically, the Agency has interpreted LAER as prohibiting consideration of these factors.[116] The restrictive new source review requirements for non-attainment areas—LAER included—are widely resented by local officials and business interests in those areas as putting them at a disadvantage in competing with attainment areas for economic development.

Part D also provides that existing sources in all nonattainment areas must achieve emissions reductions reflecting "reasonable available control technology" (or RACT).[117] In its application of RACT to emissions of ozone precursors, such as VOCs, under the 1990 Clean Air Act Amendments, the Agency has interpreted the requirement to apply independently of the requirement to adopt control measures needed to attain the standard.[118] Under this reading, RACT could require controls on existing sources regardless of whether the controls were shown as necessary for attainment.

The NAAQS implementation plan focused on areas that could expect to be newly designated non-attainment under the revised standard—i.e., areas that had been in attainment under the pre-existing standards but did not meet the new standards. Based on its program to reduce interstate ozone pollution, the plan predicted that "the vast majority of [these] areas" would be able to achieve healthful air quality without additional local controls—that is, without local controls beyond those necessary to respond to the regional NO_x reduction plan.[119] For areas that participated in the regional NO_x reduction plan, the implementation plan contemplated a series of accommodations for these areas with the general assurance that "only minor revisions to their existing programs" would be necessary.[120] Among the accommodations contemplated by the plan was that something less than LAER, as traditionally understood, and very close, if not identical, to BACT would be the control technology required for new and modified sources in these areas, despite

---

114   See 42 U.S.C. § 7503(a)(2).
115   42 U.S.C. § 7501(3)(B).
116   See 1990 Draft Manual, supra note 80, at G4.
117   42 U.S.C. § 7502(c)(1).
118   See Letter from J. Cannon, General Counsel, EPA, to Representative T. Bliley, 6 October 1997 [hereinafter 6 October 1997 letter].
   The Agency had adopted a contrary interpretation for particulates and other pollutants, reading RACT "to mean that only those measures that are needed to demonstrate attainment by the applicable attainment date are 'reasonably available' and thus required." Ibid., at 5.
119   NAAQS Implementation Plan, supra note 101, at 38,425.
120   Ibid.

their non-attainment status.[121] For existing sources in these areas, the Agency would consider RACT requirements under the revised ozone standard satisfied by measures adequate to attain the standard.

The Agency's lawyers produced a legal opinion that concluded that the new interpretation of RACT for the revised ozone standard and most of the other reinterpretations offered in the implementation plan could be accommodated within the language and intent of the statute, with some rule changes.[122] On the issue of applying BACT instead of LAER to new sources, legally the most difficult of the new interpretations, the Agency justified its reading not in the terms of the statute but as a de minimis departure from the statute's plain meaning.[123]

There were outcries from Congress and elsewhere when the standard and accompanying implementation plan were issued. Oversight hearings were held before committees in both the House[124] and the Senate[125] to address allegations that the Agency was buying off potential opponents of its new NAAQS by making promises it would not be able to fulfill legally. In House hearings, Congressman Bilrakis, Chairman of the Subcommittee on Health and the Environment of the House Commerce Committee, said: "The implementation plan either stretches the Clean Air Act far beyond its original intent or seeks, without proper authority, to make new law."[126] Congressman Dingell, no friend of the new air quality standards either, echoed the sentiment.[127] In his prior role as Committee Chairman in a Democratic Congress, Dingell had been EPA's most effective antagonist on the Hill, chastising agency officials in oversight hearings for failure faithfully to implement statutory requirements or to properly manage the Agency, and it was he, from his current position as Ranking Minority Member, who led the questioning of EPA Administrator Browner on the asserted lack of Agency authority for the implementation plan. But although the attacks were pointed, they lacked the force of past attacks, because it was clear that the critics were not in substance opposed to the regulatory accommodations in the plan. The critics of the legal basis for these accommodations were also among those who opposed the toughening of the standard, the economic effects of which the plan was designed to mitigate.

As with Project XL, committee members suggested that the plan ought to be codified by amending the Clean Air Act, in order to correct its perceived

---

[121]   See 6 October 1997 letter, supra note 118 at 6.
[122]   See ibid.
[123]   See ibid., at 6.
[124]   "Implementation of the Clean Air Act National Ambient Air Quality Standards (NAAQS) Revisions for Ozone and Particulate Matter, Subcomm. on Health and the Environment and Subcomm. on Oversight and Investigations of the House Comm. on Commerce," 105th Cong. (1997) [hereinafter House Implementation Hearings].
[125]   "Clean Air Act: Ozone and Particulate Standards, Subcomm. on Clean Air, Wetlands, Private Property and Nuclear Safety of the Senate Comm. on Environment and Public Works," 105th Cong. (1997).
[126]   House Implementation Hearings, supra note 124, at 2.
[127]   Ibid., at 5 ("[T]hrough a number of addenda and other changes which they seek to make in the way the statute would be implemented by these new regulations, it appears that we have on our hands a situation where we may be well observing the strong possibility of extralegal and improper behavior which will be challenged successfully in court").

legal weaknesses.[128] Given the plan's legal vulnerabilities, it might have been expected that the Agency would welcome the offer to codify it. But the Administrator declined the invitation, in much the same way (and presumably for much the same reasons) as the EPA had resisted statutory authorization for Project XL.[129]

In a mammoth transportation funding bill, Congress later codified the extended time frames that the Administration had advanced for implementing the new standards,[130] but no Congressional action took place on the substantive elements of the implementation plan, such as the substitution of BACT for LAER. The revised NAAQS was not overturned by Congress. Instead, for reasons unrelated to the Agency's strategic accommodations in the implementation plan, the D.C. Circuit Court of Appeals, overturned the Agency's NAAQS decision pending Supreme Court review and the outcome of Agency deliberations on remand.

Although the Agency's ozone strategy was not a collaborative undertaking of the sort that took place in the Merck example and in other XL projects,[131] it evinced similar bargaining behavior by the Agency. As in Project XL, the Agency sought to convert stringent regulatory controls into bargaining assets that could be used to gain support for its programs and advance its environmental goals. But in this case, the conversion was not confined to a reinvention "pilot." It was reinvention at the core, designed to shore up political support for a controversial national standard that (with the accompanying new standard for fine particulate matter) was probably the most significant policy decision the Agency would make this decade at least until the D.C. Circuit's intervention—and to create incentives for participation in an ambitious regional NO_x reduction plan for that standard's implementation. In the current deregulatory era, the Agency was able to advance this conversion without serious adverse political consequences.[132]

6 CONSEQUENCES AND LIMITS: A CRISIS IN LEGITIMACY?

The EPA's use of its newfound flexibility has given it the capacity for positive responses to problems—positive in the sense of advancing its goals, reducing conflict and reconciling competing interests. It also has a more

---

[128] See ibid., at 37–38 (questions by Congressman Brown); ibid., at 38–40 (questions by Congressman Burr).

[129] See ibid., at 38–39. EPA was supported in its position by a leading environmentalist, David Hawkins, testifying on behalf of the Natural Resources Defense Council. Ibid., at 128–131. Hawkins stated that he did not "see anything that violates the law" in EPA's "implementation schedule" and opposed congressional tinkering with the Clean Air Act.

[130] See Pub. L. No. 105-178, Sec. 6103(a), 112 Stat. 465 (1998), discussed in *American Trucking Ass'ns v. EPA*, 175 F.3d 1027, 1043, 1049 (D.C. Cir. 1999).

[131] EPA's approach to the ozone problem has included collaborative elements, such as the OTAG process, which informed the Agency's approach to the NO_x SIP call.

[132] Such bold moves are not confined to EPA's programs. Farber points to the implementation of the Endangered Species Act (ESA) by the Departments of Interior and Commerce as a prime example of what he calls "positive slippage." His focus is on the transformation by Interior and

problematic side, to the extent that it may affect the legitimacy of the programs that the Agency administers. And it has its limits—defined by institutional forces, judicial and otherwise, operating to assure that the legal adventurousness exhibited in the ozone setting and Project XL will be contained.

One might see the EPA's behavior as proof, once again, of Louis Jaffe's observation that "[f]rom the point of view of an Agency, the question of the legitimacy of its action is secondary to that of the positive solution of a problem."[133] The legal authority of the Agency to carry out programs such as Project XL[134] or the ozone implementation plan[135] has been questioned. Even commentators sympathetic to the Agency's collaborative impulse have stopped short of suggesting that the Agency should be free to exceed its statutory authority in its effort to reconcile interests and strike bargains.[136] Concerns are intimated about the "ambiguous legitimacy" of the leveraged interpretation of statues that can accompany aggressive bargaining.[137] In its willingness to push its statutory authority to the limits, or beyond, is the Agency compromising its legitimacy?

7   RULE OF LAW LEGITIMACY

In his indictment of the "delegalization" of administrative law (which takes to task, among other things, the current administration's "regulatory reform"), Werhan asserts that rule of law is the core requirement of legitimacy.[138] "[I]t is the rule of law that legitimates administrative service.

Commerce of the "incidental take" permit provisions of Section 10 of the Act into the "basis for a sweeping new approach to protecting endangered species." Farber, supra note 5, at 307. This approach has included regulatory inducements (such as "no surprises" assurances) designed to encourage private landowners to seek and obtain Section 10 permits, which contain conditions designed to minimize and mitigate harm to endangered species. Like EPA's XL initiative and its NAAQS strategy, the ESA reforms have helped take "the initiative away from Congress," J. Ruhl, "While the Cat's Asleep: the Making of the 'New' ESA" [Winter 1998] Nat. Resources & Env't 187, 188, and allowed Interior and Commerce to retain control in shaping a politically viable program that advances species protection. Unlike EPA under prescriptive statutes such as the Clean Air Act, Interior and Commerce are operating within a relatively open regulatory regime; Section 10 itself acts as a variance from the broad prohibition against "taking" endangered species in Section 9 of the ESA. Even in this more relaxed structure, however, and much like EPA's XL initiative and NAAQS strategy, efforts by Interior and Commerce to bring landowners to the table "stretch the agencies' authorities to the limits", ibid., at 187, and have attracted law suits from disappointed environmentalists, see *Spirit of the Sage Council v. Babbitt*, No. 1:98CV01873(EGS) (D.D.C. filed 24 October 1998).

[133]   L. Jaffe, *Judicial Control of Administrative Action* (Little, Brown & Co., Boston, 1965), p. 323.
[134]   See note 57 supra.
[135]   See L. Langworthy, "Will Transitional Ozone Nonattainment Work?" (manuscript on file with author).
[136]   See Weber, supra note 9, at 232–233.
[137]   Farber, supra note 5, at 310–311.
[138]   Werhan, supra note 2, at 460–461.

By requiring agencies to conform their actions to the law, the rule of law serves democracy by ensuring that Congress—the most representative organ of government—sets the basic outline of public policy."[139] To the extent that an agency is seen not as following the letter of the law, but instead as manipulating the law to advance its own interests, its actions, by this view, would lack legitimacy. If not guided by directives devised by "the most representative organ of government," the agency might be subject to capture or dominance by special interests, or to idiosyncratic decisionmaking by its leadership not responsive to public preferences,[140] and therefore, in some fundamental sense, anti-democratic.

Alternative views of legitimacy tend to focus not on rule of law but on wise public policy or on public acceptance.[141] In addressing legitimacy in the context of delegation to administrative agencies, Peter Shuck states that legitimacy and public policy "cannot be separated, that democratic legitimacy is a function of effective governance, desirable policy outcomes, and other political values."[142] Jody Freeman defines legitimacy as "the *acceptability* of administrative decisions to the public."[143] Freeman's formulation has the merit of explicitly capturing the connection between legitimacy and public acceptance while also recognizing that a factor in public acceptance is whether a decision seems "right" or represents "a technically optimal solution to a regulatory problem."[144]

The traditional approach allows one to assume that adherence to the rule of law serves the public interest by "disabling administrators from skewing their decisions according to the dictates of their will or the demands of interest groups" and subjecting them to the democratic will (reflected in statutory directives). The alternatives, in a sense, remove the cover provided by rule of law and demand that these questions be confronted directly: Has a decision been skewed by willful administrators or interest group demands in a way that is not publicly acceptable, to the extent that can be discerned? Strict adherence to law, although an important consideration in answering this question, may not be determinative of the answer. If an agency action that strains the bounds of its statutory authority enjoys a higher degree of support among those affected or among the public at large than it might if the law had been strictly followed, and can be fairly characterized as maximizing the public good, then it might also claim democratic legitimacy.

---

[139] Ibid., 461. But see Spence, supra note 19, at 438–446 (noting that Congress does not necessarily, follow "the will of the governed").

[140] Werhan, supra note 2, at 461.

[141] See J. Freedman, *Crisis and Legitimacy: The Administrative Process and American Government* (Cambridge University Press, 1978), pp. 262, 264; P. Selznick, *Law, Society and Industrial Justice* (Russell Sage Foundation, New York, 1969), p. 31.

[142] P.H. Schuck, "Delegation and Democracy: Comments on David Schoenbrod" (1999) 20 Cardozo L Rev 775, 779.

[143] J. Freeman, "Private Parties, Public Functions and the New Administrative Law" in D. Dyzenhaus (ed.), *Recrafting the Rule of Law* (Hart, Oxford, 1999), p. 335, n. 14 (emphasis in original).

[144] Ibid.

One's acceptance of alternative views of legitimacy may depend on how seriously one is concerned about the vulnerability of agencies to influence by private interests, to political pressure from the White House and Congress, and to their interests in protecting and enhancing their own authority.[145] These concerns are real, but it is easy to overstate them. These same characteristics of agencies might also enhance political responsiveness, as we have seen in the EPA's case. Cass Sunstein argues that "agencies have a kind of democratic pedigree, certainly a better one than the courts."[146] Jerry Mashaw goes further to suggest that agencies may be more responsive to public preferences than Congress.[147]

One might expect that, in the majority of cases, traditional rule of law principles would serve adequately to define legitimacy. In other circumstances, however, an alternative view may be necessary in order to save the rule of law from the anti-democratic consequences of its own formalistic rigidity. The circumstances under which the EPA now operates—at least with its more elaborate prescriptive statutes such as the Clean Air Act—may provide a good example of when rule of law, by itself, may be the enemy of legitimacy.

Wallace Stevens wrote: "too great an order is a disorder."[148] Mashaw has articulated the administrative law version of that poetic maxim, pointing out "[t]he extraordinary delegitimizing effect of rules that are so specific that they cannot be made responsive across either space or time.... [T]ight accountability linkages at one point in the governmental system may reduce the responsiveness of the system as a whole."[149] Although Mashaw was arguing in favor of broad delegations to administrative agencies, his point illuminates the dilemma faced by agencies such as EPA that have been tasked by Congress to administer detailed command-and-control requirements.

The Clean Air Act, which is implicated in both cases we have examined in detail, is a monument to congressional prescriptiveness—to "tight accountability linkages."[150] As previously discussed, those tight linkages were a function, ostensibly, of a pro-environment Congress' efforts to assure implementation of its environmental policies by reluctant administrations and an impotent Agency. Thus, the Clean Air Act not only specifies the ambient standards that are to be maintained for important pollutants, such as SO_x, CO, and ozone, but the Act also specifies the means by which progress toward those standards is to be made. These include the technology-based source requirements for new and modified sources, such as BACT, NSPS, and LAER. Critics of these provisions have argued that,

---

[145]   See C. Sunstein, "Is Tobacco a Drug?" (1998) 47 Duke L J 1013, 1061.
[146]   Ibid., at 1056.
[147]   J. Mashaw, *Greed, Chaos and Governance* (Yale University Press, New Haven, 1997), pp. 151–157.
[148]   "Idea of Order at Key West" in *Ideas of Order* (Alcestis Press, New York, 1935).
[149]   Mashaw, "Prodelegation: Why Administrators Should Make Political Decisions" (1985) 1985 J L Econ and Org 81, 98; Mashaw, supra note 147, at 155 (reiterating the same point).
[150]   It is also, paradoxically, characterized by some quite loose linkages. See *American Trucking Ass'ns v. EPA*, 175 F.3d 1027 (D.C. Cir. 1999).

though these standards have assisted in securing concrete progress in improving air quality, they are inefficient and unduly burdensome, discourage innovation, and may inhibit future environmental progress.[151] If subject to future applications of BACT or NSPS, at least as traditionally applied, the Merck facility might have incurred more costs and still produced more air pollution than under its XL agreement with the EPA. Thus, the "tight linkages" represented by the technology-based limitations may be seen as counterproductive, at least in certain situations, and as undermining the reasonableness and soundness of the Act itself. By loosening these linkages, in dialogue (albeit often fitful) with the White House, Congress, and constituent groups, the EPA is arguably increasing the responsiveness of the system, not decreasing it.

Legitimacy is also affected by political changes that have occurred since the most prescriptive of these requirements were enacted. In recent years Congress has signaled dissatisfaction with the regulatory apparatus as well as the goals of the Clean Air Act, and even the Administration, which strongly supports environmental goals, has signaled its willingness to move away from "command-and-control" where it can.[152] As we have seen, the Agency has appropriated the slack created by this political shift in order to advance its interests, but by doing so, it is also filling the gap that has opened between the law on the books and the working understanding among lawmakers, executive branch officials and at least some of their constituencies that some of the specific provisions of these laws may be unnecessary or even counterproductive. In the absence of action by Congress to codify this shift, EPA's implementation may better approximate the public interest, or be more acceptable to the public, than strict adherence.

The alternative views of legitimacy raise a number of issues. Are there valid notions of "desirable outcomes" or "public acceptance" that exist apart from authorized legislative enactments? Apart from the constitutionally ordained legislative process, how can we know what outcomes are desirable or are acceptable to the public, and what mechanisms assure that the administrative process is yielding these outcomes? How do the answers to these questions relate to traditional administrative law concerns such as transparency and accountability?[153] My discussion here does not to try to answer these questions. It is only to suggest that the question of legitimacy, in the circumstances in which the EPA now finds itself, is a complex one, and one not satisfactorily addressed by resorting to traditional rule of law principles.

---

[151] See B. Ackerman and R. Stewart, "Reforming Environmental Law: The Democratic Case for Market Incentives" (1988) 13 Columbia J Envtl L 171, 173–175; R. Stewart, "The Future of Environmental Regulation: United States Environmental Regulation: A Failing Paradigm" (1996) 15 J L and Comm 585, 587–591.

[152] A. Gore, *National Performance Review, Improving Regulatory Systems* (Washington, D.C., 1993), pp. 11, 24.

[153] See Farber, supra note 5, at 319 (raising issues of transparency and accountability in reinvention).

8 LIMITS OF FLEXIBILITY

Ultimately, the debate about legitimacy may be of marginal importance, because internal and external constraints ensure that the Agency's ability to stretch its authorities is limited. The most formidable external constraint, of course, is the federal judiciary—which serves institutionally to enforce traditional rule of law principles. It is before the courts that the difficulties associated with prescriptive legislation, and administrative attempts to remold it, are now most acute. The specificity of prescriptive provisions often, in the courts' view, leave little room for interpretation. Recent commentators have noted trends that would limit both the availability and scope of judicial review of EPA rulemaking and permitting decisions.[154] However, these trends have not shielded the bulk of EPA's permits and rules from judicial review.[155] The Supreme Court's decision in *Chevron U.S.A. v. Natural Resources Defense Council*[156] is similarly seen as limiting the scope of judicial review of Agency action to the extent that it makes room for the exercise of Agency discretion in interpreting regulatory statutes.[157] However, *Chevron* does not provide for Agency discretion where Congress has spoken to the issue at hand and its intent on the issue is clear.[158] In that case, Congressional intent controls.

The courts have developed doctrines that allow departures from the plain meaning of a statute under limited circumstances; chief among these are the de minimis and the absurd results exceptions. The EPA has had modest success using these doctrines. In *Environmental Defense Fund v. EPA*[159] for example, the D.C. Circuit upheld EPA's interpretations of Clean Air Act provisions (SIP conformity requirements) that departed from the plain meaning of the statute. In allowing these interpretations, the court relied on both de minimis and absurd results doctrines. "[T]he literal meaning of a statute need not be followed where the precise terms lead to absurd or futile results, or where failure to allow a de minimis exception is contrary to the primary legislative goal."[160] De minimis and absurd results doctrines are fissures in the rock of interpretation based on plain meaning or original intent; the question is how deep and how wide these fissures are. If a court were persuaded by the wisdom of EPA's actions, the court might create room within these doctrines to uphold a reading contrary to the

---

[154] Ibid., at 311–313 (citing *Chevron* doctrine and recent decisions restricting standing of those seeking to challenge Agency actions); but see *Friends of the Earth, Inc. v. Laidlaw Environmental Services, Inc.*, 528 U.S. 167 (2000) (revisiting restrictions on standing).

[155] For example, of the 23 petitions for review of EPA rules and other determinations decided by the D.C. Circuit in 1995 and 1996, only two were dismissed for lack of jurisdiction. See Environment and Natural Resource Division, U.S. Department of Justice, Reported D.C. Circuit Decisions in EDS Cases, 1995–1996.

[156] 467 U.S. 837 (1984).

[157] See ibid., at 843.

[158] See ibid., at 842–843.

[159] 82 F.3d 451 (D.C. Cir. 1996).

[160] Ibid., at 466 (quoting *Public Citizen v. Young*, 831 F.2d 1108 (1987)).

plain meaning of provisions such as those for BACT, NSPS, or LAER, just as the court sanctioned departures from strict application of the conformity provisions.[161] However, the likelihood that courts will engage in "dynamic interpretation" of regulatory provisions,[162] consistent with enhanced agency flexibility, is not great. Much more often than not, courts have rebuffed de minimis arguments by administrative agencies—including the valiant attempt by the Food and Drug Administration to read common sense into the Delaney Clause.[163] More recently, in a counterpoint to its earlier decision in the *Environmental Defense Fund* case, the D.C. Circuit invalidated newly adopted conformity provisions that sought to grant further flexibility to states with the familiar remonstration that if the legislative scheme is too onerous, it is up to Congress to change it.[164] If the question at the heart of the matter is the public interest or what the majority of people now prefer, then the courts are in a weaker position to approximate the answer than the Agency. They are also institutionally much less inclined to do so.[165] As Sunstein observes, if dynamic interpretation is to take place, it will be in agencies, with their greater political responsiveness, not in the courts.[166]

Of course, where the EPA can achieve consensus among parties that are affected by a decision and that may be in a position to seek review, the Agency may be able to insulate itself from judicial oversight, as it did in the Merck case. Thus, to the extent that it advances interpretations that have a low likelihood of being sustained judicially, the Agency has added incentive to obtain consensus, which can be legitimacy-enhancing. Finding consensus in complex regulatory settings, however, even with generous offers of regulatory flexibility from the agency, is difficult. Freeriders and holdouts abound. Even in regulatory negotiations which yielded positive agreement, for example, the Agency was frequently sued.[167]

The Agency may decide to proceed with high-risk legal positions, even in the absence of consensus, because (for reasons already discussed) the risks of reversal are outweighed by more compelling and immediate political benefits. But the uncertainties created by future litigation, and the likelihood of an adverse outcome, can undercut the usefulness of these positions to the Agency. Parties may be unwilling to alter their positions or behavior in response to the Agency's inducements precisely because of their uncertain legal footing and the prospect of future reversal. The EPA may use

---

[161] See W. Eskridge, Jr. and P. Frickey, "Statutory Interpretation as Practical Reasoning" (1990) 42 Stan L R 321, 359 (remarking that "[c]onsideration of [current public policies and] values has in fact exercised an important gravitational pull in statutory cases").

[162] W. Eskridge, Jr., *Dynamic Statutory Interpretation* (Harvard University Press, 1994), p. 11.

[163] See R. Merrill, "FDA's Implementation of the Delaney Clause: Repudiation of Congressional Choice or Reasoned Adaptation to Scientific Progress" (1988) 5 Yale J Reg 1.

[164] See *Environmental Defense Fund v. EPA*, 167 F. 3d 641, 651 (D.C. Cir. 1999).

[165] See Eskridge, *Dynamic* supra note 162, at 151.

[166] See Sunstein, supra note 145, at 1060.

[167] See Coglianese supra note 24, at 1300–1301 (finding that "at least *six* of EPA's *twelve* finalized rules developed using negotiated rulemaking have been subject to petitions for judicial review filed in federal court") (emphasis in original).

strategies to limit this. For example, it may attempt to postpone or avoid judicial review by issuing guidance or policy memoranda instead of rules, as it did in the case of the NAAQS implementation plan for ozone. But where litigation is likely, these strategies cannot promise protection for parties urged to rely on generous agency interpretations. In the case of the ozone NAAQS, for example, legal analysts have cautioned states and others against acting in reliance on the innovative interpretations embedded in the implementation plan. One might expect, if the Agency's approach is widely supported, that in the event of judicial reversal, Congress would validate the Agency's action; but Congress may or may not act, and if it does, it may or may not act in accordance with the expectations of the parties involved. Thus, the uncertainties of judicial review limit the Agency's ability effectively to trade at the limits of its statutory authority.

Another restraint on the Agency's bargaining with its statutory mandates is internal: if the Agency too easily or too often moderates requirements that it might otherwise strictly impose, it may devalue its currency at the bargaining table. To the extent that deviations from requirements come to be seen as an entitlement, the Agency may find that it receives less in return for them. Thus, it will likely be in the interest of the Agency to maintain a strong enforcement policy, to assure general adherence to its mandates, and to use deviations from requirements only in a limited and strategic manner. A strong enforcement posture is also fundamental to the Agency's general interest in maintaining its "environmentalist" reputation.

Finally, there are aspects of the Agency's culture that inhibit adventurous trading at the limits of statutory authority. The Agency is diverse. It includes program personnel who may be interested in striking bargains to reduce resistance and facilitate implementation. It also includes hundreds of attorneys—in the counseling and enforcement functions—who are, by training and by function, particularly sensitive to rule of law concerns. Enforcement attorneys, and their counterparts at the Department of Justice, have an interest in maintaining the sharp edge of regulatory requirements as the basis for a credible enforcement program. Counseling attorneys have an interest in avoiding anomalies in application that create additional complexities in legal interpretation, assuring the strength of legal arguments advanced by the Agency, and successfully defending the Agency's actions in court. Both the enforcement and counseling subcultures may function to restrain the dealmaking enthusiasm of program staff. To the extent that these subcultures are not excluded from policymaking—and the Agency's culture is to be inclusive in this regard—they may check routine resort to arrangements that challenge the legal boundaries. Such arrangements thus may be reserved for high profile cases (like ozone and Project XL), in which the EPA's leadership makes an affirmative decision to proceed in face of concerns advanced by the enforcement or counseling cadres. The new political climate, by showing a high tolerance for innovation that stretches the law's limits, or even rewarding it, may itself breed cultural changes within the Agency, but it is unclear how thoroughgoing such changes may be or how long they may take.

For all these reasons, and despite the favorable political climate, the kind of dealing that is evident in Project XL and the ozone implementation plan will remain exceptional. This falls short of a transformation of EPA programs based on principles of flexibility and collaboration in pursuit of environmental goals, if that is what is desired. We might amend the Agency's statutes to enable that transformation, if we knew exactly what changes would be adequate to the task (and would not have large downside effects). But legislative action will be difficult for a number of structural reasons well-rehearsed in the literature.[168] We have also seen why, at least in the current political alignment, the EPA and the Administration might want to avoid having the current laws reopened—even though changes could broaden the Agency's options and reduce legal risks. And we have seen why Congress might be reluctant to reopen them over the EPA's and the Administration's non-concurrence.[169]

More fundamentally it is not clear, even if the barriers to change could be overcome, that we know now what changes to make. We have seen that prescriptive requirements (such as source-by-source technology-based requirements) can impede the effort to find cost-effective, environmentally sound solutions and can even erode the legitimacy of EPA's programs. But some commentators see these same requirements as responsible for most of the environmental progress we have made to date. Although some have discerned a "consensus" supporting various environmental regulatory reforms,[170] this consensus has not proved clear enough or strong enough to drive legislative action.[171]

After exhaustive efforts to arrive at a consensus view on the future of environmental regulation, the report by former EPA Administrator Ruckelshaus's Enterprise for the Environment treads warily on the issue of legislative reform. While urging increased use of "performance-based approaches," the report cited "major obstacles" to the broader use of those approaches relating to implementability.[172] The report stopped short of recommending legislative change but encouraged the use of pilot projects and other measures as part of a transition process to a reinvented but not yet defined or definable future regulatory regime.[173]

---

[168] See R. Steinzor, "The Politics of Subsequent Environmental Legislation: The Legislation of Unintended Consequences" (1998) 9 Duke Envtl L and Pol'y F 95, 96 ("Obviously, legislative gridlock is not confined to environmental issues and is the inevitable byproduct of divided government, internally fractious political parties, interest groups with antithetical goals and evenly matched resources, the electronic age, and a slew of other factors"); M. Munger, "Pangloss Was Right: Reforming Congress is Useless, Expensive, or Harmful" (1998) 9 Duke Envtl L and Pol'y F 133.

[169] See also M. Kraft and D. Scheberle, "Environmental Federalism at Decade's End: New Approaches and Strategies" (1998) 28 Publius: J. Federalism 131, 144.

[170] E.g., C.B. Gray, "Obstacles to Regulatory Reform" (1997) U Chi Legal F 1–5.

[171] Kraft and Scheberle, supra note 169, at 144.

[172] Enterprise for the Environment, supra note 2, at 25–26.

[173] Ibid., at 29–31.

Some participants specifically sought a series of legislative changes to correct perceived shortcomings in existing laws, while others were concerned that any invitation to change might result in unwanted backsliding. None of us were so certain that we knew how to construct the new system that we were willing to recommend its immediate adoption; we recognized that a lot of care and adaptive management will be needed along the way.

Ibid., at vii (Chairman's Preface).

Munger points out that the costs of reform are high and that "real reform is generally dangerous because we can't predict its effects."[174] Although the current regime may not be the best of all possible worlds,[175] we still have much to learn from exploring alternative arrangements at the margins, such as with Project XL, and from testing new approaches devised in the crucible of high stakes policymaking, such as with the NAAQS ozone problem, and from pursuing other cooperative or collaborative ventures.[176] Since we may be condemned to it in any event, a period of further testing and experimentation will certainly be useful in future deliberations about reform. It could help protect us from reforms that, to an even greater extent than the present laws, we would find difficult to live with.

---

[174] Munger, supra note 168, at 142.
[175] But cf. Farber supra note 5, at 315–318 (suggesting possibility that present system, with its extensive "slippage" in implementation, may in fact provide efficient pollution controls).
[176] See D. Elliott, "Toward Ecological Law and Policy" in M. Chertow and D. Esty (eds), *Thinking Ecologically: The Next Generation of Environmental Policy* (Yale University Press, 1997), p. 183.

3. Environmental Contracts in the United States

*Geoffrey C. Hazard, Jr. and Eric W. Orts**

If men mean to reach agreement about the relations between themselves they treat each other civilly. If they mean to reach agreement about their relations with the natural world they build up among themselves a body of shared knowledge or opinion about things in the natural world and of traditional methods for dealing with them. ... This, then, is the essence of civilization: ... Being civilized means living, as far as possible, ... in constant endeavor to convert every case of non-agreement into an occasion of agreement. A degree of force is inevitable in human life; but being civilized means cutting it down, and becoming more civilized means cutting it down still further.[1]

1 INTRODUCTION

Environmental contracts, as we will use the term, refer to an approach to the regulation of environmental problems through negotiated and enforceable agreements among interested parties. Unlike regulatory methods that focus primarily on the traditional mechanisms of representative government—namely, statutes and administrative agencies—environmental contracts aim to include the various interested parties directly in the regulatory process and to make agreements reached through this process mutually enforceable. The various interests include businesses and their employees, environmental groups, and local community interests, as well as the government.

To be sure, government contracts of several kinds have long been used in the United States, and environmental law is no exception. First,

---

*In addition to those who commented on this chapter at a Wharton Impact Conference on Environmental Contracts, we also thank those who did the same at presentations at the Kennedy School of Government at Harvard University and an environmental regulation session of the Academy of Management's annual conference in Chicago. Michael Greenwald and Susan French assisted us also on a reference.
[1]   R. Collingwood, *The New Leviathan* (Oxford University Press, 1992), p. 326.

settlement agreements to end governmental enforcement actions or prosecutions are enforceable contracts. Approximately 90 percent of the EPA's civil enforcement actions result in a negotiated settlement.[2] Since 1991, the EPA has encouraged the use of innovative Supplemental Environmental Projects as a substitute for some portion of damages in settlements. These projects may focus on auditing, improved compliance, environmental restoration, or pollution prevention.[3] Second, litigation against the government by business or environmental interest groups is commonly used to challenge regulations or the procedures by which they were adopted. Like enforcement actions, this litigation also most often results in settlements that include promises of administrative amendment or some other compromise. In fact, litigation of regulations may be seen as a form of bargaining for the very purpose of achieving a negotiated solution by contract.[4] Third, settlements of environmental litigation among private parties in complex circumstances—such as large toxic clean-up cases—also sometimes approach the comprehensive character of regulation.[5] Fourth, pollution permits (and variances to them) at various governmental levels often involve negotiated settlements among industry, government, and environmental interests.[6] In combination, these various contractual settlements may already be said to compose a significant part of the corpus of environmental law in the United States. The background of seemingly rule-based statutes and regulations is in fact a shifting inventory of piecemeal contractual negotiations in the context of adversarial rulemaking and enforcement.[7]

There are serious drawbacks to this kind of regulation-by-litigation, however, including the expensive costs of lawsuits and the adversarial nature of the process. Those who are able most easily to bear the high costs of litigation—namely, large business enterprises, a few large environmental public interest groups, and the government itself—have a distinct advantage. Regulation-by-litigation is contentious, often insensibly so, and not

---

[2] C. Caldart and N. Ashford, "Negotiation as a Means of Developing and Implementing Environmental and Occupational Health and Safety Policy" (1999) 23 Harv Envtl L Rev 141, 187.

[3] Ibid., at 188–191. See also Final EPA Supplemental Environmental Project Policy, 63 Fed. Reg. 24,796 (5 May 1998). Most academic commentary on this innovation has been favorable, emphasizing the partnerships and collaboration with regulated businesses and communities enabled by these projects. See, e.g., L. Kaschak, "Supplemental Environmental Projects: Evolution of a Policy" (1996) 2 Envtl 465. For a dissenting view that these projects distort economic incentives for compliance by reducing damages, see D. Dana, "The Uncertain Merits of Environmental Enforcement Reform: The Case of Supplemental Environmental Projects" (1998) Wis L Rev 1181.

[4] See C. Coglianese, "Disputes and Disturbance in the Regulatory Process" (1996) 30 L & Soc'y Rev 735, 754–758.

[5] See, e.g., P. Harter, "The Political Legitimacy and Judicial Review of Consensual Rules" (1983) 32 Am U L Rev 471, 477–478.

[6] See, e.g., 3M: Negotiating Air Pollution Credits, Harvard Business School Case No. 9-897-134, -135 and -136 (as revised 29 May 1998).

[7] Yet another kind of government contracts in environmental law include grants and awards for the study of particular environmental problems and "outsourcing" of services, such as for the monitoring of air or water quality or the clean-up of toxic waste sites at public expense.

"collaborative."[8] It is difficult to see how this approach is the best possible method to solve the environmental problems that are, in the end, problems that everyone shares.

The idea of environmental contracts also shares a family resemblance with negotiated rulemaking as a method of regulation. Administrative rules adopted under the Negotiated Rulemaking Act of 1990[9] specifically involve interested parties in the process of formulating a particular regulation.[10] Regulations derived through negotiation—or "reg negs"—have been used by the EPA for approximately a dozen regulations, including some of those governing equipment leaks and reformulated gasoline.[11] Unlike settlements of litigation involving the government as a party, however, negotiated rule-making does not result in a contract enforceable against the government as well as the regulated party. It is in fact a "negotiation" only in the sense that "a limited number of identifiable interests that will be significantly affected by the rule" are convened to act as a committee when a government agency believes such a procedure would be appropriate.[12] The agency is then supposed to organize and work with this committee of interests to find a consensus for the proposed regulation. But the agency itself remains free to withdraw from the agreement and propose a different regulation.[13] "Consultation" by the government authority rather than "negotiation" more accurately describes this process of rulemaking. In any event, reg negs are relatively rare. They are required by statute in only a limited num-ber of circumstances.[14] Agencies voluntarily follow negotiated rulemaking procedures in less than two percent of cases.[15]

More serious candidates for true environmental contracts in the United States appear in some of the "government reinvention" programs sponsored by the Clinton Administration. The mostly highly visible of these experiments

---

[8]   See J. Freeman, "Collaborative Governance in the Administrative State" (1997) 45 UCLA L Rev 1.

[9]   Public L. No. 101-648, 104 Stat. 4969 (1994) (codified at 5 U.S.C. §§ 561-70). In 1996, the statute was reauthorized permanently, Pub. L. No. 104-320, § 11(a), 110 Stat. 3870, 3873.

[10]   See, e.g., P. Harter, "Negotiating Regulations: A Cure for Malaise" (1982) 71 Geo L J 1; R. Reich, "Regulation by Confrontation or Negotiation?" (1981) Harv Bus Rev, May–June 1981 issue, at 82. In its embrace of negotiated rulemaking, the United States followed European examples. See, e.g., Harter, supra note 5, at 467–477.

[11]   See C. Coglianese, "Assessing Consensus: The Promise and Performance of Negotiated Rulemaking" (1997) 46 Duke L J 1255, 1274 tbl. 1; P. Harter, "Fear of Commitment: An Affliction of Adolescents" (1997) 46 Duke L J 1389, 1400–1404. Coglianese and Harter have conflicting views about whether negotiated rulemaking has met instrumental goals of faster and less frequently litigated regulations. For a description of the negotiation of the equipment leak regulation, see Freeman, supra note 8, at 41–49.

[12]   Coglianese, supra note 11, at 1267 (quoting 5 U.S.C. § 563(a)(2)).

[13]   See *USA Group Loan Services, Inc. v. Riley*, 82 F.3d 708 (7th Cir. 1996) (referring to negotiated rulemaking as "a novelty in the administrative process" and rejecting claim by regulated entity that government withdrew from negotiated agreement in bad faith).

[14]   Coglianese, supra note 11, at 1268 and n. 75 (canvassing the statutes and agencies affected).

[15]   Even with statutory approval and the Clinton Administration's endorsement, negotiated rulemaking has occurred in the formulation of less than two percent of federal regulations. Ibid., at 1277 tbl. 2.

are called "partnerships with industry" by Secretary Carol Browner of the EPA.[16] These include Project XL (short for "excellent leadership") and the Common Sense Initiative. In Project XL, the EPA and interested parties negotiate with particular companies or other entities (which may include government agencies or even entire communities) to offer regulatory relief in return for the creation of innovative environmental management, auditing, and reporting programs. Plans that offer long-term environmental benefits may justify short-term regulatory leniency. In the Common Sense Initiative, the EPA convenes with industry groups to discuss agreements to fit regulations to particular kinds of businesses.[17] This approach, again according to Browner, "emphasizes bringing together a diverse set of interests, to reach consensus-based decisions, emphasizing pollution prevention rather than clean-up, tailored to a specific industry rather than one-size-fits-all, that are flexible in achieving tough environmental standards."[18]

Of these two experiments in regulation, Project XL has generated the most scholarly attention.[19] But its results have been decidedly mixed. Some success stories have been told.[20] At the same time, Project XL has not generated a great deal of active participation. Of the 50 experimental projects that the EPA had hoped to begin when it announced Project XL in 1995, only 14 had been approved by August 1999 and another 31 were "in negotiation or development."[21]

---

[16]   C. Browner, "Foreword: The Role of Private Parties in Resolving Public Problems" (1997) 18 U Pa J Int'l Econ L 447, 448–450. See also B. Thompson, "Foreword: The Search for Regulatory Alternatives" (1996) 15 Stan Envtl L J vii, xi (referring to an "emerging interest" in public and private "consensus partnerships" as a regulatory alternative).

[17]   See D. Fiorino, "Rethinking Environmental Regulation: Perspectives on Law and Governance" (1999) 23 Harv Envtl L Rev 441, 463–464. The six groups are automobile manufacturing, computers and electronics, iron and steel, metal finishing, petroleum refining, and printing. Ibid. Information on this initiative is available on the internet at <http://www.epa.gov/commonsense>. It would be interesting to study comparatively the industries that participate in both the Common Sense Initiative in the U.S. and Dutch environmental covenants. See D. Fiorino, "Toward a New System of Environmental Regulation: The Case for an Industry Sector Approach" (1996) 26 Envt'l L 457, 485–486 (noting that Dutch covenants were negotiated with 12 industrial sectors initially, including primary metals and printing).

[18]   Browner, supra note 16, at 449–450.

[19]   See, e.g., T. Caballero, "Project XL: Making It Legal, Making It Work" (1998) 17 Stan Envtl L J 399; M. Dorf and C. Sabel, "A Constitution of Democratic Experimentalism" (1998) 98 Colum L Rev 267, 382–386; Freeman, supra note 8, at 55–66; D. Hirsch, "Bill and Al's XL-ent Adventure: An Analysis of the EPA's Legal Authority to Implement the Clinton Administration's Project XL" [1998] U Ill L Rev 129; B. Mank, "The Environmental Protection Agency's Project XL and Other Regulatory Reform Initiatives: The Need for Legislative Authorization" (1988) 25 Ecology L Q 1; R. Steinzor, "Regulatory Reinvention and Project XL: Does the Emperor Have Any Clothes?" (1996) 26 Envt'l L 10,527; L. Susskind and J. Secunda, "The Risks and Advantages of Agency Discretion: Evidence from EPA's Project XL" (1998–1999) 17 UCLA J Envt'l L & Pol'y 67. For an extended description of Project XL, see also the contribution of Dennis Hirsch in his chapter in this book.

[20]   See, e.g., Freeman, supra note 8, at 55–66 (describing projects with Berry Corporation and Intel in favorable terms); Hirsch, supra note 19, at 143–146 (describing project with Merck & Co favorably). For further discussion of the Merck example, see also the chapter by Jon Cannon in this book.

[21]   Notice of Process Improvements under Project XL, 64 Fed. Reg. 16450 (5 April 1999); EPA, Project XL: 1999 Comprehensive Report (October 1999), at 2. According to one count in 1998,

The basic approach of Project XL is to invite proposals from a regulated person (usually a company) for a project that promises to achieve "superior environmental performance" in return for regulatory flexibility in government enforcement of standard legal requirements.[22] A Final Project Agreement is negotiated with interested parties, including community and public interest groups. The incentive for the regulated entity to participate is regulatory flexibility, which is usually given in the form of a "waiver" of permit requirements or promises of regulatory leniency; hence the quip from traditional EPA bureaucrats that "If it isn't illegal, it isn't XL."[23] In return, the regulated entity promises to engage in specified innovative programs designed to improve environmental performance.

A major weakness in Project XL lies in its uncertain legal foundation. The EPA has the authority to promise enforcement discretion (though there is no guarantee), and a "site-specific rulemaking" allows some flexibility in granting regulatory waivers.[24] However, the heavily statutory nature of many environmental obligations often do not expressly allow waivers.[25] Citizen lawsuits under many environmental statutes also remain a threat even if the government stays its enforcement hand. As a result, the legal incentives for regulated entities to participate in Project XL are severely limited. In addition, even though significant time and expense is required to negotiate a Final Project Agreement, the EPA insists on a clause indicating that the agreement is *not* legally binding as a contract.[26] In other words, even finalized XL projects are "gentlemen's agreements" that do not bind the government and rely essentially on unenforceable good faith among the parties in a regulatory environment characterized ordinarily by litigation.[27]

The Common Sense Initiative (CSI) was more ambitious than Project XL. Unlike Project XL, which operates on a case-by-case basis, CSI contemplated regulatory contracts to effect regulation industry-wide. In this sense, CSI was the closest legal development in the US to environmental covenants negotiated in some European countries such as the Netherlands.[28] Although

---

52 initial project proposals had been made, 7 of them had been approved, 9 were under negotiation, and 30 had been withdrawn or rejected. Hirsch, supra note 19, at 142–143.

[22] For an overview, see Caballero, supra note 19, at 401–408.

[23] See R. Steinzor, "Reinventing Environmental Regulation: The Dangerous Journey From Command to Self-Control" (1998) 22 Harv Envtl L Rev 103, 147.

[24] See Hirsch, supra note 19, at 146–157.

[25] Ibid., at 155. Hirsch argues that courts may find the EPA to have "implied waiver authority" even with respect to "direct statutory requirements." Ibid., at 157–168. This is a creative argument, but it is fully persuasive only in the case of de minimus departures from statutory requirements. The uncertainty of whether a waiver of an arguably significant statutory obligation would be legal considerably reduces the regulatory incentives that Project XL can offer.

[26] See Caballero, supra note 19, at 404 n. 12 (noting that all FPAs signed to date have included clauses stating that they are not legally binding as contracts).

[27] Other chapters address the European perspective in detail, but much of the European experience also seems also to involve "soft" environmental agreements rather than enforceable contracts. See *Environmental Agreements* (Environmental Law Network International, 1998), pp. 26–27.

[28] See ibid., at 54–58. See also the contributions of Van Calster and Deketelaere, Seerden, and Vedder in their chapters in this book.

ambitious in its regulatory aims, however, CSI did not live up to expectations. Of six industry initiatives begun, only three resulted in recommendations made formally to the EPA.[29] In two cases, industry groups withdrew. The metal finishing and printing groups witnessed some success, but significant "regulatory reinvention" did not occur, and CSI was abandoned.[30] The problems with CSI included inadequate definition of its goals and purposes.[31] Perhaps equally important, CSI lacked the credible threat of alternative regulatory action if an agreement was not reached.[32] Like Project XL agreements, it was also not clear that CSI agreements could be enforced against both the regulated entities and, as importantly, the government itself.

One interesting legislative development was Senator Joseph Lieberman's proposals for an Innovative Compliance Act of 1996[33] and a similar Innovative Environmental Strategies Act of 1997.[34] A bill for a Second Generation of Environmental Improvement Act that would authorize the EPA to enter into innovative strategy agreements was introduced with bipartisan support in late 1999.[35] Legislation along these lines would authorize the EPA to enter enforceable agreements with regulated entities under which the agency could waive specific regulatory requirements.[36] Legislation would not, however, authorize waivers from other statutory requirements or preempt citizen suits. This kind of legislation could give the EPA the authority, with Congressional encouragement, to pursue environmental contracts vigorously. Without such legislation to ground Project XL and CSI more firmly in the legal infrastructure, however, uncertainty about these contractual regulatory approaches will continue.

2   OF CONTRACTS AND REGULATION: ENVIRONMENTAL CONTRACTS AS A TYPE OF REGULATION

Our description of the experimental use of regulatory contracts (or at least negotiated regulations) and the prevalent role of contracts in the settlement of litigation in enforcement and challenges to regulations suggests that the

---

[29] See Caldart and Ashford, supra note 2, at 193–195 (citing GAO report).
[30] Ibid., at 198.
[31] See Dorf and Sabel, supra note 19, at 385–386; Fiorino, "Rethinking Environmental Regulation," supra note 17, at 195–196.
[32] For an argument that threatening regulated entities with something worse is often needed to drive them to their second best preferences, see E. D. Elliott, et al., "Toward a Theory of Statutory Evolution: The Federalization of Environmental Law" (1985) 1 J L Econ & Org 313. The need for a viable regulatory threat has also been recognized in some studies of European experience. See *Environmental Agreements*, supra note 27, at 128.
[33] S. 2160, 104th Cong. (1996).
[34] S. 1348, 105th Cong. (1997).
[35] Memo from Dennis Hirsch to Members of the ABA Subcommittee on Second Generation Environmental Policy, 26 August 1999 (attaching proposed bill sponsored by Reps. Dooley and Greenwood).
[36] Ibid. See also Hirsch, supra note 19, at 134–135 and nn. 31 and 32 (reviewing earlier bills).

Figure 1

Contract	Regulation
Party assent	Party submission
Participation in process	Subjugation to process
Resolution by negotiation	Resolution by direction
Adaptation of terms to specific situations	Generalized terms, applied "across the board"
Quid pro quo	Benefits from and obligations of citizenship
Fixed duration	Indefinite duration
Specified participants	General population (within legal jurisdiction)
Enforceable according to its terms	Enforceable and revocable by government
Enforceable by outside authority (courts or arbitration)	Unilateral enforcement by government

line between "contracts" and "regulation" is not always clear in practice. At a more general theoretical level as well, the difference between "contracts" and "regulation" becomes blurred. It is nevertheless conventional to consider that, as a means of social control and organization, "contract" may be contrasted with "regulation." This dichotomy involves the antinomies depicted above in Figure 1.

These differences between contract and regulation are real and important, but they are differences largely of degree rather than kind. Contracts are sometimes thought to belong in the realm of so-called "private law" and regulation in the realm of "public or administrative law." But this private/public distinction has been under assault in jurisprudence for some time, and rightly so.[37] This distinction is especially treacherous in environmental law because, as Carol Rose has argued, "the public/private divide, taken alone, misses the substantive content... of various techniques or strategies" of regulation.[38] As discussed above, government regulation through serial contracting with various groups is common. Governments also enter enforceable contracts with businesses for supplies and other products; for example, government employees serve under contracts, and the government procures through contracts all sorts of provisions from

---

[37] See, e.g., Symposium, "The Public/Private Distinction" (1982) 130 U Pa L Rev 1289; see also L. Seidman, "Public Principle and Private Choice" (1987) 96 Yale L J 1006; J. Williams, "The Development of the Public/Private Distinction in American Law" (1985) 64 Tex L Rev 225.

[38] Carol Rose, "Rethinking Environmental Controls: Management Strategies for Common Resources" 1991 1 Duke L J 8–9.

paper clips to sophisticated military weaponry.[39] At the same time, governments regulate the use of contracts in everyday life. Consumer regulation, for example, is concerned primarily with the regulation of contracting processes and outcomes with the aim of assuring that businesses with strong market power do not take undue advantage of this power in dealing with individual customers. Antitrust, civil rights, and employment law—among many other substantive areas of regulation—limit the scope of contracts. The law of contracts itself is in large part a government product.

The distinction between the respective roles of "government as sovereign regulator" and "government as contracting party" raises a difficult practical question. When may the government avoid its own contractual promises by virtue of its sovereign authority to establish the rules under which contractual promises are enforced—and to change them? Some commentators, though sensitive to fairness concerns of those persons and entities who negotiate with the government about regulations, advocate that the government should be permitted, as a democratic sovereign, to abrogate all regulatory contracts that it enters. For example, Susan Koniak and David Dana recognize that the government may be tempted to renege on regulatory agreements made with citizens, but they argue that the evils of opportunism, compromise, and capture by individuals who may usurp the government's authority through regulatory contracts are worse.[40] Regulatory contracts undermine "a fundamental norm" of legitimate "majority rule," they argue, "by entrenching the will of past legislatures and by transferring sovereign power to private parties."[41] Along similar lines, Gillian Hadfield recognizes the long-standing tension that has been perceived between the roles of "government as honest contractor" and "government as democratic legislator," but she believes that the sovereign principle should invariably override the contractual one.[42]

We disagree with these commentators and believe the distinction between "government-as-contractor" and "government-as-sovereign" merits closer analysis for a couple of important reasons.[43] First, as discussed above, the ordinary machinery of democratic government is not free from various kinds of contracting and negotiation. Lobbying, voting, and political contributions, as well as regulatory litigation, are an everyday part of democratic political life. It is not clear, without a comparative analysis of particular kinds of problems and proposed solutions, whether a broadly negotiated regulatory contract would be more or less democratic, efficient,

---

[39]   Specialized legislation often regulates government contracts. See, e.g., Contract Disputes Act, 41 U.S.C. §§ 601–613; Competition in Contracting Act, 41 U.S.C. §§ 401–412. For example, the Court of Claims is given jurisdiction in federal procurement contract disputes "notwithstanding any contract provision, regulation, or rule of law to the contrary." 41 U.S.C. § 609(a)(1).

[40]   See S. Koniak and D. Dana, "Bargaining in the Shadow of Democracy" (1999) 148 U Pa L Rev 473, 495–515.

[41]   Ibid., at 526.

[42]   G. Hadfield, "Of Sovereignty and Contract: Damages for Breach of Contract by the Government" (1999) 8 S Cal Interdisc L J 467, 467–470.

[43]   Ibid., at 537 (employing this distinction though denying its relevance).

or effective than traditional regulation composed of a patchwork of smaller contractual negotiations.

Second, there are deeper theoretical reasons to doubt the assertion that democratic sovereignty should always take primacy over contractual principles. To begin with, the example of international law demonstrates that contractual principles are applied to governments even as "sovereigns." International law is largely composed of treaties and informed by the foundational principle of *pacta sunt servanda*. Indeed, treaties may be seen as merely contracts-writ-large.[44] More fundamentally, the idea of democratic sovereignty itself, even within the framework of the nation-state, depends significantly on philosophical principles of contract and consent. From Rousseau to Rawls, modern democratic political theory has been concerned with the nature of the general social contract that binds together the will of citizens in legitimate governments.[45] The idea of "the consent of the governed" is essential in the history of democracy.[46] The fact that democratic political theories of obligation refer commonly to "tacit" or "hypothetical" consent highlights the connection between principles of democratic sovereignty and contract, rather than distinguishing them from each other.[47]

---

[44]   See, e.g., E. Benvenisti, "Exit and Voice in the Age of Globalization" (1999) 98 Mich L Rev 167, 192 and n. 107 (describing international treaties as relational contracts). The fact that treaties in international law are viewed as legitimately binding even when nondemocratic political states negotiate them has led to criticism of international law as lacking democratic legitimacy. See ibid at 194–195 and n 119 (giving sources); see also P. Lindseth, "Democratic Legitimacy and the Administrative Character of Supranationalism: The Example of the European Community" (1999) 99 Colum L Rev 628, 633–635 (arguing that delegation of supranational power is twice removed from the legitimacy of the people). The absence of an effective and representative legislator at the international level also leads to a general question of the democratic legitimacy of international law as expressed through treaties over time. Debates about the "democratic deficit" within international organizations such as the European Union are symptomatic of this larger issue as well. See, e.g., J. Weiler, "The Transformation of Europe" (1991) 100 Yale L J 2403, 2417, 2430, 2466–2474 (discussing allegations of a "democracy deficit" in the European Union). Comparative analysis is needed, of course, to assess whether international law is more or less "democratic" than national or regional variations. See R. Dehousse, "Comparing National and EC Law: The Problem of the Level of Analysis" (1994) 42 Am Comp L Rev 761.

[45]   Classic works are J. Rousseau, *The Social Contract* (M. Cranston, trans.) (Penguin Books, New York, 1987) and J. Rawls, *A Theory of Justice* (Harvard University Press, 1971). More recent applications of social contract theory are many and varied. See, e.g., T. Donaldson and T. Dunfee, *Ties That Bind: A Social Contracts Approach to Business Ethics* (Harvard Business School Press, 1999); D. Gauthier, *Morals By Agreement* (Oxford University Press, 1986); J. Hampton, *Hobbes and the Social Contract Tradition* (Cambridge University Press, 1986); T. Scanlon, *What We Owe to Each Other* (Harvard University Press, 1998); B. Skyrms, *Evolution of the Social Contract* (Cambridge University Press, 1996).

[46]   See, e.g., R. Dahl, *On Democracy* (Yale University Press, 1998), p. 22. For one important example, social contract theory, particularly in its Lockean form, strongly influenced those who founded the democratic government of the United States. See, e.g., A. Allen, "Social Contract Theory in American Case Law" (1999) 51 Fla L Rev 1, 2–3 (reviewing scholarship on this point).

[47]   Hobbes and Locke give the most famous arguments for obligation on the basis of "tacit consent." See T. Hobbes, *Leviathan* (Penguin Classics, 1982) (1651); J. Locke, *The Second Treatise of Government*, (Hacket Publishing Co., 1980) (1690), pp. 119–120. Although "historically dominant," this political and legal theory of obligation has "recently fallen on hard times." J. Feinberg, "The Right To Disobey" (1989) 87 Mich L Rev 1690, 1693 (book review).

At least in the general sense of classical and modern social contract theory, even regulations at the highest levels of government are properly conceived as types of basic political agreements.

The notion of regulatory contracts cannot therefore be easily dismissed as antidemocratic. Moreover, we believe it is useful to break down the presumed division between private contracts and public regulation. It is helpful to free the idea of contract from its usual association with private law because the concept and process of "contract" may provide some useful suggestions for public regulation. On the view that direct consent through participation and formal agreement may be seen as more democratic than the diffuse processes of representative government through the use of regulatory bureaucracies, it is possible to argue on grounds of democratic political theory in favor of a broader regulatory use of contracts. In other words, regulation through contractual processes may be superior to traditional regulation because it may better accord with democratic values. In this respect, contemporary political theories of "deliberative democracy" support arguments in favor of regulatory contracts formed through collaborative participation of relevant interests directly in the processes of the administrative state.[48]

Third, the use of contract is a paradigm of efficient agreement in contemporary economic theory. In essence, an economic view of regulation holds that, other things being equal, contracts are presumptively more efficient than other forms of mandatory regulation because the consent needed to form contracts makes them by definition "Pareto optimal" between the parties.[49] Regulation by contract may therefore often have the benefit of being presumptively more efficient as well as more democratic than traditional methods of regulation.[50]

(cont.)

For examples of criticism of theories of tacit consent, see K. Greenawalt, *Conflicts of Law and Morality* (Oxford University Press, 1987) ch. 5; H. Hurd, "Challenging Authority" (1991) 100 Yale L J 1611, 1657–1663. Theories of "hypothetical" consent based on a sense of benefits received from the government and "fair play" with respect to fellow citizens have had a stronger purchase in contemporary theory. See, e.g., Greenawalt, supra, ch. 7; J. Rawls, "Legal Obligations and the Duty of Fair Play" in S. Hook (ed.), *Law and Philosophy* (New York University Press, 1964).

[48] For collections of essays on the topic, see J. Bohman and W. Rehg (eds), *Deliberative Democracy: Essays on Reason and Politics* (MIT Press, 1997); J. Elster (ed.), *Deliberative Democracy* (Cambridge University Press, 1998); S. Macedo (ed.), *Deliberative Politics: Essays on Democracy and Disagreement* (Oxford University Press, 1999). For recent work discussing related themes from differing theoretical perspectives, see B. Barber, *Strong Democracy: Participatory Politics for a New Age* (University of California Press, 1985); J. Drysek, *Discursive Democracy* (Cambridge University Press, 1990); A. Gutman and D. Thompson, *Democracy and Disagreement* (Harvard University Press, 1996); J. Mansbridge, *Beyond Adversary Democracy* (University of Chicago, 1986); B. Williams and A. Matheny, *Democracy, Dialogue, and Environmental Disputes* (Yale University Press, 1995).

[49] For systematic discussions that explore the nuances of this intuition, see the contributions of Johnston, Delmas and Terlaak, Segerson and Dawson, and Spence and Gopala Krishnan in their chapters in this book.

[50] This does not mean, however, that careful analysis will inevitably show environmental contracts to be superior to other methods of regulation for particular problems. Several chapters in this book argue that the empirical evidence is as yet ambiguous with respect to some samples in Europe, and other chapters argue that the economic arguments are also complex.

Figure 2

Spectrum of Contracts and Regulation

| Private property with no contract rights | Private contracts | Regulatory contracts | Leviathan state of direct regulation only |

We therefore see "contract" and "regulation" better characterized as covering a variety of legal instruments that appear on a spectrum of possibilities, rather than a rigid dichotomy between "private" and "public" regimes. One way to envision the theoretical spectrum of regulation is to imagine contracts and regulation to lie between the extremes of (1) private property ownership and individual rights that do not recognize any agreements among individuals about the future (in which a brutish Hobbesian world would arguably obtain) and (2) a Leviathan state in which every type of behavior is regulated by a central administrative authority. This spectrum is depicted above in Figure 2. Intermediate options describe most contemporary legal civilizations, including not only enforceable property rights and direct regulation, but also private contracts and different forms of regulatory contracts. Contracts of different kinds in this sense fill the void between anarchy and absolutism.

Different variations may be adopted to address different problems. In some situations, individual private contracting may provide the best approach. A paradigm is a restrictive covenant between private parties governing the permissible use of a tract of land.[51] Regulatory contracts may best address other problems, particularly those involving multiple immediate interests. Yet other problems may call for direct command-and-control or informational regulation.[52] Our submission is simply a call for a close and careful consideration of the option of regulatory contracts as a private/public alternative for addressing environmental problems.[53]

Whether grounded by regulation or contract, or a regulatory contract hybrid, there are two other important dimensions of environmental problems and their legal treatment that are salient. First, environmental issues are inevitably political. The history of environmental regulation is the story of growing political awareness about the detrimental effects on the natural

---

[51] See American Law Institute, Restatement (3rd) of Property (Servitudes) §§ 1.3, 2.1, 2.2, 5.1, 5.2, 8.3 (2000).

[52] See P. Kleindorfer and E. Orts, "Informational Regulation of Environmental Risks" (1998) 18 Risk Analysis 155, 166–168 (proposing a multi-criteria approach to selecting the best form of regulation for particular environmental problems). For an economic analysis, see N. Keohane et al., "The Choice of Regulatory Instruments in Environmental Policy" (1998) 22 Harv Envtl L Rev 313.

[53] Again, we are not the first to make this argument. In addition to the European experience discussed above, see E. D. Elliott, "Toward Ecological Law and Policy" in M. Chertow and D. Esty (eds), *Thinking Ecologically: The Next Generation of Environmental Policy* (Yale University Press, 1997), pp. 170, 183–185 (describing a movement from "command and control" to "command and covenant").

environment of a growing and complex industrial economic society. These detrimental effects include damage to human health through pollution of land, water, or air and damage to the natural environment including other species, wilderness preserves, and ecological conditions of global scope, such as ozone layer depletion or climate change.[54] The science of these effects and their probabilities or "risks" is complex, dynamic, and important.[55] At the same time, the politics of what to do about environmental risks is highly charged.

A second important dimension of environmental regulation is one of the major reasons for its political nature: Environmental issues usually require some form of regulation to influence the behavior of the economic system and, specifically, business. In other words, environmental regulation is infused fundamentally with a business character. Virtually by definition, environmental law addresses the process of investment in and the use (and abstention of use) of common resources of land, water, and air. Because use of resources is involved, environmental regulation immediately poses questions of positive and negative limitations on participation and economic externalities. Environmental regulations implicate not only relationships among persons but relationships of persons in the use of specific non-human resources, and these relationships concerning resource use are as essential to the economic processes of business and markets as to environmental protection.

3   CONTRACTS, REGULATION, AND THE CONSTITUTION

The use of contracts in regulation raises interesting and difficult constitutional issues. One of the characteristics that divides "contracts" and "regulations" as we conceive them is that the parties in a contract are specified, whereas regulations apply to everyone within a particular government's jurisdiction. In addition, the time period of a contract is ordinarily defined, whereas regulations are ordinarily open-ended.[56] Unlike contracts, regulations can usually be revoked, extended, or otherwise changed at the will of one of the parties, namely, the government, as long as it acts within its legally authorized powers and according to legal procedures.

---

[54]   For historical accounts of the birth and growth of environmentalism in the United States, see, e.g., K. Sale, *The Green Revolution: The American Environmental Movement 1962–1992* (Hill & Wang, 1993); P. Shabecoff, *A Fierce Green Fire: The American Environmental Movement* (Hill & Wang, 1993). For a general introduction to the nature and scope of contemporary environmental problems, see C. Stone, *The Gnat Is Older Than Man: Global Environment and the Human Agenda* (Princeton University Press, 1993).

[55]   See the introductory chapter by Orts and Deketelaere in this book for a description of how "the science of risk" informs a reform agenda for comprehensive comparative risk analysis of regulations.

[56]   There are, of course, exceptions. Some contracts imply a "reasonable time" for a performance. Some regulations have "sunset" provisions requiring reauthorization or lapse after a specified period.

In the United States, there are additional constitutional limitations to the otherwise arbitrary power of the legislative and executive branches of government to change its mind about regulations. With respect to the criminal law, for example, the government is prohibited by the Ex Post Facto Clause from adopting laws that would impose penalties on the behavior of any citizen retroactively.[57] In civil law, the constitutional prohibition on retroactive legislation does not usually apply—as perhaps best exemplified in environmental law by the immense economic burdens imposed retroactively by the Superfund legislation for toxic clean-up liability.[58] Several constitutional limitations to civil regulation nevertheless appear under the rubric of the following: (1) the Takings Clause, which protects settled expectations in private property from government interference without monetary compensation;[59] (2) the Bill of Attainder provisions, which prevent specific legislative punishment of persons with civil penalties;[60] (3) the Due Process Clause, which protects certain rights of property, privacy, and "personhood;"[61] and (4) perhaps most importantly for our purposes, the Contracts Clause, which protects some contracts made when the government is a party.[62]

The Contracts Clause does not, of course, preclude the government from interfering with any expectations expressed in any contract. Such a radical approach would open a huge hole in the modern constitutional fabric that would enable the contractual avoidance of any foreseeable regulation. The usual rule instead is that contracts are made subject to change in the regulations as they apply generally to citizens. Thus, a contract or contractual provision that subsequently becomes illegal is ordinarily unenforceable.

However, an exception sometimes applies to contracts made by the government that involve private parties. These situations expose an interesting tension within the constitutional order between (1) the intentionally prospective reach of contracts to cover specified parties, including the government when it is a party, for a specified period of time, and (2) the effect of government regulation that modifies or destroys ordinary contractual expectations. Easy cases appear when the government acts obviously either as a contracting party (such as in an ordinary supply contract for office materials or munitions) or as a regulator (with an incidental general effect on contracts among citizens). Hard cases arise when the government acts *both* as a contracting party and a regulator. These hard cases can arise in

---

[57] US Const., Art I, § 9, cl. 3; id., § 10, cl. 1. This restriction applies to both the national government and the states.

[58] For a recent discussion of this inconsistency, see H. Krent, "The Puzzling Boundary Between Criminal and Civil Retroactive Lawmaking" (1996) 84 Geo L J 2143.

[59] US Const., Amend. V.

[60] US Const., Art I, § 9, cl. 3; id., § 10, cl. 1. See also L. Tribe, *American Constitutional Law* (2nd edn, Foundation Press, 1988), pp. 641–663.

[61] US Const., Amend. V, cl. 1; Amend. XIV, cl.1. See Tribe, supra note 60, ch. 15.

[62] US Const., Art I, § 10, cl. 1. Although the original intent of the Contracts Clause was to protect private contracts from legislative regulation, this jurisprudence passed with the *Lochner* era. The Supreme Court breathed new life into the Contracts Clause to apply to certain forms of government contracts. See Tribe, supra note 60, at 613–628. See, e.g., *United States Trust Co. of New York v. New Jersey*, 431 US 1 (1977); *Allied Structural Steel v. Spannaus*, 438 US 234 (1978).

various circumstances. For example, the government may agree to an ordinary contract as a contracting party, and then pass legislation making the contract illegal. Or the government may negotiate with parties about a new regulation, and then breach its agreement when the regulation is actually adopted or enforced. In both cases, the government in effect breaches its own contract. The regulatory breach is often justified by the government in the name of the public interest, but a conflict arises with contractual principles of keeping one's promise or at least paying damages for breaking it.

United States v. Winstar[63] illustrates a difficult case of the conflict between government-as-contractor and government-as-regulator. In *Winstar*, three Savings and Loan thrifts (S&Ls) sued the United States for breach of contract when the Financial Institutions Reform, Recovery, and Enforcement Act of 1989 (FIRREA)[64] imposed new capital requirements that contradicted agreements the S&Ls had signed with the federal Bank Board under previous legislation. Prior to FIRREA, the federal government had, through the Bank Board, encouraged failing S&Ls to merge with healthy ones. As an inducement, the Bank Board contractually approved favorable accounting treatments for "supervisory goodwill" of the acquired S&Ls, even though they were failing.[65] When S&Ls across the country continued to fail and federal insurance costs mounted, the government changed course and adopted FIRREA. This new legislation eliminated the accounting incentive allowed for supervisory goodwill in the previous deals signed and promoted by the Bank Board. Two of the three plaintiff S&Ls in *Winstar* were immediately seized by regulators and liquidated, and the third avoided the same fate only through an aggressive recapitalization to meet the new capital requirements. In a plurality opinion, the US Supreme Court upheld the Federal Circuit's decision that the government had breached its express contracts with the S&Ls and therefore was liable for damages. The Court rejected the government's defense based on the "unmistakeability doctrine," which says that the government cannot contractually surrender its "sovereign power" to regulate unless it did so "in unmistakeable terms."[66] The plurality opinion of four Justices held that a claim of damages was not barred under the facts, though a claim for an injunction may very likely have been rejected. In addition, the plurality found unmistakeable evidence of intentional "risk-shifting" in the contracts.[67] In a concurring opinion, three Justices did not agree with the distinction between damages and equitable remedies, but nevertheless found the requirements of the unmistakeability doctrine to have been met.[68] In an unusual dissenting partnership, Chief Justice Rehnquist and Justice Ginsburg argued that unmistakeability

---

[63] 518 U.S. 839 (1996).
[64] Pub. L. No. 101-73, §§ 301–308, 103 Stat. 183, 277–354 (codified as amended in scattered sections of 12 U.S.C.).
[65] A failing business may not ordinarily count goodwill as an asset, but this is only one example of creative accounting that often occurs in corporate mergers and acquisitions.
[66] 518 U.S. at 871–872 (quoting *Bowen v. Public Agencies Opposed to Social Security Entrapment*, 477 U.S. 41, 52 (1986)).
[67] Ibid., at 880–887 (Souter, J., plurality).
[68] Ibid., at 919–924 (Scalia, J., concurring).

had not been shown and claimed that a major change had been made to the sovereign acts doctrine, which distinguishes between cases in which the government acts as a sovereign regulator and cases in which it acts as a contractor.[69]

In essence, then, *Winstar* seems to stand for the following. The government's express contractual agreement to treat the S&L mergers favorably in terms of an accounting convention conflicted with the government's attempt to renege on its agreements through the adoption of FIRREA. The constitutional basis for the Court's plurality and concurring opinions is not entirely clear. The case seems to be decided on the basis of federal contract principles in cases authorized under federal tort claims legislation. But whatever the constitutional foundation, the result in *Winstar* confirms that contracts of a regulatory nature made by the government may be enforced against the government at least in some circumstances. Although the Court makes an important distinction in the case between claims for damages and injunctions, *Winstar* seems at least to indicate that some constitutional or statutory limitations may prevent the government from easily changing its mind and reneging on a contract made in a regulatory context.

Winstar is relevant for environmental contracts because a principle of prospective enforceability of regulatory contracts made by an authorized government agency would provide a significant incentive for businesses and other regulated entities to negotiate such agreements. Statutory adjustments may be required similar to those proposed in the Second Generation Environmental Improvement Act to extend authority explicitly to the EPA to make regulatory contracts through Project XL and similar programs.[70] *Winstar* itself suggests that private parties could recover damages against the EPA for breaches of regulatory contracts, but the law at present is sufficiently uncertain to provide only a weak incentive for businesses to enter negotiations. In particular, statutory authority would be required for regulatory contracts to allow for at least the possibility of changing the underlying standards for citizen suits—though in this regard it would also seem necessary to allow local community or environmental groups to negotiate free-standing citizen enforcement provisions in regulatory contracts.[71] In any event, environmental contracts as a method of regulation appear more promising in light of the principles elucidated in *Winstar*. At least in appropriate cases to be determined by the government itself through its decisions to enter collaborative negotiations with regulated parties and other affected interests, regulatory contracts may begin to supplement traditional command-and-control as a mode of "doing" environmental law in the United States. Advantages of this approach to environmental contracts may include the following: (1) periodic renegotiation of regulatory contracts in light of experience, scientific knowledge, and technology; (2) regulatory flexibility to allow economical alternatives to achieve environmental protection goals

---

[69] Ibid. at 924–934 (Rehnquist, C.J., dissenting).
[70] See supra note 35 and accompanying text.
[71] The proposed Second Generation Environmental Improvement Act does not go this far.

at lower costs; and (3) collaborative decision making that would involve government, regulated entities, and public interest groups in collective problem-solving rather than adversarial legal posturing and wasteful litigation.

Dangers are also present. They include most prominently the threat that regulatory contracts would ratchet down levels of environmental protection under the guise of legal "reinvention." Sweetheart deals might be negotiated between colluding government bureaucrats and business interests, and the check of local community and environmentalist interests could be sidelined in negotiations.[72] But the potential benefits seem large enough that it is worth thinking seriously about how these dangers of renewed "capture" might be avoided in adopting an environmental contracting approach to regulation. Environmental contracts, if properly conceived and used, may bring the benefits of both contracts—including the flexibility, direct consent, and mutual enforceability that are among the special features of contract— and the authority and public-interest focus associated with traditional forms of regulation.

4   MULTI-JURISDICTIONAL ENVIRONMENTAL ISSUES AS A SPECIAL PROBLEM AND OPPORTUNITY

Environmental contracts may also help to address the well-known failure of many ecological problems to observe human-made boundaries. Most serious environmental problems transcend the boundaries within and across nation-states. Harmful chemicals and other substances emitted into the air and water observe the laws of physics rather than those of political states. Indeed, multi-jurisdictional problems appear to be increasingly common in the environmental area, as the global economy expands and its impact is felt in problems such as biodiversity loss, deforestation, overfishing of the oceans, and climate change. The special nature of multi-jurisdictional problems invites critical reflection about the legal mechanisms needed to solve them.

The multi-jurisdictional dimension of many environmental problems suggests that creative solutions beyond traditional methods of regulation should be sought, if only because traditional regulation works effectively only within well-defined jurisdictional boundaries. Environmental contracts may provide an additional legal tool—in addition to the unwieldy and uncertain use of international regulation by inter-governmental treaties—to address this multi-jurisdictional phenomenon common to many environmental problems. A contractual approach may also offer needed flexibility to address special problems of the benefits and burdens of environmental regulation, especially in view of significant disparity in economic wealth among various legal jurisdictions, whether they are localities, states within federal national systems, or nation-states.

---

[72]   For an argument along these lines, see Koniak and Dana, *supra* note 40.

Regulatory authority is conventionally limited within national boundaries, except through multinational arrangement or at least implicit consent to the exercise of extraterritorial authority and jurisdiction.[73] This limitation of jurisdiction entails correspondingly limited authority to govern behavior either through contracts or traditional regulation. Multi-jurisdictional controls are inherently weaker, whatever regulatory tool is used. In many situations, the only feasible solution may be to negotiate direct regulation through mutually enforceable treaties or the creation of supra-national entities such as the World Trade Organization.[74] In other cases, however, it may make sense on both political and economic grounds to consider whether using international environmental contracts would prove helpful. As we discuss next, we believe that a regulatory approach of recognizing contracts may have a number of advantages, though these advantages are balanced by structural and other limitations.

The nation-state remains the fundamental building block of the world political order.[75] The nation-state is defined in terms of its supreme and exclusive authority within its geographical boundaries.[76] Each of the nearly 200 nation-states today recognizes itself as having such authority and extends similar recognition to other states.[77] The nation-state is, of course, the source of authority that is exercised in the regulatory regimes we are addressing. Federal systems are not an exception.[78] All established federal systems have internal rules to resolve allocations of regulatory authority within their constitutional structures. Because the nation-state as a political body is recognized by international law as supreme within its borders, it follows that the global system of nation-states is a major political obstacle to dealing with environmental problems that cross international borders simply because the populations of no two nation-states have precisely the

---

[73] The most well-known cases involved the attempt by the United States to exert extraterritorial authority to protect dolphins from being killed by foreign methods of fishing for tuna, which resulted in two adverse World Trade Organization (formerly GATT) opinions against the U.S. See GATT Dispute Panel Report on United States Restrictions on Imports of Tuna, 30 I.L.M. 1598 (3 September 1991); GATT Dispute Settlement Panel Report on U.S. Restrictions on Imports of Tuna, 30 I.L.M. 839 (16 June 1994). For an overview of the dispute and its current status, see C. Miller and J. Croston, "WTO Scrutiny v. Environmental Objectives: Assessment of the International Dolphin Conservation Program Act" (1999) 37 Am Bus LJ 73 (1999). See also P. Nichols, "Trade Without Values" (1996) 90 Nw U L Rev 658, 672–679 (discussing how environmental values expressed through national law may conflict with principles of international free trade).
[74] See, e.g., C. Runge, *Freer Trade, Protected Environment: Balancing Trade Liberalization and Environmental Interests* (Council on Foreign Relations, 1994), pp. 100–107 (arguing for a World Environmental Organization).
[75] For historical accounts of the rise of the nation-state, the implacable creature of post-Renaissance European politics, see E. Gellner, *Nations and Nationalism* (Cornell University Press, 1983); E. Hobsbawm, *Nations and Nationalism Since 1780: Programme, Myth, Reality* (2nd rev edn, Cambridge University Press, 1993).
[76] See, e.g., R. McIver, *Web of Government* (1965).
[77] These basic rights to equal sovereignty among and within nation-states are recited in Article Two of the United Nations Charter.
[78] Of 22 democratic governments existing since 1950, only six have federal systems, each of them for different specific historical reasons. See Dahl, supra note 46, at 119–121.

same interests in environmental controls. Some modification of nation-state sovereignty can overcome this political obstacle.

The means of modifying the sovereignty of the nation-state are various forms of international contract. The classic international contract is of course the treaty. Many treaties indeed deal with environmental problems.[79] Another form of international contract is one that creates a special-purpose governmental authority, for example, the international commissions set up to govern international rivers, such as the Meuse and the Scheldt.[80] In these arrangements, the contracting states agree to create a joint governmental body that is generally subordinate to the contracting powers, but which has supreme authority in the limited sphere of its establishment. A term conventionally used for these types of quasi-autonomous nongovernmental organizations that lie partly outside (or above) the ordinary processes of national governments is "quango."[81]

In practice, the form of arrangement identified as an international treaty or convention often merges with the special-purpose governmental authority. That is, in order to effectuate the terms of a treaty between sovereign states, it often proves practically necessary to create a special trans-border administrative body to do so. Such an administrative body or quango may be called merely a cooperative arrangement, but through operation and over time it tends to achieve a measure of semi-autonomy. Thus, it is a mistake to consider the treaty and quango as distinct types, except conceptually. In practice the two are synergistic. An example is the international law and organizations established to govern fisheries.[82]

Still another form of international contract is the "concession" granted by a sovereign state to a business enterprise. Some commentators have regarded this form of arrangement generally as disreputable, being associated with the contractual exactions obtained by imperial powers from weak

---

[79]   For a list and summary of 15 major global environmental treaties from the Antarctic Treaty to the Convention on Climate Change, see L. Susskind, *Environmental Diplomacy: Negotiating More Effective Global Agreements* (Oxford University Press, 1994), pp. 152–175, app. A.

[80]   See Agreement on the Protection of the (River) Meuse, 33 ILM 854 (26 April 1994); Agreement on the Protection of the (River) Scheldt, 33 ILM 859 (26 April 1994). Earlier river basin authorities with multi-jurisdictional authority occurred also in federal systems. An example is the Tennessee Valley Authority in the United States. See L. Teclaff, "Evolution of the River Basin Concept in National and International Water Law" (1996) 36 Nat Resources J 359, 366.

[81]   The concept originates in the United Kingdom, particularly in connection with agreements for the governance of Northern Ireland. For a recent American translation, see M. Tushnet, "The Possibilities of Comparative Constitutional Law" (1999) 108 Yale L J 1225, 1257–1264. Less colorfully, one might also refer to "transnational institutions," see Benvenisti, supra note 44, at 202–209.

[82]   See C. Joyner, "Compliance and Enforcement in New International Fisheries Law" (1998) 12 Temp Int'l & Comp L J 271. See also D. Hunter, et al., *International Environmental Law and Policy* (Foundation Press, 1998) pp. 702–731 (overview of international fisheries law). Article 118 of the UN Convention on the Law of the Sea recommends the establishment of subregional or regional fisheries organizations. Similarly, the Magnuson Fisheries Conservation and Management Act establishes eight regional fishery councils charged to prepare fishery management plans. 16 U.S.C. §§ 1801–1882.

regimes in undeveloped countries.[83] We maintain, however, that international concessions are not inevitably unfair and unjust. Indeed, they are the basis of virtually all "foreign direct investment," ancient or modern, that is not based on sheer military superiority. The basic deal in a concession is simple. The foreign source provides development capital but agrees to limitations on the development, and the domestic regime guarantees against expropriation and other legal infringements of the property and profits of the enterprise during the life of the venture. The limitations imposed on the enterprise can include environmental controls, for example, emission controls for factories, height or other restrictions in building construction, or traffic controls for large facilities. The facts that concessions may be attended by corruption and that many of the modern versions are mundane should not obscure their functional importance.

A contractual concession can also merge with the special-purpose international authority or quango. Examples include arrangements concerning tunnel construction across national borders, such as the European Chunnel,[84] and dam construction at national borders, such as the hydroelectric power facility on the Parana River at the border of Brazil and Paraguay.[85] These arrangements require not only government-to-government agreements, but also agreements with respect to private investment and operation. One can visualize similar arrangements for other projects that would have significant environmental consequences, such as the construction and operation of plants to produce electricity through fossil-fuel with enforced limitations on air pollution emissions or for fishery control operations that would include private investments for hatcheries or "aquaculture."[86]

Viewed in this way, the problem of environmental control in the multi-jurisdictional context is simply a variant of the counterpart problem in a wholly domestic setting. In any event, it seems clear that there is nothing peculiar about international multi-jurisdictional environmental problems, except that they involve greater political complexity that results from the fact that more than one sovereign state is involved. This does not mean that easy optimism should result about the feasibility of international

---

[83] See, e.g., M. Pendleton, "A New Human Right: The Right to Globalization" (1999) 22 Ford Int'l L J 2052, 2070 (rehearsing this argument, though disagreeing with it on economic grounds). This reputation may well be fully deserved. Certainly, many concessions appear in retrospect to be one-sided and often to have been obtained from local political authorities through bribery and other unethical inducements.

[84] The governments of France and the United Kingdom awarded a private contract to a consortium of 10 companies for a tunnel under the English Channel (dubbed the Eurotunnel), including a concession to the consortium to build and operate it for 55 years. See A. Valdez, "Financing High Speed Rail: Meeting the Transportation Challenge of the '90s"(1990) 18 Transp L J 173, 186.

[85] "World Record Project Completed" Engineering News Record, 27 May 1999, p. 18.

[86] For example, agreements between governments and non-governmental organizations have been used to help establish aquaculture in some developing countries. See D. Lewis, "Charity and Empowerment: NGOs, Donors, and the State in Bangladesh" (1997) 554 Annals 33; T. Dobson, "Community Participation in Natural Resources Management in Malawi: Charting a New Course for Sustainability" (1998) 153 Colo J Int'l L & Pol'y 166–169.

environmental contracts. The greater the number of players in any human "game," the more the difficult it usually is to agree to a set of rules.[87] No nation-state is a political monolith, and hence each state has internal divisions that its government must somehow accommodate. Private businesses, particularly large ones, can have similar if less obvious internal divisions. Then again, all parties must be aware that the representatives at the table may be out of office when the agreement is to be signed, and they will certainly be out of office when a long-term agreement is to be carried through. All these difficulties and obstacles to international contractual arrangements must be recognized and addressed. However, in the multijurisdictional context, given the persistence of the nation-state as a form of basic political organization, there is no other way.

5 OF REASON AND WILL

In *The Cultural Study of Law*, Paul Kahn has recently characterized law reform in modern democratic societies as driven by "the intersection of reason and will, which are thought to be the twin sources of legitimate legal order."[88] On one hand, "the legal order should satisfy a standard of reason; irrationality in legal rules and procedures always appears as a deficiency in need of correction."[89] In environmental law, the force of reason seems to drive those who argue most strongly for comprehensive comparative risk regulation and for economically sensible rules. On the other hand, according to Kahn, the legal order "should also satisfy a standard of will; law should be a product of popular consent."[90] He goes on to conclude:

Law that appears to make no contact with the popular will, either past or present, is as problematic as law without reason. The ambition of law's rule in a democratic polity is to reach a coincidence of will—popular consent—and reason. Because this ambition is never fully and finally achieved, at every moment law stands in need of reform.[91]

In environmental law, regulatory contracts may help to square the circle of democratic legitimacy requiring both "reason" and "will," though never perfectly achieving either. Recommendations for the coercive rationalization of environmental law by faceless bureaucrats, whether through a superagency or the courts, threaten to violate the principle of some degree of expression of general will and consent required in a democratic government.

---

[87] For an argument making this point in the international context, see Susskind, *supra* note 79, at 3–5.

[88] P. Kahn, *The Cultural Study of Law: Reconstructing Legal Scholarship* (University of Chicago Press, 1999), p. 7.

[89] Ibid., at 7–8.

[90] Ibid., at 8.

[91] Ibid.

By the same token, the problem of participation in environmental lawmaking is not easily solved. The European principle of "subsidiarity" recommends that environmental problems are best solved at the lowest possible government level, but this principle is not self-executing.[92] In the best of all possible worlds, perhaps environmental contracts may achieve some of the goals of deliberative democracy, which would bring together, if properly conceived and structured, the strengths of both reason and will to solve our very large and expensive modern environmental problems.[93] At least, there is room to doubt the traditional pluralists who advocate old-style democratic theories of administrative law in an era when less than half of the electorate in the United States vote even for their President.[94]

---

[92] For comparative discussions of this elusive constitutional principle, see G. Bermann, "Taking Subsidiarity Seriously: Federalism in the European Community and the United States" (1994) 94 Colum L Rev 331; E. Swaine, "Subsidiarity and Self-Interest: Federalism at the European Court of Justice" (2000) 41 Harv Int'l L J 1.

[93] See supra notes 48 and 54 and accompanying text.

[94] Statistical Abstract of the United States, (1998) tbl. 485, p. 297 (only 49 percent of the US electorate voted for President in 1996).

4. Is Consensus an Appropriate Basis for Regulatory Policy?

*Cary Coglianese**

Regulators in the United States are increasingly urged to build consensus before making policy decisions. The process of consensus-building aims to create an explicit agreement over the substance of regulatory policy among the individuals and groups who will be affected by the policy. This craving for consensus was institutionalized in 1990 with the passage of the Negotiated Rulemaking Act,[1] which authorizes agencies to establish formal negotiation processes over the terms of proposed regulations. Since that time, more than two dozen other federal statutes either compel or strongly encourage agencies to use consensus-based procedures.[2]

---

*I am grateful for the detailed comments on earlier versions of this chapter provided by Alice Andre-Clark, Curt James, and Henry Lee, as well as the helpful input offered by the participants in sessions at the University of Pennsylvania Law School, Kennedy School of Government, and the annual meetings of the Law and Society Association, the Greening of Industry Network, and Association of Public Policy and Management.

[1] 5 U.S.C. §§ 561–570 (1996). The Negotiated Rulemaking Act was permanently reauthorized by the Administrative Dispute Resolution Act of 1996, Pub. Law No. 104-320 (1996).

[2] The number of statutory provisions requiring the use of consensus-based decision-making continues to grow. For a list of a selected statutes requiring the use of negotiated rulemaking proceedings, see C. Coglianese, "Assessing Consensus: The Promise and Performance of Negotiated Rulemaking" (1997) 46 *Duke LJ* 1255, 1268 n. 75. For additional legislation requiring or encouraging consensus-based decisions, see the Transportation Equity Act for the 21st Century, Pub. Law No. 105-178 (1998); Higher Education Amendments of 1998, Pub. Law No. 105-244 (1998); VA, HUD, and Independent Agencies Appropriations Act, Pub. Law No. 105-276 (1998); Omnibus Supplemental Appropriations, Pub. Law No. 105-277 (1998); Carl D. Perkins Vocational and Applied Technology Education Amendments of 1998, Pub. Law No. 105-332 (1998); Traumatic Brain Injury Programs Authorization, Pub. Law No. 104-166 (1996); VA, HUD, and Independent Agencies Appropriations Act, Pub. Law No. 104-204 (1996); Sustainable Fisheries Act, Pub. Law No. 104-297 (1996); Omnibus Parks and Public Lands Management Act of 1996, Pub. Law No. 104-333 (1996); Fisheries Act of 1995, Pub. Law No. 104-43 (1995); Goals 2000 Educate America Act, Pub. Law No. 103-227 (1994); Marine Mammals Protection Act Amendments of 1994, Pub. Law No. 103-238 (1994); Federal Aviation Administration Authorization Act of 1994, Pub. Law No. 103-305 (1994); Federal Acquisition Streamlining Act of 1994, Pub. Law No. 103-355 (1994); Yavapai-Prescott Indian Tribe Water Rights Settlement Act of 1994, Pub. Law No. 103-434 (1994). In addition, the National Technology Transfer and

The desire for consensus has also taken an especially strong hold in efforts to adopt new approaches to environmental regulation. Nearly every major commission report and panel study issued on environmental policy in recent years has called for greater reliance on consensus-building.[3] In recent years, the United States Environmental Protection Agency has launched several consensus-based projects, such as the Common Sense Initiative and Project XL. Furthermore, a range of natural resource initiatives in the areas of ecosystem management and habitat conservation have also relied on collaborative approaches to policy-making. We are living, some might have it, at the dawn of an age of consensus.

In the face of a prevailing enchantment with what Louis Jaffe once called the "beauties of co-operation," it is worth pausing to reflect on whether consensus really is an appropriate mode of making public policy.[4] Much of what has been written so far on consensus in regulatory policy-making focuses on its advantages, with comparatively little attention having been paid to any potential hazards of consensus as a decision rule. In this chapter, I seek to broaden attention to the implications of efforts to increase the search for and reliance on consensus in the making of regulatory policy. Drawing on the experiences of several recent consensus-building processes, I examine what is to be gained from the institutionalization of consensus-building—as well as what is to be lost.

Even though I seek to raise questions about consensus in this chapter, I recognize that it does, in principle, hold a certain allure. Reaching consensus implies that people have worked out their differences and come to a collective decision. Consensus conjures up notions of teamwork, community, and harmony—all attractive ideas in themselves. Yet as alluring as consensus may be in principle, any widespread institutionalization of consensus-building as a basis for policy-making would mark a significant shift in prevailing modes of governmental decision-making in the United States. Such a shift, I argue here, appears neither necessary nor wise. It is not necessary because the benefits attributed to consensus-based processes can be obtained from other forms of public participation which do not revolve around a quest for consensus. It is not wise because reliance on consensus

---

Advancement Act of 1995, Pub. Law No. 104-113 (1996), declares that "all Federal agencies and departments shall use technical standards that are developed or adopted by voluntary consensus standards bodies ... as a means to carry out policy objectives or activities" unless doing so would be "inconsistent with applicable law or otherwise impractical."

[3]   The following reports—to name just a few—all recommend expanding the use of various forms of consensus-building: National Performance Review, *Improving Regulatory Systems* (Washington, D.C., 1993); Presidential/Congressional Commission on Risk Assessment and Risk Management, *Framework for Environmental Health Risk Management* (Washington, D.C., 1997); Carnegie Commission on Science, Technology and Government, *Risk and the Environment: Improving Regulatory Decision Making* (New York, 1993); National Academy of Public Administration, *Setting Priorities, Getting Results: A New Direction for EPA* (Washington, D.C., 1995); President's Council on Sustainable Development, *Sustainable America: A New Consensus for Prosperity, Opportunity, and a Healthy Environment for the Future* (Washington, D.C., 1996); Enterprise for the Environment, *The Environmental Protection System in Transition: Toward a More Desirable Future* (The CSIS Press, Washington, D.C., 1998).

[4]   L. Jaffe, "Law Making by Private Groups" (1937) 51 *Harvard Law Review* 201, 251.

as a decision rule exposes policy-making to new sources of failure and fosters unrealistic expectations for governance in a complex political system.

1   CONSENSUS AND REGULATORY POLICY

At the outset, it is important to be clear about what consensus means. Contemporary policy lingo can create confusion about the different ways to involve non-governmental actors in policy-making. A host of related terms are casually tossed about: "stakeholder involvement," "outreach," "partnerships," "consultation," "public participation," "constructive engagement," "collaboration," "regulatory negotiation," "policy deliberation," and "consensus." Far too seldom are these terms defined with any precision. In order to evaluate the relative contribution of consensus, it is necessary to clarify what it means and how it might differ from other, related terms.

Consensus commonly means unanimity or, at a minimum, something that everyone can "live with," even if it is not the ideal policy that everyone would want. The Negotiated Rulemaking Act defines "consensus" as a "unanimous concurrence" of the interests represented on a negotiated rulemaking committee, or any lesser agreement that has been unanimously agreed to by the committee.[5] The achievement of such a unanimous agreement is the defining feature of negotiated rulemaking. Before convening a negotiated rulemaking committee, agencies are required to consider whether a committee could be formed consisting of "persons who...are willing to negotiate in good faith to reach a consensus."[6] Once formed, the committee is legally obligated to "attempt to reach a consensus."[7]

Outside of federal negotiated rulemaking, "consensus" has also been stipulated by statute and practice to mean unanimity.[8] The EPA established the Common Sense Initiative (CSI) in 1994 as a vehicle for "reinventing" environmental regulation in six industrial sectors. The Initiative, which ran until 1998, was overseen by an advisory committee comprised of representatives from the various industrial sectors, environmental groups, and federal, state, and local government. The operating principles of the advisory committee, called the Common Sense Initiative Council, declared that the Council would "operate by consensus decision-making," which meant that decisions were "reached when all Council members at the table can accept or support a particular position."[9] Similarly, some of the EPA's Project XL

---

[5]   5 U.S.C. § 582.

[6]   5 U.S.C. § 583 (a)(3).

[7]   5 U.S.C. § 586 (a).

[8]   See Omnibus Consolidated Appropriations Act of 1997, Pub. Law. No. 104-208 § 201(a)(6) (1996) (defining "consensus" in the procedures for the Upper Klamath Basin Working Group to mean "unanimous agreement by the Working Group members present"). Where "consensus" has been defined in state negotiated rulemaking legislation, unanimity has also been the characteristic feature. See Mont. Code Anno. § 2-5-103 (1995); Tex. Govt. Code § 2008.056 (1997); Neb. Rev. Stat. § 84-923 (1994).

[9]   See US EPA, *Operating Principles of the U.S. Environmental Protection Agency Common Sense Initiative Council* (Washington, D.C., 1996).

initiatives have conceived of consensus in terms of the unanimous agreement of interests involved in the consultation processes that accompany these projects. Under Project XL, the EPA may waive certain regulatory requirements for individual firms which can demonstrate that alternative technologies or processes would allow them to achieve superior environmental performance. The EPA will approve Project XL waivers only after negotiating an agreement with the regulated firm and gaining the support of local community and environmental groups.[10]

Understood to require unanimity among designated interests, consensus specifies a decision rule. It therefore can be distinguished from other terms—such as "stakeholder involvement," "constructive engagement," and "public participation"—which describe deliberative efforts that are not dependent on a particular decision rule. Stakeholders can be "involved" by giving them a chance to be heard, giving them a vote, or giving them a veto. Only the last of these involves consensus. Consensus-based processes are those deliberative efforts that seek an agreement among all the participants. Conceived this way, the term "collaboration" can be used synonymously with consensus. For example, the Environmental Protection Agency, in a recent draft manual, defined collaboration as "a joint endeavor, a sharing in the process, and its goal is working together towards an agreement—consensus."[11]

Unfortunately, consensus is sometimes characterized in such a way that it might appear to be the only alternative to governmental fiat. Such characterizations are obviously misleading. Regulatory agencies can (and do) incorporate extensive public consultation into their decision-making processes without needing to strive for consensus.[12] Regulators can infuse the regulatory process with public deliberation in three conceptually distinct ways:

(1) *Feedback.* When public participation serves as a check on decision-making that the government has already initiated, we can consider

---

[10]   The EPA has not required formal unanimity among affected parties for all of its XL projects; however, serious opposition to an XL proposal will usually mean EPA will not approve it. For a description of the consensus-based endorsement processes used in the Intel and Merck XL projects, see US EPA, *Evaluation of Project XL Stakeholder Processes: Final Report* (Washington, D.C., 1998).

[11]   US EPA, *Better Decisions Through Consultation and Collaboration: A Manual on Consultative Processes and Stakeholder Involvement* 8 (Washington, D.C., 1998). Somewhat confusingly, "collaboration" is also sometimes used to refer to meaningful deliberation. For example, the Presidential/Congressional Commission on Risk Assessment and Risk Management, supra note 3, at 17, states that in its view "[c]ollaboration does not require consensus, but it does require that all parties listen to, consider, and respect each other's opinions, ideas, and contributions."

[12]   Policies based on consensus are certainly responsive to public input, but policies can be equally responsive—if not more so—without being based on consensus. Since it is normally impossible for policy-makers to secure the agreement of all the firms and individuals affected by a policy, especially in the area of environmental policy, consensus-based processes are inherently limited in terms of who participates. To the extent that agencies base their decisions solely on agreements reached between a limited segment of the affected public, consensus-based policy may very well turn out to be less responsive than decisions that follow a wide-ranging, open deliberation which is unconstrained by the need to reach agreement.

such public involvement to be a form of feedback. The bare bones, notice-and-comment rulemaking procedures of the Administrative Procedure Act[13] reflect this notion of public involvement. The Act merely requires agencies to provide notice of a regulatory proposal and to give members of the public an opportunity to comment on it before a regulation becomes final.

(2) *Input.* Unlike feedback, input occurs before or contemporaneously with governmental decision-making. Members of the public provide their views as the problem is being framed and possible policy solutions are being developed. Such input can be sought by the government itself or initiated by the parties. It can also be collected individually from each interested party in one-on-one conversations with government officials. Or it can be gathered collectively, in round-tables or dialogue sessions which allow multiple parties to engage each other in a conversation. However conducted, input processes aim to help government officials make more informed decisions.

(3) *Consensus.* A consensus-based process will typically involve collective input, but the ultimate aim of the conversation is different. With consensus, the goal is to establish agreement among all of the participants, with the expectation that the government will use that agreement as the basis for its policy decision.

In questioning consensus, I am not challenging the idea that public feedback or input is desirable. Rather I am asking whether we should design policy-making in such a way as to seek agreement before setting public policy. Should we, in other words, structure domestic regulatory policy-making along the lines of NATO or UN Security Council decision-making?

As I have already noted, it is increasingly suggested that we should. A recent report by the Keystone National Policy Dialogue on Ecosystem Management, for example, asserted that "[c]learly, consensus is the most desirable outcome of a collaborative process."[14] An EPA paper describing the Common Sense Initiative stated that the initiative's "first priority is to craft agreements that parties support, accept, or are neutral on."[15] Yet making consensus the goal of policy-making would markedly shift the prevailing norms of governance in two ways. First, an emphasis on consensus would "de-center" the state. The government would no longer be, in practice or in theory, the central, accountable decision-maker but would instead become more of a facilitator of bargaining between interest groups, or at most just another player in that bargaining game.[16] Second, a focus on

---

[13]   5 U.S.C. § 553.
[14]   Keystone Center, *The Keystone Center National Policy Dialogue on Ecosystem Management: Final Report* (Keystone, Colo., 1996).
[15]   US EPA, *Consensus Decision-Making Principles and Applications in the EPA Common Sense Initiative* (Washington, D.C., 1997).
[16]   See K. Werhan, "Delegalizing Administrative Law" (1996) U Ill L Rev 423. To be sure, policy-making in the United States has long involved bargaining, see R. Dahl, *A Preface to Democratic Theory* (The University of Chicago Press, 1956), and much regulatory litigation is resolved through negotiated settlement agreements, see C. Coglianese, "Litigating within

consensus would shift the aim of policy-making away from that which will serve the public interest to that which will be agreeable to those interests that are well represented in the political process.[17] Negotiators and facilitators, after all, are not analysts seeking to craft the best solutions to public problems. Indeed, sometimes they are skeptical of whether policy-makers ought to strive to make correct decisions at all.[18] As a result, when reformers describe consensus as "the most desirable outcome" and speak of securing agreement as "the first priority," they signal a significant shift away from norms which heretofore have made the development of sound public policy and the advancement of social values the most important priorities for government decision-makers.

2   IS CONSENSUS NECESSARY?

Since the frequent pursuit of consensus would mark a shift in the prevailing practice of governance in the United States, it is helpful to consider first whether making such a shift is even necessary. The argument for making such a shift hinges on various claimed benefits that consensus can bring to policy-making, namely that consensus-building holds instrumental advantages over processes based on feedback or input. Philip Harter, for example, has argued for consensus over what he calls "consultative processes"—that is, deliberative processes which do not seek consensus. The crux of his argument is that processes of consultation lack many of the benefits attributed to consensus.[19] Consensual processes, it is often claimed, will reduce conflict, increase compliance, improve public policy, and promote public participation. In this section, I consider whether the goal of reaching a consensus is necessary in order to achieve these principal benefits attributed to consensus-building. For each advantage attributed to consensus-building,

---

Relationships: Disputes and Disturbance in the Regulatory Process" (1996) 30 L & Soc'y Rev 735. However, the reliance on formal agreements to develop and implement regulatory policy has at least until now remained rather limited.

[17]   See W. Funk, "Bargaining Toward the New Millennium: Regulatory Negotiation and the Subversion of the Public Interest" (1997) 46 Duke L J 1351.

[18]   For example, Philip Harter has suggested that agencies should not think of themselves as seekers of correct decisions: "The agency retains a wide range of discretion and is called on to make choices that are inherently political. Political choices, however, have no right or wrong or even rational answer." P. Harter, "The Political Legitimacy and Judicial Review of Consensual Rules" (1983) 32 Am U L Rev 471, 475.

[19]   P. Harter, "Fear of Commitment: An Affliction of Adolescents" (1997) 46 *Duke LJ* 1389. Harter has argued that "the dynamics of the process change markedly if either the definition of consensus is modified to require less than unanimity or, if no attempt is made to reach full closure, to require a commitment to adhere to the agreement" and that "many of the benefits of the process are lost" by a reliance on consultation instead of consensus. Ibid. at 1411 and 1420. Cornelius Kerwin has similarly noted that "advocates of negotiated rulemaking are skeptical of partial substitutes and decry the loss of commitment that goes with them." C. Kerwin, *Rulemaking: How Government Agencies Write Law and Make Policy* 183 (2nd edn, CQ Press, Washington, D.C., 1999).

I conclude that the same benefits come from (or can come from) something other than a quest for consensus.

2.1   Reduced Conflict

Perhaps the most intuitive benefit attributed to consensus is the reduction of conflict. If all the interested parties can come to an agreement, or at least commit not to disagree, then it would appear that conflict should be eliminated. The intuition is that affected organizations will not subsequently challenge a policy with which they have concurred.

Coming to a consensus, however, is certainly not the only way to avoid conflict. A potential conflict arises, by definition, when a policy does not satisfy the interests of affected individuals and groups. Government officials can avoid conflict by learning the interests of the various parties and seeking to craft a policy that addresses these interests. Most sophisticated government officials already do this. That helps explain why, contrary to popular conceptions, most policy decisions are not challenged in court.[20] To avoid litigated conflict, government officials need not fully satisfy all the interests of all affected individuals and organizations. Such a task is almost always impossible anyway. Rather, they need only design a policy that those affected are willing to "live with."

Proponents of negotiated rulemaking have pointed to the averaging provision in EPA's reformulated gasoline regulation as an example of a key conflict-avoiding innovation that came about because of a pursuit for consensus.[21] The provision gave refiners more flexibility by allowing them to meet fuel standards based on the average content of entire stocks of fuel rather than on a per gallon basis. In return for this flexibility, refiners were required to meet average standards that were 10 percent more stringent, thus allaying some environmentalists' concerns. Philip Harter, one of the leading defenders and practitioners of negotiated rulemaking, has argued that the averaging approach, combined with a somewhat more stringent standard, was a significant innovation that EPA would not have developed had it not needed to find consensus.[22] Environmental regulators, though, did not need a consensus-driven process to lead them to conceive or adopt this averaging plan. The emissions trading policies that EPA adopted more than a decade before the reformulated gasoline rule all relied essentially on averaging.[23] The EPA used averaging for fuel standards at least since the 1970s, and such an

---

[20]   Despite assertions made by many knowledgeable observers that almost all EPA regulations are challenged in court, only a minority ever are. See Coglianese, supra note 2.

[21]   See E. Weber, "Successful Collaboration" (November 1998) 40 *Environment* 10. For the text of the reformulated gasoline rule, see 54 Fed. Reg. 7716 (1994).

[22]   Harter advanced this argument in remarks delivered to the administrative law section of the Association of American Law Schools at its meeting on 9 January 1998, in an effort to continue to advocate the use of negotiated rulemaking notwithstanding research showing that negotiated rulemaking has failed to achieve its purposes of saving time and reducing litigation.

[23]   For a review of emissions trading and other market-based policies, see R. Hahn and R. Stavins, "Incentive-Based Environmental Regulation: A New Era from an Old Idea?" (1991)

approach was integral to the EPA's phasedown of leaded gasoline in the 1980s.[24] Moreover, agency officials hardly needed to conduct formal negotiations to realize that environmentalists would more readily support averaging if it was accompanied by lower standards. The EPA had adopted essentially the same kind of averaging approach, with a corresponding 20 percent reduction, four years earlier in its regulations governing the trading and banking of emissions from heavy duty diesel engines.[25] In this earlier case, as with other market-based policies, EPA officials developed the averaging policy through routine, informal consultations with industry and environmental groups, not through any formal negotiation that sought consensus. Attentive and savvy government officials pursue such innovative arrangements and other strategies to reduce conflict even without formally negotiating agreements. Having groups sign on to an agreement may well be one way to determine what the parties can accept and to design policies that resolve conflicts, but it is by no means the only way.

Moreover, in the normal course of policy-making interest groups do not pursue every potential conflict they may have with an agency. A considerable amount of "lumping it" always occurs, and parties will often forgo their opportunity to contest each minute aspect of a policy with which they might disagree.[26] An organization's disagreement with an agency must be sufficiently great to justify the costs of a subsequent challenge as well as the risks of creating an adverse decision or prompting those with opposing interests to raise challenges of their own.[27] For this reason, consensus is not only unnecessary for avoiding conflict, but it can be counterproductive as well. Processes that seek out consensus can actually make conflict more protracted. In order for representatives of industry and citizen groups to "sign on" to a policy, they need to achieve an outcome which is tangibly better than what they would otherwise have received. All other things being equal, it is always harder to convince representatives of constituent-based organizations that they should affirmatively endorse a policy rather than simply forgo raising objections or legal challenges to that same policy. Thus, it is not surprising that conflicting views have arisen over the meaning of "superior environmental performance" in the EPA's Project XL negotiations, with environmentalists insisting that to gain their support firms must achieve performance superior to what their facilities have already achieved (which is often cleaner than the regulations allow) and not merely performance superior to what is legally allowable. Industry also finds it harder to make affirmative

---

18 Ecology L Q 1. Administrative lawyers should already be quite familiar with emissions averaging, as such an approach undergirded the EPA's "bubble" rule which was challenged in *Chevron v. Natural Resources Defense Council*, 467 U.S. 837 (1984).

[24] R. Hahn and G. Hester, "Marketable Permits: Lessons for Theory and Practice" (1989) 16 Ecology L Q 361.

[25] See 55 Fed. Reg. 30, 584 (26 July 1990).

[26] Cf. W. Felstiner, R. Abel, and A. Sarat, "The Emergence and Transformation of Disputes: Naming, Blaming, Claiming ... " (1980–1981) 15 L & Soc'y Rev 631.

[27] See R. Cooter and D. Rubinfeld, "Economic Analysis of Legal Disputes and their Resolution" (1989) 27 *Journal of Economic Literature* 1067.

endorsements than to offer tacit acceptance. Representatives of a utility trade association, for example, pursued difficult negotiations to secure a preliminary agreement with the Nuclear Regulatory Commission on proposed regulations, only later to balk at formally "signing on" to the agreement in the face of objections from some of the trade association's corporate members.[28]

Conflict can best be avoided if state officials listen carefully to the concerns of affected parties and craft policies that address these concerns. Once organizations are put on the spot and expected to affirm a policy, they will likely demand an even better outcome for their interests. If many of the participants in a negotiation act in this way, it will prove still more difficult under a consensus process to resolve the conflicts between groups. This helps explain why consensus-based processes tend to consume more time and resources for everyone involved.

2.2 Increased Compliance

A related benefit sometimes attributed to consensus-building is that it will increase compliance by the regulated industry. People tend to be more likely to follow through on those things for which they claim ownership. So if a regulated industry signs onto a consensus policy, it could be predicted to be more likely to comply with that policy, as well as to comply more quickly and more fully than it otherwise would.

The existence of subsequent litigation over negotiated rulemakings seems to draw this prediction into question, for it shows that a "buy in" to a consensus agreement does not necessarily mean complete "buy in" to the final policy. Environmental regulations developed using consensus-based procedures have resulted in more litigation than have comparable regulations promulgated using other forms of public participation.[29] Of course, litigation is not direct evidence of the specific compliance effects of a consensus decision rule, but unfortunately researchers have yet to study systematically whether consensus-based policies elicit greater compliance. That said, there are plausible grounds to question whether consensus is all that significant in promoting industry compliance with a policy decision.

Compliance rates are affected by a number of factors, such as industry knowledge of a standard, the cost of complying with the standard, the probability that noncompliance will be detected, and the penalties for noncompliance. When a regulation is backed by effective monitoring and the possibility of penalties of ten to twenty-five thousand dollars per day (as are many environmental regulations in the United States), it is not unreasonable to ask whether the mere fact that the policy emerged from a consensus process should matter at all. Lead has been phased out of gasoline, passive restraints have been installed in cars, and cigarette smoking in some states has been virtually eliminated from public buildings, all without

---

[28] See C. Harrington, "Howard Bellman: Using 'Bundles of Input' to Negotiate an Environmental Dispute," in D. Kolb (ed.), *When Talk Works* (Jossey-Bass, San Francisco, 1994).
[29] See Coglianese, supra note 2.

attempts at consensus-building preceding the policy decision. Effective compliance can certainly be achieved without efforts at building consensus.

At most, the "buy in" that accompanies consensual decision-making process may increase compliance at the margins. Yet we still have to wonder whether even this marginal effect exists. The "buy in" that some consensus processes require, after all, is simply a willingness to let the policy move forward. A decision that an industrial sector can "live with" is not the same as a decision it affirmatively likes. It is not altogether clear why organizations which are simply willing to "live with" a policy developed through negotiation would have all that much more incentive to comply with it than with a policy that was not negotiated.

It is also far from clear that any effects of a "buy in" by those sitting around a table in Washington, D.C., will necessarily carry through to the individuals across the country who have, at the ground level, the day-to-day responsibility for complying with government regulation. When consensus is used as the basis for industry-wide or sector-wide regulation, can we expect that the plant-level managers who carry out the implementation and monitoring of the regulation will take "ownership" of that regulation? Will they even know that the regulation was negotiated with representatives from their industry's trade association in Washington? More empirical research obviously needs to be done to answer these questions, but it clearly is not self-evident that the "buy in" to a consensus regulation will have any substantial effect on compliance.

2.3 Improved Policy

Even if the "buy in" prediction does not hold, consensus might still affect compliance indirectly by the kind of policy that is likely to emerge from a consensus process. Proponents of consensus-building have increasingly argued that consensus-based policies are simply better and more sensible because they are based on better information and a more realistic understanding of the specific demands of an industry and concerns of affected citizens.[30] The intensive discussions with regulated industry, as well as the give-and-take dialogue with the other parties, brings detailed information to the table that arguably leads to better policy decisions. A consensus-based process, it is argued, takes advantage of the collective wisdom of those who are sitting around the negotiating table, as opposed to relying mainly on agency staff's best guess of plant conditions or other technical aspects of industry operations. Consensus-building efforts are therefore thought to promote learning and yield more informed decisions.

---

[30] Harter has asserted that "[a] negotiated rulemaking forces the parties to bring an enormous amount of practical information to the table and hence expands the data base on which to build a regulation. The practical insight contributed by those with first-hand experience also allows agency staff to focus resources on areas with the greatest potential payback." Harter, supra note 19, at 1418.

Empirical evidence to sustain the claim that consensus-based processes yield systematically better policies has yet to emerge.[31] Moreover, as I discuss in Part 3 of this chapter, several pathologies can afflict consensus-based processes which will lead to inferior policy results. The existence of these pathologies alone provides reason to doubt whether consensus-based processes will tend to lead to better policies. Yet there are still other reasons to question whether structuring a dialogue around a quest for consensus will yield full disclosure and debate of policy issues. The fact that the group is charged with the task of achieving a consensus may actually inhibit some participants from raising important issues which seem at the time likely to hinder consensus-building. In his study of groupthink in government, Paul Hart writes that when policy decisions are based on consensus some participants "may refrain from voicing their concerns, either by self-discipline and a desire not to shatter group harmony (suppression of doubts) or following direct hints by the leader (compliance) or by fellow group members (mindguards; peer pressure). When consensus is no longer required, group discussion can be more open."[32] In regulatory negotiations, such inhibition does occur. In one case, for example, an EPA official told me that he knew industry was overlooking an entire category of equipment in setting consensus-based standards for equipment leaks, but that he never said a word about it during the negotiations. In another illustrative case, a citizen member of the Intel Project XL negotiation group reportedly signed the final agreement, but only reluctantly after "feeling pressure from all sides."[33] Often what decision-makers need is conflict to illuminate policy issues most fully. The full articulation of opposing views may provide more useful information on which to construct public policy than the truncated discussion that can develop when individuals feel pressured to achieve consensus.

Nevertheless, even if it could somehow be shown that consensus-building processes do yield better, more informed decisions, the question remains whether this benefit derives from, or depends on, consensus itself. On its face, it is the deliberation—not the consensus—which advocates claim yields the additional information needed to craft better policy decisions.[34]

---

[31] Langbein and Kerwin report findings that show participants in negotiated rulemakings tend to rate the quality of the final outcome higher than do participants in other rulemakings. See L. Langbein and C. Kerwin, *Regulatory Negotiation Versus Conventional Rulemaking: Claims, Counter-Claims, and Empirical Evidence* (manuscript 1998). However, it is far from clear that ratings by participants are unbiased measures of the actual quality of the policy outcomes achieved in these cases. Cognitive dissonance seems likely to explain the favorable outcome ratings participants give to negotiated rulemakings, as these proceedings involve considerably more time and effort on their part.

[32] P. Hart, *Groupthink in Government: A Study of Small Groups and Policy Failure* 293 (Johns Hopkins University Press, Baltimore, 1994).

[33] US EPA, *Constructive Engagement Resource Guide: Practical Advice for Dialogue Among Facilities, Workers, Communities and Regulators* (Washington, D.C., 1999), appendix 1.

[34] As one proponent of negotiated rulemaking has acknowledged, "[t]he potential [of negotiated proceedings] derives not from the parties' 'success' in achieving consensus rules (though they were successful) but rather from the fact that the parties engaged in a problem-solving exercise through which they were able, if only briefly or incompletely, to break out of traditional conceptions of rulemaking." J. Freeman, "Collaborative Governance" (1997) 45 UCLA L Rev 1, 40.

Consensus-based procedures certainly can demand much more time and resources on the part of participants than other procedures. If this same amount of time and effort were devoted to policy deliberations that did not aim at consensus, it seems quite plausible that the informational benefits would be the same, if not better. As we know, alternatives exist which do not aim at consensus. To the extent that public officials employ deliberative processes that lead interested parties to identify their areas of agreement and disagreement, there is no strong reason to doubt that this kind of intensive deliberation can provide comparable, if not superior, results in terms of contributing to better public policy.[35]

2.4   Expanded Participation

It has sometimes been suggested that a consensus rule, along with a commitment by the agency to implement the consensus decision, is needed in order to attract people to participate in deliberative processes.[36] Consensus, according to this argument, amounts to something like a "field of dreams." If you seek to build consensus, the players will come to the table. If consensus is not the main goal, few will engage in the sport.

While it is true that a successful policy deliberation depends on individuals being motivated to deliberate, a quest for consensus is by no means necessary in order to achieve that motivation. A few years ago I helped facilitate a pilot workshop convened by the National Performance Review and EPA's Region I office to which members of industry, the environmental community, and local government were invited. This was to be the first in a series of workshops across the country through which the EPA would "get in touch" with the grassroots. Although the goals of this particular meeting were not specified in the least,[37] and only short notice was given of the meeting, more than 50 participants crowded into the workshop room for the day-long event. They needed not the slightest assurance that they would be there to reach a consensus which the EPA would implement, but rather took advantage of this opportunity to communicate their concerns with regulators.

The possibility of influencing policy decisions is what drives participation in policy-making. It is well documented that the past thirty years have seen considerable growth in interest group representation in Washington, D.C.[38] These groups and their representatives have come to play the game

---

[35]   Cf. R. Reich, "Public Administration and Public Deliberation: An Interpretive Essay" (1985) 94 Yale L J 1617.
[36]   For example, Jody Freeman argues that "agencies must presumptively commit to agreements developed in these processes, and courts must presumptively defer to them. If not, participants will never engage in the prolonged negotiation and planning required to produce either a consensus rule or an FPA." Freeman, supra note 34, at 92. See also Harter, supra note 19, at 1411.
[37]   For a discussion of the lack of focus in the Clinton Administration's early partnership effort, see M. Sparrow, *The Regulatory Craft: Controlling Risk, Solving Problems, and Managing Compliance* (Brookings Institution Press, Washington, D.C., 2000).
[38]   D. King and J. Walker, Jr., "An Ecology of Interest Groups in America," in J. Walker, Jr., *Mobilizing Interest Groups in America: Patrons, Professions, and Social Movements* (University of Michigan Press, 1991) pp. 57, 62–64.

even though consensus has only recently become a trendy—even though still relatively infrequent—way to play. Interest group representatives already have the incentives to engage in policy deliberations without a consensus decision rule. It turns out, in fact, that most of what the EPA considers its "stakeholder involvement" projects do not formally adopt a consensus rule. What group representatives need in order to be motivated to play is an assurance that some decision is going to be made and that their input may help influence that decision.[39] Agencies can provide that assurance without requiring the parties to search for consensus and agreeing to implement a consensus that develops. Agencies can—and do—show that they have an open mind, that they have a decision yet to be made, and that they are genuinely interested in learning about the various perspectives.[40]

Participation can be sought in a collective forum which allows for a give-and-take dialogue as long as the agency demonstrates a willingness to listen and, as best it can while still pursuing its public mandate, to incorporate what it learns into its decisions. As I discuss in Part 3, consensus rules can sometimes create unrealistic expectations about what an agency is able or willing to deliver, and when these expectations are dashed it may actually lead to less willingness in the future to engage in public deliberations. Policy-making by consensus can also lead, ironically, to the exclusion of some affected parties from the decision-making process in order to facilitate agreement.[41] The best way for an agency to motivate outside groups to participate in policy deliberations seems to be to set realistic expectations, meet them, and demonstrate on a repeated basis that the deliberations have an impact on—even if they do not control—the agency's final decisions. Promises about consensus cannot stack up against an agency culture that takes deliberation and consultation with affected parties seriously, even though the agency maintains its position as the ultimate decision-maker.

When it comes to encouraging public participation—as with reducing conflict, increasing compliance, and developing better public policy—a consensus decision rule simply is not needed. Alternative forms of engagement with the public can yield the same benefits which have been attributed to consensual policy processes. Advocates of consensus-building have overstated the need for consensus by de-emphasizing alternative forms of public participation that do not depend on consensus.

---

[39] Ironically, when a consensus decision rule is adopted, the resulting dynamics may actually turn groups away from participating. Participants in some of the sector projects in the Common Sense Initiative lost interest once they saw that little would be accomplished given the requirement for unanimity imposed on the initiative.

[40] J. Applegate, "Beyond The Usual Suspects: The Use Of Citizens Advisory Boards In Environmental Decisionmaking" (1998) 73 *Indiana Law Journal* 903.

[41] D. Beardsley, T. Davies, and R. Hersh, "Improving Environmental Management: What Works, What Doesn't" (September 1997) 39 *Environment* 6, 32; J. Rossi, "Participation Run Amok: The Costs of Mass Participation for Deliberative Agency Decisionmaking" (1997) 92 *Northwestern University Law Review* 173, 231; K. Harrison, "Talking with the Donkey: Cooperative Approaches to Environmental Protection" (1998) 2 *Journal of Industrial Ecology* 51, 54, 63, 66.

3   THE PATHOLOGIES OF CONSENSUS

Just as the recent literature on regulatory consensus-building has overstated
the need for consensus, it has also tended to understate the hazards of consensus as a decision rule. Perhaps this has been because those writing about
consensus have largely sought to convince legislators and regulatory agencies of the value of formal negotiated proceedings—and possibly also of the
need for professional facilitation services which some of those writing in
this area provide.[42] For example, Philip Harter, a leading advocate for
and practitioner of regulatory negotiation, argues that consensus-building
leads to "regulatory actions [that] are often simply better by virtually any
measure. These are, indeed, powerful tools."[43]

The generally one-sided view that emerges from contemporary advocacy
of consensus-building in the regulatory process, however, is not reflected in
the broader literature on group decision-making and policy deliberation.
There is, for instance, considerable work in social psychology examining
both the strengths and weaknesses of group decision-making, one of the
latter being the potential for "groupthink."[44] In addition, the work of Jane
Mansbridge on democratic decision-making illuminates certain strengths of
consensus decision-making for small groups with relatively homogeneous
interests, but also stresses substantial disadvantages of consensus-building
used more widely.[45] Mansbridge studied participatory decision-making in
both a small workplace and the government of a small New England town
and found that decision-making by consensus presented numerous disadvantages. It demanded considerably more time, opened decisions up to
more frequent revision, generated ambiguity and imprecision, and sometimes resulted in deadlock or social coercion.[46] She also confirmed that consensus tended to bias decisions in favor of the status quo and strengthened
those who were already powerful. Mansbridge concluded that even though
consensus may be suitable for the governance of small groups of individuals who have ongoing relationships and common interests, it is not suitable
for governance of large nation-states or in highly conflictual settings.[47]

The disadvantages of consensus in the context of regulatory policy have
not received comparable consideration in the literature. However, experience is showing that the same kinds of pathologies elsewhere associated
with consensus decision-making also find their way into the regulatory
process. Even those who otherwise support consensus-building acknowledge that decisions agreed to by select groups of policy actors need not
necessarily comport with the public interest.[48] A consensus decision rule

---

[42]   See B. Rabe, "The Politics of Environmental Dispute Resolution" (1988) 16 *Policy Studies
Journal* 585, 591.
[43]   Harter, supra note 19, at 1423.
[44]   See I. Janis, *Victims of Groupthink: A Psychological Study of Foreign Policy Decisions and
Fiascoes* (Houghton Mifflin, Boston, 1972); Hart, supra note 32.
[45]   See J. Mansbridge, *Beyond Adversary Democracy* (University of Chicago Press, 1980).
[46]   Ibid. at 166–170.
[47]   Ibid. at 293.
[48]   See, e.g., Kerwin and Langbein, supra note 31, at 31–32; Weber, supra note 21, at 36.

can create or exacerbate at least six pathologies in the policy process: (1) tractability having priority over public importance; (2) regulatory imprecision; (3) the lowest common denominator problem; (4) increased time and expense; (5) unrealistic expectations; and (6) new sources of conflict. To be sure, not every consensus-based process will suffer from these pathologies, and just as surely some non-consensual processes will. Nevertheless, each of these problems, elaborated in the sections that follow, derive from a quest for consensus and their risk is increased when decision-making procedures effectively hand each participant a veto over the policy decision.

3.1 Tractability over Importance

The first pathology created by a focus on consensus relates to the nature of the issues selected for consideration. Consensus-based processes increase the likelihood that the wrong issues will receive attention. Instead of devoting time and resources to the issues of most importance to the public, a focus on consensus tends to lead to the selection of the most tractable issues, the ones most amenable to agreement.

That such a selection process occurs is evident in the paucity of cases in which consensus has been used to develop federal regulations. Proponents of negotiated rulemaking have never claimed that consensus-building would be appropriate for more than about 5 percent of all agency rulemakings, and in practice the use of the procedure has been exceedingly rare (less than one-tenth of one percent of all regulations).[49] The small fraction of rules that agencies have selected for negotiated rulemaking has not been comprised of the rules with the largest impact on the public. For example, only five negotiated rulemakings have been classified as "major" or "significant" rules according to the economic impact standards set forth by executive order.[50] The Negotiated Rulemaking Act sets forth standards for selecting rules for negotiation, most of which guide agency officials to select rules that are most likely capable of resulting in a consensus. Among other things, agency officials contemplating negotiated rulemaking are required to determine that there is "[a] reasonable likelihood that a committee will reach a consensus on the proposed rule within a fixed period of time."[51] Standards such as these favor tractability over social importance.

An emphasis on consensus not only leads to the selection of more tractable policy matters for negotiation to begin with, it also leads to a selection of the more tractable issues within the negotiating proceedings themselves. The Quincy Library Group, a high profile group organized to develop a consensus over forest policy in California, focused on those issues where agreement was possible. As two participants acknowledged, "true consensus" as a decision rule "greatly limits the range of issues the group can take on."[52] The subset of issues addressed in consensus-building are typically tractable ones, not necessarily the ones that are most important.

---

[49] See Coglianese, supra note 2, at 1277.
[50] Ibid. at 1314.
[51] 5 U.S.C. § 563(a)(4) (1994).
[52] See P. Terhune and G. Terhune, "QLG Case Study" (workshop paper, 1998).

The problem with tractability is also evidenced in the recent report of the Enterprise for the Environment initiative.[53] In 1996, former EPA Administrator William Ruckelshaus convened this initiative, dubbed "E4E" for short, in order to bring together leaders from industry, government, and the environmental community to forge a consensus about how to improve environmental policy in the United States. The project initially sought agreement on a diagnosis of the problems in the current system of environmental protection and on a set of concrete legislative solutions. Not long into the discussions, however, it became apparent to the participants that consensus would never be achieved on either the specification of current problems or the precise form of legislative proposals. Even though an illumination of existing problems and specific legislative fixes was surely what was needed, the group shifted its goals to what was more attainable (but ultimately less valuable): agreement on a broad "vision" of an ideal environmental protection system.[54]

It seems a truism that consensus will be more difficult to achieve on the most vexing problems. In evaluating policy "experiments" which rely on consensus-building, one therefore needs to be mindful of potential selection bias. This is especially true with initiatives that rely on volunteers. Not only are the firms that volunteer for initiatives such as Project XL already likely to be those that have better-than-average relationships with their communities, the types of problems that they initially choose to address are not likely to be the most complex or challenging.[55] This raises a question. If site-specific regulation of the kind envisioned by proponents of Project XL really can improve efficiency and innovation, should resources go to projects based on whether they do (or do not) draw initial support (or lack opposition) from various citizen groups? At least in the early years of the XL initiative, a community group could write a strongly worded three-paragraph letter asking the EPA "to scratch this company from the list immediately," and the project would never go forward.[56] The EPA now assures XL applicants that a single community group cannot kill an application, but the agency nevertheless maintains that stakeholder support is a critical criterion for selecting projects.[57] Certainly there will still be opportunities to make cost-saving environmental improvements in the projects that garner community support and are selected for Project XL or other reform efforts. However, to the extent that consensus (or even just the absence of controversy) drives

---

[53]   See Enterprise for the Environment, supra note 3.
[54]   For a discussion of the E4E process and report, C. Coglianese, "Limits of Consensus" (April 1999) 41 *Environment* 28.
[55]   Blackman and Mazurek have noted that the EPA's Project XL appears to have been biased against the most complex and innovative projects. See A. Blackman and J. Mazurek, *The Cost of Developing Site-Specific Environmental Regulations: Evidence from EPA's Project XL* (Resources for the Future Discussion Paper, Washington, D.C., 1999).
[56]   The quoted language comes from a letter from Denny A. Larson, Communities for a Better Environment, to President William Clinton, dated 26 October 1995, in which Larson expressed his organization's opposition to an XL proposal submitted by Citgo Corporation. The EPA did not pursue Citgo's proposal.
[57]   Notice of Modifications to Project XL, 62 Fed. Reg. 19872 (23 April 1997).

decision-making, it is likely that the opportunities for gains will be smaller than if other selection criteria were used.[58]

3.2   Imprecision

Just as a focus on tractability makes consensus easier to achieve, so too does imprecision or ambiguity. In her study of democratic decision-making, Mansbridge found that "[c]onsensual decision making … generates impreci-sion. In order to reach unanimous agreement, groups formulate their collective decision so as to blur potential disagreements."[59]

The E4E process, mentioned earlier, is a stark example of the pathology of imprecision that comes from a quest for consensus. The final Enterprise for the Environment report described the project's resulting consensus in terms with which no one could seriously disagree: "[T]he environmental protec-tion system of the next century must become as efficient and low cost as possible without compromising environmental progress."[60] Elsewhere the report offered other platitudes as recommendations: policy-makers should "adapt and adjust policies, strategies, and systems based on experience and new information;" they should "generate, disseminate, and rely on the best-available scientific and economic information;" and society should "place authority, responsibility, and accountability at the appropriate level of gov-ernment."[61] Of course, no one would seriously urge otherwise, although different people do disagree about specifically how best to achieve better environmental protection at lower cost. Rather than seek consensus for its own sake, what was needed was to illuminate areas of disagreement and to conduct further analysis that might better inform decision-making.

Admittedly, the E4E report may be an outlier in terms of imprecision, but the pressure always exists that negotiators will adopt abstract or unclear language in order to secure an agreement. It will usually be easier to achieve consensus at higher levels of abstraction, and it is always less time-consuming and less controversial to adopt imprecise language.[62] Adopting abstract principles and vague standards may serve to secure agreement in the face of conflict, but doing so will undoubtedly constrain the usefulness of the public policy that emerges from consensual processes.

---

[58]   Of course, in saying this, I am mindful that community support (or lack of significant opposition) could be thought necessary given the legal vulnerability of XL agreements and site-specific rulemakings. See T. Caballero, "Project XL: Making It Legal, Making It Work" (1998) 17 Stan Envtl L J 399. However, I am also mindful of a small survey of participants in four XL projects which resulted in at least one interesting finding: nearly half of the respon-dents thought that the deliberation process neglected issues that should have been addressed. US EPA, supra note 10, at 32. Had the EPA not placed such a priority on securing stakeholder support, there would presumably have been less pressure to truncate the deliberative processes in these cases.
[59]   Mansbridge, supra note 45, at 167.
[60]   Enterprise for the Environment, supra note 3, at 3.
[61]   Ibid. at 4.
[62]   See C. Diver, "The Optimal Precision of Administrative Rules" (1983) 93 Yale L J 65, 73.

3.3   Lowest Common Denominator

By handing each participant a veto, consensus-based processes also make it more likely that the final outcome will amount to no more than the lowest common denominator acceptable to all the parties. Consensual decision rules have the effect of giving domestic policy-making the same structural form as international policy-making. It is common for multilateral international agreements to require no more than what is acceptable to the state with the most objections to regulation. For example, initial drafts of the ISO 14001 environmental management system standards would have required public accessibility of environmental data, third party certification, and sector-specific pollution standards—requirements that some have argued are needed to make environmental management systems credible. However, these requirements were dropped in response to objections from the United States and Japan.[63] The problem with the lowest common denominator, of course, is that such a minimally-acceptable outcome will not be sufficient to achieve policy objectives. In a recent study of negotiated rulemaking, Caldart and Ashford concluded that because industry representatives will not likely "sign on" to any regulations that would force dramatic changes upon business, "negotiated rulemaking's focus on consensus can effectively remove the potential to spur innovation."[64]

3.4   Time and Resources

The lowest common denominator problem, along with the pathologies of tractability and imprecision, arise in part because it takes time and resources to achieve consensus. Deliberation takes time for everyone to present their concerns and for others to respond, and consensus demands that the deliberation continue until everyone agrees (or at least agrees to "live with" a decision). Time, in itself, is not inherently a pathology, at least not if the additional time yields valuable information and better results. All other things being equal, though, the additional time it takes to develop a decision through consensus is certainly an important drawback, especially when it takes longer to reach closure on only the most tractable issues.

Those who have participated in consensus-building processes complain about the amount of time and effort these processes take. In one study, participants in negotiated rulemakings were three times more likely to complain that the process took too much time, effort, and resources than were those respondents who participated in conventional rulemakings.[65] One of

---

[63]   N. Roht-Arriaza, "Shifting the Point of Regulation: The International Organization for Standardization and Global Lawmaking on Trade and the Environment" (1995) 22 Ecology L Q 479.

[64]   C. Caldart and N. Ashford, "Negotiation as a Means of Developing and Implementing Environmental and Occupational Health and Safety Policy" (1999) 23 Harv Envtl L Rev 141, 201.

[65]   C. Kerwin and L. Langbein, *An Evaluation of Negotiated Rulemaking at the Environmental Protection Agency* (manuscript 1997).

the most common complaints about the EPA's now-defunct Common Sense Initiative was that it took a frustratingly long time to accomplish anything.[66] EPA's Project XL has generated similar reactions.[67] No one should expect that decision-making by consensus will help speed up the policy process.

3.5   Unrealistic Expectations

By making consensus the goal of participatory processes, public officials can give rise to unrealistic expectations about how much any agreement will affect the ultimate policy decision. Even though widespread reliance on consensus would have the effect of "de-centering" the state by making it more of a player and facilitator than a decision-maker, the agreements made through collaborative partnerships are usually not self-implementing statements of policy. Government officials must still formally enact and implement these agreements. In so doing, the policy may change—even slightly—from the proposal on which the parties thought they had agreed. After a consensus is forged, maintaining that consensus throughout the remaining steps of the policy process can prove difficult. Other actors not party to the agreement, such as legislators, other interest groups, and executive branch officials, may also try to take another bite at the apple.[68]

When this happens and the policy outcome diverges from the agreement, participants in the consensus proceeding will undoubtedly have certain expectations disappointed, expectations that would have been much less likely to have developed had the process simply sought public input to assist the agency in reaching its decision. In a study of several consensus-building initiatives at the National Marine Fisheries Service, 60 percent of the participants who were surveyed reported that they were dissatisfied with the results of the process.[69] The study's authors found that much of the dissatisfaction arose because participants expected to control the outcomes much more than was realistically possible. It was also precisely such a case of dashed expectations that led to the underlying litigation in the first major appellate decision to interpret the Negotiated Rulemaking Act. In *USA Group Loan Servicers, Inc. v. Riley*,[70] participants in a Department of Education negotiated rulemaking sued the agency claiming that it had reneged on commitments made during the negotiated rulemaking. The Seventh Circuit

---

[66]   J. Todd, *Review of the Common Sense Initiative* (US EPA, Washington, D.C., 1997), 30, 52.

[67]   According to the US EPA's review of Project XL, "[m]ost stakeholders commented that the process was too long or much longer than they expected or felt was warranted." US EPA, *supra* note 10, at 41. To be sure, not all of the time and expense associated with developing XL agreements have been due to the pursuit of consensus, and only some XL projects have sought to achieve consensus from a broad range of affected parties. However, the need to reach an agreement with EPA and other governmental agencies has still contributed to a more costly and time-consuming process than participants would like.

[68]   See R. Kagan, "Political and Legal Obstacles to Collaborative Ecosystem Planning" (1997) 24 Ecology L Q 871.

[69]   RESOLVE, Inc., *The National Marine Fisheries Service Take Reduction Team Negotiation Process Evaluation* (National Marine Fisheries Service, Washington, D.C., 1999).

[70]   82 F.3d 708 (7th Cir. 1996).

held that federal agencies could not be compelled to adopt a consensus agreement nor held to positions taken during negotiations because the agency retains the ultimate decision-making authority. To the extent that it will remain possible for government officials to enact policies that depart from the precise (and not-so-precise) understandings of those involved in policy negotiations, a process centered on the quest for consensus only sets up expectations that in the end probably cannot help but be somewhat unfulfilled. In this way, an increased reliance on processes that aim for consensus could very well undermine trust and increase cynicism in the policy process.

3.6   Additional Sources of Conflict

The case of *USA Group Loan Servicers* shows that conflicts not only persist following consensus-building, but that they can even be engendered by the expectations such processes create. Consensus is not always attainable, and even when it is it may only temporarily hide underlying conflicts. Perhaps the most notable disappointment in terms of avoiding conflict has been the EPA's reformulated gasoline regulation. Heralded by some as a "successful collaboration,"[71] this negotiated rulemaking hardly succeeded at all in eliminating conflict. The final rule elicited extensive criticism in the press and from the public, prompted four legal challenges and a petition for administrative review, and resulted in an adverse ruling by the World Trade Organization.[72] The reformulated gasoline regulation is not unique. As noted earlier, environmental regulations developed through consensus-based processes overall end up being challenged in court more frequently than do comparable regulations formulated through procedures that do not depend on consensus.[73]

Consensus-based processes create new sources of conflict that do not exist with other methods of policy-making. Conflicts first arise over who participates in the negotiations. A recent set of negotiated rulemakings at the Department of Housing and Urban Development (HUD) spawned what appears to be the first legal action filed to secure a spot on a negotiated rulemaking committee.[74] HUD had originally named four public housing organizations to participate on negotiated rulemaking committees for regulations addressing subsidies and capital funds. After the housing organizations subsequently filed a petition against the agency over a separate matter, HUD officials declared that the organizations could no longer bargain in good faith and removed them from the negotiated rulemaking committees. The organizations filed for a court order reversing the agency's decision to remove them from the committee, claiming that HUD's action discriminated against them for exercising their fundamental right of

---

[71]   See Weber, supra note 21.
[72]   See Coglianese, supra note 2, at 1290–1294.
[73]   Id., at 1296–1309.
[74]   *Council of Large Public Housing Authorities, Inc. v. US Department of Housing and Urban Development,* No. 1:99CV00634 (Dist. D.C. 25 March 1999) (motion for a temporary restraining order).

petition. HUD subsequently capitulated and reinstated the organizations to the negotiated rulemaking committees, but the experience demonstrates one significant new source of conflict caused by a process designed around the search for consensus.

In addition to conflicts over who gets to participate, processes structured around consensus can create conflicts over the meaning of any agreements that are reached and over whether final government decisions comport with those agreements. Disagreements also arise over the meaning of terms in consensus statements as well as over the implications of terms or issues that are absent from these statements.[75] Just as with disputes over membership in the consensus process, neither of these additional sources of conflict arise outside the context of consensus-based processes.

4 CONCLUSION

A reliance on consensus introduces new sources of conflict and creates additional problems in the policy process. It leads to unrealistic expectations, increased time and resources, lowest common denominators, imprecision, and a focus on tractability over importance. We should therefore not engage in any wishful thinking about consensus-based processes. Even though public officials, scholars, and policy advocates seem to be converging on a new vision of policy-making based on consensus, we should not expect that simply by organizing policy around consensus, defined variously as requiring either unanimity or a decision everyone "can live with," we will indeed achieve a more timely, less conflictual, and higher quality system of regulation.

The widespread establishment of a consensus-based approach to regulation would constitute a shift in the prevailing mode of governance in the United States, amounting to a "decentering" of the state and a retreat from the public interest as the primary goal of government officials. In this chapter, I have argued that such a shift is neither necessary nor wise. All the purported benefits of consensus-building can be achieved through other participatory processes which do not aim for consensus. Moreover, basing decision-making on a search for consensus introduces new pathologies into the policy process. Enthusiastic calls for consensus, and in particularly those efforts to compel agencies to employ consensus-building, are at best premature. Environmental regulators can—and many do—seek to engage in public deliberation in ways that do not impose consensus as a constraint on decision-making. In doing so, they can achieve the same kinds of benefits that have been attributed to consensual decision-making without introducing the pathologies of consensus as a decision rule.

---

[75] For examples of the range of conflicts engendered by attempts to build consensus, see Coglianese, *supra* note 2, at 1322–1327.

5. Understanding Project XL: A Comparative Legal and Policy Analysis

Dennis D. Hirsch*

1 INTRODUCTION

This chapter describes the leading American experiment with environmental contracting, known as Project XL, and places that description in the context of European approaches to environmental contracting—in particular, the approach taken in the Netherlands. The chapter is intended both for a European audience that does not yet know much about Project XL and for an American one with some knowledge of this innovative regulatory program. It will attempt to describe the policy context in which Project XL arose, how the program is structured, how it compares to Netherlands' model of environmental contracting, and the main policy and legal issues that presently confront Project XL. It will conclude with some thoughts on the future of environmental contracting in the United States.[1]

2 PROJECT XL: A BRIEF DESCRIPTION

In order to understand Project XL, it is important first to understand the problems that this innovative program was designed to address. These are the problems of "command-and-control" regulation.

---

* Associate Professor, Capital Law School, Columbus, Ohio, USA. I would like to thank Professor Michael Faure and my other European colleagues for suggesting that I write this chapter. I am indebted to Professor Rene Seerden of the University of Maastricht, and Peter Verkerk, Counselor for the Environment to the Royal Netherlands Embassy (Washington, D.C.), for their willingness to read the portions of this chapter that discuss the Dutch approach to environmental contracting. All errors are my own and are not the product of their useful review.
[1] I describe the legal issues confronting Project XL in more detail in my article, "Bill and Al's XL-ent Adventure: An Analysis of the EPA's Legal Authority to Implement the Clinton Administration's Project XL" [1998] U Ill L Rev 129. That earlier article did not address the policy issues confronting the program, recent legislation intended to resolve the initiative's legal

2.1 The Problem with Command and Control; or, How the Americans Came to be Interested in Environmental Contracting

Most federal environmental regulation in the United States today consists of specific governmental requirements that mandate how businesses should go about reducing pollution.[2] These regulations are of two basic types: design standards and performance standards.[3] Design standards require all facilities in the target industrial category to install a specific type of pollution control technology.[4] Performance standards establish the levels at which facilities can emit pollutants[5] and often require each covered plant to obtain a permit that legally binds it to that emission rate.[6] In practice, performance standards often function as de facto design standards since cautious companies eager to prevent any misunderstanding about their compliance status tend to mimic the "reference technology" that the U.S. Environmental Protection Agency (EPA) used in order to set the performance standard.[7] The end result is a nationally-uniform system of specific design and performance standards (many of which function as design standards) that dictate the degree to which facilities must control their pollution and, in many cases, how they should go about doing so.

This nationally-uniform, "command-and-control" system of regulation suffers from two main weaknesses: it is inefficient; and it discourages innovation. The inefficiency stems largely from the inability of a "one size fits all" approach to take into account variations in the benefits and costs of a given pollution control requirement as applied to different facilities. Such variations may occur because the costs of pollution control are greater at one facility than at another due to plant design; or because the benefits of pollution control are greater at one facility than at another due to the sensitivity of the environment in which the facility is located. Due to these variations, a regulation may be efficient as applied to some targeted facilities (i.e. the benefits

---

issues, and the future of environmental contracting in the United States, all of which are discussed in this chapter. It also did not compare Project XL with the Dutch approach to environmental contracting, as this piece attempts to do.

[2]   E. Orts, "Reflexive Environmental Law" (1995) 89 Nw UL Rev 1227, 1235.

[3]   R. Percival, et al., *Environmental Regulation: Law, Science and Policy* (2nd edn, 1996), pp. 154–155.

[4]   Ibid.

[5]   Ibid.

[6]   Orts, supra note 1, p. 1235. Often, the level of performance is set at the level of emissions achievable through use of the "best available control technology" (BAT), i.e., the most stringent control technology then available that the company could implement and still stay in business. B. Ackerman and R. Stewart, "Reforming Environmental Law: The Democratic Case for Market Incentives" (1988) 13 Colum J Envtl L 171, 172.

[7]   R. Percival, et al., supra note 3, p. 155. EPA generally uses a pollution control technology, known as the "reference technology," as the basis for setting the required level of performance. Regulated entities frequently decide that the safest way for them to ensure compliance with the "performance" standard is to install the reference technology (the standard, after all, was based on that technology). Should anyone later assert that technology fails to achieve the required level of performance the facility can argue that it relied on *EPA's own determination* that the technology *would* achieve that amount of emissions. Thus, even "performance" standards that EPA promulgates tend to function in practice as "design" standards. Ibid.

of pollution control exceed the costs of achieving that pollution reduction) but highly inefficient as applied to others (i.e. the environmental benefits are far less than the control costs).[8] Nationally-uniform command-and-control regulations, by their very nature, cannot take these differences into account. Such regulations "waste many billions of dollars annually by ignoring variations among plants and industries in the costs of reducing pollution and by ignoring geographic variations in pollution effects."[9]

The other main problem with command-and-control regulation is that it provides little incentive for—and even may be said to discourage—the development of more effective approaches to pollution control. Most command-and-control regulations require facilities to apply "best available control technology," i.e. the most stringent control technology currently available and feasible. They offer no rewards for exceeding this benchmark, and hence no incentive for doing so.[10] The incentive to innovate is further diminished by the constantly changing nature of "best available control technology."[11] The control technology that a company invests in today could be displaced tomorrow by one that is "better." This takes away the incentive to invest in the first place.[12]

2.2   Project XL as an Answer to the Problems of Command-and-Control

Project XL (for eXcellence and Leadership) is a U.S. EPA pilot project, initiated in 1995,[13] that uses environmental contracting to address the above-described problems with command-and-control regulation.[14] As initially conceived, Project XL consisted of four, semi-independent programs: Project XL for Facilities; Project XL for Sectors; Project XL for Government Agencies; and Project XL for Communities (XLC). XL for Facilities is the most developed of these programs, and has effectively incorporated XL for Sectors and for Government Agencies.[15] XL for Communities still exists as its own program, but has not been as active as XL for Facilities. Accordingly, this chapter focuses on Project XL for Facilities which is referred to, for the sake of simplicity, as "Project XL."

Project XL can be distilled into four main components. First, it is a *site-specific* approach in that it seeks to tailor regulatory requirements to the conditions that exist at a particular facility. Second, it involves *regulatory*

---

[8]   J. Krier, "The Irrational National Air Quality Standards: Macro- and Micro-Mistakes" (1974) 22 UCLA L Rev 323, 326–327.
[9]   B. Ackerman and R. Stewart, *Reforming Environmental Law,* supra note 6, at 173.
[10]   R. Stewart, "Regulation, Innovation, and Administrative Law: A Conceptual Framework" (1981) 69 Cal L Rev 1256, 1283–1284.
[11]   Ibid.
[12]   Ibid., at 1284.
[13]   U.S. Environmental Protection Agency, "Regulatory Reinvention (XL) Pilot Projects" 60 Fed. Reg. 27,282 (1995) (announcing Project XL).
[14]   President William J. Clinton and Vice President Al Gore, "Reinventing Environmental Regulation" (16 March 1995), in *Bureau of National Affairs Daily Environmental Report* (17 March 1995).
[15]   See B. Mank, "The Environmental Protection Agency's Project XL and Other Regulatory Reform Initiatives: The Need for Legislative Authorization" (1998) Ecology L Q 1, 20 and note 94.

flexibility in that EPA agrees to lift existing regulatory requirements and substitute in their place a site-specific compliance plan. Third, it requires that the contracting entity achieve *superior environmental performance* through the new approach. Fourth, it seeks to increase *stakeholder* involvement in the regulatory process.[16]

2.2.1 Site-Specific Approach

The program's principal innovation is to move from the top-down, "one size fits all" approach of command-and-control to a site-specific, facility-driven one. Rather than telling regulated entities how they should go about reducing pollution, as is typical of command-and-control regulation, the EPA in Project XL challenges such companies to come up with their own, more cost-effective means of achieving pollution reduction goals at their plant.[17]

Companies submit these ideas to the agency in the form of a project proposal that the EPA evaluates in accordance with eight criteria.[18] Once a proposal has been selected, the Agency and the project participant negotiate a Final Project Agreement (FPA) that sets out the terms of the innovative strategy.[19] The FPA is the "environmental contract" for Project XL purposes. Once it has been signed, it becomes the governing regulatory requirement for that facility, replacing any conflicting command-and-control standards. At the time that it announced the program in 1995, the EPA intended to create 50 XL projects in the four XL program areas.[20] Nearly five years into the program, the Agency has fallen well short of this goal. As of February 2000, only 18 XL projects were being implemented.[21]

The site-specific approach of Project XL attempts to address the problems of inefficiency and deterring innovation that plague command-and-control. It addresses the efficiency concern by allowing for tailored compliance plans that take into account the particular characteristics of a facility and its environment.[22] Companies that face inordinate compliance costs due to the specific design of their facility, or for whom the benefits of environmental

---

[16]   U.S. EPA, supra note 13, at 27,283.
[17]   Ibid., at 27,282.
[18]   The EPA evaluates project proposals according to whether they will: (1) "achieve environmental performance that is superior to what would be achieved through compliance with current and reasonable anticipated future regulation;" (2) "produce cost savings or economic opportunity" and/or result in a decrease in paperwork; (3) receive "the support of parties that have a stake in the environmental impacts," such as community members, local or state governments, local businesses, and public interest environmental groups; (4) "test innovative strategies for achieving environmental results;" (5) be "transferable" to other similar facilities or industrial sectors; (6) be technically and administratively feasible; (7) have "clear objectives and requirements" that will be easily measurable; and (8) not transfer environmental impacts or risk to poor or minority communities. Ibid., at 27,287.
[19]   Ibid., at 27,284.
[20]   Ibid., at 27,283.
[21]   U.S. EPA, "Project XL Web Site," <www.epa.gov/projectxl/implemen.htm> <www.epa.gov/projectxl/projdev.htm>, 14 February 2000.
[22]   U.S. EPA, supra note 13, at 27,286 (by "[t]aking account of facility-specific circumstances" XL projects will "result in ... reduced compliance costs").

control are minimal due to the characteristics of their environment, can now propose to the EPA alternative methods of compliance through Project XL.

The site-specific approach promotes innovation by giving facilities the license and the incentive (through potential cost savings) to experiment with new approaches to pollution reduction, and by offering public recognition for these efforts. To further encourage innovation, the EPA has made the use of new environmental technologies one of the criteria on which it will base its evaluation of project proposals.[23]

2.2.2 Regulatory Flexibility

The site-specific solutions developed under Project XL are bound to conflict with existing nationally-uniform command-and-control requirements that dictate how pollution reductions are to be achieved. Out of this tension is borne the second main element of Project XL: regulatory flexibility.

As part of their project proposal, participants can request that the EPA lift any binding regulatory requirement that conflicts with the company's XL project, and replace it with the company's site-specific compliance plan.[24] Where the Agency believes that the overall result will benefit the environment, and other program criteria are also met, it authorizes such departures from the regulatory norm.[25] The regulatory flexibility offered by Project XL is one of the main selling points of the program as far as participating businesses are concerned and provides part of the incentive for the innovations that the program promotes.

2.2.3 Superior Environmental Performance

Project XL assumes that since participants can reduce pollution more cheaply through regulatory flexibility, they should also be able to protect the environment *better* than they would have under traditional, command-and-control requirements. In order to get their proposal approved, participating companies must accordingly demonstrate that their innovative compliance strategy will result in *superior environmental performance* than the existing command-and-control requirements would have achieved.[26]

2.2.4 Stakeholder Participation

To further ensure the protection of the environment, give communities a voice in decisions that affect them, and expand civic participation in environmental issues, Project XL also requires participating companies to work with and gain the support of stakeholders. EPA will approve only those proposals that "have the support of parties that have a stake in the

---

[23] Ibid., at 27,287 (including innovation as one of the eight criteria by which project proposals will be evaluated); U.S. EPA, "Regulatory Reinvention (XL) Pilot Projects" 61 Fed. Reg. 47,929 (specifically requesting project proposals that feature innovative environmental technologies).
[24] U.S. EPA, supra note 13, at 27,283.
[25] Ibid., at 27,283 and 27,287.
[26] Ibid., at 27,283.

environmental impacts."[27] As defined by the EPA, this category includes "communities near the project, local or state governments, businesses, environmental and other public interest groups, or other similar entities."[28] This requirement gives stakeholders a larger role in corporate environmental planning than is generally the case under traditional regulatory methods.[29] Moreover, it gives stakeholders a say in the environmental contract negotiated between EPA and the participating company (although stakeholders generally are not signatories to the agreement).

The designers of Project XL hoped that the four elements described above would, together, lead to a more protective, less expensive and more accountable system of environmental regulation; or, as the Clinton Administration likes to call it, a "cleaner, cheaper and smarter" approach.[30]

2.3   Two Representative Projects

To get a better sense of how the program addresses the core problems of command-and-control regulation it is helpful to look at some specific projects. The Merck & Co. XL project provides a good example of how the program attempts to deal with variation and encourage efficiency. The Weyerhaeuser XL project demonstrates how the program attempts to promote innovation.

2.3.1   *The Merck & Co. XL Project*

Merck & Co. manufactures pharmaceutical products at a plant in rural Virginia near Shenandoah National Park.[31] The plant makes frequent process changes and, when it does, it often increases its emissions of an air pollutant known as Volatile Organic Compounds, or VOCs.[32] This VOC increase, in turn, generally triggers a Clean Air Act requirement that the facility obtain a permit prior to making the desired change.[33] The six months to a year that it takes to get such a permit slows the company down and hurts its competitiveness.[34]

In most regions of the country, VOC is a harmful pollutant that contributes to the ozone problem and, under these circumstances, the VOC permitting requirement makes environmental sense. But the Merck case is

---

[27]   Ibid., at 27,287.
[28]   Ibid.
[29]   T. Mohin, "The Alternative Compliance Model: A Bridge to the Future of Environmental Management," (1997) 27 Envtl L Rep 10,345 (in its XL project, the Intel Corporation "conducted perhaps the most inclusive stakeholder process of any industrial permitting project in history").
[30]   "EPA Aims to Sign First Detailed 'Project XL' Agreements in May" (28 February 1996) *Waste Business* at 4.
[31]   U.S. EPA, "Project XL Site-Specific Rulemaking for Merck & Co., Inc., Stonewall Plant" 62 Fed. Reg. 15,304, 15,305 (1997) [hereinafter, Merck Proposed Rule].
[32]   Ibid., at 15,305–15,306.
[33]   Ibid., at 15306.
[34]   Merck & Co., "Project XL for Facilities: Final Project Agreement Application" (19 July 1995), p. 2 (unpublished proposal on file with author).

different. Due to the specific meteorological conditions that prevail in the rural area where the facility is located, the VOC emissions from the plant do not lead to an increase in ozone.[35] Thus, in this instance, the permitting process—with its attendant delays and great costs—serves little environmental purpose. This is a clear example of how a nationally-uniform command-and-control requirement (here, the federal permitting requirement for VOC emission increases) cannot take into account a variation in the sensitivity of the environment in which a regulated facility operates (here, the fact that the VOC increases at Merck's location cause little or no environmental harm) and thereby results in a regulatory inefficiency.

Merck's XL project seeks to resolve this inefficiency in a way that will lead to more—not less—environmental protection. Under the terms of the project, the EPA allows Merck to carry out its process changes without having to apply for a new permit (so long as the VOC emissions increases do not exceed a specified level).[36] This is the "regulatory flexibility" component of the project. In exchange, Merck has agreed greatly to reduce its emissions of two other air pollutants, sulphur dioxide and oxides of nitrogen,[37] which do seriously impact the environment in nearby Shenandoah National Park (SO_2 contributes to acid rain; NO_x contributes to ozone formation).[38] Merck can achieve this by switching from a coal-fired to a natural gas-fired boiler.[39] This alteration, which will require a capital investment of approximately $10,000,000 as well as an additional $1,000,000 per year in increased operational costs, is not required under existing regulations.[40] The SO_2 and NO_x reductions accordingly constitute "beyond compliance" reductions. The end result is better for the company and for the environment—all because EPA was able to use Project XL in order to tailor regulatory requirements to the specific characteristics of the facility and its environment.

2.3.2 The Weyerhaeuser Co. XL Project

Weyerhaeuser operates a large, bleached kraft pulp manufacturing facility in Oglethorpe, Georgia near the Flint River.[41] The plant's most significant pollution consists of wastewater discharges containing bleach, emissions of certain hazardous air pollutants, and pollutant runoff from timbered lands.[42]

The company's XL project experiments with a number of innovative approaches to pollution control. For example, the plant has adopted a holistic, multi-media approach to pollution reduction. This contrasts with the

---

[35] U.S. EPA, "Project XL Site-specific Rulemaking for Merck & Co., Inc., Stonewall Plant" 62 Fed. Reg. 62, 52,622, 52,627 (1997).
[36] Merck Proposed Rule, supra note 31, 62 Fed. Reg., at 15,309.
[37] Ibid., at 15,306.
[38] Ibid., at 15,306–15,307, 15,310.
[39] Ibid., at 15,306.
[40] Ibid., at 15,311.
[41] Weyerhaeuser Co., "Project XL Proposal" p. 1 (13 September 1995) (unpublished proposal on file with author).
[42] Weyerhaeuser Co., "Final Project Agreement Fact Sheet" pp. 1–2 (January 1997).

medium-specific approach of traditional regulation which can result in the transferring of pollution loads from one medium to another rather than true reductions.[43] On another front, the facility is substituting pollution prevention approaches for end-of-pipe, technology-based controls on hazardous air pollutants.[44] Weyerhaeuser has also committed to voluntary adoption of an environmental management system consistent with ISO 14001 standards,[45] in exchange for which it will be subject to reduced regulatory inspections and consolidated, streamlined reporting obligations.[46] The facility hopes that these strategies will significantly reduce the pollution it creates.[47]

Each of the strategies that Weyerhaeuser is employing in its XL project—the multi-media approach to pollution reduction, the substitution of pollution prevention for end-of-pipe controls, and the use of environmental management systems as part of a facility's reporting obligations—represent innovative, and potentially more effective, approaches to environmental control. Weyerhaeuser's XL project allows the EPA to test these strategies in a limited setting with the possibility of extending them to other facilities if they prove to be productive.[48]

3   PROJECT XL AND DUTCH ENVIRONMENTAL COVENANTS: A COMPARISON

Project XL differs in a number of ways from European environmental covenanting initiatives. We can best appreciate these distinctions by comparing it to the Dutch model of environmental covenants, the best-known of the European approaches.[49]

The Dutch interest in voluntary agreements between government and business preceded the American, and grew from a somewhat different set of circumstances. The Dutch received a "wake up call" on the state of their environment in a watershed 1988 report by the National Institute for Public Health and the Environment entitled *Concern for Tomorrow*.[50] The report demonstrated that, in order to achieve sustainable environmental quality in the Netherlands, emissions reductions of 70 to 90 percent for many types of pollutants would be necessary.[51] It further concluded that existing regulatory requirements and policies were insufficient to achieve this goal, and

---

[43]   Weyerhaeuser Co., supra note 41, at 6.
[44]   U.S. Environmental Protection Agency, "XL Project Progress Report: Weyerhaeuser Flint River Operations" p. 3 (March 1999).
[45]   Ibid., at 4.
[46]   Weyerhaeuser Co., supra note 41, at 3, 9.
[47]   Ibid., at 4.
[48]   U.S. Environmental Protection Agency, supra note 44, at 3.
[49]   For further information on and an analysis of voluntary agreements in Europe, see the chapters by Deketelaere and Van Calster, Seerden, Delmas and Terlaak, and Vedder in this book.
[50]   P. de Jongh, "The Netherlands' Approach to Environmental Policy Integration" (Center for Strategic and International Studies, Washington, D.C., 1996), pp. 3–4.
[51]   Ibid., at 27.

that a new and qualitatively different set of regulatory strategies was needed.[52]

In the aftermath of this report, there was strong public support in the Netherlands for dramatic further reductions in environmental pollutants.[53] Business interests in the Netherlands became concerned that a stringent and onerous set of new environmental regulations was in store. Industry and other economic sectors accordingly approached the government about the possibility of negotiating new policy approaches that would achieve the desired (and significant) environmental improvements while minimizing their economic impact.[54] The Dutch Environmental Ministry, recognizing that it could only achieve the ambitious goals set out in *Concern for Tomorrow* by involving all sectors of society on the project and that new forms of regulation were needed in order to reach these objectives, agreed to work together with business.[55] It drew on a method that it had already applied with some success in a few instances: voluntary agreements between the government and industry, also known as "environmental covenants."[56] In short order, environmental covenants became the main instrument for achieving the ambitious goals set out in *Concern for Tomorrow*, elaborated in the first Dutch National Environmental Policy Plan in 1989.[57]

Environmental covenants in the Netherlands are generally negotiated, in the first instance at least, between the national government and a regulated sector (e.g., the printing industry, or the chemicals production industry).[58] On occasion, provincial governments will also sign the agreement if it covers areas over which they have authority to regulate.[59] Dutch environmental covenants can be divided into two basic types: those that govern homogeneous sectors, and those that govern heterogeneous ones.

Homogeneous sectors are those in which all generating facilities share the same basic operating conditions and emissions.[60] Under these conditions it is possible to apply the same performance and operating standards to all facilities within the sector. Environmental covenants for these sectors attempt to do just that. They set emission reduction goals and operating conditions for the entire industry.[61] All facilities within the industry must comply with these standards, which are generally negotiated on their behalf by an industry trade association.

---

[52] Ibid.

[53] Ibid., at 4.

[54] Ibid., at 3.

[55] Ibid., at 6, 54; Royal Netherlands Embassy, "Working with Industry: The Way Towards Covenants" <www.netherlands-embassy.org/c_envcov.html>, 10 November 1999, pp. 1, 4 [hereinafter Embassy-Covenants].

[56] P. de Jongh, supra note 50, at 53.

[57] Ibid., at 34.

[58] D. Fiorino, "Toward a New System of Environmental Regulation: The Case for an Industry Sector Approach" (1996) 26 Envtl L 457, 485–486.

[59] Telephone interview with Pieter Verkerk, Counselor for the Environment, Royal Netherlands Embassy (21 December 1999).

[60] P. de Jongh, supra note 50, at 8.

[61] D. Fiorino, supra note 58, at 486.

Heterogeneous sectors display more variation in operating conditions and emissions.[62] Environmental covenants for these industries generally set emission reduction targets on sector-wide basis,[63] but leave the precise implementation strategies for reaching these goals up to provincial or municipal governments to negotiate, within predetermined limits, with individual companies.[64] The resulting individual agreements, known as Company Environmental Plans, serve as the basis for the issuance of facility permits.[65] Thus, government negotiations with heterogeneous sectors generally lead to both sector-wide and company-specific environmental covenants.

Together, the environmental covenants with homogeneous and heterogeneous sectors seek to achieve far greater emission reductions than previously, but to do so in a flexible, cost-effective way.[66] Moreover they seek to encourage business investment in new pollution control technologies by establishing a long-term regulatory framework to govern the industry. This allows industry to take a strategic perspective towards environmental planning and to time their pollution control investments to work in concert with other needed changes at their facilities.[67]

There are some strong similarities between the Dutch approach, as outlined above, and Project XL.[68] Both use voluntary agreements between government and business to increase regulatory efficiency and spur the creation of new approaches to pollution control. Both also seek to achieve greater environmental protection than traditional regulation allows. But there are a number of important differences as well.

To begin with, most Dutch covenants seek to go beyond the scope of existing environmental regulation so as to achieve dramatic, new pollution reductions across a variety of regulated sectors. By contrast, Project XL agreements are pilot experiments that address environmental problems that are already subject to regulation. They do not expand beyond the reach of existing regulation the way that most Dutch covenants do. We might think of this central difference between Dutch environmental covenants and Project XL as a difference of "scope" between the two initiatives.

The approaches also differ in terms of the parties that the government chooses to negotiate with. In the Netherlands, the government primarily enters contracts with *sectors* of regulated entities. While it is true that individual Company Environmental Plans play a role in the covenants with heterogeneous sectors, they are preceded by a sector-wide covenant and must be negotiated within a framework set in the larger agreement. Thus, it is

---

[62]   Ibid.

[63]   Embassy-Covenants, supra note 55, at 3.

[64]   Ibid., P. de Jongh, "The Netherlands Approach" supra note 50, at 9.

[65]   Ibid., Embassy-Covenants, supra note. 55, at 2–3.

[66]   H. van Zijst, "A Change in the Culture" (May/June 1993) Envtl F, at 15.

[67]   D. Fiorino, supra note 58, at 486. Verkerk interview, supra note 59.

[68]   For a more in-depth discussion of Dutch environmental covenants, including the legal context within which they operate, see Rene Seerden's valuable contribution to this book, titled "Legal Aspects of Environmental Agreements in the Netherlands, in particular the Environmental Agreement on Packaging and Packaging Waste."

fair to say that the emphasis in Dutch covenants is on *sector-based* negotiations. In Project XL, on the other hand, the emphasis is on negotiations with individual regulated entities, primarily companies. The United States has engaged in some sector-based negotiations, such as Project XL for Sectors and the Common Sense Initiative,[69] but these experiments have not flourished.[70] Project XL for Facilities, in which the EPA negotiates environmental contracts with individual entities, has been a more significant program.

The different levels at which the Dutch covenants and Project XL agreements are primarily negotiated—one with sectors, the other with individual entities—may be a reflection of the "scope" difference alluded to above. An environmental covenant aimed at developing an entirely new layer of environmental regulation, intended to lead to dramatic reductions in environmental pollutants, will have far reaching effects on regulated entities and should be negotiated with the regulated sector as a whole. By contrast, the more limited ambitions of Project XL are appropriately achieved through negotiations with individual companies.

A third difference between the two approaches is that one employs "regulatory flexibility," whereas the other does not. As described above, regulatory flexibility is central to Project XL. It allows the program to achieve its main goals of reducing inefficiency and promoting innovation. Moreover, regulatory flexibility, and the cost savings that arise from it, provide the principal incentive for businesses to participate in the program. By contrast, environmental covenants in the Netherlands do not provide regulatory flexibility insofar as the term refers to the lifting of binding regulatory requirements.[71]

This distinction, too, may reflect the "scope" difference. One of the central motivations for Project XL has been to bring flexibility to areas already covered by rigid, command-and-control rules. To do this, it is necessary to lift these existing regulations. The Dutch covenants, on the other hand, generally go beyond the scope of existing regulation in order to map out new areas of pollution control (although some serve more to accelerate the implementation of existing legislation). Consequently, one would not expect them to come as often into conflict with existing standards. Regulatory flexibility (in the sense used above) should not be as necessary.

---

[69] See U.S. EPA, supra note 13, at 27,286 (discussion of Project XL for Sectors); B. Mank, supra note 15, at 14 (discussing the Common Sense Initiative, a program that preceded Project XL and attempted to develop innovative multimedia regulation for industrial sectors through a consensus-based process).

[70] Project XL for Sectors never developed to nearly the extent that Project XL for Facilities did. T. Caballero, "Project XL: Making it Legal, Making it Work" (1998) 17 Stan Envtl L J, at 403, note 5 (in practice, EPA combined XL for Facilities, Government Agencies and Sectors into one category, with most activity concentrating on XL for Facilities). In 1998, the EPA discontinued the Common Sense Initiative amid criticisms of its huge demands on participants' time and modest outcomes, and folded it into the National Advisory Council for Environmental Policy and Technology. Bureau of National Affairs, "Regulatory Reform: Final CSI Meeting to Review Progress; Role of NACEPT to be Examined by Council," *Daily Environment Report* (15 December 1998).

[71] P. de Jongh, supra note 50, at 9, 55, 70; Embassy-Covenants, supra note 55, at 1.

As one top Dutch environmental official has put it: "covenants do not replace regulations; instead, they are precursors of sensible regulation."[72]

A fourth difference has to do with the ways in which Project XL and Dutch covenants are enforced. Dutch environmental covenants, especially the more recent covenants, are intended be legally binding documents that are enforceable under Dutch civil contract law.[73] Project XL Final Project Agreements, by contrast, are not enforceable as contracts.[74] Instead, if a XL participant deviates from the terms of its XL agreement the EPA will enforce the underlying command-and-control regulations that it lifted for "regulatory flexibility."[75] The facility, which has been relying on EPA's offer to lift these requirements, is likely to be in violation of them. (Consider, for example, the VOC permitting requirements in the Merck example described above.)[76] Alternatively, some FPA's are codified into regulations (through site-specific rulemaking) or incorporated into permits, which are directly enforceable.

Fifth, Project XL and Dutch covenants differ in terms of the role of environmental and other non-governmental organizations (NGOs). In the Netherlands, environmental groups were active in setting the agenda for the recent effort to achieve sustainability through greater pollution reductions.[77] However, they play little role in the development or negotiation of the covenants themselves.[78] In Project XL the situation is quite different. The EPA requires, as a condition of EPA approval, that NGOs and other members of the public be brought into the XL project planning process and endorse the project. Thus, while NGOs are usually not signatories to the Final Project Agreement, they can play an important role in the shaping of the agreement.

4   CONTROVERSY OVER PROJECT XL

A final major difference is that initial reviews of the Dutch efforts show it to be a success,[79] and even environmental groups in that country have started to support covenants,[80] whereas Project XL has been a lightning rod for

---

[72]   P. de Jongh, supra note 50, at 70.
[73]   D. Fiorino, supra note 58, at 486.
[74]   See Memorandum from James Nelson, Associate General Counsel, Cross-Cutting Issues Division, U.S. EPA, to Lisa Lund, Deputy Associate Administrator, Office of Reinvention, U.S. EPA, "Legal Principles for FPA Drafting," at 1 (18 December 1997).
[75]   See Memorandum from Steve Herman, Assistant Administrator for Office of Enforcement and Compliance Assurance, "OECA's Operating Principles for Project XL Participants," (2 October 1995), ("EPA's statement of intent not to enforce certain statutory and regulatory requirements is expressly conditioned upon the participant's compliance with the terms of the agreement").
[76]   See supra notes 31–40 and accompanying text.
[77]   P. de Jongh, supra note 50, at 48.
[78]   H. van Zijst, supra note 66, at 17; P. de Jongh, supra note 50, at 48.
[79]   P. de Jongh, supra note 50, at 6.
[80]   Ibid., at 57.

criticism by environmentalists and business groups alike.[81] This disparity is odd in that, on its face at least, Project XL is a far less ambitious program than the Dutch covenants. One would expect it to be less controversial, not more.

There is no single, clear explanation for why environmental contracting has been so much more controversial in the U.S. than in the Netherlands. It may be that Project XL promises "regulatory flexibility," whereas the Dutch covenants do not. Notwithstanding EPA's intent that regulatory flexibility result in greater protection of the environment, some environmental groups in the U.S. have had a hard time seeing it as anything other than a loophole that allows business to avoid binding regulations. The fact that the Dutch covenants go *further* than existing regulations, and do not provide regulatory flexibility, may help to avoid the appearance that they favor business.

Another possible explanation might be cultural differences between the Netherlands and the United States. Holland is a small country, a significant portion of which is below sea level.[82] Since the Middle Ages, people have had to work together to maintain a system of dikes that protect against floods from the sea. These centuries of close cooperation have spawned a culture of negotiation and consensus,[83] sometimes referred to as the "polder" model[84] after the "polders" or units into which the dike system was divided.[85] This cultural disposition may explain why business and government have been able to work so well together on environmental covenants and why environmental groups, while voicing some objections, have ultimately come to support the process.[86]

The United States, on the other hand, is a large, heterogeneous nation with many competing interests that is known more for its litigiousness than its spirit of compromise. This is especially true with respect to environmental debates which implicate fundamental values as to which compromise is often difficult.[87] In contrast to the "polder" model at work in the Netherlands, one might say that the culture that surrounds environmental issues in the United States is "polarized." In this societal context, it is little wonder that environmentalists, industry and government have been unable to come together to support Project XL.

Finally, it may be that XL projects are simply not as well designed as their Dutch counterparts and thus are more deserving of criticism. However, such a comparative study has not yet been done.

---

[81] T. Caballero, supra note 70, at 451–452 (describing environmental and industry objections to the program).
[82] Telephone interview with Pieter Verkerk, Counselor for the Environment, Royal Netherlands Embassy (22 November 1999).
[83] P. de Jongh, supra note 50, at 11.
[84] Netherlands Ministry of Housing, Spatial Planning and the Environment, (1998) *Silent Revolution*, at 9.
[85] Verkerk interview, supra note 82.
[86] P. de Jongh, supra note 50, at 71; H. van Zijst, supra note 66, at 13.
[87] Percival, et al., *Environmental Regulation*, supra note 3, at 68 (describing the "moral outrage" that informs debate over many environmental issues).

4.1   Areas of Controversy

Project XL has come under fire with respect to all four of its main elements.

4.1.1   *Site-Specific Regulation*

Environmentalists and industry competitors of XL participants point out that the practice of negotiating site-specific alternative compliance plans may result in "anti-competitive effects."[88] The concern here is that participating companies would experience cost savings that would give them an unfair advantage over their competitors who remain subject to traditional regulatory requirements.

On another front, environmental groups have also expressed concern that the increasing use of site-specific regulation could drain scarce EPA resources away from its "core mission" of promulgating and enforcing command-and-control requirements and could thereby undermine the regulatory system as a whole.[89] For these reasons, some have recommended that the EPA abandon the site-specific approach to environmental contracting in favor of an industry-wide, sector-based approach, or that it give up on environmental contracting altogether.[90]

4.1.2   *Superior Environmental Performance*

The question of what counts as "superior environmental performance" has been a serious bone of contention among industry, environmental groups, and the government. Business representatives have argued that the concept should include such things as increased stakeholder participation or increased disclosure of facility environmental information, even where there has been no actual reduction in pollutants as compared to what would have been achieved under traditional, command-and-control regulation.[91] As chronicled in Alfred Marcus's chapter in this volume, business interests and the EPA have also disagreed over whether the "baseline" from which superior environmental performance is judged should, or should not, include "beyond compliance" reductions achieved prior to the initiation of the XL project.[92] This divisive issue effectively killed the 3M XL project.[93]

Environmentalists, for their part, have questioned whether it is always possible to determine whether the pollution reductions achieved under the XL project are "superior" to those that would have been achieved under the

---

[88] R. Steinzor, "Reinventing Environmental Regulation: The Dangerous Journey from Command to Self-Control" (1998) 22 Harv Envtl L Rev 103, 185

[89] Ibid., "EPA's Project XL in Need of Adjustments to Ease Participation, Forum Participants Assert," *Bureau of National Affairs Environment Reporter* (3 January 1997).

[90] R. Steinzor, supra note 88, at 201.

[91] U.S. Environmental Protection Agency, "Project XL Roundtable: Final Summary" <http://www.epa.gov/ooaujeag/projectxl/archivl.htm>, 18 December 1999.

[92] See Marcus et al. chapter in this book.

[93] Ibid.

traditional regulation. They are principally concerned with the relatively large number of XL projects that contemplate cross-pollutant trades (e.g., reduction of NO_x and SO_2 emissions to the air in exchange for the ability to increase VOC emissions to the air in the Merck & Co. XL project) and cross-media trades (e.g., reduction of emissions to the air in exchange for the ability to increase discharges to water). They point out that the EPA lacks the necessary experience and data to evaluate accurately the environmental and health impacts of such trades.[94]

4.1.3 Stakeholder Involvement

The stakeholder negotiation process, too, has come under fire. Industry has maintained that it is too time-consuming and expensive and that it greatly increases the transaction costs of participating in an XL project.[95] Environmental groups, for their part, maintain that it is unrealistic to expect national NGO's to participate effectively in the development of dozens of XL projects all around the country. They maintain that the XL concept stretches NGO resources too thinly, making effective stakeholder participation extremely difficult, if not impossible.[96]

4.1.4 Regulatory Flexibility

Environmentalists are even more critical of the regulatory flexibility component of Project XL. Some believe that the Agency has been too liberal in granting exemptions, thereby creating "a regulatory free-for-all" in which companies ask for exemptions that bear no relation to the environmental improvements their XL proposals promise to achieve.[97] Others go even further and accuse the EPA of using regulatory flexibility as a pretext for granting "sweetheart deals" that allow industry to avoid regulatory requirements.[98] In their view, "XL" does not stand for "eXcellence and Leadership," but for "Xtra Leniency."[99]

While these claims are dramatic, the most significant challenge to the program is the claim that the EPA lacks proper legal authority to grant regulatory flexibility. This brings us to the legal controversy over Project XL.

5 PROJECT XL: THE LAW

The central legal issue is whether the EPA can lift binding regulatory requirements for certain parties (i.e., those participating in Project XL),

---

[94] R. Steinzor, supra note 88, at 136–137.
[95] U.S. EPA, supra note 91.
[96] R. Steinzor, supra note 88, at 144–145.
[97] Ibid., at 138–139.
[98] American Political Network, "Spotlight Story on Project XL: EPA Officials Move to Save Troubled Program;" (4 December 1996) 6 *Greenwire* No. 149.
[99] C. Skrzycki, "Critics See a Playground for Polluters in EPA's XL Plan" Washington Post (24 January 1997), at D1.

while at the same time enforcing those very same requirements against all other covered parties. Does such behavior comport with the "rule of law" pursuant to which all like parties are supposed to receive the same treatment? Is it irrational for the EPA to interpret the same environmental statute as simultaneously requiring two wholly different compliance approaches? If so, does regulatory flexibility violate the Administrative Procedure Act which instructs courts to strike down agency action that is "arbitrary" or "capricious"?[100]

These legal questions have bedeviled Project XL.[101] They may soon find their way into court. Recently, a public interest environmental group filed a legal challenge against an XL project that will presumably raise these or related issues.[102]

5.1 The EPA's Legal Mechanisms

The EPA has identified four legal mechanisms that it believes allow it to implement regulatory flexibility. However, as we will describe below, none of these approaches fully meets the needs of Project XL and several of them threaten to undermine the policy foundations of the program.[103]

5.1.1 Enforcement Discretion

The EPA initially decided to implement regulatory flexibility through the exercise of "enforcement discretion," the Agency's prerogative *not* to enforce environmental regulations in certain situations.[104] Under this mechanism, the EPA provides flexibility by promising not to enforce certain regulations (the ones being "lifted") so long as the participating company honors the terms of its XL agreement. The EPA's authority to do this is well-established[105] and bears a strong resemblance to the "prosecutorial discretion" commonly exercised by criminal prosecutors.

The Agency's use of "enforcement discretion" in the environmental regulatory context runs into a roadblock that criminal prosecutors need not contend with. Most federal environmental statutes give private citizens standing to sue to enforce regulatory requirements where the EPA has failed to do so.[106] This right of action is intended to operate as a check on the

---

[100] Administrative Procedure Act, 5 U.S.C. § 706(2)(A) (1994) (requiring courts to "hold unlawful and set aside agency action, findings and conclusions found to be ... arbitrary, capricious, an abuse of discretion or otherwise not in accordance with law").

[101] D. Hirsch, "Bill and Al's XL-ent Adventure," supra note 1, at 131–136; T. Caballero, "Project XL: Making it Legal, Making it Work," supra note 70, at 412.

[102] *Atlantic States Legal Foundation, Great Lakes United, and New York Rivers Unlimited v. U.S. EPA*, No. 14-909 (D.C. Circuit, 1999).

[103] For a more detailed discussion of these issues, see D. Hirsch, supra note 1, at 146–164.

[104] Memorandum from Steve Herman, supra note 75, at 4.

[105] See *Heckler v. Chaney*, 470 U.S. 821, 831–82 (1985).

[106] See, e.g., Clean Water Act § 505(a), 33 U.S.C. § 1365(a) (1994) (authorizing citizen suits to enforce CWA regulations); Resource Conservation and Recovery Act § 7002, 42 U.S.C. § 6972 1994) (authorizing citizen suits to enforce RCRA regulations); Clean Air Act § 304, 42 U.S.C. 7604 (1994) (authorizing citizen suits to enforce CAA regulations).

agency and is not diminished by an agency's exercise of its enforcement discretion. Thus, the EPA's promise to the XL participant amounts to no more than an assurance that the EPA itself will not pursue the violation. It does not prevent a citizen from suing the XL participant for the very violations that the EPA had promised to ignore as part of the XL project. Citizen suits can accordingly negate the flexibility that EPA promises to deliver through enforcement discretion, rendering this legal mechanism inadequate for Project XL.

5.1.2 Flexible Interpretations

The EPA has accordingly developed a number of other legal mechanisms for implementing regulatory flexibility. The main virtue of these other legal methods is that they absolve the XL participant of any violation and thereby insulate it against the threat of a citizen suit (if there is no violation, there is nothing for the citizen to enforce).[107] One of these, "flexible interpretations of regulatory requirements," would exempt an XL participant from a regulatory standard by interpreting the rule in such a way that it no longer applies to the participant. For example, the EPA could use this approach in the *Merck & Co.* case by interpreting the Clean Air Act's VOC permitting rules as not applying to facilities that benefit the environment by agreeing to "beyond compliance" reductions of NO_x and SO_2.

The main problem with this approach is that it only works for those regulations that are susceptible of reinterpretation. It would not allow the EPA to provide regulatory flexibility with respect to unambiguous regulations. Another problem is that the "flexibility interpretation" approach leaves the EPA susceptible to the legal charge that it has acted "arbitrarily" or "capriciously" by simultaneously interpreting the same statute in two different ways (one interpretation for the XL participant; the other for all other regulated entities). As one court has stated, "[the] law does not permit an agency to grant to one person the right to do that which it denies to another similarly situated. There may not be a rule for Monday, another for Tuesday, a rule for general application, but denied outright in a specific case."[108] Perhaps due to these drawbacks, the EPA has not made wide use of the "flexible interpretation" approach in Project XL.

5.1.3 Express Waiver Authority

Another mechanism, "express waiver authority," utilizes statutory provisions that expressly authorize the EPA to "waive" requirements in certain circumstances. For example, Section 111 of the Clean Air Act, which establishes technology-based performance standards for new sources of air

---

[107] EPA's intent to use these mechanisms is described in an Agency guidance document, see U.S. EPA, Regulatory Reinvention (XL) Pilot Projects, 62 Fed. Reg. 19,872, 19,876–877 (1997).
[108] *Mary Carter Paint Co. v. FTC*, 333 F.2d 654, 660 (5th Cir. 1964) (concurring opinion).

pollution, provides that "[a]ny person proposing to own or operate a new source may request the Administrator for one or more waivers from the requirements of this section for such source...to encourage the use of an innovative technological system or systems of continuous emission reduction."[109]

While the express waiver approach appears promising, in practice its usefulness is limited. Many XL projects do not fall within the narrow confines of statutorily-provided express waiver authority.[110]

5.1.4 Site-Specific Rulemaking

The EPA has accordingly decided to rely primarily on yet another legal mechanism: "site-specific rulemaking." Under this approach, the EPA promulgates a new regulation that expressly authorizes the XL project as an alternative means of complying with the statute (albeit an alternative available only to the XL participant).[111] So long as the XL participant operates within the bounds of the new regulation, it does not "violate" the regulations or statute and is not vulnerable to a citizen suit. The EPA utilized this mechanism in the *Merck & Co.* case, promulgating an amendment to its PSD regulations that expressly authorizes the Merck XL project.[112]

While this approach provides XL participants with some measure of legal protection, it creates problems of its own. Under the site-specific rulemaking approach, the EPA must simultaneously interpret a statute in two different ways—one way for the XL participant's site-specific rule, and another for the generally applicable rule. This opens the agency to the charge that it is acting "arbitrarily" or "capriciously" in violation of the law.[113]

Another, and potentially more serious, drawback of the site-specific rulemaking approach is that it is very expensive. The Administrative Procedure Act requires that agencies go through a multitude of steps in order to promulgate a rule. These generally include: drafting of preamble and regulatory language for the proposed rule, publishing the proposed rule, holding a public hearing on the rule, maintaining a docket to receive comments on the rule, analyzing each comment, drafting preamble and regulatory language for the final rule, and publishing the final rule.[114] Often, at the conclusion of this protracted process, an interested party challenges the final rule and the agency must defend it in court. The rule is then in limbo for several additional years while the litigation proceeds.

---

[109]   Clean Air Act § 111(j), 42 U.S.C. § 7411(j) (1994).

[110]   "Regulatory Reinvention (XL) Pilot Projects" 62 Fed. Reg. 19,872, 19,876 (1997) ("[T]he flexibility tools needed for many projects will not be found within the range of discretion afforded by existing federal and state regulatory mechanisms").

[111]   Ibid., at 19,876–19,877.

[112]   See "Project XL Site-specific Rulemaking for Merck & Co., Inc. Stonewall Plant" 62 Fed. Reg. 52,622, 52,627 (1997).

[113]   See *Chevron, U.S.A., Inc. v. NRDC*, 467 U.S. 837, 843–844 (1984). This problem is similar to the one described above with respect to "flexible interpretations" of existing rules, except that there the issue arose from simultaneous yet conflicting interpretations of a rule, whereas here it arises from simultaneous yet conflicting interpretations of a statute.

[114]   Administrative Procedure Act, 5 U.S.C. § 553 (1994).

The site-specific rulemaking process accordingly involves a great investment of time and administrative resources. This threatens to undermine Project XL's goal of providing superior environmental protection at *less* cost to society. It also denies participating companies the early assurance and security that they need to justify expending significant resources of their own on the XL project.[115]

Business groups have cited the legal issues surrounding regulatory flexibility as one of the main reasons for their less than enthusiastic embrace of Project XL.[116] The lower-than-expected rate of participation in the program, coupled with the various points of controversy outlined above, has clouded the future of this once-vaunted initiative. As the Clinton Administration draws to a close, there are questions as to whether Project XL, or environmental contracting by a different name, will continue to exist as part of the regulatory framework in the US.[117]

6 THE FUTURE OF ENVIRONMENTAL CONTRACTING IN THE UNITED STATES

If the United States is to continue its experiment with environmental contracting it will need to find a way to address the issues described above.

6.1 Resolving the Legal Doubts about Project XL

There are at least two possible solutions to the legal questions that have been raised about the program. The first is for the US Congress to pass a statute that provides the EPA with legal authority to replace binding regulatory requirements with site-specific agreements. Such a statute would clear up any questions as to whether Project XL fits within the current statutory framework. The second is for the EPA to resurrect the little-used administrative law doctrine of "implied waiver authority."

6.1.1 Legislation

Over the past few years there have been several attempts to authorize Project XL through legislation. The first of these was the "Innovative

---

[115] According to the U.S. General Accounting Office, in a report on Project XL, "[s]ome industry representatives have specifically questioned whether EPA's strategy of using site-specific rulemakings will provide industry with the assurance it desires that actions taken under a reinvention project will not extend the approval process for reinvention projects for months or years, because it may take years to implement a rule and additional years to litigate it." U.S. General Accounting Office, "Environmental Protection: Challenges Facing EPA's Efforts to Reinvent Environmental Regulation" (1997), p. 52.
[116] R. Steinzor, supra note 88, at 149–150.
[117] As mentioned above, the Clinton Administration ended its other main environmental contracting program, the Common Sense Initiative, and incorporated the remnants of it into another organization.

Compliance Act of 1996," a bill introduced in the United States Senate by Senator Joseph Lieberman (a Democrat from the State of Connecticut).[118] The legislation would have allowed any owner or operator of a facility to petition the EPA to lift any federal environmental regulatory requirement and substitute, in its place, an "alternative compliance strategy."[119] It would have authorized the Agency to grant the petition where the alternative compliance strategy would: (1) "achieve better overall environmental results than would be achieved under the current regulatory requirements;"[120] (2) provide for "accountability, monitoring, enforceability, and public and Agency access to information at least equal to that provided under the Agency rule that is modified or waived;"[121] and (3) be the result of a "stakeholder participation process" that was "balanced and representative of interests likely to be affected by the proposed alternative compliance strategy."[122] This is, in essence, the Project XL environmental contracting approach.

The Senate Committee on the Environment and Public Works never reported the bill out of committee, and it consequently died before being voted on by the full Senate. The following year, Senator Lieberman introduced a similar bill, the Innovative Environmental Strategies Act of 1997,[123] that also failed to make much progress.

On 18 November 1999, a bi-partisan group of legislators introduced a new statute in the House of Representatives that would authorize Project XL. The "Second Generation of Environmental Improvement Act of 1999"[124] empowers the EPA to enter into "innovative strategy agreements" which it defines as "an agreement ... that allows flexibility in meeting environmental standards in return for greater transparency and accountability."[125]

The new bill resembles the Lieberman legislation in several respects. It contemplates that regulated entities will generate the ideas for innovative strategies and will propose them to the EPA.[126] Moreover, it authorizes the EPA to enter into a proposed innovative strategy agreement (ISA) only where the ISA: (1) "can reasonably be expected to produce better environmental results;"[127] (2) "includes a detailed, feasible monitoring plan

---

[118]   S. 2160, 104th Cong. (1996). As is further explained below, this bill was not passed. Senator Lieberman introduced a slightly modified version of the bill in October, 1997 (the Innovative Environmental Strategies Act of 1997, S. 1348, 105th Cong. (1997)), which also was not passed. My discussion will focus on Lieberman's first bill.

[119]   The Innovative Compliance Act of 1996, S. 2160, 104th Cong. (1996) § 102.

[120]   Ibid., § 105(a)(2).

[121]   Ibid., § 105 (a)(1).

[122]   Ibid., §§ 104(b)(1), 105(a)(11).

[123]   S. 1348, 105th Cong. (1997).

[124]   The Second Generation of Environmental Improvement Act, H.R. 3448, 106th Congress (1999).

[125]   Ibid., § 4(4).

[126]   Ibid., § 201. The proposals must identify the "expected environmental benefits and any other expected benefits to the public" as well as "any Agency rule, requirement, policy, or practice or which a modification or waiver is sought and any alternative requirements that is proposed." Ibid., § 202(a) & (b).

[127]   Ibid., § 203(a)(1).

that ... will provide the Agency and the public with better data to gauge the state of the environment;"[128] and (3) "reflects the results of a stakeholder process" in which the "applicant has consulted adequately with interested national, State and community groups and the general public."[129] With some small adjustments, these are essentially the same three approval criteria that the Lieberman bill would have required.

The Second Generation of Environmental Improvement Act also goes beyond the Lieberman effort in an important way. It attempts to improve and expand the EPA's collection of environmental information, especially measures of environmental performance, and to make this information more accessible to the public. In the jargon of environmental policy, it pushes the EPA to make environmental regulation more "transparent."

It does this in five ways. First, the bill would require the EPA, in consultation with the States and other interested parties, to propose a set of "national environmental performance indicators."[130] These indicators must be "quantitative measure[s] designed to provide data on the quality of the environment over time."[131] They should be designed so that the public can use them to evaluate the nation's "progress towards meeting environmental goals" and the success (or failure) of ISA's in helping to achieve these objectives.[132]

Second, the bill would require the EPA to publish, each year, a "State of the Environment" report in which it presents and analyzes the current levels of each of these environmental indicators.[133]

Third, within two years of its enactment, the bill would require the EPA to publish a "unified plan" for all of the Agency's information collection activities.[134] The plan would seek to facilitate information collection and distribution by, among other things, establishing "standard data formats," setting up procedures to ensure "data quality, timeliness and accuracy," and creating a system of data indexing and retrieval that will ease public access.[135]

Fourth, the bill would provide additional incentives for the creation and utilization of improved monitoring technologies that improve the ability to track environmental conditions and facility emissions.[136]

Finally, the bill would require the EPA Administrator to designate a Chief Information Officer at the level of Assistant Administrator to coordinate these activities.[137]

The portion of the bill that deals with the collection and disclosure of environmental information (Title I) and the section that authorizes innovative strategy agreements (Title II) are each interesting and important in their own right (although by no means perfect). But the real contribution of the

---

[128]   Ibid., § 203(a)(2).
[129]   Ibid., §§ 202(a)(3), 203(a)(3).
[130]   Ibid., § 102.
[131]   Ibid., § 4(3).
[132]   Ibid., § 102(a)(2).
[133]   Ibid., § 102(d).
[134]   Ibid., § 103(a).
[135]   Ibid., § 103(b).
[136]   Ibid., § 106(a).
[137]   Ibid., § 101.

Second Generation of Environmental Improvement Act lies in its decision to combine these two aspects. The bill recognizes that regulatory flexibility can only occur in an atmosphere of accountability (otherwise the appearance, if not the practice, of abuse would be too great). By helping to ensure accountability, information disclosure makes regulatory flexibility possible. In this way, regulatory flexibility and increased information disclosure are connected. By tying these two elements together into a single statute, the Second Generation of Environmental Improvement Act advances the legislative effort to authorize environmental contracting.

A possible weakness of the bill is that it may place too many limits on the types of agreements that can serve as ISAs.[138] The bill defines "better environmental results" mainly in terms of reductions in "actual emissions."[139] Moreover, it prohibits any ISA that would "result in an increase in emissions, discharges or other releases above those allowable under the otherwise applicable regulatory requirements."[140] These requirements could be read to preclude virtually all cross-pollutant trades, even those that allow a small and environmentally insignificant increase in one pollutant (above either actual or allowable levels, or both), in exchange for a much larger decrease in another.

While these limits may be intended for a good purpose, i.e. to prevent the creation of greater environmental risks under the guise of flexibility, they go too far. The blanket restrictions on virtually all cross-pollutant trades, even those that are environmentally beneficial, will preclude some useful environmental contracts. For example, they could be read to preclude the Merck & Co. XL project which allows small VOC increases above allowable levels in exchange for large, beyond compliance NO_x and SO_2 decreases.[141] A more narrative definition of better environmental results which focuses on the overall environmental benefits and drawbacks as compared to a baseline, might be a better solution.

The bill further limits the EPA's environmental contracting options by creating a closed list of innovative strategies that the Agency may pursue. As set out in the bill:

Under innovative strategy agreements, the Administrator may—(A) modify, waive or replace otherwise applicable agency rules, requirements, policies, or practices; (B) allow a tiered approach under which monitoring and reporting requirements are loosened initially when emissions are significantly below those allowable under the agreement and then those requirements increase as actual environmental performance gets closer to the emission, discharge and other limitations stipulated in the agreement; (C) extend permit terms, expedite permit reviews, or provide multi-media permits; (D) establish facility-wide limitations on overall allowable emissions and discharges; (E) allow third-party or self-certification in lieu of

---

[138] The following discussion of the bill's weaknesses is the product of a series of conversations that I had with Timothy Malloy of UCLA Law School and Elliott Stern of Eastman Kodak Co.

[139] Ibid., § 203(c).

[140] Ibid., § 204(b).

[141] See supra notes 36–40 and accompanying text.

frequent inspection, provided the sponsor has a credible environmental management program in place; and (F) employ market-based strategies, including pollution trading credits.[142]

While this list contains a number of useful ideas for ISAs, it is by no means exhaustive. For example, it could be read to exclude ISAs that involve innovative approaches to land use or to site remediation—areas that are not expressly mentioned on the list.[143] Such limits do not belong in a statute that is intended to promote innovation. The whole idea is to encourage regulated entities to come up with new and different strategies that have not yet been thought of. Creating a closed list of options can only serve to constrain this process. This problem could be solved by adding a catch-all provision to this section of the bill, leaving the door open to ISAs other than those listed if they meet the other criteria set out in the bill (e.g. result in better environmental performance).

Like the Lieberman legislation before it, the Second Generation of Environmental Improvement Act is unlikely to be passed by the present Congress. The reasons for this lie more with the politics, than the merits, of the legislation. For better or worse, Project XL is tied to the Clinton Administration which launched it, and especially to Vice President Gore. In the coming election year, the Republican-controlled Congress is unlikely to do anything that a Democratic candidate might use to his advantage in his campaign for the Presidency. Thus, the chances for a legislative solution to Project XL's legal problems are slim, at least for the short term.

For present purposes, including its defense of Project XL in the recently-filed lawsuit,[144] the EPA needs to think about other legal solutions that do not require a special Act of Congress. The little-discussed administrative law doctrine of implied waiver authority may prove useful.

6.1.2   Implied Waiver Authority

As I have discussed at greater length in another article,[145] case law supports the idea that, under certain circumstances, federal administrative agencies in the US may possess inherent legal authority to waive their own binding regulations even where Congress has not expressly given them power to do so.[146] This authority is commonly referred to as "implied waiver authority,"

---

[142]   Second Generation of Environmental Improvement Act, H.R. 3448, 106th Cong. (1999) § 204(a)(1).
[143]   I owe these examples to Timothy Malloy. See supra note 138.
[144]   See supra note 102 and accompanying text.
[145]   D. Hirsch, supra note 1.
[146]   Ibid., at 157–167. Some of the key cases that support this proposition include: *Chemical Manufacturers Association v. NRDC*, 470 U.S. 116 (1985); *United States v. Allegheny-Ludlum Steel Corp.*, 406 U.S. 742, 755 (1972); *Alabama Power Co. v. Costle*, 636 F.2d 323, 357 (D.C. Cir. 1979); *Basic Media, Ltd. v. FCC*, 559 F.2d 830, 833 (D.C. Cir. 1977); *WAIT Radio v. FCC*, 418 F.2d 1153, 1157 (D.C. Cir. 1969). For excellent scholarly discussions of this agency authority, see A. Aman, "Administrative Equity: An Analysis of Exceptions to Administrative Rules" (1982) Duke L J 277; P. Schuck, "When the Exception Becomes the Rule: Regulatory Equity and the

although some commentators have termed it "administrative equity"[147] or "regulatory equity."[148]

The policy behind this inherent agency authority begins with the idea that no drafter of a generally applicable rule can, at the time of drafting, foresee all the applications of that rule. It follows that every general rule, no matter how well drafted, will result in some applications that undermine the very purposes for which the rule was drafted, or create unintended and severe hardships, inequities, or inefficiencies. These are often referred to as "bad fit" applications since the rule does not "fit" the circumstances to which it is being applied. In these "bad fit" cases the implementing agency should have the discretion to waive the rule and devise a flexible alternative that better comports with the drafter's intent.[149]

Implied waiver authority could be used as a legal mechanism for implementing the regulatory flexibility component of Project XL. To do so, the EPA would need to show that the regulations to be lifted create a "bad fit" as applied to the XL participant. Once it had made this showing, the Agency could use its implied waiver authority to "waive" the existing regulation and substitute the flexible compliance plan in its place.

This mechanism would serve the EPA better than would its current mechanism of choice, site-specific rulemaking, since it would not require expensive rulemaking proceedings. Instead, EPA could grant flexibility simply by issuing a written waiver.[150] The courts would have the power to review the Agency's decision, thereby creating a check on the process that would help to counter any abuse.[151] To employ this mechanism, the EPA will need to identify a "bad fit" between the regulation to be lifted and the XL participant. This is not as easy as it sounds. Agencies only possess implied waiver authority where they can show that strict application of the rule would result in unintended and severe hardship[152] or inequity,[153] unintended and gross inefficiency,[154] or a manifest subversion of the purpose for which the rule was initially created.[155] There is some authority for the proposition that, even where one of the above conditions is not found,

Formulation of Energy Policy Through an Exceptions Process" (1984) Duke L J 163; K. Davis, *Discretionary Justice: A Preliminary Inquiry* (1969).

[147]   A. Aman, supra note 146, at 280.

[148]   P. Schuck, supra note 146, at 169.

[149]   See the cases cited supra note 146. For a representative case that states this reasoning in a clear and compelling way, see *Chemical Manufacturers Association v. NRDC*, 470 U.S. 116 (1985).

[150]   See *Basic Media Ltd. v. FCC*, 559 F.2d 830, 833 (D.C. Cir. 1977); *WAIT Radio v. FCC*, 418 F.2d 1153, 1159 (D.C. Cir. 1969).

[151]   See *International Union v. Mine Safety and Health Admin.*, 830 F.2d 289, 292 (D.C. Cir. 1987); *Basic Media Ltd. v. FCC*, 559 F.2d 830, 833 (D.C. Cir. 1977).

[152]   See, e.g., *Permian Basin Area Rate Cases*, 390 U.S. 747, 784–787 (1968); *Alabama Power Co. v. Costle*, 636 F.2d 323, 357 (D.C. Cir. 1979).

[153]   See, e.g., *WAIT Radio v. FCC*, 418 F.2d 1153, 1159 (D.C. Cir. 1969).

[154]   See, e.g., *Chemical Manufacturer's Association v. NRDC*, 470 U.S. 116, 120 n. 7, 129–134 (1985); *Alabama Power Co. v. Costle*, 636 F.2d 323, 360–361 (D.C. Cir. 1979).

[155]   See, e.g., *Chemical Manufacturers Association v. NRDC*, 470 U.S. at 129–133; *Alabama Power Co. v. Costle*, 636 F.2d at 360.

an agency may waive rules in order to experiment with new regulatory approaches,[156] but this is not as well established in the law.

Given these limits, implied waiver authority will work better as a legal mechanism for some XL projects than for others. For example, the EPA could probably rely on implied waiver authority to grant regulatory flexibility to Merck & Co. for its XL project. The Agency would point out that since Merck & Co.'s VOC increases do not create more ozone, the costly VOC permitting requirements create an "unintended and gross inefficiency" as applied to this facility. Under the implied waiver authority doctrine, the EPA should be able to correct this "bad fit" by granting an exemption to Merck & Co. and substituting a tailored compliance plan. By contrast, it will be harder for the Agency to maintain that the Weyerhaeuser XL project corrects a "bad fit." This project is more purely about experimentation with new regulatory approaches. Implied waiver authority does not apply as clearly to such cases.

In sum, the EPA should be able to cobble together legal authority for most of its XL projects by employing implied waiver authority, site specific rulemaking, and the other legal mechanisms described above. A statute expressly authorizing Project XL would clearly help the situation. But even in the absence of such a statute, the legal obstacles to the program should not prove insurmountable.

6.2 Addressing Other Areas of Controversy

If environmental contracting is to succeed in the US, the EPA will also have to address the policy issues outlined above.

6.2.1 Is Project XL Anti-competitive?

The Agency should be able to develop an effective response to the claim that Project XL is anti-competitive. It may be true that participating companies benefit economically from their environmental contracts, as compared to their competitors. But this benefit does not come to them free of charge. In order to join Project XL, participating companies have had to invest considerable sums in, among other things, researching innovative strategies, carrying on a stakeholder participation process, negotiating the final project agreement with the EPA, and implementing the project. Moreover, they have had to make many of these expenditures prior to the EPA's approval of their proposal and without any guarantees that the Agency ultimately would approve the project. Looked at in this context, it does not seem so unfair that XL participants, who have made the investments and borne the risks, should receive the early benefits of Project XL.

Further bolstering this view is the fact that the EPA intends to "transfer" the lessons learned in successful XL projects to other facilities in the same

---

[156]   See *WAIT Radio v. FCC*, 418 F.2d at 1159; A. Aman, *supra* note 146, at 293.

industry, thereby making the innovative strategies available to all. Thus, the current XL participants are bearing the start-up costs for experiments that their competitors will later benefit from. These arguments suggest that the EPA should be able to address the anti-competitiveness challenge.

6.2.2   Would Project XL Drain Resources from Core Programs?

Reasoning alone cannot resolve the complaint that site-specific regulation is resource-intensive and will take resources away from the development and enforcement of traditional command-and-control regulations. This is a dollars and cents issue and must be addressed as such. While site specific regulation and regulatory flexibility are designed to save societal resources in the long term (by allowing for more cost-effective methods of pollution control) they require a governmental investment in the short term. It simply takes more EPA resources to negotiate a host of innovative, site-specific agreements than to develop a single, one-size-fits-all, command-and-control rule.

If American society believes that such agreements are important, then it will need to foot the bill for them. More regulatory flexibility and more site-specific regulations must mean larger EPA budgets, at least in the near term. Those who support alternative forms of regulation should get squarely behind this idea. That said, it remains to be seen whether, in this era of "less government," the Congress will provide the necessary resources to underwrite environmental contracting. If it does not, there will likely be a budgetary tug of war between traditional and alternative forms of environmental regulation, and it may well turn out that the traditional approaches will win out.

6.2.3   Does Project XL Result in Superior Environmental Performance?

The questions raised about superior environmental performance pose the greatest challenge to environmental contracting in the U.S. For some XL projects, the EPA cannot know with certainty whether environmental performance will be superior or, indeed, whether it will even be equal to that which would have been achieved under traditional approaches. This creates a major issue for the program.

If Project XL-type environmental contracting is to go forward, the EPA will need to compile better and more accessible data to document the environmental improvements associated with these innovations. As the Second Generation of Environmental Improvement Act correctly suggests, the fate of regulatory flexibility and of information disclosure are intimately linked. The information management provisions of this legislation are a step in the right direction.

But even where the EPA cannot prove with absolute certainty that an environmental contract will provide superior environmental results, this does not mean that the Agency should therefore forego further experiments. In some instances, the environmental benefits are so manifest that, even if they cannot be measured precisely, the information we have is "good enough" to justify going forward.[157]

The Merck & Co. project, in which the company is trading small VOC emission increases for dramatic NO_x and SO_2 reductions, is an example of such a project. There is good evidence to suggest that VOCs do not create ozone in Merck's region, while NO_x and SO_2 are very harmful to the environment. While we cannot document with absolute certainty what the effects of such a cross-pollutant emissions trade will be, we should not let this keep us from moving in a direction that all available evidence tells us is good for the environment. The EPA's best strategy for dealing with the uncertainty issue might be to start with "easy cases" such as this one and use them to build the trust, information and experience and that will allow it to tackle the harder cases later on.[158]

Building such a spirit of trust may well be the key to the future of EPA's experiment with environmental contracting. The United States is different from Netherlands. It has many more interest groups vociferously advocating for their points of view. This great diversity of interests can make it hard to reach the consensus needed to move forward with innovative approaches to regulation. On the other hand, if properly channeled, this diversity could constitute an advantage when it comes to environmental contracting. More public involvement creates more accountability and this, in turn, can allow for more flexibility without compromising environmental values.

---

[157] For a useful discussion of this approach in the context of emission "bubbles," see E.D. Elliott and G. Charnley, "Toward Bigger Bubbles" (1998) *Forum for Applied Research and Public Policy*, pp. 51–52.

[158] Ibid.

6. The Quest for Cooperative Environmental Management: Lessons from the 3M Hutchinson Project XL in Minnesota

Alfred A. Marcus, Don Geffen, and Ken Sexton

1   INTRODUCTION

The Clinton administration initiated Project XL (eXcellence and Leadership) on 16 March 1995. It was one of 25 actions the administration took "to produce a new era of cleaner, cheaper, and smarter environmental management." XL was one of a series of regulatory reinvention initiatives that the administration started in order to put an end to adversarial regulation and begin a new era of cooperative approaches. This chapter uses a case study of the XL pilot at 3M's world-class manufacturing facility in Hutchinson, Minnesota to examine the barriers encountered in an attempt to move towards a new competence in environmental regulation. Caring and committed people with different beliefs and opinions worked diligently and in good faith over a two-year period to forge a cooperative, mutually agreeable pilot project that would result in a series of "win-win" outcomes.[1] Unfortunately, their efforts resulted in a stalemate.

This chapter reviews some of the classic criticisms of adversarial command-and–control regulation. It describes efforts to move toward a new competence in environmental management and tries to explain the reasons for the Minnesota setback and its implications. This chapter looks at the prospects for reform now that the dust has settled on the EPA's early reinvention initiatives.

2   CRITICISMS OF THE ADVERSARIAL SYSTEM

For over 20 years, the underlying assumptions of a command-and-control regulatory system were seldom challenged. Under a command-and-control

---

[1]   The authors were both participants and observers in this multi-organizational, bipartisan effort to design and undertake an experiment in flexible, performance-based, facility-wide environmental permitting at the facility.

system, regulators tell polluters what they should do and how they should do it on a source-by-source basis. But how can regulators determine the best actions to control diverse sources in different industries throughout the country? Economists criticized command-and-control regulation for being costly and rigid and for suppressing innovation. They called for a system that would make greater use of market mechanisms such as pollution charges. These mechanisms would give plant managers and employees increased freedom to devise best solutions on a site-by-site basis. They would be a stimulus for making decisions where the information was best.

The basic principle underlying the system the economists advocated is that the polluter should pay for the damages.[2] Markets that fail to internalize the price of pollution are defective. They can be fixed by assigning an appropriate price for pollution. Aware of this price, the polluter has the opportunity to choose the most cost-effective response, as well as an incentive to innovate and reduce pollution at the lowest cost.

No matter how reasonable the economists' argument, regulated businesses never accepted it.[3] Although US businesses criticized environmental regulations, they also opposed pollution charges or other market mechanisms. The business community preferred the certainty of regulation to the uncertainty of a new approach. It feared that the economists' idea of introducing pollution charges and markets was a euphemism for more taxes.

Businesses tended to agree that one-size-fits-all command-and-control regulation was costly and rigid and that it suppressed innovation. They were politically active in opposing different kinds of pollution control legislation and fought many regulatory initiatives. They often claimed that the public benefit from EPA programs did not justify the cost. They pointed out that the EPA oversaw the most expensive federal regulatory program.

Rather than being a proponent of a system constructed according to economists' abstract models, members of the business community tended to concentrate on specific instances of regulatory error and mismanagement. A common source of complaints was the record keeping requirements the EPA imposed. These requirements kept pollution control staff at a company busy with the minutia of compliance. The staff could not engage in the more important task of reducing waste.

Historically, most environmentalists had a different perspective.[4] For them, the effectiveness of pollution control laws was more important than their efficiency. They often maintained that existing laws did not go far enough in regulating dangers. They also believed that the enforcement of these laws was lax. More, rather than less, government intervention was needed. Most environmentalists maintained that reform was needed, but what they really meant was strengthening government intervention not weakening it.

---

[2] A. Marcus, *The Adversary Economy* (Quorum Books, Westport, 1984).
[3] Ibid.
[4] Ibid.

This stance in the environmental community started to change in the early 1990s. The Environmental Defense Fund (EDF) was probably the most outstanding example of an environmental group that started to see the benefits of economic approaches that economists had proposed and of working collaboratively with business firms.

3   ASSESSING THE EPA

Meanwhile, the EPA appeared to be doing a fairly good job.[5] Since its creation, available indicators suggested that the environment was in better shape than that it had been prior to the birth of the agency. Taking into account population growth and the economy's expansion, this accomplishment—whether entirely due to the EPA or not—could not be dismissed.

The question was how much of this improvement would have occurred in any event because of the changing nature of production in the US in an increasingly global economy. The US economy was moving away from heavy industries like steel and petroleum refining towards a service economy of white-collar jobs and workers. A study done by Davies and Mazurek found that changes in the composition of manufacturing and weather patterns had more effect on declines in air pollution in cities like Pittsburgh, Baltimore, and Cleveland than mandated pollution control programs.[6] A broad movement toward dematerialization—using less material to produce the same economic value—played an important role in the decline of pollution per unit of GNP.[7]

Even granting that the EPA had an important role to play in this process, questions could be raised about the costs of what it did and whether more could have been accomplished had environmental problems been conceived differently and a different set of policy instruments been used. Alhough the US was a world leader in rigorous regulatory programs, it consistently ranked among the highest in the world in emissions of sulfur oxides and nitrogen oxides per capita.[8] Miles driven per capita outstripped that of any other nation, and the US was the world's leading contributor to greenhouse gases. Part of the problem was that the EPA did not have a mandate from Congress to address these kinds of underlying issues.

---

[5]   J. Davies and J. Mazurek, *Pollution Control in the United States: Evaluating the System* (Resources for the Future, Washington, D.C., 1998).

[6]   Ibid.

[7]   L. Schipper, "Lifestyles and the Environment: The Case of Energy" (1996) 125 Daedalus 113; V. Weizsacker, et al., *Factor Four: Doubling Wealth, Having Resource Use—The New Report to the Club of Rome* (Island Press, Washington, D.C., 1994); I. Wernick, et al., "Materialization and Dematerialization: Measures and Trends" (1996) 125 Daedalus 171.

[8]   A. Van de Ven and M. Poole, "Explaining Development and Change in Organizations" (1995) *Academy of Management Review* 510.

4   TOWARDS A NEW COMPETENCE IN
ENVIRONMENTAL MANAGEMENT

The EPA's opportunities for developing new approaches to environmental regulation were limited. Although its experiments went back almost to its beginning, they were piecemeal in nature and grafted onto the existing command-and-control structure.[9] They also differed in important ways from the theoretical systems economists constructed.

4.1   Emission Trading Schemes

The EPA's most well-known experiments were with emission trading schemes.[10] It started to introduce various forms of emission trading in the late 1970s. The simplest explanation of how they worked was that they allowed emission reduction rights to be exchanged externally between firms and internally within a facility by means of a single performance standard and a so-called "bubble" over the facility's sources. If a firm decreased pollution below a standard, it created a right that it could hold for future use (i.e., "bank" the right, in the EPA's terminology), or trade either internally among its own pollution sources or externally with other firms. One of the earliest bubbles involved a steel mill dampening piles of coal rather than installing expensive electrostatic precipitating equipment to control the spread of particulate matter (i.e., dust). As long as the particulate matter standard for the facility was met, the EPA did not care how it was done, but this right to exchange emissions was not easily won. It involved years of administrative hearings and judicial controversy.[11]

The experiments with market approaches that the EPA tried were grafted on to the existing command-and-control structure. They relied on the existing air, water, and other environmental quality standards to establish benchmarks and determine to what extent facilities and individual sources were above or below them. By conducting these experiments, the EPA discovered how difficult it was to establish benchmarks and decide how far a firm was below them, a problem that later plagued Project XL.[12]

A disincentive for firms to participate in the incentives trading schemes was the problem they had attaining recognition for their reductions.[13] The EPA was slow to develop rules and to approve bubbles, banking of pollution rights, and other parts of the emissions trading system. Nonetheless, assessments showed potential for substantial gains. A 1985 EPA estimate suggested that the 42 bubbles that it had approved had resulted in savings

---

[9]   See Marcus, supra note 2.
[10]   D. Dudek and J. Palmisano, "Emissions Trading" (1980) Column J Envtl L 217–54; R. Hahn and G. Hester, "Marketable Permits" (1989) 16 Ecology L Q 361.
[11]   See R. Hahn and G. Hester, "Where Did All the Markets Go? An Analysis of EPA's Emissions Trading Program" (1989) 6 Yale J on Reg 109.
[12]   Ibid.
[13]   Ibid.

of more than $300 million.[14] Other EPA studies suggested that these gains had been achieved without additional harm to the environment.[15]

4.2 SO₂ Trading under the 1990 Clean Air Act

The 1990 Clean Air Act Amendments had unique provisions for the creation of trading rights in sulfur dioxide emissions from power plants.[16] Representatives from the Environmental Defense Fund supported this initiative, which was a breakthrough in the environmental communities' attitude toward market approaches. Under the 1990 Act, the government set an aggregate performance emission cap and granted utilities emission allowances, based on about half their total annual emissions in 1985–87. The utilities could reduce emissions below these allowances by any means they chose—switching to low sulfur coal, installing scrubbers, or closing down plants. Reducing emissions below this level created credits they could bank or sell to other utilities. The purpose was to set up an active market in which many external trades took place. The hope was that a host of brokers, utilities, and environmentalists would participate in this market.

In the first phase of the Clean Air Act, which lasted until 1995, only 9 percent of compliance came about because of the trades utilities made with each other.[17] The 1990 Clean Air Act provisions dealing with sulfur dioxide generally were successful not only because of trading in pollution rights, but also because of the use of performance based rather than technology-forcing standards.[18]

4.3 Voluntary Programs

In the late 1980s and early 1990s, the EPA tried many voluntary programs.[19] A number of their features were incorporated into Project XL, especially the idea of transparency—companies being moved through an open and accessible process to improve environmental performance to enhance their public image—as a stimulus to change. The community right-to-know provision of the 1986 Superfund Amendments Reauthorization Act (SARA)

---

[14] Ibid.

[15] Ibid.

[16] A. Marcus and D. Geffen, "The Dialectics of Competency Acquisition: Pollution Prevention in Electric Generation" (1998) 19 Strategic Mgmt J 1145.

[17] J. Davies and J. Mazurek, *Industry Incentives for Environment Improvement: Evaluation of U.S. Federal Initiatives* (Resources for the Future, Washington, D.C., 1996).

[18] See Marcus and Geffen, supra note 16.

[19] See D. Fiorino, "Toward a New System of Environmental Regulation" (1996) 26 Envtl L 457; P. Gruss, "Any Volunteers?" (1998) 8 *Tomorrow* 38; D. John, "Community Based Environmental Protection" (National Academy of Public Administration, 12 May 1997); P. Kleindorfer and E. Orts, "Informational Regulation of Environmental Risks" (1998) 18 *Risk Analysis* 155; K. McDonald, "Project XL: An Experiment in Environmental Regulatory Reform" Plan B Paper, HHH Institute of Public Affairs, University of Minnesota, 1997; N. Vig and M. Kraft (eds), *Environmental Policy in the 1990s: Reform or Reaction?* (CQ Books, Washington, D.C., 1996).

was the legal framework that authorized creation of the Toxic Release Inventory (TRI). Companies had to let the public know what chemicals were emitted at specific sites. In 1991, the EPA launched the 33/50 program. The top 8,100 TRI emitters were asked to reduce 17 of the most toxic chemicals 33 percent by 1992 and 50 percent by 1995. About 1,300 firms voluntarily signed up to participate in this program, for a participation rate of about 16 percent.[20] The cumulative reduction of emissions from these firms from 1988–1993 was about 46 percent.[21]

In 1990, Congress passed federal pollution prevention (P2) legislation. More symbolic than substantive, the main intention of the 1990 (P2) Act was to expand the amount of information available to the public.[22] As part of this effort, the EPA also started an awards program. In addition, industry had to include toxic chemical source reduction and recycling reports in its TRI reports.

Another voluntary program the EPA started was the Green Lights program.[23] In 1991, it asked companies to install high-efficiency lighting that would pay for itself within five years. In exchange, the EPA gave technical support and information about financial assistance programs, products, and energy service companies. The EPA started a similar program in 1993 called Energy Star, which certified energy-efficient equipment in the electronics industry. By 1995 the EPA had concluded agreements with 90 percent of US computer, printer, and monitor manufacturers.[24] These programs started to move the EPA incrementally away from the command-and-control model.

4.4   Corporate Environmentalism

Along with these trends at the EPA, the 1990s saw a maturing of corporate environmentalism.[25] This maturation came about for many reasons. The encouragement of the EPA helped, as did assistance from private consultants. There were also generational changes in most companies. Top management began to change their thinking, many citing their children as motivating them toward a greater concern. Increasingly, corporate environmental staff people became less resistant to environmental regulation and more interested in positive outcomes that would benefit both business and the environment. Increasing numbers of companies became proactive as

---

[20]   See Davies and Mazurek, supra note 17; Vig and Kraft (eds), supra note 19.
[21]   See Davies and Mazurek, supra note 17.
[22]   See Vig and Kraft (eds), supra note 19.
[23]   Ibid.
[24]   Ibid.
[25]   See T. Galdwin, "The Meaning of Green" in J. Schot and K. Fischer (eds), *Environmental Strategies for Industry: International Perspectives on Research Needs and Policy Implications* (Island Press, Washington, D.C., 1993), p. 37; B. Piasecki, et al., *Environmental Management and Business Strategy* (John Wiley and Sons, Danvers, 1998); N. Roome (ed.), *Sustainability Strategies for Industry: The Future of Corporate Practice* (Island Press, Washington, D.C., 1998); M. Russo, *Environmental Management: Readings of Cases* (Houghton Mifflin College, Boston, 1998).

they discovered win–win solutions that improved profitability as well as the environment.[26] Another change was more technical knowledge and experience within the typical company. Knee-jerk, negative reactions to environmental concerns were no longer as prevalent. The opposition to specific environmental proposals, if it occurred, was likely to be more thoughtful and positive.

In addition to these internal trends in the firm, disasters such as the massive toxic chemical release and loss of life at Bhopal and the huge Exxon oil tanker leak with its vast environmental degradation made most companies more vigilant.[27] They better understood the consequences of corporate laxness. They began to calculate more carefully how best to manage in order to prevent disasters.

4.5 Self-Regulation and Other Collaborative Efforts

In some instances, trade associations played a leading role. The Responsible Care program adopted by the Chemical Manufacturers Association (CMA) in 1988 was a prime example. Started after Bhopal, it emphasized among other matters pollution prevention and helped to stimulate the adoption of P2 programs in many companies. The chemical industry's efforts bore some resemblance to the nuclear power industry's responses to Three Mile Island.[28] However, the self-regulatory apparatus it set up had less teeth because the ability to discipline errant companies was more limited.

There were other examples where elements within the business and environmental communities showed signs that they had grown weary of old positions and were willing to experiment. An example was the EDF's work with the McDonald Corporation. Still another example was the drawn-out but successfully completed negotiations between the EPA, Amoco, and environmentalists for pollution prevention reductions at the Yorktown refinery.[29] Long and Arnold document 12 cases of collaboration that were carried out in the 1990–95 period.[30] Though difficult to put together and to sustain, these cooperative ventures suggest that a start had been made in the United States toward more cooperative environmental regulation.

---

[26] See R. Florida, "Lean and Green: The Move to Environmentally Conscious Manufacturing" (1996) 39 *California Management Review* 80; A. King. "Improved Manufacturing Resulting From Learning-From Waste" (Paper presented at the annual meetings of the Academy of Management, 1994); M. Porter and C. Van der Linde, "Green and Competitive" (1995) 73 Harv Bus Rev 120; N. Walley and B. Whitehead, "It's Not Easy Being Green" (1994) May–June Harv Bus Rev 46.

[27] See A. Hoffman, *From Heresy to Dogma: An Institutional History of Corporate Environmentalism* (Lexington Books, San Francisco, 1997).

[28] Ibid.

[29] See B. Raffle and D. Mitchell, "Effective Environmental Strategies: Opportunities for Innovation and Flexibility Under Federal Environmental Laws, Draft for Discussion" (1993) AMOCO.

[30] See F. Long and M. Arnold, *The Power of Environmental Partnerships* (Dryden Press, Fort Worth, 1998); D. Wallace, *Environmental Policy and Industrial Innovation: Strategies in Europe, the USA and Japan* (Royal Institute of International Affairs, London, 1995).

4.6   European Models

US policy makers increasingly looked to Europe for models of environmental policy that were more cooperative and less adversarial in nature. In Europe, the Dutch model was the most prominent one to come to the attention of US policy makers.[31] There were many features in the Dutch experience and the experience of other countries that could be the basis for experiments in the US, including:[32]

1. broad performance standards as alternatives to conventional regulation, rather than narrow technology-based ones;
2. the use of flexibile and iterative processes to reach pollution reduction goals;
3. innovative initiatives at the local as well as just the national level;
4. greater reliance on cooperation and voluntarism and less on adversarialism and confrontation.

Analysts in the US started to discuss these alternatives.[33] Some sharply attacked the US government's adherence to technology-based command-and-control standards.[34] They argued that these standards were inefficient because they did not take into account plant, industry, and geographic variations. The standards also worked to the disadvantage of new industry, which had to comply with more exacting prevention-of-significant-deterioration and best-available-control-technology standards. Requiring industry to comply with these standards had the potential to retard industrial innovation. Others defended the existing system, maintaining that other goals besides efficiency had to be considered.[35] In the face of high uncertainty and strategic behavior by regulated firms, uniform technology-based standards were said to be preferable to more flexible approaches.

Still others admitted that the US system had made great strides in controlling conventional pollution from large industrial facilities and motor vehicles, the main problems of the 1960s and 1970s.[36] However, the system now was outdated. A better system would be more flexible. It would vary control levels in accordance with control costs and the harm pollution causes. It would be result-oriented and focus on ends rather than means (i.e., technology). It would be more integrated and less dependent on the medium-based approach (air, water, solid waste, etc.). It would rely more

---

[31]   See E. Orts, "Reflexive Environmental Law" (1995) 89 Nw U L Rev 1227; F. Van den Akker, "Environmental Policy: Legislation and Sustainable Development" (1996) Ministry of Housing, Spatial Planning and the Environment, the Netherlands.
[32]   D. Wallace, *Environmental Policy and Industrial Innovation: Strategies in Europe, the USA and Japan* (Royal Institute of International Affairs, London, 1995).
[33]   See Fiorino, supra note 19; D. Fiorino, "Will There Be a New Environmental Regulation?" Unpublished manuscript (1996).
[34]   See, e.g., R. Percival (ed.), *Law and the Environment: A Multidisciplinary Reader* (Temple University Press, 1997).
[35]   B. Thompson, "The Search for Regulatory Alternatives" (1996) 15 Stan Envtl L J 8.
[36]   See Percival (ed.), supra note 34.

on experiments designed to continuously improve the system and on citizen participation. It would evaluate these experiments as they were carried out to determine what worked and what did not. These ideas were part of an evolving consensus about the substance and direction of a new cooperative approach to environmental regulation.

4.7 Responses

In 1996, the President's Council on Sustainable Development issued a report called "Sustainable America: A New Consensus-Building Framework for a New Century" in which it argued that the nation had to go beyond the command-and-control structure that had proved effective in the past.[37] The lessons of this experience, according to the President's Council, were as follows:

1. the adversarial nature of the current system was counter-productive;
2. collaboration and cooperation among past adversaries were needed;
3. pollution prevention was better at encouraging technological innovation than technology-based standards;
4. if compliance were assured, enhanced flexibility for achieving environmental goals could be provided; and
5. many of the most creative and lasting solutions came from partnerships and collaborations at the state level.

Similar proposals were put forward by the Office of Technology Assessment (OTA) in 1996.[38] OTA called upon policy makers to experiment with different approaches and to learn more about the strengths and weaknesses of less-often used tools. It called for state and regional experiments in using instruments with which the US has had little experience.

5 HOW ONE EFFORT FARED

In 1995 the Clinton administration proposed a series of regulatory reinvention initiatives that called for wide-scale experimentation with new forms of cooperative regulation. Clinton and Gore's March 1995 plan to reinvent environmental regulation had 25 "high experiments". These were divided into two categories: 18 "improvements to the current system" and 7 "building blocks for a new system."[39] This approach revealed an admirable commitment to change, but was inherently flawed because it called for action before extensive analysis was undertaken. Important details and specifics were left to the implementation stage, where potential disagreements and stalemates might prevent specific experiments from being carried out.

---

[37] Ibid., Vig and Kraft (eds), supra note 19.
[38] See Percival (ed.), supra note 34; Vig and Kraft (eds), supra note 19.
[39] See D. Osborne and T. Gaebler, *Reinventing Government: How the Entrepreneurial Spirit is Transforming the Public Sector* (Plume Books, New York, 1993).

The Clinton-Gore initiatives emphasized partnerships that would rely on teamwork and trust[40] to mitigate concerns that different sides would take advantage of each other. For a new competence in environmental management to be realized, a higher level of trust would have to be achieved among communities, states, companies, and the EPA.[41] The boundaries between sectors historically at odds would have to become more permeable. Inspired by greater degrees of civic activism and public spiritedness, the one-way traffic—from government to society—would have to become a two-way street.

Project XL, one of the more amitious of these initiatives, stood for excellence and leadership. The intent was to create innovative alternatives to present regulation that would enhance environmental protection and promote vibrant economic growth.[42] The Clinton-Gore administration wanted to give flexibility to good corporate citizens who would develop creative ways to achieve superior environmental performance. The EPA's goals in asking for proposals under this program were the following:[43]

1. environmental performance superior to that which could be achieved under current and reasonably anticipated future regulation;

---

[40]   See W. Clinton, Press Release and President's Comments on Project XL, Washington, D.C., 3 November 1995 <www.epa.gov>; W. Clinton and A. Gore, "Reinventing Environmental Regulation" USEPA, Office of Policy Analysis and Review, Office of Air and Radiation, Washington, D.C., 1995.
[41]   See L. Hosmer, "Trust" (1995) 20 *Academy of Management Review* 379; R. Mayer and J. Davis, "An Integrative Model of Organizational Trust" (1995) 20 *Academy of Management Review* 709; W. Ruckelhaus, "Trust in Government: A Prescription for Restoration" National Academy of Public Administration, Webb Lecture, Washington, D.C., 15 November 1996; C. Sabel, "Studied Trust: Building New Forms of Cooperation in a Volatile Economy" in F. Romo and R. Swedberg (eds), *Human Relations and Readings in Economic Sociology* (Russell Sage, New York, 1991); W. Wittkopf, "Trust Development in Temporary Teams" Unpublished paper (1996).
[42]   See K. Sexton, et al. (eds), *Better Environmental Decisions: Strategies for Governments, Businesses, and Communities* (Island Press, Washington, D.C., 1999); C. Sparrow, "Regulatory Reform: Putting the Pieces Together" (1998) *State Environmental Monitor* 2, February, at 30.
[43]   C. Buelow, "An Experiment in Flexible Permitting: Project XL" Master's Project, Nicholas School of the Environment, Duke University, 1996; C. Buelow, "Barriers to Regulatory Reform as Experienced in the 3M Project XL Pilot" Master's Project, Duke University, 1997; E. Dawson, "Looking at Voluntary Participation Programs: A Case Study of Project XL at the Weyerhaeuser Flint River Facility" Senior Honors Thesis, University of Michigan, 1998; F. Dews, "A Project XL Pilot Summary: 3M" Brookings Institution Government Studies Program, Washington, D.C., 1997; G. Ginsberg and C. Cumis, "EPA's Project XL: A Paradigm for Promising Regulatory Reform" (1996) 26 *ELR News and Analysis* 10059; A. Marcus and D. Geffen, "XL Project at 3M" Paper presented at EPA Pollution Prevention/Green Manufacturing Conference, Atlanta, 17 November 1998; K. McDonald, supra note 19; Minnesota Pollution Control Agency, "Facts About Project XL" Air Quality Division, November 1995; A. Ronchak, "Project XL Overview" Presented to M2P2 Permitting Project Conference, Baltimore, 8 November 1995; A. Ronchak, "3M XL Pilot History, 7/30/96–12/24/96" (1997); R. Steinzor, "Regulatory Reinvention and Project XL: Does the Emperor Have Any Clothes?" (1996) 26 *ELR News and Analysis* 10527; Fed. Reg. Notice (FRL 5197-9), Environmental Protection Agency, "Regulatory Reinvention (XL) Pilot Projects, Solicitation of Proposals and Request for Comments" 23 May 1995 27283.

2. cost savings and paperwork reductions for regulators and the affected firms;
3. stakeholder support;
4. innovative environmental management strategies;
5. multimedia pollution prevention;
6. transferability, feasibility, and clearly defined objectives, measures of success, and time-frames;
7. easily understandable information, including performance data, made available by participating firms to stakeholders;
8. consideration of risk to worker health and safety; and
9. cooperative relations between regulators, the facility, and the community.

As EPA originally conceived Project XL, individual companies that wanted to participate would design and submit proposals to the agency.[44] If a proposal was accepted, the company would draft a permit and Final Project Agreement (FPA), working in collaboration with the state pollution control agency, the EPA regional office, local stakeholders, and the EPA national office. Before implementation, the permit and the FPA would have to be agreed to by all the parties involved in the negotiations.

5.1 Superior Environmental Performance

Project XL was based on the premise that in exchange for superior environmental results, regulated entities should be granted greater regulatory flexibility. The question that plagued Project XL Minnesota was how to apply the concept of superior environmental performance (SEP) to the Hutchinson facility and how to guarantee it over the life of a long-term permit. In 1996, allowable emissions at the facility for the main category of air pollutants in question, Volatile Organic Compounds (VOCs), were 33,989 tons per year. Since 1987, 3M had reduced its emissions of VOCs by 87 percent, while production grew by nearly 70 percent. Consequently, by 1995, actual emissions of VOCs at Hutchinson were reduced to 2,307 tons per year, well below what regulations required. The company intended to expand production at Hutchinson at a rate similar to the past (i.e., nearly 70 percent). To allow for this increased production and in light of the large gap between current actual VOC emissions and allowable emissions, 3M proposed a ten-year XL permit with a cap on VOC emissions of 4,500 tons per year. The XL permit and FPA that was developed by the Minnesota stakeholders adopted this facility-wide cap. The XL permit and the FPA also included an advanced environmental management system, multi-media pollution prevention, greater transparency, and stakeholder involvement.

---

[44] EPA, "Principles for Development of Project XL Final Project Agreements" <www.epa.gov>, 1 December 1995; EPA, "Project XL-Process for OECA Involvement and Review of Final Project Agreements" 27 February 1996.

In addition and in contrast to existing regulations, the permit and FPA required that VOC emissions from all significant sources at the facility be controlled. The Minnesota Pollution Control Agency (MPCA), its stakeholder group, called the Pilot Project Committee (PPC), and 3M anticipated that the company would make reductions in pollution that it otherwise would not make under existing laws.

In EPA's 2 July 1996 comments on the proposed XL permit and FPA for the Hutchinson facility, the agency expressed its concern. The main worry was that the proposed XL permit would allow 3M to emit more VOCs than would be allowed under future, more stringent regulations. The agency wanted annual regulatory analyses comparing actual emissions at the facility to what would have been emitted under otherwise applicable requirements. The EPA suggested that performance should be at a minimum 10 percent better than the Clean Air Act would have mandated. The agency also wanted stronger enforcement provisions in the proposed permit and FPA. The Agency sought clarification of the consequences if 3M violated the emissions caps, and stated its belief that violation should result in unilateral termination and a speedy return to compliance with the Clean Air Act. Finally, the EPA maintained that under the Clean Air Act it could not grant such a permit for longer than five years.

In its negotiations with 3M, the EPA maintained that if facilities were to be granted more flexibility, they must provide a guaranteed level of SEP—the greater the economic benefit, the greater the SEP required. 3M disagreed with the EPA about how much SEP should be required and about the way in which the company would have to guarantee SEP in advance. 3M also argued that the large voluntary reductions in emissions it had previously made at Hutchinson already demonstrated SEP. The MPCA and its stakeholder group maintained that the purpose of an experiment was to test new ideas and that SEP was a many faceted concept, including: pollution prevention; advanced environmental management systems; multi-stakeholder involvement; simpler permits; greater transparency; public understanding; and cost savings as well as emission reductions. The parties failed to reach an agreement at Hutchinson mainly because 3M did not offer what EPA thought were enough guaranteed emission reductions to justify the flexibility the company was seeking.

5.2   The Results of Project XL Minnesota

Although the 3M Hutchinson project was not successful, it did help to set the boundaries for future reform. Policy makers and analysts sitting above the fray and contemplating what the best approach should be did not finalize XL policies before-the-fact. Instead, these policies evolved out of cases and controversies where contestants had real stakes, pondered how they would be affected, developed rationales and arguments for their positions, and engaged in debate. Because the issue-rich controversy surrounding 3M's manufacturing facility in Hutchinson occurred relatively early, the debate it engendered played an important role in the subsequent development of policy. The reactions that the EPA had to 3M's facility set the tone for positions the Agency subsequently took on Project XL in general.

The conclusions that the agency reached included the following:

1. Because projects like 3M Hutchinson had been so expensive, the public had to be assured that there would be a large environmental payback from each pilot.

2. A facility had to offer more environmental benefits than it was currently providing. It could not be rewarded for past environmental performance.

3. Since the EPA's primary purpose was to make environmental progress, experiments like the one proposed at Hutchinson had merit only if they assisted the agency in meeting this goal.

4. The pilots were meant to gather data that would help the EPA decide how to modify current regulatory processes so that the agency would be able to produce better environmental results in a more streamlined, cost-effective, and efficient manner in the future.

5. Project XL, along with other reinvention programs, was a potential step towards a new form of regulation, but it was not itself necessarily a component of that new form of regulation.

6. For now, the EPA's main goal was to learn lessons that could be applied within the existing regulatory framework and environmental laws. Reinvention did not mean the wholesale restructuring of this system.

7. Project XL was a laboratory in which the EPA, state and local governments, and other stakeholders could experiment with alternative environmental strategies from which future environmental protection strategies *might* evolve.

6   DIFFICULTIES IN MOVING FORWARD

After the collapse of the 3M negotiations, the EPA had difficulties in moving forward with Project XL. The impasse made additional companies less eager to be involved. The MPCA and its stakeholder group did not share the EPA's conclusions about this reinvention effort. They had more ambitious and far reaching goals, and regarded XL as an opportunity to experiment with some of the possible components of a new, more cooperative regulatory system. The incremental changes the EPA sought did not seem to be worth the considerable effort that an XL project would require. Other companies watching the 3M experience agreed.

In 1995, President Clinton and Vice President Gore asked for 50 signed Project XL agreements in one year. As of April 1999, the EPA had ten signed agreements, and 31 had been rejected or withdrawn. The EPA had facilitated six non-full-fledged projects, nine projects were in development, and five were proposed.

Some of the approved projects (Weyerhaeuser and Lucent) had the potential, when implemented, to provide the participating companies a fair amount of flexibility. The approval of these projects suggested that the EPA was willing to take some risks, albeit ones that were well-defined. The EPA, however, was concerned about the unwillingness of additional companies to come forward with proposals. The limits it established meant that XL was not an easy program within which companies could operate. The EPA's top leadership maintained that a reason companies did not step forward was because they were not creative and forthcoming about superior environmental performance. The companies argued, in response, that projects languished because of the lengthy and difficult selection and approval process. Painful negotiations with companies like 3M had made them reluctant to bring forward new proposals.

6.1 Trying to Achieve Greater Clarity

Companies like 3M had wanted to see more rapid progress. They were looking for operational business advantages that would come from more open interactions with the government and a streamlining of the regulatory system. They had hopes that Project XL could show how the system could be stretched and probed for reform. With fewer regulatory barriers, they believed that win–win solutions would be more possible.

3M suggested that, in the future, Project XL should have:

1. a clearer definition of the role SEP would play so that companies would understand the ground rules better and the extent to which they could make changes;
2. consistent expectations from different players inside EPA and out, including state agencies, national environmental groups, local stakeholders and other interest;
3. a distinct definition of the rules—who is to be involved and what decision making authority they would have;
4. high-level policy guidance and decision making from a team of top EPA officials that would work closely with companies, state governments, and stakeholders;
5. a well-defined and efficient management structure for staff reporting to the top officials so that decisions could be made and implemented expeditiously; and
6. early discussion of the risks, of possible surprises and how to avoid them; and a communication plan about who would make information public, when, and under what circumstances.

6.2 Redefining Superior Environmental Performance

After the stalemate, the EPA's top leaders made efforts to obtain feedback and make changes. They argued that XL was in its formative stages and that it should evolve. The Agency's April 1997 Federal Register Notice redefined SEP in a way that showed the influence of the aborted attempt to reach agreement with 3M.[45] The EPA established a new distinction between what it called Tier 1 and Tier 2 hurdles:

1. A Tier 1 hurdle was a baseline defined by what a facility's environmental performance would have been under existing law if the XL proposal had not gone forward.
2. A Tier 2 hurdle was a determination of future environmental performance if the project went forward. The key question was how much improvement would there be over the baseline?

Only after determination of how much environmental improvement a proposal would deliver would EPA consider other, secondary issues, such as: innovative environmental management strategies; pollution prevention; stakeholder support; and cost savings—the elements to which the MPCA and its stakeholder had appealed when they had argued for the 3M pilot. In the original statement that President Clinton and Vice President Gore made about Project XL, these elements had received more equal standing. Though it was listed first, better environmental performance than could be achieved under existing and future regulations was only one of many attributes Clinton and Gore had said they were seeking.

The EPA also directly addressed the issue of obtaining credit for past voluntary controls. It tried to provide an understanding of how it would respond to a situation similar to 3M Hutchinson where a company had voluntarily made substantial progress in the past, and therefore had to establish SEP using a higher environmental performance baseline. It rejected the idea, attributed to 3M, that pre-existing voluntary measures should be credited to the project. EPA maintained that companies could not create "bank accounts" based on their existing voluntary controls, upon which they then could potentially draw, because doing so would result in lower environmental performance. In effect, this policy deterred companies with recognized histories of excellence in environmental leadership, like 3M, from seeking XL permits. The EPA tried to provide some reward for past voluntary achievement in future cases by granting that in the Tier 2 analysis facilities that had significant pre-existing voluntary controls would not have to show as much environmental improvement in order to qualify. The Tier 2 criteria, however, were qualitative and vague, so companies were uncertain whether, after devoting considerable resources to designing an XL proposal, they would meet the Tier 2 requirement.

6.3 Clarifying How Decisions Would Be Made

In October 1997, the EPA began a process to reengineer the way it made XL decisions. Although it modified the approach it originally took, the new approach it adopted still relied on a series of linear interactions and

---

[45]   62 Fed. Reg. 19,872 (1997).

multiple iterations with many offices and programs within the EPA. Decision-making under the reengineered system continued to use a consensus process as the basis for making decisions within the Agency. The EPA's intention was that this process would take no more than six months, but a problem with the revised system was that it was still very complex. It depended on sequential decision-making in which formal documents flowed back and forth many times between the Agency and the applicant in an iterative cycle that compounded the possibilities for objections, modifications, delay, and deadlock. EPA's management insisted that such procedures were necessary because each individual XL pilot was potentially precedent setting in nature.

This process was not likely to satisfy applicants who were looking for a crisper management structure and more rapid decision-making. The process was not likely to inspire confidence in potential applicants that stalemate was less likely to occur. The reengineered process, through a step in the right direction, did not grapple forcefully enough with the potential for impasse. Although the Agency brought greater clarity to the process established to approve an XL project, it did not use a parallel team approach in which all the parties including state governments, local stakeholders, and national environmental organizations had the chance simultaneously to work out agreements in face-to-face discussions. The EPA's revised process also did not provide clear decision-making authority, deadlines, on accountability.

7   WHY THE IMPASSE TOOK PLACE

Why was impasse the outcome of so many of the attempts to reach agreement under Project XL? We believe that there were numerous reasons:

1. The goals of Project XL were not clear and consistent; nor did various people in the different organizations involved understand them in a similar way.
2. The means, especially the legal ones, were not adequate to the task.
3. The activities of the many participants from different organizations and different units in these organizations were not well coordinated.
4. The key participants did not anticipate many of the major barriers that developed and were not in a position where they could effectively deal with them.
5. Although trust grew among some of the participants, the overall level was not high enough for those engaged in the process to work together effectively.
6. External political conditions also impeded the efforts to reach an agreement.

Here we briefly discuss two of these factors—trust and external political conditions. We then consider the prospects for further reform and give our recommendations about how to achieve it.

7.1 Trust

Project XL demonstrates that without trust the evolution of new forms of cooperative regulation may be thwarted. Trust is the foundation upon which agreements must be built,[46] and without it, progress is difficult, if not impossible. However, at the national level, as a precedent-setting challenge to the status quo, the 3M pilot bore symbolism that aroused strong emotions. The issues were not confined to limits on VOCs that could be emitted from the facility. The debate was not confined to rational assessment and rejoinder about minor points; as evidenced in many exchanges and interactions it was often about first principles. Dialogue and negotiations were often, either implicitly or explicitly, about basic values behind environmental goals and matters of who should have the power to decide. Participants sometimes disagreed regarding answers to important questions. What role should economic considerations play when making decisions about environmental protection? If a trade-off between these competing values has to be made, as is often implicitly the case, how are reasonable solutions best achieved? Who can be trusted to make these important, precedent-setting judgments about the future?

7.2 External Political Conditions

External conditions also did not help ease the parties into an agreement.[47] The favorable conditions, which initially stimulated and contributed to the creation of Project XL, did not last. In 1994 the Republican Party's "Contract with America" proclaimed it wanted to protect US citizens from "overzealous regulators."[48] In response to this attack on the existing system, the climate of opinion in the environmental community changed. On the one hand, environmentalists throughout the 1990s had shown a greater receptivity to more cooperative approaches.[49] The best example is the Environmental Defense Fund. Of course, parts of the environmental community did not share this view. However, evidence that the view was gaining ground comes from the widespread participation by environmentalists in various dialogues and government-sponsored initiatives.[50]

---

[46] P. Ring and A. Van de Ven, "Structuring Cooperative Relationships Between Organizations" (1992) 13 Strategic Mgmt J 483; P. Ring and A. Van de Ven, "Developmental Processes of Cooperative Interorganizational Relationships" (1994) 19 *Academy of Management Review* 90; E. Weber, *Pluralism by the Rules: Conflict and Cooperation in Environmental Regulation* (Georgetown University Press, 1998).

[47] A. Marcus, et al., "The 3M/EPA Project XL Stalemate" Unpublished paper (1997); A. Marcus and D. Geffen, "XL Project at 3M" Paper presented at EPA Pollution Prevention/Green Manufacturing Conference, Atlanta, 17 November 1998.

[48] K. Sexton and B. Murdock (eds), *Environmental Policy in Transition* (Center for Environment and Health Policy, School of Public Health, University of Minnesota; 1996); Long and Arnold, supra note 30.

[49] Aspen Institute, "The Alternative Path: A Cleaner, Cheaper Way to Protect and Enhance the Environment" (The Aspen Institute Program on Energy, the Environment, and the Economy, Queenstown, 1996).

[50] See EPA, "The Common Sense Initiative: Lessons Learned" Office of Reinvention, EPA 100-R-98-011, December 1998.

Reactions by the environmental advocacy community to the election of the Republican-controlled Congress in 1994 varied considerably. Some members of this community may have been more willing to compromise with the business community in order to preserve the gains environmentalists believed they had achieved over the years. Other environmentalists saw the election of the Republican-controlled Congress as a major threat to these achievements and a sign that no compromises should be made. According to these environmentalists, the initial movement toward reconciliation with business had to be reconsidered, rather than expanded.

Many in the environmental community saw Project XL as a stopgap measure that the Clinton administration proposed in order to prevent a far worse setback.[51] These elements did not view Project XL as the natural culmination of the 1990s discussions of how to work together with business to create a more sustainable future. They did not perceive it as the next essential stage in creating new forms of cooperative regulation. Nor did they see it as an experiment designed to build the competence needed to contend with the next important set of global environmental issues, such as the buildup of greenhouse gases in the atmosphere, the loss of biodiversity, overpopulation, and resource scarcity. Project XL was seen instead as an attempt to blunt Republican criticism of the environmental regulatory system by eliminating or reducing some of what the business community regarded as its most onerous features.

Some within the environmental community saw Project XL as a misguided response to a political attack on the existing regulatory framework.[52] So long as a Republican threat seemed real, reform efforts such as Project XL were a reasonable gambit for the Clinton administration. XL was meant to provide business with flexibility, and in return business was expected to demonstrate a commitment to a higher level of environmental protection. Because both business and environmentalists got some of what they wanted, Project XL was seen by many as a way to stifle regulatory rollback that many Congressional Republicans wanted.

However, as the challenge posed by the Congressional Republicans receded, there was no longer any need to keep Project XL at the top of the policy agenda. Democratic Party circles and elements in the environmental movement were no longer interested in an accommodation with industry in order to defend the status quo. They wanted a stiffening of existing environmental statutes and regulations to make them more protective of the public health and ecosystems. They perceived less need for new forms of cooperative regulation, arguing, for instance, that the EPA

---

[51] See e.g., Public Interest Representatives Letter to Al Gore—Common Sense Initiative Input on Project XL Proposals, San Francisco, 21 September 1995.

[52] See Public Interest Representatives, "Joint Statement on the Clinton Administration's Project XL Announcement" 3 November 1995; Natural Resources Defense Council (NRDC), Letter from van Loben Sels to the Keystone Center, 21 March 1996; Natural Resources Defense Council (NRDC), Letter from Hawkins and van Loben Sels to Hansen (EPA) and Laughlin (Council on Environmental Quality) on poor initial results on superior environmental performance, 1 July 1996.

should not waste its valuable resources in regulating industry more efficiently and at lower cost. Instead, it should enhance its enforcement capabilities and move more vigorously against recalcitrant violators. It should
investigate additional environmental threats and impose new requirements on polluters that were threatening human health and the planetary
ecosystem.

Environmentalists saw less justification and urgency for the kinds of
compromises they believed they would have to make in Project XL, and
saw an increased opportunity to pursue their agenda of strict regulatory
enforcement and a broadening of the scope of regulation to include more
health and ecological problems. According to environmental advocates, the
EPA should not have as its first priority providing flexibility to business.
Instead, it should refocus its efforts on new threats such as non-point source
pollution, bio-persistent compounds, and greenhouse gases.

8   THE PROSPECTS FOR REFORM

The system of environmental regulation in the United States came into being
because of a series of historical events and legislative responses, each of
which made sense at the time. The EPA and state pollution control agencies
invested years in developing and administering a complex body of laws and
regulations.[53] They engaged in policies of command-and-control, setting
and enforcing standards largely based on the technological capabilities of
individual sources and end-of-pipe controls. They policed errant companies
and municipalities. The structure they created was deep and durable and in
some ways very effective. To a great extent, however, this structure has now
become locked in.[54]

The environmental regulatory system created by the EPA and state
agencies has many excellent features, but it is in need of renewal and
reform.[55] A vision for new cooperative regulation has emerged. It involves

---

[53] See M. Landy, et al., *The Environmental Protection Agency: Asking the Wrong Questions*
(Oxford University Press, 1990).
[54] D. Foray and A. Grubler, "Introduction to Special Issue on Technology and the
Environment" (1996) 53 *Technological Forecasting and Social Change* 3; Davies and Mazurek,
supra note 17; Davies and Mazurek, supra note 5; Fiorino, supra note 19; Fiorino, supra note
33; Hahn and Hester, supra note 11; Hahn and Hester, supra note 10; R. Hall "A Framework
Linking Intangible Resources and Capabilities to Sustainable Competitive Advantage" (1989)
14 Strategic Mgmt J 607; M. Landy and L. Cass, "U.S. Environmental Regulation in a More
Competitive World" in P. Nivola (ed.), *Comparative Disadvantages* (Brookings Institution,
Washington, D.C., 1997); Marcus, supra note 2.
[55] See Aspen Institute, supra note 49; Collaborating for a Better Environment and Economy in
Minnesota, "Recommendations of the Pollution Prevention Dialogue" (The Minnesota
Environmental Initiative, Minneapolis, 1996).

experimentation that will yield greater innovation, efficiency, and continuous improvement.[56] A new system would:[57]

1. break down the media by media focus of regulatory laws, rules, and enforcement so that environmental impact, production, and use are dealt with holistically;
2. permit emission trading within and between facilities;
3. allow for facility-wide performance standards that could be extended to suppliers and customers;
4. establish, to the extent possible, standards based on environmental outcomes and not on current technical solutions;
5. make these standards harm-based and responsive to the latest advances in scientific thinking;
6. encourage system-wide approaches like life-cycle analysis, design for the environment, and total product responsibility;
7. provide the public with clear, understandable information;
8. allow stakeholders to play a greater role as watchdogs and guardians of the public interest and to establish priorities for the kinds of environmental protection that, consistent with national standards, best fit the circumstances and needs of the local community and region;
9. encourage an ecosystem-based approach to ecological problems;
10. reduce business and government compliance costs; and
11. use pollution taxes and other market-like measures when feasible.

This vision has a results orientation, and embraces flexibility, holism, and stakeholder involvement. There is no broad-based consensus, however, about how best to put these principles into practice.

8.1   Recommendations for Improvement

The EPA continues to make changes and fine-tune Project XL and its other reinvention programs. These ongoing efforts are commendable. They are needed to allow for breakthroughs in a policy still too prone to impasse. To realize a new competence in environmental management, this process of assessment and change must continue.

1. The EPA should clearly redefine the vision and goals of reinvention pilots and adopt a more ambitious agenda for reinventing environmental regulation.
2. The vision should downplay the precedent-setting nature of individual pilots, while emphasizing their experimental value.

---

[56]   Aspen Institute, supra note 49; Collaborating for a Better Environment and Economy in Minnesota, supra note 55; D. Geffen and A. Marcus, "Environmental Regulation for Sustainable Development" (report prepared for Minnesota Environmental Quality Board, 1997).
[57]   See M. Tushman and P. Anderson (eds), *Managing Strategic Innovation and Change* (Oxford University Press, 1997).

3. A new statute that authorizes experiments in regulatory innovations is needed; but without this statute, the EPA should be more aggressive in the use of its discretionary authority within existing laws to seek alternative solutions and approaches.

4. In forging XL agreements, EPA should rely on teams that consist of individuals from the affected community, the state pollution control agency, the regulated facility, EPA headquarters, EPA regions, and national environmental organizations.

5. The agency should delegate final decision-making authority to its designated working groups.

6. It should have fixed timetables for reaching decisions and adopt the goal of identifying, developing, and approving as many projects as possible.

A new competence in environmental management depends critically on the pragmatic sharing of information and perspectives in face-to-face encounters among people from groups traditionally kept at a distance. In the business world, it has been proven that this type of sharing can make processes more fluid and efficient. Project XL Minnesota achieved some sharing among the groups—3M, the MPCA, and other stakeholders in Minnesota. Doing so was not easy, but it enabled the parties to work together with sufficient trust to seek innovative solutions. It is time for the EPA to consciously work towards the adoption of these processes.

Alone, however, the sharing and pooling of information are not sufficient. To overcome the threat of impasse, a new competence also requires clear lines of decision-making authority. When it comes to experiments, the EPA should delegate authority for decision making to its working groups. To build the foundation for new forms of regulation, it should decentralize power. It should permit its staff, which has knowledge of local conditions and national law and policy, to make decisions about win-win experiments that provide information and understanding about how new forms of regulation will work. An a priori insistence on a guaranteed level of superior environmental performance for each XL pilot is a self-defeating proposition that greatly limits the learning that can be achieved from such experiments.

8.2 Experiments that Foster Innovation

Reflection is needed on the kinds of experiments that should be conducted to foster innovation.[58] At one extreme is the model suggesting the widest range of variation should be encouraged. This model holds that learning cannot take place unless a large number of different kinds of experiments are carried out. There is too little information and too much uncertainty to be very careful about selecting experiments in advance. Many experiments should be launched, the results should be monitored and evaluated, and another new round of experiments should be launched in iterative fashion based on what has been learned.

---

[58] Ibid.

At the other extreme is a model in which only a few—the very best—experiments are carried out. Only those that clearly show superiority are worth pursuing. Only the fittest ideas that survive a rigorous process of prior assessment, refinement, and careful sorting should be tried.

When designing its overall reinvention program, the EPA opted for the first approach. Under the Clinton–Gore reinvention initiatives, it expanded the original list of 25 projects into more than 60 included under the reinvention umbrella.[59] By March 1997, it had numerous initiatives in many different areas underway.[60] The categories it used to describe what it was doing included cutting red tape, partnerships, flexibility for results, and facility compliance. The actual programs included one-stop reporting, auditing, risk-based enforcement, emission and effluent trading, small business assistance, brownfields, electronic public access, and green chemistry. No list, EPA claimed, could "capture the full range of reinvention activity underway."[61] Integration and the capacity to manage all these projects at once had to be challenging, and the number of experiments the Agency could carry out in any one category was limited by practical realities.

It seems logical that conducting many experiments in a single category would provide more information about how to implement a new approach to environmental regulation. Indeed, there is some evidence from the EPA's most recent descriptions of its reinvention efforts that it is moving in this direction.[62] The Agency is committing itself to fewer categories of reform and is showing a willingness to probe more deeply in each of the categories.

In sum, reforming environmental regulation is a longstanding yet elusive goal for US environmental policy. It should transcend partisan politics and temporary setbacks.[63] Its aim is to channel scarce societal resources into achieving higher levels of environmental protection in the face of ever more pressing local, regional, international, and global challenges. Simply to maintain environmental amenities at the current level in the face of a rapidly growing world population and economic development is difficult enough. Both the environment and the world economy will suffer if business and government cannot learn how to better manage their relations and collaborate to achieve cooperative environmental solutions.

---

[59] See EPA, "New Directions: A Report on Regulatory Reinvention" Office of the Administrator, EPA 100-R-97-001, January 1997; EPA, "Managing for Better Environmental Results: A Two Year Anniversary Report on Reinventing Environmental Protection" Office of the Administrator, EPA 100-R-97-004, 1997; EPA, "Regulatory Plan and Semiannual Agenda of Regulatory ad Deregulatory Action"' Policy, Planning, and Evaluation, EPA 230-Z-97-002, 1997.

[60] EPA, "New Directions," supra note 59; EPA, "Managing for Better Environmental Results," supra note 59; EPA, "Regulatory Plan and Semiannual Agenda of Regulatory and Deregulatory Actions," supra note 59.

[61] EPA, "New Directions," supra note 59.

[62] See EPA, "Reinventing Environmental Protection—EPA's Approach" Office of Reinvention, EPA 1000F-98-010, 1998; EPA, "New Directions: A Report on Regulatory Reinvention" EPA 100-R-98-04, 1998; EPA, "The Changing Nature of Environmental and Public Health Protection" Office of Reinvention, EPA 100-R-98-003, 1998; EPA, "Project XL Preliminary Status Report" Office of the Administrator, EPA-100-R-98-008, 1998; EPA, "Reinventing Environmental Protection: 1998 Annual Report" Office of the Administrator, EPA 100-R-99-002, March 1999.

[63] See M. Chertow and D. Esty (eds), *Thinking Ecologically* (Yale University Press, 1997); E. Weber, supra note 46.

Part II
Environmental Agreements and
Regulation in Europe

7. Environmental Contracts: A Flemish Law and Economics Perspective

Michael Faure

1 WHY CONTRACTS?

Many chapters in this book deal with the American experience concerning environmental contracts.[1] They not only provide an interesting overview and classification of the various types of contracts that have been used in the US, but also address the theoretical framework within which one must examine these environmental contracts. In that respect, a lot of attention is paid to the important question of whether environmental contracts should be considered as regulation or as contracts. If one reads these chapters carefully, it becomes clear that environmental contracts have so far not been very popular in the US, though many of the authors believe that there is room for an increased use of these contracts.[2] Indeed, the frequency of rising environmental contracts seems to be an important difference between the US and Europe, especially Belgium and the Netherlands, where environmental contracts have become relatively popular.[3]

1.1 Advantages

From an environmental policy perspective, the first question which must inevitably be addressed is obviously: Why should a regulator choose to use environmental contracts at all? A naive lawyer (or, some would argue, a smart one) could argue that if the government believes that a certain subject in

---

[1] See, e.g., the chapter in this book by Geoffrey Hazard and Eric Orts.
[2] For a similar conclusion, see J. Davidson, "Voluntary Agreements in the USA" in J. van Dunné (ed.), *Non-Point Source River Pollution: The Case of the River Meuse* (Kluwer Law International, London, 1996), pp. 217–230.
[3] For an overview of the use of environmental agreements in Europe with a description of recent studies, see ELNI (ed.), *Environmental Agreements. The Role and Effect of Environmental Agreements in Environmental Policies* (Cameron May 1998); P. Bailey, "The Creation and Enforcement of Environmental Agreements" (1999) Eur Envtl L Rev 170.

environmental policy merits regulation, then that is precisely what the government should do: take responsibility and regulate, using the full array of command-and-control or economic instruments that have been described in the literature.[4] Why would it be better in some cases to negotiate with the regulated industry, resulting in the "reg negs"[5]? Many arguments are advanced traditionally in the literature to favor environmental contracts, including environmental contracts are consensus based; they emphasize pollution prevention rather than clean up; they allow for regulatory flexibility in light of changes in scientific knowledge; and they offer the opportunity of fruitful, collaborative decision making.

One could also approach environmental contracts in light of economic analysis of law.[6] On one hand, a law and economics scholar should be enthusiastic hearing the idea that, for example, optimal abatement techniques or standards would be fixed as a result of voluntary agreements between government and industry. One would be tempted to think that this may result in a optimal allocation of resources as predicted by Ronald Coase.[7] However, Coase's theory obviously applies primarily to negotiations between victims and polluters, and the government can hardly be considered as a representative of victims in a Coasean bargaining framework. One might counter that if a government intervention in environmental policy is deemed necessary, for instance because of prohibitive transaction costs, it would be wiser from an economic point of view to look primarily to market-based instruments, such as emission trading systems rather than direct regulations, even in the form of "environmental contracts." Still, an economist could respond that if the government regulates environmental standards, the result is likely to be more efficient when the government negotiates with industry. At least in theory, the advantage of this bargaining process would be that the often poorly informed government would obtain adequate information about the environmental risks involved and about the abatement techniques to reduce those risks.[8] The resulting regulation would be nicely tailored to the specific situation of industry and would thus "mimic" a market solution. This approach to environmental regulation may therefore prove better than command-and-control regulations that are simply imposed upon the regulated community. Command-and-control regulation always entails the risk of the government imposing regulatory standards without conducting a proper cost-benefit analysis.[9]

---

[4] For a recent survey of the available instruments for pollution control see N. Gunningham and P. Grabosky, *Smart Regulation. Designing Environmental Policy* (Clarendon Press, Oxford, 1998).
[5] See the terminology used by Hazard and Orts in their chapter.
[6] See the chapters collected in Part III of this book.
[7] R. Coase, "The Problem of Social Cost" (1960) JL & Econ 1.
[8] In the words of Gunningham and Grabosky: "Voluntarism has the considerable virtue of being non-interventionist, having high industry acceptability and raising minimal equity concerns." Gunningham and Grabosky, supra note 4, at 58–59.
[9] On the importance of cost-benefit analysis for regulatory appraisal, see generally A. Ogus, "Regulatory Appraisal: A Neglected Opportunity for Law and Economics" (1998) Eur JL & Econ 53. On the regulation of risk in particular, see A. Ogus, "Risk Management and 'Rational Social Regulation'" in R. Baldwin (ed.), *Law and Uncertainty: Risks and Legal Processes* (Kluwer Law International, London, 1997), pp. 139–153.

1.2 Dangers

Although the idea of a regulation that results from free negotiations with market participants sounds very appealing at first glance, the major danger is obviously that it could result in a regulation of the kind in which the contents are simply determined by industry. In that case, environmental contracts would be nothing but another technique for industry to lobby for lenient environmental standards.[10] Indeed, industry could behave strategically in its negotiations with a government agency when it comes to providing adequate information on the environmental risks at stake and the possibilities for reducing them. Industry's incentives for disclosing such information during negotiations of environmental contracts may well be very limited, especially when this information could be used to impose extra costs on industry. Naturally, this risk of regulatory capture is recognized in the literature on environmental agreements.[11] When discussing environmental contracts, one will inevitably have to address the question of how one can avoid the risk of these so-called public choice effects. Neglecting this danger would run the risk that an environmental contract would simply result in the nightmare of institutionalized capture rather than the wonderful fairy tale of market-based voluntary compliance. The question therefore arises whether it is possible to construct a framework to encourage an environmental policy that enjoys the advantages of negotiated contracts without the disadvantages of administrative capture.

2 A LEGAL FRAMEWORK

One possible way to enjoy the undoubtedly existing benefits of environmental contracts and to limit the inherent risks is to adopt legislation that would identify the kinds of cases in which the government may use environmental contracts. This type of legislation, indicating the conditions under which a regulator could waive specific regulatory requirements, would clearly establish the limits and potential benefits of environmental contracts for all market participants.[12] In considering such legislation, the US could benefit from European experience. For example, a Draft Decree on Environmental Policy prepared in the Flemish region of Belgium by an Interuniversity Commission for the Reform of Environmental Law sets forth strict criteria concerning the use of environmental covenants.[13]

In 1989, the former Flemish minister for environmental policy installed a commission of academics, under the presidency of Hubert Bocken, and

---

[10] See generally M. Maloney and R. McCormick, "A Positive Theory of Environmental Quality Regulation" (1982) JL & Econ 99; J. Adler, "Rent Seeking Behind the Green Curtain" (1996) *Regulation* 26.

[11] See Hazard and Orts, supra note 1.

[12] See P. Gilhuis, *Milieurecht op weg naar de jaren negentig* (W.E.J. Tjeenk Willink, Zwolle, 1989), pp. 22–28.

[13] The text of this draft is included in an appendix to this chapter.

asked it to draft a comprehensive code on environmental law and policy.[14] The first report of this commission was presented in December 1991,[15] and the final draft was presented in 1995.[16]

Many parts of this Draft Decree, including the chapter on environmental agreements have now been implemented in the Flemish legislation.[17] Indeed, even before the Interuniversity Commission presented its final draft, the Flemish authorities had implemented the proposals of the commission in 1994.[18] In the remainder of this chapter, I will primarily discuss the text of the Draft Decree and indicate where the provisions can be found in a good English translation.

The Flemish (Draft) Decree contains several interesting provisions. Article 4.7.2, for example, states that environmental covenants cannot replace existing legislation or regulations and cannot depart from their general terms.[19] Such a legislative framework seems useful and necessary in order to make the rules of the game explicit both for the government and for the contracting partners.[20]

The Draft Decree also contains a few other provisions which are worth mentioning. One crucial issue is to make clear who has representative power for industry to negotiate an environmental contract. Another is to indicate whether the contract has binding force upon an entire industry. One difference between a contract and regulation is that contracts, in principle, only bind the parties, whereas regulations may be enforced upon all those for whom they apply.[21] This obviously raises the question of the representative force of an industry organization that agrees to a regulatory contract. In Flanders, the Flemish government may conclude the environmental agreement with one or more umbrella organizations that represent enterprises faced with a common environmental problem.[22] In principle, the

---

[14] See Besluit van de Vlaamse Executieve van 5 juli 1989 houdende Oprichting van een Interuniversitaire Commissie tot Herziening van het Milieurecht in het Vlaamse Gewest, *BS*, 25 August 1989.

[15] See H. Bocken and P. Verbeek (eds), *Voorontwerp decreet milieuhygiene*, Seminarie voor Milieurecht, 1991.

[16] Interuniversitaire Commissie tot Herziening van het Milieurecht in het Vlaamse Gewest, *Voorontwerp Decreet Milieubeleid*, Bruges, Die Keure, 1995, also available in English: H. Bocken and D. Ryckbost (eds), *Codification of Environmental Law. Draft Decree on Environmental Policy* (Kluwer Law International, London, 1996), pp. 2–158. For an outline, see H. Bocken, et al., "The Flemish Draft Decree on Environmental Policy: An Outline" in H. Bocken and D. Ryckbost (eds), *Codification of Environmental Law. Proceedings of the International Conference* (Kluwer Law International, London, 1996), pp. 11–40.

[17] For an overview, see K. Deketelaere, "Belgium" in R. Seerden and M. Heldeweg (eds), *Comparative Environmental Law in Europe. An Introduction to Public Environmental Law in the EU Member States* (Maklu, Antwerp, 1996), p. 38.

[18] Decree concerning environmental contracts of 15 June 1994, *Moniteur Belge*, 8 July 1994.

[19] Article 3 of the Decree of 15 June 1994.

[20] For a discussion of the framework for environmental agreements in this Flemish Draft Decree, see H. Bocken, et al., "The Flemish Draft Decree on Environmental Policy: An Outline," supra note 16, at 22, and K. Deketelaere and M. Faure, "Environmental Law in Belgium" in N. Koeman (ed.), *Environmental Law in Europe* (Kluwer Law International, The Hague, 1999), p. 76.

[21] See Hazard and Orts, supra note 1.

[22] Article 4.7.1 of the Draft Decree; Article 2 of the Decree of 15 June 1994.

agreement binds only the members of that particular organization, but this approach runs the risk of non-members acting as free riders.[23] It hardly seems effective to supplement a covenant with command-and-control regulation in order to exclude free riding. In that case, many of the advantages of using covenants would disappear. To remedy some of these problems, the Flemish regulation on environmental covenants stipulates that the region shall be empowered to convert an environmental covenant, either wholly or in parts, into regulations, even during the period that the covenants are applicable. Thus the covenant in fact becomes transformed into a regulation, a process which confirms that the difference between covenants and regulations may not be as large as one might first expect. In any case, it is certainly important to guarantee the representative qualities of an industrial or branch organization in order to prevent a covenant from creating an artificial barrier to entry.[24] This may occur if certain standards had been negotiated with the government to which only a particular branch of industry could comply, thus enabling this group to drive their competitors out of the market.

3   BINDING FORCE?

The issue of binding force, which is crucial in any contract, not only plays a role for the representative branch organization, but also for the governments who negotiate with industry. The "reg negs" have apparently not been very popular in the United States, and one reason may be that these types of negotiated agreements have not resulted in a contract that is enforceable against the government. If the government agency is free to withdraw from the agreements, the question then arises what incentives industry would have to conclude the agreement with the government in the first place. A contract which is only binding for one party can hardly be considered a contract. In the American context, this problem has apparently been remedied to some extent through the *Winstar* doctrine which prevents the government from easily changing its mind on a contract made in regulatory context.[25]

The European experience indeed shows that these types of environmental agreements will only be successful if the result of the negotiations are somehow binding for the government. Again, referring to the Flemish example, Article 4.7.4 of the Draft Decree clearly states that environmental covenants shall be legally binding on the parties.[26] Moreover, Article 4.7.3 states that during the applicable period of an environmental covenant, the

---

[23]   On this free riding risk, see N. Gunningham and P. Grabosky, *supra* note 4, at 433.
[24]   On the use of standards to erect barriers to entry, see R. Hahn, "The Political Economy of Environmental Regulation: Towards a Unifying Framework" (1990) *Public Choice* 21; A. Ogus, *Regulation, Legal Form and Economic Theory* (Clarendon Press, Oxford, 1994), pp. 55–75.
[25]   See Hazard and Orts, *supra* note 1.
[26]   Article 5 of the Decree of 15 June 1994.

Flemish Region shall not issue any regulation imposing more stringent requirements than those in the covenant. Furthermore, Article 4.7.4 stipulates that environmental covenants shall be binding not only for the parties, but also for all members of the organization. Environmental covenants in Flanders are therefore binding in principle for a certain period, but they can be terminated. A termination is possible with six months notice or through common agreement between the parties.[27]

4   ENFORCEMENT

A major problem with environmental contracts is how the covenant can be enforced. Public prosecutors in Europe generally do not like these types of self-control mechanisms in environmental law, because they fear that they cannot easily monitor compliance.[28] In Flanders, this problem is to some extent solved because environmental agreements cannot depart from existing regulations. The covenant itself is also binding for members of the organization that have concluded the covenant, but the Flemish Draft Decree is silent about how compliance shall be monitored. It does stipulate, however, that where provisions of an environmental covenant are infringed, any party who is bound by it may claim specific performance or damages from the person who has committed the violation.[29] Thus, the Flemish Draft Decree clearly provides for remedies of a contractual sort. It is, again, in the best interest of all parties to the contract that members of a representative branch organization comply in order to exclude free riders.

Obviously, public law remedies such as fines do not apply in the case of violation of a contract. This kind of remedy is available only when the government has converted the contents of the covenant into a regulation. Then the covenant can be enforced by means of public law. Again, this process indicates that there is in fact only a thin line between a covenant and a regulation. The government must be careful that covenants do not simply turn into regulations whereby industry has the luxury of determining the contents of regulation for itself.

5   TRANSPARENCY

It is also important to address the transparency of the procedure through which covenants are drafted. In this respect, it is important to publicize any proposed discussions about a project agreement with interested parties, including providing motive to community and public interest groups. It is

---

[27] Articles 4.7.8 and 4.7.10 of the Draft Decree; Articles 9 and 11 of the Decree of 15 June 1994.
[28] See, e.g., A. de Lange, "Trias Politica in de Polder" (1998) *Nederlands Juristenblad* 866.
[29] Article 4.7.9 of the Draft Decree; Article 10§2 of the Decree of 15 June 1994.

important to guarantee notice and participation rights to third parties precisely in order to avoid the risk of regulatory capture. The Flemish Draft Decree provides for the publication of a draft of any environmental covenant and for mandatory consultation with the public at large.[30] At the same time, if the same guarantees of public involvement in standard setting and licensing procedures are extended to environmental contracts, then many of the advantages of speedy decision-making and flexibility may soon disappear. Again, this demonstrates that if one wishes to give a covenant the same qualities as regulation, such as a binding force upon third parties and public rights of participation, the differences with regulations become smaller.

6   TRANSBOUNDRY CONTRACTS

There is perhaps one field where there might be a great deal of room for environmental agreements, namely the area of transboundry pollution. Many of these covenants or treaties do exist, and some law and economics scholars such as Cohen and van den Bergh, for example,[31] see the application of the Coase theorem to apply even more directly in this context of transboundry pollution. But though it is certainly true to say that some of these covenants which have been concluded sound like fairy tales,[32] it is equally true to state that they would probably never have come into being without the support of institutional arrangements such as the European Directives issued in the framework of European environmental law. The incentives to agree to a covenant would not have been as great if there had not been the threat of regulation under European environmental law, which might even have been a factor for a non-Member state such as Switzerland. Although no formal enforcement of European law is possible against Switzerland, the Swiss compliance with the *acquis communautaire* seems important. Another interesting example is the river contract of 1996, concerning the upper-Meuse which is, however, confined to the Belgian territory. Some skeptics contest the effectiveness of this non-binding instrument, since it remains closely linked to the existing command-and-control instruments, and the environmental results are poor when one considers the time and money expended.[33]

---

[30]   Article 4.7.5; Article 6 of the Decree of 15 June 1994.
[31]   M. Cohen, "Commentary" in E. Eide and R. van den Bergh (eds), *Law and Economics of the Environment* (Juridisk Forlag, Oslo, 1996), pp. 67–171; R. van den Bergh, *Economics in a Legal Strait-Jacket: The Difficult Reception of Economic Analysis in European Law*, paper presented at the workshop Empirical Research and Legal Realism. Setting the Agenda, Haifa, 6–9 June 1999.
[32]   For the case of the river Rhine, see J. van Dunné (ed.), *Transboundary Pollution and Liability: The Case of the River Rhine* (Lelystad, Vermande, 1991).
[33]   See D. Misonne, "The River Contract of the Upper-Meuse," in ELNI, *Environmental Agreements* (Cameron May, 1998), pp. 25–26.

7 NEED FOR EMPIRICAL RESEARCH

This chapter will finally address the importance of empirical research in this area. The first results seem promising: several Dutch scholars have compared the efficiency of environmental covenants with the results achieved under market-based instruments and they are, once more, relatively enthusiastic concerning environmental covenants.[34] One of their conclusions is that the likelihood of compliance with the terms of a covenant is higher if, during the application period of the covenant, the government guarantees that it will not intervene with more stringent measures, such as the adoption of new taxes. Industry thus complies if they can achieve some gain by doing so. Still, scholars conclude that in comparison, market-based instruments such as tradeable pollution rights, may be more efficient than environmental contracts. In addition, the Rhine covenant seems to be an example of a success story for environmental agreements.

A study of the use of environmental agreements in many European countries performed by the Environmental Law Network International (ELNI) recommended, on the basis of empirical research, the use of environmental agreements to complement the weaknesses of existing environmental policy tools. According to this study, environmental contracts work best in combination with other policy instruments.[35] Therefore, ELNI recommends further research on the effects of different combinations of instruments.[36] On the basis of this future empirical research, one might finally be able to judge the usefulness of the environmental contracts.

In addition, there are some basic legal questions that remain to be examined. In the European context, one must question whether the increasing use of environmental contracts by Member States is compatible with the requirement that European directives should be implemented by clear and enforceable legislation. However, a tendency towards the increasing use of European-wide covenants is also perceptible.[37] The future use of environmental contracts largely depends upon these experiences.

---

[34] See R. Wit, et al., *Kosten en baten van milieuconvenanten in vergelijking met marktconforme instrumenten* (Ministerie van Economische Zaken, The Hague, 1999).
[35] The same conclusion is reached by N. Gunningham and P. Grabosky, supra note 4, at 432–433.
[36] ELNI, supra note 3 at 163–170.
[37] See ibid., which contains a discussion of the Commission Communication on Environmental Agreements of 1996.

ANNEX: FLEMISH DRAFT DECREE ON ENVIRONMENTAL POLICY

Title 7   Environmental Covenants

Article 4.7.1

For the purpose of applying this title, the term "environmental covenant" shall be understood as meaning an agreement concluded between, on the one hand, the Flemish Region, represented by the Flemish Government—hereinafter referred to as The Region—and, on the other hand, one or more umbrella organizations—hereinafter referred to as The Organization—having legal personality and representing enterprises which either operate in the same field of business or are faced with a common environmental problem, or are located in the same area, for the purpose of preventing environmental pollution, limiting or removing the consequences thereof, or of promoting effective management of the environment.

Article 4.7.2

Environmental covenants can not replace the existing legislation or regulations nor depart from them in a less strict sense.

Article 4.7.3

§1   During the period of applicability of the environmental covenant, the Region shall not issue any regulations imposing by means of an Executive Decision, in relation to subjects dealt with by the covenant, more stringent requirements than the latter. However, the Region shall remain entitled to adopt measures or issue regulations, both in cases of urgency, and in order to meet obligations imposed by the international law or European law. The Region shall be empowered to convert an environmental covenant, either wholly or in part, into regulations, even during the period of applicability of the covenant.

§2   Environmental covenants can not reduce nor limit the authority of any other public body.

Article 4.7.4

Environmental covenants shall be binding on the parties. Depending on the clauses contained in them, they shall also be binding on all the members of the organization or on a group of its members, to be defined in general terms.

Article 4.7.5

§1   'A summary of the draft environmental covenant shall, on the initiative of the Region, be published in the Official Journal or in any other medium designated for that purpose. This summary shall at least describe the subject-matter and the general purpose of the environmental covenant. The full proposed version of the draft covenant shall be available for consultation for a period of thirty days in a place to be stated in the published version of the agreement.

§2 Within a period of thirty days of the date on which the summary was published, any person may submit his objections and observations in writing to the competent departments of the Flemish Government, designated for that purpose in the published summary. These departments shall examine the objections and observations submitted and transmit them to the Organization.

§3 The draft environmental covenant shall be communicated to the Flemish Social and Economic Council and to the Flemish Council for the Environment and Nature, who shall issue a properly reasoned opinion within a time limit of thirty days following the date of receipt of the draft. This opinion shall not be binding.

Where one of the aforementioned advisory organs issues a negative opinion on the draft, the Region shall, in a report to be added to the published version referred to in §5, justify its decision nevertheless to conclude the covenant.

§4 Where the draft environmental covenant is amended in the light of the objections or opinions submitted, the agreement may be concluded without there being any need to initiate once again the procedure described in §1 to §3.

§5 Environmental covenants shall, following their signature by the parties, be published in full in the Official Journal, where appropriate preceded by the report referred to in §3.

§6 Save where express provision has been made to the contrary, environmental covenants shall enter into effect ten days after the date of publication thereof in the Official Journal.

Article 4.7.6

Only where the region and the organization give their consent may an organization of enterprises which meets the condition set out in Article 4.7.1, accede to an environmental covenant, in accordance with the procedure to be determined by a decision of the Flemish Government. Any such accession shall be published in the Official Journal. As from the date of the notification, the environmental covenant in question shall be binding on the acceding organization. Depending on the relevant clauses of the deed of accession, the agreement shall also be binding on all the members of the acceding organization or on a group of its members defined in general terms. By virtue of its accession, the acceding organization shall become a party to the covenant.

Article 4.7.7

§1 Environmental covenants shall be concluded for a certain period. Save where express provision has been made to the contrary, this period shall be two years. No environmental covenant may be extended tacitly.

§2 The Region, as well as one or more of the affiliated organizations, may extend the validity of an environmental covenant in unamended form. The Region shall, at least two months prior to the expiry of applicability, propose any such extension to the advisory bodies referred to in Article 4.7.5

§3 The latter shall submit their opinion within a time limit of thirty days. This opinion shall not be binding. Where one of the aforementioned advisory bodies submits a negative opinion on the extension of an environmental covenant, the Region shall, in a report to be added to the published version of the extension, justify its decision nevertheless to proceed to extend the covenant. Any extension of an environmental covenant shall be published in the Official Journal, where appropriate preceded by the report referred to in the previous paragraph.

§4 In the course of its period of validity, the parties may agree to amend an environmental covenant, provided that neither its contents nor its objectives be influenced thereby to any significant extent. Any such amendments shall be published in the Official Journal. They shall be binding for all the parties who where previously bound by the covenant.

Article 4.7.8

The parties may at all times terminate, subject to notice, an environmental covenant, subject to observing a period of notice of six months. Where the notice of termination is not given by the Region, it must be made jointly by the other parties. The procedure to be followed when issuing this notice of termination shall be laid down by the Flemish Government.

Article 4.7.9

Where the provisions of an environmental covenant are infringed, any party who is bound by it may claim specific performance or damages from the person committing the violation.

Article 4.7.10

Environmental covenants shall terminate either by common agreement between the parties, by the expiry of a specified period, or by notice of termination. The adaptation of regulations in accordance with Article 4.7.3 shall not have the effect of terminating the covenant.

Article 4.7.11

The parties shall report to the Flemish Parliament on the implementation of the environmental covenant. The formalities and conditions which are to be observed in making these reports shall be determined by a decision of the Flemish Government.

Article 4.7.12

The provisions of this title shall be mandatory. They shall apply to the environmental covenants which will be concluded after the entry into force of this Decree.

8. Legal Aspects of Environmental Agreements in the Netherlands, in Particular the Agreement on Packaging and Packaging Waste

René Seerden

1. INTRODUCTION

At the beginning of the year 2000 approximately 30 environmental agreements concluded between the central government (the Minister for the Environment) and branches of industry or business groups are in force in the Netherlands.[1] Since the 1980s, these types of collective environmental agreements have played a role of increasing importance for the realization of environmental policy. In the Netherlands, these environmental agreements are usually termed environmental covenants (*milieuconvenanten*), but other terminology is also used, such as declarations of intent, policy agreements, and protocols. In this chapter, I refer to *milieuconvenanten* as environmental agreements.

One of the more recent Dutch environmental agreements is the Environmental Agreement on Packaging and Packaging Waste (*Convenant Verpakkingen II*, hereafter the Environmental Agreement on Packaging). It consists of a general integration agreement and several additional agreements. It is intended to implement the European Community Directive on Packaging and Packaging Waste (hereafter the Packaging Directive) in conjunction with or in lieu of the Dutch Ministerial Regulation on Packaging and Packaging Waste (*Ministeriële Regeling Verpakkingen en Verpakkingsafval*, hereafter the Ministerial Regulation on Packaging).

Because environmental agreements are increasingly important instruments for environmental protection, it is useful to elaborate on how environmental agreements may complement or even replace more traditional command-and-control legislation. This chapter focuses on the place, function, and legal status of environmental agreements in the Netherlands and,

---

[1]   The annex to this chapter lists the various Dutch environmental agreements.

in particular, the Environmental Agreement on Packaging. In that regard, I first offer some general remarks about environmental agreements in the Netherlands, especially their legal status. Then the implementation in the Netherlands of the Packaging Directive through the Ministerial Regulation on Packaging and the Environmental Agreement on Packaging are addressed. I discuss the most relevant legal aspects of this agreement, such as its scope of application, its public or private law status, the parties to it, and the connection of this agreement with relevant legislation. Finally, I conclude with a summary and some general comments.

2 ENVIRONMENTAL AGREEMENTS: POSSIBILITIES, TYPES, LEGAL FRAMEWORK, AND DEVELOPMENT

2.1 Possibilities: Private Law Actions or Administrative Law Actions by the Government?

In the Netherlands, there is no specific statutory framework for dealing with the conclusion, contents, or implementation of agreements between public authorities and private parties. When they are intended to be legally binding, such environmental agreements have private law status and are governed by the general rules for contracts laid down in the Dutch Civil Law Code (*Burgerlijk Wetboek*).[2] In the Netherlands, the use of private law instruments by the administrative authorities, such as actions under tort law or the conclusion of contracts, is not always allowed when public law competencies also exist. Private law contracts that violate statutory requirements are void under section 3:40 BW of the Dutch Civil Law Code.

The Windmill case is one of the leading cases concerning the possible use of private law competencies parallel to or instead of existing public law competencies for the purpose of realizing public aims.[3] In this case, the Supreme Civil Court decided that when public law provisions do not address a matter—this is the use of private law competencies parallel to or instead of the use of the respective public law authority—these public law provisions may not be crossed out in an unacceptable way. In this respect, the content and meaning of the public law regulation and the way in which and the extent to which this public law regulation protects the rights of citizens (in the light of other written and unwritten rules of public law) has to be taken into account. According to the Supreme Civil Court, it is also important to establish whether the government could achieve a similar result by exercising the public law authority instead of exercising civil law

---

[2] I use private law and civil law as synonyms here.

[3] Supreme Civil Court (*Hoge Raad*) 26 January 1990, Administratiefrechtelijke Beslissingen 1990, 408. After the Windmill case several other judgements were given by this court in which the Windmill criteria were used. See also R. Seerden and M. Heldeweg, "Public Environmental Law in the Netherlands" in R. Seerden and M. Heldeweg (eds), *Comparative Environmental Law in Europe, An Introduction to Public Environmental Law in the EU Member States* (Maklu/Blackstone/Nomos, 1996), pp. 306–307.

competence. If so, then the Court seems to indicate that there is no place for a private law action by the government. For instance, the court seems to imply that where governmental bodies have public law authority to apply penalties, the use of similar civil law competence under tort law would not be allowed. Of course, the government is free to use private law competencies to achieve public goals, where statutes or delegated legislation explicitly state that this is allowed.

Case law of the Supreme Administrative Court concerning the relationship between agreements and environmental permits or enforcement decisions also supports this conclusion. For instance, in a case in which an environmental organization requested administrative enforcement measures against illegal pollution by several greenhouses, the President of the Supreme Administrative Court decided that an administrative non-enforcement decision by the competent authority could not be set aside by an agreement between the competent public authority and an organization representing the greenhouses.[4] The Supreme Administrative Court also ruled that promises made by the competent public authority in an agreement or otherwise do not fit into the legal framework of environmental permitting.[5] One of the main reasons for the Court's view is that guaranteed public participation rights concerning the handing out of permits would be eliminated. The fact that a government body has discretionary authority to hand out permits or enforce decisions is therefore not sufficient to confer the power to conclude environmental agreements on matters of policy.

Although this case law mostly deals with agreements between public authorities and individual companies, it is also applicable to private law environmental agreements between the central government and branches of industry or other business sectors. The bottom line is that environmental agreements cannot set aside existing statutes, delegated legislation, or general administrative law powers.

2.2 Types of Environmental Agreements

Generally speaking there are three categories of environmental agreements in the Netherlands:

(1) those concluded between the central government, primarily the Minister for the Environment, and branches of industry or other business sectors to collectively reduce environmental pollution;

(2) agreements between the central government and decentralized authorities or their representing organizations to handle environmental

---

[4] *Voorzitter Afdeling Geschillen van Bestuur van de Raad van State* 7 July 1992, Milieu en Recht 1993/1, nr. 1. For a similar ruling of the Supreme Administrative Court, *Afdeling bestuursrechtspraak Raad van State* of 1 September 1992 concerning a non-enforcement agreement, Administratiefrechtelijke Beslissingen 1996, 288.

[5] *Afdeling Geschillen van Bestuur van de Raad van State*, 1 September 1992, Milieu en Recht 1993/1, nr. 2. The case law mentioned here reflects the opinion of the Central Government. See Second Chamber of Parliament 1993–1994, 23.400 XI, nr. 53, p. 5.

problems, often involving financial arrangements for the implementation of environmental policy (to this category also belong agreements between merely decentralized authorities, e.g., in the field of environmental enforcement); and

(3)   those concluded between a single administrative authority and an individual company, entailing actions to reduce pollution caused by the company that are often linked to a permit or enforcement decision.

In this chapter, I address only the first category of collective agreements mainly because these agreements play the most important role in achieving environmental policy goals.[6] Although public participation is not legally required, in practice environmental organizations often observe their negotiation and implementation. This first type of collective environmental agreements also seems to be more accepted than the third category of individual agreements. The total number of these individual agreements is uncertain because there is no formal registration and they are sometimes not reduced to written documents. However, these individual agreements could eventually become more important if legislative provisions give more scope for them to be negotiated. So far, however, this has not been the case for agreements linked to permits or enforcement decisions.[7] In other areas, there are some possibilities. For example, the Dutch Soil Protection Act explicitly allows for co-financing agreements for the decontamination and cleanup of polluted areas.[8] I do not address the second category of agreements because these agreements do not involve private parties and, in that respect, are less interesting as compared to the first and third categories, which may arguably be said to replace command-and-control instruments of regulation with more consensual instruments.

Collective environmental agreements between the central government and branches of industry or other business groups play a role parallel to the more traditional legislative instruments for the realization of public policy, expressing the internalization of environmental protection in the private sector. Collective environmental agreements are said to be self-regulatory, though they are often bargained for or negotiated in light of (legislative) principles such as proportionality. Collective environmental agreements result from communication and cooperation rather than legislation. In the Netherlands, the use of collective environmental agreements may also reflect a culture of bargaining: There are many political parties in Parliament and at the decentralized state level. In addition, there are a lot of people living in a relatively small territory in the Netherlands, which causes a great deal of cooperation to take place. A strong movement

---

[6]   For some comparative remarks about Dutch and American environmental agreements, see the chapter in this book by Dennis Hirsh.

[7]   See also supra notes 4 and 5 and accompanying text.

[8]   As of this writing, a circular is under preparation at the Ministry for the Environment on this topic. See the Dutch chapter in R. Seerden and K. Deketelaere (eds), *Legal Aspects of Soil Pollution and Decontamination in the EU Member States and the United States* (Intersentia, 2000).

of environmental groups participating in environmental policy and overseeing the negotiation of and compliance with environmental agreements
contributes as well.

2.3   Instructions for Collective Environmental Agreements

In the Netherlands, there is no act of Parliament or delegated regulation that specifically addresses the use and negotiation of environmental
agreements between central government and various business sectors.
However, there are the so-called Instructions for Agreements (*Aanwijzingen
voor convenanten*)[9] that generally cover the conclusion of these kinds of
policy agreements.

There are 24 Instructions for Agreements. Although they are given in a
formal decision of the Prime Minister, they are formulated in such a way
that they have no direct legal force for the parties of the agreements or third
parties. They can, perhaps, be therefore classified as a kind of "soft law."

The Instructions for Agreements contain rules for choosing agreements
rather than other instruments. Rules also apply to the formal contents and
the procedure of policy agreements. The Instructions for Agreements are
addressed to the central government ministers and subordinate civil servants (Instruction 2).

In Instruction 1, an agreement (*convenant*) is defined, as:

an agreement, whatever its name, between the central government and one or more
parties involving or related to the application of public law powers or in another
way dealing with the realization of central government policies.

Whether or not the conclusion of an agreement is appropriate depends on
the following considerations (Instruction 3):

(1)   whether involvement of the central government is necessary and
      whether governmental policy goals can be achieved by self-regula-
      tion of the respective sectors or other public authorities; and
(2)   the preference for other instruments taking into account the extent to
      which central government policy will be realized, the practicability
      and enforceability of an agreement, and the protection of the inter-
      ests of third parties.

Instruction 4 states that there is a preference for legislation when the choice
between legislation and an agreement must be made, unless the latter is
more effective and efficient. In this respect, it is indicated that agreements
may be made in the following cases: (1) to achieve results prior to the enactment of legislation, (2) as a substitute to legislation that will be canceled

---

[9]   Decision of 18 December 1995, No. 95M009543. In this respect, there is also a similar preliminary Code of Conduct of 1992, that is not further described here.

in the near future, (3) in order to provide for investigations for possible future legislation, or (4) as a means of supporting legislative provisions.

Instruction 5 points out that an agreement, in principle, is not used to implement European directives. However, it states that in certain circumstances implementation through a legally binding agreement may be possible, provided that, among things: (1) the agreement is in keeping with the directive and secures correct and timely implementation; (2) the agreement is binding for all parties and can be enforced in court; and (3) when the directive constitutes rights and obligations for third parties, the latter have access to justice.

Instructions 6 to 20 deal with the contents of the agreement. Apart from the general rule that agreements are in writing, they concern the following items:

(1) the binding, representation, accession of, and signing by the parties (Instructions 7 and 8);
(2) the goals, legal duties, and obligations of the parties (Instruction 9);
(3) conformity with international and national law and the relation to relevant legislation (Instruction 10);
(4) taking into account rules on public participation and advice (Instruction 11);
(5) the indication and the weighing of third-party interests (Instructions 12 and 13);
(6) compliance with the agreement, if it is intended to impose rights and obligations, and dispute resolution procedures (Instructions 14, 15 and 16);
(7) the duration and evaluation of the agreement (Instructions 17 and 18); and
(8) amendment and termination of the agreement (Instructions 19 and 20).

Instructions 21 to 24 focus on procedural requirements, such as consultation of the legal department of the respective ministry and the European Commission. For agreements with significant financial consequences for the government, the relevant minister of the Cabinet, must be involved in a decision making capacity. On occasion, the Parliament should be informed or involved. In principle, an agreement or at least a summary of its contents should be officially published in the Dutch *Staatscourant* or in another suitable manner.[10]

2.4   The Use of Collective Environmental Agreements in Practice

From the middle of the 1980s onwards, the conclusion of collective environmental agreements has become increasingly important in the Netherlands. In the beginning, the central government made use of them incidentally.

---

[10]   The decision of the Prime Minister also holds an annex with several sample provisions, which are not set forth here.

It was an ad hoc approach, but lessons were learned: for instance, that the goals to be achieved must be clear; that the environmental agreements must fit with the system of environmental legislation; that legislation can not be ignored or overriden.[11]

Since the beginning of the 1990s, environmental agreements have gradually become an increasingly strategic, legally binding instrument for the central government to implement mid-range and long-term environmental policy goals.[12] These "modern" environmental agreements, share a common ideological basis and structure for accountability.[13] There is also a link to other systems of decision making and more openness, for example, through reporting. The Environmental Agreement on Packaging, which is discussed below, is not an ad hoc instrument that precedes legislation or fully replaces it. It, partly, is a replacement for legislation but moreover it supports legislation and may be successful due to the process of covenanting and not just because of its formal way of conclusion and its legal status of a private law contract.

Before this chapter continues to discuss the Environmental Agreement on Packaging, another Dutch environmental covenant that uses this modern approach is briefly highlighted, namely, the Environmental Agreement Benchmarking Energy Efficiency (*Convenant Benchmarking Energie-efficiency*), which is close to entering into force. The parties to this Agreement are the Minister for the Environment, the Minister for Economic Affairs, the 12 Dutch provinces, and approximately 80 energy-intensive enterprises.[14] The purpose of the Agreement is to effectively reduce CO_2 and thereby implement obligations under the Kyoto Protocol regarding climate change.[15] It differs from most other agreements so far, in the way that not one specific branch as the total but several individual companies have to fulfill obligations. This is achieved by the requirement of the drawing up of energy-efficiency plans that need the approval of the competent authority. The necessary measures are in principle to be decided by the company but a change of the environmental permit is possible. If the competent authority does not approve the plan, the required permit under the Environmental Management Act can be adjusted. The principle of pollution prevention adopted in section 8.11 of the Environmental Management Act remains applicable.[16] Again, in principle, enforcement is possible through both

---

[11] On the general use and legal status of agreements (*convenanten*), see "De staat van het convenant," Nederlands Juristenblad 1993/14.

[12] See P. Glasbergen, "Milieusturing op maat, Over de karakteristieken en relevantie van het covenanting proces", Bestuurswetenschappen 1999/1, pp. 4–19.

[13] The place and function of environmental agreements is explicitly dealt with in the National Environmental Policy Plans. The first integrated National Environmental Policy Plan dates from 1989.

[14] In my opinion, this agreement could be regarded as a mix of all three categories mentioned above. See supra section 2.2

[15] See J. van den Broek and J. Niezen, "Convenant Benchmarking Energie-efficiency," Milieu en Recht 1999/6, pp. 152–159.

[16] It states that permit provisions should prevent pollution of the environment. If that is not possible, the permit must protect the environment to the greatest extent reasonably possible.

the Agreement and the environmental permit. So far, however, energy-efficiency has not been addressed in environmental permits, and the Dutch Supreme Administrative Court has expressed some skepticism about the impact of energy-efficiency requirements on individual companies.[17] Nevertheless, the Environmental Agreement Benchmarking Energy Efficiency may yet have a significant influence as the field of energy-efficiency law develops.

3   IMPLEMENTING THE EUROPEAN PACKAGING DIRECTIVE THROUGH LEGISLATION[18]

3.1   Introduction

On 20 December 1994, the European Parliament and the Council of the European Union enacted the Directive on Packaging and Packaging Waste (Packaging Directive).[19] The main purpose of this directive, which must be implemented in the legislation of the EU Member States before 30 June 1996, is to reduce the amount of packaging and to encourage the re-use and recycling of packaging waste.[20] Five years after this directive comes into force on 30 June 2001, a minimum of 50 percent and a maximum of 65 percent of the weight of the packaging needs to be recovered. Between 25 and 45 percent must be recycled, including at least 15 percent of each type of packaging material (e.g., paper/cardboard, glass, synthetics, metal and wood). In addition, the Packaging Directive prescribes limit values for concentrations of heavy metals in packaging. Also, all the EU Member States must set up return, collection, and recovery systems for packaging and packaging waste. In general, prevention of packaging materials and packaging waste must be promoted.

To implement the Packaging Directive, the Dutch central government enacted legislation at the end of 1997, namely, the Ministerial Regulation on Packaging and Packaging Waste (*Ministeriële Regeling Verpakkingen en Verpakkingsafval*, hereafter the Ministerial Regulation on Packaging).[21]

---

[17] See, e.g., the judgement of the Dutch Supreme Administrative Court (*Afdeling bestuursrechtspraak Raad van State*) 3 April 1998, Milieu en Recht 1998/11, p. 104.
[18] My discussion of the implementation of the Packaging Directive in the Netherlands is based on research that I conducted together with Marleen Hertoghs and Jürgen Lefevere for the European Commission. The final research report was offered to the European Commission on 29 January 1999. For the Dutch implementation of the Packaging Directive, see also W. Th. Douma, "Het Nederlandse verpakkingenbeleid gerecycled", Milieu en Recht 1998/9, pp. 208–214.
[19] EC Official Journal, 31 December 1994, L 365.
[20] Ibid. In addition, there are two other objectives that focus on economic issues, namely, to harmonize national measures in order to prevent restriction of competition, and to ensure free movement of packaged goods. These economic objectives are not treated here.
[21] *Staatscourant* 1997, 125, p. 14.

I review some of the details of this ministerial regulation and then discuss its legal context, mainly the Environmental Management Act and delegated regulations.

3.2 The Ministerial Regulation on Packaging

According to the Dutch central government, the Ministerial Regulation on Packaging, which consists of 16 sections, is a full and almost literal implementation of the Packaging Directive. It adopts the maximum percentages for packaging recovery and recycling given in this directive. It goes beyond the scope of this chapter to address all the provisions of the Ministerial Regulation on Packaging. I limit myself to a few remarks to clarify the relationship between the Ministerial Regulation on Packaging and the Environmental Agreement on Packaging. The Agreement is addressed in section 4.

The Ministerial Regulation on Packaging adopts almost the same definitions as the Packaging Directive. It also establishes various obligations for individual producers and importers of packaging material and packaged goods, such as the drawing up of monitoring reports.[22] For other participants in the packaging chain who are not producers or importers, the Regulation creates a duty of care to take reasonable measures to assure that producers and importers meet their obligations.[23]

The Ministerial Regulation on Packaging states that if binding agreements are made about the collective realization of the obligations, mainly reduction and recycling targets, then an exemption may apply to the various individual obligations that constitute a significant administrative burden on an enterprise.[24] This exemption is provided through the Environmental Agreement on Packaging of 1997. In addition to issues that can and are worked out in this Agreement, the Ministerial Regulation applies separate standards to the collection of domestic packaging waste, the establishment of limit values of heavy metals in packaging materials and the labeling of packaging.[25]

3.3 The Environmental Management Act

The Ministerial Regulation on Packaging forms part of a broader environmental legal framework. This chapter is not the place for detailed elaboration

---

[22] Ibid., sections 3–9.
[23] Ibid., section 4.
[24] Ibid., section 2. Such an explicit reference makes the conclusion of an agreement less problematic from a legal point of view. See supra section 2.1. Of course, the contents of the agreement may not conflict with other rights and duties established in legislation. In the Dutch legislative hierarchy, ministerial regulations are subordinate to crown decrees, statutes (Acts of Parliament), the Constitution (*Grondwet*), and directly applicable provisions of international treaties and decisions of international organizations. Ministerial regulations are superior to provincial and municipal regulations.
[25] Ministerial Regulation on Packaging, supra note 21, sections 11–13.

on this legal framework of environmental legislation, but it is appropriate to emphasize the public law dimensions of related legislative provisions and their enforcement.[26] This public law framework is not applicable to private law agreements. For the latter, only general private law liability rules apply under the Dutch Civil Code.

Provisions related to the prevention of packaging waste and the re-use and recycling of packaging waste are found in various chapters of the Dutch Environmental Management Act (*Wet milieubeheer*). In particular, the chapters on environmental planning (chapter 4), licensing (chapter 8) and waste (chapter 10) are relevant. The Ministerial Regulation on Packaging is based on various provisions in chapter 10, dealing with the prevention of waste and the processing and removal of waste. A broader set of delegated legislative instruments on the central, provincial, and municipal state levels are based in part on this chapter.

This legal foundation in the Environmental Management Act, together with other legislation like the General Administrative Law Code (*Algemene wet bestuursrecht*), makes possible the establishment of legal duties and obligations in the fields of inspection and enforcement by administrative authorities. Apart from the administrative law enforcement of general regulations and individual permits through fines and administrative orders, the use of criminal sanctions also becomes available because of a legal connection between the Environmental Management Act and the Economic Offenses Act (*Wet op de economische delicten*).[27]

4   IMPLEMENTING THE EUROPEAN PACKAGING DIRECTIVE THROUGH THE ENVIRONMENTAL AGREEMENT ON PACKAGING

4.1   Introduction

As previously stated, the individual obligations of sections 3–9 of the Ministerial Regulation on Packaging do not apply to individual producers and importers if binding agreements are made about the collective realization of these obligations, such as in the Environmental Agreement on Packaging and Packaging Waste (*Convenant Verpakkingen II*). This Environmental Agreement on Packaging consists of a general integration agreement and several additional agreements, namely, the Agreement for Producers and Importers and five Sectoral Agreements dealing with the recycling and re-use of paper/cardboard, glass, metal, synthetics, and wood.[28]

---

[26]   See R. Seerden and M. Heldeweg (eds), supra note 3, at 269–290.
[27]   For a general elaboration on the administrative and penal enforcement of Dutch environmental legislation, see ibid., at 297–299 and 308–310.
[28]   *Staatscourant* 1997, 247, at 38.

First, this chapter briefly describes the contents of these agreements. Second, it outlines their legal context and present status. Third, the section discusses the European Union's approach to the use of environmental agreements and its relevance for the Environmental Agreement on Packaging.

4.2   The Integration Agreement

The integration agreement was concluded on 15 December 1997 among the following: the Minister for the Environment acting on behalf also of the Ministers of Economic Affairs and Agriculture, the Association of Dutch Employers (*VNO-NCW*), the Association of Small Enterprises (*MKB*), and the Foundation for Packaging and Environment (*Stichting Verpakking en Milieu*). The latter was a business organization charged with the realization of an earlier agreement on the same topic that originated in 1991, prior to the entry into force of the European Packaging Directive.[29] In the new Environmental Agreement on Packaging, this organization is renamed *SVM-PACT*. The framework of the first agreement of 1991 involved approximately 2000 enterprises. The second agreement of 1997 represents around 325 thousand enterprises.

The integration agreement begins with the definition of legal concepts and then deals with several issues, such as stating the targets for packaging and packaging waste reduction in industry and trade, introducing a system for monitoring that is detailed in a supplementary protocol, and requiring monitoring and other reports. Smaller enterprises of four or less employees or producing less than 50 thousand-kg packaging per year are exempt from the monitoring and reporting requirements. It should be noted that the targets for re-use are more stringent than the maximum targets for re-use under the Ministerial Regulation on Packaging and the Packaging Directive.

The integration agreement further includes sections concerning consultation of the parties, information sharing, and the amendment and termination of the agreement. Dispute resolution is through an arbitration commission. The additional agreements have similar provisions.

The integration agreement also sets up the Commission on Packaging (*Commissie Verpakkingen*). The Commission consists of four members of the business community, four state representatives, and one independent chairperson. It is responsible for overseeing compliance with the integration Agreement and reviewing the various reports of the business participants and the Minister for the Environment. The Commission summarizes this information in an annual report and has the authority to make recommendations for improvement to the parties.

---

[29]   *Convenant Verpakkingen*, 6 June 1991. In this agreement, an environmental organization (*Stichting Natuur en Milieu*) and a consumer organization (*Consumentenbond*) had the status of observers. The annual report of the Commission on Packaging indicates that these organizations were also consulted about the implementation of the Agreement on Packaging in 1997. See Annual Report, infra note 31, at 29.

Additionally, the integration agreement explains the relationship between the integration agreement and the additional agreements and limits its duration through 31 December 2002. The final section states that both the integration agreement and the sectoral agreements constitute private law agreements, implying that the relevant provisions for agreements of the Dutch Civil Code apply.[30]

4.3   The Additional Agreements

The additional agreements consist of the Agreement for Producers and Importers and five sectoral agreements addressing the recycling and re-use of paper/cardboard, glass, metal, synthetics, and wood. The additional agreements include many of the same terms in the integration agreement, such as the consultation of parties, amending of the agreement, and dispute resolution. However, the Minister for the Environment is mostly responsible for contracting with different parties. For example, parties to the Agreement on Paper are the Minister for the Environment, the Dutch Consultative Association of Municipalities (*Vereniging Nederlandse Gemeenten*), and the Foundation for Paper Recycling (*Stichting Papierrecycling*). Although not discussed here, the subject matter of the additional agreements and certainly the sectoral agreements differs, which can lead to alternative methods of reducing and recycling packaging waste. However, there is one aspect worth mentioning: It is the competence of the Minister for the Environment to come to a decision by which an agreement, between enterprises to come to a payment for the removal of waste, is declared generally binding (and obtains a public law status). This is done for an agreement about the removal contributions for paper and cardboard, that is resulting from the Sectoral Agreement on Paper.

4.4   The Legal Context

The Ministerial Regulation on Packaging is enforceable on the basis of the respective provisions in the Environmental Management Act and annexed legislation. In the case of violation of the Environmental Agreement on Packaging, however, the administrative and criminal legal enforcement instruments are not applicable. Only when provisions of this agreement have been incorporated into general regulations or individual permits may they be legally enforced by the government.

The Environmental Agreement on Packaging, as a private law contract, can be enforced in cases of violation by the parties to the Agreement in the manner specified in the Agreement. Other persons cannot invoke public law enforcement instruments. They may start legal actions based on tort law, but these are more difficult and more expensive than administrative legal actions, such as the enforcement of legislative provisions, under the Ministerial Regulation on Packaging.

---

[30]   See supra note 28, section 22.

The fact that, contrary to the Ministerial Regulation on Packaging, the Environmental Agreement on Packaging does not constitute a generally legally binding and enforceable instrument causes problems from the perspective of European law. Before addressing this European law dimension, however, it is helpful to provide some additional information about the Environmental Agreement on Packaging as it works in practice.

Currently, in the fall of 1999, not every company that falls under the scope of the Environmental Agreement on Packaging actually joins this agreement. Only about 75 percent do so, and those that join are mostly larger companies. At present, the Ministry for the Environment and *SVM-PACT*, the representative business organization under the Agreement of the business sector, are taking an inventory. The *SVM-PACT* has a duty to bring as many companies as possible into the Environmental Agreement on Packaging. *SVM-PACT* has set up a management system, together with the Chambers of Commerce and organizations of branches of companies, and has drawn up a blueprint for participation. It states that, when individual or clustered companies do not fulfill the conditions of an agreement, it will be excluded from the Environmental Agreement on Packaging and fall under the application of the Ministerial Regulation on Packaging.

In two years, an estimated 80 to 90 percent of all the companies in the Netherlands will be taking part in the Environmental Agreement on Packaging. At that time, the inspection by the Ministry for the Environment (specifically, the *Inspectie Milieuhygiëne*) will no longer focus on compliance with the Environmental Agreement on Packaging, but instead concentrate those provisions of the Ministerial Regulation on Packaging that are not replaced by the Agreement. It is the responsibility of the *SVM-PACT* and the Commission on Packaging to assure that the reduction targets are achieved.

In October 1999, the annual report by the Commission on Packaging for 1998 was released. It states, among other things, that without extra effort the aims of the integration agreement will not be achieved (though minimum standards will be met). This is especially true for the reduction targets of paper/cardboard and synthetics.[31]

4.5 European Law Aspects

The implementation in the Netherlands of the Packaging Directive has caused some problems from the European law perspective. EU Member States are, in principle, free to choose the form and manner of implementation of European directives, as indicated in section 249 of the EC Treaty.[32] According to the case law of the European Court of Justice, not all provisions of directives must be adopted literally by Member States. However, when a European directive creates rights and duties for individuals, then

---

[31] Annual Report 1998, Commission on Packaging (*Commissie Verpakkingen*), October 1999, p. 8.
[32] Before the coming into force on 1 May 1999 of the Treaty of Amsterdam, this was section 189 EC Treaty.

these rights and duties must be made enforceable through legally binding instruments. Although a Dutch ministerial regulation fulfills this requirement, an environmental agreement is not necessarily sufficient, especially when the respective directive does not explicitly refer to an environmental agreement as a permissible means of implementing rights and obligations. The Packaging Directive (contrary to its predecessor) does not refer to environmental agreements in this way.

According to the European Commission, it must be possible to enforce a European directive through a combination of legislative measures and voluntary agreements.[33] However, legislative measures must provide a minimum standard and a back-up for those who do not comply with voluntary agreements.

The European Commission has informed the Dutch Government that it must change the Ministerial Regulation on Packaging so that the exemption to several provisions of the Ministerial Regulation is not applicable if the goals laid down in the Packaging Directive are not achieved.[34] In other words, negotiations under the framework of the Environmental Agreement on Packaging may not endanger the minimum standards of the Ministerial Regulation on Packaging and the Packaging Directive. But as long as minimum standards are met, the use of an environmental agreement is not necessarily in conflict with European law.[35]

5   CONCLUSION

The purpose of this chapter has been to focus on the place, function, and legal status of environmental agreements in the Netherlands and, in particular, the Environmental Agreement on Packaging. I have shown that environmental agreements in the Netherlands do not necessarily have a legal status. At times they are simply gentlemen's agreements or expressions of intentions. But in other cases, such as in the case of the Environmental Agreement on Packag-ing, the parties to environmental agreements qualify them as private law agreements. Whether or not they are legally binding and enforceable by the government or third parties, those agreements are intended to achieve environmental policy goals.

In the Netherlands, there are three types of environmental agreements: (1) those concluded between central government, primarily the Minister for the Environment, and branches of industry or other business sectors; (2) agreements between central and decentralized authorities; and (3) agreements between one authority and an individual company. Occasionally

---

[33]   See the chapter of Deketelaere and Van Calster in this book for a more complete description of European law in this respect.
[34]   The Ministerial Regulation on Packaging was changed in this respect by decision of 6 June 1999.
[35]   For other issues not involving the use of environmental agreements, see the research report mentioned supra note 18, at 22–36.

there is a mix of the three categories. This chapter addressed only the first category of collective agreements given their great importance in the Dutch practice of environmental protection.

Although environmental agreements between central government and branches of industry or other business groups have become increasingly important, neither the Environmental Management Act nor the General Administrative Law Code offer a general legal framework for this type of instrument. There are some non-legally binding instructions, such as in a decision of the Prime Minister (*Aanwijzingen voor Convenanten*). And when environmental agreements are intended to be legally binding, they are considered to be private law contracts governed by the Dutch Civil Code.

Private law contracts, including environmental agreements, that violate statutory requirements are void. There is some case law available concerning the question of whether or not public authorities can use private law instruments, like agreements, to complement or replace public law instruments in order to realize public aims. Private law instruments may not be used in such a way that public law authority is undermined. For instance, agreements cannot set aside legislation, statutes, or delegated regulations. This limitation applies to collective agreements between the central government and branches of industry, but also for the other categories of environmental agreements, including the agreements between an individual company and a public authority.

In large part, the success of using collective environmental agreements in the Netherlands seems to result from the fact that they are strongly embraced by both industry and other business sectors and the central government to be a worthwhile and innovative instrument to internalize environmental protection. The fact that a specific environmental agreement is legally binding or, in other words, can be regarded as "hard law" is relevant in cases of disputes. Enforcement is available through private law mechanisms under the contractual terms of the agreement. To my knowledge, however, there have been so far no court actions concerning the implementation of environmental agreements. This paucity of litigation may owe in part to the fact that many agreements, though formally written as private law contracts, function also as an expression of internalized behavior. In addition, if the goals of environmental agreements are not achieved, there is always the possibility that the government will come forward with stricter (and more expensive) legislative measures.

Whatever the case may be, environmental agreements between central government and branches of industry and other business sectors are used in various situations: (1) to accomplish something when there is no previous legislation; (2) to prevent legislation; (3) to accelerate the implementation of legislation; and (4) to parallel legislation, but express the intent to achieve higher goals. In general, environmental agreements are more concerned with preventing legislation than waiving or lifting legislative requirements. They focus on particular environmental protection standards and pollution reduction goals. If they are linked to legislation, the goals are the same or even higher. In large part, the Environmental Agreement on Packaging (*Convenant Verpakkingen II*) can be seen as an alternative to legislation for certain provisions such as monitoring requirements of the

Ministerial Regulation on Packaging (*Ministeriële Regeling Verpakkingen en Verpakkingsafval*). In addition, the Environmental Agreement on Packaging adopts higher protection/reduction goals than the Ministerial Regulation on Packaging and the European Packaging Directive. The Ministerial Regulation on Packaging explicitly states that some of its provisions may be replaced by the use of environmental agreements. At the same time, the Ministerial Regulation states that other provisions cannot be waived or replaced by an agreement. Thus, the Environmental Agreement on Packaging does not stand alone. It fits into a broader legal framework, including not only the Ministerial Regulation but also the Environmental Management Act. Using an agreement does not necessarily cause the government to lose influence.

The Ministerial Regulation on Packaging and the Environmental Agreement on Packaging thus work together. The Regulation sets a minimum standard, and free riders under the Agreement fall under the application of the Regulation. The same is true for parties who do not meet their obligations under the Agreement. In the Netherlands, this mix of legislation and environmental agreements works quite well, combined as it is with annual reports that give objective and accessible information, such as the annual report of the Commission on Packaging issued under the Environmental Agreement on Packaging. The central government, remains a party to an agreement and in any event retains its public law authority to intervene if the goals and terms of the agreement are not achieved. Thus, there is no permanent shift of authority under the agreement to the parties or, in particular, the private sector.

Given that the approach in the Netherlands involves a combination of legislation measures and agreements, some of the problems inherent to environmental agreements also become less problematic. These include the role of third parties such as nonprofit environmental associations, the democratic dimension, and the lack of general public law enforceability. The approach in the Netherlands may also balance collective obligations with the encouragement of individual achievements towards improving environmental protection. Conflicts with European law are not inevitable though it is important to consider when a Member State chooses to mix environmental agreements or legislation to implement European directives.

Certain kinds of environmental issues where health and safety are not directly at stake, such as the reduction of packaging waste and energy efficiency, are especially well suited for a more consensual approach. The same may be true for experiments with environmentally protective measures that go beyond existing legislative provisions, provided that the consensual approach conforms with this legislation. The transparency of environmental agreements to the public is especially important. Sufficient openness of the terms of agreements and explicit links between legislation and collective environmental agreements seem more and more to describe the situation in the Netherlands.

However, it is difficult, if not impossible, to draw general conclusions about the use and legal status of all collective environmental agreements concluded in the Netherlands. One cannot speak of a single environmental agreement because environmental agreements differ in a number of respects, including: the number of parties involved, the subject matter, the organization, the implementation techniques, whether or not they are part of an extensive legislative framework, whether or not they are legally binding, and whether and how they are enforceable. All these aspects require further research. In addition, empirical questions remain as to whether businesses comply with environmental agreements to a greater extent than with legislation and, partially as a consequence, whether environmental agreements are more effective and efficient in achieving environmental protection than the traditional legislative instruments. These questions extend beyond the purpose of this chapter.

ANNEX OF DUTCH ENVIRONMENTAL AGREEMENTS IN FORCE OR UNDER REVISION OR EVALUATION (WITH THE YEAR OF CONCLUSION)

This list is derived from a list of February 1998 of the Coordination Office Environmental Agreements that forms part of the Dutch Ministry for the Environment. Approximately ten environmental agreements are now out of force.

The coordination Office stated in a telephone conversation on 5 January 2000 that this list is under revision and that the total number of environmental agreements in force at the beginning of 2000 is not exactly known. Some of the environmental agreements included in this list are under revision, will be evaluated, will loose force in 2000. A few new agreements will be concluded in the near future.

In addition to environmental agreements with several branches of industry to prevent environmental pollution, there are also ten agreements that deal with the environmental protection of specific regions.

1. Environmental Agreement on Detergents (*Wasmiddelenconvenant*, 1987)
2. Environmental Agreement on Crates (*Krattenconvenant*, 1988)
3. Environmental Agreement on Crop Protection Products (*Gewasbeschermingsmiddelenconvenant*, 1988)
4. Environmental Agreement on Asbestos (*Asbest-frictie-convenant*, 1989)
5. Environmental Agreement on Waste Problems in the Inland Shipping (*Convenant Afvalstoffenproblematiek Binnenvaart*, 1989)
6. Environmental Agreement on Air Pollution caused by Tank Storage Firms (*VOTOB-convenant*, 1989)
7. Environmental Agreement on Reduction of CO_2 and NO_x of Heating Installations and Electricity Production Companies (*SEP-convenant*, 1990)
8. Environmental Agreement on Cargo Waste of Flat-bottom Crafts (*Intentieverklaring ladingresten uit duwbakken*, 1991)
9. Environmental Agreement on the Decontamination of Soil at Petrol Stations (*Bodemsaneringsprotocol Tankstations*, 1991)
10. Environmental Agreement for the Basic-metal Sector (*Milieuconvenant Basismetaal*, 1992)
11. Environmental Agreement on Green-lable Stables/Sheds (*Convenant Groen-Label Stallen*, 1993)
12. Environmental Agreement on Synthetic Waste in the Agricultural Sector (*Convenant Kunststofafval Land- en Tuinbouw*, 1993)
13. Environmental Agreement on Synthetic Waste in Industry (*Convenant Kunststofafval Industrie*, 1993)
14. Environmental Agreement on Paper Isolated Cable Waste (*Convenant Papiergeïsoleerde Kabelresten*, 1993)
15. Environmental Agreement for the Chemical Industry (*Milieuconvenant Chemische Industrie*, 1993)
16. Environmental Agreement for the Graphic Industry and Packaging Printing Business (*Milieubeleidsovereenkomst Grafische Industrie en Verpakkingsdrukkerijen*, 1993)

17. Environmental Agreement for the Building Industry (*Beleidsverklaring Milieutaakstellingen Bouw*, 1993)
18. Environmental Agreement on Crop Protection (*Bestuursovereenkomst Uitvoering Meerjarenplan Gewasbescherming*, 1993)
19. Environmental Agreement for the Dairy Industry (*Intentieverklaring Uitvoering Milieubeleid Zuivelindustrie*, 1994)
20. Environmental Agreement for the Oil and Gas industry (*Intentieverklaring Uitvoering Milieubeleid Olie- en Gaswinningsindustrie*, 1994)
21. Environmental Agreement for the Metal and Electronic Industry (*Intentieverklaring Uitvoering Milieubeleid Metaal- en Elektrotechnische Industrie*, 1995)
22. Environmental Agreement for the Flower Bulb Sector (*Overeenkomst Uitvoering Milieubeleid Bloembollensector*, 1995)
23. Environmental Agreement for the Collection and Processing of Used Paper and Cardboard (*Intentieverklaring Inzamel- en Verwerkingssyteem Oud-papier en -karton*, 1995)
24. Environmental Agreement for the Decontamination of Soil Pollution at Railway Stations (*Convenant inzake Bodemsanering NS-percelen*, 1995)
25. Environmental Agreement on Used Package Glass (*Convenant Gebruikt Verpakkingsglas*, 1995)
26. Environmental Agreement for the Textile and Carpet Industry (*Intentieverklaring Uitvoering Milieubeleid Textiel- en Tapijtindustrie*, 1996)
27. Environmental Agreement for the Paper and Cardboard Industry (*Intentieverklaring Uitvoering Milieubeleid Papier- en Kartonindustrie*, 1996)
28. Environmental Agreement for Greenhouses Horticulture (*Convenant Glastuinbouw en Milieu*, 1997)
29. Environmental Agreement on Packaging and Packaging Waste (*Convenant Verpakkingen II*, 1997)

The following Dutch Environmental Agreements (with the year of conclusion) have been expired:

1. Mercury-oxide Batteries (*Kwikoxydebatterijencode*, 1985)
2. Drinking Packaging (*Drankverpakkingenverklaring*, 1985)
3. PETP-bottles (*PETP-flessen*, 1987)
4. Trucks (*Vrachtwagenconvenant*, 1987)
5. Alkaline Batteries (*Alkalinebatterijen*, 1987)
6. Waste Transport (*Afvaltransportverklaring*, 1987)
7. Sprayers (*Spuitbussenconvenant*, 1988)
8. Nickel and Cadmium Batteries (*Gedragscode nikkel-cadmium batterijen*, 1989)
9. Packaging I (*Convenant Verpakkingen*, 1991)
10. Energy Efficiency existing Houses (*Energiebesparing bestaande Woningvoorraad*, 1992)
11. Timber Stairways (*Convenant Houten Binnentrappen*, 1993)
12. Tropical Timber (*Convenant Tropish Hout*, 1993)
13. Youth Information (*Jongerenconvenant*, 1994)

9. The Use of Voluntary Agreements in the European Community's Environmental Policy

Geert Van Calster and Kurt Deketelaere

1 AIM AND SCOPE OF THE ANALYSIS

This chapter discusses the role of voluntary agreements in European Union (EU) environmental policy. It assesses whether the European Commission in particular has embraced this "new" instrument of environmental policy, or whether it follows a rather unsure route, neither heralding nor rejecting voluntary agreements. We take the most complete policy document with respect to voluntary agreements, a Commission Communication of 1996, as a starting-point for our analysis.

In general, the Commission's Communication on Voluntary Agreements[1] signalled a cautiously positive view of their use at the national level. With respect to European-wide voluntary agreements, however, the text was much more skeptical. The authors argue that the limited use of such EC-wide agreements is to an important extent outweighed by the considerable access that European industry has to the legislative process, through official consultation and lobbying. The genesis of both a voluntary agreement and formal legislation in the automobile sector serves as an example in this respect.

This chapter does not offer a complete overview of voluntary agreements at the national and/or European level.[2] Instead, offering a cross-section of the theory and practice of voluntary agreements in the EU, we aim to clarify their role in European environmental policy.[3]

---

[1] COM(96) 561, OJ [1996] L333/69.
[2] Some more specific aspects of voluntary agreements in the EU are addressed by other authors in this volume.
[3] This chapter chiefly employs the term "voluntary agreements." "Environmental agreements," "negotiated agreements" and "covenants" have likewise been used to identify the trend, and we may use them interchangeably. See also P. Bailey, "The Creation and Enforcement of Environmental Agreements" [1999] Eur Env L Rev 170–179.

2   THE BLEAK PICTURE IN 1995

Preceding the 1996 Communication, the EC Commissioner for the Environment at the time, Ms Bjerregaard, had shown serious hesitation as to the use of voluntary agreements in EU environmental policy. At a seminar organized by Union of Industrial and Employers' Confederations of Europe (UNICE) the Commissioner expressed unmistakable skepticism.[4] That seminar turned out to be something of a stocktaking exercise, focusing minds from the perspective of the European Commission, the industry, and the European Parliament (EP) perspective.

The UNICE seminar noted the relative success of *national* agreements in such countries as the Netherlands where by 1997 at least 70 such agreements had been concluded between industry and the authorities. In the Netherlands, these agreements seemed to contribute to an effective reduction of environmental degradation in a number of areas.[5]

At the European level, one has to take account of the case law of the European Court of Justice (ECJ), which holds that Community secondary legislation is to be implemented at the national level by formal statutory instruments, unless the legislation at issue specifically provides that other instruments may be used, including voluntary agreements, *or* where the legislation does not create rights and obligations for individuals.[6] Such a provision in the legislation is, however, rare. We submit[7] that the Packaging and Packaging Waste Directive[8] is the only Directive to date where a voluntary agreement to reach the goals of the Directive, in particular the recycling and recovery targets, is seriously put forward as an instrument to further the goals of an EC Directive. (Even though the Directive does not expressly mention voluntary agreements, it is generally understood that the reference in Article 7 with respect to return, collection, and recovery systems, together with the need to involve the economic operators of the sectors concerned in the design and operation of such systems, is a reference to voluntary agreements.)

Industry lobbied heavily with the European Commission to upgrade the status of voluntary agreements within the executive's environmental services. The chemical industry in particular proved keen to change the Commission's mind and channelled its initiative through UNICE. Right through the seminar and, more generally, in any assessment of voluntary

---

[4] "EC institutions lay down criteria for environmental agreements," *The E.N.D.S.-Report*, No. 243, April 1995, 42.

[5] See "Environmental policy in the Netherlands—The role of industry," Den Haag, VNO-NCW, 1995 (describing the situation as of 1995, listing the agreements, and assessing their success).

[6] See F. Vogelaar, "Verpakkingen en verpakkingsafval. De Richtlijn 94/62 en haar tenuitvoerlegging in Nederland" in K. Deketelaere and L. Wiggers-Rust, *Actualiteiten Europees Milieurecht* (Brugge, Die Keure, 1997), 95,123.

[7] But we expressly invite comments as to this assertion.

[8] Directive 94/62 of 20 December 1994, OJ [1994] L365/10. This Directive's predecessor provided the ECJ with the clearest opportunity so far to assess the use of voluntary agreements for the implementation of Directives; see note 69 below.

agreements, it became obvious that one has to distinguish between the levels of industry involved in negotiations and actual policy decisions on voluntary agreements. Agreements between the European Commission and the car industry in particular have, rightly, received a lot of media attention. However, one of the necessary conditions for the success of voluntary agreements at any level is the representativeness of the industry involved in the negotiations. This makes voluntary agreements at the European-wide level most likely in industries such as car manufacturing or the chemical industry. The wide range of environmental issues that affect and interest small and medium-sized enterprises (SMEs) may not be easily tackled by EC-wide agreements because the SMEs lack a forum to speak with one voice in Brussels, even if speaking with one voice would be possible given the wide variety of environmental interests affecting SMEs.

The UNICE seminar originated in a survey with its members, which showed that Members were skeptical about the chances of success for voluntary agreements that are directly negotiated between industry and the European Commission.[9] UNICE Members expressed a preference for agreements at the national level with an element of European coordination, in particular with respect to the goals that are to be reached by the voluntary effort. Coinciding with this view, industry urged the Commission and the Council to increase the number of Community Directives that may be implemented by voluntary agreements.

2.1 UNICE's List of Conditions

From the results of the survey, UNICE compiled a list of conditions for the success of voluntary agreements: the goals of the exercise have to be clearly defined; the negotiating process has to be transparent; top management of the sectors or enterprises concerned have to be involved in the process; free riders have to be discouraged; and a number of measures has to ensure compliance with the agreement (including tax advantages, subsidies for research and development, and the option to introduce stricter legislation for those who do not participate in the agreement).

UNICE identified the Commission as crucial for the fulfilment of a number of these conditions. Because of its right to initiate European legislation, the Commission could first of all identify a set of general goals for the entire EU, in a given sector. The Commission could subsequently serve as the clearing-house for the national agreements that implement the overall goals. Finally, the Commission could monitor the implementation of the agreements and the effect on the environmental challenge at issue.

UNICE expressed the view that parliamentary control (both by the national parliaments and by the EP) is possible without infringing the voluntary nature of the agreements. It suggested that this goal could be

---

[9] "Negotiated agreements between public authorities and industry: a complementary instrument for EU environmental policies—Some considerations on the role to be played by the different actors", Brussels, 17 March 1995.

achieved by having the national or European parliaments draft a general framework for voluntary agreements. Clearly, UNICE does not want parliaments to assess each and every agreement.

2.2 The Commission's Reply

Commenting on these suggestions in 1996, the Commissioner for the Environment was very cautious. She formulated three questions which need to be answered prior to getting engaged in voluntary agreements at the European level:

(1) What are the criteria for the acceptance, by the European Community, of voluntary agreements concluded at the national level?

This issue concerns the relationship between these agreements and EC competition law, as well as between the agreements and subsequent Community legislation. The Commissioner suggested that the EC should issue a set of guidelines in both respects, but did not comment on the possible contents of any such guidelines.

(2) Can environmental objectives that are defined at the European level be implemented by national voluntary agreements?

The Commissioner referred to the case law of the ECJ, recalled above.[10] Replying to industry's request to increase the number of Community Directives that may be implemented by voluntary agreements, the Commissioner said that this may be considered on a case-by-case basis, but there could be no general policy of including this clause in each and every Directive. She nevertheless referred to the Fifth Environmental Action Plan, which encourages experiments with voluntary agreements. The plan seems to adopt the old truism *quid leges sine moribus*: regulatory intervention does not suffice to change people's behaviour.

Under this heading, the Commissioner enumerated the following conditions for voluntary agreements to be acceptable: the goals of the agreement have to be clearly defined, if possible in quantitative terms; precise time limits have to be set out; the parties' responsibilities have to be clearly defined; the implementation of the agreement has to be closely monitored, linked to reporting duties of the parties; free riders have to be discouraged; and the agreement itself and the reports contemplated by it have to be open to the public.

(3) What are the criteria for the acceptance, by the European Community, of voluntary agreements concluded at the European level?

Obviously, the conditions set out above for the acceptance of environmental agreements at the national level (including transparency, reporting duties, etc.), extend to agreements at the European level. Commissioner Bjerregaard set out some additional requirements for these agreements.

---

[10] See supra note 6 and accompanying text. See also the analysis of the 1996 Communication below.

First, the Commissioner's view was that the aims of such agreements should relate to a core element of the Community Environmental Action Programs. Second, agreements should only be concluded where the regulatory approach would fail; in other words, voluntary agreements should not be the first port of call. Finally, the sector concerned should involve a limited number of market players only (viewed from the production side), and the sector should be comprehensively represented at the European level. The Commissioner insisted that an agreement covering these and possibly other points should form the subject of an agreement between the Council of Ministers, the Commission, and, last but not least in the Commissioner's view, the European Parliament.

2.3   Reply by the European Parliament

The European Parliament was represented at the UNICE meeting by Ken Collins, who was the then president of the Parliament's environment committee. He clarified that the Commission and industry would have a tough job convincing the EP members to support the use of voluntary agreements. In particular, the EP is concerned that these agreements are not transparent, and it objects to the lack of democratic accountability of the negotiators of the agreements. These issues are not only political and philosophical. If the negotiations falter, or if the aims are not achieved, then the negotiators are also not legally accountable. This fact, the EP argues, undermines the incentives for negotiators to reach successful agreements.

In this respect, Collins identifies a classic argument against voluntary agreements, namely, that they constitute a licence to pollute, allowing industry to keep the authorities at bay with long-lasting negotiations.

2.4   The Commission's Conclusion

Commissioner Bjerregaard ended her contribution at the UNICE seminar by saying that the Commission would be prepared to draft a set of guidelines with respect to environmental agreements, but only if it received a specific proposal from UNICE. That the Commission would wait with undertaking an initiative until industry presented a proposal clearly indicated that the Commission would not actively pursue a policy in this area.

3   THE 1996 COMMUNICATION

The 1996 Communication on Voluntary Agreements[11] is not a direct reply to UNICE's quest, but it does reflect most of the concerns expressed by Commissioner Bjerregaard at the UNICE seminar. The Communication's policy considerations reflect the ideas contained in the Fifth Environmental

---

[11]   See supra note 1.

Action Program,[12] which suggests a new line of cooperative efforts with industry:

Whereas previous environmental measures tended to be prescriptive in character with an emphasis on the "thou shalt not" approach, the new strategy leans more towards a "let's work together"approach. This reflects the growing realization in industry and in the business world that not only is industry a significant part of the (environmental) problem but it must also be part of the solution. The new approach implies, in particular, a reinforcement of the dialogue with industry and the encouragement, in appropriate circumstances, of voluntary agreements and other forms of self-regulation.[13]

Not only the Commission, but also the Council has explicitly recognised the need to broaden the range of instruments and to involve all levels of society in a spirit of shared responsibility.[14] The catch-phrase is that industry is not just part of the environmental problem, but also of its solution. However, broadening the range of instruments has proved to be more difficult than envisaged. When reviewing the Fifth Action Program, the Commission therefore suggested this issue as one of five key priorities. According to the Commission, special attention should be given to environmental charges, to the encouragement of fiscal reform, to the concept of environmental liability, and to voluntary agreements. The Commission had already presented a communication on environmental levies in the Member States, which seeks to facilitate the introduction of such levies at the national level by clarifying the possibilities and limitations of the use of these measures.[15] The Commission has also already stimulated the public discussion on better implementation and enforcement of environmental legislation by way of a communication to Parliament and Council.[16]

Below, we set out the main elements of the Commission's 1996 Communication and add our comments. The Communication defines "environmental agreements" as "agreements between public authorities and industry on the achievement of environmental objectives."[17] Prior to examining the advantages that environmental agreements may include, the Commission emphasises that regulatory action will remain the backbone of the EU's environmental policy. This statement does not pre-judge the analysis which the Commission subsequently undertakes. It does, however, reduce the enthusiasm that one may otherwise perceive in more general policy instruments, such as the Fifth Environmental Action Program.

---

[12]   Approved by Resolution of the Council, OJ [1993] C138/1.
[13]   Ibid.
[14]   Resolution 93/C138/0 of the Council and Representatives of the Governments of the Member States, meeting within the Council, February 1993, OJ [1993] C138/1.
[15]   Commission Communication of 29 January 1997 on environmental taxes in the Single Market, COM(97) 9, OJ [1997] C224/6.
[16]   Communication from the Commission to the Council on implementing Community environmental law, November 1996, COM(96) 500.
[17]   See supra note 1.

3.1   The Benefits of Environmental Agreements

Generally, comparing voluntary agreements with regulatory action has to be done with caution. There is a tendency to over-simplify or over-idealise both. The advantages of the actual regulatory system are rarely as good as those of the model. The same is true of voluntary environmental agreements.[18]

3.1.1   *The Encouragement of a Pro-active Approach from Industry*

In its approach to legislation, industry is often involved at a late stage, according to the Commission and even then its participation is usually limited to more or less formal consultations.

This is likely to lead to a defensive rather than an open and pro-active response. The dialogue and negotiations on "what to do" and "how to do it" in order to achieve certain goals will help to overcome this defensive attitude. Moreover, the negotiation processes as such, regardless of the actual agreement, can lead to a common understanding of environmental problems and mutual responsibilities. Such a common understanding is in itself an advantage which helps to shape sensible environmental policy and which should not be underestimated. This also implies that agreements should be seen as the continuation of the partnership between authorities and industry rather than just the result of it.[19]

Although this consideration is undoubtedly fair with respect to voluntary agreements, this quotation indicates that the Commission may underestimate the involvement of the industry in formal consultation in legislative processes. As we discuss in more detail below, industry is very actively involved in shaping EU environmental law. The Commission's exhortation in its Communication may in fact already be true for both voluntary agreements and the participation of industry in the regulatory process, at least at the EU level.

Moreover, the active involvement of industry is at the same time one of the main objections against voluntary agreements. Environmental non-governmental organizations and the European Parliament are deeply suspicious that industry employs negotiations as a means to delay justified regulatory action.

3.1.2   *Cost-Effectiveness*

An important benefit of environmental agreements, according to the Commission, is that they leave greater freedom to industry at the company or sectoral levels to decide on how to reach specified environmental targets. This allows industry the freedom to find cost-effective solutions adapted to its specific situation, taking into account, for instance, previous investments. It also allows environmental permits to be more flexible, reducing the need for excessive detail. Flexibility, argues the Commission, encourages

---

[18]   See Bailey, supra note 3, at 173.
[19]   Commission Communication, supra note 1, at 7.

creative solutions and technological innovations which may not only reduce compliance costs but also entail spin-off benefits. Innovative solutions to environmental problems may yield competitive advantages.

Allowing industry the freedom to adapt its on-site technology and know-how to reach environmental goals is undoubtedly cost-efficient. Likewise, the task of governmental authorities in drawing up environmental permits would be less burdensome if they were not obliged to formulate site-specific technological requirements.

However, even when environmental goals are set by legislation, and subsequently translated into permit requirements, these permits do not always contain a detailed set of technical rules on how to achieve the permit's requirements. The legislation itself often includes a significant amount of technical detail, thus obviating the need for the administrative authorities to formulate such details in the permits. Although permits are often very specific in terms of the emission levels sought, European legislation ordinarily leaves specification of the means for reaching these goals to the enterprises involved.

One could also argue that flexibility in permits merely serves to shift the timing of costs borne by the government. Enforcement and control are arguably easier and less expensive when the government has already specified all details at the moment of drawing up the permit. Flexibility in the means to reach more generally specified goals may mean that the government may later face additional costs in having to assess the effectiveness of various methods used to reach these goals.

Finally, the development of new technologies, and innovation generally, are part of the industrial cycle. Market mechanisms should ensure that enterprises that do not innovate will be driven out of the market. Therefore, one could argue that it would be wrong to credit environmental agreements with innovation. This economic argument has also played a role in Commission decisions on state aid for environmental protection (discussed below).

3.1.3   Faster Achievement of Objectives

The Commission argues that particularly in situations where the targets to be reached concern a limited number of companies, the conclusion of voluntary agreements can be considerably quicker than the adoption of legislation.

(T)he average time between the Proposal for an environmental Directive and its adoption is well over two years with usually another two-year period for transposition by the Member States. Once a Directive is transposed, which in quite a number of cases happens belatedly, it still has to be implemented and applied. For that reason, according to the Commission, agreements might be a quicker and thus potentially more effective way of action, even if the negotiation and conclusion of an agreement takes more than a couple of months.[20]

---

[20]   Ibid., at 8.

This alleged advantage of voluntary agreements is now far from certain. Recent experience with negotiations at the European level shows that the conclusion of such agreements takes more than just "more than a couple of months."

Moreover, opponents of voluntary agreements have always argued that the advantage of speed is lost when negotiations fail. When negotiations falter, the legislative process has to be initiated after months if not years of delay. Experience has also shown that one possible solution—the parallel negotiation of legislative measures as well as voluntary agreements—is not feasible.

3.2   Risks Associated with Environmental Agreements

The Communication of 1996 does not contain a heading of "disadvantages." The Commission does warn, however, of "certain risks," which include: (1) the need to define clear objectives from the outset, which would also aid transparency and would create room for all stakeholders to have their voice heard; (2) the provision of clear enforcement mechanisms and sanctions; and (3) avoiding the risks of freeriders.[21]

3.3   Guidelines for the Use of Environmental Agreements

The core of the Communication of 1996 consist of a set of "guidelines for the use of environmental agreements."[22] The guidelines are designed both for agreements in the application of Community law, and those that are totally independent of Community law. In what follows, we refer in the footnotes to the most important corresponding provisions of the 1994 Decree of the Flemish Region on voluntary agreements, which we also discuss in more detail below. Even though this Decree may not necessarily have been a direct source of inspiration to the Commission, its provisions nevertheless provide for a legislative instrument in which the conditions and reservations regarding voluntary agreements are directly addressed.

3.3.1 Substantial Conditions

All interested circles stakeholders have the opportunity to comment on the draft of a voluntary agreement. "In addition to those actually negotiating the agreement, all relevant business associations or companies concerned, environmental protection groups, local or other public authorities concerned should therefore be appropriately informed and comments should be taken into consideration in the final negotiation of the agreement."[23]

---

[21]   Ibid.
[22]   Ibid., at 11 onwards.
[23]   Bailey (note 3 above, at 173) notes that in most voluntary agreements, local authorities are involved (this only applies, of course, to national environmental agreements, not to those negotiated at the European level); local authorities have first-hand knowledge of quite a number of environmental issues.

The Commission believes that *a contract is the best format for concluding environmental agreements.* Contracts are binding for both parties[24] and provide a clear framework, which may include sanctions in the case of non-compliance and are enforceable through court decisions. The effect on third parties is of course more controversial and depends on national law. An understanding is often implicit that no legislative action will be proposed as long as the agreement works satisfactorily.[25] Such an understanding would serve to enhance the enforcement of the agreement.

Choosing the route of a contract means that all the classical elements of this instrument should be present, including the clear determination of the rights and obligations of both parties. The Commission strongly urges the inclusion of quantitative targets, rather than an obligation to reach a certain but open-ended goal. In practice, this means that either absolute numbers will have to be set out (e.g., emission limits) or relative numbers (e.g., a percentage of reduction of emissions compared to a base year).

The Commission also urges the *definition of interim goals*, not so much to impose interim obligations on industry, but rather to detect problems before they become unmanageable. Legislation may then be necessary.

The results are to be monitored and collected centrally.[26] The Commission does not believe monitoring and data collection require additional Community initiatives. Existing Community instruments could prove very useful in this respect. In particular, the Commission identifies the Eco-management and audit scheme (EMAS)[27] and the European Environment agency (EEA).[28] EMAS could help companies measure their environmental performance. The Commission is language with respect to the EEA is very cautious. This is quite surprising. The EEA is indeed controversial particularly because a number of Member Sates suggested, in the early 1990s, that the EEA should adopt the role of "enforcer" of Community environmental law, a suggestion that was rejected outright by other Member States. However, the collection, dissemination, and interpretation of data would seem to fall precisely within the EEA's jurisdiction.

All voluntary agreements have to be transparent and public.[29] The Commission suggests that voluntary agreements should be published either in the Official Journal of the Communities or in an equally accessible medium. A central register ought to serve as a central database for all agreements. Again, the EEA could take this role. The Commission also suggests that

---

[24] See, e.g., Article 5 of the Flemish Decree.

[25] This is stated explicitly in Article 4(1) of the Flemish Decree.

[26] In Article 10 of the Flemish Decree, each agreement itself determines specific provisions with respect to monitoring and control. Article 11 provides that each party to the agreement must report annually to the Flemish Parliament.

[27] Council Regulation 1836/93 of 29 June 1993 allowing voluntary participation by companies in the industrial sector in a Community eco-management and audit scheme, OJ [1993] L168/1.

[28] Regulation 933/1999 amending Regulation (EEC) No. 1210/90 on the establishment of the European Environment Agency and the European environment information and observation network, OJ [1999] L117/1.

[29] Article 6 of the Flemish Decree provides for publication of both the draft and the final version of the agreement.

the Community should consider amending the Directive on access to environmental information,[30] in order to oblige the enterprises or organisations that are a party to the agreement to grant access to all information that could be relevant in the context of the agreement to any individual. This suggestion is put forward with little elaboration; if it were to be pursued, however, it would most certainly rustle a few feathers.

The *independent verification of results*, the Commission argues, may be appropriate in certain cases, particularly where the measuring methods differ (because of the lack of Community harmonization) or where the disclosure of business secrets has to be avoided. However, the Commission does not anticipate that Community legislation would be introduced for this purpose. Instead, the Commission sees independent verification as a responsibility of the parties to the agreement.

The Commission is vague when it comes to setting out *measures to ensure the effective implementation of the agreement*. In addition to the possibility of enforcing agreements through the courts or arbitration, the Commission mentions the following:[31] fines and penalties in the case of non-compliance;[32] amendments to the relevant permits, when they come up for renewal or in the event of non-compliance with the agreement; and the determination of the authorities to introduce regulatory measures if agreements fail to reach the set target.

3.3.2 Formal Conditions

As to the form of the agreements, the Commission enumerates a number of what it calls "general provisions" which need to be included in all agreements.[33]

(1) There must be an express indication of the parties to the environmental agreement. Where business associations are involved, it should be indicated whether they act on behalf of their members or on their own authority.

(2) It has to be made clear who does what to achieve the objectives. For instance, where business associations are party to the agreement, it is necessary to clearly distinguish between their own obligations and the obligations of their members.

(3) The agreement has to provide a definition of the most important terms, especially technical terms, taking into account existing definitions in relevant legislation.

(4) Third parties, including those who are not members of a business or trade association, should have thes right to join. The conditions and procedure for adherence should therefore be defined.

(5) The duration of the environmental agreement must be indicated.

---

[30] Directive 90/313 on the freedom of access to information on the environment, OJ [1990] L158/56.
[31] Commission Communication, supra note 1, at 14.
[32] Under Article 10(2) of the Flemish Decree, each party has the right to force others to comply with the provisions of the agreement.
[33] Commission Communication, note 1, at 14 et seq.

(6)   A revision of the environmental agreement must be possible so that new findings, adaptations to technical progress, or changed market conditions can be taken into account.[34]

(7)   Unilateral termination of a binding agreement must be allowed by either party in response to non-compliance. Industry may also be allowed to revoke its commitment if, contrary to the common understanding when the agreement was concluded, additional regulatory measures or taxes directly relating to the subject of the agreement are introduced.

(8)   The agreement must specify a dispute settlement procedure.

3.3.3   *Compatibility with the EC Treaty*

Environmental agreements must comply with the EC Treaty and its derived legislation. The relevant areas of law include the creation of the internal market, EC competition law, and rules regarding permissible state aid.

3.3.3.1   INTERNAL MARKET

First, a voluntary agreement may not hinder the provisions with respect to the internal market, in particular the EC Treaty Articles with respect to the free movement of goods, i.e., Articles 28–30 (formerly Articles 30–36). If an agreement hinders the free movement of goods, it must be justified under the conditions of Article 30 or the so-called rule of reason. Moreover, if an agreement includes product standards or other technical specifications, the Commission must be notified. Other Member States are then given the opportunity to inform the State concerned of any objections they may have.[35]

All trading rules enacted by Member States that are capable of hindering, either directly or indirectly, actually or potentially, intra-Community trade constitute measures having an effect equivalent to quantitative restrictions within the meaning of Article 28 (previously Article 30).[36] Hence, the effect of a national measure and not its aim is determinative for the application of Article 28.[37] Generally, one can distinguish between three types of measures which fall under Article 28.[38] First, formally discriminatory measures, such as those which discriminate prima facie against imports; second, measures amounting to material or de facto discrimination, such as those which do not

---

[34]   See, e.g., Article 8(3) of the Flemish Decree.

[35]   Directive 98/34 of 22 June 1998 laying down a procedure for the provision of information in the field of technical standards and regulations, OJ [1998] L204/37.

[36]   See Judgment of the Court of 11 July 1974 in Case 8/74, *Procureur du Roi v. Benoit and Gustave Dassonville*, ECR [1974] 837, at 5. Where pre-Amsterdam judgments of the ECJ are quoted, reference will be made to the old numbering: Articles 30–36. The Treaty of Amsterdam replaced Articles 30–36 with Articles 28–30.

[37]   See D. Geradin, "Trade and Environmental Protection: Community Harmonization and National Environmental Standards," in A. Barav, and D. Wyatt, *Yearbook of European Law—1993* (Clarendon Press, Oxford, 1994), p. 153, citing P. Oliver, "Measures Having Equivalent Effect: A Reappraisal" Common M L Rev [1982] 223.

[38]   See D. Geradin, *Trade and the Environment—A Comparative Study of EC And US Law* (Cambridge University Press, 1997), p. 10. See also K. Lenaerts, "L'égalité de Traitement en Droit Communautaire" *Cahiers de Droit Européen* [1991] 3–41.

formally discriminate against imports but in practice have a discriminatory effect;[39] and third, measures which do not discriminate prima facie nor in their effect, but which nevertheless have a trade-restrictive effect.[40]

When Member States introduce measures restricting the free movement of goods, the policy goal of those measures needs to fall within the exceptions of Article 30 or the "rule of reason," further discussed below. Moreover, the ECJ will appraise whether these measures serve the policy goal sought and whether the means are proportionate to the end. Finally, the measures must not arbitrarily discriminate against or amount to a disguised restriction of trade.

According to the principle of proportionality, the ECJ first decides whether the regulatory measure truly serves the stated policy goal.[41] For instance, an absolute import ban on certain goods that harm human health when taken in very high doses is very effective when trying to protect the health of a Member State's citizens.

Second, the measures need to be proportionate to the objective to be attained. The ECJ assesses whether there are other means reasonably available to the Member State that would equally efficiently serve the objective without infringing to the same extent on the free movement of goods.[42] For example, one might avoid having to introduce an absolute import prohibition by using adequate labelling and relying on the consumer's common sense.[43]

The proportionality test is influenced by the degree of Community harmonization present in the policy field concerned. The less common or harmonized rules governing the policy measures concerned, the greater the Member State's discretion to define the policy objective and select the means to attain it.

To benefit from the exceptions provided for in Article 30, a national provision must not constitute a means of arbitrary discrimination against or a

---

[39] The classic example is the imposition of product standards to which national products all or nearly all conform (e.g., because of traditional manufacturing processes) and that imported products universally fail.

[40] Typically, the introduction of new product standards or other requirements, for which national production does not have the kind of historic advantages as in the situation described supra note 39, but that—because, for example, of geographic circumstances (transport and distance) or the duty and related costs of having to adhere to a variety of national standards— impose a heavier burden on foreign manufacturers.

[41] See e.g., Judgment of the Court of 25 July 1991 in Joined Cases C-1/90 and C-176/90, *Aragonesa de Publicidad Exterior SA and Publiva SAE v. Departamento de Sanidad y Seguridad Social de la Generalitat de Cataluña* [1991] ECR I-4151, at 14, et seq.

[42] See e.g., Judgment of the Court of 13 July 1994 in Case C-131/93, *Commission v. Germany*, [1994] ECR I-3303, at 18 (national measures restricting intra-Community trade cannot be covered by the derogation provided for in Article 30 if the policy aim may be achieved just as effectively by measures having less restrictive effects on intra-Community trade) See also Somsen, H., [1995] Eur Env L Rev 214–217; Judgment of the Court of 13 July 1994 in Case 124/81, *Commission v. UK* [1983] ECR 203, at 16: "can the same result be achieved by means of less restrictive measures?".

[43] Examples of this approach are abundant in the foodstuffs sector, for protection of the consumer. For a typical application, see Judgment of the Court of 11 May 1989 in Case 76/86, *Commission v. Germany* [1989] ECR 1021, and judgment concerning the German *Rheinheitsgebot*, Judgment of the Court of 12 March 1987 in Case 178/84, *Commission v. Germany* [1987] ECR 1227.

disguised restriction on trade between Member States. Once necessity and proportionality have been established, this condition is not normally an insurmountable hurdle. The function of the second sentence of Article 30 is to prevent restrictions on trade on the grounds mentioned in the first sentence from being diverted from their proper purpose and used to discriminate against goods originating in other Member States or indirectly to protect certain national products.[44]

Trading rules constitute a means of arbitrary discrimination whenever they discriminate between national products and imported products on grounds which are neither objective nor justified.[45] Any decision by the Court as to whether this is the case is somewhat arbitrary,[46] and the ECJ therefore tries to link its decisions as much as possible to scientific evidence, procedural requirements, and factual circumstances. "Common sense" also enjoys a high ranking in this assessment. Importantly, the Community has not adopted a "likeness" test of economic interchangeability.

Trading rules may indicate a disguised restriction on intra-Community trade when the restrictive effect of the rules on trade is not limited to what is necessary to protect the interests referred to by the rules. The necessity and the proportionality tests apply here as well. However, just because measures are proportional does not mean that they are ipso facto not a disguised means for restricting trade. The disguised restriction test refers to abuse of the Article 30 exceptions,[47] while the proportionality requirement focuses more on factual circumstances.

Generally, there is no magic formula to decide whether this extra "no disguised restriction" test is fulfilled. National legislation that does not distinguish between products based on their origin may be an indication that there is no disguised restriction,[48] but this is not conclusive.

Apart from the exceptions under Article 30, the ECJ has added the concession of the "rule of reason." This doctrine amounts to a recognition of the social reality in the Community and adopts a teleological interpretation of Article 28. The context of Article 28 leads one to conclude that the exceptions it enumerates provide an exhaustive list of interests which may justify an exemption from the free movement of goods restriction.[49] A few years

---

[44]   See, e.g., Judgment of the Court of 14 December 1979 in Case 34/79, *Regina v. Henn and Darby* [1979] ECR 3795, at 21.

[45]   See Van Gerven AG in his Opinion of 11 June 1991 in Joined Cases C-1/90 and C-176/90, *Aragonesa de Publicidad Exterior SA and Publiva SAE v. Departamento de Sanidad y Seguridad Social de la Generalitat de Cataluña* [1991] ECR I-4151, at 9, referring to Judgment of the Court of 8 July 1975 in Case 4/75, *Rewe-Zentralfinanz v. Landwirtschaftskammer* [1975] ECR 843, at 8.

[46]   See ibid.

[47]   See Opinion of Van Gerven AG of 18 May 1994 in Case C-131/93, *Commission v. Germany* [1994] ECR I-3303, at 17, in fine. If the "real aim" (see Judgment of the Court of 15 July 1982 in Case 40/82, *Commission v. United Kingdom* [1982] ECR 2793, at 37) of the national measures is not to enhance the policy goal included in Article 30, the measure will be struck down.

[48]   E.g., in Joined Cases C-1/90 and C-176/90, supra note 41, at 25.

[49]   See e.g., Judgment of the Court of 17 June 1981 in Case 113/80, *Commission v. Ireland* [1981] ECR 1625, at 7.

after the Community was set in place, the ECJ observed that a number of interests emerged that society looked upon as being of equal importance as those listed in Article 30. Their non-inclusion in Article 30, however, seemed to exclude all national measures aimed at protecting these interests.

The ECJ allowed non-discriminatory measures that aimed at protecting a number of "mandatory requirements" in the changing society. Environmental protection was recognised as one of these requirements. National measures concerning the environment are still subject to the necessity and the proportionality tests. The *Cassis de Dijon* case held that obstacles to movement of goods within the Community relating to the marketing of products must be accepted in so far as these provisions are necessary to satisfy mandatory requirements relating "in particular" to the effectiveness of fiscal supervision, the protection of public health, the fairness of commercial transactions, and the defence of the consumer.[50] The protection of the environment was later recognised as one of the Community's "essential objectives" which could justify a derogation from Article 28,[51] with the caveat that measures adopted to protect the environment must not "go beyond the inevitable restrictions which are justified by the pursuit of the objective of environmental protection."[52]

The rule of reason does not extend the scope of Article 30, but defines the limits of Article 28. When the rule of reason applies and its conditions are fulfilled, Article 28 does not apply at all.

Under the rule of reason, the measures taken must be "indistinctly applicable" in form and in substance to domestic producers and to producers from other Member States.[53] This principle remains the foremost implication of non-inclusion in the list of Article 30. Although the conditions governing the applicability of the *Cassis de Dijon* doctrine and of Article 30 are the same (i.e., absence of harmonization, examination of the criteria of necessity and proportionality, and prohibition of arbitrary discrimination against or disguised restriction on trade), the mandatory requirements under the rule of reason come into play only in the event of "indistinctly applicable" measures.

After and to the extent that a certain area of law has been harmonized, Member States no longer have recourse to Articles 30 and 28 types of

---

[50] See Judgment of the Court of 20 February 1979 in Case 120/78, *Rewe-Zentral AG v. Bundesmonopolverwaltung für Branntwein* [1979] ECR 649 at p. 662, at 8. See on the *Cassis de Dijon* principle (the product at issue): S. Weatherill and P. Beaumont, *EC Law* (Penguin, London, 1995), pp. 490 et seq.

[51] See Judgment of the Court of 7 February 1985 in Case 240/83, *Procureur de la République v. Association de Défense des Brûleurs d'Huiles Usagées* [1985] ECR 531. The insertion of a specific environmental heading in the Treaty, by the Single European Act, strengthened the case for environmental protection being a ground for derogation from the Treaty's economic principles and objectives.

[52] Ibid.

[53] Abundant case law supports this proposition, including Case 113/80, *Commission v. Ireland* [1981] ECR 1625, at 10; Case 6/81, *Industrie Diensten Groep v. Beele* [1982] ECR 707, at 7; Case 207/83, *Commission v. United Kingdom* [1985] ECR 1201, at 19–22; Joined Cases C-1/90 and C-176/90, supra note 41, at 13.

arguments that would restrict the free movement of goods.[54] The interests that are protected in these Articles are then presumed to have been taken into account in the harmonizing Directives.[55] Provision does however have to be made for the so-called "environmental guarantee" included in Articles 95 and 176 of the EC Treaty, which will not be discussed here.

In summary, voluntary environmental agreements with governmental authorities are often likely to restrict the free movement of goods. Abundant case law of the ECJ with respect to this fundamental freedom has recognised environmental protection as one of the general interests that may override free movement. One must consult this case-law, to assess the legality of each voluntary environmental agreement individually.

3.3.3.2   EC COMPETITION LAW

Further, voluntary environmental agreements must not be incompatible with EC competition law. This issue is extensively dealt with elsewhere in this collection.[56] The freedom of contractual cooperate is limited by the requirement to maintain effective competition. Environmental agreements on the one hand present a number of classic concerns for EC competition law, such as firms negotiating with each other on topics that will inevitably influence their common future strategy and information sharing and effective cooperation among firms. On the other hand, the positive influence of such agreements on environmental protection, suggests that they may deserve to be exempt from the normal working of EC competition law. Both the EC Treaty (Article 81(3)) and Commission case law provide room to take these considerations into account, but this subject is beyond the scope of this chapter.

3.3.3.3   RULES ON STATE AID

EC law on state aid is also relevant. Where financial contributions from public authorities or other benefits such as tax exemptions or a redistribution of revenues from levies are part of a voluntary agreement, compliance with Article 87 of the Treaty (previously Article 92) has to be ensured. To this effect, the Commission has issued guidelines specifically for the environmental sector.[57]

EC rules on state aid center around Article 87 (previously Article 92), which provides that

(1)   Save as otherwise provided in This Treaty, any aid granted by a Member State or through State resources in any form whatsoever which distorts or threatens to distort competition by favouring certain undertakings or the

---

[54]   See P. Slot, "Harmonisation" [1996] Eur L Rev 382.
[55]   See Judgment of the Court of 10 July 1984 in Case 72/83, *Campus Oil Limited and others v. Minister for Industry and Energy and Others* [1984] ECR 2727, at 27, 49: "Recourse to Article 36 is no longer justified if Community rules provide for the necessary measures to ensure protection of the interests set out in that Article."
[56]   See the chapter by Hans Vedder in this book.
[57]   For more details G.Van Calster, "State Aid for Environmental Protection: Has the EC Shut the Door?" *Environmental Taxation & Accounting*, 1997, No. 3, 38–51.

production of certain goods shall, in so far as it affects trade between Member States, be incompatible with the common market.

(2) The following shall be compatible with the common market:
  (a) aid having a social character, granted to individual consumers, provided that such aid is without discrimination related to the origin of the products concerned;
  (b) aid to make good the damage caused by natural disasters or exceptional occurrences;
  (c) ...[and aid relating to the division of Germany].

(3) The following may be considered to be compatible with the common market:
  (a) aid to promote the economic development of areas where the standard of living is abnormally low or where there is serious underemployment;
  (b) aid to promote the execution of an important project of common European interest or to remedy a serious disturbance in the economy of a Member State;
  (c) aid to facilitate the development of certain economic activities or of certain economic areas, where such aid does not adversely affect trading conditions to an extent contrary to the common interest ...;
  (d) aid to promote culture and heritage conservation ...;
  (e) such other categories of aid as may be specified by decision of the Council acting by a qualified majority on a proposal from the Commission.

Community guidelines on state aid for environmental protection adopted in 1994 aim to inform Member States of the policy that will be pursued by the Commission with regard to this specific kind of aid.[58] State aid in the environmental sector is of course subject to all standard state aid regulation, and the 1994 Guidelines are merely meant to set out the Commission's policy in this specific area. The "normal procedures" include notification requirements, and a de minimis level below which state aid is presumed not to have an effect on the Common Market.[59] The application of Article 87 has been reorganized following a double initiative of the Commission. The first initiative formalizes the communications, guidelines and notices that the Commission has used to communicate its policy with respect to state aid in specific areas, including environmental aid. The Commission's discretion in individual cases, however, remains.[60] The second initiative is procedural.[61]

The first policy instrument of the Commission on state aid for environmental protection dates back to 6 November 1974.[62] The initial view of the Community toward state aid was that its use had to be a transitional stage,

---

[58] OJ [1994] C72/3.

[59] See Commission Decision of February 1990, OJ [1990] C40/2; amended by the Communication of 2 July 1992, OJ [1992] C213/10 and by the notification to the Member States of March 1996, OJ [1996] C68/9.

[60] Regulation 994/98 of 7 May 1998 on the application of Articles 92 and 93 (now 87 and 88) of the EC Treaty to certain categories of horizontal aid, OJ [1998] L142/1.

[61] Regulation 659/1999, OJ [1999] L83/1.

[62] See letter from the Commission to the Member States S/74/30807 from 7 November 1974, with the Communication from the Commission to the Member States from 6 November 1974 in annex.

paving the way for the gradual introduction of the "polluter pays" principle. State aid in this area was to disappear gradually, because it would
prevent an effective, long-term Community environmental policy. During a
transitional period, existing firms were permitted to adapt themselves with
Member State support to Community and national environmental regulations if such regulation imposed an extraordinary financial burden on the
firms. However, both the Fifth Action Program and the 1994 Guidelines, as
well as subsequent practice, would seem to indicate that state aid for environmental protection is now more widely seen as one of the "new" instruments of environmental policy, and an instrument that is here to stay. The
rules on state aid are in this respect correctly seen as a safeguard against
abuse. Despite the cautious language in the introductory part of the
guidelines,[63] the Commission leaves the door open for conditional, non-
discriminatory policies in the Member States to speed up environmental
protection through the provision of governmental incentives.

The heading in the Commission's 1994 Guidelines under which voluntary agreements would fit best is the one that refers to aid to encourage
firms to improve on mandatory environmental standards. Such aid is
authorized up to 30 percent gross of the eligible costs, provided that (1) the
investment allows significantly higher levels of environmental protection to
be attained than those required by mandatory standards, and (2) the level
of aid actually granted is proportional to the improvement of the environment achieved. For Community and national mandatory standards that
apply to the same measure of environmental protection, the stricter one
applies to evaluate the improvement achieved. When a project partly
involves adaptation to standards and partly improvement on standards, the
eligible costs belonging to each category are separated and the relevant
limit applied. The Member State must provide the Commission with convincing figures that mandatory environmental standards will effectively
be met and improved upon significantly. In the absence of mandatory
standards, the same rules as for the aid encouraging improvement apply.

Tax relief, reductions in charges, and various tax benefits are subject to the
Guidelines in the same way as direct financial support.[64] Specific issues include the determination of the extent of the tax benefit and compliance with
the EC rules on tax discrimination under Article 90 (previously Article 95).

3.3.4   Compatibility with WTO Rules

The Commission also emphasises that Member States must not disregard
the rules of the World Trade Organization relating to free trade in goods and
technical barriers to trade.[65] It refers in particular to the principle of non-discriminatory national treatment of GATT Article III, which requires imported
goods to be treated in the same way as domestically produced goods, and
to the requirement that technical specifications for products, whether
mandatory "technical regulations" or merely non-mandatory "standards,"

---

[63]   In the Commission's words: "Aids are not encouraged; aids are a second-best solution."
[64]   For details, see W. De Wit [1997] *Nationale Milieubelastingen en Het E.G.-Verdrag*, 360–415.
[65]   Commission Communication, supra note 1, at 17.

must comply with the rules governing consultation and non-discrimination in the WTO Agreement on Technical Barriers to Trade. The provisions of the Agreement on Subsidies and Countervailing Measures, designed to discourage, inter alia, subsidies which favor the use of domestically produced goods or which subsidise exports, may also be relevant. An extended treatment of international trade law, however, is out of the scope of this chapter.

4   ENVIRONMENTAL AGREEMENTS TO IMPLEMENT CERTAIN PROVISIONS OF COMMUNITY DIRECTIVES

Community Directives were designed to be a flexible instrument for the implementation of Community law. Directives are binding as to the results to be achieved, but leave to the national authorities the choice of form and methods. The only reference in the Treaty to voluntary agreements as a means of implementation, is in the agreement on social policy,[66] which explicitly refers to agreements between management and labor as a means of implementing Directives adopted in that field.

It follows from the binding nature of Directives that Member States need to ensure their full and timely transposition and application. The crucial consideration in reviewing the implementation of Directives, is whether the corresponding national measures guarantee legal certainty and effective implementation. Moreover, when Directives intend to create rights and obligations for individuals, the transposing acts need binding force and appropriate publicity.[67]

What does this mean for voluntary agreements in environmental policy? When Directives intend to create rights and obligations for individuals, it is generally not possible to implement the relevant provisions through voluntary agreements because Member States will not be in a position to ensure that these provisions are applicable to everyone.[68] On the other hand, when a provision of a Directive provides for setting up general programs or for general targets, the full achievement of the set objectives or targets does not necessarily require regulatory action. For such provisions, binding voluntary environmental agreements would be an appropriate and adequate implementation tool. They contain undertakings given by the public authorities and may therefore constitute an appropriate implementation measure for Member States to fulfil their obligations under Community Directives.[69]

---

[66]   OJ [1992] C224/127.
[67]   Commission Communication, supra note 1 at 18. Established case law of the ECJ is to the same effect. See, e.g., Case 29/84, *Commission v. Germany* [1985] ECR 1661.
[68]   Commission Communication, ibid.
[69]   Ibid., referring to Case C-225/93, *Commission v. France* [1994] ECR 4949. Directive 85/339/EEC on containers of liquids for human consumption required Member States to draw up programmes for reducing the tonnage and the volume of such containers. The French authorities had concluded agreements with the relevant industry circles in order to establish such reduction programmes. The Court of Justice found that these agreements contained undertakings by the authorities and could therefore, in principle, be considered as programmes for the purpose of that Directive.

The Commission asserts that in some cases, the Community legislator may provide that Member States may chose to reach the objectives either through environmental agreements or through national legislation.[70] It gives the example of a Directive that provides for setting limit values in order to achieve a defined reduction in emissions of certain substances. Member States could be allowed to achieve these targets through agreements rather than through limit values. This approach, the Commission argues, is particularly appropriate in view of agreements put in place by a Member State prior to the adoption of a Directive. However, the Commission takes the view that the Community legislator should restrict this possibility to clearly defined circumstances and make it subject to expressly stated and verifiable conditions in order to ensure legal certainty and efficient enforcement of Community Directives throughout the Community. In other words, the Commission believes very strongly that voluntary agreements can never be a general tool of implementation for environmental Directives.

Also according to the Commission, the requirement of legal certainty normally implies that, when used, environmental agreements are combined with the transposition of a Directive by national legislation. The transposing legislation could exempt parties to a voluntary agreement from the relevant provisions, as long as they comply with the terms of the agreement. Such a legislatory fallback provides an effective basis to prevent free-rider profits and also a guarantee for compliance with Community legislation. The Commission argues that providing for such a legislative fall-back should not be too cumbersome: "[S]ince the implementation of all provisions of a Directive will require national legislation, the fall-back legislation can easily be adopted together with the transposition of the Directive."[71]

Obviously, when Directives allow for implementation by voluntary agreements, the usual procedures apply, including the duty of Member States to ensure that the agreement is concluded in a timely fashion, i.e., before the implementation date, and the reporting duties of the Member States with respect to required information.

5 ENVIRONMENTAL AGREEMENTS AT THE COMMUNITY LEVEL

5.1 Considerations in the Communication

The Commission does not oppose the use of environmental agreements at the European level in principle. It does warn against high expectations. The crucial reason for the Commission's caution is the lack of an established track record of negotiations between government and industry throughout

---

[70] Commission Communication, supra note 1, at 18.
[71] Ibid.

Europe. Not all sectors of industry in Europe are represented by some form of an association. Such associations, however, are identified by the Commission as the only possible partners in negotiations for pan-European agreements.

There are a number of sectors for which the Commission sees the potential for EC-wide environmental agreements, namely, those areas that are suited for comprehensive, long-term objectives or that may act as a transitory complement to an economic instrument. In particular, the Commission names the following sectors as promising in this repect: the reduction of CO_2 emissions from passenger cars, the reduction of SO_2 and NO_x emissions from electricity suppliers, and the reduction of energy losses in the stand-by phases of electronic devices such as televisions and video-recorders.[72] These topics are by no means exhaustive, as they seem to be limited to topics that were current at the time the Communication was adopted.

The Commission also considers it necessary to base non-binding agreements on objectives already endorsed by the Community institutions, for instance through the Fifth Action Program, Parliament and Council resolutions, or international conventions. It considers these instruments to be proof of "the institutional balance,"[73] a guarantee for equitable results, and providing industry with an element of stability. Where Council and Parliament have confirmed clear policy objectives and the Commission has negotiated how to best implement these objectives, additional regulatory measures in the same field are unlikely to be necessary.[74]

5.2 Conditions—Form and Contents

As regards environmental agreements at Community level, the aforementioned criteria and requirements apply, the only exception being the contractual form.

5.3 The Impact of the Principle of Subsidiarity

One consideration may prove crucial for the conclusion of voluntary agreements at the Community level, namely, the principle of subsidiarity. This issue is not addressed in the Commission Communication, but, in our view, it merits special attention.

Voluntary agreements will only be possible when the Community is in principle competent to deal with the problem at issue. In determining whether the Community is competent to act in a given sector, the principle of "subsidiarity" is paramount. Originating in papal doctrine, the principle of subsidiarity essentially means that power has to be exercised at the level where it achieves the most added value. In the context of the division of

---

[72] Ibid., at 21.
[73] Ibid.
[74] Ibid.

powers (or "competencies" in Euro jargon) within the European Community, the principle of subsidiarity acts as a kind of consitutional check: the Community can only regulate or otherwise act if and to the extent that such regulation is of added value compared to action by the Member States.

Article 5 EC of the EC Treaty (previously Article 3b), which contains the principle, reads:

The Community shall act within the limits of the powers conferred upon it by this Treaty and of the objectives assigned to it therein. In areas which do not fall within its exclusive competence, the Community shall take action, in accordance with the principle of subsidiarity, only if and insofar as the objectives of the proposed action cannot be sufficiently achieved by the Member States and can therefore, by reason of the scale or effects of the proposed action, be better achieved by the Community. Any action by the Community shall not go beyond what is necessary to achieve the objectives of this Treaty.

In view of the confusion that had arisen with respect to this principle, the Treaty of Amsterdam added a Protocol to the Treaty.[75] This Protocol reads, in relevant part:

The High Contracting Parties ... have agreed on the following provisions which shall be annexed to the Treaty establishing the European Community:

(1) In exercising the powers conferred on it, each institution shall ensure that the principle of subsidiarity is complied with. It shall also ensure compliance with the principle of proportionality, according to which any action by the Community shall not go beyond what is necessary to achieve the objectives of the Treaty.

(2) The application of the principles of subsidiarity and proportionality shall respect the general provisions and the objectives of the Treaty, particularly as regards the maintaining in full of the *acquis communautaire* and the institutional balance; it shall not affect the principles developed by the Court of Justice regarding the relationship between national and Community law, and it should take into account Article F(4) of the Treaty on European Union, according to which "the Union shall provide itself with the means necessary to attain its objectives and carry through its policies."

(3) ... The criteria referred to in the second paragraph of Article 3b of the Treaty shall relate to areas for which the Community does not have exclusive competence ... .

(4) For any proposed Community legislation, the reasons on which it is based shall be stated with a view to justifying its compliance with the principles of subsidiarity and proportionality; the reasons for concluding that a Community objective can be better achieved by the Community must be substantiated by qualitative or, wherever possible, quantitative indicators.

(5) For Community action to be justified, both aspects of the subsidiarity principle shall be met: the objectives of the proposed action cannot be sufficiently achieved by Member States' action in the framework of their national constitutional system and can therefore be better achieved by action on the part of the Community.

---

[75] OJ [1997] C340/105.

The following guidelines should be used in examining whether the afore-mentioned condition is fulfilled:

—the issue under consideration has transnational aspects which cannot be satisfactorily regulated by action by Member States;

—actions by Member States alone or lack of Community action would conflict with the requirements of the Treaty (such as the need to correct distortion of competition or avoid disguised restrictions on trade or strengthen economic and social cohesion) or would otherwise significantly damage Member States' interests;

—action at Community level would produce clear benefits by reason of its scale or effects compared with action at the level of the Member States.

(6)   … Other things being equal, directives should be preferred to regulations and framework directives to detailed measures …

(9)   Without prejudice to its right of initiative, the Commission should:

—except in cases of particular urgency or confidentiality, consult widely before proposing legislation and, wherever appropriate, publish consultation documents; …

The subsidiarity principle and its application have resulted in a string of opinions and academic articles.[76] Here, we point to those elements in the Protocol which are of particular relevance for environment policy. The limitation of the principle of subsidiarity to non-exclusive EC competencies is imposed by Article 5. These competencies include the area of environment policy.

The Protocol reaffirms the kind of specific motivation which is needed as to the subsidiarity argument. The Community (in practice, the Commission) is supposed to substantiate the reasons for concluding that a Community objective can be better achieved by the Community, through qualitative or, wherever possible, quantitative indicators.

In a related development, DG XI (i.e., the Directorate-General with responsibilities for the environment, now officially called "the Environment DG") has been looking at ways to introduce economic analysis into its Proposals. In the wake of a continuing battle with DG III, responsible for industry, DG XI is hoping that by introducing a detailed economic breakdown of its Proposals, industry might oppose fewer of its new initiatives. Calculating the costs and benefits of environmental legislation is a difficult undertaking. Although the economic costs of a regulatory Proposal might be more or less foreseeable, the environmental benefits are often more difficult to ascertain, as are the environmental costs of not regulating. In addition, though calculating the costs of environmental legislation might

---

[76] See L. Brinkhorst, "Subsidiarity and European Community Environment Policy" [1993] Eur Env L Rev, 16–24; G. Cross, "Subsidiarity and the Environment" in A. Barav and D. Wyatt, *Yearbook of European Law* (Clarendon Press, Oxford, 1996), pp. 107–134; K. Lenaerts, "The Principle of Subsidiarity and the Environment in the European Union: Keeping the Balance of Federalism" in F. Abraham, K. Deketelaere, J. Stuijck (eds), *Recent Economic and Legal Developments in European Environmental Policy* (Leuven University Press, 1995), pp. 11–48; K. Lenaerts and P. Van Ypersele, "Le Principe de Subsidiarité et son Contexte: Etude de L'article 3B du Traité CE" [1994] *Cahiers de Droit Européen* 3–85; P. Van Nuffel, "Gebruiksaanwijzing Voor Subsidiariteit—Een Bijsluiter Bij de Eerste Toepassing Door Het Hof van Justitie", [1997–1998] *Rechtskundig Weekblad* 273–297; P.W. Wils, "Subsidiarity and EC environmental policy: taking people's concerns seriously," [1994] J En L, 85–91.

be necessary to improve relations between DG XI and DG III, OECD studies suggest that the cost factor of environmental legislation is not a predominant factor in the investment choices made by industry.

The Protocol clarifies the relationship between the two elements which Article 5 mentions as part of the subsidiarity principle. For Community action to be justified, both aspects of the subsidiarity principle have to be met: the objectives of the proposed action cannot be sufficiently achieved by a Member State's action in the framework of their national constitutional system *and* it can be better achieved by action on the part of the Community. Article 5 adds to the latter part of the exercise "by reason of the scale or effect of the proposed action." The Protocol includes this element in guidelines which should be used in examining whether the conditions are fulfilled.

(1) The subsidiarity argument denying regulatory authority to the community may not apply when the issue under consideration has transnational aspects which cannot be satisfactorily regulated by Member States. One has to be careful not to claim this is always the case in environmental matters. Environmental issues are not necessarily transnational. Environmental resources such as air and water certainly have transnational potential. This is not the case, however, for say noise regulation, spatial planning, and a significant part of household waste management.

(2) The subsidiarity argument does not apply when actions by Member States alone or a failure of the Community to act would conflict with the requirements of the Treaty (such as the need to correct distortion of competition, avoid disguised restrictions on trade, strengthen economic and social cohesion) or would otherwise significantly damage Member States' interests. This would seem to provide a basis for most EC environmental legislation. It was used as the legal basis for EC environmental policy prior to the introduction of an environment chapter in the Treaty, and it remains an essential part of the Commission's rationale, for regulation in areas such as waste management, emission standards, and environmental liability.

(3) The subsidiarity argument also does not disqualify action at Community level when it would produce clear benefits by reason of its scale or effects compared with action at the level of the Member States. This is probably true for most instances of international environmental policy that do otherwise fall under (1) above. Noise regulation may serve as an example for a type of problem not falling under (1), but under (3).

The Protocol states that Member States should, when possible, be given the freedom to enforce Community policy and regulation through the means they prefer, taking into account their traditions and legal systems. Directives are therefore generally preferable to regulations, and framework Directives are generally preferable to Directives giving detailed requirements. The Community's preference to work with Directives rather than Regulations in the environmental field is empirically confirmed. Environmental Regulations are very rare. The Protocol's suggestion to employ framework Directives rather than more detailed ones might be at odds with attempts to try to achieve a higher rate of implementation within the Community of Directives in general and environmental legislation in particular. The Commission singled out the widespread use of Directives as one of the obvious causes for delays in implementing Community environmental law. The relatively vague and open character of a substantial part of Community environmental legislation, combined with an increasing trend toward differentiated obligations, have contributed to significant delays in implementation of EC environmental law and policy.

Turning to the specific issue of voluntary agreements, industry itself sometimes claims that a problem is local in nature and can therefore be tackled by local initiatives, including voluntary agreements.[77] Arguably, however, a plethora of voluntary agreements at the national or local level would serve to revive the Community's competence. Because most of these agreements in one way or another include product regulations and because a wide variety of such agreements at the national or local level may endanger the objectives of the Internal Market, national and local voluntary agreements may give the Commission good reason to address the issues itself under good old Internal Market rationale.

Foreign competition is another consideration often raised by industry when the use of voluntary agreements is considered.[78] When a market in goods is characterized by a substantial level of imports, competitive considerations may force European manufacturers out of the market if an agreement leads to extra costs for the industry involved. This simultaneously prevents the environmental goal from being reached (assuming the imports do not posses the environmental qualities of the European products that comply with the obligations of the agreement). In such cases, the use of harmonizing legislation seems to be the only option.

6 CONCLUSIONS FROM THE COMMUNICATION

The Commission itself concludes that environmental agreements with industry have an important role to play within the mix of policy instruments sought by the Commission since the adoption of its Fifth Environmental Action Program.[79] However, the Communication failed to kick-start the use of voluntary agreements at the Community level, and the Commission remains skeptical of their use in implementing Community Directives. The Communication's Guidelines are mostly commonplace. For instance,

---

[77] See e.g., "Phosphate Review Splits Industry", December 1998 *European Voice* 10–16.
[78] See, e.g., the agreement with the car manufacturers, analysed below. See also "Proposal for a Directive on Energy Efficiency Requirements for Ballasts for Fluorescent Lighting," IP/99/435.
[79] "Taking into account the reactions to the Communication, the Commission will consider on a case by case basis whether environmental agreements are an appropriate instrument for the purpose of achieving environmental objectives ... .

the Commission mentions the tension between the Treaty Articles on competition and voluntary agreements, but it fails to set out a precise view of how it proposes to reconcile this tension.

The explanation for the Commission's reluctance to issue a more specific set of general guidelines most probably lies in its belief that all voluntary agreements ought to be case-specific, starting with the question of whether such an agreement is acceptable in a specific sector or with respect to specific Directives. Thus, the Commission can do nothing but communicate general observations.

The Council reiterated the conclusions of the Communication. Like the Commission, it emphasized that each agreement must be judged on its merits.[80] The Council noted that the Commission guidelines on how environmental agreements could be used to implement Community Directives needed more work. It also expressed its wish for a formal procedure of environmental agreements at the European level, which has yet to be agreed to. In short, the Council seems to regard the Commission's Communication to be more of a stock-taking exercise than a policy document.

Not surprisingly, the European Parliament also went along with the suggestion that environmental agreements may provide a useful tool to further environmental protection in specific cases. However, it firmly identified binding legislation as the backbone of the European Union's environmental policy.[81]

7   RECOMMENDATION OF 9 DECEMBER 1996 CONCERNING ENVIRONMENTAL AGREEMENTS IMPLEMENTING COMMUNITY DIRECTIVES

The Commission's Communication on the use of voluntary agreements generally was followed by a Recommendation of 9 December 1996 concerning Environmental Agreements Implementing Community Directives.[82] This text

---

—With respect to environmental agreements concluded at Member State level, the Commission, as guardian of the Treaty, will ensure their compliance with the Treaty and in particular internal market requirements and competition rules.

—Whenever regulatory action becomes necessary for the Community, the Commission will carefully consider whether certain provisions of these legislative measures will allow for implementation by binding environmental agreements and will include, if appropriate, such provisions in its proposals.

—The Commission addresses a Recommendation to the Member States which provides a clear framework for the use of environmental agreements as a means of implementing certain provisions of Community Directives.

—In recognizing environmental agreements at Community level, the Commission will ensure their transparency and credibility. It will therefore ask for quantified objectives, a staged approach, appropriate monitoring and reporting. The Commission will make such commitments public and report to the Council and the European Parliament on the results achieved." Commission Communication, supra note 1, at 22.

[80]   Council Resolution of 7 October 1997 on environmental agreements, OJ [1997] C321/6.

[81]   See Resolution on the Commission Communication, OJ [1997] C286/254.

[82]   OJ [1996] L333/59.

is also somewhat ambiguous. In its considerations, the recommendation refers to the need for a deepening and broadening of the range of instruments to *complement* legislation; it considers environmental agreements to be a policy instrument which can cost-effectively contribute to achieving environmental objectives by encouraging a pro-active approach from industry; and it suggests that environmental agreements might in certain circumstances complement legislation or replace otherwise more detailed legislation when they are used as a means for implementing certain provisions of directives. For the most part, the Commission's Recommendation recalls the conclusions of its Communication with respect to environmental agreements as a means of implementing Community Directives in the field of the environment:

Where provisions in Directives in the field of the environment explicitly allow for implementation by way of Environmental Agreements, Member States should observe the following guidelines.

... Agreements should in all cases
(a) take the form of a contract, enforceable either under civil or under public law;
(b) specify quantified objectives and indicate intermediary objectives with the corresponding deadlines;
(c) be published in the national Official Journal or as an official document equally accessible to the public;
(d) provide for the monitoring of the results achieved, for a regular reporting to the competent authorities and for appropriate information to the public;
(e) be open to all partners who wish to meet the conditions of the agreement.

... Agreements should, where appropriate,
(a) establish effective arrangements for the collection, evaluation and verification of the results achieved;
(b) require the participating companies to make available the information regarding the implementation of the agreement to any third person under the same conditions applying to public authorities under Council Directive 90/313/EEC of 7 June 1990 on the freedom of access to information on the environment...
(c) establish dissuasive sanctions such as fines, penalties or the withdrawal of a permit, in case of non-compliance.

... In concluding environmental agreements, the competent authority should make provision for examining the progress reached under the agreement and for taking additional measures in due time, if this is necessary to fulfil the obligations under the Directive.
... As a party to the agreement, the national authority should also ensure its compatibility with the Treaty and in particular with the Treaty's internal market requirements and competition rules and also with Directive 83/189/EEC.
... When used as a means of implementing Community directives, Environmental Agreements, together with all relevant information concerning them, should be notified to the Commission at the same time as other national measures taken to implement the directive, in order to allow verification of their effectiveness as a means of transposition.

8   ENVIRONMENTAL AGREEMENTS AND THE FIFTH ENVIRONMENTAL ACTION PROGRAM

As noted above, the Fifth Environmental Action Program emphasises that only by replacing the command-and-control approach with shared responsibility among governments, industry, and the public can commit to agreed measures to be achieved.[83] In January 1996, the Commission approved a progress report on the implementation of the Fifth Action Program.[84] It examines progress in relation to a number of key elements and trends within each of the five target sectors—agriculture, energy, manufacturing industry, transportation, and tourism—as well as international developments, widening the range of regulatory instruments, and the development of structures for shared responsibility. Based on the conclusions of this progress report, and on the updated State of the Environment Report published by the European Environment Agency in November 1995, the Commission adopted a draft Decision of the European Parliament and the Council on the Review of the Program in January 1996.[85] The draft Decision identified five priority areas in which Community action needed to be stepped up. These priority areas included the use of a wider range of policy instruments, including market-based instruments and "horizontal" instruments. Following legislative progress, the Commission issued amended proposals.[86] In July 1998, 30 months after the Commission first presented the proposal, the European parliament and the Council finally agreed in conciliation to the text of the Co-Decision on the Review of the Fifth Environment Action Program "Towards Sustainability."[87]

General policy instruments tend not to include much detail. The review of the Fifth Environmental Action Program therefore did not add much to the

---

[83]   For an assessment of the Fifth Environmental Action Program, see the Commission's website: <http://www.europa.eu.int/comm/dg11/actionpr.htm>

[84]   COM(95) 624.

[85]   OJ [1996] C140/5.

[86]   OJ [1997] C28/18.

[87]   OJ [1998] L275/1. "In relation to the development, at an appropriate level, of effective market-based and other economic instruments as a means of implementing policy, special attention will be given to:

    (a)   environmental accounting;

    (b)   examining constraints on the introduction of economic instruments and identifying possible solutions;

    (c)   the use of environmental charges;

    (d)   identifying subsidy schemes which adversely affect sustainable production and consumption practices with a view to their reform;

    (e)   encouraging the application of the concept of environmental liability at Member State level;

    (f)   voluntary agreements which pursue environmental objectives while respecting competition rules;

    (g)   encouraging the use of fiscal instruments to achieve environmental objectives, inter alia by considering possible legislative initiatives in this area during the course of the Programme and continuing the study of the potential wider benefits of such instruments, notably in the context of the general economic objectives of the Community, such as employment, competitiveness and growth." Ibid., at 6.

findings of the 1996 Communication of the Commission. However, the revised Environmental Action Program does indicate that the EU has not accomplished its stated goals to broaden the range of regulatory instruments, or to encourage Member States to do so. As a matter of policy, the jury is still out with respect to whether the EU is truly committed to moving in this direction.

9   OVERVIEW OF VOLUNTARY AGREEMENTS AT THE NATIONAL LEVEL

The 1996 Communication[88] includes an overview of voluntary agreements at the national level. We reproduce this overview as an Annex. The overview given by the Commission represents the situation in 1996. Over 200 of the 300 agreements concluded at the national level in 1996 had been agreed in The Netherlands and Germany, though practice seems to be picking up in other Member States, particularly in the waste sector.

In most Member States, voluntary agreements are not regulated by formal legislation. The Flemish Region of Belgium[89] seems to be a notable exception. Its legislation provides for specific consideration of most of the Commission's reservations and conditions expressed in its Communication. The Flemish decree of 15 June 1994 concerning environmental policy agreements[90] defines an environmental policy agreement as every agreement between the Flemish Region, represented by the Flemish Government, and one or more representative umbrella organizations of companies, with the goal to prevent environmental pollution, to limit or to avoid its con-sequences, or to promote sound environmental management.[91] An envi-ronmental policy agreement may not replace or be less stringent than prevailing legislation or regulations. During the valid period of the agreement, the Flemish Region commits itself not to issue more stringent regulations relating to the issues dealt with by the agreement. However, the Flemish Region remains competent to issue new regulations in cases of urgent necessity, or in order to meet international or European legal obligations. An environmental policy agreement is limited in time and may not extend for more than five years.

This decree has led to a number of agreements, all of them in the waste sector. It arguably includes all the Commission's precautions and conditions, even though the decree's enactment preceded the Commission's Communication of 1996. Practice in Flanders arguably reflects what may in the future come to be regarded as the European approach: the benefits of

---

[88]   See supra note 1.
[89]   In the federal structure of Belgium, environmental policy is the responsibility of the Flemish, Brussels, and Walloon Regions.
[90]   Belgian State Gazette, 8 July 1994. For an English version of this text see Title 7—Environmental covenants, in H. Bocken, and D. Ryckbost, *Codification of Environmental Law—Draft Decree on Environmental Policy* (prepared by the inter-university commission for the revision of environmental law in the Flemish Region) (Kluwer Law International, London, 1995), pp. 191–194.
[91]   For details, see G. Van Hoorick and C. Lambert, "Het Decreet Betreffende de Milieubeleidsovereenkomsten" *Tijdschrift voor Milieurecht* [1995] 1–10.

voluntary agreements are recognised, but its pitfalls lead to a cautious approach that results in the conclusion of agreements in certain specific sectors only. However, the authorities consult widely with the industry involved when considering legislation, and this would seem to ensure that industry's views are sufficiently taken into account.

As practice develops, the advantages and disadvantages of the use of environmental agreements should become clearer. Experience will show whether these agreements will effectively become a viable alternative for legislation, and whether they can be used effectively to enforce existing law.

10   THE AGREEMENT WITH EUROPE'S CAR MANUFACTURING INDUSTRY ON CO_2 EMISSIONS BY CARS[92]

The agreement between the Commission and the European car manufacturers is the leading example of a European-wide environmental agreement to date.

10.1   Genesis of the Agreement

The Kyoto Protocol to the United Nations Framework Convention on Climate Change includes targets for the reduction of CO_2 emissions. The EC has of course laid down a strategy to reduce these emissions. According to the Commission, 15 percent of these emission reductions can be contributed by reducing CO_2 emissions from passenger cars and improving fuel economy. The Commission decided that the major portion of these two targets could be met through an environmental agreement with the automotive industry.[93] Reaching the agreement with the car industry was part of an overall Community strategy to reduce CO_2 emissions from passenger cars which was proposed by the Commission in 1995.[94]

Negotiations started in September 1996 and were completed in June 1998. After an initial series of proposals by the European Automobile Manufacturers Association (ACEA), which were rejected by the Commission for not going far enough, a breakthrough occurred in March 1998. The automobile industry made an offer to commit itself to reduce the average CO_2 emissions of its new cars sold in the EU to 140 g/km by 2008.[95] The industry's proposal included the following main elements: 140 g/km by 2008 measured on the new test cycle, 120 g/km models to be available by the

---

[92]   We thank Chris Pickup of S J Berwin & Co's Brussels office for his research on this agreement.

[93]   See Commission Communication on an environmental agreement with the European automobile industry, COM(98) 495.

[94]   COM(95) 689.

[95]   This measurement corresponds to 6 l/100 km for petrol cars and 5.3 l/100 km for diesel cars.

year 2000, a review of the situation in 2002/2003 to evaluate the potential for further reductions by 2012, and formation of a Joint ACEA/Commission to monitor implementation of the agreement. However, the ACEA's offer also included conditions that no negative measures would be taken against diesel-fuelled cars and that improved fuels in particular with low sulphur content would be made fully available by 2005. The latter restriction required the adoption of strict measures with respect to petrol production, which were the subject of negotiations within the framework of the Auto-Oil Program discussed below in section XI of this chapter. The ACEA also assumed that importers would make equivalent commitments and that the major car-manufacturing countries would adopt similar policies.

The Commission carefully welcomed ACEA's move.[96] It was under strong pressure from environmental ministers to either conclude a far-reaching deal with the industry before June 1998 or propose stricter legislation itself.

The Council then accepted the ACEA's proposal, but only as a basis for future negotiations. It requested the Commission to continue discussions with the industry to clarify details of the proposal, particularly with respect to the following: including intermediate targets, monitoring progress towards meeting the targets, clarification of the ACEA's assumption "that the main car manufacturing countries implement similar policies," and explanation of how non-ACEA manufacturers and importers would be included.

The Council asked the Commission to report on these and other matters before the Environment Council in June.[97] The European Parliament was told that it would be briefed on progress, though the Council did not say to what extent and how it would be done. The EP had consistently been critical of the negotiation.

In June 1998, the ACEA issued what became the basis of the final agreement. It contained a commitment to a CO_2 emission limit of $140 \, g/km$ for 2008. The Commission immediately pronounced it acceptable. Among other things, the new proposal included an intermediate goal, which both the Commission and the Council had called for. The text put forward an estimate that ACEA could reach an average CO_2 emission figure of 165 to 170 g/km by 2003. The proposal still included a number of assumptions concerning the availability of fuels of a certain quality, the competitive position of European car manufacturers compared with non-ACEA manufacturers, the market penetration of fuel-efficient engine technologies, and the inclusion of new vehicle concepts.[98]

Since new fuel quality specifications were the subject of the conciliation procedure between the Council and the EP in the Auto-Oil Program (discussed below), the Commission believed it had to wait for the outcome of this procedure before making a final decision on an agreement with the ACEA. The ACEA also insisted that, especially for the improvement of environmental fuel standards, an agreement with the Commission was crucial.[99]

---

[96]   IP/98/234.
[97]   2076th Council meeting—*Environment*—23 March 1998, 6894/98 (Presse 78).
[98]   IP/98/499.
[99]   *European Voice*, 28 May–3 June 1998.

In June 1998, the final agreement was reached. The ACEA will reduce CO_2 emissions to 140 g/km by 2008.[100] ACEA also committed itself to a review in 2003. Although the agreement ends with the meeting of its aims (140 g/km by 2008), the potential exists for additional CO_2 emission reductions by 2012.

This agreement was endorsed by the Council in October 1998. The debate in the Council centred upon the need to ensure that the agreement is not a licence to pollute. Some delegations suggested that the Commission ought to prepare a draft directive to assure realization of the agreement. Should it become clear that industry would not meet its target, then the Community's legal institutions would be able to act swiftly. The Commission, however, strongly opposed such parallel legislation. It argued that the forbearance of regulatory action was essential to getting the industry to agree to the strict limits. The Council finally decided that the Commission should assess the need to develop legislation in 2003, when the agreement will be reviewed.

Ministers also emphasized that the agreement with the car industry is only one element in the climate change strategy which the EU has to pursue in order to meet its Kyoto Protocol commitments. In this connection, the Council noted that manufacturers that are not members of the ACEA are not bound by the agreement. Non-EU manufacturers are likewise not covered.[101]

The ACEA's main commitment under the agreement is the reduction of the average CO_2 emission figure of 140 g/km by 2008 for all new cars sold in the EU, according to the EU's test procedure.[102] To be sure, the commitment does not relate to each individual car: the members of ACEA should collectively achieve a CO_2 emission target of 140 g/km, as an average of their new cars sold in the Community. Non-emitting cars (i.e., those using alternative fuels) will count as a contribution towards this objective. The intermediate target of 165 to 170 g/km by 2003 has eased the European Parliament's worries, and a review at this time will decide whether the ACEA has carried out this reduction, effectively, thus preserving the threat of potential legislation if the terms of the agreement are not met.

The Commission accepted that external factors could affect the ACEA's ability to honor its commitments. The agreement is therefore linked to a number of assumptions, such as the availability of appropriate fuels and the ability to develop new fuel-efficient technologies. The most important of these assumptions, however, is that non-European manufacturers, especially Japanese and Korean automobile manufacturers, could be persuaded by the EU to adopt similar policies.

The discussions between the EU and the Japanese and Korean car industries were complex. The Council has endorsed the voluntary agreements that the Commission eventually reached with the Korean and Japanese car manufacturers.[103] The Koreans and Japanese have made commitments to

---

[100] This compares with the Community's general objective of 120g/km by 2010. See Commission Recommendation of 5 February 1999 on the reduction of CO2 emissions from passenger cars, OJ [1999] L40/49.

[101] 2121st Council meeting—Environment—Luxembourg, 6 October 1998, PRES/98/323; EIS Europe Environment, 20 October 1998.

[102] See Commission Directive 93/116, OJ [1993] L329/39.

[103] 2207th Council—Environment—12 October 1999, Presse 299.

cut back CO_2 emissions from passenger cars similar to those agreed by European manufacturers. The agreement has also cleared EC competition rules.[104]

10.2 Legal Form

The automobile agreement on CO_2 emissions with the EU Institutions eventually took the form of a Commission Recommendation addressed to the ACEA, which endorses the ACEA's commitments under the agreement.[105] The Recommendation does not include a commitment by the EU to refrain from introducing legislation unless the ACEA fails to live up to its commitments (even though this is part of the understanding). A similar route was adopted when the Commission endorsed commitments by the Association of Detergent and Cleaning Product Industries in the Community. This commitment concerned "good environmental practice" for household laundry detergents, including the total amount of energy used per wash cycle, reduction of consumption, advertising, and biodegradable organic ingredients.[106]

There is a more formal, legalistic side to the agreement, however. The Commission explicitly exempts the automobile agreement on CO_2 emissions from the EC's competition rules. The Commission reasoned that industry's commitment does not impose a target on individual manufacturers, but only an overall average target for all ACEA members. Car manufacturers will develop and introduce new CO_2 efficient technologies independently and in competition with one another.[107]

10.3 Assessment of the Agreement

Does the agreement with ACEA present the advantages which the Commission presented in its 1996 Communication (set out above), including the indentified "advantages" of active involvement of the industry cost-effectiveness, or the fast achievement of environmental objectives?

First, the agreement most definitely involves the car manufacturers actively in the shaping of the agreement. However, industry was arguably just as deeply involved in the legislation that arose out of the Auto-Oil Program discussed next, even though that program resulted in legislation rather than in a voluntary agreement.

Second, with respect to cost-effectiveness, the agreement includes little detail on what type of technologies should be devised to reach the targets. Industry is left very much to itself to develop these technologies. We do not

---

[104] IP/99/922 (1 December 1999).
[105] See Commission Communication of 29 July 1998, "Implementing the Community Strategy to Reduce CO_2 Emissions from Cars: an Environmental Agreement with the European Automobile Industry," COM(98) 495.
[106] Commission recommendation of 22 July 1998 concerning good environmental practice for household laundry detergents, OJ [1998] L215/73.
[107] IP/98/865.

see any reason why standard legislation could not have followed the same route.

Third, the agreement took only two years to be finalized, which is faster than comparable legislation. However, before the agreement actually kicked in, a similar agreement with the Japanese and Korean manufacturers was required. Work on those issues took additional time. One would arguably have to add this delay to the time frame of the agreement, even though the European industry should already have been working on improving its standards in the interim.

In summary, we conclude that the automobile agreement on CO_2 emissions shows that in certain specific sectors, negotiations with industry can indeed lead to favorable results, even at the European level. However, we can see no reason why the legislative process itself cannot be improved to offer these advantages as well. The truth most probably lies somewhere in the middle. Voluntary agreements may present advantages in a number of sectors, but they cannot serve as the *deus ex machina* policy makers had hoped for when environmental policy started to stumble in the early 1990s.

11 THE AUTO-OIL PROGRAM: THE THIN LINE BETWEEN "VOLUNTARY" AND "REGULATORY"

European institutions have traditionally adopted an open attitude towards lobbying by interest groups, including representatives of industry. This is not just a reflection of a general attitude of European administration. It is also explained by pure necessity. The number of civil servants working for the European Union in Brussels is now close to 20,000. This is still less than, for example, the French Ministry for Agriculture. Of these 20,000 civil servants, only about one-fourth operate at A-level and are responsible for developing policy. In practice, this means that very often only one civil servant is responsible for one particular policy issue. As a result, EU officials tend to warmly welcome any input from interested parties who have expertise in the matter.

Consultation with industry and nonprofit organizations is widespread in the environmental sector. The Auto-Oil Program is a prime example in this respect. Even though the final text of the program was adopted in the Council, and thus subject to traditional Community diplomacy (including trade-offs based on national preferences), industry's voice was preponderate throughout the process. It makes one wonder whether it would really have made a difference if the initiative had taken the route of a voluntary agreement rather than legislation.

11.1 Genesis of the Legislation

The legislation that resulted from the so-called Auto-Oil Program does not amount to a voluntary agreement. It is straightforward legislation. Nevertheless, the lobbying undertaken to influence the legislation, and the origins of the regulations, show clearly that even where no voluntary agreement *sensu stricto* is negotiated, the voice of industry in shaping EU environmental policy can remain very important and powerful.

In September 1996, the Commission presented its Proposals with respect to the control of atmospheric emissions. The Proposals were the result of the so-called Auto-Oil Program, which began at the end of 1992 and brought together the Commission and industry representatives to identify the problems with the aim of lowering atmospheric pollution and to suggest possible solutions.

The key elements of the Auto-Oil Program, were as follows. First, it sought to fill the gap of existing knowledge by carrying out extensive vehicle emission tests. Second, air quality was monitored in representative European cities (Athens, Cologne, The Hague, London, Lyon, Madrid, and Milan). Based on the outcome of the monitoring operation, the Commission set air quality standards. These standards were also influenced by, among other things, the emissions limits set by the World Health Organization.

The outcome of the Auto-Oil Program was criticized by the motor industry when they realized that the bulk of the costs would fall on them. In response, the Commission proposed to set up a second Auto-Oil Program to address fuel quality.[108]

Two legislative Proposals were a direct outcome of the second Auto-Oil Program.[109] The Proposal to amend Directive 93/12 relating to the quality of gasoline and diesel fuels was not very ambitious.[110] The limits set in fact reflected the then existing current market situation. The second Proposal amended Directives 70/156[111] and 70/220[112] with respect to air pollution by emissions from motor vehicles. Emission standards for passenger cars would be tightened. Passenger cars would have to be equipped with technology to monitor emission performance and to indicate malfunctions to the driver (so-called "on board diagnostics"). It is the second Proposal that alarmed the motor industry. Fierce lobbying to amend the Commission Proposals resulted.

First on the lobbying list was the European Parliament. Successive changes to the European Treaty have given the EP a larger influence in environmental legislation. In general, the EP was unhappy with the Auto-Oil Program. Many Members of the EP felt that the Program had departed from its intended function as an information gathering exercise and evolved into a lobbying operation that lacked transparency and accountability.[113] The EP hosted a meeting with the Commission and with the trade associations of the industry to prepare for the EP's first reading of the text of the proposals.[114]

---

[108]   See The ENDS-Report, May and June 1996.
[109]   COM(96) 248.
[110]   OJ [1993] L74/81.
[111]   OJ [1970] L42/1.
[112]   OJ [1970] L76/1.
[113]   *European Voice*, 14–20 November 1996.
[114]   Ibid.

The meeting was polarized. The car industry claimed that improving the quality of fuels would have an immediate effect on the environment. The oil industry argued for scrapping end-of-life vehicles and renewing the fleet, better vehicle inspection systems, traffic management programs, and improvement in energy efficiency.[115] The position of the EP remained unclear. Although it appeared that the EP wanted stricter emission standards than those proposed by the Commission, it remained unclear whether it shared the car industry's view that fuel quality should also be addressed more urgently.

The EP voted on the measures in May 1997. With respect to *fuel standards*, it demanded radically lower limits on the sulphur content of gasoline and diesel fuel beginning in 2000. It also proposed that two grades of diesel should be marketed beginning in 2000: a grade with a very low sulphur content and a transitional grade with a higher sulphur content that would be prohibited by 2005. The *car emission limits* proposed by the EP were more stringent for nitrogen oxides and particulates from diesel cars and for hydrocarbon emissions from gasoline vehicles. In addition, the EP proposed a number of measures such as allowing fiscal incentives aimed at encouraging people to meet the standards set prior to their effective entry into force.[116]

The Commission indicated that it would not include many of the amendments by the EP in its Proposal to the Council. The Council had to act by unanimity if it wished to adopt the EP's amendments at this stage, and this was not likely. Commentators suggested that the EP's tough stance was an initial bargaining position giving scope for compromise in later conciliation talks between the EP and the Council.[117]

The Council reached its first formal agreement in July 1997 (adopting it formally in October 1997.)[118] It included specifications on the composition of gasoline and diesel fuels, to be reached by the year 2000, as well as indicative values for objectives to be attained by 2005. (The latter figures were to be confirmed by the Commission before 30 June 1999.) The sale of leaded gasoline would be completely prohibited by 2000 (this element has remained almost unchanged). Exceptions could be made for old-timers. Moreover, Member States could ask for an extension of this prohibition until 2005 if they could prove that a total ban would cause serious socio-economic problems or would not result in any environmental or health benefit due, for example, to the country's climate conditions. The agreement also included emission limit values for carbon monoxide, hydrocarbons, nitrogen oxide, and combinations of these pollutants. The emission limits were to take effect on 1 January 2000.[119] The EP reacted unenthusiastically. It considered the proposals to be too lax. Industry, not surprisingly, considered them to be too stringent.[120]

---

[115] *EIS Europe Environment*, 3 December 1996.
[116] *Environment Watch Western Europe*, 18 April 1997; *EIS Europe Environment*, 22 April 1997.
[117] *European Voice*, 3–9 April 1997; *Financial Times*, 10 April 1997.
[118] *EIS Europe Environment*, 14 October 1997; *Communication à la Presse* 9132/97 (Presse 204).
[119] *EIS Europe Environment*, 24 June 1997.
[120] *EIS Europe Environment*, 8 July 1997.

In February 1998, the Environment Committee of the EP adopted a report. First, in EP tradition, the Committee argued for stricter standards for unleaded gasoline and diesel beginning in 2000. Second, the Committee agreed with the Council's Proposal to allow for exemptions for southern Member States in particular.[121] In March, the EP in plenary session voted to follow the advice of its *Rapporteurs* and rejected the Council's common position.[122]

In April 1998, the Commission published a report that was not specifically concerned with the Auto-Oil Program but serves as a reminder of its importance. The report gave an overview of the proposed, planned, and existing Community measures to combat the CO_2 emissions of from transportation. The overview was intended to assist the Council and the Commission in defining its strategy for the implementation of the Kyoto Protocol. CO_2 emissions from transportation currently make up 26 percent of overall emissions. The Commission's report set out a policy that should cut the increase in CO_2 emissions in half by 2010. The proposed measures focused on four areas: action on passenger car fuel economy, progress with fair and efficient pricing in transportation, completion of the internal market in rail transportation, and measures to integrate various modes of transportation and develop intermodal transport systems.[123]

The Commission's report did not introduce any new measures. It reminded the Member States and industry that the Commission would actively pursue progress in areas such as the Auto-Oil Program and the creation of a more environment focused price structure in the transportation sector.

Meanwhile, as the Council discovered that not all of the changes proposed by the EP would be supported by the Member States,[124] the proposals regarding the Auto-Oil Program went into so-called "conciliation talks." This is a step in the legislative procedure whereby Parliament and Council together try to trash out an agreement. Agreement was finally reached in June. The conciliation centred around the following elements.

(1) With respect to *emissions from passenger cars*, the core of the agreement is that the EP agreed to accept the limit values on emissions to be applied beginning in 2000 and 2005, respectively, which reflected the Council's common position. In return, the Council accepted mandatory standards (instead of "indicative" ones) to apply beginning in 2005.

(2) Similarly, with respect to *emissions from light vans*, the Council accepted mandatory standards for light vans beginning in 2005. In return, the EP accepted the limit values for 2000 and 2005, respectively, as reflected in the Council's common position.

---

[121] *European Voice*, 12–18 February 1998; *EIS Europe Environment*, 10 February 1998.
[122] EP Decision A4-0038/98 and A4-0044/98.
[123] IP/98/307; COM(1998) 204.
[124] 2094th Council Meeting—Internal Market—8528/98 (Presse 148).

(3) Finally, as to the *quality of gasoline and diesel fuels,* the EP accepted the limit values set by the Council for the year 2000 as well as the Council's position that 2005 limit values (other than for sulphur and aromatics) should be set through the Auto-Oil II process. In return, the Council accepted that its 2005 indicative standards would be mandatory. Member States may, however, in certain circumstances, seek extensions for the 2005 standards until 2007. The Commission stated that when it comes to considering such requests, it will ensure that any extension is compatible with EU law, including competition law, taking into account the availability in the EU of sufficiently good quality fuels in adequate quantities.[125]

The EP did not manage to force the Council to take a clear position on the use of fiscal instruments to reach the goals of the Directives. The final agreement simply recalls that negotiations on an EU-wide minimum levy on energy products are in progress and that the Commission will monitor the implementation of the Auto-Oil legislation with a view to proposing amendments where needed.[126]

11.2 Appraisal

The outcome of the first leg of the Auto-Oil Program is important from two points of view. First, the environmental content of its texts will significantly reduce the emission of harmful substances by transportation and thereby help the EU reach its Kyoto commitments. Second, and with particular interest for the topic of this chapter, the procedure followed in the Auto-Oil Program is seen by many observers as a model for future environmental legislation, including the direct involvement of industry as a central feature. However, a number of elements of the procedure have also been criticized. They include the long delays (it took ten years from the initiation of the Program to its result) and the bypassing of the normal legislative process, that tended to exclude the EP in the preparatory stages of the legislation.

Immediately after the completion of the Auto-Oil Program, the Commission announced that it had started work on a Proposal to improve the transparency and institutional accountability of such negotiations in future. These include the "Auto-Oil II" Program, which is anticipated to include even tougher targets for road transportation, as well as other sectors such as factories and power stations.[127]

In our view, negotiations such as those within the Auto-Oil Program avoid some of the disadvantages of both the standard regulatory approach and of voluntary agreements.

---

[125] 2106th Council meeting—Environment—Luxembourg, 16–17 June 1998.
[126] *EIS Europe Environment,* 7 July 1998.
[127] *European Voice,* 4–10 June 1998.

12 CONCLUSION

Quid leges sine moribus. Industry and some academics have opposed the preponderant reliance of the EC's environmental policy on standard regulatory action, claiming that one cannot substantially improve our environment if one of the principal actors, industry, does not go along voluntarily. Looking at the policy documents issued by the Commission, and given the Commission's reluctance to let the Member States implement EC environmental legislation through voluntary agreements (with exception of the waste sector), it is clear that the Commission does not really believe voluntary agreements will be a major tool of environmental policy in the EU. The Council is at most lukewarm towards the use of agreements in most sectors, and the EP is outrightly hostile.

It would seem, therefore, that the EU Institutions rely more on the convincing force of *leges* to change *mores*. This may in the future make the compatibility of *national* environmental agreements, whether or not in implementation of Community law, more important than the use of voluntary agreements at the European level. From the perspective of the policy documents of the European Commission and the Council, there are strong indications that the EC policy on voluntary agreements has not met with plenty of enthusiasm.

First and foremost, the 1996 Communication does not indicate any kind of enthusiasm for such agreements. Furthermore, within the EC's legal framework, there are a number of legal obstacles to the widespread use of voluntary agreements both at the national and the EC level. At the national level, voluntary agreements cannot be used to implement Community legislation, if the EC legislation confers rights and obligations upon individuals or the use of voluntary agreements as an implementation measure has not been specifically authorized. In addition, Article 81 (on competition), Article 87 (on state aid) and Articles 28–30 (on the free movement of goods) impose a number of limitations to voluntary agreements, requiring specialized lawyers to check them for compatibility with EC law. At the EC level, the Commission requires industry to have a degree of EC representativeness before it will sit down to negotiations. The subsidiarity principle may bode further limitations in the future.

Despite the apparent absence of widespread potential for the use of voluntary agreements in EC environmental policy, we do not believe that this means that the advantages of such agreements are not being realized in the EC. Industry's participation in shaping EC environmental policy is considerable whether in voluntary agreements in the automobile sector or legislative initiatives in the same sector.

Finally, the increasing involvement of European industry in molding actual environmental legislation raises the important question of whether the environmental and consumer lobby is involved to a similar degree. The chapter hopes to kick-off further research in this area.

ANNEX—THE USE OF ENVIRONMENTAL AGREEMENTS AT THE NATIONAL LEVEL—AS OF 1996*

I Belgium

In all, 14 agreements have been concluded in Belgium since the late 1980s concerning the reuse, recovery and recycling of waste (packaging and household), the phasing out of CFC (aerosol, refrigerators, plastics) and the substitution of polluting substances in products such as batteries. Two sectoral agreements ("accords de branche") have been concluded in order to reduce emissions from the electricity suppliers (SO_2 and NO_x, satisfactorily implementing Directive 88/609/EEC on large combustion plants) and the furnaces for smelting glass.

Since the competence in this field is shared between the federal state and the regions, this sectoral agreement is signed by the federal state together with the three regions. The regions also entered into regional agreements: The Brussels Capital Region (Ministry of the Environment) has established with commercial offices agreements regarding the sorting, recycling and recovery of office waste. In the Walloon Region, agreements concern the preservation of natural resources and the reduction of solid waste. Flanders had made negative experience with agreements which lacked binding character. On 15 June 1994, the Flemish Parliament therefore adopted the decree concerning the environmental policy agreements which is of public order. According to Article 2 of the decree of 15 June 1994, an environmental policy agreement is every agreement between the Flemish Region, represented by the Flemish Government on the one hand, and one or more representative umbrella organizations of companies on the other, with the goal to prevent environmental pollution, to limit or to take away the consequences of it or to promote a more effective environmental management. An environmental policy agreement can not replace, or be less stringent than, the prevailing legislation or regulations. During the validity period of the environmental policy agreement, the Flemish Region can not issue regulations, by means of execution decisions, which are, relating to the topics dealt with by the environmental policy agreement, more stringent than this last one. However, the Flemish Region remains competent to issue regulations, either in case of urgent necessity, or in order to fulfil compelling obligations of an international or European legal nature. An environmental policy agreement is closed for a certain period, which in no case can be longer than five years. No agreement has yet been concluded pursuant to this decree, although a few are now in preparation in the framework of the Flemish waste policy where environmental agreements serve as an (temporarily) alternative for take-back-obligations.

Source: The European Commission, 1996 [COM(96) 561, OJ [1996] L333/69].

II Denmark

In Denmark, sixteen voluntary environmental agreements have been concluded since 1987, relating to energy saving, waste management (e.g., controlled recycling or disposal of refrigerants containing chlorofluorocarbons (CFC) and hydrochlorofluorocarbons (HCFC), fire protection equipment, batteries, packaging, tires), the phasing out of specific substances (e.g., organic solvents used in paints and varnishes, volatile organic compounds, PVC, heavy carbon hydrates in diesel) and the clean-up of contaminated sites. Current initiatives also relate to waste management (electronics, vehicles, demolition waste). Parties to the agreements are usually the Minister for Environment and Energy or the Danish Environmental Protection Agency and the industry sectors concerned (companies or their organizations). The agreements generally take the form of a declaration of intend or an action plan, which are not legally binding but which the parties perceive as being binding. A main feature of agreements concluded in Denmark is their combination with economic incentives such as tax reductions or with deposit funds.

The Environmental Protection Act of 1991 introduced the possibility for the Minister of the Environment to make agreements with enterprises or associations thereof to meet national targets for pollution-reduction. The Minister can also lay down rules on the basis of which agreements are made and on general agreements terms including penalties for delaying or otherwise violating the agreement. The Minister is also empowered to lay down requirements similar to those of the agreements for enterprises not covered by the agreement, i.e., he can react to "free-riders." Before implementing such an agreement, it shall be negotiated with the most relevant national trade and environment organizations, with organizations of local authorities and with other state authorities involved. The first agreement concluded on the basis of the Environmental Protection Act in April 1996 relates to the collection and recovery of lead accumulators. Another agreement on electric and electronic waste is in preparation.

III Germany

In Germany, industry has issued about 80 self-commitments in the field of the environment since the late 1970's. They mainly cover waste management (e.g., batteries, paper, packaging, end of life vehicles), the phasing out of specific substances (asbestos, CFC in a number of appliances, certain substances in detergents), discharges of dangerous substances into the water (ammonium, safety concept for chemical installations) and CO_2 emissions (fuel consumption from cars and a variety of industry sectors). Bavaria has recently concluded a formal agreement with industry, trade and commerce associations, covering a range of general issues such as participation of companies in the eco-management and audit scheme, waste reduction, energy efficiency and an increased use of railways as a means of transportation.

With the exception of the latter agreement, public authorities are not formally involved in these commitments which take the form of unilateral declarations. However, these declarations are often the outcome of intensive discussions with the competent ministries (environment, economic affairs) and recognized in an informal way, for instance a press release or a press conference of the ministry concerned. Virtually all of them contain reporting requirements of industry.

The use of such informal agreements has recently attracted more attention, the discretion of the parties as to the design of the commitments being limited, however, by the Law against restraints of competition. A number of commitments have been issued in 1996 (end of life vehicles, chemical industry, paper industry and editors). The commitment of industry to reduce CO_2 emissions, undertaken in view of the 1995 Berlin Climate Conference, has recently been extended and clarified (more participants, unequivocal objective, independent evaluation of results). Eighty percent of the energy consumption by the German industry is covered by this revised commitment.

The latter commitment as well as the Bavarian agreement seem to indicate a shift to a more formal and public approach in Germany.

IV   Spain

To date, a total of 6 agreements has been established in Spain. Numerous agreements are currently under discussion, and it appears as though they will gain importance in meeting environmental goals.

The agreements concluded by the Ministry of Public Works, Transportation and Environment (MOPTMA) relate to the phase-out of chlorofluorocarbons in aerosols (by the year 1989) and to waste management. The latter agreements aim at facilitating the implementation of the Ministry's National Master Plan for Waste Management and Disposal; industry and regional Governments at each Autonomous Community must implement the plan at a regional basis; Municipalities are the final responsible for waste collection, treatment and disposal. Financing at each administrative level is included.

Recent agreements relate to end-of-life vehicles and used tires. A waste management levy on new tire sales is to raise money for the collection, recycling and disposal of tires. Current initiatives concern electric and electronic equipment, 12 types of equipment where agreements could be used have been identified. Other areas (solvents, chlorine products, paints, construction wastes) are also being considered.

Direct reference to the use of agreements has also been made in the Royal Decree 484/1995 on waste water regulation and control. Recognizing the deficit in industrial waste water treatment and control, the new regulation empowers watershed authorities (Confederaciones Hidrográficas) to negotiate and conclude with industrial associations sectorial plans for waste water control. The Decree also includes a provision of financial aid to industries to facilitate reaching these goals.

In its Strategy for Energy and Environment, 1995–2000, the Ministry of Industry and Energy has identified agreements as one of the tools to meet environmental goals at short and medium terms. These agreements will aim at creating a framework to encourage environmental investments so as to promote environmental retrofitting of industries. Enforcement of existing regulations will not be restricted by these agreements. Several financing programs for industry environmental retrofitting (PITMA, PAE) recognize agreements between Industry and Public Authorities as the preferred way to obtain financial contributions.

V France

France appears to be the first Member State to have concluded an agreement in the field of environmental protection: an "accord de branche" was concluded between Ministry of Environment and the cement sector in August 1971. The agreement established a time-table for taking corrective actions through a sector-wide program for existing facilities (program de branche). New facilities were required to meet emissions standards.

About twenty agreements were issued for the major polluting industrial sectors in the ensuing decade. These agreements had different functions and names (e.g., contrat de branche, program de branche, contrat d'entreprise, program d'entreprise, plans sectoriels anti-pollution). A limiting factor are legal requirements protecting the authority of the State and third party rights. For instance, the Administrative Court (Conseil d'Etat) ruled that a facility contract from 1975 between the Ministry for the environment and a paper manufacturer was illegal because it restricted the State's authority and the required protection of third parties. Ultimately, most of the early agreements served as a basis for developing national legislation and emission standards which replaced them.

Recent agreements relate to packaging waste and end-of-life vehicles. About ten agreements concerning CO_2 emissions from industrial sectors (smelting, chemical, paper, welding, glass, plaster, sugar, cement) are being prepared, a corresponding agreement with the aluminium sector has recently been signed.

VI Greece

At present, there are no environmental agreements in Greece. The general assessment of public authorities and industry seems to be that regulatory measures are necessary and sufficient for the protection of the environment. However, because agreements may succeed in fostering partnership between industry and public authorities, some representatives of industry start appreciating the potentials of agreements.

VII Ireland

In Ireland, agreements usually take the form of business "initiatives" welcomed but not signed by the Irish Government. An agreement on packaging waste, called REPAK, was signed in February 1996 by the department of the environment and business associations (Irish Business and Employers Confederation as well as the associations of retail grocers, soft drinks and beer bottlers, plastic industries, food drink and tobacco, and wine and spirits).

The latter agreement was initiated in 1994, when the Department of the Environment published a recycling strategy, including targets for the recycling of waste such as packaging, beverage containers, composting. The strategy document went on to invite industry to propose agreements.

The Irish Business and Employers Confederation (IBEC) set up an industry task force which reported back to the Minister in December 1995 and proposed REPAK, as one element in their response. The Society of the Irish Motor Industry is currently drafting an agreement on car batteries. Other possible target sectors for future agreements include waste newspaper, detergents, pharmaceutical and chemical manufacturing.

The Waste Management Bill, which was adopted in mid-1996, gives the Minister wide powers to specify how packaging might be recycled, how it should be marked, how refund systems might work and what collection mechanisms might be required. By signing up to REPAK, industry avoids such prescriptive rules, because the Act allows the minister to approve an agreement which exempts participants from other requirements.

VIII   Italy

Eleven agreements have so far been concluded in Italy, both at federal and at regional level. In the late 1980's, the Ministry of Environment and the Fiat group exchanged a letter of intend concerning air pollution and noise reduction in the metropolitan areas. Following this initiative, a protocol "Environment and Development" was concluded, covering not only the depollution of metropolitan areas but also waste reduction, the development of non-polluting vehicles and environmental research programs.

In the waste sector, "REPLASTIC," which started as a voluntary consortium before becoming compulsory, deals with the separate collection, sorting out and reuse of plastic liquid containers. The recovery of discarded lead batteries is the subject of an agreement signed in 1995 between the Ministry of Environment, the municipalities (ANCI—Associazione Nazionale Comuni d'Italia) and Federambiente (Federation of Public Services of Environmental Hygiene) on the one hand and industry associations on the other hand. Examples of agreements concluded at regional level regard the recovery of toner cartridges (Lombardia) and the collection of paper and cardboard.

IX   Luxemborg

Five agreements have been concluded in the field of the environment and energy. The first agreement, dealing with industrial waste, was introduced in 1989. An agreement on energy efficiency within the industrial sector has just been concluded (1996) and some more are to come up, involving banking, insurance, medical care and trade sectors.

Agreements in the waste management field were developed from the Directory Program of the Ministry of Environment and relate to construction waste, hazardous waste, packaging waste from beverages and industrial waste.

X   Netherlands

More than hundred agreements have been concluded in the Netherlands. They mainly cover waste management (e.g., packaging, recovery of asbestos, plastics), the reduction of emissions (e.g., volatile organic compounds, SO_2 and NO_x from electricity suppliers, ammoniac from livestock), clean-up of contaminated soil (petrol stations), energy saving or reduction strategies for industrial noise. Some of the agreements specify comprehensive programs for the integrated pollution control in various sectors of industry (base metals, chemical, print, dairy). Current initiatives relate, for instance, to the paper and cardboard industry. Usually, such written and signed agreements, used as a policy instrument and with public authorities as one party are summarized under the title covenant, although they can actually be entitled declaration of intend or code of conduct.

The general background for the increased use of covenants is provided by the National Environmental Policy Plan (NEEP) and the NEPP Plus, published in 1989 and 1990. These plans set out a strategy for achieving sustainable development by the year 2010. The plans establish quality objectives across a number of environmental issues and translate these into over 200 quantified targets. In this context, covenants represent a commitment by industry sectors to play their part in meeting the established environmental objectives. To date, declarations of intent set environmental objectives for 16 industry sectors, involving some 12,000 companies responsible for over 90 percent of industrial pollution in the Netherlands

While most of the first generation of covenants are not enforceable by law, more recent covenants take the form of a contract enforceable under civil law and are part of an overall strategy of the Government.

Although the procedure is not defined by law, covenants are usually concluded according to the following procedure: The competent Minister informs both Houses of the States General of his intention to conclude a covenant. An integrated target plans is established for the sector in question pursuant to negotiations between public authorities (including provincial and municipal government) and the industry sector (sometimes including employer's and trade unions). On the basis of this plan a covenant is drawn up at branch level if the sector uses similar processes allowing for a standardized approach. In heterogeneous sectors, company environmental plans are prepared in close co-operation with the licensing authority. Signed covenant are published in the Official Journal (Staatscourant).

The Ministry of Housing, Spatial Planning and the Environment has issued guidelines for the conclusion of covenants in the form of a code of conduct. An administrative direction, issued by the Prime Minister in December 1995, gives instructions on content and procedure of covenants in general.

XI   Austria

In Austria, some 25 agreements have been concluded since the early 1980's. Most of the agreements concern the recycling of waste (end of life vehicles, paper, tires, building material, car batteries, electronics, plastics, packaging), others aim at introducing vapour recovery units at petrol stations (to reduce hydrocarbons emissions) or at reducing the import of tropical timber. A particular voluntary agreement is the climate coalition founded in 1994. It primarily comprises municipalities and states commitments with respect to supply of public services and procurement, but is also open to industry.

Two types of agreements can be distinguished: Self-commitments by industry, where public authorities are not formally involved although the commitments are normally the outcome of intensive negotiation with the competent ministry, and agreements concluded between industry and government. Self-commitments are predominant.

Parties to the agreements are usually the competent ministry and the national industry association (Federal Economic Chamber) or national branch associations (subdivisions of the Federal Economic Chamber), in some cases also individual firms.

Almost all voluntary self-commitments and agreements have been concluded at national level.

XII   Portugal

Portugal's first experience with voluntary agreements dates from 1984 with the setting of targets on water discharges, air pollution and waste reduction from the pulp sector. In all, around 10 agreements have been reached, mainly relating to waste reduction and elimination of substances.

In 1994, the government has pursued the application of agreements through its publication of the Global Agreement Protocol on Environment and Sustainable Development. This document summarizes the Government's orientation towards environmental challenges faced, and outlines an approach towards achieving them.

Based on this protocol, the government has issued a framework for Sectorial Voluntary Agreements. This framework was derived through negotiations between the Ministries of Environment, Agriculture and Industry on the government side and several national and regional confederations of Portuguese agriculture and industry. The Sectoral Protocol requires Industry to develop an environmental plan for reaching compliance with environmental laws according to their particular situations. This plan must receive approval from the public authorities. The Government commits itself not to impose new environmental standards for the duration of the agreement. If new community regulations are issued, the government agrees to a phased imposition of these.

The Sectoral Protocol includes provisions for renegotiating the agreement in such a case, and for proposing specific measures if required after diagnosis studies. It also provides for the creation of a steering committee representing signatory parties in order to monitor whether objectives are met and, if necessary, to formulate new measures. It should also resolve problems as they are encountered—one anticipated problem is that some industrial facilities may lack an environmental permit. Agreements concluded in the framework of the Sectoral Protocol terminate by the end of 1999, provide for periodic governmental reporting and include free rider provisions.

XIII Finland

Agreements concern the phasing out of chlorofluorocarbons and the energy saving. The latter agreements are based on the Council of State Programs on Energy Conservation, which the government established in 1992 as part of its efforts to curb energy consumption. The main goal of these agreements is to diminish energy consumption 10–15 percent by 2005. A new program on energy conservation was presented in December 1995. This program promotes agreements which would support monitoring energy efficiency, the preparation of conservation plans, energy audits, investments in conservation, the introduction of new technologies, and mechanisms to provide consumers with information and guidance on their energy consumption.

Agreements are usually concluded between the competent ministry and business associations; two of the agreements relating to energy conservation have been concluded between the Ministry of Trade and Industry and local municipalities (the City of Helsinki and the Association of Finnish Local Authorities).

The Ministry of the Environment has recently (1995) concluded an agreement with the packaging industry. Negotiations regarding certain product groups (cars, tires, car batteries, electronics, household appliances) have been started in an overall strategy to proceed with voluntary agreements in waste management.

XIV Sweden

The thirteen agreements concluded in Sweden relate to waste management (car tires, construction products and materials, magazine paper and packaging materials), energy conservation (cars and individual companies), the phasing out of certain substances (lead in petrol and in paints), research and development (alternative fuels for vehicles) and the heavy metal contents of sludge from sewage treatment plants.

In practice, most agreements could be characterized as gentlemen's agreements or letters of intent by industry. Individual industries can not be held responsible if the industry organization which developed and administered the systems fails to achieve the targets. The failure of industry to meet a target would typically lead to the introduction of taxes, or to a sharing of the regulatory responsibilities with local municipalities instead.

Agreements in the energy sector have been made with individual companies and thus allow recourse to sanctions if industries fail to comply.

XV United Kingdom

The United Kingdom has used a wide range of voluntary approaches rather successfully, for instance in the form of Best Practice Programs relating to energy efficiency (e.g., Making a Corporate Commitment—"MACC"), environmental technology or producer responsibility initiatives or initiatives to encourage a dialogue between Government and business (e.g., advisory committee on business and the environment, local green business clubs).

Eight agreements have been concluded since the early seventies, relating to the storage and transportation of pesticides ("BASIS," its standards and certification of staff selling pesticides being formally recognised by the Control of Pesticides Regulation of 1986), the banning of certain substances in domestic and industrial washing products (alkyl phenol ethoxylates and for domestic use nitrilo tri-acetic acid), the collection of plastic film from farms and the use and the emissions of hydrofluorocarbons (HFCs). In order to reduce HFCs, which present an important alternative to chlorofluorocarbons (CFCs) but still have a high global warming potential, the British Government concluded in January 1996 three separate agreements and one declaration of intend with associations of the aerosol, air conditioning and refrigeration, fire protection and foam industries.

10. Competition Law and the Use of Environmental Agreements: The Experience in Europe, an Example for the United States?

*Hans H.B. Vedder**

1 INTRODUCTION

Agreements among businesses and business groups, whether or not they concern environmental issues, tend to be regarded critically by antitrust authorities. Early US experience with the automobile manufacturing industry in the so-called Smog case is a notorious example that may justify this critical attitude.[1] The critical attitude of the competition authorities is not always shared by the governments and academia.[2] The use of environmetal agreements as an environmental policy instrument is considered to have certain advantages over the use of traditional regulatory instruments. The European Commission, for example, has issued a recommendation indicating that it encourages self-regulation.[3] Furthermore, the European Commission is party to an environmental agreement with the European Car Manufacturers Association (ACEA).

*The author would like to thank professors Hanna G. Sevenster and Floris O.W. Vogelaar, both of the University of Amsterdam, for their valuable remarks. The author would also like to thank Mr. Franz Heistermann for his comments during the conference. Any remaining errors are the author's sole responsibility. Because of the deadline for submission the author was unable to take into account the Court's judgment in the *Sydhavens* case, infra note 91, of 23 May 2000 and the Commission decision in the CECED case, [2000] OJ L 187/47.
[1] This case concerned the agreement by the Automobile Manufacturers Association to cooperate on the research into the reduction of exhaust emissions. In the end, it was suspected that the real purpose of the agreement was to slow down the research. Because the case ended with a consent decree, it is unclear whether this was true. See *United States v. Automobile Manufacturers Association*, 307 F. Supp. 617 (C.D. Cal. 1969) and 1969 CCH Trade Regulation Reports, Nos. 45, 69 and 72, 907.
[2] Cf. see F. Vogelaar, "Towards an Improved Integration of EC Environmental Policy and EC Competition Policy: An Interim Report" in B. Hawk (ed.), *Annual Proceedings of the Fordham Corporate Law Institute 1994* (New York, 1995), p. 546.
[3] Commission Recommendation 96/733/EC, [1986] OJ L 333/59. See also Commission Communication on Environmental Agreements, COM (96) 561.

It is outside the scope of this chapter to compare the advantages and disadvantages of environmental agreements with those of regulatory instruments. Suffice it to say that several European governments as well as European Union institutions have expressed a preference for the use of environmental agreements. With this preference, it is also stated that such agreements should accord with the rules on competition. The ease with which this is stated belies the often complex problems that surface when environmental benefits are to be considered in the process of applying competition law. Competition law generally prohibits restrictions of competition, with some important exceptions, in order to attain certain objectives. The structure of the European anti-cartel provision, Article 81 of the EC Treaty, exemplifies this through its bifurcation in a prohibition clause and an exemption clause. Article 81 reads in relevant part:

(1) The following shall be prohibited as incompatible with the common market: all agreements between undertakings, decisions by associations of undertakings and concerted practices which may affect trade between Member States and which have as their object or effect the prevention, restriction or distortion of competition within the common market [...]
(3) The provisions of paragraph 1 may, however, be declared inapplicable in the case of: any agreement or category of agreements between undertakings; any decision or category of decisions by associations of undertakings; [...] any concerted practice or category of concerted practices, which contributes to improving the production or distribution of goods or to promoting technical or economic progress, while allowing consumers a fair share of the resulting benefit, and which does not: impose on the undertakings concerned restrictions which are not indispensable to the attainment of these objectives; [...] afford such undertakings the possibility of eliminating competition in respect of a substantial part of the products in question.[4]

In a similar fashion, most other modern competition laws balance the restrictions of competition with the advantages of certain forms of cooperation between undertakings. Extensive litigation and myriad academic works devoted to antitrust law show that striking this balance is often very difficult. If reaching a bilan economique proves difficult, how can a balance possibly be struck between the protection of the environment and competition? Should an agreement with an environmental objective pass the competitive test just because of its objective or should the environmental target of an agreement play no role at all in the competitive appraisal?

Apart from cartel law, environmental considerations may also play a role in the competition rules that apply to governments. Some Member States prefer the use of these agreements as instruments of environmental policy. This has led them to encourage the use of such agreements or to undertake measures to increase their effectiveness. This leads to another encounter with competition rules. Apart from the rules on the competition between business enterprises, EC competition law also concerns government influences on

---

[4]   The enumeration of restrictions of competition in the first paragraph as well as the second paragraph, declaring prohibited agreements to be void, have been omitted.

competition. One aspect of the latter group of competition rules[5] concerns government actions that diminish the *effet utile* or useful effect of the EC's competition rules for businesses.[6] Member States that encourage environmental agreements that restrict competition may violate this rule.

When a Member State decides to encourage the use of environmental agreements to solve environmental problems, it may consider this method as an alternative to the more traditional regulatory approach. Whereas national regulatory environmental measures are judged by their compatibility with the European rules on the free movement of goods,[7] Member State's environmental policy based on environmental agreements must comply with European competition rules. It is submitted that the two tests (i.e. the free movement and competition tests) should lead to the same outcome both materially and procedurally. This is called the seamless web approach.[8] This chapter considers whether this seamless web approach is actually followed in the EC.

This chapter also attempts to give some suggestions for competition policy regarding environmental agreements in the United States. The search for an integration of environmental concerns and competition law is taking place with respect to EC and Dutch competition law. Before attempting to answer these questions, however, it seems useful first to contemplate why and how environmental agreements came about in the first place and to understand their connection to competition law.

2 ENVIRONMENTAL AGREEMENTS: THE INTEGRATION PRINCIPLE AND THE POLLUTER PAYS PRINCIPLE

From an economic perspective, environmental pollution is the result of the fact that use of the environment constitutes external costs to the individual actor. Consequently, there is no incentive for any economically rational actor to limit its use of the environment. A cure to this problem is presented by the Polluter Pays Principle. According to this principle, the costs for the use of the environment are to be borne by the polluter, which then has an economic incentive to limit its use of the environment. This approach, however, is still very much utopian because environmentally friendly production methods and products remain much more expensive than their polluting counterparts. Moreover, traditional environmental policy instruments originate from a command-and-control philosophy by which environmental protection is to be achieved through the setting of standards.

---

[5] The others concern distortions of competition through state aids (Article 87 EC) and the granting of exclusive rights to certain business undertakings (Article 86 EC).
[6] Cases C-2/91, *Meng* [1993] ECR I-5751, C-245/91, *Ohra* [1993] ECR I-5851, C-185/91, *Reiff* [1995] ECR I-5801 and Case C-35/96, *Commission v. Italy* [1998] ECR I-3851.
[7] Article 28-30 EC (ex Article 30-36).
[8] This term was coined by L. Gyselen, "The Emerging Interface Between Competition Policy and Environmental Policy in the EC" in J. Cameron, et al. (eds), *Trade & the Environment: The Search for Balance* (William Gaunt & Sons, London, 1994), p. 245.

The principle that the polluter should pay plays only a minor role in command-and-control instruments.

As it gradually became clear that environmental protection through the use of command-and control instruments could only be achieved at high costs, a solution was proposed to actively involve the regulated entities (usually businesses) in the process of protecting the environment.[9] Only with this change in perspective did the implementation of the polluter pays principle become an end in itself.[10]

Because environmental costs are external costs, there is no reason for any economically rational actor to voluntarily internalize environmental costs. Because environmental benefits constitute an often intangible benefit to the whole society, and yet represent actual costs to the polluter wishing to improve its environmental performance, there is a strong incentive for individual economic actors to free ride.

Furthermore, the regulated enterprises themselves have realized that some of the costs flowing from compliance with environmental legislation can be reduced if the enactment of such legislation is prevented.[11] On many occasions an industry itself has tackled the environmental problems. Because economies of scale exist in environmental protection as well as other business activities, enterprises may want to cooperate in solving the environmental problems to reduce costs. To prevent free-rider problems and in order to achieve the benefits flowing from the economies of scale, businesses may enter agreements to cooperate that may entail some restriction of competition. These restrictions of competition bring the environmental agreements into possible conflict with competition law.

This brings us back to the questions above: Should environmental considerations play a role in competition law and, if so, what should this role be? For the EC, the answer to the first question is straightforward. The EC Treaty explicitly contains a provision stating that "environmental protection requirements must be integrated into the definition and implementation of the Community policies and activities…"[12] This provision can hardly be understood as other than requiring an integration of environmental concerns.[13] In the end, this is a political argument that is often criticized for leading to the "politicization" of competition law.[14] Irrespective of the precise scope of competition law and policy objectives, allegations of

---

[9] These costs may be economic (e.g., high enforcement costs) as well as ecological (e.g., limited compliance with standards and protracted procedures to adopt these standards).

[10] See, e.g., the European Community's Fifth Action Programme [1993] OJ C 138/1.

[11] As happened in the FKS-case, note 78 infra. A variation on this theme exists where legislation exists and prescribes an expensive environmental obligation that can be avoided by creating or joining a collective system as occurred in the DSD-case, note 41 infra.

[12] Article 6 EC. Before the Treaty of Amsterdam came into force, a comparable provision could be found in Article 130 R (2) EC.

[13] See J. Jans, *European Environmental Law* (Kluwer Law International, Den Haag, 1995), p. 25; M. Doherty, "Analysis of Cases C-284/95 and 341/95, Safety High-Tech and Bettati" (1999/2) J Envtl L 378 et seq.

[14] This "politicization" or "instrumentalization" (or, in German, *instrumentalisierung*) is based on the premise that the maintenance of a certain intensity or degree of competition is

politicization must be put into perspective. To ask whether or not environmental protection is included in the objectives of competition policy[15] implicitly follows from the traditionally perceived antagonism between competition and environmental protection. However, competition and environmental protection are not intrinsically opposed, just as environmental pollution is not immanent in competition but only follows from the fact that harm to the environment represents external costs. Indeed environmental concerns, when they are properly integrated into competition law, may not necessarily lead to any restriction of competition at all.

The inclusion of environmental concerns may actually intensify competition as a new field of economic activity is created where competition is possible. This is true for static conceptions of economic competition, but it is even more significant when dynamic aspects of competition are considered. Moreover, where exemptions from competition law are seen to be necessary to achieve certain environmental benefits, a natural monopoly often results. In these cases, competition may not even be possible, so there may be no restriction of competition in the first place.[16] All things considered, there are some strong reasons to support an integration of environmental considerations and competition law. A valid objection to the integration of environmental concerns that nevertheless remains is that competition authorities may be asked to judge the environmental merits of an agreement. It is doubtful that the expertise of competition law experts extends to this area.

The second question relates to what integration of environmental considerations should entail. Answering this question requires an appreciation of the role of competition in connection with the Polluter Pays Principle. If this principle is meant to work effectively, the polluter must feel some competitive pressure. If the use of the environment has a price but actors are able simply to pass this cost on to others, then these actors will lack an incentive to make less use of the environment. This, in turn, will reduce the incentive to undertake research and development of better and more efficient methods for environmental protection. The presence of competitive pressure that internalizes environmental costs is necessary. For example, the absence of competitive pressure to recycle and develop recycling systems will likely result in less innovation in this field. Competition law should thus not completely withdraw from the field of environmental agreements. In order to provide the right economic incentives, such agreements will need some shelter from the rigor of competition law. Cooperation among parties for environmental protection requires some departure from the normal competitive regime.

---

objective of competition law and policy. Instrumentalization or politicization takes place when other objectives (a very popular one being employment) are ascribed to competition policy. In these cases, there may very well be a true conflict between the objectives of competition policy and those of other policies.

[15] See R. Jacobs, "EEC Competition Law and the Protection of the Environment" (1993) *Legal Issues of European Integration* 1, 46.

[16] For example, this argument has been advanced in connection with the DSD-system. See note 40 infra. Prior to this system there was no competition at all (the collection and treatment of waste was publicly regulated) and the nature of the market was considered to allow only one competitor; cf. Gyselen, p. 253, note 8 supra.

A general definition of what this integration should entail cannot be provided, given that environmental agreements may concern a multitude of different objectives,[17] means,[18] parties,[19] and other factors.[20] In my opinion environmental agreements should not be granted an *a priori* exemption from competition law. In the terms of Article 81 of the EC Treaty, an environmental cartel should not fall outside the scope of the prohibition in Article 81(1) solely because of its environmental objective. A general exception for environmental agreements would deny the positive role that competition may play in achieving environmental protection, as mentioned above.[21] In the framework of Article 81, the analytical emphasis should be given to the exemption clause in its third paragraph.[22] Below, both European and Dutch cartel law will be scrutinized to determine whether and to what extent this approach is followed.

3 ENVIRONMENTAL AGREEMENTS AND ARTICLE 81 EC

Article 81 of the EC Treaty is considered to be not only an instrument for ensuring effective competition, but also an instrument for promoting the establishment of the European internal market.[23] Therefore, in its application of this provision, the Commission is concerned with preventing any business enterprise from erecting barriers to intra-community trade.

This is one of the reasons why the prohibition of restrictive agreements and practices, contained in the first paragraph of Article 81, is interpreted broadly. Article 81 applies to agreements that intend or have the effect of restricting of competition. The fact that an agreement has a purely environmental objective and does not intend to restrict or distort competition does not remove the agreement from the scope of Article 81 if it nevertheless has an effect on competition.[24]

In order to violate Article 81, the effect on competition must be appreciable. The Commission has substantiated this notion of "appreciability" through various notices.[25] The "appreciability" criterion employed in these

---

[17] Some examples of different objectives of environmental cooperation are better research and development into environmental protection methods, prevention of waste, better collection and recycling of waste, and prevention of various forms of pollution.

[18] One broad distinction may be made between horizontal and vertical cooperation.

[19] The number of parties to environmental agreements varies from six (VOTOB) to over 550 in the case of DSD. See infra notes 49 and 41.

[20] Examples of such other factors include the relevant national and/or European legislation, the presence or absence of competing systems and general economic circumstances. See also Vogelaar, supra note 2, at 545.

[21] See the European Commission's 25th competition report (1995) paras 83–85.

[22] See Vogelaar, supra note 2, at 542.

[23] D. Goyder, *EC Competition Law* (Clarendon Press, Oxford, 1998), p. 16.

[24] See Case 56/65, *Société Technique Minière*, [1966] ECR 235.

[25] Most recently, the 1997 Notice on agreements of minor importance that do not fall under Article 85(1) of the Treaty establishing the European Community, [1997] OJ C 372/13.

notices is a quantitative one. Whether or not an agreement has an appreciable effect is determined by, among other things, the relative market shares of the parties. The notice also indicates the existence of another form of appreciability, namely, qualitative appreciability. Certain types of agreements are deemed to have an appreciable effect on competition despite the fact that market shares may remain below the quantitative thresholds.[26] These types of agreements may be said to have a *per se* appreciable effect on competition. Qualitative appreciability appears also to have been applied to exclude agreements from the scope of Article 81 as well. The Belgian Association of Pharmacists' scheme to affix a quality label to certain pharmaceutical products was found to fall outside the scope of Article 81.[27] One of the reasons for this negative clearance[28] was that "the quality of pharmaceutical products is only one means of competition among others."[29] In other words, an agreement on the environmental quality of a product concerning, for example, eco-labels would most probably have no appreciable effect on competition.[30] The notice on agreements of minor importance also indicates a *per se* appreciability for horizontal agreements on price fixing, limiting production, limiting sales, sharing markets, or sharing sources of production.[31] An example of this kind of appreciability can be found in the *VOTOB* case, where the horizontal fixing of an environmental charge, constituting less than 5 percent of the total costs, was considered to violate Article 81.[32]

The prohibition of Article 81 therefore applies to environmental agreements. This conclusion also follows from the Commission's practice and statements.[33] Furthermore, the Commission has repeatedly expressed concerns that environmental agreements are used to create barriers to trade, indicating that the Commission is likely to act against such agreements.[34] Apart from the exemption clause in Article 81(3), there are only two ways to escape from the prohibition of Article 81: the exceptions offered for certain sectors of the industry and the application of a "rule of reason."

Sectoral exceptions exist for the agricultural and transport industries. They appear of little value as a vehicle for integration. The scope of these exceptions is construed narrowly, which is one argument against using a sectoral approach for environmental agreements. Environmental agreements can already be found in a multitude of different sectors of industry.

---

[26]   Ibid., para. 11.

[27]   Commission Decision 90/33/EEC in the *APB* case, [1990] OJ L 18/35.

[28]   This is the term for an official declaration by the Commission that an agreement falls outside the scope of Article 81.

[29]   Para. 41 of the APB decision, note 27 supra.

[30]   See Vogelaar, supra note 2, at 547.

[31]   See para. 11 (a) of the notice on agreements of minor importance, supra note 25.

[32]   See infra note 49.

[33]   See European Commission's 22nd Competition Report (1992), para. 77. See the European Commission's 25th Competition Report, supra note 21.

[34]   Examples include the *IFCO, DSD,* and *GDB* cases, infra note 41. All three cases concern German environmental agreements that have a nationwide effect. The Commission was concerned that membership to such agreements might become necessary to compete in the market. See also Decision 82/371/EEC in the *NAVEWA/ANSEAU* case, infra note 41.

It would be contrary to the horizontal nature of environmental policy to adopt an approach to environmental agreements that would encourage them only in particular sectors of industry.

The notion of a rule of reason is familiar to competition lawyers in the US. In the EC, however, this notion is much debated and sometimes misunderstood.[35] Its existence as well as its content are subject to discussion. In my view, some Commission decisions and judicial rulings may be seen as an application of a rule of reason within the interpretation of the first paragraph of Article 81. The prohibition contained in this paragraph refers to agreements or decisions "which have as their object or effect the prevention, restriction or distortion of competition." Substantively, there must be a restriction of competition. In determining whether or not there is such a restriction of competition, the European authorities have, on some occasions, balanced a restriction of competition with an increase in competition.[36] Whether or not practice in EC law regarding the rule of reason is comparable with its use in US antitrust law is outside the scope of this chapter. Suffice it to say that US antitrust and the EC competition provisions are fundamentally different.[37]

The misunderstanding surrounding the rule of reason in EC law stems from, among other things, the fact that European law also has a "rule of reason" in connection with the different context of rules on the free movement of goods. The mandatory requirements that the European Court of Justice has adopted as an exception to the free movement of goods are generally referred to as the "rule of reason."[38] This misunderstanding becomes especially important when it is understood that this "rule of reason" has functioned as a vehicle to integrate environmental concerns into the law on free movement of goods.[39]

The "rule of reason" in competition law has quite a different function. On some occasions, initial restrictions of competition were considered to be justified if competition would be increased in the long run. Within competition law, the rule of reason is thus strictly confined to balancing present restrictions of competition with increases in future competition: a *true bilan economique*.

Hence, the competition law rule of reason should not be confused with the free movement rule of reason. To this day, European practice suggests that both the European Court of Justice and the Commission have applied a strictly economic rule of reason in competition law. The rule of reason, therefore, fails as an instrument to integrate environmental concerns into competition law.

---

[35] See Goyder, pp. 117 et seq., supra note 23; P. Craig and G. De Burca, *EU Law* (Oxford University Press, 1998), p. 905.

[36] Such balancing has been applied to ancillary restraints, selective distribution systems, and franchising agreements.

[37] For one thing, the Sherman Act lacks the bifurcated structure that characterizes Article 81.

[38] P. Kapteyn and P. VerLoren van Themaat, *Introduction to the Law of the European Communities* (Kluwer Law International, London, 1998), p. 674.

[39] Case 302/86, *Commission v. Denmark (Danish Bottles)* [1988] ECR 4607, C-2/90, *Commission v. Belgium (Walloon Waste)*, [1992] ECR I-4431.

This leaves only the third paragraph of Article 81 of the EC Treaty. According to this paragraph, the Commission may exempt certain agreements from the prohibition. It may do this in individual cases or, for a specified category of agreements, through a group exemption. Below, I first examine the integration of environmental concerns through individual exemptions. I then consider whether group exemptions can play a role in integrating environmental concerns and competition requirements. Finally, an exception for environmental agreements will be considered.

3.1 Integration in Practice: Individual Exemptions

To qualify for an individual exemption, an agreement must contribute to improving production or distribution or contribute to promoting technical or economical progress. At the same time, the agreement must allow consumers a fair share of the benefit. Furthermore, the agreement should not go beyond what is necessary to attain its objectives and should preserve an effective level of residual competition.

At first glance, the third paragraph of Article 81 seems to be focused on economic considerations as exclusively as the competition law rule of reason. The European Community has recognized that it is possible to acquire an environmental competence even when the EC Treaty was silent on this score. In a similar manner, the Commission has interpreted Article 81(3) to include environmental benefits in several decisions. It has also stated that it considers environmental benefits to constitute an element that contributes to the improvement of production or distribution, and contributes to technical and economical progress.[40] A more exact determination of the heading under which environmental improvements are to be considered is absent.

This chapter does not discuss in their entirety the approximately 20 occasions on which the protection of the environment has played a role in the Commission's decisions.[41] These consist of formal decisions and public

---

[40] See Commission's 25th Competition Report, supra note 21, para. 85.
[41] Commission Decision 68/319/EEC, IV/26045 *ACEC/Berliet* [1968] OJ L201/7; Commission Decision 76/248/EEC, IV/26.940/a *United Reprocessors* [1976] OJ L51/7; Commission Decision 82/371/EEC, IV29.995 *Navewa Anseau* [1982] OJ L167/39; Commission Decision 83/669/EEC, IV/29.955 *Carbon Gas Technologie* [1983] OJ L376/17; Commission Decision 88/541/EEC, IV/32.368 *BBC Brown Boveri* [1988] OJ L301/68; Commission Decision 91/38/EEC, IV/32.363 *KSB/Goulds/Lowara/ITT* [1991] OJ L19/25; Commission Decision 91/301/EEC, IV/33.016 *Ansac* [1991] OJ L152/54; Commission Decision 92/96/EEC, IV/33.100 *Assurpol* [1992] OJ L37/16; Commission Decision 93/49/EEC, IV/33.814 *Ford Volkswagen JV* [1993] OJ L20/14; Notice pursuant to Article 19(3), IV/34.781 *EEIG EFCC* (European Fuel Cycle Consortium) [1993] OJ C351/6; Commission Decision 94/322/EC, IV/33.640 *Exxon Shell JV* [1994] OJ L144/20; Commission Decision 94/986/EC, IV/34.252 *Philips Osram JV* [1994] OJ L378/37; Notice pursuant to Article 19(3), IV/34.415 *IFCO* [1997] OJ C48/4; Notice pursuant to Article 19(3), IV/34.493 *DSD* [1997] OJ C100/4; Notice pursuant to Article 19 (3), IV/F1/36.172 *ZVEI/Arge Bat* [1998] OJ C172/13; Notice pursuant to Article 19(3), IV/F2/35.742 *EUCAR* [1997] OJ C185/12; Notice pursuant to Article 19(3), IV f. 11 36.718 CECED, [1998] OJ C38216; Notice pursuant to Article 19(3), IV/C-3/36.494 *EACEM* [1998] OJ L12/2.

notices pursuant to Article 19(3) of Regulation 17.[42] In addition, the Commission has unfortunately added the practice of merely mentioning its informal decisions in press releases or in the annual competition reports. In my opinion, no complete or direct integration of environmental concerns and competition law has taken place to date. When an exemption has been granted from the prohibition, economic grounds alone have been found to be sufficient. The environmental benefits were mentioned, as Gyselen once put it, *ad colorandum* or as *obiter dicta*.[43]

I do not know of any decision to exempt an agreement on purely or primarily environmental grounds. The most recent officially published decision on the topic was in 1994 and is thus over five years old. Any comment on the role of environmental considerations in the Commission's recent practice therefore requires some speculation. It can, however, be said confidently that political influences are not completely alien to the Commission's competition policy.[44] Environmental agreements that are in line with European policy and agreements that involve substantial government funding seem to have a better chance of being exempted. For example, the United Reprocessors Agreement concerned a plan in a field where the European Community had already encouraged cooperation.[45] The research in the *BBC/Brown/Boveri* case had received substantial government funding, and the Carbon Gas Technologie Agreement concerned research into a problem that the European Community had considered very important.[46]

At the same time, when the Commission seems to have wanted to deny the exemption, it played down the environmental benefits. The *NAVEWA/ANSEAU* and *ANSAC* cases both presented examples of this approach.[47] The *NAVEWA/ANSEAU* case concerned a scheme that would make parallel imports, which are an important tool for creating the internal market, more difficult if not impossible. The erection of barriers to entry to a national market was considered so severe that it could not be justified. The outcome of the *ANSAC* case may very well have been influenced by the fact that anti-dumping measures had recently been enacted against the US soda industry. ANSAC represented the US soda industry, which was the European soda industry's major competitor. Although the Commission did not deny the environmental benefits of ANSAC's products, it considered an export cartel to be a disproportionate instrument.[48]

Reasoning along the lines of an integration of environmental concerns and competition law can be found in the Commission decision in the

---

[42] These notices consist of a short description of the agreement, an invitation to submit comments and the Commission's preliminary opinion.
[43] See Gyselen, supra note 8 at 256; Vogelaar supra note 2, at 547.
[44] See D. Ehle, *Die Einbeziehung des Umweltschutzes in das Europäische Kartellrecht* (Carl Heymanns Verlag, Köln, 1996), pp. 140 et seq.
[45] See supra note 41.
[46] Ibid.
[47] Ibid.
[48] See Vogelaar, supra note 2, at 548, 549.

VOTOB case.[49] Although this case did not grant an exemption to the agreement, the Commission was clearly trying to make competition policy work for the environment. VOTOB is the Dutch association of independent tank storage enterprises. Its members offer storage facilities to the chemical industry. In order to anticipate legislation, VOTOB concluded a covenant with the Dutch authorities to reduce emissions. Initially, it appeared that the costs for VOTOB's plans would be partly subsidized by the Dutch government under a general investment scheme, because the business enterprises had shown that they would be unable to bear the full costs themselves. Six months after signing the covenant, the government aid scheme was withdrawn. VOTOB decided nonetheless to continue the implementation of its covenant obligations and to collect the extra environmental costs from the real polluters, namely, the chemical industry. To this end, a scheme was conceived that consisted of a uniform fixed environmental surcharge that would compensate for the loss of the subsidy. Furthermore, the environmental charge was to be listed separately on invoices. VOTOB considered these measures necessary, first because the market for tank storage facilities is a "buyers market"[50] and second because, from an environmental point of view, the VOTOB members would be considerably ahead of their German and Belgian competitors, but as a result VOTOB would face extra costs. In general, the market for tank storage can be characterized as one where profit margins are limited. Moreover, storage does not add much value to the product. In these circumstances, the VOTOB members wanted to prevent competition with regard to the costs for environmental protection that would result in less effective protection of the environment.

The Commission decided that VOTOB's scheme amounted to price fixing. It rejected the VOTOB's argument that the surcharge was de minimis.[51] Although VOTOB considered separate invoicing necessary to implement the Polluter Pays Principle, the Commission viewed the fixed and uniform surcharge as in obvious contradiction with the Polluter Pays Principle. VOTOB argued that separate invoicing would make the chemical companies aware of the environmental costs of their activities. The Commission contended that the enterprises involved had made significantly different investments to meet their obligations, and the uniform character of the surcharge therefore meant that the real environmental costs remained hidden.

The Commission clearly reasoned in environmental terms when it considered the role of the Polluter Pays Principle in VOTOB's scheme. Unfortunately, the Commission's attempts to make competition for the environment in this case left VOTOB standing out in the cold, having invested in pollution abatement techniques and facing a potential financing

---

[49] Unfortunately, this case was decided without the issuance of a formal decision. Some attention is devoted to this case in the Commission's 22nd Competition Report (1992), paras 177–186. For an account of the *VOTOB* case see Vogelaar, supra note 2, at 549 et seq.
[50] This refers to a market where the buyers (industrial giants in the chemical industry) have considerable power.
[51] The environmental charge amounted to approximately 5 percent of the total costs.

deficit at the same time. Perhaps the Commission's virtually *per se* prohibition of multilateral price fixing actually fails to make competition and the
Polluter Pays Principle work simultaneously.

The Commission's position may be evolving, as indicated in the Commission's comfort letter in the *Stibat* case.[52] This case is in many respects
identical to the *VOTOB* case, yet the Commission authorized an exemption.[53] The Dutch competition authority was of the opinion that Stibat's
comfort letter could be explained by the lack of effect on intra-community
trade. Given that *Stibat* and *VOTOB* both concerned purely national agreements in an international industry, it remains to be seen whether *Stibat*
indeed differs from *VOTOB* in this respect to such an extent that it justified
a departure from the strict *VOTOB* reasoning. Because the precise contents
of comfort letters and the reasons for issuing them are unknown, it seems
impossible to draw any further conclusions that would be based on anything other than guess work.

3.2   Group Exemptions

Apart from the possibility of individual exemptions, EC competition law
also allows for so-called group or block exemptions. These provide a procedurally easier way to obtain an exemption, and it therefore may be considered advantageous for an agreement to qualify for such an exemption.[54]
The prospects of integration of environmental concerns in group exemptions, however, are not bright for several reasons. First and foremost,
there is no group exemption for environmental agreements. Second,
the group exemptions that do exist contain no reference to environmental
agreements and thus serve only as an indirect instrument for integrating
environmental concerns. Third, experience shows that the Commission is
unwilling to enlarge the scope of group exemptions to accommodate environmental agreements. The *BBC/Brown/Boveri* and *KSB/Goulds/Lowara/ITT*
cases both provide examples where the Commission has denied that a
group exemption is applicable, though it nevertheless granted individual
exemptions.[55]

Thus, the Commission's practices to this day show that no integration
of environmental considerations with competition law has taken place.
Neither the European Court of Justice nor the Court of First Instance has
ruled on a case involving the integration of environmental considerations
and Article 81. However, the Court of First Instance has ruled on the integration of social considerations and on the rules concerning corporate

---

[52]   The decision by the Dutch competition authority mentions this comfort letter. It must be
said that the reason for the comfort letter remains unclear. See decision in *Stibat*, infra note 76.
[53]   Stibat also involved a multilaterally fixed environmental charge that had to be passed on
and was invoiced separately.
[54]   For an account of group exemptions and their advantages see Goyder, supra note 23, at 55
et seq.
[55]   See supra, note 41.

concentrations.[56] The rules on concentration are found in Regulation 4064/89.[57] From the outset, the Commission has stated that it would apply a pure competition test in decisions that form the basis of this Regulation. The Court of First Instance ruled, however, that the Regulation "requires the Commission to draw up an economic balance for the concentration in question, which may, in some circumstances, entail considerations of a social nature ..." It appears uncertain whether this result can be applied by analogy to questions of antitrust and the environment. The Court based its discussion on the preamble that refers to the objectives of Article 2 of the EC Treaty, notably the strengthening of social cohesion. Of course, questions of a social nature are more closely related to competition rules on concentration control than environmental questions are related to competition law on anti-competitive agreements. In this respect, some consideration for the social aspects in the concentration context seems more likely than consideration of environmental concerns in an antitrust context. It is also important to note that the Court's decision involved the procedural issue of the admissibility of certain parties rather than substantive issues.

3.3 Exceptions

Furthermore, the European Court of Justice has recently ruled on the role of social considerations in connection with, among other things, Article 81.[58] In this case the Court decided that the "decision taken by the collective organizations representing employers and workers, in the context of a collective agreement, to set up [...] a single pension fund responsible for managing a supplementary pension scheme and to request the public authorities to make affiliation to that fund compulsory" fell outside the scope of Article 81(1).[59] The EC has competition as well as social policy,[60] said the Court, and in its social policy the Community actively encourages cooperation and the conclusion of collective agreements.[61] The Court's reasoning appears to be applicable to environmental agreements as well.[62] The Community has an environmental policy and actively encourages the conclusion of environmental agreements. However, I do not advocate this approach because it does not provide for a proper appreciation of how environmental agreements fit within the framework of Article 81(3). This approach would also make it difficult to apply a proportionality test that could balance competition and the environmental policy.

---

[56] Case T-12/93, *CCE de Vittel v. Commission* , ECR [1995] II-1247.
[57] Regulation 4064/89 Concerning the Control of Concentrations between Undertakings, amended by Regulation 1310/97, [1997] OJ L 180/1.
[58] Judgment of 21 September 1999 in Case C-67/96, *Albany International, n.y.r.*
[59] Ibid., paras 52–64.
[60] Ibid., para. 54.
[61] Ibid., paras 55–59.
[62] See E. Loozen, "CAO's, bedrijfspensioenfondsen en het EG-mededingingsrecht" 11/1999 *Nederlands Tijdschrift voor Europees Recht*, p. 279; K.J.M. Kortelmans, "Milieubeleid en mededingingsrecht: onvermijdelijke confrontatie en gewenste integratie" 1/2000 *Nederlands Tijdschrift voor Europees Recht*, p. 24.

I conclude that the notion of an integration of environmental concerns and competition floats subconsciously though the Commission's various statements of policy. There is, however, no positive example of this integration. This may change in the near future because the Commission has indicated that it seeks to develop case law in the area of environmental protection.[63] The recent rulings by the Court of Justice attempt to reconcile the objectives of competition and other policies, but this does not qualify as integration in the form that I would advocate.

3.4 Possibilities for Integration

The absence of evidence of actual integration does not mean that the integration of environmental concerns is impossible for EC competition law. Although an exemption of a restriction of competition has not yet been granted on environmental grounds, the Commission's practice shows that it is beginning to think along the lines of an integration approach.

The Commission considers itself able to take environmental benefits into account within the appreciation of an agreement under Article 81(3).[64] Environmental considerations may be taken into account within the first requirement of Article 81(3). In my opinion, this does not stretch the meaning of improving production or distribution or improving technical or economical progress unreasonably.[65] Improvements in the environmental aspects of the production or distribution of products or services can certainly be considered as constituting technical improvements. The internalization of environmental costs can similarly be regarded as economic progress.[66]

The second requirement that there be a fair share of the benefits for consumers also seems possible for environmental agreements. The purpose of this requirement is to ensure that only benefits that extend beyond the parties' interests are exempted. This condition may be fulfilled because improvements in environmental protection inherently provide benefits for an open group and not just to parties to an agreement. Even if this improvement in environmental protection entails extra costs for consumers, those costs might also be fairly apportioned. Taking into account the rules for abuse of a dominant position, it appears that only unreasonable increases in price are prohibited.[67] The mere transfer of costs for environmental protection to the consumers would not appear unreasonable. Indeed, any requirement contrary to this would deviate from the Polluter Pays Principle.[68]

Traditionally the most difficult hurdle to pass in competition law has proven to be the proportionality requirement, which dictates that any restriction of competition must be necessary to attain the objective. The

---

[63] European Commission, 28th Competition Report (1998), para. 348.
[64] Commission's 25th Competition Report, supra note 21, para. 85.
[65] See Vogelaar, supra note 2, at 543.
[66] See Jacobs, supra note 15, at 53 et seq.
[67] See, e.g., C-27/76, *United Brands v. Commission*, [1978] ECR 207, paras 235 et seq.
[68] See Commission, 22nd Competition Report (1992), para. 185.

Commission has indicated that it will be especially vigilant where direct, across-the-board restrictions such as price fixing or market divisions are involved.[69] Experience suggests that this vigilance has resulted in an almost *per se* prohibition, though the Commission indicates that it does not completely reject the possibility of an exemption in these circumstances.[70] The Commission has indicated that through the proportionality requirement, it will balance the environmental concerns with the competitive concerns. However, I would submit that in applying the traditional, rather crude,[71] proportionality requirement to environmental agreements in an unmitigated fashion would not do justice to the nature of the problem. At least, the strict proportionality requirement with respect to direct, across-the-board restrictions such as price-fixing or market divisions should be relaxed.[72]

The fourth requirement, that some residual competition remains, has not been a problem until now. The cases mentioned all leave the impression that, once the first three hurdles have been passed, the fourth will not be the stumbling block. However, problems can be expected when an agreement becomes so successful that it can act as a virtual monopoly. One wonders, for example, how much residual competition is left in the German market for packaging waste after the arrival of DSD. On the other hand, the Commission seems at least willing to take potential competition into account when determining if there is sufficient residual competition.[73] In this respect, the Commission appears to sometimes allow rather thorough restrictions of competition because an intensification of competition is expected.[74]

All things considered, the Commission's practice with regard to Article 81 shows that it is definitely possible to integrate environmental concerns. It is possible for environmental agreements to satisfy all of the different elements of the third paragraph of Article 81. The Commission, however, has been reluctant to admit that the fulfillment of all these elements should lead to a standard exemption.

4 INTEGRATION OF ENVIRONMENTAL CONCERNS IN DUTCH COMPETITION LAW AND PRACTICE

Dutch practice is going further than that of the European Commission in recognizing that environmental benefits may serve as legitimate and independent justifications for restrictions of competition. This is perhaps surprising given that the Dutch Competition Act was actually modeled on

---

[69] Commission, 25th Competition Report (1995) para. 85, 2nd section.
[70] Ibid., 3rd section.
[71] See Gyselen, supra note 8, at 252, 257.
[72] See Vogelaar, supra note 2, at 559, et seq.
[73] See, e.g., Commission decision concerning Assurpol, supra note 41.
[74] In its decision to allow the VALPAK-scheme, the Commission seemed to attach some importance to the fact that the market was still emerging and VALPAK was a newcomer on this market, 28th Competition Report (1998), paras 133, 134.

European competition rules and policy. Substantively, the provisions of the Dutch Competition Act are identical to those of the EC Treaty.[75] During the Dutch parliamentary debates, an amendment was proposed to include a provision addressing environmental agreements. In the end, the amendment was not adapted, however, because European competition law was considered to leave sufficient room for accommodating environmental concerns. Indeed, as discussed above, environmental considerations had played at least an implicit role in European competition law. However, these considerations have never resulted in the exemption of such severe restrictions of competition as existed in the *FKS* case. Prior to the decisions made in the *FKS* case which is examined below, the Dutch competition authority had already ruled on several other environmental agreements.

The first substantive ruling concerned the *Stibat* case.[76] The Stibat scheme is very similar to the *VOTOB* scheme. The *Stibat* case was decided by the authorities by analogy to the Commission's decision in *VOTOB*. The role of the environmental concerns in the *Stibat* case provides evidence of an uncomfortable relation with competition law. In the *VBN* case, the competition authority exempted a scheme on primarily environmental grounds.[77] The competitive problems resulted from a general supply requirement. This requirement prescribed that packaging material for supplies had to conform to the VBN's policy on packaging waste. In the end, the Dutch competition authority decided that this policy contributed to technical improvements because it would encourage the re-use of packaging materials and would minimize the environmental impact of packaging. The competition authority took the long-term cost savings into account only as a secondary consideration.

4.1   The *FKS* Case

The case concerning the Dutch Association of Manufacturers of Plastic Pipes (FKS) provides another example of what integration of environmental consideration in competition law could entail.[78] The agreement in this case concerned a system to collect, sort, and recycle plastic pipe waste. The association devised this system to prevent the enactment of legislation that would compel producers of the waste to take responsibility for it. Most plastic pipe waste is generated when buildings are constructed or demolished. The nature of this waste makes it very difficult if not impossible to

---

[75]   There are some changes due to jurisdictional differences.

[76]   See decision in case 51, *Stibat* of 18 December 1998, and the decision of 31 May 1999 on the notice of objection in case 51. The *Stibat* saga continues as Stibat has filed an appeal against the decision to reject its notice of objection. The decisions of the Dutch competition authority can be found at <http://www.nma-org.nl>.

[77]   Decision in Case 492, *Vereniging van Bloemenveilingen in Nederland* (Association of Flower Auctions) of 9 July 1999.

[78]   Decision of 23 July 1999 in Case 12; *Vereniging van Fabrikanten van Kunststofleidingsystemen* (Association of Manufacturers of Plastic Pipes) [hereinafter the FKS decision].

identify the producer. Sorting the plastic waste according to the producer would only create extra costs, and the FKS therefore decided that it made sense to divide the generated waste according to fixed shares. These shares are based on historical market shares. Furthermore, the FKS agreed that a fixed price would be charged to demolition and building contractors. Contractors opting into the scheme would be charged nothing, and they would even receive a bonus to encourage collection when special containers were used. Lastly, limits were placed on the ways in which secondary raw materials could be used. Overall, these restrictions of competition seemed quite severe from a competition law perspective.[79]

The Dutch competition authority decided that the environmental benefits—including savings on primary raw materials and reduced waste for incineration—justified the restriction of competition. Considering the fact that the recycling of plastic waste is currently unprofitable and the fact that the collection system would be an efficient way to solve this problem, the competition authority decided that these relatively severe restrictions of competition were necessary for the scheme to work. If the fixed price requirement for waste had been abandoned, the FKS members could have charged a higher price to discourage the use of the system by the contractors thereby avoiding their costly obligations. Although the distribution of waste according to market share may not completely reflect the actual producer's responsibility for the waste, the collection system was more efficient than a more refined one would have been. Although it is impossible to know for certain however, one wonders whether the goals of environmental protection would have been better met if the FKS had simply waited for a legal obligation. If so, then plastic waste would at least not be recycled as it is today because the legislative process is too slow for that to have happened yet.

The *FKS* case provides an example of a creative solution to an environmental problem and an integration of environmental concerns and competition policy. A restriction of competition is allowed on environmental grounds because it is necessary for the system to function. Moreover, the exemption was granted for a limited period only. This allows the competition authority to strike a different balance when, for example, the recycling of the waste becomes profitable. In such a case, the market for plastic pipe waste would become a normal market, subject to normal competitive forces. However, the restriction on the use of the secondary raw materials precludes the coming about of a competition for the environment. The competition authority believed this restriction to be justified because it would prevent the use of these materials in unduly low-tech applications. However, I think that this restriction limits innovation in the use of these secondary raw materials. More competition in this market may also lead to better or cheaper ways to recycle the plastic waste, thus increasing the chances of a faster normalization of the market for recycled waste.

---

[79] The Commission has indicated that it considers such restrictions so severe that they will be very difficult to justify under EC competition law; Commission, 25th Competition Report (1995), para. 85.

The examples of environmental agreements mentioned above show that the advent of these agreements did not result in a complete withdrawal of government authorities from the scene. Often, the Dutch governments actually contributed to the emergence of these agreements. Government influence presents another important connection between competition law and the environment.

5   GOVERNMENTS, ENVIRONMENTAL AGREEMENTS, AND THE *EFFET UTILE* RULE

The competition rules of the EC Treaty are divided into parts that contain rules for business enterprises and parts that govern distortions of competition through state aids given to particular programs. This analytical division cannot be strictly maintained, however, because the rules that govern enterprises also have an effect on the Member States' freedom to intervene in the market. The general rule is that the Member States must be loyal to the Community,[80] a rule which the European Commission and Court of Justice have applied to the competition rules.[81] Regarding the prohibition of restrictive agreements, Member States may not encourage such agreements, reinforce the effects of such agreements, or transfer the public character of a regulation to private parties by giving them the responsibility for acting under this regulation. For environmental agreements, the government's encouragement and reinforcement of its effects seem particularly relevant.

A Member State's regulations may encourage environmental agreements that have anti-competitive effects by requiring a minimum scope. The German Packaging Ordinance, for example, requires that the agreement cover at least one Bundesland.[82] This requirement would inevitably result in the creation of large-scale collective systems. The German Packaging Ordinance suggests the option of a cheaper collection system to avoid costly responsibilities for individual producers. This option encourages cooperation among enterprises.[83] The Dutch practice of declaring an agreement generally binding for all producers or importers obviously reinforces the effects of an agreement.[84] Problems with Dutch and European competition law and policy are not expected because such declarations are subject to approval by the competition authorities. In other words, the substantive test is therefore that of Article 81 or the corresponding provision in the Dutch Competition Act.

---

[80]   See Article 10 of the EC Treaty (ex Article 5 EC).
[81]   See, e.g., the cases mentioned in supra note 6.
[82]   § 6 Verpackungsverordnung, BGBl, p. 1234.
[83]   See M. Bock, "Entsorgung von Verkaufsverpackungen und Kartellrecht" (1996) *Wirtschaft und Wettbewerb* 3, 201 et seq.
[84]   Article 15.36 Wet milieubeheer (Environmental Management Act).

As of yet, there is no case law on the application of the *effet utile* rule in an environmental setting.[85] The experience gathered in the application of Articles 82 and 86 of the EC Treaty could be applied by analogy.[86] Articles 82 and 86 apply to the distortion of competition that is caused by a state measure with regard to public enterprises.[87] The rules on public enterprises can be seen as a lex specialis as compared to the *effet utile* rule.[88] As such, the integration of environmental concerns in the rules on public enterprises could serve as an example for the integration of environmental concerns in the *effet utile* rule.

In a case some years ago, the European Court of Justice has held that, in determining whether or not a restriction of competition was necessary to ensure the proper functioning of a public enterprise, account should be taken of the environmental regulations that apply to this enterprise.[89] This approach offers some perspective for the integration of environmental concerns with respect to environmental agreements. In the recent Dusseldorp case, the environmental objectives of the public measure seemed to play no role at all.[90] In this case, the restriction of competition would probably have had no positive effects on the protection of the environment. The public entity's exclusive right to treat certain dangerous wastes, together with the prohibition to export these wastes, precluded export of wastes to Germany where they could have been treated in an equally environmentally friendly manner, but at a lower price. The public entity in the case also had no incentive to innovate or to research cheaper treatment methods. Perhaps other methods for treating waste more effectively than the German company does will be discovered which would increase competition for the environment. In this field at least, there are a number of interesting cases waiting to be decided.[91]

If these cases are applied by analogy to the *effet utile* rule, there may be some extra room for governments to encourage or reinforce environmental agreements that pass the competition test. However, the primary substantive legal standard remains Article 81, and the application of this legal standard to governmental measures leads to the question of whether or not a "seamless web" may be said to exist in the regulatory structure at issue.

6   A SEAMLESS WEB?

One of the EC's most important goals is the creation of an internal market. As such, it is concerned with the erection of barriers to intra-community

---

[85]   The Commission, however, certainly considers this possible. See 22nd Competition Report (1992), para. 77.
[86]   Before the Treaty of Amsterdam, Articles 86 and 90.
[87]   For a somewhat more detailed description of this matter, see Vogelaar, supra note 2, at 562.
[88]   See the opinion of A. Jacobs of 28 January 1999 in cases C-67/96, C-115-117/97 and 219/97, *Albany et al., n.y.r*, para. 371.
[89]   Case C-393/92, *Almelo* [1994] ECR I-1477.
[90]   Case C-203/96, *Dusseldorp* [1998] ECR I-4075.
[91]   See, e.g., case C-209/98, *Sydhavens Sten & Grus*, pending [1998] OJ C234/22.

trade by governments and businesses alike. As the Dusseldorp case shows, the danger of these barriers being erected is still acute, and the protection of the environment may sometimes be used as a pretext for such barriers.

Other forms of barriers to trade result from regulatory measures, and the Commission and other European institutions seek to abolish these barriers through the enforcement of the rules meant to assure the free movement of goods. Insofar as a Member State's environmental policy may affect trade, two sets of rules apply.

When a Member State decides to protect the environment through regulatory actions, it must comply with the rules governing the free movement of goods. If the Member State chooses to encourage environmental agreements, it is subject to the Community's competition rules. This chapter argues that both tests should lead to the same outcome; there should be a "seamless web."

European law as it stands today does not provide a seamless web. The rules on the free movement of goods appear to leave the Member States more leeway than the competition rules provide for businesses and Member States.[92] There are several reasons for this state of affairs.

First, though environmental protection has been recognized as a valid exception to the fundamental rule on the free movement of goods, no such recognition has been given in EC competition law.

Second, as shown above, there is no integration of environmental concerns and EC competition law. Environmental concerns have, in contrast, been integrated with the rules on the free movement of goods.

Third, Article 81 is more likely to apply to environmental agreements than the rules on free movement are to apply to environmental regulations. Article 81 applies to agreements that are purely internal to one Member State, and the rules on the free movement do not usually apply to such internal situations.[93] Article 81 does not recognize a "*Keck* exception" for sales modalities, which is yet another aspect of its greater scope when compared to the rules on free movement.[94]

From a procedural point of view, the competition provisions also appear to be ill-suited to take environmental concerns into account. The exemption under Article 81(3) can be granted by the Commission for a limited period only. Furthermore, the procedure for obtaining an exemption is often protracted. The DSD saga serves as an example in this respect. The German DSD was approach extensively examined by both the Bundeskartellamt and the Commission. The result was that the DSD was limited in its

---

[92] See H.G. Sevenster, "De Geoorloofdheid van Milieubeleidsafspraken in Europees Perspectief," in M. Aalders and R. van Acht, *Afspraken in het milieurecht* (W.E.J. Tjeenk Willink, Zwolle, 1992), pp. 87–88.

[93] The statement that the rules on the free movement of goods do not see to purely internal situation may require some refining as a result of the *Pistre* ruling by the European Court of Justice. See Case C-159/91 and C-160/91, *Poucet and Pistre* [1993] ECR I-637.

[94] The *Keck* exception applies to government rules on sales modalities; these are not governed by the rules on free movement of goods. See Cases C-267/91 and C-268/91, *Keck and Mithouard* [1993] ECR I-6097.

activities and otherwise faced severe restraints. A comparable, purely regulatory governmental system would probably have fared better.

This bias in favor of governmental intervention in the competitive process can also be seen within the EC competition rules themselves.[95] Environmental concerns have been integrated with the rules on state aid and these rules appear to leave much more room for state intervention in the competitive process than other competition rules.[96]

The difference between the legal standards applied to private and state environmental initiatives cannot easily be explained. The EC itself has stated a preference for the use of private environmental initiatives. Furthermore, the subsidiarity principle implies that Member States are basically free to choose the policy instruments that they like the best.[97] Moreover, the reasoning behind the advent of environmental agreements is their increased effectiveness from both economic and environmental points of view. These reasons, together with the principles that underlie the EC's environmental policy, should lead to a preference for the use of environmental agreements. If environmental protection can be obtained more cheaply or more effectively through the use of environmental agreements, then the use of this instrument should be encouraged. At the very least it should not be more difficult to use environment agreements than other regulatory instruments.

The conclusion must therefore be that an integration of environmental concerns and competition would benefit both competition and the protection of the environment. Such an integration may very well entail some initial restrictions of competition and the competition authorities are right to be vigilant. Their vigilance should not, however, make the use of environmental agreements impossible. A limit to this critical attitude also follows from the seamless web approach that I advocate. With this in mind, the experiences today in Europe can only be characterized as a step in the right direction.

7   AN EXAMPLE FOR THE UNITED STATES?

If the experience with environment agreements is a step in the right direction for Europe, it would seem to follow that they might also represent an equally worthwhile approach that US antitrust law should accommodate. However, given that the voluntary approach to environmental problems is still rather uncommon in the US, the competition problems that have arisen in Europe have not yet surfaced in the US. Moreover, the fact that a price-fixing scheme was upheld by a competition authority in Europe[98] must sound strange to American antitrust lawyers who are used to the *per se* rule with regard to price fixing. The Dutch competition authority's ruling,

---

[95] Gyselen, supra note 8, at 257.
[96] Community Guidelines on State aid for environmental protection, [1994] OJ C 72/3.
[97] Article 5 of the EC Treaty.
[98] See in the *FKS* case, supra note 78 and accompanying text.

however, seems logical and justified from both a competition law as well as an environmental perspective. Thus, it seems both possible and necessary to contemplate the effectiveness of a per se rule in these matters.

It seems that neither environmental nor other non-competitive considerations play a role in US antitrust law. For example, the US Supreme Court has ruled that: "the purpose of the analysis [under the rule of reason] is to form a judgment about the competitive significance of the restraint; it is not to decide on whether a policy favoring competition is in the public interest or in the interest of the members of an industry."[99] The Court went on to state that "the statutory policy precludes inquiry into the question whether competition is good or bad."

In the end, the only way of integrating environmental concerns and competition law that follows from the Sherman Act may be to loosen up the rule of reason. This does not necessarily have to involve asking the question whether competition is good or bad. Certainly, competition is a good thing. One may properly wonder, though, to what extent competition is possible in certain markets in the first place. Likewise, it may be asked whether certain initial restrictions may not actually intensify competition in the long run. In a recent paper, Herbert Hovenkamp shows that US antitrust law is reluctant to take environmental concerns (as well as other non-economic policies) into account.[100] When the benefits resulting from environment agreements are taken into account, part of the conclusion should be that environmental concerns need to be integrated with competiton law. In this respect, experience in Europe could serve as an example for future American policy. Eventually, the question becomes whether protection of the environment is considered a common cause for various interests a within society or one that only the government is competent to address.

---

[99] *National Society of Professional Engineers v. United States*, 435 U.S. 678.
[100] H. Hovenkamp, "Competition Law Implementation at Present—Working Paper IV" in C. Ehlermann and L. Laudati, *1997 European Competition Law Annual—The Objectives of Competition Policy* (Hart Publishing, Oxford, 1998), pp. 426 et seq.

Part III
The Law and Economics of Environmental Contracts and Regulation

11. The Law and Economics of Environmental Contracts

Jason Scott Johnston

1 INTRODUCTION

In both Europe and the United States, environmental regulators over the past decade have promoted a package of regulatory reforms commonly referred to as "voluntary approaches." This term includes a broad range of commitments by regulated firms to improve their environmental performance.[1] Such commitments do not, of course, require regulatory involvement, and there are many examples of firms that have unilaterally announced that they will improve their environmental records. There have been plenty of collective efforts by groups of firms or industry associations to promulgate and comply with private environmental standards. Finally, more formal agreements between regulated firms and environmental regulators have been negotiated.[2] In this paper, I analyze this final version of the voluntary approach—what I shall refer to as an "environmental contract."

Environmental contracts are typically "voluntary" in a formal legal sense and yet negotiated against the background of the status quo regulatory outcome that would otherwise obtain. A basic lesson from both game theory and the economic analysis of contracts is that the status quo or default outcome that will obtain if the parties don't reach agreement on a particular point will be a crucial determinant of their strategic behavior in bargaining to reach agreement. Environmental contracts are both contractual and regulatory. Because they are intended to be legally enforceable agreements, analytical tools drawn from the economic analysis of contract law (such as the default rule paradigm) promise to generate substantial insight into both

---

[1] For a very useful classification and general economic overview of voluntary environmental agreements, see C. Carraro and F. Leveque, "Introduction: The Rationale and Potential of Voluntary Agreements" in C. Carraro and F. Leveque (eds), *Voluntary Approaches in Environmental Policy* (Kluwer Academic Publishers, The Netherlands, 1999), 1–17.
[2] This typology is taken from Rinaldo Brau and Carlo Carraro, Voluntary Approaches, Market Structure and Competition, Fondazione. E. Mattei WP (March 1999).

the process by which such contracts are negotiated and the significance of their substantive terms. But environmental contracts are also an alternative to traditional regulation. Regulators and regulated firms behave strategically both in negotiating environmental contracts and in shaping status quo regulatory outcomes through legal and political conflict. Unless we have some theory of how strategic regulators determine this status quo, we cannot begin to assess the normative desirability of environmental contracts relative to the status quo.

We also cannot begin to explain and evaluate environmental contracts without first having a very concrete notion of just what such agreements look like. Toward this end, section 2 of this chapter surveys some recent and important instances of environmental contracting in the United States: Habitat Conservation Plans under the Endangered Species Act; EPA's Project XL; federal and state Brownfields redevelopment programs; and, more briefly, wetlands mitigation banks under section 404 of the federal Clean Water Act. My survey shows that environmental contracts are responsible for three major shifts in environmental regulation: a relative transfer in power and influence from national to local interest groups; a move toward multimedia, outcome-oriented regulation (versus traditional media-specific approaches); and, perhaps most significantly, the delegation to present regulators of the power to legally bind and limit the discretion of future regulators.

In section 3 of the chapter, I informally develop a model for analyzing the likely effects of these shifts on the behavior of regulators and regulated firms. I first employ the default rule paradigm drawn from the economic analysis of private contract law to identify some of the key factors—such as the information available to and the identity of the contracting parties— which determine the social desirability of environmental contracts. Then I sketch a theory of strategic environmental regulation. These two are then used to analyze the likely effects of excluding national interest groups from the negotiation of environmental contracts and allowing cross-media trade-offs to be made in such agreements. Finally, I discuss how the introduction of binding regulatory contracts is likely to influence the incentives of both present and future regulators and the firms they regulate.

My goal is primarily to supply an analytical framework for understanding environmental contracts. I reach few definite normative conclusions. Among these, however, is the recommendation that while participation in the negotiation of environmental contracts should be as broad as possible, national interest groups that participate in the negotiation process ought not necessarily to be parties to the agreements. This may, however, require yet another kind of environmental contract: binding agreements by such groups not to challenge environmental contracts in court under statutory citizen suit provisions. Environmental contracts are also likely to generate better present day environmental performance, at the expense of making certain types of future regulatory change much more costly. In particular, future shifts in environmental policy designed to provide large benefits to a relatively small and geographically dispersed national group will be deterred by the potential contractual liability one gets with formal, legally binding agreements.

2 HOW ENVIRONMENTAL CONTRACTS ALTER THE FORM AND SUBSTANCE OF ENVIRONMENTAL LAW

In this section of the chapter, I survey three important types of environmental contracts. This survey is not exhaustive, but it does reveal the major ways in which environmental contracts have the potential for changing federal environmental regulation in the United States.

2.1 Environmental Contracts in the 1990s

2.1.1 *Habitat Conservation Plans under the Endangered Species Act*

During the first decade of the Endangered Species Act (ESA), the prohibition in section 9 of the Act against the "taking" of endangered species by private parties applied even when the taking was incidental to otherwise lawful activities such as land development. In 1982, Congress amended the ESA by adding section 10(a). This gives U.S. Department of the Interior the authority to permit "incidental" private takings when they are pursuant to habitat conservation plan (HCP) which will minimize the impact of the taking and ensure "that it will not appreciably reduce the likelihood of the survival and recovery of the species in the wild."[3] Section 10 and private HCPs originated with the San Bruno HCP. In 1978, the U.S. Fish and Wildlife Service (USFWS) proposed listing the callippe silverspot butterfly as endangered under the ESA, and in 1980, the Service issued a proposed critical habitat designation for the butterfly which included most of the remaining developable areas of San Bruno Mountain near San Francisco.[4] Environmentalists, developers, and local government officials negotiated an agreement covering 3,000 acres of habitat which protected in perpetuity over 90 percent of the butterfly's habitat. The plan provided a trust fund to permanently fund butterfly population monitoring and habitat restoration efforts, and it sets up the county as the ongoing habitat manager, required to make annual reports to the Service. The San Bruno HCP was implemented by an agreement between USFWS, the California Department of Fish and Game, the California Department of Parks and Recreation, the county, three cities, and four major landowners. The landowners participating in the plan demanded a promise, included in the implementing agreement, that no landowner would be required to take habitat mitigation steps beyond those set forth in the HCP.

Although section 10 of the ESA was modeled after the San Bruno plan, the section had very little practical impact prior to the early 1990s simply because the USFWS never enforced the section 9 takings prohibition against

---

[3] ESA § 10(a)(2)(B).
[4] D. Bauer and K. Donovan, "The No Surprises Policy: Contracts 101 Meets the Endangered Species Act" (1997) 27 Env'l Law 767, 771–773.

incidental takings. Only 38 HCPs were approved between 1982 and 1994.[5] In 1994, however, as part of the Clinton Administration's effort to make the Endangered Species Act a more effective, "user friendly" regulatory device, Secretary of Commerce Brown and Secretary of the Interior Babbitt announced the "No Surprises Policy."[6] The objective of the No Surprises Policy was both to encourage non-federal participation in the negotiation of HCPs and to provide certainty for participating landowners by assuring them that the federal government "would not come back ten years from now and say you have to pay more or give more."[7] More precisely, under the policy, "No Surprises" means that a developer holding an HCP permit gets "long-term assurances ... that the terms of the plan will be adhered to and that further mitigation requirements will only be imposed in accordance with the terms of the plan."[8] The developer with an HCP permit cannot be required to commit more land or money to habitat conservation than promised in the HCP unless "extraordinary" and "unforeseen" circumstances arise. The policy does not provide clear safe harbor rules regarding what might constitute such unforeseen circumstances. It instead list a number of factors which the Service will look to in determining whether an HCP permitee will be required to take additional mitigating steps:

1) the size of the current range of the affected species; 2) percentage of range adversely affected by the HCP; 3) percentage of range conserved by the HCP; 4) ecological significance of that portion of the range affected by the HCP; 5) level of knowledge about the affected species and the degree of specificity of the species conservation program under the HCP; 6) whether the HCP was originally designed to provide an overall net benefit to the affected species and contained measurable criteria for assessing the biological success of the HCP; and 7) whether failure to adopt additional conservation measures would appreciably reduce the likelihood of survival and recovery of the affected species in the wild.[9]

The No Surprises Policy has been crucial in the Clinton Administration's push to use HCPs to encourage voluntary ecosystem protection. As of late 1999, over 250 HCPs had been negotiated, with more than 200 new plans in the negotiation process.[10–11] Several of these HCPs set aside areas of more than 100,000 acres, and USFWS expects tens of millions of additional acres

---

[5] Ibid., at 782.

[6] Ibid., at 776. The policy applied both to the Endangered Species Act, administered by Interior, and to the Marine Mammal Protection Act (which has a similar prohibition against private takings of protected species) administered by Commerce.

[7] Ibid., at 777 (quoting Secretary Babbitt).

[8] Ibid., at 777.

[9] *Endangered Species Habitat Conservation Planning Handbook*, pp. 3–31.

[10–11] "Who's Stopping Sprawl? The Endangered Species Act Goes to Town" (1999) 31 *High Country News* 16 (30 August 1999), p. 1.

to be protected under HCPs in the coming years. Roughly half of the HCPs negotiated over the past five years contain No Surprises assurances.[12]

2.1.2 Multimedia Regulatory Reform

In the early 1990s, the EPA and Amoco cooperatively produced a study showing that it would be possible to reduce pollution at Amoco's Yorktown refinery at less cost than was then possible under existing regulatory requirements.[13] The EPA and the company found that by spending $6 million, the refinery could reduce more benzene emissions at its unregulated marine loading docks than would be reduced by spending $31 million to rebuild its wastewater treatment system. The study revealed other ways that emissions could be reduced more cheaply than under statutory or regulatory requirements, and it recommended that Congress or the EPA should create the flexibility for firms to conduct facility-wide assessments to enable multimedia pollution reduction strategies.

The Yorktown study encouraged the EPA to begin several multimedia alternative compliance programs, and in 1993 EPA Administrator Browner announced that the EPA would begin organizing rulemaking on an industry-by-industry, multimedia basis, instead of the traditional media-based rules.[14] Soon thereafter, EPA proposed a regulation that would have integrated Clean Air Act and Clean Water Act requirements in seeking an "ecosystem-wide" reduction in dioxin and other toxic emissions in the pulp and paper industry. Environmentalists criticized the rule because it did not totally eliminate the use of chlorine (which is turned into dioxin in the paper bleaching process).[15]

There have been a number of similar initiatives over the past several years. In 1996, EPA's Permits Improvement Team (PIT) recommended that both federal and state regulators should focus plant-specific monitoring and reporting requirements on the most serious pollutants, reduce paperwork compliance burdens for less serious emissions, and interpret permits to allow firms to make a variety of plant and physical changes without triggering violations of technology-based permit requirements.[16] In 1995, the EPA signed an agreement with states to develop the National Performance Partnership System under which state and tribal permitting authorities are to have greater permitting discretion, and by 1997 the EPA had signed performance partnership agreements or grants with 48 states designed to encourage regulatory innovation at the state level.[17]

Of all these recent initiatives, the Project XL program goes the furthest in replacing the default command-and-control regime of limits on emissions

---

[12]   Bauer and Donovan, supra note 4, at 782.
[13]   See B. Mank, "The Environmental Protection Agency's Project XL and Other Regulatory Reform Initiatives: The Need for Legislative Authorization" (1998) 25 Ecology L Q 1, 12–13.
[14]   Ibid., at 13.
[15]   Ibid., at 14.
[16]   Ibid., at 17.
[17]   Ibid., at 19.

to specific media with more flexible, site-specific regulation.[18] Under the Project XL program, if a firm goes beyond regulatory requirements in reducing some emissions that are especially locally harmful, then it may forego other emissions reductions which would otherwise be required but which are not especially efficacious. As some Project XL critics have been quick to point out, Project XL works by allowing firms to violate some environmental laws in exchange for doing more than other environmental laws require.[19] The centerpiece of these exchanges are "no action assurances" by which the EPA promises not to pursue enforcement actions against the firm provided that it complies with all of its obligations under the Final Project Agreement.[20] Under such an agreement, the EPA will bring an enforcement action only in the event of an unanticipated risk posing an imminent environmental hazard or unacceptably human health risk.[21]

Agreements between Intel and the EPA illustrate the operation of Project XL. Computers and electronics are one of six industrial sectors targeted by EPA under the Common Sense Initiative (CSI), a Project XL precursor. CSI was intended as a way of eliminating conflicting and contradictory regulations, promoting pollution prevention, and creating incentives for industry to develop new, environmentally cleaner technologies.[22] The electronics sector ranked third in 1995 in toxic releases and transfers, and chip and computer firms use a constantly changing set of process chemicals which makes relatively static conventional regulation almost inevitably both an inefficient and ineffective means of creating incentives for emissions reductions.[23] As with other sectors, the EPA initially envisioned very broad participation in the CSI process—bringing together industry, local and state agencies, and representatives from environmental, labor, and environmental-justice organizations. The difficulty, however, with any such process is that the larger the number of groups involved, the lower the probability of achieving consensus. During 1996, the EPA dismissed a non-profit representative in the computer industry group for being consistently uncooperative and obfuscatory, while representatives of some environmental-justice groups resigned on the grounds that their views were being underrepresented.[24] Absent enforceable confidentiality agreements and agreements by nonprofits not to sue, participating firms were reluctant to disclose production and business information, but without such disclosures, public interest groups complained that they did not have the technical data or ability necessary to critically analyze firm proposals.[25] Beyond a 1997 conference on how to foster

---

18   Ibid., at 20.
19   See R. Steinzor, "Regulatory Reinvention and Project XL: Does the Emperor Have Any Clothes?" (1996) 26 Env'l L Rep 10,527; R. Steinzor, "Reinventing Environmental Regulation: Back to the Past by Way of the Future" (1998) 28 Env'l L Rep 10,361.
20   See Mank, supra note 13, at 23, and 23, n. 111.
21   Ibid., at 23, n. 111.
22   J. Mazurek, *Making Microchips: Policy, Globalization, and Economic Restructuring the Semiconductor Industry* (1999) 153.
23   Ibid., at 155.
24   Ibid., at 157.
25   Ibid.

the recycling of used computers, the CSI initiative in the computer and electronics industry achieved few concrete agreements.[26]

Against the background of the relative failure of the CSI, Intel's November 1996 Project XL agreement was held forth by EPA Administrator Browner as exemplifying successful regulatory reform.[27] The five-year agreement among Intel, ten regulatory agencies (local, state and federal) and five local residents covers operations at Intel's 720 acre Ocotillo site in Chandler, Arizona. It allows Intel to make routine process changes at its new Pentium microprocessor manufacturing facility at the site, as well as adding a second wafer fabrication facility without the need to get an additional air permit. It also includes a city permit for Intel to recharge the local groundwater aquifer with treated wastewater. In exchange, Intel promised to recharge the wastewater through its existing $28 million reverse osmosis water purification plant (which the company built originally to purify the city water it used as a production input), to donate computers and equipment to local schools and libraries, and to cap conventional and hazardous air emissions at the facility below the levels required for a facility to be classified as a minor source.[28] From Intel's point of view, the agreement had the potential to greatly reduce its regulatory compliance cost: in realizing the constant improvements in microprocessor speed for which it has become famous, Intel modifies its process chemistries between 30 and 45 times per year, and the type and location of its equipment between one and three times per year. These modifications cause variations in the type and quantity of hazardous and non hazardous facility emissions. According to Intel, the conventional Clean Air Act permitting process was far too slow and costly to give it the flexibility it needed if it was to continue to locate and expand facilities in the United States.[29] Under Intel's Project XL permit, the emission of only two pollutants—phosphine and sulfuric acid—exceeded Arizona's risk-based guidelines. For these, Intel's XL permit established separate limits to be included in the aggregate site limit. Importantly, the parties agreed that in the absence of historical or benchmark industry data, Intel's air emissions under its permit would be judged against what would be required under "reasonably anticipated future regulation," which the parties interpreted as the minor source limits under the 1990 Clean Air Act amendments.

---

[26] Ibid., at 158–164.

[27] Browner described the Intel agreement as the "crown jewel" in the Project XL program. Ibid., at 167.

[28] This and the following discussion of the Intel Project XL agreement is drawn from Mazurek at 167–197.

[29] Local Maricopa County Air Quality Management District officials had already allowed Intel the flexibility to make routine process changes and even to expand the Ocotillo facility without seeking permit re-approval. Intel's problems with Clean Air Act stemmed primarily from its own 1994 air permit, which promised emissions reductions that Intel discovered it was unable to achieve because scrubber removal efficiencies were much lower at lower waste concentrations than it had anticipated.

The EPA deliberately excluded national environmental groups from the lengthy (11 months) and costly (over 100 meetings) negotiation of the Intel Project XL agreement. Those groups criticized the agreement on a number of counts: they alleged that it was impossible to estimate the health effects of the aggregate hazardous air pollutant limits allowed by Intel's permit (the Clean Air Act addresses hazardous air pollutants individually because they have unique exposure pathways, thresholds, and properties); it was impossible to say whether the agreement actually generated "superior environmental performance" relative to command-and-control because there were no benchmark data for the semiconductor industry; finally, the Natural Resources Defense Council (NRDC) criticized the permit as implicitly allowing Intel to use increasingly hazardous substances over time and for measuring pollutants on an annual basis, thus missing potentially harmful spikes and for failing to contain explicit pollution prevention commitments from the company. Non-local environmental groups eventually persuaded the EPA to ensure that emissions from the plant would increase at a rate less than or equal to the rate of increase in plant output, but remained critical of the EPA's failure to require specific commitments from Intel to reduce the absolute level of pollutants over time.

Perhaps the most persistent criticism of the Intel Project XL agreement is that nonprofit environmental interests were not effectively represented in the negotiation process. Major national environmental groups such as the NRDC were not directly included, and the local public participants relied upon regulators and Intel for all of their technical information, with little or no opportunity to get expert advice in evaluating what the regulators and Intel gave them. Another complaint was that the public participants were selectively chosen and included only those—such as the planning director for the City of Chandler and all five community representatives drawn from an existing Intel Community Advisory Panel—who had a vested interest in keeping Intel in town. Even before adding the new plant, Intel employed 4,800 people and Chandler residents in general view Intel as an "outstanding corporate citizen."[30] Non-local citizen groups from Silicon Valley and New Mexico such as the Silicon Valley Toxics Coalition and the Campaign for Responsible Technology maintained that Intel's environmental record outside Arizona has been less than exemplary, but local groups did not welcome non-local participation, and the EPA and Intel argued that local citizens were most affected by the agreement and hence most important to include in the process. Eight widely advertised local public hearings were held on the agreement, which both Intel and regulatory parties say was a far more inclusive than traditional administrative permitting processes.

Environmentalists have criticized Project XL as fine in theory but terrible in practice. As the Intel agreement illustrates, they decry the vagueness of the EPA's standard that Project XL agreements must "achieve environmental performance that is superior to what would be achieved

---

[30]   Mazurek, supra note 22, at 188.

through compliance with current and reasonably anticipated future regulation,"[31] especially insofar as many of the agreements (such as those at Weyerhaeuser's Flint River, Georgia facility and 3M's Hutchinson, Minnesota plant) not only impose facility-wide air emission caps, but also grant a variety of other non-air regulatory relief with no apparent substantive justification. As is also illustrated by the Intel agreement, another general environmentalist complaint is there is no agreed-upon baseline for determining whether environmental performance is truly "superior." Actual emissions or allowable emissions may be too lenient a standard for old facilities or old standards, while a standard based upon anticipated emissions from new, expanded facilities needs to be made conditional on the expansion actually occurring to avoid giving the firm a windfall.[32] This failure to define a baseline is argued to be especially damaging, given that the facility-based emissions caps under Project XL agreements aggregate chemical discharges of various toxicities and allow firms to increase the amount of more dangerous substances over time.[33]

Again as illustrated by Intel, the main environmentalist complaint about the Project XL agreement negotiation process has been that the EPA has given firms far too much control in selecting which local public residents get to be at the bargaining table, and the Agency has not done enough (either by providing the information itself or requiring firms to disclose what they know) to ensure that local representatives are fully informed about the risks entailed by various terms of the agreement.[34] One commentator who has studied the Intel agreement in great detail has argued as follows:

At least in the case of the Intel effort—an experiment that involved a multi-national corporation and a set of novel permitting strategies—it is clear that national environmental and environmental-justice groups should have been included in the official stakeholder process. Excluding non-local groups and interested individuals might be a legitimate strategy in cases where the scope and the consequences of a project are confined to a single community, but not in the case of a path-breaking federal environmental experiment involving a multi-national corporation. Non-local environmental and environmental-justice groups sought to participate in Intel's experiment to keep the company from using its enormous influence to co-opt local residents and regulators—something that federal environmental laws were presumably designed to prevent.[35]

---

[31] R. Steinzor, Regulatory Reinvention and Project XL, supra note 19, at 10,529–10,530.
[32] Ibid., at 10,531.
[33] Rena Steiznor, for instance, has argued that for Project XL purposes, "superior" environmental performance is achieved only when: (1) the agreement reduces actual emissions of currently regulated pollutants, (2) it does not increase any emission above the level allowed under existing technology-based standards, (3) pollutants should not be aggregated into classes, but trades between specific pollutants should be allowed, (4) the firm carries the burden of producing scientific evidence that cross-media or cross-pollutant trading will reduce risk to human health and the environment and that any regulatory exemptions will not increase such risk. Ibid., at 10,531–10,532.
[34] Ibid., at 10,533.
[35] Mazurek, supra note 22, at 192.

What makes the lack of substantive standards and procedural safeguards for Project XL agreements especially troubling, say critics, is that these agreements are not understood by regulators as special demonstration projects, but rather as precedents for a national policy.[36]

2.1.3   *Brownfields Redevelopment*

Federal hazardous waste law—Superfund (or CERCLA) and RCRA—is generally acknowledged to have had at least two major failings. The first problem is that statutory cleanup standards are too stringent, going far beyond the point where marginal cleanup costs are justified by marginal reductions in risk to human health.[37] Because it is so costly for potentially responsible parties (current and past owners of contaminated land, past generators, and disposers of hazardous waste) to meet these cleanup standards, it is actually cheaper for such parties to spend vast sums on lawyers and litigation to avoid or delay cleanup. Thus the stringent cleanup standards end up defeating the statutory goal of prompt site cleanup. A second failure of federal hazardous waste law is caused by the fact that the law imposes potentially enormous liability (the average cleanup bill as of 1999 is about $15 million) on *current* landowners. This liability scheme has significantly chilled private incentives to acquire and redevelop contaminated sites. This is an obvious problem for sites that are known to have such serious contamination problems that they have been listed for cleanup by state and federal regulators. The uncertainty surrounding potential future listing is a problem of even greater magnitude. Many sites which suffer from less serious contamination could be viably redeveloped but for the risk that the site will turn out to be much worse than the new owner thought, triggering astronomical potential cleanup cost liability when and if the site is listed.

One way to overcome these adverse incentive effects would be to amend the hazardous waste laws. Given that such legislative reform seems hopelessly stalemated, the EPA announced in its 1995 "Working Draft of the Brownfield Action Agenda" a multipronged plan to improve the performance of the federal Superfund program and to encourage the cleanup and re-use of contaminated sites.[38] One part of this program involved removing sites at which no further cleanup would be required from the Superfund database and providing funds for demonstration projects for the reclamation and re-use of abandoned hazardous waste sites. In addition to these relatively direct measures, the EPA announced that it would use prospective-purchaser agreements and comfort-status letters to improve the marketability of such sites.

---

[36]   Steinzor, Regulatory Reinvention and Project XL, supra note 19, at 10,535–10,536.
[37]   In assessing cancer risks at Superfund cites, for instance, EPA assumes that residential development will take place at the site, regardless of how low the actual probability that such development will occur. See J. Hamilton and W. Viscusi, "The Benefits and Costs of Regulatory Reforms for Superfund" (1997) 16 Stanford Envt'l L J 159, 166.
[38]   See M. Dennison, *Brownfields Redevelopment: Programs and Strategies for Rehabilitating Contaminated Real Estate* (1998), 2.

Under a prospective-purchaser agreement (PPA), the EPA promises not to sue a purchaser of contaminated property for cleanup costs under section 107 of CERCLA,[39] and, in exchange, the purchaser cleans up the site or provides money to reimburse EPA's cleanup costs. Moreover, by developing the site, the purchaser provides indirect benefits to the local community in the form of employment and enhanced local tax base. Prior to 1995, the EPA would enter into a PPA only if the agency was planning on taking an enforcement action and the purchaser provided a benefit to the agency which would otherwise be unavailable.[40] In 1995, EPA's policy changed. The agency will now negotiate a PPA with a financially sound purchaser at any site where it is either taking or anticipating taking enforcement action,[41] provided that the agency receives a "substantial" benefit (such as funds for cleanup greater than those it would otherwise net out an enforcement action) and provided that the new development will not exacerbate health risks from the site.[42] Perhaps most importantly, under its new policy, the EPA is willing to trade-off lower direct benefits to the EPA for bigger indirect benefits to the local community. What this means is that by reducing risk while providing local jobs and public goods (recreational space, reducing urban blight, facilitating improved transportation), a developer may get the advantage of a PPA even if it pays relatively little to the EPA.

Prospective purchaser agreements are clearly intended to be legally enforceable, binding contracts between the developer, federal EPA, and state hazardous waste regulators. The agencies formally promise not to take any civil action against the purchaser for the reimbursement of response costs under sections 106 and 107 of CERCLA, and the purchaser agrees not to sue the agencies for any claim arising from the site or the agreement. The regulatory parties retain, however, the right to sue the developer if it fails to comply with the terms of the agreement or if any new contamination or exacerbation of contamination is caused by the purchaser.[43]

As noted, PPAs are employed for those sites where federal or state cleanup and enforcement either has already occurred or is likely to occur. They do not address the more general Brownfields problem—where the fear that a contaminated site *may* someday become the subject of regulatory action chills its purchase and redevelopment. To deal with this problem— what might be called the penumbral uncertainty associated with potential Superfund liability—the EPA initiated its Comfort-Status Letter policy in early 1997. When a developer has asked an EPA regional office about the current status of a particular property, the office may respond by giving the developer some assurance regarding future enforcement action at that location, provided that it determines there is a realistic probability that the site

---

[39] After the purchase, that is, when the prospective purchaser becomes a current owner subject to section 107 liability.
[40] Dennison, supra note 38, at 8.
[41] Hence EPA will enter into PPAs at sites listed or proposed for listing on the National Priority List or sites where it is taking a response action under CERCLA.
[42] Dennison, supra note 38, at 8–9.
[43] Ibid., at 17.

might someday trigger CERCLA liability.[44] The assurance may range from a formal covenant not to sue to more general policy statements regarding the Agency's exercise of enforcement authority, and the assurance will typically include information as to whether the site has been, is, or is anticipated to be the subject of an EPA or state response action.[45]

For less seriously contaminated sites, the most important action in recent years has occurred at the state level. Two distinct programs have been developed: voluntary cleanup programs and Brownfields remediation programs.[46] Although the distinction is blurry and varies across states, voluntary cleanup programs focus on encouraging private efforts to cleanup contaminated properties, while Brownfields programs focus on providing incentives for redevelopment and reuse of contaminated properties.[47] Most states (25 of the 44 with voluntary cleanup programs) exclude sites that are subject to enforcement actions under their voluntary cleanup programs. For less contaminated sites, state voluntary cleanup programs innovate by basing the cleanup standard for a particular property on its expected land use. If a site is going to be used as an industrial or commercial facility, then contaminated groundwater or soils may simply be left in place, on the theory that the proposed use will itself minimize contamination pathways.[48] The main incentives provided by state voluntary cleanup programs are cleanup standards under which redevelopment may itself be viewed as a way to mitigate future harm and some form of assurance that no more cleanup will be required. The degree of assurance varies. Some states provide a formal covenant not to bring an enforcement action based on contamination remedied by the voluntary cleanup, while others provide "No Further Action" letters that do not provide relief for future liability.[49]

By the end of 1997, roughly half of all states had Brownfields programs (roughly half again of which are part of state voluntary programs).[50] Although the criteria for inclusion vary somewhat—with Brownfields eligibility typically contingent upon underutilization and potential for redevelopment—cleanup standards are generally the same under both Brownfields and voluntary cleanup programs. When there is a difference, Brownfields cleanup standards tend to be even more flexible in basing required cleanup on local risk-assessment. For instance, "risk-based" Brownfields cleanup standards in North Carolina and Florida focus on how the redevelopment may itself remove exposure pathways.[51]

---

[44] Ibid., at 18–19.
[45] Ibid., at 20.
[46] See L. Breggin and J. Pendergrass, "Voluntary and Brownfields Remediation Programs: An Overview of the Environmental Law Institute's 1998 Research" (1999) 29 Envt'l L Rep 10,339. See also Dennison, supra note 38, at 53–139 (describing individual state Brownfields programs).
[47] Breggin and Pendergrass, supra note 46, at 10,340.
[48] Ibid., at 10,341.
[49] Ibid., at 10,343.
[50] Ibid.
[51] Ibid., at 10,345.

2.1.4 Wetlands Mitigation

A well-established feature of federal wetlands regulation in United States under section 404 of the Clean Water Act is the requirement that developers create new wetlands to mitigate wetland losses caused by their development activities. To this extent, wetlands regulation has always had a contractual component: in exchange for a permit from the Army Corps of Engineers allowing development, the developer agrees to create new wetlands. Under such an arrangement, the failure to provide in-kind mitigation constitutes a violation of the permit.

In-kind payment is the natural corollary to medium-specific regulation: to offset wetlands loss, a new wetlands must be created. But in-kind exchange is inherently limited. Some, perhaps many, developers have neither the expertise to mitigate themselves nor access to mitigation banks that possess mitigation credits for purchase. An increasingly popular alternative is what has become known as "in-lieu" mitigation. Under such an arrangement, the permit to develop and destroy a wetland is made contingent upon the payment of money to a fee administrator, who then uses the funds to undertake wetlands mitigation elsewhere.

In the absence of either explicit statutory authority or general federal regulatory policy, in-lieu mitigation, like other instances of environmental contracting, has arisen as a primarily local regulatory initiative. It represents a delegation by district Corps administrators of substantial authority to the fee administrator, who is responsible for determining how much money should be paid by the developer in exchange for the right to develop and using that money typically to acquire valuable wetland habitat elsewhere. Very often, the fee administrator is a local Audubon Society or Nature Conservancy chapter.[52]

Rather than having the developer dig a pond surrounded by cattails (a very common although technically illegal form of in-kind mitigation), in-lieu-fee mitigation gives local environmental groups with substantial expertise and interest the opportunity to realize gains from trade. In southeast Louisiana, for instance, the Nature Conservancy as in-lieu-fee administrator has received more than $3.5 million in mitigation payments for losses of roughly 1,470 acres of pine wetland. With this money, the group has acquired and initiated restoration on 2,565 acres of pine wetlands and associated habitats on which more than 30 species of plants and four species of animals in the rare, threatened, or endangered categories have been observed.[53] As this example illustrates, in-lieu-fee mitigation can use the expertise and interest of highly informed local environmental groups to ensure that mitigation efforts generate superior *outcomes* in terms of the goals of wetlands protection. Indeed, in-lieu-fee mitigation offers the possibility of shifting development to areas of great economic but little ecological

---

[52] J. Chowning, "In-Lieu-Fee Programs Belong Among Mitigation Options" [July–August 1999] 21 *National Wetlands Newsletter* 4.

[53] R. Martin, "In-Lieu-Fee Programs Belong Among Mitigation Options" [August–September 1999] 21 *National Wetlands Newsletter* 4, 6–7.

value and then using the surplus from such development to acquire, restore, and preserve wetlands of much greater local ecological value.

2.2   Environmental Contracting and Regulatory Reform

In all of the areas surveyed in this chapter—Habitat Conservation Plans, Project XL, Brownfields, and in-lieu-fee wetlands mitigation—environmental regulatory reform is founded on the negotiation of contracts between regulators and individual facility or site owners. Developers would not enter into HCPs without the "No Surprises" assurance that preserving and enhancing habitat today buys the developer a highly certain guarantee (barring "extraordinary" circumstances) that no similar steps will be required in the future. Project XL's flexible approach to facility-wide bubbles would not be attractive to firms if they were not assured that the technical non-compliance permitted by a Project XL agreement will not be the basis for future charges of non-compliance. Brownfields redevelopment efforts at both the federal and state level are premised upon the supposition that redevelopment of contaminated sites will not happen unless purchasers are given some very solid assurance that they will not be liable for additional cleanup expenditures in the future. In-lieu-fee wetlands mitigation rests upon memoranda of agreement under which the regulator promises that payment of a specified amount of money to the fee agent will satisfy the developer's mitigation obligation.

Environmental regulatory reform thus involves an exchange. Firms get the regulator's assurance limiting future regulatory enforcement. The regulator gets, at least in theory, a higher actual level of compliance than it would otherwise get. There is an additional party and an additional benefit. Whether it is a real estate venture that eats up critical habitat of endangered species or an industrial facility, development activities enabled by environmental contracts generate local benefits in the form of jobs and enhanced local revenues for public goods. Hence localities—both local residents and government officials—also receive benefits from environmental contracts.

For this reason, one potential criticism of environmental contracting is that it simply represents a return to inefficient local competition for jobs and tax revenues at the expense of the environment. That is, if uniform federal environmental standards are justified in large part because states would otherwise degrade their environmental standards to attract industry, then environmental contracting may simply be a back door form of destructive devolution. Much of the force of this criticism vanishes as soon as one takes a look at the federal statutory structure against which environmental contracting is taking place. It is true, for example, that section 9 of the Endangered Species Act absolutely prohibits the taking of any endangered species, and Interior Department regulations that define "take" to include "significant habitat modification or degradation" have been upheld by the Supreme Court.[54] However, section 4(b) of the ESA explicitly states that

---

[54]   See 50 C.F.R. § 17.3; *Babbitt v. Sweet Home Chapter of Communities for a Great Oregon*, 115 S. Ct. 2407 (1995).

the designation of critical habitat is to "take into consideration the economic impact, and any other relevant impact of specifying any particular area as critical habitat."[55] Moreover, as described earlier, Congress specifically authorized HCPs when it amended the ESA in 1982. Similarly, Brownfields reform may be viewed simply as a new, sensible aspect of the longstanding joint implementation of Superfund by state and federal regulators. The federal EPA has always had broad discretion in determining Superfund cleanup standards, and (through section 121(d)(2)) state law standards have always played a role in determining CERCLA cleanup standards.[56] Moreover, state law voluntary programs affect primarily sites that have not been and foreseeably will not be subject to federal action in any event. Project XL has not been explicitly authorized by federal statute, but neither do Project XL agreements typically permit clear violations of federal air or water pollution standards.[57] In any event, both federal and state regulators are parties to those agreements.

If regulatory contracts do represent a form of devolution, then it is not because they give authority to state regulators that they do not now possess or that Congress intended to take from them. Neither is it because environmental contracts somehow replace federal substantive standards with state standards. State regulators have always been at the bargaining table, and federal law has always in fact permitted significant regional and state variation in environmental standards as actually implemented.[58] Environmental contracts do implement regulatory reform, but not in the way they superficially appear to do. The important process shift made by environmental contracts is in replacing *national environmental groups* with *local community representatives*. The important substantive shift made by these contracts is in breaking down *media-specific* environmental controls in favor of *outcome-oriented* controls. Finally, and perhaps most importantly, if environmental contracts really are legally enforceable, then they mark a fundamental shift in *temporal regulatory scope*: a regime founded upon environmental contracts seems intended to create obligations that are legally binding on future regulators.

3   THE POLITICAL ECONOMY OF ENVIRONMENTAL CONTRACTING

To analyze the impact of the policy shifts made by environmental contracts, one must take account of the fact environmental contracts are both contractual and regulatory. That is, they are contracts negotiated in the shadow of what regulators can credibly threaten to do if contractual agreement is not

---

[55]   ESA § 4(b).
[56]   See R. Percival, et al., *Environmental Regulation: Law, Science and Policy* (2d edn 1996) 395.
[57]   Even critics such as Steiznor concede this point. See supra note 19.
[58]   See J. Krier, "On the Topology of Uniform Environmental Standards in a Federal System—and Why it Matters" (1995) 54 U Maryland L Rev 1226.

reached. The next section of this chapter uses an analytical framework drawn from the economic analysis of private contract law—the default rule framework—to identify the determinants of the social desirability of environmental contracts qua contracts. I then draw from positive political theory an account of strategic regulatory behavior. This account is used to compare the likely outcomes under environmental contracts with those that will obtain under the status quo regulatory regime. Together, the default rule paradigm and the theory of strategic regulation allow us to identify the factors that will determine the normative desirability of the policy shifts made by environmental contracts. Finally, I turn to the rather distinct set of issues raised by the fact that environmental contracts may bind future regulators in a very different way than would be true without formal contractual commitments.

3.1   The Default Rule Paradigm

Let us borrow a paradigm from private contract law scholarship and begin by thinking of status quo environmental regulation as a default that the parties are considering bargaining around with an environmental contract.[59] On the default rule approach to private contract, rules of contract law—such as the rule that the measure of contract damages should be set so as to make the victim of breach as well off as he or she would have been had the contract been performed—are understood as applying only when the parties have not explicitly contracted otherwise. If the parties do not like the default rule on contract damages, for instance, then they are free (at least in theory) to contract around it by specifying a liquidated damage amount when they contract. Such a term will not appear in the contract unless (perhaps in combination with other terms, such as a covenant not to compete) both parties are better off by including it than living under the default rule which would otherwise prevail.

Now consider environmental regulatory reform. Clearly the benefits to a regulated firm from changing the status quo regime increase as its costs under that regime increase, while the costs to the regulator fall as its benefits under the existing regime decrease. On a contractual model, however, it is not merely the costs or benefits of the status quo regime which determine whether it will be contractually reformed. Environmental contracts, unlike other regulatory reforms, really do represent agreements that all parties must believe to be preferable to the status quo. Hence from a positive point of view, the greater the inefficiency under a particular regulatory regime, the greater will be the gains to be realized from bargaining around that regime. In other words, the more inefficient the existing regime, the greater the rents to be realized from altering that regime.

---

[59]   On the law and economics of this contract law paradigm, see J. Johnston, "Strategic Bargaining and the Economic Theory of Contract Default Rules" (1990) 100 Yale L J 615; I. Ayres and R. Gertner, "Strategic Contractual Inefficiency and the Optimal Choice of Legal Rules" (1992) 101 Yale L J 729.

This suggests that environmental contracting is a simple solution to the much-decried inefficiency of nationally uniform federal environmental standards. In localities where the federal standards require inefficiently high pollution control or environmental preservation, local parties will bargain around the standards and mutually agree upon lower standards and/or less preservation. In localities where federal standards are too lax, the parties will mutually agree to tougher standards. Like standard (or Coasean) contract law default rules, uniform federal standards should be set to minimize the costs incurred in contracting around them. This requires that they be set at a level that is optimal for the average or typical locality.[60]

This might seem to carry the analogy between uniform federal environmental standards and contract law default rules too far. After all, contract law default rules emerge from the process of common law decision-making. We don't know what motivates judges to do what they do, but a fair case can be made that the common law contract default rules come pretty close to what is optimal for typical contracting parties.[61] Moreover, because contract law in the United States falls under the jurisdiction of state court judges rather than federal judges, the system permits interstate variation. Uniform federal environmental standards, by contrast, emerge from the interplay between Congress, the federal EPA, and national environmental and industry interest groups. There is no particular reason to think that these standards are efficient for anybody anywhere. They may, as with the Clean Air Act's scrubber requirements, simply represent the triumph of particular interest groups.[62] Moreover, the argument may continue, a primary justification for federal environmental standards may be to prevent interstate variation.

The difference between judge made contract law and environmental regulation is not, however, between nationally uniform regulation and particularistic common law outcomes. In practice, supposedly uniform federal standards conceal tremendous interstate variation.[63] The ozone and fine particulate standards in Los Angeles will never be what they are in Portland, Maine. The most direct and likely explanation for such variation is that it reflects regional and local variations in the costs and benefits of compliance with supposedly uniform federal standards. The distinction between private contract law and public environmental regulation is blurry on the contract law side as well. When a particular type of ostensibly private contract—such as the insurance, lending, or sale of goods agreement—is sufficiently ubiquitous and important, it has invariably become subject to uniform legislative and regulatory control. It is difficult to argue that such uniform legislation is invariably efficient: the private legislative bodies such as the American Law Institute and Commissioners on Uniform State Laws

---

[60]   On optimal uniform regulatory standards, see Steven Shavell, "A Model of the Optimal use of Liability and Safety Regulations" 15 Rand J. Econ. 271 (1984).
[61]   For the encyclopedic exposition of this view, see R. Posner, *Economic Analysis of Law* (4th edn 1992).
[62]   See B.A. Ackerman and W.T. Hassler, *Clean Coal, Dirty Air* (1981).
[63]   For more on this theme, see Krier, supra note 58.

that develop uniform legislation are arguably subject to much more interest group pressure and control than national and state legislatures.[64]

What distinguishes environmental contracts from private contracts is that one of the parties to the environmental contract—the environmental regulator—is also responsible for implementing the default outcome, the status quo regulatory regime. Moreover, the expected regulatory outcome is a product of efforts by both the regulator and the other parties to the contract. Parties to private contracts bargain in the shadow of expected legal outcomes, and they may well expect to affect those outcomes through litigation. But unlike the regulatory context, neither of the parties makes the default decision. One cannot predict or assess the likely outcome of environmental contracts without explaining first what the regulators who are parties to the contract will do if agreement is not reached. Only if regulators will actually implement inefficient uniform federal standards could it be the case that environmental contracts represent efficient localized bargaining around inefficient uniform standards.

There is another consequence of the fact that regulators are both parties to formal environmental contracts and responsible for the default regulatory outcomes that shape the terms of those contracts. Due to the power of political appointment, today's regulators are not, at least in the United States, likely to be tomorrow's regulators. The history of both federal and state environmental regulation in the United States reveals enormous variation across political cycles. The temporal duration of an environmental contract may far exceed the temporal duration of the regulatory status quo against which that contract is negotiated. It is not just that unforeseen events may occur during the performance of the contract. That is as much true of private contracts as it is of public environmental contracts. Allowing today's regulators to enter into binding contracts with regulated firms permits today's regulators to bind future regulators in a way which arguably is in direct conflict with the existence of a partly political (and partly career) executive agency. On the other hand, those future regulators will be responsible for interpreting and enforcing the contract. No such conflict arises in the case of private contracts, where judges are not parties to the contract, but just ex post interpreters and enforcers.

Pursuing the default rule paradigm a bit further reveals two final factors that will determine the social desirability of environmental contracts. The first of these is information. The efficiency of legal enforcement of private contracts presumes that the bargaining process was such that parties were well informed (or at least could have become well informed) at the time they contracted. The second factor is whether the contract generates non-pecuniary externalities.

Whether parties efficiently bargain around contract default rules hinges upon the information available to them at the time of the bargain. Indeed, default rules may themselves sometimes create incentives for parties to

---

[64] See A. Schwartz and R.E. Scott, "The Political Economy of Private Legislatures" (1993) 143 U Pa L Rev 595.

reveal their private information, as well as the possibility of gains from trade which might otherwise go unrealized.[65] On the other hand, if information is radically asymmetric, then agreement may not occur or may be inefficient.[66]

This is also true of environmental contracts. Without adequate information as to the probable effects of habitat modification or cross-media emission trade-offs, local citizens may well agree to environmental contracts that generate negative net benefits. If all benefits and costs were local, then we might well expect that local parties would have the appropriate incentive to gather information about potential risks and benefits before signing environmental contracts with regulators and firms. But local parties will generally have an inadequate incentive to gather information relevant to contractual payoffs when the contract generates non-local benefits and costs.

Indeed, a fundamental (perhaps the fundamental) justification for federal environmental regulation is that only at the federal level will there be appropriate incentives for the production and distribution of information about environmental costs and benefits. This is due to a number of factors. There may be economies of scale in environmental research: in particular, federal level environmental science may have systematically lower observational costs because there is greater environmental variation and hence more information than at more local levels. Moreover, assuming it is available on a free access basis (and is not protected by private property rights), knowledge of general processes and relationships, as opposed to purely local phenomena, is a global public good. The smaller the governmental unit sponsoring research, the smaller the share of the benefits from research that will accrue to residents of the unit, and the greater will be the shortfall in research funding relative to the globally optimal level.

For this reason, local environmental contracts must rely upon knowledge generated at a more centralized political level. Even with adequate information, environmental contracts may be much more likely than private contracts to generate externalities. This emerges most clearly when a cross media trade-off effectively reduces emissions within the locality but increases total emissions by shifting emissions outside the locality. Environmental agreements of this sort generate harmful spillovers across jurisdictions. They may nonetheless be efficient. It may be that the cost saving realized by allowing Intel to increase its total emissions is so great that the move generates a net efficiency gain, even though it redistributes pollution from the town where Intel's fabrication plant is located to nearby towns. On the other hand, there is no guarantee that the gains from such a cross-media transfer outweigh its costs.

Our confidence that the gains do exceed the losses should be greater, the greater our certainty that the people who bear the costs of the cross-media

---

[65] See Ayres and Gertner, supra note 59.
[66] To be more precise, the parties may reach an agreement that is in their mutual interests given their incomplete information at the time of contracting but which turns out, upon the revelation of all payoff-relevant information, to be inefficient ex post.

exchange have been effectively represented in the local contractual bargaining process. Strictly speaking, to ensure that the contract takes account of all harmful effects of the proposed exchange (i.e., eliminates all externalities), we must be assured that all of the individuals affected by the agreement have been included (either directly or by representation) as parties to the agreement.

This proposition is true of all contracts. With standard market transactions, however, the market itself ensures internalization. If alternative buyers would be willing to pay a great deal for the object up for sale, then the successful buyer must compensate the seller for this lost opportunity in order to succeed in acquiring ownership of the object. The seller's opportunity cost is precisely what another buyer would have paid, what they have lost by not getting the object. (And if there are indeed many other potential buyers, the seller will have a great incentive to produce more of the same object, or to partition a unique object into use rights or shares and create multiple ownership.) With respect to free access public resources—air, water, groundwater, animal species—the difficulty is that there is no market mechanism to ensure that the effects of a particular transaction on other resource users will be internalized by the transacting parties. Interjurisdictional competition can be at best a partial surrogate for the thick, low transaction cost markets which dominate private contracting. If residents of one community strike a deal which gives them the benefits of economic development while externalizing costs to other jurisdictions, mobility may actually cut against internalization by increasing expected future relative property values in the externalizing jurisdiction.[67]

More problematically, it is often difficult to determine which people will be affected by a localized environmental contract. When Intel negotiates a package of cross-media pollution controls with local community representatives, which communities should be included in the bargaining process? In general, the larger the number and greater the geographic range of the communities which directly participate in an environmental agreement, the lower is the risk that the agreement inefficiently externalizes harm, but the higher are the transaction costs of negotiating the agreement. There is therefore an inevitable trade-off between the costs of externalization from environmental contracts and the transaction costs incurred in their negotiation.

Pursuit of the default rule analogy thus reveals that the differences between environmental contracts and status quo environmental regulation identified by the survey above in section 2 are likely to be of great normative importance. Substantively, once one understands environmental agreements as bargains around the existing status quo regulatory outcome, it becomes clear that the desirability of such agreements cannot be assessed without some theory of how the very same regulators who are parties to the

---

[67] To see this, imagine that residents of community one could simply destroy all local public goods in community two. The gain to community one includes the direct benefits of the destruction plus the incremental value that community one residents get when they disable a local competitor. Given that location is a fixed attribute in the non-cyber world, there are obviously precisely the sort of entry barriers that make such predation profitable.

environmental agreement determine regulatory outcomes. Secondly, while contract default rules are made by a third party (i.e., a court), one of the parties to the environmental contract is a generation of regulators whose future replacements will determine both whether to perform by its terms and whether to alter the default regulatory environment.

3.2   Contracting in the Shadow of Strategic Regulation

One of the biggest puzzles regarding federal environmental regulation in the United States is the apparently bizarre combination of both vast vagueness and absurd precision in federal environmental statutes. I argue elsewhere the this system makes perfect sense once one understands the ways in which environmental goods are created, distributed, and paid for.[68] The upshot of that argument is that regional and local variation in the implementation of ostensibly uniform federal environmental laws is precisely what Congress intended. Variation reflects what I call "perceived" or "communicated" benefits and costs, where perceived benefits and costs are a function not only of actual benefits and costs but of the relative strength of interest group advocates in courts and in Congress.[69]

On this theory, regulators implement and enforce regulations based on the perceived net benefit of regulation. That is, even if promulgated regulations apply to a particular industry, they will not be enforced as promulgated if the regulator perceives low net benefits of enforcement. One thing that can account for low perceived net benefits is high perceived costs. On this model, costs include not only direct compliance costs but also threatened job losses and impaired international competitiveness. That is, at the federal level, the threat of impaired international competitiveness is just as effective as a threat of impaired state competitiveness with state regulators. Hence the greater the *national* significance of an industry, the greater its clout with federal regulators. Now consider the benefit side of regulation. National environmental groups specialize in advocating the national environmental benefits of proposed regulations. This accounts not only for the increasing focus of such groups on general health risks, but health risks which affect urban and suburban populations and land preservation issues which similarly are of interest to those populations. Most simply put, relative to rural residents, rural and suburban residents are much more numerous and significant politically (especially in the U.S. House of Representatives).

The predominance of national interest groups in shaping the actual implementation of environmental regulations has a number of consequences, but three in particular create potential gains when these groups

---

[68]   See J. Johnston, "The Political Economy of Environmental Legislation" (mimeo, January 2000).
[69]   For a simple formal model of how political influence determines expected regulatory outcomes, thus creating a motive for preemptive voluntary compliance, see J. Maxwell et al., "Self-Regulation and Social Welfare: The Political Economy of Corporate Environmentalism" (March 1998).

are excluded from the negotiation of localized, site, plant, or habitat-specific contracts. First, and somewhat paradoxically, the political economics of environmental regulation generates a tendency for regulatory stalemate at the federal level whenever both perceived national benefits and costs are substantial and relatively uniformly distributed across states. Big national benefits and costs mean that the stakes in federal litigation and political lobbying are high, warranting large and largely offsetting expenditures by both sides. The second situation arises when national benefits are relatively uniform but local costs vary (both by types of cost and across industry groups). In this case, federal regulation will tend to be enforced at a level that is often locally too tough. Finally, when benefits are local and heterogeneous or diffuse, but costs are national and uniform, regulation will tend to be enforced at a level that is locally sub-optimal.

What is taking place in the latter two cases is that national interest groups have an issue—whether it is jobs in the auto industry, the fate of imperiled species, or the health effects of elevated ozone levels—that makes them very effective in national political and legal contests. Costly environmental compliance (and its economies of scale) may be a way for nationally established firms to exclude smaller and more efficient rivals. Similarly, local environmentalists get only a small portion of the benefits of preserving endangered species habitats, but as local citizens they bear virtually all of the cost in terms of lost jobs and housing. A national environmental group, by contrast, enables non-local residents to realize the benefits of land preservation while bearing none of the costs. The group may be reasonably certain that it will prevail over a single municipality in court or in the political contest to influence an agency. There is no reason for such a national group to compromise and give up potentially valuable habitat so that the local community gets some of the benefits of development, even if local environmentalists are better off under the compromise proposal.

Now recall that environmental agreements will not be reached unless both parties perceive that they are better off than under the existing status quo regulatory outcome. Moreover, one of the recent lessons from the experimental economics literature is that fairness norms may be an important constraint on bargaining.[70] Experimental subjects will often fail to play the strategies that game theory identifies as optimal if they are too "hard-nosed" or tough relative to prevalent norms. In the environmental contracting context, this suggests that an agreement will be reached only if the parties feel they have split the surplus from agreement in a way that more or less mirrors the split that they would have gotten under the default regulatory outcome. In other words, even though both sides may recognize that the regulatory conflict will be costly and that there will gains from avoiding the transaction and reputation costs that such conflict may entail, they may well fail to reach an agreement unless they both feel that the terms are fair relative to the expected split given conflict.

---

[70] For a good overview of the evidence, see C. Camerer and R. Thaler, "Anomalies: Ultimatums, Dictators and Manners" (1995) 9 J Econ Perspectives 209.

The implication of this model of the environmental contracting process is that environmental contracts will tend to *replicate* rather than eliminate existing regulatory inefficiencies. What drives this result is my underlying assumption that only *credible* regulatory threats can affect the terms of environmental contracts. This assumption is implicit in the behavioral model of regulators as net perceived benefit maximizers. The net perceived benefits of regulation take account of the existing political structure. On this model, even if an environmental regulator's own preferences completely ignore the costs of regulation, actual regulatory outcomes are determined by the game between Congress and the administrative regulator. If the regulator pushes too far in the environmental direction, members of Congress who represent groups bearing the cost of this regulatory push will react with oversight hearings, budget reductions, and perhaps even substantive legislation.[71] The regulator is constrained by the influence and political clout of the regulated entity with Congress and the White House. But if the regulator is a strategic actor, then what the regulator will anticipate if he or she fails to reach an environmental agreement is not some sort of legislative reaction, but a regulatory outcome (a "deal" loosely speaking) that precludes legislative reaction.[72] Hence the greater a regulated firm's strategic power in this game, the better the terms it would get in any such deal, and the better will be the terms it demands in any environmental contract.

It is important to stress that this is a *political* model of regulation and regulatory contracting in its shadow. Recent economic analyses of regulatory contracting have focused instead on how the presence of transaction and enforcement costs creates room for potential Pareto-improving bargains between the regulator and the regulated firm.[73] This approach generates some interesting results—such as Amacher and Malik's demonstration that bargaining outcomes are better when the regulator is an advocate who ignores the firm's cost than when the regulator considers both costs and benefits. This literature recognizes that incredible threats to regulate (or enforce) will not affect bargaining outcomes. What it does not explore is

---

[71] On the variety of instruments of Congressional control, see M. McCubbins and T. Schwartz, "Congressional Oversight Overlooked: Police Patrols versus Fire Alarms" (1984) 28 Am J Political Sci 165–179; E. Tiller and P. Spiller, "Strategic Instruments: Legal Structure and Political Games in Administrative Law" (1999) 15 JL Econ & Org 349–377.

[72] One may derive this result formally within the context of a simple model where both the regulator and the legislature have simple Euclidean preferences. See, for instance, J. Ferejohn and C. Shipan, "Congressional Influence on Bureaucracy" (1990 Supp.) 6 JL Econ & Org 1–20; R. Gely and P. Spiller, "A Rational Choice Theory of Supreme Court Statutory Decisions with Applications to the *State Farm* and *Grove City* Cases" (1990) 6 JL Econ & Org 263–296. This is a fundamental difference between the model that I develop informally here and the model in K. Segerson and T. Miceli, "Voluntary Environmental Agreements: Good or Bad News for Environmental Protection?" (1998) 36 J Envtl Econ & Mgmt 109. They model a non-strategic regulator subject to legislative override. I presume that regardless of the regulator's particular preferences over policy outcomes, the regulator behaves strategically.

[73] See K. Segerson and T. Miceli, supra note 72; G. Amacher and A. Malik, "Instrument Choice when Regulators and Firms Bargain," (1998) 35 J Envtl Econ & Mgmt 225; G. Amacher and A. Malik, "Bargaining in Environmental Regulation and the Ideal Regulator," (1996) 30 J Envtl Econ & Mgmt 233. See also the chapters by Segerson and Dawson and Delmas and Terlaak in this book.

how the political process determines the credibility of alternative regulatory threats. On my approach, credible congressional oversight determines credible regulation, which in turn establishes the threat or disagreement point against which environmental contracts are negotiated.

As a positive matter, this model explains both when and why environmental contracting has risen in prominence in the United States. Federal environmental regulatory agencies have a media-based organizational structure. The Department of the Interior regulates land-based activities. The Corps of Engineers deals with navigable waterways. The EPA program offices are all medium-based (air, water, hazardous waste). My model predicts that within each agency (or office) potential regulatory targets are prioritized according to the communicated costs and benefits with respect to the particular medium of concern to that agency or office. Efficient trades across agencies or offices—e.g., a big, cost effective decrease in air pollution in exchange for more water pollution from a facility—are not consistent with the incentives of program officers who are subject to media-specific Congressional and bureaucratic oversight. If an officer is evaluated on the basis of his or her performance in cleaning up a specific medium, then it will be difficult to realize political gains from efficient cross-media trades.

This explains the general hostility of environmental program officers toward environmental contracting. It suggests that the incentive for environmental contracting must have developed at a higher, more political level within American environmental agencies. Both general historical and anecdotal evidence bears out this prediction. Structurally, environmental contracting has arisen during a somewhat unique period in the history of federal environmental regulation in the United States. Over the last eight years, the strongly pro-environmental Clinton Administration has faced (after 1994) a Congress dominated by Republican members from the southern and western United States who were intensely attuned to the many costs of federal environmental regulation.[74] Over this period, key Congressional gatekeepers have repeatedly threatened to make cost-benefit analysis a statutory requirement in all federal environmental legislation. Environmental contracts are a way for regulators to take site-specific costs and benefits into account, thus preserving executive control over the implementation of environmental policy and forestalling Congressional action to actually re-write federal environmental statutes.

3.3   Process and Substance in Environmental Contracts

This model illuminates two of the more controversial features of environmental contracts revealed by the survey in section 2: the exclusion of some national interest groups from the process by which environmental contracts are negotiated, and the substantive shift from a regulatory focus on remedial inputs to a contractual concern with concrete environmental outputs. Rather than looking at emissions of, say, benzene on a medium-by-medium

---

[74]   See Jon Cannon's chapter in this book.

basis with the goal of imposing particular abatement technologies, Project XL agreements allegedly attempt to target the most serious pathways of contamination. Increased airborne emissions may be traded off for reductions in wastewater effluent if waterborne contamination is judged the more serious problem. Rather than treating habitat as a fixed variable and imposing an absolute ban on development that alters existing habitat or (as in wetlands) requiring ineffective on-site mitigation, HCPs and in-lieu-fee mitigation recognize that the *quality* of habitat may matter more than the quantity. Hence they allow some reductions in quantity to be traded-off for improvements in quality. Finally, Brownfields agreements recognize that moderate cleanup expenditures coupled with commercial development will often generate a greater reduction in the risk of exposure to site-based contamination than will the continuing fruitless demand for a return to pristine conditions, a demand which only exacerbates exposure risks by leaving sites abandoned and contaminated.

The substantive flexibility underlying all of these environmental contract types rests on a common perception that local development may sometimes be necessary to restore and preserve environmental values. If this is so, then it is not immediately apparent how environmental contracting allows local development that would not otherwise occur under the default regulatory option. The model of strategic regulatory behavior that I have sketched above tells us that local development interests are unlikely to get more from an environmental contract than they would from regulation as it is actually implemented in equilibrium. But this model presumes that the same interest groups which play the regulatory implementation game also are parties to the environmental contract. Here, the shift in process wrought by environmental contracts is inseparable from the shift in substance. Environmental contracts generally reduce the role of national trade and environmental interest groups in the negotiation process (at least relative to their role under the default regulatory regime). Local development that benefits local environmental, civic, and industry groups but does not benefit corresponding national interest groups would potentially be allowed under an environmental agreement when it would not under the default regulatory regime. In particular, insofar as national interest groups have become specialists in input or technology-based command-and-control environmental regulation, they will oppose regulatory reform, which shifts the focus to environmental outcomes. Environmental contracts are founded upon the notion that it is often better to weaken environmental requirements and to allow development (or redevelopment) where environmental harm is relatively small in order to acquire the surplus funds to generate big environmental benefits elsewhere rather than to insist upon uniform requirements.

It is thus a positive prediction of my model that the enhanced flexibility achieved by environmental contracts could not have been realized without a relative decline in the role played by at least some national trade and environmental groups. It is equally important, however, to stress that my model of strategic regulation does not imply that it is normatively desirable to exclude such national groups. If most of the environmental costs of development are external to the local community that *is* represented in the environmental contract bargaining process, then excluding regional or national environmental groups may make the contract an instrument of inefficient externalization of environmental harm. Similarly, if local citizens have very little information about the environmental consequences of the proposed agreement, and there is no institutional mechanism to replace national environmental advocates as suppliers of such information, then the agreement may fail even to be locally efficient. On the other hand, by including local development interests and local environmental groups, the environmental contracting process can be made more efficient. A new, environmentally innovative firm may threaten its competitors with pollution abatement or sustainable development strategies that are both more effective and lower cost than the existing way of doing things. Local environmental groups may have an interest in the use value of local environmental goods, as opposed to the focus of national environmental groups on the non-use or existence value of these goods. Including local interest groups may indeed be a path to more flexible and efficient regulation.

In other words, the efficiency of any particular environmental contracting process depends upon its context: the type of harms or benefits generated by the agreement, the information needed to assess those harms and benefits, and their geographic extent. Were the sole purpose of HCPs to ensure that habitat is conserved and protected, then a panel of scientists who have spent their professional lives studying the concerned species might ensure the adequacy of the agreement. But many HCPs have clearly been intended as much to provide local recreational open space as to protect endangered species.[75] Local environmental groups with these interests at stake must then be included as participants in the negotiating process. Were the goal of wetland regulation to prevent *any* loss of wetlands, then it might be appropriate to include national environmental groups with this goal in the formulation of mitigation policy. But when the focus shifts to the quality of preserved wetlands—in terms of species habitat, and more general ecological service value—then, groups with such a broadened focus should appropriately be included at the bargaining table.

Of course, on a statutory level, national interest groups can only be excluded from the ex ante process of negotiating an environmental contract. They cannot be prevented from bringing citizen suits under the liberal statutory environmental citizen suit provisions. If national interest groups aren't allowed to participate in negotiating an environmental contract, then they can go to court afterward and make the arguments they would have made ex ante. This tends to make one a bit suspicious about the outright exclusion of such groups. Purely as an analytical matter, it would seem that the better approach would be to allow national interest groups to participate in the negotiation of environmental contracts by advising the local parties, but to exclude them as actual parties to the agreement.

---

[75] See T. Beatley, *Habitat Conservation Planning: Endangered Species and Urban Growth* (1994), pp. 54–68 (discussing the San Bruno HCP).

The difficulty with including such groups is that regulated entities may well be unwilling to reveal private information that is necessary to negotiate an efficient and effective environmental agreement if that information can later be used either by dissatisfied national environmental groups in future citizen suit litigation or by their competitors. For this reason, participation in the negotiation of such an agreement may be made contingent upon a contractual waiver of the right to bring a suit challenging the agreement and upon agreement to keep confidential information revealed during the negotiation process. This will not prevent the agreement from being challenged by groups who were excluded from the negotiation process. But my analysis provides direct guidance to courts in reviewing such challenges. The first thing any court should ask of the challenging party is to show what information it would have provided or what interests it would have protected in the negotiations. If the information is not germane and the interests are not affected in a reasonably direct way by the agreement, then the court should find that the challengers lack standing under the prudential or "zone of interests" prong of standing analysis. In effect, challenges to environmental agreements would be allowed only if the court found that the plaintiffs had interests and information directly relevant to statutory goals but that their information and interests were not represented by any of the parties to the agreement.

It is important to stress the distinction between including parties to the negotiation and parties to the agreement. One of the advantages that environmental contracts have over private contracts is that because they are negotiated under an existing statutory framework, the informational and representational value of inclusion can be achieved even without granting rights to veto the contract. A national environmental group might well question whether it is worth its time to participate in a negotiation when it will not be a party to the ultimate agreement. But environmental statutes give such a group the opportunity to challenge agreements ex post. A party to a private contract has to be included in the ex ante negotiation process (in theory at least) in order to have manifested assent to its terms and must give up valuable consideration to make the contract binding. Interest groups may effectively assent to the terms of an environmental contract by participating ex ante, and what they give up is an otherwise credible threat to challenge the agreement ex post. By giving up the right to bring suit for statutory violations, national interest groups would greatly improve incentives for the parties to reveal information in the bargaining process and thus overcome one of the main normative problems with environmental contracts, which is the information deficit faced by citizen and local parties to the agreement. A legally enforceable agreement not to bring a subsequent citizen suit thus benefits both local interests—by generating information they would otherwise not possess—and national interests—by giving them place at the bargaining table and a continuing representative interest in the performance of the contract.

As with the exclusion of national interest groups, the adoption of cross-media trades in environmental contracts allows the parties to get something that they could not otherwise get in the regulatory game. Again as with the exclusion of national interest groups, the normative desirability of cross-media exchanges cannot be assessed in general. Moreover, just as the efficiency of substantive terms in private contracts depends upon the process under which they were negotiated, so too the likely efficiency of cross-media trading in environmental contracts depends upon the information available to and the identity of the contracting parties. If the parties are fully informed as to the relative efficacy of targeting alternative media for emissions control or preserving and restoring some patches of habitat while losing others to development, then we may have greater assurance of the social desirability of the trade. If all the parties likely to be affected by the trade were included in the negotiation process, then again we can be more confident of the social desirability of the substantive trade-offs reached in that process.

The trade-offs found in environmental contracts necessarily reflect the regulatory status quo. Historical accident may explain why environmental regulation in the United States was initially organized by medium of contamination, but it does not explain the persistence of such an organizational form. If regulators implement regulations based on perceived net benefits, then they should look first to an industry's major emissions problem. An industry whose production process generates primarily airborne emissions will be targeted first by the Clean Air Act office. Large and established firms within an industry will be targeted first simply because they are the biggest polluters with the greatest compliance potential. Installing abatement technologies which reduce airborne emissions may initially be the cheapest and quickest way of achieving large emissions reductions. The option of devising or adopting new production technologies which actually generate fewer adverse emissions in any form is not likely to be considered initially, simply because the amount of environmental harm is so great that relatively crude command-control-directives are actually superior on cost-benefit grounds to production modification. Similarly, preserving the so-called charismatic megafauna such as whooping cranes, bald eagles, and grizzly bears may not require any serious changes in how developers do business, just better management of public lands and prohibitions on directly harmful private actions, such as deliberate killing and trading in endangered species.

Times and standards change. Cleaner and cleaner air and water becomes more and more costly on the margin. Preserving the habitat of endangered insects and mollusks extends the coverage of the ESA to vast, potentially developable private lands. The benefits to be gained from direct, and admittedly crude instruments such as media-specific technological mandates and bans on killing endangered species begin to run out. As environmental policy becomes more outcome or goal oriented, improvement can only be accomplished by exchange. In terms of my earlier model, this is to say that the costs of further enhancement in habitat quantity and quality for both human and non-human species have become so high that conventional regulatory threats have lost credibility. Once costs exceed a certain threshold level, there is no amount of spending on regulatory enforcement and no politically viable penalty structure that will induce compliance. At this point, there must be carrots as well as sticks in the regulatory tool kit.

The very inefficiency of the existing media-based regime creates the opportunity to use environmental contracts to create such carrots. By both reducing the regulated firm's costs and providing improved final environmental outputs—less risk to human health and the non-human environment—cross-media trades give something to both regulators and the regulated community. Inasmuch as they allow local development that would not otherwise occur, they also give something to local (as opposed to national) interest groups.

3.4 The Temporal Dimension: Regulatory Commitments versus Regulatory Contracts

An important distinction between environmental contracts and environmental regulations is that environmental contracts represent an attempt to bind the regulator in a way that is not possible with ordinary regulation. There is an open legal issue regarding the extent to which regulators can in fact bind subsequent regulators and legislators by making them liable to pay damages if the contract is breached.[76] Here, I assume that binding regulatory contracts will be enforced and analyze why regulators might have an incentive to enter into such agreements and the factors determining the normative desirability of such binding agreements.

Like legally binding private contracts, a major function of regulatory contracts may be to eliminate risk. When a buyer and seller contract ahead for the delivery of grain at a fixed price, they have effectively allocated the risk of market fluctuations. When a regulated firm obtains a binding commitment from a regulator, that firm has effectively shifted away the risk of changes in political preferences and changes in the information available to regulators. If the firm is risk averse but the regulator is not, then both the firm and the regulator may gain when non-binding regulations are replaced by binding regulatory contracts. For a risk averse firm, spending $100 today with a 20 percent probability of spending an additional $500 in the future is worse, and perhaps far worse, than spending $200 today. With an assurance that no further cleanup expenditure will be necessary, such a firm may agree to spend far more today (double, in this example) than it otherwise would. The regulator thereby obtains a higher level of cleanup today in exchange for giving up the opportunity to demand even more cleanup in the future. Moreover, in the Brownfields context an additional benefit is realized by state government and state residents when such agreements facilitate redevelopment of abandoned sites that would not occur without the commitment to limit future demands.

What such binding agreements sacrifice is the flexibility that regulators would otherwise have to demand further cleanup (or, more generally, tougher standards) in the future. This would not be an especially serious problem if today's regulators were certain to be tomorrow's regulators and felt the same way about future contingencies as do citizens. But the typical

---

[76] Due to the decision in *United States v. Winstar Corp.*, 518 U.S. 339 (1996).

regulator spends only a few years as a regulator and afterward is quite likely to be employed by the very industry that he or she has regulated. Thus while regulators may have the same *present* incentives as environmental groups or non-industry persons more generally, their *future* interests are likely to diverge from those of environmentalists and correspond much more closely to those of the regulated industry. Under these circumstances, the compliance standards demanded by a series of short-term regulators will diverge from the long-term standards agreeable to any one of them. Today's regulator will benefit from tying the hands of tomorrow's regulator in a way that will not be optimal for tomorrow's regulator when tomorrow rolls along.

Somewhat surprisingly, this is not necessarily normatively undesirable. Its normative desirability depends upon how today's generation feels about future harms and upon the size of the "future" generation.[77] Suppose, for instance, that the society has a very low birth rate and is in fact declining, and suppose that the present generation strongly discounts the future: an impatient generation uninterested in reproducing. Since it really attaches very little weight to the future, such a present population will be more than willing to trade-off big decreases in present environmental harm for the commitment not to demand further decreases in the future. A future regulator—albeit one representing a very small future generation—might well demand further decreases in environmental harm. If the present regulator were unable to tie the hands of such a future regulator, then the polluting industry would fail to agree to reductions in present harm that would serve the interests of the future generation.

It is also possible, however, that the interests of even the present generation conflict with those of the short-term regulator. This conflict may arise for a number of distinct reasons. Suppose, for instance, that the regulator is an attorney who expects to represent polluting industries after he or she leaves the agency. This regulator may have an incentive to reach agreements that subsequent regulators will find to be overly lax in their treatment of those industries. Indeed, the terms of the regulator's subsequent employment may implicitly depend upon the kind of regulatory contract terms that he or she gives her future clients today. A less sinister possibility is that the regulator simply attaches less weight to the future than do others in the society. The legal right to stiffen regulatory standards if and when new information about the causes and consequences of environmental changes becomes available may be less valuable to such a myopic regulator than it is to the society. Such a regulator will demand smaller increases in present environmental quality in exchange for a commitment to demand no further increases than the median voter would prefer.

It may be objected that the potential divergence between the regulator's interests and those of the median voter is a general problem which affects

---

[77]   This is in fact a version of the time inconsistency problem. For a discussion in this context, see R. Brau and C. Carraro, "Voluntary Approaches, Market Structure and Competition" (revised, March 1999).

the social optimality of regulation just as much as it affects the optimality of regulatory contracts. This objection ignores the crucial distinction between environmental regulation and a binding environmental contract. Even if one accepts my view that regulations, like regulatory contracts, result from a process of strategic bargaining among interest groups, the default rule for regulations is that they are subject to renegotiation by future regulators. Provided that the future regulator follows the required notice and comment procedures for rulemaking, and in the absence of more explicit instructions from the regulatory principal (i.e., Congress) the regulator has vast discretion over the substantive reason for revising the regulations. Under current American administrative law, once the court concludes that Congress has indeed conferred discretion upon the agency, it is very difficult for the regulated industry to succeed in getting the court to strike down new regulations as beyond the limits of reasonableness. Thus there are few direct legal constraints on regulatory renegotiation.

It is true that environmental statutory structure provided by Congress has increasingly limited the EPA's discretion by setting deadlines by which the Agency must act or else watch as detailed statutory commands—which are effectively legislative regulations—kick in. Examples of such statutes include not only the "deadline" and "hammer" provisions found in many vintage 1980's statutory revisions such as RCRA but also more recent legislation, such as the hazardous air pollutant title of the 1990 Clean Air Act. However, as a practical matter, there is very little that a court can do actually to force an agency to act. The ultimate sanction in cases where an agency fails to comply with a court order *to regulate* is to throw regulators in jail for contempt. Such a coercive step brings the executive and judicial branches into open conflict, a conflict that is likely to be more costly politically for the judge than for the regulator. After all, if regulators are dragging their feet in implementing statutory deadlines, then it is either because they would like to write regulations but are simply overburdened and are triaging programs in order of descending net perceived benefits or because their net perceived benefits of implementing the regulations are negative. If regulators are overburdened then it is hard to see how throwing them in jail will actually increase their already inadequate productivity. If they are actually responding to an interest group's argument that regulation is not a good idea, then it would seem that whatever credit regulators are getting for not regulating an industry will only increase when they demonstrate a willingness to go to jail rather than regulate.

This leaves the possibility that extralegal sanctions constrain the regulatory renegotiation. It may well be that career bureaucrats at the EPA or Department of Interior have an interest in establishing long term cooperative relationships with concerned interest groups. To develop a reputation for being cooperative and trustworthy, such bureaucrats might well have an incentive to resist attempts to renegotiate regulatory deals they helped negotiate in the first place. However attractive this story might be in general terms, it is likely to be far too simplistic. Neither the EPA nor the Department of Interior is monolithic. Within the ranks of career regulators, there are spectrum of types: some steadfastly sympathetic to environmental interest groups, others much more moderate, still others generally sympathetic to the cases made by regulated entities. Career regulators who perceive themselves as advocates for a particular interest group will tend to view regulations as compromise between their interests and those represented by other bureaucrats both within and outside (especially in the White House and Office of Management and Budget). Regulatory advocates will seize opportunities to renegotiate compromise regulations to get more for the group or groups they represent.

Like private contracts, such renegotiation opportunities will often arise because of unforeseen circumstances: a catastrophic accident that reveals the inadequacy of current regulatory standards, new scientific information on environmental risks or harm, or new economic data on the cost of regulatory compliance. Rather more often than is the case with private contracts, renegotiation opportunities also arise because the principals to the deal change. When a new administration arrives in Washington, the political appointees who run environmental agencies often have policy preferences that are very different than those of earlier regulators. When the preferences of top level, political appointees change, the relative power of career regulators changes as well. Regulators who advocate the views of environmental groups will have an incentive to renegotiate regulations adopted under a previous, relatively anti-environmental administration. External litigation by environmental groups will tend to complement such internal efforts to renegotiate: the greater the likelihood that a court will strike down a regulation, the easier it will be to get a party that was on the whole pleased by the regulation to sit down and renegotiate it.

What drives regulatory renegotiation is political change. The American system of executive democracy is subject to greater swings in policy direction than European parliamentary democracy. It takes only a small shift in median voter sentiment on a bundle of issues for a change in the executive, a change that may mean a substantial shift in environmental policy and regulation. As during the Reagan administration, previously promulgated regulations may be revised or simply go unenforced while a moratorium is placed on new regulations. The Browner EPA, by contrast, has written volumes of new regulations and new legislation against the background of repeated and explicit congressional complaints that these efforts represent a renegotiation of the existing regulatory deal. Especially in an executive democracy, environmental regulations are often subject to substantial renegotiation both up—toward tougher standards and more vigilant enforcement—and down—with little enforcement and more lenient, less costly standards.

The renegotiation of binding regulatory contracts is likely to be quite a different matter. To see how and why this is so, consider what might occur when a relatively pro-environmental administration replaces a relatively anti-environmental, pro-development administration. The existence of a regulatory contract does not prevent the new administration from asking for and spending more money on environmental enforcement. But if environmental contracts are actually legally enforceable agreements, then the new political leaders of the EPA can renegotiate existing environmental contracts to toughen the standards for some industries in some places only if they pay damages for any increase in cost borne by industry. That is, assuming that the contract does not give such a renegotiation right to the government, the government must pay regulated entities for the cost to those entities of any further reduction in environmental harm.

By analogy to the law of takings and just compensation, it might be argued that a compensation requirement improves incentives both ex ante and ex post. If a regulated firm is compensated for taking additional costly steps to reduce pollution or restore ecosystem health, then it will be much more willing to take those steps than if it was not compensated. Even if compensation is imperfect, leaving the firm with some of the cost, compensation reduces the firm's incentive to lobby and litigate against the proposed regulatory revision relative to what it would if there were no regulatory contract and no compensation requirement. As already shown, the binding agreement may be used to induce the firm to spend more on compliance at the ex ante stage than it otherwise would have done. Thus legally enforceable environmental contracts may both increase a regulated firm's present level of environmental remediation or control and reduce its resistance to further improvements in the future.

Analogies to the law of takings also apply to the other party to an environmental contract, the government. If the government can violate with impunity a contractual promise not to require a regulated firm to spend more than an agreed upon amount for environmental compliance, then the government will fail to internalize the costs it imposes on the firm and hence will regulate too stringently. Moreover, from an ex ante point of view, if the government's promise is not enforceable, then the regulated firm will be less willing to rely upon and make costly investments in pollution abatement that it would not otherwise make. This matters most with those firms and industries that lack political power. Powerful regulated entities may be able to effectively litigate and lobby to prevent regulators from violating earlier promises and toughening regulations. It is politically weaker firms and industries that will be most susceptible to government efforts to renegotiate environmental agreements if they are not effectively enforceable with damages.

This argument suffers from a serious flaw, a flaw that is also found in the economic literature dealing with the law of regulatory takings. The argument for a governmental compensation requirement rests on the uncontroversial idea that the relative costs and benefits of a government regulation determine its social desirability. But the argument implicitly assumes the net benefits from a regulation determine its political feasibility as well, so that the legislature will approve funding for projects with big net benefits and disapprove those with small or negative net benefits. This implicit assumption is false. Whether a bicameral legislature approves funding for a project depends in part upon the project's net benefits, but primarily upon the distribution of benefits and costs. When the government is made to pay for regulatory change, it has to find the funds from somewhere. Other things equal, taxes must be raised to pay for the regulatory change. When general taxes rather than beneficiary taxes are used, the distribution of costs and benefits is radically altered relative to what it would be without a compensation requirement. In particular, voters who would otherwise be indifferent between the regulatory status quo and the new regulation now bear an additional tax burden and will oppose the change.

For this reason, the compensation requirement is unlikely to block regulatory revision when those revisions generate widely distributed and widely appreciated benefits. But when a regulatory revision is perceived as benefiting only a relative minority of voters who are diffusely distributed across states, requiring compensation to those who lose from the change imposes a new tax burden that will lead a majority of voters to oppose the regulatory revision. Of course, the government may implement the costly regulatory change and simply pay for it sub rosa by reducing expenditures on other programs and policies. Still, a wholesale shift to a regime of compensated regulatory change will systematically slow the pace of regulatory change. The more costly the (compensated) change, the greater and more widely distributed must the benefits be for a majority of voters to benefit by the change.

By contrast, environmental contracts will probably leave unaffected the cost of relaxing standards. Relaxation of environmental standards is only rarely justified on the ground that compliance with the standard actually generates no benefits or even perversely increases environmental harm. More often, it is instead that relaxing the standard will generate cost savings to regulated firms that are bigger than any increase in environmental harm to citizens more generally. Sometimes the regulator will allow a regulated firm to cause more environmental harm at one site provided that it mitigates harm elsewhere. (Section 404 wetlands mitigation exemplifies such a trade and does represent a kind of liquidated damage agreement that arises under the current regulatory system.) The important point is that environmental contracts impose no further requirement upon the regulator. It is up to the regulator to determine whether the firm must make a side payment of some sort in exchange for renegotiating the regulatory contract in the firm's favor. The contract itself will not require compensation to the regulator: indeed, as argued above, the incentives of the regulator who negotiated the contract ex ante were to guarantee the firm that standards would not be stiffened in the future, not to include a clause requiring the firm to compensate the treasury if standards were relaxed.

Thus the net effect of intertemporally binding environmental contracts should be to slow the pace of many regulatory shifts toward more stringent environmental standards and development limitations. Whether this is normatively desirable or not depends upon the explanation for such shifts. To provide such an explanation is, however, a task beyond the scope of this chapter.

12. The New Political Economy of Regulation: Looking for Positive Sum Change in a Zero Sum World

David B. Spence and Lekha Gopalakrishnan

1 INTRODUCTION

The last few years have seen an explosion of popular and scholarly interest in a very old topic; namely, regulatory reform. After many decades of crying in the wilderness, critics of traditional command-and-control regulation—primarily economists—have persuaded the federal government to experiment with alternative regulatory procedures—primarily collaborative, bargaining processes—that are designed to promote more efficient regulation. That success, in turn, has heightened scholarly interest in the topic of regulatory efficiency generally. Of course, the efficiency critique of regulation has been particularly unrelenting in the field of environmental regulation, where economists have criticized the barriers to efficient pollution control posed by environmental statutes and regulations. Their arguments have spurred calls for reform of environmental regulation[1] and a wave of regulatory reform experiments at the US Environmental Protection Agency (EPA).[2] Many of the EPA's reform experiments are aimed at overcoming legal or statutory barriers to efficiency, yet after more than a half-decade of experiments, pilot projects, and "reinvention" efforts, the EPA

---

[1] Indeed, regulatory reform legislation has occupied a place on the legislative agenda of late. See, e.g., "Washington Clarifies Lender Liability" 26 Env't Rep. (BNA) 235 (1995) (discussing legislation "already passed by the House as part of the 'Contract With America,' including regulatory reform bills with an emphasis on cost-benefit analysis"); "Property Rights Measure Most Visible of Several Proposals to Curb Regulation" 25 Env't Rep. (BNA) 2502 (1995) (discussing Republicans' reform agenda generally); "House Pledges Progress on Reform, Says Help from EPA Would be 'Welcome'" 27 Env't Rep. (BNA) 1656 (1996) (discussing House Republicans' regulatory reform agenda).

[2] EPA's own reform efforts are numerous and varied. They can be tracked via EPA's "reinvention" web page, at <http://www.epa.gov/reinvent/>.

seems uncertain where to go next. Many of its reinvention programs have stalled or failed to meet expectations, and the Agency seems unable or unwilling to draw larger lessons from the successful experiments. This chapter attempts to understand and explain why.

We begin by outlining the efficiency critique of regulation, as well as economists' prescription for reform—the argument that all available positive sum changes from the status quo will be achieved through bargaining. We then explore the EPA's disappointing experience to date with a series of reforms that aim to put that bargaining prescription into practice. Next we outline some of the traditional explanations for the failure of these reforms to produce the expected benefits, and we offer an alternative explanation drawn from the traditional neoclassical economic literature. We argue that in the larger context of long-term, repeated political conflict over environmental regulation, reforms that economists would view as positive sum changes are viewed by important stakeholders in zero sum terms. Those stakeholders, primarily environmental interests inside and outside of the EPA, veto proposed reforms that would neither harm nor benefit them but would benefit their adversaries, primarily industry. We show that stakeholders exercise this veto power rationally, not simply because they suspect that proposed reforms would harm their interests, but also because this approach maximizes their ability to extract further concessions from their adversaries. We conclude with some thoughts on the implications of this analysis for the future of regulatory reform.

2   THE EFFICIENCY CRITIQUE OF REGULATION

While studies of regulations and regulatory agencies have filled scholarly journals for more than a century,[3] the call for regulatory reform has grown stronger in the last three decades, producing a succession of presidential reform initiatives. First, beginning with the stagflation and malaise of the Carter Administration and culminating in the Reagan–Bush era, the United States has seen a groundswell of opposition to regulation as part of the prescription for economic growth, particularly within the Republican Party.[4] Second, this period witnessed a general trend toward increasingly centralized White House review of regulations culminating in the Bush Administration's Competitiveness Council headed by Vice President

---

[3]   For a discussion of the early scholarly debates over administrative reform, see M. Spicer, *The Founders the Constitution and Public Administration: A Conflict of World Views* (Georgetown University Press, 1995), pp. 26–40. For a discussion of early reform debates within the federal government, John A. Rohr, *To Run a Constitution: The Legitimacy of the Administrative State* (University Press of Kansas, 1986), pp. 55–167.

[4]   This trend is chronicled in R. Harris and S. Milkis, *The Politics of Regulatory Change: A Tale of Two Agencies* (Oxford University Press, 1996), chapters 1–4, 10. See also D. Spence, "Administrative Law and Agency Policymaking: Rethinking the Positive Theory of Political Control" (1997) 14 Yale J on Reg 407, 430–432.

Dan Quayle.[5] The combination of regulatory *reform* with regulatory *relief* during the Reagan–Bush years led to some confusion of these two analytically distinct notions. The elevation of another Democrat, Bill Clinton, to the presidency in 1992 brought a retreat from the regulatory relief efforts of the Reagan–Bush years. But the Clinton Administration did not slow the movement for regulatory reform. To the contrary, it continued to press for further regulatory reform.

The distinction between regulatory relief and regulatory reform is a distinction between ends and means—between simply reducing the regulatory burden on industry by lowering standards, on the one hand, and addressing the question of how best to achieve a given standard, on the other. Though some have pushed unsuccessfully for reform under the guise of the relief,[6] we are interested only in regulatory reform. The persistent and broad-based impulse toward regulatory reform has been fed not only by politicians and interest groups, but by a scholarly critique of the regulatory system that has continued to develop alongside the political debate. That scholarly critique has coalesced along two dimensions: one that focuses on the *substantive efficiency* of regulatory policies and another that focuses on *procedural efficiency*, or rather the inefficiencies that stem from the process by which agencies make policy. The former critique is led by economists, the latter by public administration scholars, and both have allies among legal scholars. We will briefly outline those critiques now.

2.1 Substantive Efficiency

Economists' critique of inefficient government regulations is well known, as is their prescription for inefficiency; namely, the replacement of regulatory

---

[5] The Council was roundly criticized for providing extra-legal opportunities for input to the regulatory process for industry, and Congress ultimately voted to remove the Council's funding. See "House Votes to Cut Funds of Quayle Council" 23 Env't Rep. (BNA) 776 (1992).

[6] Indeed, Resources for the Future's Paul Portney has labeled these efforts "cartoon reform." See P. Portney, "Cartoon Caricatures of Regulatory Reform" (Fall 1995) 121 *Resources for the Future* 21. We would place the efforts of the Competitiveness Council and some parts of the 1994 House Republicans' environmental agenda in this category as well. It is worth noting that some critics of reform do not make this distinction or suspect that most regulatory reform is a disguised attempt at regulatory relief. See, e.g., Heinzerling, "Reductionist Regulatory Reform" (1997) 8 Fordham Envtl L J 459, 460–461 ("the express purpose of the laws regulating pollution in this country is the protection of human health and natural resources") (coupling the 1994 "Contract with America" with risk-based regulatory reform); E. Geltman and A. Skroback, "Reinventing the EPA to Conform with the New American Environmentality" (1998) 23 Colum J Envtl L 1, 25–26 (describing 1994 House Republicans anti-environmental agenda). Of course, we acknowledge the existence of good faith arguments that regulatory standards (the ends of regulation) may be inefficiently stringent from a social welfare point of view. This argument is often associated with advocacy of risk analysis as a guide to spending on environmental protection. For a good summary of this large literature, see F. Cross, "The Subtle Vices Behind Environmental Values" (1997) 8 Duke Envtl L and Pol'y F 151; C. Sunstein, "A Note on 'Voluntary' versus 'Involuntary' Risks" (1997) 8 *Duke Envtl L and Pol'y F* 173. We do not address those arguments here; rather, we are concerned only with reform arguments aimed at the means of achieving regulatory goals.

mandates with market incentives. Since at least the early twentieth century and the writings of A.C. Pigou,[7] economists have favored regulation that is minimally prescriptive, leaving to regulated firms the task of determining the means of complying with regulatory limits and goals. That preference for cost-efficiency has led to sustained criticism of so-called "command-and-control" environmental regulation, under which (1) all regulated firms must meet uniform, technology-based pollution control standards and (2) regulators often specify not only the firm's pollution control goal, but the means of achieving it as well.[8] Economists contend that by specifying *how* individual firms must contribute to pollution control goals we make pollution control unnecessarily costly. This is because command-and-control regulation ignores opportunities for gains from technological innovation and gains from trade.

First, leaving the means of pollution control to the discretion of the firm provides an incentive for firms to develop less costly control technologies; conversely, specifying control technologies destroys that incentive.[9] EPA regulations are replete with examples of prescriptions that force firms to use inefficient means to achieve a regulatory goal. Perhaps the most frequently-cited testimonial to the fact is the celebrated Yorktown Pollution Prevention Project, a multi-year collaborative effort between Amoco and the EPA that yielded an agreement to permit Amoco to reduce pollution from its Yorktown, Virginia refinery using more cost-effective approaches than those specified in EPA rules. Edward Weber, who has studied the Yorktown Project, described how project participants identified the gains to be had from regulatory flexibility:

[Stakeholders] discovered a number of instances in which regulations were poorly matched to the emissions profile of the facility. For example, in the particular case of benzene, ... EPA rules issued in 1990 required Amoco to build a $31 million water-treatment system to capture benzene vapors emanating from the wastewater. But data gathered by the [project participants] showed "that EPA's basic assumptions in requiring such a system ... were wrong for this refinery ..." At the same time, the project's monitoring efforts uncovered a far more serious, and unregulated, benzene

---

[7] Pigou, *The Economics of Welfare* (AMS Press, 1922). Most environmental economics texts contain good descriptions of Pigou's ideas. See, e.g., T. Tietenberg, *Environmental Economics and Policy* (Addison-Wesley Publishing Co., 1998); R. Turner and D. Pearce, *Economics of Natural Resources and the Environment* (John Hopkins University Press, 1990); W. Baumol and W. Oates, *Economics, Environmental Policy, and the Quality of Life* (Ashgate Publishing Co., 1979).
[8] This literature is far too extensive to summarize here. For good summaries of the argument, see Tietenberg, supra note 7, at 362–369; and Turner and Pearce, supra note 7, at 84.
[9] While most federal air and water emissions standards are "technology-based," most such standards do not legally require that firms actually use the technology on which the standard is based. See, e.g., 40 C.F.R. Parts 60–63 (permitting standards under the Clean Air Act) and 125, 129 (permitting standards under the Clean Water Act). Sometimes, however, permitting agencies include such specifications in permits. Furthermore, firms may deem it in their best interests to use the technology in order to minimize the chances of harsh regulatory treatment in the event of a future problem. Finally, other parts of the federal environmental regulatory structure specify in detail *how* firms must accomplish regulatory goals. See discussion of the Amoco Yorktown facility, in the text above.

problem at the refinery's loading docks...Given the estimated $6 million capital construction cost of controlling barge-loading emissions, the refinery could have saved $25 million while concurrently cleaning up five times more pollution...[10]

Second, pollution control can be made less costly by allowing those firms that can reduce pollution more inexpensively to bear the lion's share of the control burden. Command-and-control regulation may specify that firms A and B must each reduce their pollution by 10 units. If firm A can reduce pollution at a flat cost of $10 per unit of pollution, and if firm B's pollution reduction costs are $50 per unit, then the firms provide 20 units of pollution reduction at a total cost of $600. However, if firm A provided all 20 units of pollution reduction, the cost would be $200. A system of pollution taxes or marketable permits would allow these gains to be realized[11] and would provide a further incentive for firms to develop less costly pollution control methods.[12] Despite some incremental movement toward market-based approaches in the first three decades of modern American environmental regulation, the United States continues to rely mostly on command-and-control approaches. Hence the continuing calls for greater substantive efficiency in that regulatory regime.

2.2 Procedural Efficiency

Since the inception of the modern environmental movement, the EPA has relied overwhelmingly on rulemaking to make and administer environmental policy, far more than most other federal agencies.[13] Scholars trace this predilection to the political environment under which the EPA was created, noting that modern environmental laws were enacted at a time of heightened concern over the problem of agency capture by industry.[14] The EPA

---

[10] E. Weber, *Pluralism by the Rules: Conflict and Cooperation in Environmental Regulation* (Georgetown University Press, 1998), p. 201.

[11] Of course, under a marketable permit system, firm B would be willing to purchase 10 units of pollution reduction from firm A for some amount greater than or equal to $100. Likewise, at any tax rate greater than $20 per unit of pollution reduced, firm A will choose to reduce pollution by 20 units (or more), while firm B will choose to pay the pollution tax.

[12] It is easy to see how, under either system, firms will try to devise less expensive pollution reduction methods to further reduce their own costs.

[13] Some agencies eschew rules, preferring to make decisions on a case-by-case basis. Others adopt broad policies but choose not to promulgate them formally as rules. Of course, the Administrative Procedures Act (APA) requires that all "rules" be promulgated through APA rulemaking procedures. But as others have noted, many broad policies that appear to meet the definition of a "rule" under the APA are not formally memorialized as rules. For a discussion of these policy-making options, see Spence, "Administrative Law and Agency Policymaking," supra note 4. In any case, EPA's relative preference for rulemaking has been well chronicled. See, e.g., C. Kerwin, *Rulemaking: How Government Agencies Write Law and Make Policy* (CQ Press, Washington D.C., 1994).

[14] Among the many prominent academics voicing this concern were E. Schattschneider, *The Semisovereign People: A Realist's View of Democracy in America* (1975); M. Olson, *The Logic of Collective Action* (Harvard University Press, 1965); R. Stewart, *The Reformation of American Administrative Law* (1975); and T. Lowi, *The End of Liberalism* (W.W. Norton & Company, 1979).

was designed specifically to resist this kind of capture.[15] Even with its tamper-resistant design, however, EPA's policy-makers have remained acutely aware of the possibility that industry might nevertheless capture the agency by persuading a sympathetic future President to appoint leaders who might try to undermine the Agency's mission. Rulemaking is a logical *ex ante* response to that risk. Memorializing policy choices in regulations makes it more costly for future agency policy-makers to reverse those choices.[16] Indeed, agencies face the question of whether to memorialize policies in formally promulgated regulations continually (when facing new policy choices) and continuously (with respect to each existing informal policy). In making that decision the agency balances the benefits of rulemaking against the transaction costs. Therefore, the probability that current policy-makers will choose to formalize a policy in the form of a rule is partly a function of their assessment of future policy-makers' hostility to the policy. Thus, the EPA's attachment to rulemaking testifies to its (and its environmental constituents')[17] omnipresent concern over possible future capture by industry.[18]

Of course, there are all sorts of other reasons to engage in rulemaking, not the least of which is the desire to strengthen the effect of favored policies by giving them the force of law. In addition, Kenneth Culp Davis has made the case for rulemaking as an objectively superior process that maximizes fairness, access, and certainty in administrative law.[19] However, scholars from a variety of disciplines have identified some of the drawbacks and unintended consequences of rulemaking as a policy-making device. One group of critics argues that overuse of rulemaking has slowed agency decision-making and multiplied interest group opportunities to challenge agency decisions in court, causing an explosion of administrative litigation and a consequent reordering of administrative priorities. This, in turn, has made agencies gun-shy and produced an "ossified" agency decision-making process that is less flexible, less rational, and less

---

[15] Thus, the Agency's mission was defined clearly in pro-environmental terms in enabling legislation, in part to attract environmentally concerned professionals to the agency, and also to facilitate legal challenges by environmental interest groups in the event the agency swayed from this path in the future. See Alfred Marcus, Promise and Performance: Choosing and Implementing an Environmental Policy (1980).

[16] For an argument to this effect, see, e.g., T. Moe, *The Politics of Structural Choice: Toward a Theory of Public Bureaucracy, in Organization Theory: From Chester Barnard to the Present and Beyond* (1990), pp. 116–153; T. Moe, "Political Institutions: The Neglected Side of the Story" (1990) 6 JL Econ & Org 213 (Special Issue). This does not mean, of course, that future agencies cannot reverse the policy; they can. That is what happened (and what the Supreme Court approved) in *Chevron U.S.A., Inc. v. Natural Resources Defense Council, Inc.* 467 U.S. 837 (1984).

[17] We should note Congress often specifies that particular policies must be embodied in formally promulgated rules. This too can be explained as a precautionary device against capture instigated by environmental interests and their Congressional allies. See Moe, *The Politics of Structural Choice*, supra note 16.

[18] The term "capture" is beginning to fall into disfavor, primarily because it is vague and because of its conspiratorial or pejorative connotations. For a discussion of the varieties of capture, see D. Spence, "Agency Discretion and the Dynamics of Procedural Reform" (1999) 59 *Public Administration Review* 425.

[19] See K. Davis, *Discretionary Justice* (Greenwood Publishing Group, 1969).

effective.[20] Another group of critics argues that rulemaking necessarily begets certain varieties of substantive inefficiency because the task of writing an "optimally specific" rule is difficult if not impossible.[21] Most of the time, one size does not fit all. For this reason, crafting a rule that simultaneously provides meaningful guidance to private sector actors *and* accommodates the myriad circumstances that the rule will encounter over the course of its lifetime is a Herculean task. The attempt to accommodate specific situations (either at the drafting stage or in subsequent revisions) can make rules complicated and unwieldy, as the previously cited Yorktown Project illustrates.[22] This kind of problem has led some scholars to propose that agencies rely only minimally on rules, or that agencies instead make rules on a case-by-case basis, in the same way that common law "rules" emerge from a body of case law.[23] Others recommend ways to make rules more adaptable and accommodating, such as writing less specific rules, authorizing waivers, and the like.[24] Indeed, it is this need to make exceptions to

---

[20] This argument has sparked a lively debate. See, e.g., Spicer, supra note 3; T. McGarity, "Some Thoughts on Deossifying the Rulemaking Process" (1992) 41 Duke L J 1385; T. McGarity, "A Cost-Benefit State" (1998) 50 Admin L Rev 7, 26; C. Sunstein, "Congress, Constitutional Moments, and the Cost-Benefit State" (1996) 48 Stan L Rev 247 (advocating more adaptive rules); M. Seidenfeld, "Demystifying Deossification: Rethinking Recent Proposals to Modify Judicial Review of Notice and Comment Rulemaking" (1997) 75 Tex L Rev 483; and M. Siedenfeld, "Bending the Rules: Flexible Regulation and Constraints on Agency Discretion" Unpublished Paper, Florida State University School of Law (1999) (on file with authors) (arguing, among other things, that the ability of agencies to evade procedural mandates helps ameliorate the ossification problem); T. McGarity, "The Courts and Ossification of Rulemaking: A Response to Professor Seidenfeld" (1997) 75 Tex L Rev 525; R. Anthony and D. Codevilla, "Pro-Ossification: A Harder Look at Agency Policy Statements" (1996) 31 Wake Forest L Rev 667, 676–680; R. Pierce, Jr., "Seven Ways to Deossify Agency Rulemaking"; (1995) 47 Admin L Rev 59, 82–86; J. Freeman, "Collaborative Governance in the Administrative State" (1997) 45 UCLA L Rev 1, 18 (arguing that "adversarialism ... has contributed to a rigid rulemaking and implementation process that fails to encourage creativity, adaptation, and cooperation in solving regulatory problems").

[21] See C. Diver, "The Optimal Precision of Administrative Rules" (1983) 93 Yale L J 65 ("The degree of precision appropriate to any particular rule depends on a series of variables peculiar to the rule's author, enforcer, and addressee. As a consequence, generalizations about optimal rule precision are inherently suspect."); Spicer, supra note 3; C. Sunstein, "Problems With Rules" (1995) 83 Calif L Rev 953, 1021 ("A system dedicated to the rule of law is committed to limiting official discretion, but it is not committed to the unrealistic goal of making every decision according to judgments specified in advance."); P. Howard, *The Death of Common Sense: How the Law Is Suffocating America* (Warner Books, 1993) p. 27 ("Once the idea is to cover every situation explicitly, the words of law expand like floodwaters that have broken through a dike. Rules elaborate on prior rules; detail breeds greater detail. There is no logical stopping point in the quest for certainty").

[22] See supra note 10 and accompanying text. For an exploration of this phenomenon in federal regulations, see Howard, supra note 21, at 17–18 (describing legal impediments to "sensible" mass transit policy in New York).

[23] This is what Spicer, supra note 3, proposes. Likewise, Sunstein prescribes a system of "causuistry" and "privately adaptable rules ... that allocate initial entitlements but do not specify end states." Sunstein, supra note 21, at 958. Freeman prescribes "provisional" rules that allow for adaptation of the rule to new, unforeseen circumstances. Freeman, supra note 20, at 22.

[24] *WAIT Radio v. F.C.C.*, 418 F.2d 1153 (D.C. Cir., 1969) stands for the proposition that the right to waive regulations is implied by the delegation to the agency of the right to create regulations. Likewise, the US Supreme Court has authorized EPA to grant waivers, absent explicit

rules that lies at the root of many of the EPA's reform initiatives, a subject to which we turn now.

3   THE BARGAINING PRESCRIPTION IN THEORY AND PRACTICE

Neoclassical economics prescribes a framework for solving the kind of inefficiency problems facing the regulatory system. At the heart of that framework is the concept of Pareto optimality. Pareto optimality measures alternatives according to the satisfaction, or utility, each alternative would produce among affected individuals. In other words, given a status quo position or distribution, if no change in that position or distribution can be made without making at least one individual worse off, then the status quo is said to be "Pareto optimal." Similarly, any change from the status quo that makes one individual better off without making another worse off is "Pareto superior." It is a fundamental axiom of neoclassical microeconomics that under certain conditions a Pareto optimal distribution should be achieved through bargaining.[25]

This notion is commonly illustrated through the use of a so-called "Edgeworth Box."[26] Consider Figure 1, which depicts the standard Edgeworth Box bargaining process in a two-person, two-good economy. Every point in

---

statutory authority to do so, in at least one instance. See *Chemical Mfrs. Ass'n v. N.R.D.C.*, 470 U.S. 116 (1985) (upholding EPA's variance program under the Clean Water Act as a reasonable way of ensuring that the agency's "necessarily rough-hewn" rules do not impose a hardship on atypical firms). The Supreme Court's opinion in *Heckler v. Chaney*, 470 U.S. 821 (1985), which hold that an agency decision *not* to take enforcement action was unreviewable, sparked a debate over the reviewability of waiver decisions. For a good discussion of the legal authority for granting waivers to rules and the reviewability of waiver decisions, see J. Rossi, "Waivers, Flexibility and Reviewability" (1997) 72 Chi-Kent L Rev 1359. See also, C. Caldart and N. Ashford, "Negotiation as a Means of Developing and Implementing Environmental Policy" (1998) Unpublished Working Paper, MIT, 22–23 (on file with author) (discussing the legal authority for waiving regulatory requirements in existing environmental statutes and EPA's reluctance to use its waiver authority); D. Hirsch, "Bill and Al's XL-ent Adventure: An Analysis of the EPA's Legal Authority to Implement the Clinton Administration's Project XL" (1998) U Ill L Rev 129, 160–165 (arguing that EPA has a broad implied waiver authority to make exceptions to regulatory requirements); B. Mank, "The Environmental Protection Agency's Project XL and Other Regulatory Reform Initiatives: The Need for Legislative Reauthorization" (1998) 25 Ecology L Q 1, 24–26, 31–34.

[25]   Indeed, this basic notion underlies the First Fundamental Theorem of welfare economics, which says that *if* given a perfectly competitive market economy: (1) consumers maximize utility and consumer preferences are "convex" (see definition of convexity, infra note 28); (2) consumer preferences satisfy nonsatiation, i.e., "more is better"; and (3) there are no "market failures," that is, markets exist for all goods, there are no externalities and increasing returns to scale (and natural monopolies) do not exist; then the competitive market equilibrium is Pareto optimal. See, e.g., D. Kreps, *A Course in Microeconomic Theory* (Princeton University Press, 1990), p. 199.

[26]   This device is named after Francis Ysidro Edgeworth, an English economist. The Edgeworth box assumes a two-person, two-good economy, and it uses the microeconomic concept of "indifference curves" to illustrate why private bargaining among individuals should lead to a Pareto optimal distribution of goods in the usual case.

Figure 1   The Standard Edgeworth Box Analysis

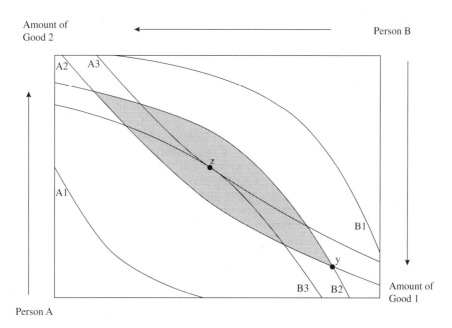

the Box represents a potential division of the total amount of goods 1 and 2 between persons A and B. Assume that A's utility increases moving from indifference curve[27] A1 to A3, and that B's utility increases from B1 to B3.[28] It is easy to demonstrate that point y in Figure 1 is Pareto inferior or

---

[27]   Of course, as the name implies, the indifference curve represents the various combinations of goods 1 and 2 between which person A is indifferent. In other words, at every point on indifference curve A1, person A has the same level of utility as she would at any other point on that curve; that is, she is indifferent between the various combinations of goods represented by that curve. In this way, the shape of the curves shows A's marginal rate of substitution between the two goods—that is, the rate at which person A is willing to exchange an amount of good 1 for an amount of good 2—over a range of possible combinations. The marginal rate of substitution is actually the slope of the indifference curve.

[28]   Curves that are farther from the origin represent higher levels of utility; thus, A would be happier with a distribution on curve A2 than curve A1. In the usual case, indifference curves look like those shown in Figure 1: that is, they are monotonic, with a decreasing slope as x (or the amount of good one in person A's bundle) increases. This means simply that over the range of choice examined, more of each good is better, implying a negative slope to the curve. This is also sometimes referred to as the property of "convexity." Hence, economists say that "well-behaved" indifference curves are convex to the origin. Convexity implies that the marginal rate of substitution for a good decreases over increasing amounts of that good. This assumes away the notion of satiation—i.e., that there are distributions of goods at which a person may not prefer more of a particular good. While the assumption of monotonicity assumes away the notion of satiation, the assumption of convexity reflects the decreasing marginal utility of a good at higher amounts of the good. This is, of course, true for many goods.

suboptimal. Indeed, all the points in the shaded area represent distributions that are Pareto superior to y, because the parties can move to higher indifference curves (and greater levels of utility or satisfaction) by voluntarily engaging in trades that take them into the shaded areas from these initial distribution points. Given an initial distribution at point y, trades that place the parties at point z will put each party on a higher indifference curve; hence, point z is Pareto superior to point y. In fact, point z represents a Pareto optimal distribution because it, like all Pareto optimal distributions within the Edgeworth Box, is at a point in which the indifference curves of A and B are tangent to each other.[29] At these points of tangency, any trade that moves one person to a higher indifference curve will move the other to a lower one. Hence, these points are Pareto optimal.

This basic idea, which motivated much of the economic critique of environmental regulation for decades, was given voice in the Clinton Administration, primarily through the Gore report on "reinventing government" and subsequent agency initiatives to reinvent administration at the federal government level.[30] The move to reinvent the EPA was also spurred on by a series of reports by the National Academy of Public Administration (NAPA) that focused exclusively on reforming environmental regulation.[31] Like the scholarship that preceded them, these reports identified problems in both the product and process of environmental regulation. They concluded that, as a product, environmental regulation was sometimes too prescriptive and too detailed. Overly detailed prescriptions sometimes foreclosed opportunities for more efficient and effective ways to achieve regulatory goals.[32] The reports urged the EPA to explore the further use of market incentives, risk-based decision making, and opportunities for greater cooperation with states, local governments, citizens, and industry.[33]

For its part, the EPA did not wait for the Gore and NAPA reports before undertaking its own in-house reforms. The Agency undertook a series of regulatory initiatives designed to promote pollution reduction by industry, including experiments with more cooperative approaches to regulation[34] and a series of voluntary programs designed to persuade industry to move

---

[29] This generalization holds true assuming well-behaved preferences for both parties.

[30] See A. Gore, "From Red Tape to Results: Creating a Government that Works Better and Costs Less" (7 September 1993) The Report of the National Performance Review.

[31] See NAPA, "Setting Priorities, Getting Results: A New Direction for EPA" (1995); and NAPA, "Resolving the Paradox of Environmental Protection: An Agenda for Congress, the EPA and the States" (1997).

[32] See, e.g., Gore, supra note 30, Executive Summary, Appendix A, Recommendations EPA01, EPA02, and EPA04; and NAPA, "Setting Priorities, Getting Results," supra note 31, at 97–104.

[33] NAPA, "Setting Priorities, Getting Results," supra note 31, at 100–104. Indeed, the Gore report explicitly urged agencies to make more and better use of negotiated rulemaking and other consensus based processes. Gore, supra note 30.

[34] The Administrative Procedures Act authorizes the use of negotiated rulemaking at 5 U.S.C. Subchapter III. Shortly after the Gore report, the President signed Executive Order 12,866, which directed executive branch agencies to explore the use of "consensual mechanisms for developing regulations" and to use negotiated rulemaking where possible.

"beyond compliance" in pollution control.[35] The Clinton EPA initiated a wide variety of pilot programs and regulatory experiments addressing nearly every element of the modern critique of regulation.[36] We briefly summarize the progress of two reforms, each of which (1) embodies a more cooperative, less formal, and less adversarial approach to regulation as a means to achieve existing environmental goals more efficiently; (2) seeks to enable regulators to take advantage of the specialized knowledge of industry in order to avoid regulatory inefficiencies; and (3) has met considerable resistance and criticism from opponents of reform. One reform is the EPA's Project XL program, which has been widely promoted by the Clinton Administration as an example of its new approach to regulation. Its focus is narrow, attacking regulatory inefficiency on a firm-by-firm basis. The second reform is the EPA's use of negotiated rulemaking, which offers an example of the Agency's attempts to apply cooperative or collaborative processes on a broader scale.

The Project XL program was first announced by the Clinton administration in March 1995 as the most highly-touted of a package of initiatives aimed at encouraging rational regulatory reform without rolling back or compromising environmental quality objectives.[37] The EPA had high ambitions for Project XL, promising to implement 50 pilot projects by mid-1997.[38] The EPA initially established eight criteria for selecting companies for Project XL: (1) superior environmental performance;[39] (2) cost savings; (3) support of interested stakeholders, including local communities and governments; (4) testing of new and innovative processes that prevent the generation of pollution; (5) testing of new approaches that could be incorporated into other EPA programs; (6) technical and administrative feasibility; (7) making information about the project available to interested parties for evaluating success; and (8) ensuring compliance with Executive Order 12898 on environmental justice.[40] Despite high hopes that the program would provide an avenue for consensus-based, positive sum change in environmental policy, the program experienced an early set back on 5 September 1996, when the sponsor of one of the program's most

---

[35]   For analyses of EPA's voluntary programs, see T. Davies and J. Mazurek, "Industry Incentives for Environmental Improvement: Evaluation of U.S. Federal Initiatives" Prepared for the Global Environmental Management Institute (1996); M. Gearhart, "Case Studies in the Implementation of Voluntary Environmental Management System Standards" *Rosenbaum News & Views*, <www.lawinfo.com/law/ca/environmentallaw/Gearhart.htm>; M. Khanna and L. Damon, "EPA's Voluntary 33/50 Program: Impact on Toxic Releases and Economic Performance of Firms" (1997) University of Illinois at Urbana-Champaign Envtl and Resource Econ Working Paper No. 8; J. McCarthy, "Voluntary Programs to Reduce Pollution" (1995) Congressional Research Service Report for Congress.

[36]   These various initiatives are described at the EPA's reinvention web site at <http://www.epa.gov/reinvent/>.

[37]   See US EPA, Regulatory Reinvention (XL) Pilot Projects, 60 Fed. Reg. 27,282 (23 May 1995).

[38]   Ibid.

[39]   Ibid. at 27,287. The notice stated that projects must deliver "environmental performance that is superior to what would be achieved through compliance with current and reasonably anticipated future regulation."

[40]   Ibid. at 27,287.

promising early proposals—the Minnesota-based 3M Company—notified the EPA that it was withdrawing from the Project XL process. As late as June 1996, the EPA, 3M, and the state had seemed close to an agreement on the project, and company representatives seemed confident that the 3M plant was in line to receive the first-ever multimedia permit.[41] One of the reasons cited for 3M's withdrawal was a dispute over whether 3M's proposal would satisfy the the Agency's requirement to achieve superior environmental performance.[42]

The 3M experience led the agency to reevaluate the XL process. In early 1997 the EPA revised its decision criteria by stating that in the future the Agency would emphasize three factors in deciding whether to approve an XL proposal: (1) whether the proposal would achieve superior environmental performance (which it also defined more precisely); (2) whether the types of regulatory flexibility proposed were appropriate and might serve as a model for other projects; and (3) whether the proposal contained adequate opportunities for involvement by stakeholders.[43] Since the 1997 notice, several high-profile companies have secured approval for their XL proposals. However, progress in the XL program has not kept pace with expectations. The program has succeeded in identifying opportunities for positive sum change,[44] but it appears that only a small subset of these opportunities are being realized. As of this writing, the EPA has approved only 11 projects for implementation; in the same time period, three times as many projects have either been rejected or have been withdrawn from consideration by the sponsoring company.[45] Perhaps more importantly, the XL program has been treated with scorn within the Agency,[46] where its legality

---

[41] See "3M Decides to Drop out of Project XL Process After Disagreement Over Performance Guarantees" (1996) 27 Env't Rep (BNA) 1045, 1046; C. Buelow, "Barriers to Regulatory Reform as Experienced in the 3M Project XL Pilot 18–21" (May 1997) (unpublished Master's thesis, Duke University) (on file with authors).

[42] 3M proposed reductions in the allowable emission levels under its air permit, a benefit that participants in the bargaining process appeared to believe satisfied the criterion. Some at EPA disagreed, however, apparently because 3M's actual emissions had been below even the reduced levels. See Beulow, supra note 41. The 3M Project XL case is further discussed in the chapter by Alfred Marcus et al., in this book.

[43] Regulatory Reinvention (XL) Pilot Projects, Notice of Modifications to Project XL, 62 Fed. Reg. 19,872 (23 April 1997).

[44] In addition to the 3M example, other XL proposals (such as the Berry and Intel projects) would involve emissions reductions coupled with increased compliance flexibility for industry. For an in-depth study of the Intel proposal, see J. Boyd et al., "Intel's XL Permit: A Framework for Evaluation" (1998) Resources for the Future Discussion Paper 98-11. The Merck XL project addressed a prototypical example of rule-based inefficiency. Under applicable ozone regulations, small changes in emissions of volatile organic chemicals (VOCs) at the Merck facility would have triggered costly permitting requirements even though the change would not increase ozone concentrations due to the unusual characteristics of the area (low levels of nitrogen oxides, a necessary precursor of ozone). See Hirsch, supra note 24, at 143–146. See also Hirsch's chapter in this book.

[45] See <http://yosemite.epa.gov/xl/xl_home.nsf/all/homepage>.

[46] An internal EPA newsletter quoted an unidentified EPA staffer as saying the "if it isn't illegal, it isn't XL." This quotation has been reproduced in a number of places. See, e.g., R. Steinzor, "Regulatory Reinvention and Project XL: Does the Emperor Have Any Clothes?" 26 Envtl L Rep 10,527 (citing "What's Up With Project XL" Week of 11 March 1996, Project XL update).

and wisdom have been questioned. Environmental interest groups[47] and commentators[48] have echoed these concerns, particularly with respect to (1) the fear that XL projects will result in environmental harm and (2) the concern that the projects often require variances or exemptions from legal requirements.[49] However, despite a recent groundswell of criticism, the program continues; indeed, compared to many of the EPA's other reform initiatives, its future is relatively secure.

Negotiated rulemaking can be conceived of as Project XL writ large, in that it employs the same goals and methods but on a broader scale. While negotiated rulemaking takes place throughout the executive branch, nowhere has it been used as frequently and extensively as it has at the EPA.[50] In theory, negotiated rulemaking is designed to bring stakeholders into the regulation development process earlier, to promote the sharing of information and perspectives among stakeholders and the agency, and thereby to produce better and less controversial rules.[51] Given the amount of resources the EPA devotes to rulemaking and litigation in defense of its rules,[52] it is perhaps not surprising that the Agency has also been a frequent user of negotiated rulemaking. Indeed, if negotiated rulemaking can produce less controversial rules, there is good reason to expect that the EPA would be a frequent user of the process. However, despite its eager embrace of negotiated rulemaking, the EPA's experiences with the process have met with a decidedly mixed reaction. Its critics contend that the process (1) has not produced better, more widely-accepted regulations; (2) has not saved agency resources;[53] (3) has not helped the agency avoid

---

[47] See C. Skrzycki, "Critics See a Playground for Polluters in EPA's XL Plan" Washington Post (24 January 1997) D1 ("Environmental and citizens' groups have their own names for what the Environmental Protection Agency's Project XL stands for: Instead of Excellence and Leadership, they call it 'Extra Leniency'").

[48] The scholarly criticisms of the XL program, are also discussed infra section 3.

[49] See R. Steinzor, "Reinventing Environmental Regulation: The Dangerous Journey from Command to Self-Control" (1998) 22 Harv Envtl L Rev 103, 134–136; Geltman and Skorback, supra note 6 at 33–34 (contending that Project XL operates "contrary to" the law); Mank, supra note 24, at 24–28, and 70–88 (arguing that the XL program lacks the statutory authority to waive regulatory requirements, and urging legislative reform to authorize XL); B/Wechsler, "Note: Rethinking Reinvention: A Case Study of Project XL" (1998) 5 *Environmental Lawyer* 255, 275 (arguing that XL's "tenuous legal foundations" will limit its effectiveness).

[50] For a summary of EPA and other agencies' use of negotiated rulemaking, see C. Coglianese, "Assessing Consensus: The Promise and Performance of Negotiated Rulemaking" (1997) 46 Duke L J 1255, especially Appendices A and B. For a summary of EPA's negotiated rulemaking experience, see L. Langbein and C. Kerwin, "Regulatory Negotiation Versus Conventional Rulemaking: Claims, Counter-claims, and Empirical Evidence", Unpublished Manuscript (1998) George Washington University School of Public Affairs (on file with authors).

[51] Philip Harter is sometimes cited as the leading force behind APA's endorsement of negotiated rulemaking. His arguments in its favor are summarized in P. Harter, "Negotiating Regulations: A Cure for Malaise" (1982) 71 Geo L J 1. See also Freeman, supra note 20 at 33–40.

[52] For two good analyses of the litigation process that follows EPA rulemakings, see R. O'Leary, *Environmental Change: Federal Courts and the EPA* (Temple University Press, 1993); and C. Coglianese, *Challenging the Rules: Litigation and Bargaining in the Administrative Process* (Book Manuscript, Harvard University, 1995).

[53] Coglianese, "Assessing Consensus," supra note 50, at 1321 (arguing that there is little or no difference in the likelihood that a negotiated rule will be challenged in court compared with a

litigation;[54] and (4) represents an abdication of the Agency's decision-making responsibilities to private sector participants in the negotiation process.[55] Its defenders dispute these contentions[56] and argue that negotiated rulemaking has produced some benefits that are difficult to quantify or measure.[57] Whatever the ultimate verdict, it is safe to say that the process remains controversial, particularly among environmental groups.

It seems clear that neither Project XL nor negotiated rulemaking has been an unqualified success, though perhaps this is an unrealistic goal in the contentious and polarized world of environmental policy making. In both examples, the EPA was able to bring together industry and environmental interests (from inside and outside the agency) to share information and seek positive sum change through consensus. However, consensus was not always forthcoming, even in support of what appeared to be clear Pareto improvements. Critics of reform are at least partially correct when they ascribe the disappointing performance of the EPA's reforms to legal and political impediments. That is, some regulatory reforms run up against statutory and other legal constraints, and those constraints reflect (at least, in part) policy values other than cost-effectiveness and flexibility. Likewise, these regulatory reforms effect at least a putative transfer of decision-making initiative from regulators to the regulated. However, these arguments beg the more general question: why do these legal and political impediments exist? Why might environmental interests resist efficiency

---

traditionally promulgated rule and that promulgating negotiated rules consumes no fewer resources than traditional notice and comment rulemaking). See also Caldart and Ashford, supra note 24, at 10–11 (arguing that negotiated rulemaking has not delivered on its primary promised benefits of reduced rulemaking time and reduced litigation).

[54] Coglianese, "Assessing Consensus," supra note 50, at 1321 (concluding that negotiated rulemaking "actually creates new sources of potential conflict in the regulatory process" by providing additional opportunities "to disrupt the consensus…").

[55] See W. Funk, "Bargaining Toward the New Millenium: Regulatory Negotiation and the Subversion of the Public Interest" (1997) 46 Duke L J 1351, 1374–80. For further detailed discussion of this issue, see infra section 4.

[56] Langbein and Kerwin, supra note 50, offer a defense to many of these criticisms. Based on a survey of participants in negotiated rulemakings, they conclude that rules selected for negotiated rulemaking tend to be more complex and controversial to begin with. They also question whether comparisons like Coglianese's, supra note 50, are fair. Langbein and Kerwin, supra note 50, at 35. Coglianese disputes this conclusion; Coglianese, "Assessing Consensus," supra note 50. Langbein and Kerwin also find no support in their data for the notion that EPA abrogates its decision-making authority in negotiated rulemakings. See Langbein and Kerwin, supra note 50, at 35–36.

[57] Freeman, for example, argues that negotiated rulemaking cannot be judged fairly according to traditional regulatory goals, such as litigation avoidance. Rather, by allowing participants to "transcend the public–private divide," the process enables participants and policymakers to discover flexible solutions to problems that would not otherwise have been discovered. Freeman, supra note 20, at 33–54. See also P. Harter, "Fear of Commitment" (1997) 46 Duke L J 1389, arguing that the "rules that emerge through reg neg reflect a shop-floor insight and expertise…[and they] take account of issues that would likely escape the attention of an agency in a traditional rulemaking…". Ibid., at 1403. See also Langbein and Kerwin, supra note 50, who contend that the negotiated rulemaking process produces "better" rules irrespective of the probability of subsequent litigation, because participants (1) are more satisfied with negotiated rules, and (2) clarify more disputed issues in negotiated rulemakings. Ibid., at 35–36.

improvements apart from any concern over the environmental effects of those improvements? In the following section, we discuss potential answers to these questions.

4   BARGAINING, COLLABORATION, AND STRATEGIC BEHAVIOR

4.1   Assessing Consensus:[58] Some Diagnoses of the Problem

Not everyone has mourned the relative lack of success of the regulatory reform initiatives in the United States. To the contrary, in recent years defenders of traditional regulatory approaches have answered the pro-reform critique with their own vigorous critique of reform generally and cooperative approaches to regulation in particular. Their critique boils down to two basic, overlapping arguments. The first challenges the goals of regulatory reform, particularly its emphasis on "efficiency" as an evaluative criterion for regulation. It argues that the very inefficiencies about which reform advocates complain serve other important purposes that trump the goal of efficiency. The second argument is that by seeking new ways to inte-grate stakeholders into the policy process, cooperative regulation amounts to an abdication of decision-making responsibility by regulatory agencies. Critics of reform contend (or fear) that these collaborative processes are leading the EPA to cede its authority to stakeholder groups, thereby elevat-ing the interests of these ad hoc groups over the public interest. Proponents of each of these arguments see regulatory reform as undermining the "rule of law," and they contend that traditional means of making law—statutes and regulations—better reflect these important values than the collabora-tive or ad hoc decision-making processes used in the EPA's various reform initiatives.

4.1.1   What Price Efficiency?

Even if the EPA's reform initiatives were to achieve their twin goals of sub-stantive and procedural efficiency, one might ask whether those goals are worth pursuing or, more specifically, whether the pursuit of these goals entails unacceptable costs. Defenders of traditional regulation contend that each of these goals holds a relatively low place in the list of environmental regulatory priorities—and for good reason. With respect to substantive inef-ficiencies, there are reasons why environmental interests might sincerely prefer regulation that is relatively cost-inefficient. After all, defenders of tra-ditional approaches may say, the primary goal of the current system is not cost-efficiency but environmental protection. Hence, we ought to be careful about modifying the system, particularly in ways that divert the focus

---

[58]   This is the title of a recent article reviewing the use of negotiated rulemaking in the federal government. See Coglianese, *supra* note 50.

from that central goal or elevate other goals, like efficiency or flexibility, to an equal station.[59] Indeed, environmental interests argue that certain inefficient attributes of regulation—like technology-based standards—are easier to enforce than more efficient alternatives.[60] This argument has long been a central pillar in the case against reform. Environmental interests may also fear that increased efficiency or flexibility may bring hidden environmental costs. Several commentators have lamented that while EPA reforms may yield overall environmental gains, they may allow specific environmental losses in the context of those overall gains.[61] There is also a general suspicion that reform in the name of efficiency may bring laxity.[62] Thus, critics of reform argue that statutory admonitions compelling inefficient regulation reflect, at least in part, a social choice in favor of giving priority to these other goals, even at the cost of substantive inefficiency.[63]

Critics of reform also challenge the reformers' concern with and prescription for procedural inefficiencies. The critics' argument tracks closely the original justification for using rules, and it reflects a continuing concern with the problem of regulatory capture and a deep suspicion of the motives and trustworthiness of business participants in collaborative policy processes.[64] Rena Steinzor, for example, sees virtue in the "transparency" of rules. Rules enable environmental interests to know with greater certainty what the law is and what it requires.[65] By introducing the possibility of individual variances into the regulatory process—indeed, by promoting that possibility—reform initiatives make it more difficult for environmental groups to keep track of the legal requirements to which regulated firms are subject.[66] The relative resource disadvantages of environmental groups exacerbate the problem.[67] It is difficult for national environmental groups to monitor developments in a more decentralized regulatory process.[68] Critics of reform note also that rules promote objectivity by treating regulated

---

[59]   This theme runs throughout several of the critiques of regulatory reform. See, e.g., Steinzor, supra note 46, at 105 (stressing the need to remain cognizant of EPA's "overarching mission" of environmental protection); Heinzerling, supra note 6.

[60]   See R. Percival et al., *Environmental Regulation* (Little Brown & Co., New York, 1992), p. 161. See also Mank, supra note 24.

[61]   This is analogous to the argument that using marketable permits to regulate air pollution can create "hotspots" of concentrated emissions. See Steinzor, supra note 46, at 112, 115, and at 131–135, making a similar argument in connection with Project XL.

[62]   Ibid. See also Mank, supra note 24, at 4–10 (summarizing these arguments).

[63]   This is part of the argument raised in opposition to regulation based on risk. For a survey of that literature, see Cross, supra note 6; Heinzerling, supra note 6.

[64]   Steinzor, for example, argues that statements of support for environmental protection by business interests are usually disingenuous, and systematically so. See Steinzor, supra note 46, at 156–162.

[65]   Ibid., at 135.

[66]   Steinzor says that in this way Project XL promotes a "regulatory free for all." Ibid., at 138.

[67]   For a detailed treatment of interest group theories of environmental politics, see D. Farber, "Politics and Procedure in Environmental Law" (1992) 8 JL Econ & Org 59, 60–61; and D. Spence, "Paradox Lost: Logic, Morality and the Foundations of Environmental Regulation" (1996) 20 Colum J Envtl L 145, 149–150 and 168–171.

[68]   This is a problem primarily for individual national environmental groups trying to keep track of or participate in individual bargaining processes. Local environmental groups may be

firms equally.[69] By institutionalizing departures from rules, even in the name of efficiency improvements, reform increases the opportunity for regulated firms to subvert the regulatory process—that is, to capture it.[70] Only "rigorous transparent standards," according to critics of reform, can prevent capture and adequately protect the environment.[71]

4.1.2 Reform as Abdication

The specter of regulatory capture also hangs over the second general argument raised against reform; namely, that collaborative policy processes represent a de facto cession of decision-making authority by the EPA to private parties.[72] According to this view, collaborative processes lack legitimacy, at least relatively so, for a variety of reasons. First, reform initiatives that are designed to promote collaboration and cooperation between private stakeholders assume an interest group bargaining model of the policy process[73] and, in so doing, ignore the notion of a "public interest" apart from the collision of private interests.[74] Perhaps the most vigorous proponent of this view is William Funk, who sees some collaboration-based reforms as "perversions" of the public interest.[75] He argues that the primary purpose of administrative law is to promote the rule of law and that agencies' actions are justified and legitimized by their faithfulness to statutory directives.[76] This view contends that group consensus is a poor substitute

---

included in XL negotiations and negotiated rulemaking sessions as well. Steinzor claims that local environmental groups lack the sophistication to hold their own in the XL process. See Steinzor, supra note 46, at 180 ("local citizen activists ... lack confidence in their ability to negotiate with experts in regulatory debates. ... [and] are forced to rely on an intuitive sense of which players are trustworthy in [disputes], recognizing that their intuitions can fail").

[69] Steinzor, supra note 46, at 135.

[70] That concern over capture lies at the core of Steinzor's argument seems clear, even if she does not use the term "capture" to describe her concerns. Ibid. See also, Funk, supra note 55, at 1383–1385.

[71] Steinzor, supra note 46, at 182.

[72] Advocates of this view include Funk, supra note 55; S. Linder, "Deconstructing the Public–Private Partnership", Unpublished Paper presented at the Annual Meeting of the American Political Science Association Boston, 3 September 1998. See also Steinzor, supra note 46, at 104 (who seems to endorse this view when she calls consensus-based regulation "self-regulation," but who also acknowledges that EPA retains final decision-making authority under these collaborative processes). For a good summary of the abdication argument in a larger theoretical context, see Freeman, supra note 20, at 82–90 (noting that fears of collusion and capture sometimes drive this argument).

[73] For a good discussion of the relevance of interest group bargaining models of politics to the environmental policy process, one that precedes the literature on regulatory reform, see D. Farber, "Contract Law and Modern Economic Theory" (1983) 78 Nw U L Rev 303.

[74] This view implicitly assumes the existence of a "public interest" apart from the pull and tug of private interests, contrary to the views of most law and economics scholars who, citing Kenneth Arrow, dispute the notion of the "public interest." For a discussion of public interest model of administration and its relationship to the "Arrow problem," see Spence, "Administrative Law and Agency Policymaking," supra note 4.

[75] Funk, supra note 55, at 1374 (arguing that the Administrative Procedures Act "reflects the notion of an agency acting consequentially, not politically, in an exercise of instrumental rationality" and that consensus-based processes contradict that notion).

[76] Ibid.

for statutory authority as the basis for legitimacy; indeed, collaborative policies stray even further from traditional sources of legitimacy by viewing statutory directives as impediments to or constraints on policy-making.[77] This substitution contradicts notion of the "agency as sovereign decision-maker,"[78] and several commentators have implied that it raises potential constitutional problems under the nondelegation doctrine.[79]

A second and closely related criticism is that collaborative processes lack legitimacy because they almost invariably omit important interests from the bargaining table. This has been a persistent criticism of negotiated rulemaking in particular[80] and, as we have seen, of Project XL as well. Because environmental problems are complex and implicate many diverse interests, it is often impossible to convene all important stakeholders in negotiation meetings. This, in turn, raises the possibility of collusion between the agency and included interests (presumably business) at the expense of excluded interests.[81] As a result, omitted interests see the process as illegitimate—or at least less legitimate than traditional regulatory policymaking methods.[82]

In sum, the defense of the traditional regulatory system and the corresponding critique of reform are picking up steam. In the next section we offer a framework for evaluating the progress of collaboration-based reform initiatives that sheds some light on the debate over those initiatives. We turn to that framework now.

4.2   Reform and the Dynamics of Bargaining

4.2.1   *Re-creating the Reform Debate*

We have suggested that the Edgeworth Box can be used to analyze bargaining conflicts in the context of regulatory reform. Indeed, within the field of

---

[77]   Funk argues that while the APA has "accommodated" negotiated rulemaking, "it has done so in an insidious way, by having agency preamble writers make up rationalizations for decisions made on other grounds." This process, he says, "masks the reality of bargained for exchanges." Ibid., at 1375. For a dispassionate summary of the legitimacy critique of collaborative approaches to policymaking, including Funk's argument, see Freeman, supra note 20, at 82.

[78]   Funk, supra note 55, at 1377. Steinzor, while criticizing collaborative processes, seems to acknowledge that EPA retains final decision-making authority over policy choices. Steinzor, supra note 46, at note 306. See also Freeman, supra note 20, at 87 (agreeing with Steinzor and contradicting Funk's view). For an interesting discussion of this issue in a larger context, see J. Rossi, "Participation Run Amok: The Costs of Mass Participation for Deliberative Decisionmaking" (1997) 92 Nw U L Rev 174, 203–205.

[79]   See Freeman, supra note 20, at 82 (discussing the "subdelegation" issue generally).

[80]   See Coglianese, supra note 50, at 1321–1324 (arguing that disputes over who participates in negotiations make negotiated rulemaking more conflictual than traditional rulemaking).

[81]   See Freeman, supra note 20, at 83. For a particularly skeptical view of business-government collaboration, including in the environmental context, see Linder supra note 72 ("The idea of government and business partnering for some common purpose ... seems to draw on communal traditions of cooperation that are, at once, vaguely familiar and socially valued. Of course, when we scratch the surface of these arrangements ... , the spectacle of machine politics of graft and corruption shine through").

[82]   See Coglianese supra note 50, at 1321 (arguing that this dynamic encourages omitted interests "to disrupt the consensus").

law and economics it is common to conceive of laws and policies in this way,[83] and many of the EPA's reforms seek to facilitate exactly this kind of bargaining. Thus, by reconceiving of regulatory reforms in these terms, we may be able to shed some light on the debate. Figure 2 illustrates one view of bargaining over regulatory reform, that we might ascribe to proponents of reform. In Figure 2, the "goods" at issue are attributes of regulation; namely, the legally mandated total amount of pollution reduced, on the *x*-axis, and the mandated cost per unit of pollution reduced, on the *y*-axis.[84] We can think of the *y*-axis as representing the means of environmental regulation—or legal mandates about *how* to reduce pollution (that is, the substantive or cost-efficiency of regulation). The *x*-axis represents the ends—or legal mandates about *how much* to reduce pollution. In Figure 2 (as in Figure 1), conflict on the *x*-axis is a zero sum conflict, given that we typically expect industry and environmental interests to clash over the question of how much to reduce pollution. However, in Figure 2 (unlike Figure 1), proponents of reform do not necessarily conceive of conflict on the *y*-axis as zero sum. Although industry presumably desires greater efficiency, proponents of reform might believe that greater efficiency for

Figure 2   Edgeworth Box Analysis of Regulatory Reform Bargaining—Industry View

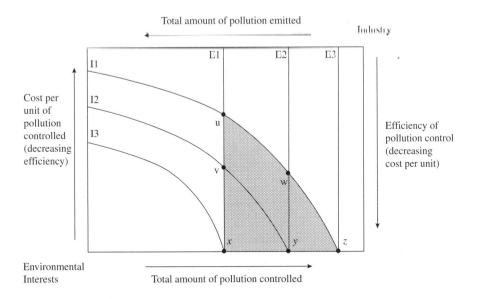

---

[83]   See, e.g., Farber, supra note 73.
[84]   Of course, most pollution control laws do not specify directly the cost of pollution control, but they sometimes do so indirectly by specifying how emissions goals must be met. Indeed, many of EPA's regulatory reform initiatives are aimed at overcoming or changing mandates that require inefficient means to reach agreed ends.

industry should not to be viewed with disfavor by environmental interests.[85] We might infer from the various efficiency critiques that proponents of reform believe that environmental interests care or should care only about the amount of pollution controlled and not about the cost per unit controlled borne by industry. Thus, in Figure 2 we depict industry's indifference curves to reflect this view of the conflict.[86]

Given an initial policy at point u, industry and environmental interests alike may be expected to prefer any point in the shaded area to u. Indeed, we would expect that bargaining between industry and environmental interests would leave them somewhere on the line that runs between x and z, which represents the set of maximally efficient (and Pareto optimal) policies. The EPA's incentives-based regulatory programs and many of its reform initiatives are designed to produce just that kind of movement into Pareto superior outcomes.[87] Yet, as we have seen, policy proposals that seem to fit this description have not found their way into existing laws, and they have been rejected by the EPA and stakeholders under the Agency's regulatory reform initiatives. Given the bargaining environment depicted in Figure 2, it is easy to see why proponents of reform find this result inexplicable.

Critics of reform respond that opposition to efficiency improvements is not surprising at all, because Figure 2 does not accurately represent bargaining over environmental policy generally. Defenders of traditional regulation appear to posit a bargaining environment more like that depicted in Figure 3, in which bargaining in both dimensions (over how much to reduce pollution and over how to reduce pollution) is zero sum bargaining. In other words, in Figure 3, environmental interests sincerely prefer inefficient regulation to efficient regulation, perhaps because they see the inefficiency of regulation as inextricably intertwined with other valued attributes of the regulation. In that case, we should not necessarily expect that the result of such bargaining will be cost-efficient regulation.[88] For example, if environmental interests believe that incentives-based regulation

---

[85]   In fact, environmental groups have not spoken with one voice on this issue in the past. Unlike most other environmental interest groups, the Environmental Defense Fund, for example, has long advocated efficiency improvements in regulation, including the use of incentives-based regulation. See, e.g., "SO_2 Trading Program Offers Answers for Other Pollution Problems, Group Says" (1997) 28 Env't Rep. (BNA) 1408.

[86]   That is, environmental interests' indifference curves are vertical, reflecting the assumption that environmental interests would be unwilling to trade any amount of pollution control for "gains" on the y-dimension. In Figure 2, only industry cares about both "goods;" the environmental interests' utility is a function only of gains on the x-dimension (amount of pollution controlled).

[87]   Of course, Project XL offers a structured process that attempts to identify Pareto superior policies compared with the status quo. Likewise, we can think of negotiated rulemaking as an attempt to find policies that are Pareto superior to those that would have been adopted under traditional notice and comment rulemaking.

[88]   The Edgeworth Box analysis still predicts that the outcome will be Pareto optimal. However, if environmental interests' value less efficient regulation, then their indifference curves will not be perpendicular to the x-axis (as in Figure 2), and we would not expect a corner solution (as in Figure 2).

Figure 3   Edgeworth Box Analysis of Regulatory Reform Bargaining—Environmental Interests' View

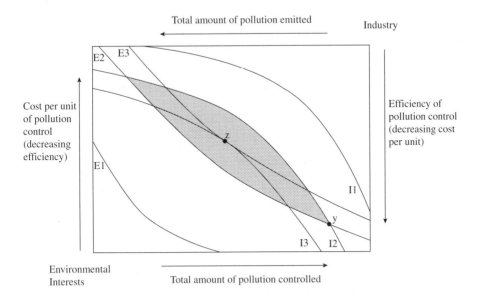

is inherently more difficult to monitor and enforce than technology-based regulation, they may resist movement to the more efficient method not because they object to efficiency, but rather because efficiency cannot be separated from other dimensions of the problem. Likewise, national environmental groups may view ostensible efficiency improvements in zero sum terms because (1) they cannot adequately monitor the bargaining processes, (2) they fear that the proposal may be a Trojan horse carrying unseen environmental harm, and (3) they cannot trust local environmental groups to represent their interests.

We find much of this argument against the use of collaborative processes to identify positive sum policy changes unpersuasive; indeed, the argument grows less persuasive by the day. First, it does not explain problems with negotiated rulemaking, which is merely one way of developing a broad-based rule or of establishing the status quo policy. The process need not be any more resource-intensive for environmental groups than traditional notice and comment rulemaking. Groups may or may not choose to participate in the early stages of negotiated rulemaking, and they would forfeit no rights to comment or to litigate by opting out of the negotiation process. Second, the EPA has designed and implemented most of its consensus-based regulatory reforms so as to ensure that environmental interests are well represented in the process. Indeed, given the strength of environmental interests within the Agency itself, it seems unlikely that environmentally harmful changes to the status quo would slip into effect unnoticed. Thus, the argument that regulatory reforms allow business to disguise environmentally harmful changes as Pareto improvements looks like a red herring. Third, the argument that technology-based standards are easier to enforce has been eclipsed by advancements in monitoring technologies[89] and increasingly cooperative and open business approaches to environmental compliance.[90] As self-reporting of violations becomes more routine[91] and monitoring becomes easier, there is less of a trade-off between regulatory flexibility and regulatory transparency. For that reason, regulation that prescribes inefficient control technologies seems to make less sense now than ever before.

However, there is another possible explanation for why bargaining may not produce Pareto improvements that comes from the experimental literature on bargaining. Experimental economists have noted that experimental simulations of Edgeworth Box bargaining often do not produce Pareto optimal outcomes.[92] Players in a two-person bargaining game often forgo clear Pareto improvements.[93] The common supposition is that such refusals are traceable to one or both players' belief that the proposed division of the gains was unfair.[94] Players recognize that each has the power to deny the other desired gains; that is, each can veto potential changes from the status quo.[95] Thus, each player tries to use that veto power to extract as many

---

[89] For example, in the case of opacity, there are now continuous emission monitors (CEMs) that use lasers to measure the opacity of plumes coming out of a plant stack. The readings produced by these monitors are often more frequent and in many cases more reliable than the estimates prepared by even the best-trained human observers called for in the EPA opacity reference test. In addition to CEMs, there are often physical process parameters related to plant emissions—such as the temperature, pressure, and speed of gas flows—that can be used reliably to estimate plant emissions of certain pollutants. See G. Van Cleve and K. Holman, "Promise and Reality in the Enforcement of the Amended Clean Air Act Part I: EPA's 'Any Credible Evidence' and 'Compliance Assurance Monitoring' Rules" 27 Envtl L Rep 10,097 (1997).

[90] The last decade has brought a sea change in industry's relationship with outside groups who are interested in environmental compliance issues. Spurred in part by right-to-know laws, their own changing attitudes toward pollution regulation, and EPA policies promoting openness, more and more companies are institutionalizing information-sharing relationships with citizens' groups. For a sampling of the extensive multi-disciplinary literature discussing this trend, see T. Sullivan (ed.), *The Greening of American Business: Making Bottom-Line Sense of Environmental Responsibility* (1992); Geltman and Skroback, supra note 49; M. Cohen, et al., "Environmental and Financial Performance: Are They Related?" (1995) Unpublished Paper, Vanderbilt University; D. Lober, "Evaluating the Environmental Performance of Corporations" (1995) *Journal of Managerial Issues*; B. Smart, "Beyond Compliance: A New Industry View of the Environment" (World Resources Institute, 1992); E. Orts, "Reflexive Environmental Law" (1995) 89 Nw U L Rev 1227.

[91] For a discussion of self-reporting of environmental violations, see Spence, "Paradox Lost," supra note 67.

[92] For a summary of this literature, see Kreps, supra note 25, at 551–573.

[93] Typical is an experiment where players must agree on how to divide a dollar provided by the experimenter. It is not atypical for players to refuse to accept divisions (and therefore to receive nothing rather than something) proposed by the other player. See, e.g., A. Roth and F. Schoumaker, (1983) 73 *American Economic Review* 362.

[94] See Kreps, supra note 25, at 556 ("bargaining outcomes depend upon individual's expectations as to what the outcomes should be"). For a more up to date treatment of this issue, see I. Erev and A. Roth, "Predicting How People Play Games: Reinforcement Learning in Experimental Games with Unique Mixed Strategy Equilibria" (1998) 88 *American Economic Review* 848.

[95] In the literature on bargaining games, this is called the "bilateral monopoly" problem.

gains as possible from the opponent; this, in turn, results in competition to see which player can improve his or her relative position the most. If one player believes the other's offer is not reasonable or fair, the player may refuse the offer even if it represents a Pareto improvement.[96]

In the context of regulatory reform, environmental interests may veto proposed positive sum changes in the status quo (such as reductions in the cost of compliance coupled with modest pollution reductions) based on the belief that industry has not done enough to control pollution. Thus, under the EPA's regulatory reform initiatives, the Agency will grant industry regulatory flexibility only in exchange for *significant* environmental improvements. If the ostensible environmental improvements an industry offers are deemed insufficient by environmental interests inside or outside the EPA, or if those interests view the pollution reductions that an industry offers as something for which they should not to have to pay (in the form of compliance cost reductions),[97] then the environmental interests will refuse the deal. This appears to be what happened in connection with 3M's XL proposal. The long history of distrust between industry and environmental interests feeds this dynamic in ways that interfere with positive sum change. From this perspective, the EPA's administration of the XL program seems aimed at divesting itself of the discretion to force positive sum changes on stakeholder groups. Thus, for example, the EPA's 1997 revision of Project XL evaluation criteria, which highlighted the importance of environmental benefits and stakeholder consensus, strengthened the leverage of environmental interests' in the bargaining process and ensured that the Agency would not be called upon to override any stakeholder veto of a proposed XL project.

4.2.2 The Implications of Strategic Bargaining

Returning to Figures 2 and 3, we might infer that Figure 2 reflects environmental interests' sincere preferences, and Figure 3 represents their strategic posture.[98] It is of course impossible to know with certainty whether environmental interests' opposition to reform is sincere, strategic, or some

---

[96] This is precisely what Ochs and Roth found in a series of experiments in which players sometimes chose to receive nothing rather than to acquiesce to a division of gains that seemed unfair. See J. Ochs and A. Roth, "An Experimental Study of Sequential Bargaining" (1989) 79 *American Economic Review* 355.

[97] Indeed there is a rich literature supporting the view that pollution is wrong and ought not to be commoditized. See Spence, "Paradox Lost," supra note 67, for a summary. This view, and an unwillingness to pay industry for pollution reductions, might be buttressed by the belief that the status quo policy is biased toward industry's preferences by its improper or unfair advantages in the political process.

[98] This is akin to the notion of "nonseparable" or "conditional" preferences, which social scientists have studied in other contexts. See, e.g., D. Lacy and E. Niou, "Nonseparable Preferences, Issue Linkage, and Economic Sanctions" Unpublished Paper presented at the Annual Meeting of the American Political Science Association, Boston, 3 September 1998 (on file with authors). Here, we might hypothesize that environmental interests' de facto preferences are strategic and guide their behavior, even if their sincere preferences would not lead

combination of the two. However, conceiving of the bargaining process in this way reveals some other interesting implications for the bargaining process. It may also help explain the trajectory of regulatory reform initiatives to date. First, the bargaining model implies that environmental interests may view bargaining with individual firms (as in the Project XL context) differently than bargaining over broad policy choices (as in the negotiated rulemaking context). In the former situation, we might expect participants in the process to be able to get a sense of just how many pollution reduction gains can be extracted from individual firms in exchange for efficiency improvements. As a consequence, we might expect these smaller bargaining groups to be more likely to reach consensus than larger groups. If environmental interests use bargaining to extract the maximum possible pollution reduction gains from firms in return for efficiency improvements, then bargaining will be extremely difficult in any negotiation that involves multiple firms, such as a negotiated rulemaking. Indeed, the task of agreeing on a policy change (in other words, writing a rule) that extracts the maximum possible gains from each firm confronts the familiar procedural inefficiency problems inherent in the rule writing process.[99]

Second, this view of bargaining suggests another, competing explanation for the problem of in-group/out-group disagreement over the outcome of bargaining. Recall that nonparticipants in negotiated rulemakings and Project XL negotiations tend to be less satisfied with the outcomes of those negotiations than participants. While nonparticipants in the bargaining process may be suspicious of hidden environmental dangers in the outcome of the process, nonparticipants may also suspect that the participants set the price of efficiency improvements too low by failing to extract the maximum amount of pollution reduction gains from industry. If that concern motivates nonparticipants, we would expect them to be more likely to oppose proposals produced by bargaining, even if the proposals represent Pareto improvements.

Third, if environmental interests can trade efficiency improvements for environmental improvements beyond those required under the law, environmental interests may prefer inefficient regulations precisely because those regulations hamstring industry. This is true in cases of bargaining over efficiency improvements for either individual firms or entire industries. The costlier the status quo is to industry, the greater will be industry's willingness to pay (in terms of environmental improvements) to eliminate those inefficiencies. This offers another reason why, in the context of bargaining-based regulatory reform, environmental interests' preferences over the how to reduce pollution (the x-axis) are conditional on their preferences

---

them to oppose efficiency improvements. That is, they would not object to efficiency improvements but for the fact that objecting permits them to extract highly-valued gains from industry. In this way, their preferences over outcomes on the efficiency dimension are conditioned by their preferences over outcomes on the pollution reduction dimension.

[99] Indeed, this may be possible only when the price extracted from industry, in terms of pollution reduction, is very high. This is one possible explanation of the bargaining process that produced the acid rain trading program under 1990 Clean Air Act Amendments.

over how much to reduce pollution (the *y*-axis). In Figure 2, recall that the most cost-efficient pollution control policies lie on the *x*-axis. If the status quo policy lies a great distance from the *x*-axis (say at point u rather than point v in Figure 2), then environmental interests should be able to extract larger pollution reduction gains from industry.[100]

Fourth, this analysis also offers a competing explanation for why national environmental groups might be more likely than local citizens' groups to oppose collaborative reforms, even if the reform processes can be used to extract environmental benefits from individual firms. It is not that national environmental groups place little value on such benefits; to the contrary, they value them highly. However, they seek the same gains for the environment on a broader scale. National environmental groups are engaged in the same bargaining process over changes to the status quo, but on a policy-wide basis. Their lobbying efforts involve a continuous process of trying to move broad policy—that is, the rule itself, not just its application in a single or set of instances—toward a more preferred position. For example, if the status quo policy is somewhere on indifference curve E1 in Figure 2, national environmental groups are trying always to move it to somewhere on E2 or E3. We can view the long process that preceded the 1990 acid rain marketable permits program in this way. Environmental interests consented to allow the acid rain allowance trading program, which is an incentives-based approach to sulfur dioxide pollution, to become law only in exchange for an additional 10 million tons in annual reductions of sulfur dioxide emissions beyond those required under the existing regulatory regime. In seeking positive sum changes at the broad policy level, national environmental groups also benefit if the status quo policy lies at a greater rather than lesser distance from the *x*-axis—that is, if it is more inefficient rather than less. The more inefficient the policy, the more industry will be willing to pay (in further pollution reductions) to change it or to realize efficiency gains. The important point is as follows: to the extent that individual firms or sets of firms can realize efficiency improvements through reform initiatives, national environmental groups lose their leverage over those firms, thereby decreasing the likelihood of arranging a positive sum change at the broad policy level. Thus, national environmental groups have reason to resist collaborative reforms apart from any concerns over the motives of industry or the ability of local environmental groups to participate effectively in the process.

5 THE FUTURE OF COLLABORATIVE REGULATORY REFORM

We believe that the strategic bargaining dynamic we have outlined here explains industry's impatience with, and environmental interests' wariness

---

[100] If the status quo is at point v, the best that environmental interests can expect to do is to move to indifference curve E2; if the status quo is at point u, there is the potential to move to indifference curve E3.

toward, regulatory reform. Believing that environmental interests have or should have preferences over policy outcomes like those shown in Figure 2, industry wonders why environmental interests veto proposals that would combine efficiency improvements with improvements in environmental conditions, even when the former are more modest than the latter. Industry approaches the bargaining process by accepting the ends of the status quo policy (that is, its prescription for how much pollution will be reduced) and challenging the means (the status quo prescription for how to achieve that pollution reduction goal). For their part, environmental interests take the opposite view: they are more inclined to challenge the ends of the status quo policy and to accept the means. Moreover, environmental interests' view of the status quo is colored not merely by their preference for more pollution reduction than the status quo policy requires, but by their belief that industrial interests were over-represented in the process by which that policy was created (that they captured the process) in the first place. Those predispositions, coupled with the opportunity to achieve highly valued pollution reduction gains, offer a powerful incentive for strategic behavior in negotiations with industry. In the presence of these forces, the inability of industry and environmental interests to realize positive sum gains seems less surprising.

The question remains, however, whether existing collaborative regulatory reform experiments can or should succeed. Commentators seem to be split over this two-pronged question. On one hand, those who favor collaborative regulatory reform fear that it is unworkable under the current legal regime. On the other hand, those who oppose collaborative regulatory reform argue that bargaining represents an abdication of authority by agencies. We have two responses to those who oppose collaborative reform on this ground. First, the argument says nothing about the substantive critique of traditional regulation. Rather, it is an attack on the process of making policy, not its content. If there are positive sum gains to be had, the presence of flaws in the process of realizing those gains does not imply that we should forgo those gains entirely. Rather, arguments over the merits of the bargaining process should be addressed on their own terms.

Second and more importantly, the bargaining-as-abdication argument attacks a straw man model of the administrative process. As we have explained, one need not subscribe to a pure interest group bargaining model of the policy process in order to favor collaborative regulatory reform of the kind discussed here. Conversely, these experiments in collaboration involve no cession of authority by agencies to private actors. In each case, the EPA retains ultimate policy making authority, and it has not been hesitant to use that authority to veto policy proposals endorsed by stakeholder groups.[101] For example, the EPA vetoed the 3M Project XL proposal even though it was endorsed by the stakeholder bargaining group.

---

[101] William Funk argues that EPA has ceded policy making initiative, if not policymaking authority, to private groups. See Funk, supra note 55, at 1382. If so, it is hard to see how this represents a change from traditional policy making processes, whether legislative or agency-based. Interest groups are a common source of policy intiatives and always have been.

The EPA has done the same in the context of negotiated rulemakings as well. In fact, contrary to the claims of critics of reform, there is no inherent inconsistency between collaborative regulatory reform and the various public interest models of the administrative process.

There is a strong argument that collaborative regulatory reform improves agencies' pursuit of the public interest—and not simply by identifying positive sum policy changes. Collaborative bargaining can be seen as an embodiment of a more deliberative and less adversarial policy process, one that comports with the constitutional model of deliberative democracy. Indeed, some scholars have argued that elected officials can no longer deliberate in the way the founders intended and that agencies do a better job of deliberating over policy change in the modern world.[102] It is does not stretch this notion to argue that collaborative regulatory reforms embrace deliberation better than their more adversarial and legalistic alternatives. This is what some defenders of collaborative processes have argued. Jody Freeman, for example, rejects interest group bargaining models of policymaking, but she is an advocate of flexible policies produced by "collaborative governance," including negotiated rulemaking and processes like Project XL.[103] Jim Rossi offers a more self-conscious version of this argument. He sees "consensus solutions" as more consistent with deliberative democracy than traditional alternatives.[104] For these reasons, the normative argument against collaborative reform as an abdication of authority seems weak.

However, though there are strong normative arguments in favor of collaborative regulatory reform, even proponents of reform tend to offer a negative (or at best a qualified positive) response to the question of whether collaborative reform can succeed. Most proponents of reform see important legal and political obstacles to success, and they advocate legislative changes that would ease restrictions on the EPA's ability to pursue positive sum change. Freeman, for example, advocates legislation that would authorize the EPA to waive legal requirements that would otherwise preclude positive sum policy changes.[105] Others have issued similar calls for lifting statutory constraints to policy proposals produced by consensus bargaining.[106] Policy proposals produced by collaborative regulatory

---

[102] See, e.g., Rohr, supra note 3, making this general argument outside of the context of regulatory reform.

[103] Freeman, supra note 20, at 82–90.

[104] Rossi, supra note 78, at 239 ("consensus solutions are more legitimate than mere preference aggregations ..."). In fact, Rossi's view is the opposite of William Funk's. Where Funk sees agencies as making policy through a process of "instrumental rationality" (see supra note 55), Rossi sees the administrative process as neither "solely instrumental [n]or strategic ...". Rossi, supra note 78, at 205–206. Like Funk, Rossi sees government as responsible for "defining virtue," but he argues that this can best be achieved through consensus processes. For a good discussion of the deliberative democracy model generally, see Seidenfeld, "Demystifying Deossification," supra note 20.

[105] Freeman, supra note 20, at 90.

[106] See Geltman and Skroback, supra note 49, at 33–34; Mank, supra note 24, at 70–88. For a slightly different view, see Hirsch, supra note 24, who argues that EPA's existing implied authority to waive legal requirements is sufficient.

reforms are sufficiently new that we do not yet know how courts will resolve disagreements over their legality. However, to the extent that the existing legal regime impedes positive sum change, the argument in favor of a granting the EPA a general waiver authority is persuasive, especially because there appear to be unrealized positive sum gains to be realized. On the other hand, our analysis implies that environmental interests have an incentive to resist any such legislation, irrespective of whether it would facilitate positive sum change or not. We have shown that there is a clear political logic to regulatory inefficiency, one that, in all likelihood, has sustained some of the inefficiencies in the present system and will continue to promote a determined resistance to their elimination.

13. An Institutional Analysis of Environmental Voluntary Agreements in the United States

*John W. Maxwell and Thomas P. Lyon**

1   INTRODUCTION

The use of environmental voluntary agreements (EVAs) began in the United States in the early 1990s. To date there are more than 30 such agreements in effect.[1] The increased popularity of EVAs has prompted a small, but growing, body of academic literature aimed at examining various efficiency and social welfare aspects of voluntary agreements.[2] Although these studies suggest several reasons why regulated firms and regulatory agencies might benefit from voluntary agreements, none explains why these supposed benefits have lead to the adoption of EVAs only recently. In fact, when one reads the existing literature on voluntary agreements one is struck by the following question regarding US EVAs: "Why is it that EVAs were only adopted in the early 1990s, when the economic justifications for EVAs seem timeless?" This chapter develops a preliminary answer to this question.

Voluntary agreements are an example of institutional change in US environmental regulations. Here, we are speaking of institutions in the sense employed by North.[3] That is, institutions are the "rules of the game." Put

---

*We thank Clifford Russell, and participants at the Third Concerted Action on Voluntary Agreements workshop in Copenhagen, Denmark, and the Workshop in Political Theory at Indiana University for helpful comments and discussions; as always, all errors remain our own.
[1]   For an overview of the environmental voluntary agreements now in effect in the United States, see J. Mazurek, "Voluntary Agreements in the United States: An Initial Survey" CAVA Working Paper No. 98/11/1, January 1999.
[2]   For a review of the current economics literature on voluntary agreements, see T. Lyon and J. Maxwell, "'Voluntary' Approaches to Environment Regulation: A Survey" in M. Franzini and A. Nicita (eds), *Economic Institutions and Environmental Policy* (Ashgate Publishing, Aldershot Hampshire, forthcoming).
[3]   D. North, *Institution, Institutional Change and Economic Performance* (Cambridge University Press, 1990).

another way, institutions are humanly devised constraints, both formal and informal, that shape human and organizational interactions. EVAs represent an institutional change away from traditional command-and-control regulation, which has dominated (and continues to dominate) US environmental policy. We will use the institutional framework set out in North's work to analyze the rise of environmental voluntary agreements in the US in the early 1990s.[4]

Institutional change arises when relative prices change, making existing institutional arrangements suboptimal for at least some of the organizations that are powerful enough to bring about change. Thus, in order to examine the rise of EVAs in the US, we must first identify those organizations that are both heavily affected by environmental regulations and in the position to shape environmental rules and regulations. In the next section we discuss these groups, focusing in particular on how they have benefited from command-and-control regulation.[5] The groups we identify are regulated industries, national environmental groups, the Environmental Protection Agency (EPA), state-level regulatory agencies, and the Congress. By understanding the benefits each group derives from traditional regulation we are able to contrast these benefits with those that arise from voluntary agreements.

In section 3 we review three recent articles on corporate voluntary initiatives, focusing in particular on which groups benefit most from voluntary agreements and why. In section 4 we turn our attention to the question of why US EVAs arose in the early 1990s. That is, we identify internal and external shocks to the existing command-and-control framework that prompted the EPA and regulated firms to promote the use of EVAs. The shocks we point to are the following: increasingly complex and unrealistic regulations, technological change and scientific discoveries that made existing laws practically unenforceable, shrinking regulatory budgets, and the rise of citizen action lawsuits that targeted both polluters and the EPA. We posit that the EPA and regulated firms proposed the use of voluntary agreements chiefly to wrestle power from national environmental groups and the Congress.

Our chapter serves merely as an initial investigation into the institutional factors that prompted the use of EVAs in the United States. As such, in the concluding section we discuss various areas of future research arising from this work.

---

[4] Ibid. Our analysis has also benefited from exposure to the Institutional Analysis and Development (IAD) framework developed by Elinor Ostrom and others at the Workshop in Political Theory at Indiana University. Polski and Ostrom provide an overview of the IAD framework and discuss how one might apply it to the study of policy analysis. M. Polski and E. Ostrom, "An Institutional Framework for Policy Analysis and Design" Workshop in Political Theory and Policy Analysis, Indiana University, WP No. W98-27, 1998.

[5] Groups that derive no benefit from the dominant form of regulation generally lack the power to change the regulatory regime, unless there has been a significant shift in the political climate since the enactment of the original regulations.

2   THE ORGANIZATIONS THAT SHAPE US ENVIRONMENTAL REGULATIONS

The economic organizations (and their entrepreneurs) that are affected by an institution are the agents of institutional change. Thus, to understand how EVAs came about in the US we must first examine those organizations that are both affected by environmental policy *and* have the ability to bring about changes in the policy. We identify four such organizations: regulated firms, national environmental groups, the EPA and state regulatory agencies, and lawmakers (primarily the US Congress).[6]

It comes as no surprise to economists that the current system of command-and-control regulation is not only inefficient, but, despite this inefficiency, difficult to change. Stigler's theory of "regulatory capture" provides one explanation: "[A]s a rule, regulation is acquired by the regulated industry, and is designed and operated primarily for its benefit."[7] By this Stigler means that the industry is able to write the rules to suit its own desires. One can extend Stigler's idea beyond the regulated industry. As Peltzman points out in his generalization of Stigler's theory, if other organizations have the power to write or influence regulation, the regulated industry will have to share the benefits arising from regulation.[8] Once all organizations with power to change the regulation agree on how to share the surplus that the regulations generate, change will be rare. In fact, change will arise only from external shocks that alter the bargaining power of the affected organizations, making it beneficial for some organizations to seek to rewrite the rules.

We identify four organizations that are powerful enough to influence US environmental regulation and enforcement. We examine each of these organizations in turn, taking care to illustrate the surplus they capture from the current command-and-control system. In section 4 we examine how shocks during the middle to late 1980s altered the relative bargaining power of these organizations, causing a subset of the organizations to attempt to rewrite the rules in the form of voluntary agreements.

2.1   Regulated Industry

Industry has fought strenuously against many major pieces of environmental legislation. If legislation is inevitable, however, industry may have

---

[6] This section of the paper has benefited from a careful reading of T. Zywicki, "Environmental Externalities and Political Externalities: The Political Economy of Environmental Regulation and Reform" (1999) 73 Tul L Rev 845. Zywicki focuses on explaining the lack of change in US environmental policy. The interested reader is encouraged to consult Zywicki for a more detailed presentation of the discussion we provide in this section.

[7] G. Stigler, "The Theory of Economic Regulation" (1971) 2 *Bell Journal of Economics and Management Science* 1, 3.

[8] S. Peltzman, "Toward a More General Theory of Regulation" (1976) 19 JL & Econ 211.

perverse incentives to support inefficient forms of regulation. When introductory environmental economics textbooks compare command-and-control regulation to incentive-based alternatives, such as marketable permit systems or pollution taxes, they focus on the efficiency of the latter. All the firms in an industry may benefit from more efficient forms of regulation, because incentive-based regulations involve lower total compliance costs. In practice, however, environmental regulation—just like any other regulation—creates winners and losers. Naturally, those firms that benefit from a particular form of environmental regulation have powerful incentives to resist regulatory change.

Industries can benefit in several ways from existing, inefficient command-and-control regulations. In some instances, certain industries benefit directly from command-and-control regulations, e.g., the waste disposal industry benefits directly from federal regulations that favor end-of-pipe waste disposal solutions rather than front-of-pipe process changes. More broadly, as Buchanan and Tullock point out, many regulated industries likely prefer direct command-and-control regulation over incentive-based regulation.[9] Buchanan and Tullock show that incentive-based regulations work to price pollution as an input in production, which encourages efficient use of the input. As a result, the "rights" to pollute tend to flow to firms and industries that can use them most efficiently. Firms, however, must pay for these rights, in addition to the increased production costs they must incur to reduce emissions. As a result, though overall pollution costs would be lower under incentive-based regulations, firms may oppose them anyway due to the increased transfer of rents to the government that would result. Hence firms may prefer a command-and-control regulatory regime.

An additional benefit from command-and-control regulation often goes to incumbent firms in an industry: command-and-control regulations may serve as an effective barrier to entry. Empirical studies have found support for this notion. Maloney and McCormick provide some empirical evidence that both OSHA and EPA regulations of cotton dust and copper smelting served as barriers to entry.[10] Portney reinforces the point in the environmental area by noting the National Ambient Air Quality Standards (NAAQS) disallow the deterioration of air quality in regions that currently exceed the standards.[11] This protects existing firms from entry by new firms and ensures that industries will not shift their location even if such shifts would improve air quality generally. Finally, Pashigian finds that politicians from existing and declining industrial regions voted for environmental legislation that tended to protect home-state industries against competition from regions experiencing rapid growth.[12]

---

[9] J. Buchanan and G. Tullock, "Polluters' Profits and Political Response: Direct Controls Versus Taxes" (1975) 65 *American Economic Review*.

[10] M. Maloney and R. McCormick, "A Positive Theory of Environmental Quality" (1982) 25 JL & Econ 99.

[11] P. Portney (ed.), *Public Policies for Environmental Protection* (Resources for the Future, Washington, D.C., 1990).

[12] P. Pashigian, "Environmental Regulation: Whose Self-Interests Are Being Protected?" (1985) 23 *Economic Inquiry* 551.

In general, command-and-control regulations, as written, tend to favor established larger firms over smaller start-ups. Often abatement capital is lumpy, requiring installation of expensive equipment (e.g., scrubbers) no matter the scale of production. More broadly, the quantity and complexity of environmental regulations along with the uncertainty of environmental liability serve as an effective barrier to entry by smaller producers.

2.2   National Environmental Groups

The primary concern of national environmental interest groups is to ensure that government and industry undertake actions to improve the environment; economic efficiency is a secondary concern, at best. These groups prefer centralized command-and-control regulation for a number of reasons. First, although command-and-control regulations may be less efficient than market-based or tax-related forms of regulation, they are generally a quicker means of attacking pollution problems. Second, command-and-control regulations are effective at "locking in" environmental improvements. As Moe argues:

By directing bureaucratic behavior themselves via detailed formal requirements— even if these requirements were technically ill advised and took a toll on agency performance—the [environmental] groups were removing crucial decisions from the realm of future influence by business. This was tremendously valuable, and they were willing to pay a price for it. As a result, they purposely created bizarre administrative arrangements that were not well suited to effective regulation.[13]

Third, it is easier to monitor compliance with command-and-control regulations than with other forms of regulation. This feature is of special importance to national environmental groups because almost every federal environmental statute contains "citizen suit" provisions that allow for citizens or groups to sue private parties for noncompliance with statutes.[14] Several environmental groups have been increasingly successful in suing under these provisions. While in many cases environmental groups do not receive direct compensation from suits won, their legal fees are often covered, strengthening incentives to pursue legal actions. Not surprisingly, environmental groups have been very active in lobbying for "technology-forcing" regulations that have become a common feature of command-and-control regulations. As Portney notes, these regulations are increasingly unrealistic and non-compliance is inevitable.[15] Once non-compliance occurs, however, environmental groups sue for compensation or remedial action, and often have their legal fees covered as part of the judgment.

For all of the foregoing reasons, command-and-control regulations tend to be favored by national environmental groups.

---

[13]   T. Moe, "The Politics of Bureaucratic Structure" in J. Chubb and P. Peterson (eds), *Can the Government Govern?* (The Brookings Institution, Washington, D.C., 1989), pp. 325–326.
[14]   The increasing frequency of lawsuits against the EPA has been an important factor motivating the adoption of voluntary agreements. We elaborate on this point in section 4 below.
[15]   See Portney, supra note 11.

2.3   The EPA and State Regulators

Under most federal environmental legislation (including the Clean Air and Clean Water Acts) the EPA is charged with setting standards that will result in the attainment of regulatory goals. For the most part, state regulatory agencies are charged with monitoring and enforcement of federal regulations. The EPA, along with the Department of Justice, serves as an enforcement back-stop.

The EPA and its state level counterparts, like any government bureaucracy, are concerned with seeking larger budgets and greater power. In order to justify their budgets, these environmental agencies must show themselves to be active and useful. As Hahn notes, "[T]he EPA recognized that the key to its growth lies in expanding the list of environmental issues that need attention and in writing regulations is such a way as to provide a greater need for the EPA."[16] Traditional regulation provides such a role for the EPA and its state-level counterparts. Firms engage in self-reporting of emissions to the EPA, and these reports are backed up by monitoring and enforcement by state agencies and in some cases the EPA. In addition, since the EPA's primary role under much existing legislation is focused on environmental benefits, not overall economic efficiency, the EPA (like environmental groups) often has incentives to support command-and-control regulation for reasons of speed and ready monitoring.

2.4   The Congress

Lawmakers have two main constituencies: voters and organizations directly affected by proposed laws. Congress acts to please both constituencies. To please voters (and environmental groups), regulations are written with absolutist goals in mind. The federal clean water and air laws, for example, dictate that lakes and streams should quickly be made "swimable" and "fishable" and generally that the environment should be made "safe." These types of legislation, along with low budget allocations for monitoring and enforcement, tend to favor command-and-control regulations. Although command-and-control regulation imposes large costs on industry, this legal structure may be hard to change because once imposed it may create rents for incumbent firms.

At a secondary level, Congress may have perverse incentives to write inefficient rent-creating laws, because members of Congress may later be able to engage in rent extraction by threatening to replace existing legislation. Direct rent extraction occurs, for example, when affected parties contribute to Congressional campaigns through political actions committees or when affected firms lobby Congressional members, providing them with honoraria, free trips to conferences, etc.

---

[16]   R. Hahn, "United States Environmental Policy: Past, Present and Future" (1994) 34 Nat Resources J 305.

2.5 Summary

We have detailed the various ways in which organizations powerful enough to shape the writing and enforcement of environmental regulations are affected by those regulations. Our analysis of voluntary agreements as an institutional change in US environmental policy now proceeds in two steps. First, we show that some organizations with the ability to effect such change in the regulatory arena benefit from the changes embodied in environmental voluntary agreements. Second, we show that those potential benefits had arisen within a reasonable time interval prior to the early 1990s (when most voluntary agreements were established in the US).

In the subsequent section we review three papers that identify the organizations that benefit from voluntary agreements and how these organizations benefit. In section 4 we explain why the benefits arose in the middle to late 1980s, prompting the establishment of EVAs.

3   THE BENEFICIARIES OF ENVIRONMENTAL VOLUNTARY AGREEMENTS

The academic literature on EVAs is small, but growing. We review some findings of three recent theoretical papers in this section. Although each paper devotes considerable space to analysis of the welfare effects of EVAs, we focus on what the papers tell us about the relative power of our four organizations in an EVA relationship.

Maxwell, Lyon and Hackett present a model of preemptive self-regulation in which political action is costly for consumers to undertake.[17] In this model, individuals must inform themselves of the implications of pollution control for their well-being, and also inform themselves of the efficacy of various feasible policy remedies. Individuals with similar interests must then coordinate a mutual strategy for gaining political influence. These various costs are collectively referred to as organizing costs. Even after individuals are organized, they must incur expenses to wield political influence, which might be attained through a variety of means, including lobbying, election campaign contributions, and tolerated forms of bribery such as revolving-door arrangements, junkets, and honoraria. Costs that are required after consumers are organized are referred to as influence or lobbying costs.[18]

---

[17]   J. Maxwell, et al., "Self-Regulation and Social Welfare: The Political Economy of Corporate Environmentalism" (forthcoming) JL & Econ.

[18]   Firms face similar tasks, but their organizing costs are typically less than those of consumers, because assessing the costs of regulation to the firm is usually much easier than assessing the health and aesthetic benefits to consumers, and the number of firms in an industry is typically very small relative to the number of consumers. Without loss of generality, then, one can normalize firms' cost of organizing to zero, though they still must incur influence costs to persuade politicians to support corporate positions.

The political costs faced by consumers drive a wedge between the consumer benefits of voluntary abatement and the benefits of mandatory abatement, and firms can take advantage of this wedge to preempt regulation. Naturally, if consumers' costs of political action are too high then consumers are effectively "blockaded" from the political process, and self-regulation becomes an unnecessary expenditure and will not be observed. As consumer costs of gaining political influence fall, however, the model predicts that corporate self-regulation will intensify. In other words, an increasing threat of government regulation induces firms to voluntarily reduce pollution emissions.[19] The theory predicts that government actions that significantly lower the information costs faced by consumer and environmental groups would thereby increase the threat of regulation faced by firms and increase the incentives for self-regulation. Similarly, exogenous shifts that raise the cost of new regulations to industry would prompt increased self-regulation.

Although this model of preemptive self-regulation downplays the role of the EPA, it makes clear that firms desire EVAs so as to preempt the legislative process (when the Congress and national environmental groups hold relatively more power). We shall see that the idea of preemption is a common theme in other papers that address EVAs.

Segerson and Miceli present a model in which legislation is threatened if corporations do not produce satisfactory results "voluntarily."[20] Their model considers a new piece of environmental legislation mandating pollution reductions that is forthcoming with positive probability, though its passage is not certain. The welfare-maximizing regulator cannot unilaterally impose new binding regulations, but possesses delegated authority to offer the firm a voluntary agreement calling for a greater level of pollution reduction. If the firm accepts the offer, the background threat of legislation is assumed to be removed. Both the physical and the transaction costs of compliance on the part of the firm are assumed to be lower under a voluntary agreement. In addition, the transaction costs faced by the regulator are lower under the voluntary agreement. The costs of legislation are not modeled explicitly.

While Segerson and Miceli highlight the efficiency of EVAs, it is the threat of legislation that prompts the EVA choice. The authors clearly assume that both the regulator and the firm have power to shape (and benefit from) the EVA. Presumably this power is related to how much harm each organization encounters if the inefficient legislation is imposed.

Hansen presents a model in which voluntary agreements involve direct negotiation between industry and a regulatory body, thereby bypassing the legislative process.[21] Like the papers discussed earlier, Hansen's model

---

[19]   In theory, the cost of preemption may be prohibitive if the threat of regulation is too high. Thus, government policies that subsidize consumer involvement in the political process could, paradoxically, reduce the level of voluntary environmental improvement.

[20]   K. Segerson and T. Miceli, "Voluntary Approaches to Environmental Protection: The Role of Legislative Threats" (1998) 36 J Envtl Econ & Mgmt 109.

[21]   L. Hansen, "Environmental Regulation Through Voluntary Agreements" in C. Carraro and F. Lévêque (eds), *Voluntary Approaches in Environmental Policy* (Kluwer Academic Publishers, Dordrecht, 1999).

views voluntary agreements as supported by the threat of mandatory regulation. However, Hansen's regulator (which he terms Government) and legislator (Congress) differ in the relative weights they place on firm profitability, revenues from a pollution tax, and environmental improvement. The utility function of Congress is taken to represent social welfare throughout most of the paper, and Government's divergent interests may lead it to take actions that reduce social welfare. Voluntary agreements produce no tax revenue, and compliance with them may be more or less costly than compliance with legislative requirements. Such agreements come about through Nash bargaining between firms and the regulator, each of whom aims to achieve higher utility by preempting Congressional legislation.

Hansen also presents an extension of the model in which various interest groups wield extra influence by applying ex post "public criticism" to the actors responsible for a decision, the impact of which is assumed to be a linear function of the actual harm suffered by the interest group. In this setup, both political branches have incentives to avoid responsibility by eschewing action and avoiding criticism. Of course, the benefits of avoiding responsibility drive a wedge between the utility function of Congress and social welfare. This opens up new opportunities for welfare-reducing voluntary agreements that weaken environmental standards and lower tax revenue. It is easy to see how welfare reductions can result from criticism by corporate interests. Hansen shows that welfare reductions can also follow from environmental group influence. He allows for criticism of both Congressional goals ex ante and legislative achievements ex post. In this context, Congress again benefits from ducking responsibility, and welfare may be reduced.

Hansen's analysis highlights the political struggles between the Congress and the regulator over EVAs. Although he is less concerned about the power of industry, Hansen makes it clear that EVAs are prompted by legislative threats which are costly to both industry and the regulator—and possibly costly to Congress itself!

All three of the foregoing models suggest two stark features of environmental voluntary agreements. First, the agreements arise under outside threats of either new regulations or direct criticism. Regulation is threatening because it is either costly, inefficient, or may generate ex post criticism. In reality each is likely true, at least to some degree. Second, the models highlight the fact that EVAs by their nature involve only two of the four organizations outlined in section 2 above, namely the regulated industry and the EPA. Thus, in contrast to command-and-control regulation, EVAs shift power away from Congress and national environmental groups towards the EPA and the firms directly involved in the agreement.[22]

---

[22] It is worth noting here that examples of national environmental groups protesting and blocking agreements made between local industry and local environmental groups are relatively easy to find. See, for example, Mazurek's discussion of the failed Intel Project XL initiative, Mazurek, supra note 1, and Zywicki's discussion of difficulties encountered by the Quincy Library group, Zywicki, supra note 6, at 879.

4   THE RISE OF ENVIRONMENTAL VOLUNTARY AGREEMENTS

According to Dixit, institutions are generally designed to reduce uncertainty and to minimize transactions costs.[23] However, it is clear that the establishment of institutions and institutional change does not occur behind a veil of ignorance. Dixit makes this point with a striking example. While the authors of the US Constitution strove to establish the principle of equality among men in order to preempt the establishment of the rigid class system they had just fought to escape, they saw fit to leave the lucrative practice of slavery untouched.

North describes the process of institutional change as follows.[24] There is first a change in relative prices. This change leads one or more of the parties to an exchange to perceive that they could do better with an altered agreement or contract. Changes in relative prices usually result from an outside shock. This shock may help or harm all parties involved in an agreement, but more than likely the shock will affect each party differently. Such shocks tend to alter the relative bargaining power of the parties involved and impose extra transaction costs on a subset of parties. These changes then lead to a desire to rewrite the rules, formal or informal, that govern the interaction of the parties.

The change we focus on here is the rise of EVAs in the early 1990s in the United States. In section 3, we argued that the two organizations most involved (i.e., those organizations rewriting the rules) are the EPA and the firms it regulates. We must therefore answer the following question: What change or changes occurred that prompted the EPA and the firms it regulates to explore EVAs as an alternative to traditional regulation? We identify four such changes: (1) mounting and increasingly complex legislation, (2) technological innovation and scientific discoveries, (3) regulatory budget cutbacks, and (4) the increasing use (and effectiveness) of "citizen suits."

While some of these changes, such as mounting legislation, have evolved gradually, we argue that the confluence of these four changes reached critical proportions in the middle to late 1980s, leading to the adoption of EVAs in the early 1990s. Portney's review of US environmental policy between 1970 and 1990 provides an excellent description of the four changes we have enumerated.[25]

4.1   Mounting Legislative Pressure

From its inception, the EPA has been charged with implementing the tremendously complex environmental laws passed by Congress. The complexity of these laws often lies in the simplicity of their wording. As mentioned earlier,

---

[23]   A. Dixit, *The Making of Economic Policy: A Transaction-Cost Politics Perspective* (MIT Press, 1996).
[24]   See North, supra note 3.
[25]   See Portney, supra note 11.

Congress tends to be absolutist in its approach to environmental legislation. Federal air and water laws, for example, required the setting of literally thousands of discharge standards, the establishment of comprehensive monitoring standards, and other important tasks while at the same time allowing only 180 days for the completion of many of these tasks.[26] As Portney notes, many of these assignments were left undone 17 years after legislation was passed, and he offers the following characterization of the EPA: Every year the EPA works harder and harder to stay on top of the laws passed by Congress, while at the same time falling further and further behind.

4.2　Technological Innovation and Scientific Discoveries

Since the formalization and centralization of US environmental policy in 1970, technological progress has affected firms and regulators in numerous ways. Abatement equipment has become increasingly sophisticated, yet given the nature of the regulatory process these advances have tended to lag innovations in monitoring technology. The innovations in monitoring technology, along with a growing body of literature on the physiological and toxicological effects of industrial pollution, lead to two stark conclusions. First, current levels of industrial emissions are "unsafe," and second, there may be no "safe" level of emissions! These facts, especially the latter, cause the EPA tremendous difficulty in carrying out its mission. As Portney notes, "Since Congress did not contemplate such [possibilities], the EPA administrator is caught between the apparent mandate of the law and the realities of science and economics."[27]

4.3　Budget Cutbacks

Although one optimal response to many scientific discoveries may be to rewrite existing pieces of legislation, another possible treatment may be to increase the EPA's monitoring and enforcement budget. At least then one might ensure that harmful emissions were trending downwards. In fact, with respect to the EPA's budget, the opposite occurred. As Table 1 illustrates, both the size of the EPA labor force and its overall budget declined in the early years of the Reagan Administration (the early to middle 1980s), which almost certainly hampered the EPA's enforcement capabilities. In 1983, the General Accounting Office (GAO) delivered a critical report of the EPA's enforcement record.[28] The report notes that in some cases enforcement action was not taken for years after non-compliance had begun.

---

[26]　Ibid., at 22.

[27]　Ibid.

[28]　General Accounting Office, *Waste Water Dischargers Are Not Complying with EPA Pollution Control Permits*, RECED-84-53 (Washington, D.C., 1983).

Table 1   EPA Budget and Employment Data

Fiscal Year	*Budget*	*Workforce*
FY 1970	$1,003,984,000	4,084
FY 1971	$1,288,784,000	5,744
FY 1972	$2,447,565,000	8,358
FY 1973	$2,377,226,000	9,077
FY 1974	$518,348,000	9,743
FY 1975	$698,835,000	10,438
FY 1976	$771,695,000	9,481
FY 1977	$2,763,745,000	11,315
FY 1978	$5,498,635,000	11,986
FY 1979	$5,402,561,000	12,160
FY 1980	$4,669,415,000	13,078
FY 1981	$3,030,669,000	12,667
FY 1982	$3,676,013,000	11,402
FY 1983	$3,688,688,000	10,832
FY 1984	$4,067,000,000	11,420
FY 1985	$4,353,655,000	12,410
FY 1986	$3,663,841,000	12,892
FY 1987	$5,364,092,000	13,442
FY 1988	$5,027,442,000	14,442
FY 1989	$5,155,125,000	14,370
FY 1990	$5,461,808,000	16,318
FY 1991	$6,094,287,000	16,415
FY 1992	$6,668,853,000	17,010
FY 1993	$6,892,424,000	17,280
FY 1994	$6,658,927,000	17,106
FY 1995	$6,658,227,000	17,663
FY 1996	$6,522,953,000	17,081
FY 1997	$6,799,393,000	17,951
FY 1998	$7,360,946,000	18,283
FY 1999*	$7,771,275,000	18,375

* Presidential budget.
Source: EPA Budget Authority, EPA Budget Division.

Note that the figures in Table 1 actually understate the extent of cutbacks at the EPA during the 1980s, because the post-1980 figures include spending and personnel devoted to the administration of the Superfund program. Portney estimates that, excluding Superfund spending, the EPA's budget had fallen 15 percent by 1990. Figure 1 illustrates the trend in the EPA's budget and labor force assuming this 15 percent reduction.

4.4   The Rise of Citizen Lawsuits

Shortly after the publication of the 1983 GAO report, several major environmental groups, citing lax enforcement by the EPA, lobbied for the use of self-monitoring data (which are public information) as the basis of citizen lawsuits against non-compliant polluters. Russell reports that these law

Figure 1   EPA Budget and Workforce Excluding Superfund

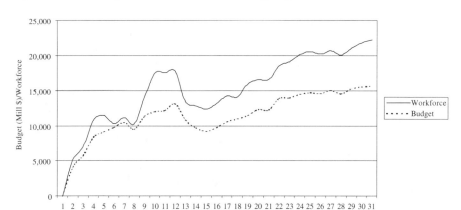

Time12 = 1981, Time 21 = 1990

suits were generally successful.[29] Through a series of cases, the courts ruled against defendant firms on most legal challenges designed to block the use of self-monitoring data. Also, following the release of the GAO report, national environmental groups began to sue the EPA for failure to enforce its own regulations. As Farber notes, "[t]he major environmental groups, most notably the Sierra Club and the Natural Resources Defense Council, have participated in scores of major law suits against the EPA and other government agencies ... "[30] This body of law shifted the balance of power in the political economy game towards national environmental groups and the Congress (because its laws are enforced), weakening the positions of both the EPA and industry. While Russell does not provide details of timing, it is quite reasonable to postulate that if environmental groups began suing for the right to use self-reported data in 1984, a sufficient body of legal precedent could not have emerged for a number of years.

The four changes that took place during the middle to late 1980s, we believe, prompted the EPA and the industries it regulates to attempt to reform US regulatory institutions. If one examines the structure of most US EVAs, one observes at least four regularities. First, EVAs necessitate a role for the EPA. Most EVAs involve membership certification by the EPA. In addition, EVAs often include information-sharing among participating firms, the EPA, and environmental abatement experts. Second, because EVAs are not legally binding they, by their very nature, present litigation

---

[29]   C. Russell, "Monitoring and Enforcement," in P. Portney (ed.) *Public Policies for Environmental Protection* (Resources for the Future, Washington, D.C., 1990).
[30]   D. Farber, "Politics and Procedure in Environmental Law" (1992) 8 JL Econ & Org 59, as quoted in Zywicki, supra note 6.

difficulties. Third, EVAs leave in place existing regulations, and therefore leave in place the rents created by existing regulations, as detailed above in section 2. The one exception to this rule is Project XL which, at least in one case, sought to relax existing regulations.[31] However, Project XL is focused at the individual firm level. Therefore, any regulatory relaxation that takes place would be firm-specific and would not repeal the general anticompetitive effects of existing regulations. Finally, most EVAs seek community input rather than the input of large national environmental groups. Indeed, several voluntary agreements have been widely criticized by national environmental groups and smaller environmental watchdogs.

As predicted by proponents of institutional change theory, EVAs appear to reduce the transaction costs and uncertainty associated with EPA-industry interactions, while leaving in place previous regulations. Although the EPA and industry might like to rewrite existing regulations, such change would likely require the active participation of Congress. This participation is unlikely because Congress would derive little benefit from revisions of current laws and would be left open to the criticism that existing laws were being weakened. At the same time, political realities make it extremely unlikely that Congress would legislate against the use of EVAs unless they were proven to be ineffective. It is interesting to note that in addition to two stated toxic emissions reduction goals of the voluntary 33/50 program, the EPA's third stated goal was to prove that voluntary agreements work. Although the EPA claims to have met all of its stated 33/50 program goals, several environmental groups, academics, and the GAO have criticized the EPA for overstating the success of the program.[32]

A major benefit that EVAs deliver to the EPA is the ability to alleviate outside pressure from environmental groups. These pressures are particularly severe when the EPA's budget is tightly constrained. In this case, money spent on litigation has a high opportunity cost. At the same time, EVAs reduce the power of the EPA in its relationship with the industries it regulates. One might therefore expect that as budgets become less constrained EVAs would lose favor. In this vein, it is interesting to note that for at least this one of the four reasons we cite for prompting EVAs, reversal was observed in the early to middle 1990s. Given a reasonable bureaucratic lag, one might expect to see a recent decline in the use of EVAs. Mazurek's findings are consistent with this prediction. As Table 2 illustrates, most EVAs arose during the early 1990s with the vast majority beginning between 1992 and 1994. Furthermore, there has been a dramatic drop in the initiation of new EVAs since 1995.

---

[31] For more information on the Project XL proposal by Intel Corporation see J. Boyd et al., "Intel's XL Permit: A Framework for Evaluation" Discussion Paper 98-11, January 1998, Resources for the Future, Washington, D.C.

[32] For an overview of EPA's 33/50 program and a discussion of various criticisms of the program by environmental groups and government agencies, see T. Davies and J. Mazurek, *Industry Incentives for Environmental Improvement: Evaluation of U.S. Federal Initiatives* (Washington, D.C., Global Environmental Management Initiative, 1996).

Table 2 Number of Voluntary Agreements Established in the United States by Year

Year	Number of VAs Established
1991	3
1992	4
1993	12
1994	5
1995	6
1996	0
1997	1
1998	0
1999	0

Source: Mazurek (1999).

5 CONCLUSIONS

Voluntary agreements represent a change in the existing institutional structure of environmental regulation in the United States. In this chapter we took an initial step in examining this change by appealing to the economic theory of institutions and institutional change. This theory tells us that the first step in examining institutional change is to examine the players that have the power to effect change. To this end, we have identified four such groups: regulated firms, the EPA and its state counterparts, national environmental groups, and the Congress. Keeping in mind that EVAs arose in the US in the early 1990s, we identified several external factors that worked to alter the relative returns these four groups derived from the existing regulatory institutions. We argued that these factors—mounting legislative pressures, budget cutbacks, citizen lawsuits, and scientific discoveries—combined to shift the balance of power in the existing institutions towards national environmental groups and the Congress, and away from the other two groups.

Institutional change analysis suggests that when outside shocks upset the balance of power in an existing institution, affected players will work to alter the rules, that is, to change the institution. It appears that the EPA and affected members of regulated industries may be attempting to use EVAs as a way to win back some of the power they have lost under the traditional regulatory structure. It is clear that EVAs grant these two groups much more power than the Congress or national environmental groups, both of whom are blocked from participation in many EVAs.

Although our analysis appears to accord reasonably well with the rise of US EVAs in the early 1990s, its fit with the apparent decline of EVAs since 1995 is debatable. Several reasons might be given to explain this decline. First, neither institutional change nor regulation itself is a smooth process.

The recent decline of EVAs may simply reflect a temporary downturn rather than a trend. Second, EVAs may have failed to strengthen the EPA and industry substantially in the regulatory dynamic. Anecdotal evidence suggests that EVAs have increased the amount of litigation involving industry, the EPA, and environmental groups, with the latter challenging the legality of some EVAs. Finally and perhaps most interestingly, other factors may have been at work in prompting the adoption of EVAs and these factors may better explain their apparent decline.

Prominent among the factors we have not included here are political changes. The tremendous spike in EVA activity in 1993 suggests that the election of a new President from a different political party, and the corresponding change in leadership at the EPA, may have been an important factor explaining EVA activity. Along these same lines, developments in the Congress, including the possibility of gridlock in the passage of new environmental legislation, may have contributed to the rise of EVAs and may also provide insight into its decline. With these factors firmly in mind, we caution the reader to view the conclusions presented here as preliminary, though we remain convinced that the tools of institutional analysis are critical to uncovering the reasons for the rise of environmental voluntary agreements in the United States.

14. Voluntary Agreements for the Environment: Institutional Constraints and Potential for Innovation

Magali A. Delmas and Ann Terlaak

1 INTRODUCTION

In the 1990s, Environmental Voluntary Agreements (EVAs) emerged as the promise of the future in environmental policy circles. EVAs are institutional arrangements between firms and regulatory agencies, which increasingly complement traditional environmental command-and-control measures. To date, more than 300 EVAs have been concluded in the European Union.[1]

A voluntary agreement is "an agreement between government and industry to facilitate voluntary action with a desirable social outcome, which is encouraged by the government, to be undertaken by the participant based on the participant's self interest."[2] In EVAs, the desirable social outcome is an improvement in the natural environment. Regulators can establish EVAs with industry associations or individual firms.[3] EVAs aim at negotiating specific regulatory targets (such as emission reduction

---

[1] For detailed typologies of EVAs see P. Börkey and F. Leveque, "Voluntary Approaches for Environmental Protection in the European Union" (1998) OECD, ENV/EPOC/GEEI(98)29/FINAL, Organization for Economic Co-operation and Development; E. Croci and G. Pesaro, "Voluntary Agreements in the Environmental Sector – The Italian Experience" (1999), CAVA Working Papers No. 98/11/5, European Research Network on Voluntary Approaches for Environmental Protection; K. Harrison, "Talking with the Donkey: Cooperative Approaches to Environmental Protection" (1999) 2 *Journal of Industrial Ecology* 3, 51–72.

[2] M. Storey, et al., "Voluntary Agreements with Industry: Summary of Annex I Expert Group on the United Nations Framework Convention on Climate Change" (Organization for Economic Co-operation and Development), p. 3.

[3] E. Croci and G. Pesaro, "Voluntary Agreements in the Environmental Sector: The Italian Experience" (1999) CAVA Working Papers No. 98/11/5, European Research Network on Voluntary Approaches for Environmental Protection; S. Labatt and V. Maclaren, "Voluntary Corporate Environmental Initiatives: A Typology and Preliminary Investigation" (1998) 16 *Government and Policy* 191–209.

targets) or implementing predetermined targets.[4] Unlike interfirm agreements, EVAs bind partners of unequal nature. Within constitutional limitations regulators have legitimate authority to coerce private actors.[5]

Firms are starting to recognize that environmental efforts may improve their industrial performance.[6] They are shifting the emphasis of their activities away from reactive responses toward proactive and innovative approaches.[7] The complexity of today's environmental concerns calls for solutions that combine knowledge from different disciplines and actors. It requires firms to find innovative solutions to environmental issues. According to the Dynamic Capability Approach, cooperative agreements are appropriate to combine required knowledge and develop new competencies.[8]

EVAs are cooperative structures that may serve as a learning opportunity for firms by providing access to complementary competencies of partners, encouraging information sharing and supplying technical assistance.[9] EVAs are one possibility to reduce pollution levels through flexible, pro-active, and cost saving strategies.[10] Further, they may also provide public recognition.[11] Through EVAs, firms can make the public counterpart aware of their willingness and ability to offer processes and products with improved environmental performance. For the public values these environmental efforts, participating firms may gain a competitive advantage with respect to other firms that are excluded from the EVA.[12]

---

[4]   EEA 1997, "Environmental Agreements" (1997) Environmental Issues Series 3, European Environmental Agency; M. Storey et al., "Voluntary Agreements with Industry: Summary of Annex I Expert Group on the United Nations Framework Convention on Climate Change" (1997) Organization for Economic Co-operation and Development.

[5]   W. Stanbury, *Business-government Relations in Canada* (Scarborough, Canada, 1999).

[6]   M. Porter and C. van der Linde, "Green and Competitive: Ending the Stalemate" (1995) 73 Harv Bus Rev 5, 120–123.

[7]   P. Groenewegen and P. Vergragt, "Environmental Issues as Threats and Opportunities for Technological Innovation" (1991) 3 *Technology Assessment and Strategic Management* 1, 43–55; S. Hart, "Beyond Greening: Strategies for a Sustainable World" (1997) 75 Harv Bus Rev 1, 66–76; A. Hoffman, *From Heresy to Dogma: An Institutional History of Corporate Environmentalism* (The New Lexington Press Management, San Francisco, 1997); J. Schot and K. Fischer, "The Greening of Industrial Firm" in *Environmental Strategies for Industry: International Perspectives on Research Needs and Policy Implications* (Island Press, Washington, D.C., 1993), pp. 3–36; R. Welford (ed.), *Corporate Environmental Management, Systems and Strategies* (Earthscan, London, 1996).

[8]   R. Langlois and N. Foss, "Capabilities and Governance: The Rebirth of Production in the Theory of Economic Organization" (1998) DRUID Working Paper No. 97-2, Danish Research Unit for Industrial Dynamics; D. Teece, et al., "Dynamic Capabilities and Strategic Management" (1997) 18 Strategic Mgmt J 7, 509–533.

[9]   See Harrison, supra note 1; J. Mazurek, "The Use of Voluntary Agreements in the United States: An Initial Survey" (1998) OECD, ENV/EPOC/GEEI(98)27/FINAL, Organization for Economic Co-operation and Development.

[10]   CEC, Communication from the Commission to the Council and the European Parliament on Environmental Agreements (1996) COM(96) 561, 27 November; Labatt and Maclaren, supra note 3; EEA 1997, supra note 4; D. Wallace, *Environmental Policy and Industrial Innovation, Strategies in Europe, the USA and Japan* (Earthscan Publications Ltd., London, 1995).

[11]   See S. Arora and T. Cason, "An Experiment in Voluntary Environmental Regulation: Participation in EPA's 33/50 Program" (1995) 28 J Envtl Econ & Mgmt 3, 271–286; Labatt and Maclaren, supra note 3.

[12]   Croci and Pesaro, supra note 1.

For regulators, EVAs may improve firms' environmental performance in situations where command-and-control regulation would fail due to the complexity of the environmental issue at stake.[13] EVAs can offer regulators the possibility to learn about firms' innovative responses, thereby enhancing their regulatory abilities.[14] Regulators receive further benefits as industry assumes ownership of the problem, which can result in reduced enforcement costs.[15]

However, both regulators and firms face risks when venturing into EVAs. Regulators may be afraid of poor compliance because EVAs lack traditional monitoring and enforcement mechanisms. They may also fear being captured by one specific industry.[16]

For firms, it is yet unclear how EVAs affect corporate performance. The New Institutional Economics and Transaction Costs Economics suggest that collaborative arrangements such as EVAs may be associated with high transaction costs caused by information leakage or free-riding partners.[17] From the perspective of firms, opportunistic behavior may thus undermine potential benefits. Because little is known about the conditions that determine success and failure of EVAs, firms may be reluctant to participate in them.

Institutional arrangements arise and persist when they confer benefits greater than the transaction costs incurred in creating and sustaining the arrangements. EVAs may bring innovative solutions for firms as well as society. These benefits have to be weighed against the costs of acquiring new environmental competencies. The focus in such an institutional analysis would be on rule-setting, monitoring, and sanctions.

Due to the novelty of the phenomena, research on EVAs has only just started and has primarily focused on the effectiveness of EVAs in preventing pollution. The results of these studies are unclear, because empirical

---

[13] See Harrsion, supra note 1; T. Whiston and M. Glachant, "Voluntary Agreements Between Industry and Government—the case of Recycling Regulations" in F. Leveque (ed.), *Environmental Policy in Europe: Industry, Competition and the Policy Process* (Edward Elgar, Cheltenham, 1996), pp. 143–174.

[14] See F. Aggeri and A. Hatchuel, "A Dynamic Model of Environmental Policies: The Case of Innovation Oriented Voluntary Agreements," Paper presented at the International Conference on Economics and Law of Voluntary Approaches in Environmental Policy, Venice, 18 November 1996; H. Imura, "The Use of Voluntary Agreements in Japan: An Initial Survey" (1999) OECD, ENV/EPOC/GEEI(98)28/FINAL, Organization for Economic Co-operation and Development.

[15] See J. Moffet and F. Bregha, "An Overview of Issues with Respect to Voluntary Environmental Agreements," (1999) CAVA Working Papers No. 98/11/3, European Research Network on Voluntary Approaches for Environmental Protection.

[16] See Börkey and Leveque, supra note 1; R. Kemp, *Environmental Policy and Technical Change: A Comparison of the Technological Impact of Policy Instruments* (Edward Elgar, Cheltenham, 1997); Mazurek, supra note 9.

[17] See D. North, *Institutions, Institutional Change, and Economic Performance* (Cambridge University Press, 1990); O. Williamson, *The Mechanisms of Governance* (Oxford University Press, 1996).

evidence is scarce.[18] A comprehensive theoretical framework of EVAs that analyzes the impact of EVAs on innovation and organizational change is still missing.[19]

This chapter analyzes the costs and benefits for firms to acquire new environmental competencies via EVAs. The chapter is organized as follows. First, we use the Dynamic Capability Approach and the New Institutional Economics to assess the impact of EVAs on firms' acquisition of new environmental competencies. Second, we view the two approaches as complementary and combine their insights to design a framework that aligns the potential for innovative outcomes and transaction costs to EVAs. Third, we illustrate our framework with examples. The last section is a concluding discussion.

2   A FRAMEWORK FOR ANALYZING EVAs AND INNOVATION

2.1   Dynamic Capability Approach

The Dynamic Capability Approach (DCA) may be seen as an outgrowth of several streams of research. These include evolutionary economics, the resource-based view of the firm, and the knowledge-based view of the firm.[20] These approaches concentrate on knowledge as a key competitive

---

[18]   See EEA 1997, supra note 5; Labatt and Maclaren, supra note 3; M. Rietbergen et al., "Quantitative Evaluation of Voluntary Agreements on Energy Efficiency" (1998) Paper presented at the International Workshop on Industrial Energy Efficiency; Mazurek, supra note 9; Storey, et al., supra note 4.

[19]   See J. Albrecht, "Environmental Agreements and Sectoral Performance: Cases of the CFC Phase-Out and the US Toxic Release Inventory" (1999) CAVA pp. 1–28; N. Ashford, "The Influence of Information-based Initiatives and Negotiated Environmental Agreements on Technological Change" (1996) Paper presented at the International Conference on Economics and Law of Voluntary Approaches in Environmental Policy, Venice, 18 November 1996; C. Caldart and N. Ashford, "Negotiation as Means of Developing and Implementing Environmental Policy" (1998) Milan Working Paper No. 38.98, Fondazione Eni Enrico Mattei; C. Carraro and D. Siniscalco, "Voluntary Agreements in Environmental Policy" in A. Xepapadeas (ed.), *Economic Policy for the Environment and Natural Resources: Techniques for the Management and Control of Pollution* (Edward Elgar, Cheltenham, 1996), pp. 80–94; T. Graedel and B. Allenby, *Industrial Ecology* (Prentice Hall, Englewood Cliffs, 1995); R. Zoboli, "Implications of Environmental Regulation on Industrial innovation: The Case of End-of-Life Vehicles" (1998), report carried out under the IPTS-DGIII framework project "Impact of the EU Regulation on Innovation of European Industry," Office for Official Publications of the European Communities.

[20]   See G. Dosi and R. Nelson, "An Introduction to Evolutionary Theories in Economics" (1994) *Evolutionary Economics* 153–172; R. Nelson and S. Winter, *An Evolutionary Theory of Economic Change* (Belknap Press, Cambridge, 1982); J. Barney, "Firm Resources and Sustained Competitive Advantage" (1991) 17 *Journal of Management* 99–120; M. Peteraf, "The Cornerstones of Competitive Advantage: A Resource-based View" (1993) 14 Strategic Mgmt J 3, 179–193; R. Grant, "Toward a Knowledge-based Theory of the Firm" (1996) 17 Strategic Mgmt J (Winter Special Issue) 109–102; B. Kogut and U. Zander, "Knowledge of the Firm and the Evolutionary Theory of the Multinational Corporation" (1993) 24 J Int'l Bus Studies 4, 625–645.

asset and emphasize the capacity of the firm to integrate tacit knowledge.[21] The DCA focuses on the importance of organizational learning to create and maintain unique resources as sources of sustained competitive advantage.[22] In this context, dynamic capabilities refer to a firm's ability to integrate, build, and reconfigure internal and external competencies to address rapidly changing environments.[23]

Firms' competencies in acquiring new competencies are bound by their capabilities' path-dependency.[24] Choice is informed by the ways in which knowledge is constructed, and pre-existing knowledge and rule systems empower or constrain firms.[25] Today's environmental problems are highly complex and more difficult to address than earlier environmental issues. Given this complexity, the knowledge necessary for the development of environmental innovations is likely to be dispersed among different types of industry and firms.[26] This holds specifically true for environmental issues, which require changes in technological trajectories. Altering technological trajectories might exceed the capabilities of individual firms. Linkages to technological information, new skills, and complementary assets must be established if innovation is to be successful.[27] The DCA demonstrates how collaborative governance structures provide a unique mechanism for partners to establish such linkages and acquire new competencies.[28] This proposition can be formalized as follows:

P1: The more the targets of EVAs require changes in technological trajectories, the more likely firms will embark in collaborations to develop new technologies.

---

[21] See K. Conner and C. Prahalad, "A Resource-based Theory of the Firm: Knowledge Versus Opportunism" (1996) 7 *Organization Science* 5, 477–501; J. Spender, "Making Knowledge the Basis of a Dynamic Theory of the Firm" (1996) 17 Strategic Mgmt J (Winter Special Issue), 1745–1762.

[22] See R. Langlois and P. Robertston, *Firms, Markets and Economic Change: A Dynamic Theory of Business Institutions* (Routlege, London, 1995).

[23] N. Foss, "Capabilities and the Theory of the Firm" (1996) *Revue d'Economie Industrielle* pp. 7–29; Teece et al., supra note 8.

[24] See R. Langlois and N. Foss, "Capabilities and Governance: The Rebirth of Production in the Theory of Economic Organization" (1998) DRUID Working Paper No. 97-2, Danish Research Unit for Industrial Dynamics; Teece, et al., supra note 8.

[25] See W. Scott, "Institutions and Organizations" SAGE Publications (1995).

[26] Environmental innovations can consist of technological and/or organizational changes. The development of greener technologies often entails reshaping organizational relationships in order to fully exploit potential gains from new technologies. See Kemp, supra note 16; S. Clarke and N. Roome, "Managing for Environmentally Sensitive Technology: Networks for Collaboration and Learning" (1995) 7 *Technology Analysis & Strategic Management* 2, 191–215.

[27] See M. Dodgson, "Learning, Trust and Inter-firm Technological Linkages: Some Theoretical Associations" in R. Coombs, et al. (eds), *Technological Collaborations* (Edward Elgar, Cheltenham, 1996); B. Kogut, "Joint Ventures: Theoretical and Empirical Perspectives" (1988) 9 Strategic Mgmt J 4, 319–332; M. Lyles, "Learning Among Joint Venture Sophisticated Firms" (1988) 28 *Management International Review* (Special Issue) 155–174.

[28] Y. Doz and G. Hamel, *Alliance Advantage: The Art of Creating Value through Partnering* (Harvard Business School Press, 1998); K. Eisenhardt and C. Schoonhoven, "Resource-based View of Strategic Alliance Formation: Strategic and Social Effects in Entrepreneurial Firms" (1996) 7 *Organization Science* 2, 136–150; Langlois and Robertston, supra note 22; Teece, et al., supra note 8.

Furthermore, collaborations can be employed as a learning vehicle to acquire and share tacit knowledge.[29] Tacit knowledge, unlike explicit knowledge, is difficult to formalize. While explicit knowledge is revealed through communication, tacit knowledge is revealed through its application. Tacit knowledge is thus slower, more costly, and more uncertain to transfer than explicit knowledge.[30] Because tacit knowledge is difficult to formalize and communicate, it cannot be transferred via market transactions. Collaborative arrangements, on the contrary, provide a governance structure that facilitates the transfer of tacit knowledge. From this perspective, EVAs allow firms to overcome their boundaries through accessing the capabilities and knowledge of its partners.[31] The effect of exchanging tacit knowledge in EVAs can be formalized as follows:

P2: The more an EVA entails the exchange of tacit knowledge among participating partners, the higher the innovative outcomes.[32]

The DCA offers some helpful insights on how EVAs can provide strategic opportunities to firms. However, limiting the analysis to the DCA is likely to overstate the net-benefits arising from EVAs, because this approach neglects the potential for transaction costs related to this new institutional arrangement. In the next section, we therefore use the New Institutional Economics to analyze EVAs in terms of potential drawbacks.

2.2   New Institutional Economics

The New Institutional Economics (NIE) links the costs of transacting under different governance modes to the institutional environment.[33] The institutional environment describes the legal and political rules of the game. In the case of EVAs, the rules—such as monitoring or sanctioning mechanisms—are negotiated within the agreement and thus become part of the arrangement rather than an externally established scheme.

Transaction cost economics (TCE) as one branch of the NIE suggests that the efficiency of different governance modes can be examined in relation to

---

[29]   See S. Berg, et al., *Joint Venture Strategies and Corporate Innovation* (Gunnand Hain, Oelgeschlager, 1982); R. Osborn and J. Hagedoorn, "The Institutionalization and Evolutionary Dynamics of Interorganizational Alliances and Networks" (1997) 40 *Academy of Management Journal* 2 pp. 261–278.

[30]   Kogut and Zander, supra note 20.

[31]   See Ashford, supra note 19; S. Georg, "Regulating the Environment: Changing from Constraint to Gentle Coercion" (1994) 3 *Business Strategy and the Environment* 2 pp. 11–20; Aggeri and Hatchuel, supra note 14.

[32]   Note that propositions 1 and 2 are closely related: targets requiring changes in technological trajectories will challenge present knowledge and the boundaries of individual firms. This is likely to result in collaboration between firms and/or regulators (P1). Collaboration entails the exchange of knowledge, which in turn increases the potential for innovative outcomes (P2). We can therefore expect that "ambitious" targets trigger collaboration and thus innovative outcomes.

[33]   See North, supra note 17; O. Williamson, *Economic Institutions of Capitalism* (The Free Press, New York, 1985); Williamson, supra note 17.

the attributes of the transaction.[34] In this chapter the transaction under study is the acquisition of new environmental competencies.

Transaction costs are primarily determined by the asset specificity of the transaction. Asset specificity creates bilateral dependency. As TCE departs from the notion that human behavior is subject to bounded rationality and opportunism, exchanging specific assets increases contracting hazards and thus transaction costs. Asset specificity can take different forms. One of these is human-asset specificity, knowledge that arises through learning by doing. As discussed before, innovations under EVAs may require firms to exchange such knowledge.[35]

Consequently, EVAs may be associated with high transaction costs. Transaction costs may be caused by information leakage.[36] Partners may imitate and replicate the core knowledge of the firm, which was exposed in order to develop new competencies.[37] Transaction costs may also be caused by free-riding partners that are not willing to exchange knowledge but still benefit from the development of new technologies.

The potential for transaction costs associated with the exchange of specific assets can be controlled by the governance structure chosen for the transaction. The governance structure of EVAs is comparable to a hybrid governance mode. Hybrid governance structures such as collaborations represent "intermediate" governance modes. These "intermediate" modes are positioned between the hierarchical, fully integrated, and the market coordinated contractual extremes of the governance scale.[38]

Hybrid governance modes like EVAs tend to be less stable than command-and-control regulations, which are more hierarchical.[39] The benefits of EVAs, such as improved public image of the industry sector or preemption of regulatory measures, are often of a collective nature. Therefore participants have a strong incentive to free ride.[40] Free-riding firms impose additional costs on complying firms because the success of an EVA may depend on a joint effort of all participating firms. With free riders engaged in an EVA, complying firms have to increase their efforts to attain overall

---

[34] Williamson, supra note 33.
[35] In EVAs, the way information is exchanged may be different than in collaborations among firms. The exchange of knowledge can be administered and facilitated by the regulator. The regulator may provide the institutional setup (e.g., knowledge networks between partners), and centralize or diffuse information. See EEA 1997, supra note 5; EPA 1998, "A catalogue of the Agency's Partnership Programs" (1998) EPA 100-B-97-003 [hereinafter EPA 1998]; Harrison, supra note 1.
[36] See Williamson, "Comparative Economic Organization," supra note 33.
[37] See G. Hamel, "Competition for Competence and Inter-partner Learning Within International Strategic Alliances" (Summer 1991) 12 Strategic Mgmt J 83–103.
[38] See Williamson, supra note 33.
[39] Command-and-control regulation is similar to a hierarchical governance mode as it exhibits the "ordering manner" typical for such hierarchical structure. Yet it is important to note that hierarchy can not fully describe command-and-control regulation. In the NIE, the hierarchical structure generally involves vertical integration, i.e., it characterizes a transaction undertaken within a firm or organization. This obviously limits the comparability, as regulator and industry are not vertically integrated.
[40] See Mazurek, supra note 9.

targets.[41] Free-riding can thus jeopardize the overall success of EVAs and provoke stricter regulations for all (and not only the defecting) firms. Free-riding firms may also undermine the commitments of those firms initially inclined to participate.[42] Generally, EVAs are legally non-binding and rarely provide legal sanctions against defecting firms.[43] The success of an EVA is therefore based on trust between partners.[44] The situation is different with command-and-control regulations, where defecting firms do not affect other firms and where legal sanctions are available to penalize non-compliance.

The effect of exchanging specific assets such as knowledge under EVAs can be formalized as follows:

P3: The higher the specificity of the assets exchanged in an EVA, the higher the potential for transaction costs associated with this EVA.

North has discussed how the institutional environment can impact the transaction costs of different governance structures.[45] An appropriate institutional environment can stabilize hybrid governance forms and reduce the potential for transaction costs. The institutional aspects that primarily influence the transaction costs of acquiring new competencies within EVAs are monitoring and sanctioning mechanisms, regulatory credibility, and protection of property rights.

2.2.1 *Monitoring*

Monitoring compliance with and progress of the EVA may be achieved through a number of mechanisms. Some EVAs employ self-conducted monitoring where firms collect, evaluate, and report the data themselves. Other EVAs may assign the monitoring responsibility to the regulator or to third parties such as research or certification institutes.[46] Monitoring mechanisms are crucial in controlling the achievement of environmental targets.[47] They increase the credibility and the political acceptance of EVAs since they can provide proof of firms' improved environmental performance.[48]

---

[41]   See EEA 1997, supra note 5; Moffet and Bregha, supra note 15.

[42]   See Harrison, supra note 1.

[43]   EVAs in the Netherlands are an exception, as 90 percent of these agreements are legally binding. See V. Ingram, "An Environment for Consensus?" CAVA Working Papers No. 98/11/5, European Research Network on Voluntary Approaches to Environmental Protection; Börkey and Leveque, supra note 1; K. Rennings, et al., "Voluntary Agreements in Environmental Protection—Experiences in Germany and Future Perspectives" (1997) Discussion Paper No. 97-04 E, Zentrum für Europäische Wirtschaftsforschung.

[44]   See Croci and Pesaro, supra note 1; Ingram, supra note 43.

[45]   See North, supra note 17.

[46]   See Storey, et al., supra note 4.

[47]   Although monitoring mechanisms serve to reduce transaction costs, they might also run the risk of increasing transaction costs. This may be the case if monitoring mechanisms cause information leakage. This can occur if they do not appropriately address firms' confidentiality concerns. See Storey et al., supra note 4.

[48]   For certain types of EVAs, such as those that primarily aim at spurring the development of new technologies, monitoring mechanisms may be difficult to implement because research

To effectively deter free-riding, sanctioning mechanisms that penalize defecting firms must complement monitoring mechanisms.[49] Without such sanctioning systems, free-riding—though detected—would not result in negative consequences for the defecting firm and would therefore be likely to persist. As already mentioned, most EVAs do not have a lawful basis to allow legal sanctions against defecting firms. Sanctions are thus restricted to excluding firms from the EVA or disclosing the free-riding behavior to the public, which could damage the firm's image.[50]

Because the majority of EVAs includes monitoring mechanisms and because monitoring is ineffective unless complemented by a sanctioning system, we focus our next proposition on the role of sanctioning:

P4: The more stringent the sanctioning system of the EVA, the smaller the potential for transaction costs associated with this EVA.

2.2.2 Regulatory Credibility

Regulatory credibility is another institutional aspect that influences transaction costs associated with EVAs. The regulator must credibly guarantee its own commitment to the EVA. Regulatory credibility might be difficult to achieve if the implementation of the EVA requires approval from different institutional levels.[51] It is also important that the regulator does not change the rules of the game once firms are engaged in the EVA. Lastly, the regulator must provide a credible threat to undertake more stringent regulations if the overall goals of the EVA are not met.

Uncertainty about future regulatory regimes affects the degree of commitment firms are willing to make and, more specifically, their innovative behavior.[52] Reduced uncertainty generally favors innovation. It reduces the potential for transaction costs because it limits the technical and organizational risks of technological development. Regulatory credibility may enhance trust between regulator and firms.[53] This can reduce the likelihood for defecting parties, lessening the potential for transaction costs.

---

activities often lack clearly defined targets. For most EVAs, however, monitoring mechanisms to control the potential for transaction costs can be effective. See Mazurek, supra note 9; Moffet and Bregha, supra note 15.

[49] These sanctioning mechanisms refer to measures undertaken in response to individually defecting (free-riding) firms. This is distinct from possible sanctions the regulator might undertake if the overall goals of the agreement are not attained.

[50] EEA 1997, supra note 5.

[51] As other chapters in this book discuss, the success of U.S. EPA's Project XL (which promises firms regulatory relief from existing regulation in exchange for environmental performance superior to status quo standards), for example, is hampered due to uncertainties regarding the program's legality. See Mazurek, supra note 9; Croci and Pesaro, supra note 1.

[52] See Ashford, supra note 19.

[53] See B. Levy and P. Spiller, "The Institutional Foundations of Regulatory Commitment: A Comparative Analysis of Telecommunications Regulations" (1994) 10 JL Econ & Org 2, 201–246; Wallace, supra note 10; M. Delmas et al., "Institutional Environment Effects on Transaction Costs: A Comparative Analysis of the US and French Nuclear Power Industries" in H. Thomas, et al. (eds), *Strategy, Structure and Style* (John Wiley & Sons, New York, 1997), pp. 283–299.

P5: The higher the regulatory credibility associated with an EVA, the lower the potential for transaction costs.

EVAs may be backed with a threat of stricter regulation in case of non-cooperation. The threat may be a stimulus to engage in an EVA.[54] A credible threat of stricter regulation can also reduce the potential for transaction costs, provided that the number of participants is sufficiently small for individual firms to realize that free-riding may jeopardize the overall success of the EVA. We consequently expect that:

P6: The stronger the regulatory threat, the lower the potential for transaction costs associated with an EVA.

2.2.3   *Property Rights*

The stringency of property rights should also impact the transaction costs related with possible appropriation of innovations by competitors. Legislation can respond to this issue by enacting and enforcing suitable protection for copyrights and patents. A tight system of property rights is expected to support firms' innovative behavior.[55] However, allocating and securing property rights is outside the scope of most EVAs, thus we will refrain from formulating a proposition on this topic.

In summary, we draw on the DCA to argue that developing complex environmental technologies requires firms to exchange knowledge through collaboration. EVAs may offer firms the possibility to venture into collaboration with other firms and regulators. NIE suggests that such collaborations may be costly. Exchanging specific assets such as knowledge under unstable hybrid modes like EVAs may be subject to the opportunistic behavior of partners. The configuration of an appropriate institutional environment may reduce the potential for transaction costs, but not eliminate it entirely.

Table 1 summarizes the propositions. The left-hand column shows the attribute of the transaction. The potential for transaction costs and innovative outcomes are indicated in the last two rows. The attributes of the transaction increase the potential for transaction costs and innovative outcome, which is marked by a $+$, or decrease the potential, which is marked by a $-$.

Table 1 presents four simplified cases.[56] It differentiates EVAs in terms of their potential for innovative outcomes and transaction costs. These four basic types of EVAs can be placed in the matrix shown in Figure 1.

---

[54]   See K. Segerson and T. Miceli, "Voluntary Approaches to Environmental Protection: The Role of Legislative Threats" (1997) Paper presented at the International Conference on Economics and Law of Voluntary Approaches in Environmental Policy, Venice, 18 November 1996; Whiston and Glachant, supra note 13.

[55]   See D. Teece, "Capturing Value from Technological Innovation: Integration, Strategic Partnering and Licensing Decisions" (1986) 15 *Research Policy* 6, 65–95.

[56]   More complex situations are, of course, possible. For example, the attributes influencing the potential for innovative outcome or transaction costs might not all have the same weight. Also note that our symbols indicate general tendencies only.

Table 1 Summary of Propositions

Attributes of the transaction

Changes in technological trajectory required by target (P1)	High	High	Low	Low
Degree of knowledge exchange (P2 and P3)	High	High	Low	Low
Institutional environment: sanctioning mechanism (P4), regulatory credibility (P5), and regulatory threat (P6)	High	Low	High	Low
Potential for innovative outcome	+	+	−	−
Potential for transaction costs	−	+	−	+

+ = Increase in the potential, − = decrease in the potential.

Figure 1

Potential for innovative outcome	High potential for innovation, low potential for transaction costs	High potential for innovation, high potential for transaction costs
	• High changes in technological trajectory	• High changes in technological trajectory
	• High degree of information exchange	• High degree of information exchange
	• High sanctioning, regulatory credibility and threat.	• Low sanctioning, regulatory credibility and threat.
	Low potential for innovation, low potential for transaction costs	Low potential for innovation, high potential for transaction costs
	• Low changes in technological trajectory	• Low changes in technological trajectory
	• Low degree of information exchange	• Low degree of information exchange
	• High sanctioning, regulatory credibility and threat.	• Low sanctioning, regulatory credibility and threat.

Potential for transaction costs

2.3   Framework for Categorizing EVAs

2.3.1   *High Potential for Innovation, Low Potential for Transaction Costs*

This cell corresponds to the first column on the left in Table 1. EVAs in this cell "combine the best of all" and optimize trade-offs between the potential for transaction costs and innovative outcomes. The targets of these EVAs entail changes in the technological trajectory and a high degree of exchange of knowledge between firms and regulators. An appropriate institutional setup reduces the potential for transaction costs that arises due to the exchange of specific assets. This setup includes suitable monitoring of participants, high sanctions against defecting firms, and high regulatory credibility and threat.

The Dutch Declaration on the Implementation of Environmental Policy in the Chemical Industry can be an example of an EVA which may be placed in this field.[57] In 1993, the Dutch government and the chemical industry established an agreement on the implementation of environmental policy in order to meet pollution reduction targets set forth in framing national policy plans.[58] Every four years, each participating company has to provide a Company Environmental Plan that identifies tasks intended to meet the targets.[59] The environmental effectiveness of this EVA has yet to be fully evaluated.[60] The agreement is thought to have increased trust and cooperation between firms and the Dutch regulatory agency. One of the driving forces for progress under this EVA is the exchange of information between companies and the regulator. The high level of exchange of knowledge favors the development of new competencies. The long term targets are considered ambitious and may therefore require changes in technological trajectories.[61] This should also have a positive impact on the potential for innovative outcomes. We thus place the Dutch EVA in the upper part of our framework. Empirical evidence suggests that the overall impact of the EVA on technical change is positive and supports this placement.[62]

In the Dutch EVA, the potential for transaction costs due to free-riding behavior is low. The agreement provides for yearly monitoring, which adequately addresses the confidentiality concerns of participating firms, as well as a sanctioning mechanism to punish defecting firms. If a firm produces an unacceptable Company Environmental Plan, the legal authority that permits the licensor to operate the plants can require this firm to comply with a stricter licensing procedure.[63]

The agreement does not contain a threat of stricter regulation in case of non-attainment of overall targets. This might increase the potential for transaction costs due to free-riding behavior. However, because of the monitoring and sanctioning mechanisms, we place this EVA in a quadrant indicating a low potential for transaction costs.

---

[57] Note that data on innovative outcomes and transaction costs associated with EVAs is scarce. In this chapter, we use the available evidence to reconstruct collaborative development efforts and institutional environments of different EVAs and estimate the likely potential for innovative outcomes and efficiency.

[58] The National Environmental Policy Plan and the Integrated Environmental Target Plans stated 61 quantitative emission reduction targets with 40 of those to be achieved by 1994/1995, the rest by 2000 and 2010. See EEA 1997, supra note 5.

[59] The plan covers an eight-year period and is to be approved by the regular licensing authority. VNCI (Vereniging van de Nederlandse Chemische Industrie), 1993, Declaration of intent on the implementation of environmental policy for the chemical industry [hereinafter VNCI 1993]. For further elaboration and discussion of the Dutch approach see the chapters by Hirsch and Seerden.

[60] See EEA 1997, supra note 5.

[61] See Börkey and Leveque, supra note 1.

[62] See EEA 1997, supra note 5

[63] See VNCI 1993. Declaration of intent on the implementation of environmental policy for the chemical industry. The Hague, April; Börkey and Leveque, supra note 1; Wallace, supra note 10.

2.3.2 High Potential for Innovation, High Potential for Transaction Costs

EVAs in this field have a high potential for innovative outcomes. This potential is triggered through targets requiring changes in the technological trajectory and/or an intensive exchange of knowledge between partners. However, this high potential for innovative outcomes is linked to a high transaction cost potential, because the institutional environment does not adequately stabilize the hybrid governance mode.

The French End-of-Life-Vehicle (ELV) Agreement represents an example of an EVA placed in this field. In 1993, the French Ministry of the Environment and the Ministry of Industry, car manufacturers, and trade associations (covering, e.g., dismantlers, shredders, recyclers, and material producers) agreed on specific objectives for reducing ELV disposal.[64] So far, there is no quantitative data available to assess the environmental effectiveness of the ELV agreement.[65]

Players within the ELV chain decided to engage in collaborations as they thought that the ELV problem was too complex and concerned too many parties to be handled by a single firm or industry.[66] The ELV agreement is a coordination mechanism, which promotes learning and exploratory action.[67]

The targets of the ELV agreement require changes in technological trajectories and an intensive exchange of knowledge between firms. This raises the potential for innovative outcomes, placing the ELV agreement in the upper part of our framework. Preliminary results indicate innovative outcomes.[68]

The institutional environment of this EVA, however, provides few safeguards to limit the potential for transaction costs. The agreement does not contain any explicit threats of alternative regulation.[69] It also lacks explicit sanctions for defecting car manufacturers.[70] It therefore seems that this institutional environment cannot reduce the potential for high transaction costs.

---

[64] The agreement stated that by 2002, no more than 15 percent of total car weight (no more than 10 percent for new cars) and a maximum of 200 kg are to be landfilled. No more than 5 percent should be landfilled in the (undated) long term. From 2002 on, new models must allow 90 percent recovery, re-use, or recycling. See EEA 1997, supra note 5.

[65] See ibid.

[66] See Aggeri and Hatchuel, supra note 14.

[67] See F. Den Hond, "The 'Similarity' and 'Heterogeneity' Theses in Studying Innovation: Evidence from the End-of-Life Vehicle Case" (1998) 10 *Technology Analysis and Strategic Management* 4, 529–543.

[68] See R. Zoboli, "Implications of Environmental Regulation on Industrial Innovation: The Case of End-of-Life Vehicles" (1998), report carried out under the IPTS-DGIII framework project "Impact of the EU Regulation on Innovation of European Industry," Office for Official Publications of the European Communities.

[69] However, firms might face an implicit threat of stricter regulation. Germany has implemented a stricter regulation concerning the ELV issue, and the French automobile industry might fear that the French regulators will copy this stricter scheme. See, EEA 1997, supra note 5; Börkey and Leveque, supra note 1; Whiston and Glachant, supra note 13; Zoboli, supra note 68.

[70] Only shredders and dismantlers may face commercial sanctioning if they do not cooperate and acquire certification. Car distributors and insurance companies have signaled that they might use certified sites only. See EEA 1997, supra note 5.

EPA's Design for the Environment Program (DfE) represents an EVA that is also marked with a high potential for innovative outcomes and transaction costs. DfE was initiated in 1992 by the EPA's Office of Pollution Prevention and Toxics. Through DfE, the EPA develops and provides businesses with information on how to incorporate environmental considerations into the design of products, processes, and management systems.[71] The program does not contain a clearly defined target other than to disseminate knowledge and to spur and coordinate research efforts.

In DfE, partnerships are formed with a variety of stakeholders such as industry, research institutions, and environmental groups in order to develop solutions to specific environmental issues. EPA usually initiates and coordinates the research efforts. It also disseminates information within DfE and assists businesses in implementing new technologies and processes. Innovative outcomes of DfE can be expected to be high. DfE bundles expertise of various stakeholders to develop new solutions and encourages the exchange of knowledge.

The institutional setup of DfE is not appropriate to reduce the high transaction costs that would be associated with the exchange of specific assets. DfE projects are negotiated without regulatory background threats. In addition, there are no monitoring or sanctioning mechanisms to deter free-riding behavior. Thus, firms could benefit from the efforts of the other firms in the agreement without having invested in DfE.

2.3.3 Low Potential for Innovation, Low Potential for Transaction Costs

EVAs in this field have target levels that are sufficiently low to be achieved without shifts in technological trajectories and without challenging firms' capabilities. Collaborative behavior is therefore unlikely. It follows that the potential for transaction costs tends to be low because firms do not exchange core knowledge. Hence, the institutional environment becomes less important. Two EVAs, the German Declaration on Global Warming Prevention and the Danish Agreement on Recovery of Transport Packaging, may serve as examples of EVAs located in this field.

In March 1996, Germany's industry and trade updated and extended its one-year old Declaration on Global Warming Prevention. The updated declaration stated overall CO_2 reduction targets, and every participating association stated its reduction goal, a timeframe, and measures to be undertaken.[72] The agreement may be evaluated as effective since some of the reduction goals have already been achieved.[73]

---

[71] See EPA 1998, supra note 35.

[72] Specifically, the declaration stated that "German industry and trade are prepared to make a special effort on a voluntary basis to reduce their specific CO_2 emissions or their specific energy consumption by 20 percent in the period up to the year 2005 (base year 1990)." See Bundesverband der Deutschen Industrie, "Updated and Extended Declaration by German Industry and Trade on Global Warming Prevention" (Cologne, 1996).

[73] Note that a thorough evaluation of the effectiveness would also include the assessment of the target levels and a comparison with alternative regulatory scenarios. See B. Hillebrand

The declaration was initiated by German industry; government involvement was limited and no specific contract between regulator and industry was signed.[74] So far, there is no evidence that the declaration has induced any meaningful collaboration between participating firms.[75] The target levels are unlikely to induce changes in the technological trajectory because they are expected to be equal to or even lower than the reduction levels a business-as-usual path would have generated.[76] The potential for innovative outcomes is therefore small, which places the German agreement in the lower part of Figure 1. In fact, the European Environmental Agency states that to date, there is no evidence that the declaration has resulted in significant technical changes.[77]

German industry adopted the EVA in order to avoid the implementation of an energy tax or waste heat ordinance.[78] Yearly monitoring is assigned to an independent economic research institute. There are no legal sanctions for defecting firms, but the publication of the monitoring reports may cause "public disgrace" for free-riding firms or trade associations.

The institutional environment of this EVA may reduce the potential for transaction costs. However, in this EVA, the importance of the institutional environment is limited. The majority of CO_2 reductions have been achieved without a significant exchange of knowledge between firms, and transaction costs are therefore expected to be low.

The Danish Agreement on Recovery of Transport Packaging was established in 1994. The Danish Government and the Federation of Danish Industries signed an agreement that targets the recycling and re-use of transport packaging material. The overall target was derived from the 1992 Government Action Plan for Waste and Recycling.[79] Specific recycling rates, staged timetables, and allocations of responsibilities were the subject of negotiations between regulator and industry. So far, no data is available to assess the environmental effectiveness of this EVA.

Government participation was limited to negotiating the agreement with other parties. The literature available does not suggest that any significant exchange of knowledge took place between firms and regulators once the EVA was established. According to the DCA, the potential for innovative

---

et al. (1997) "First Monitoring Report: CO_2-Emissions in German Industry 1995–1996", RWI-Paper No. 50, Rheinisch-Westfälisches Institut für Wirtschaftsforschung.

[74] See E. Jochem and W. Eichenhammer, "Voluntary Agreements as an Instrument to Substitute Regulating and Economic Instruments: Lessons from the German Voluntary Agreements on CO_2 Reduction," (1996) Paper presented at the International Conference on Economics and Law of Voluntary Approaches in Environmental Policy, Venice, 18 November 1996.

[75] However, greater collaboration efforts are likely to evolve as firms increasingly realize the reduction potential through integrated supply strategies. See Hillebrand, et al., supra note 73.

[76] See S. Ramesohl and C. Kristof, "The Declaration of German Industry on Global Warming Prevention: A Model for Effective and Self-improving Climate Processes?" (1999) CAVA Working Papers No. 98/11/6, European Research Network on Voluntary Approaches for Environmental Protection.

[77] See EEA 1997, supra note 5.

[78] Börkey and Leveque, supra note 1; K. Rennings, et al., supra note 43.

[79] By the year 2000, 80 percent of the volume of transport packaging in Denmark should be collected and recycled.

outcomes is therefore limited. This might be linked to the nature of the targets: the agreement focuses on transport packaging. This type of packaging is easier to collect and manage than other types of packaging waste.[80] Shifts in technological trajectories might not be required to solve this specific recycling problem and joint research might not be necessary.

The agreement was negotiated under the implicit threat of stricter regulation. It does not include explicit sanctions, but public and peer pressure is expected to provide moral sanctions for defecting firms.[81] As with the German EVA, the potential for transaction costs in the Danish agreement is very low. Firms did not engage in major collaborations to develop solutions. Therefore, they did not risk opportunistic behavior and its associated transaction costs. Background threats and public pressure might further reduce the (already low) transaction cost potential.

2.3.4   Low Potential for Innovation, High Potential for Transaction Costs

EVAs in this field correspond with the far right column in Table 1. We have suggested that EVAs with a low potential for innovative outcomes also have a low potential for transaction costs because these EVAs do not involve collaborative development efforts. However, if the institutional

Figure 2   Examples Illustrating Our Framework

	High potential for innovation, low potential for transaction costs	**High potential for innovation, high potential for transaction costs**
Potential for innovative outcome	Dutch Declaration on the Implementation of Environmental Policy in the Chemical Industry	French ELV Agreement EPA's DfE
	Low potential for innovation, low potential for transaction costs	**Low potential for innovation, high potential for transaction costs**
	The German declaration on Global Warming Prevention Danish Agreement on Recovery of Transport packaging	

Potential for transaction costs

---

[80]   See EEA 1997, supra note 5.
[81]   Börkey and Leveque, supra note 1; EEA 1997, supra note 5.

environment is poorly designed, it is possible that the transaction costs will increase. Inappropriate handling of confidential issues when monitoring, for example, may cause information leakage and impose additional costs on firms. Empirically, we do not find such EVAs to exist because firms have no incentive to participate in EVAs with both a low potential for the acquisition of new competencies and a high potential for transaction costs. Figure 2 summarizes our examples.

3 CONCLUSION

In the late 1960s and early 1970s, regulatory agencies made extensive use of command-and-control regulations with prescribed standards and technologies. In the mid-1980s, they started to employ market-based strategies and tools such as pollution taxes or tradable permits.[82] In the 1990s, values and beliefs have changed, making room for a shift away from adversarial and legalistic regulatory measures towards more cooperative actions. In Europe especially, regulators and firms are increasingly turning to Environmental Voluntary Agreements to protect the environment.

Preliminary evaluations suggest that the environmental impact of EVAs may be positive.[83] Yet environmental effectiveness is not the only attribute determining whether EVAs are successful. The innovative potential of EVAs as well as their costs need evaluation. Those attributes will determine firms' willingness to participate in EVAs. To become a valuable regulatory tool, the potential benefits of EVAs need to be fully explored. However, in the context of an emerging regulatory scheme, regulators might opt to experiment. So far, they have only a rudimentary framework to guide their actions. This creates uncertainties and costs for firms which might impede participation. In the United States, for example, EVAs are still marginal to the environmental agencies' regulatory activities.[84]

This chapter characterized the conditions for successful agreements that lead to organizational change and technological innovation. Specifically, we explored EVAs in terms of their potential for transaction costs and innovative outcomes. Drawing on the Dynamic Capability Approach, we argued that EVAs with targets that require changes in technological trajectories challenge firms' boundaries. This should induce firms to engage in

---

[82] See B. Long, "Environmental Regulation: The Third Generation" (1997) 206 *OECD Observer* June/July pp. 14–18.
[83] Assessing the environmental impact of EVAs raises the question of which baseline to compare the environmental performance to. Compared to a situation without an agreement or regulatory measures, EVAs seem to enhance environmental protection. EVAs might also be assessed to be effective, because the majority of EVAs reach their targets. However, no data is available to assess the environmental effectiveness of EVAs as compared to other regulatory instruments. See Öko Institut e.V., (1998) "New Instruments for Sustainability: The Contribution of Voluntary Agreements to Environmental Policy"; Ingram, supra note 43; Börkey and Leveque, supra note 1; EEA 1997, supra note 5; Storey, et al., supra note 2.
[84] See, for example, the chapters in this book by Jon Cannon and Cary Coglianese.

collaborative development efforts with other firms and the government. Collaborative development offers partners the opportunity to exchange tacit knowledge required for acquiring new environmental solutions. Building on the New Institutional Economics, we also showed that EVAs may entail high transaction costs. This is because partners expose their core knowledge and might be subject to opportunistic behavior. Consequently, firms have to manage the tradeoff between the benefits and costs of acquiring new competencies through EVAs. We discussed how this tradeoff may be alleviated through an appropriate institutional setup. We derived four basic types of EVAs with different potentials for innovative outcomes and transaction costs. The attributes of these four types differ according to the levels of targets of the EVA, the degree of exchange of knowledge between partners, and the features of the institutional environment, including sanctioning mechanisms, regulatory credibility, and regulatory threat.

EVAs with a high potential for innovative outcomes and a relatively low potential for transaction costs present the best case. They optimize the tradeoff between innovation and cost. The Dutch EVA on the Implementation of Environmental Policy in the Chemical Industry is an example of such an EVA. A second type of EVA is associated with a high potential for innovative outcomes but also linked to a high potential transaction costs because the institutional environment does not successfully stabilize the hybrid governance mode. The French ELV agreement and EPA's DfE illustrate this type of EVA. The German Declaration on Global Warming Prevention and the Danish Agreement on Recovery of Transport Packaging serve as examples of a third type of EVAs. This type is marked by a low potential for both innovative outcomes and transaction costs. The fourth type might theoretically, but not empirically, be relevant. EVAs of this type would be associated with a low potential for innovative outcomes and high transaction costs. Firms have no incentive to participate in such an EVA.

These examples illustrate our propositions. The French ELV agreement, for instance, shows how an intensive exchange of tacit knowledge between partners enhances innovative outcomes. The examples of the German and Danish agreements show how a lack of collaboration may result in little innovation.

The level of targets of EVAs may also influence innovative outcomes. The target level of the French EVA is higher than the levels of the German and Danish EVAs. Higher targets require changes in technological trajectories. Therefore, they are more likely to trigger collaboration and innovation than lower targets. Both target levels and exchange of knowledge influence the potential for innovative outcomes. It is difficult to estimate the differentiated effects of the two factors because they interact with each other.

When assessing our propositions concerning the potential for innovative outcomes of different EVAs, it is important to note that innovations are likely to be influenced not only by target levels and degrees of exchange of information, but also by numerous other factors. Technological opportunity, appropriability, and complementarity as well as managerial discretion determine innovation processes and choices to partner (or not) with others.[85]

---

[85]   See Den Hond, supra note 67.

In particular, industry specific cycles of innovation or collaboration-friendly cultures may impact the actual innovative outcomes. In the case of the French ELV agreement, for example, the automobile industry has traditionally been marked by strong cohesion, and durable links within the industrial system were present prior to the EVA.[86] Such a cooperative and homogeneous system is very different to the one under the German agreement, which covers a variety of heterogeneous sectors. Thus, industry specific features need to be considered when evaluating possible links between the characteristics of EVAs and actual innovative outcomes.[87]

Assessing our propositions concerning the potential for transaction costs proves challenging. A comparison with empirical evidence, i.e. with actual transaction costs arising through free-riding behavior and information leakage, requires measuring these costs. However, their quantification is difficult and so far, studies mostly focus on administrative costs when assessing the efficiency of different EVAs.[88]

Drawing on our propositions, we are able to discuss the potential for innovative outcomes and transaction costs associated with different EVAs. However, the lack of empirical data allows for only a preliminary assessment of our propositions. Additional data on perceived regulatory credibility as well as data on different levels of innovative outcomes (incremental or radical) is needed to provide a clearer picture of the constraints and opportunities EVAs provide. To better evaluate the effectiveness of threats to deter free-riding behavior, further research should, for example, also consider the number of participants in EVAs.

Institutions arise and persist when they confer benefits greater than the transaction costs incurred to create and sustain them. This chapter suggests testable propositions to assess the benefits and costs of voluntary agreements for the environment. Our conceptual framework should be useful to assist regulators in designing more efficient voluntary agreements.

---

[86] See Aggeri and Hatchuel, supra note 14.
[87] See Moffet and Bregha, supra note 15.
[88] See Labatt and Maclaren, supra note 3.

15. Environmental Voluntary Agreements: Participation and Free Riding

Kathleen Segerson and Na Li Dawson

1 INTRODUCTION

Historically, policy makers have relied on regulation as the primary means of providing environmental protection. However, this approach has been heavily criticized for its lack of flexibility and high costs,[1] prompting a search for lower cost alternatives. One alternative that has received considerable attention recently is the use of voluntary approaches to environmental protection.[2] These approaches can take a variety of forms, including (1) unilateral initiatives by firms or industries ("business-led initiatives"), (2) negotiated agreements between environmental authorities and individual firms or industry groups, and (3) voluntary programs designed by environmental agencies to induce participation by individual firms.[3] The hope is that a voluntary approach will yield cost savings (among other things) by increasing flexibility (and thereby reducing abatement costs) or reducing transactions costs and regulatory lags.[4] Examples of recent voluntary approaches include the Chemical Manufacturers Association's (CMA)

---

[1] See, e.g., R. Hahn, "United States Environmental Policy: Past, Present, and Future" (1994) 34 *Natural Resources Journal* 2, 305–348.

[2] For a recent survey of research on the use of voluntary approaches to environmental protection, see K. Segerson and N. Li, "Voluntary Approaches to Environmental Protection," in H. Folmer and T. Tietenberg (eds), *The International Yearbook of Environmental and Resource Economics 1999/2000* (Edward Elgar, Cheltenham, 1999), pp. 273–306.

[3] See C. Carraro and F. Lévêque, "Introduction: The Rationale and Potential of Voluntary Approaches," in C. Carraro and F. Lévêque (eds), *Voluntary Approaches in Environmental Policy* (Kluwer Academic Publishers, Dordrecht, 1999), pp. 1–15; Segerson and Li, supra note 2.

[4] Commission of the European Communities, *On Environmental Agreements*, Communication from the Commission to the Council and the European Parliament, Brussels, 1996. Some of these cost advantages could also be realized under a regulatory approach simply by moving from a command-and-control system to one based on performance standards. See, e.g., D. Burtraw, "The SO_2 Emissions Trading Program: Cost Savings Without Allowance Trades" (1996) 14 *Contemporary Economic Policy*, 79–94.

Responsible Care Program in the US,[5] the energy production sector's voluntary declaration to reduce CO_2 emissions in Germany,[6] and the French automobile industry's agreement with the French government to reduce car waste disposal.[7] Agreements have also been negotiated in the context of wildlife habitat protection. For example, the State of Oregon entered into a memorandum of agreement with the US National Marine Fisheries Service (NMFS) to protect and restore coho salmon habitat through (among other things) voluntary landowner and community action.[8]

A key component of the success of any voluntary approach to environmental protection is the extent of participation by polluting firms.[9] If the voluntary approach is to be successful, firms must have a sufficiently strong incentive to participate. In this chapter, we consider the incentives that firms have to undertake environmental protection measures voluntarily or to participate in voluntary environmental programs. The first section of the chapter briefly discusses various participation incentives, which can be classified as either market-driven incentives or government inducements. Market-driven incentives include responses in either the output or input markets to the environmental performance of a firm. If a firm's environmental record directly affects its profitability through market forces, the firm may have an incentive to undertake protective measures voluntarily. In addition, government policies can affect participation incentives. Government inducements include both positive inducements, such as financial subsidies, and negative inducements, such as the threat of imposition of environmental regulation or taxation.

---

[5] See S. Batie, "Environmental Issues, Policy, and the Food Industry," in B. Schroder and T. Wallace (eds), *Food Industry and Government Linkages* (Kluwer Academic Publishers, Boston, 1997), pp. 235–256.

[6] See E. Jochem and W. Eichhammer, "Voluntary Agreements as an Instrument to Substitute Regulations and Economic Instruments: Lessons from the German Voluntary Agreements on CO_2 Reduction" in C. Carraro and F. Lévêque (eds), *Voluntary Approaches in Environmental Policy* (Kluwer Academic Publishers, Dordrecht, 1999), pp. 209–228; M. Storey, et al., "Voluntary Agreements with Industry" in C. Carraro and F. Lévêque (eds), *Voluntary Approaches in Environmental Policy* (Kluwer Academic Publishers, Dordrecht, 1999), pp. 187–208.

[7] See F. Lévêque and A. Nadaï, "A Firm's Involvement in the Policy-Making Process" in H. Folmer, et al. (eds), Principles of Envtl and Resource Econ (Edward Elgar, Cheltenham, 1995), pp. 299–327; F. Aggeri and A. Hatchuel, "A Dynamic Model of Environmental Policies", in C. Carraro and F. Lévêque (eds), *Voluntary Approaches in Environmental Policy* (Kluwer Academic Publishers, Dordrecht, 1999), pp. 151–186. For other examples, see Commission of the European Communities, supra note 4; International Energy Agency (IEA), "Voluntary Actions for Energy-Related CO_2 Abatement", Energy and Environment Policy Analysis Series, 1997; Storey, et al., supra note 6.

[8] S. Mooney and L. Eisgruber, "The Influence of Riparian Protection Measures on Residential Property Values: The Case of the Oregon Plan for Salmon and Watersheds", Working Paper, Trade Research Center, Montana State University, 1999.

[9] Of course, the overall success of a voluntary program in providing environmental protection depends not only on the number of firms that participate but also on the amount of environmental protection provided per firm. In this chapter, we focus on participation. For a model that focuses on the endogenous determination of the amount of environmental protection provided, see K. Segerson and T. Miceli, "Voluntary Environmental Agreements: Good or Bad News for Environmental Quality?" (1998) 36 *Journal of Environmental Economics and Management* 2, 109–130.

Both the theoretical and empirical literature suggests that firms respond to both market-based benefits from voluntary environmental protection and government inducements.[10] However, when government inducements take the form of a regulatory threat against an industry, individual firms may have an incentive not to participate in the program in the hope that other firms within the industry will engage in a sufficient amount of voluntary activity to preempt the regulation. If the others do, the non-participating firm will enjoy the benefits of averting the regulation without incurring the associated costs.

An important question is whether this incentive to "free ride" on the participation of other firms in the industry will undermine the success of the voluntary approach. We address this question in the second section of this chapter, where we analyze the implications of free rider incentives for participation in voluntary environmental programs using a simple economic model of firm behavior. We focus specifically on a scenario where a group of polluting firms (or an industry group) is offered the opportunity to avoid regulation by voluntarily meeting a given environmental target. If the industry as a whole meets the target, the regulation will not be imposed. Thus, while there is an incentive for participation in the voluntary approach to avoid the regulation, there is also an incentive not to participate, i.e., to free ride. We use an economic model to characterize the equilibrium industry response to this opportunity for the voluntary provision of environmental protection. In particular, we ask whether some subset of the firms will choose collectively to meet the target voluntarily (i.e., to participate in a voluntary program) and to allow the remaining firms to free ride (i.e., not participate), or whether instead the potential for free riding will destroy the viability of the voluntary approach. In addition, we ask whether the free rider problem dissipates any potential welfare gains that could be realized as a result of the lower costs of the voluntary approach. Finally, we examine how the equilibrium outcome is affected by industry size. Specifically, we ask whether the free rider problem is likely to be more severe when the industry is comprised of a large number of firms rather than when it is small and whether the potential welfare gain from the use of a voluntary approach is affected by industry size.

Our results suggest that, despite the existence of free riding, it is still possible to have a successful voluntary program, i.e., a program under which a subset of firms participate and meet the environmental target voluntarily. Thus, the free rider problem does not necessarily destroy the viability of the voluntary approach. In addition, if the voluntary approach offers greater flexibility and lower costs per firm, then even with free riding the voluntary approach will be more efficient than the use of mandatory controls to meet the target. Finally, we show that whether the free riding problem and the efficiency gain from use of a voluntary approach are greater or less with larger industries will depend on the cost structure of the firms under the voluntary and mandatory approaches.

---

[10] See Segerson and Li, supra note 2, for a survey of recent theoretical and empirical literature on voluntary environmental approaches.

2 PARTICIPATION INCENTIVES

There are a number of reasons why industries might voluntarily agree to improve environmental quality. These reasons can generally be divided into two categories, market-driven benefits from environmental initiatives and government inducements. Both the theoretical and the empirical literature on voluntary approaches suggest that both types of incentives can be effective in inducing voluntary environmental improvements.[11]

Market-driven benefits can take a number of forms. For example, there is evidence of consumer demand for "green" products that reduce exposure to hazardous substances or reduce the environmental consequences of production.[12] Because consumers are often willing to pay a price premium for green products, firms that produce these products through voluntary adoption of environmental protection measures can increase market shares and profits. A growing number of eco-labeling programs allow firms to identify and advertise their products as environmentally-friendly.[13] Recent empirical work suggests that firms that produce products for final consumption are more likely to feel consumer pressures and hence more likely to adopt environmental measures voluntarily.[14] In some cases, pressure comes not from consumers of the firm's product but from local communities.[15]

Firms might also be driven to invest in environmental protection by other market forces, such as pressure from suppliers of capital and other inputs.[16] For example, stock prices can be responsive to information about the

---

[11] See Segerson and Li, supra note 2.

[12] See T. Tietenberg, "Disclosure Strategies for Pollution Control" (1998) 11 Envtl and Resource Econ 3–4, 587–602.

[13] See US Environmental Protection Agency, Office of Pollution Prevention and Toxics, *Status Report on the Use of Environmental Labels Worldwide,* Washington, D.C., EPA742-R-9-93-001, September 1993; US Environmental Protection Agency, Office of Pollution Prevention and Toxics, *Determinants of Effectiveness for Environmental Certification and Labeling Programs,* Washington, D.C., EPA742-R-04-001, April 1994.

[14] S. Arora and T. Cason, "An Experiment in Voluntary Environmental Regulation: Participation in EPA's 33/50 Program" (1995) 28 J Envtl Econ & Mgmt 3, 271–286; S. Arora and T. Cason, "Why do Firms Volunteer to Exceed Environmental Regulations? Understanding Participation in EPA's 33/50 Program" (1996) 72 *Land Economics* 4, 413–432; M. Khanna and L. Damon, "EPA's Voluntary 33/50 Program: Impact on Toxic Releases and Economic Performance of Firms" (1999) 37 J Envtl Econ & Mgmt 1, 1–25.

[15] See I. Henriques and P. Sadorsky, "The Determinants of an Environmentally Responsible Firm: An Empirical Approach" (1996) 30 J Envtl Econ & Mgmt 3, 381–395; A. Blackman and G. Bannister, "Community Pressure and Clean Technology in the Informal Sector: An Econometric Analysis of the Adoption of Propane by Traditional Mexican Brickmakers" (1998) 35 J Envtl Econ & Mgmt 1, 1–121.

[16] See D. Esty, "Clean and Competitive: Business-Led Environmental Management," in S. Batie, et al. (eds), *Business-led Initiatives in Environmental Management: The Next Generation of Policy?* Special Report (SR) 92, Proceedings of Pre-conference Workshop to the AAEA Annual Meeting, Toronto, 26 July 1997; Tietenberg, supra note 12.

environmental performance of a firm,[17] and concerns about liability for environmental contamination can affect access to capital.[18]

Firms will also have an incentive to undertake environmental protection measures voluntarily if those measures also contribute directly to profitability, i.e., if they generate a "win-win" situation. Measures that reduce waste or increase efficiency will also reduce production costs. For example, some environmentally-friendly agricultural production practices, such as conservation tillage, nutrient management, and irrigation water management, can simultaneously improve environmental quality and reduce costs.[19] Firms may also be environmentally proactive in a strategic attempt to gain market share and penalize rivals.[20]

Even in the absence of market-driven benefits, firms may choose to undertake voluntary environmental protection in response to government inducements. Those inducements can be either positive (a "carrot" approach) or negative (a "stick" approach). The most direct positive inducements are often financial subsidies or cost-sharing programs designed to provide direct compensation to firms that undertake voluntary measures. The use of financial inducements has historically been the mainstay of environmental policy in the agricultural sector.[21] Empirical evidence suggests that participation rates in voluntary programs are affected by financial inducements.[22] However, subsidies are generally viewed as economically

---

[17] See, e.g, J. Hamilton, "Pollution as News: Media and Stock Market Reactions to the Toxics Release Inventory Data" (1995) 28 J Envtl Econ & Mgmt 1, 98–113; S. Konar and M. Cohen, "Information as Regulation: The Effect of Community Right to Know Laws on Toxic Emissions" (1997) 32 J Envtl Econ & Mgmt 1, 109–124; M. Khanna, et al., "Toxics Release Information: A Policy Tool for Environmental Protection" (1998) 36 J Envtl Econ & Mgmt 3, 243–266.

[18] See S. Garber and J. Hammitt, "Risk Premiums for Environmental Liability: Does Superfund Increase the Cost of Capital?" (1998) 36 J Envtl Econ & Mgmt 3, 267–294.

[19] See, e.g., G. Fox, et al., "Comparative Economics of Alternative Agricultural Production Systems: A Review" (1991) 20 *Northeastern Journal of Agricultural and Resource Economics* 1, 124–142; L. Bull and C. Sandretto, "The Economics of Agricultural Tillage Systems," in *Farming for a Better Environment* (Ankeny, IA: Soil and Water Conservation Society of America, 1, 1995), pp. 35–40.

[20] See Lévêque and Nadaï, supra note 7; H. Gabel and B. Sinclair-Desgagné, "Corporate Responses to Environmental Concerns," in H. Folmer, et al. (eds), Principles of Envtl and Resource Econ (Edward Elgar, Cheltenham, 1995), pp. 328–346.

[21] See K. Reichelderfer, "National Agroenvironmental Incentive Programs: The U.S. Experience" in J. Braden and S. Lovejoy (eds), *Agriculture and Water Quality: International Perspective* (Lynne Reinner Publishers, Boulder, 1990), pp. 131–146; M. Ribaudo, "Lessons Learned about the Performance of USDA Agricultural Nonpoint Source Pollution Programs" (1998) 53 *Journal of Soil and Water Conservation* 1, 4–10; M. Ribaudo, et al., *The Economics of Water Quality Protection from Nonpoint Sources: Theory and Practice*, US Department of Agriculture, Economic Research Service, Agricultural Economic Report Number 782, November 1999.

[22] E.g., L. Lohr and T. Park, "Utility-Consistent Discrete-Continuous Choices in Soil Conservation" (1995) 71 *Land Economics* 4, 474–490; J. Cooper and R. Keim, "Incentive Payments to Encourage Farmer Adoption of Water Quality Protection Practices" (1996) 78 *American Journal of Agricultural Economics* 1, 54–64.

inefficient, because they can induce excessive entry into an industry[23] and the funds generally must be raised through distortionary taxation.[24]

Rather than reducing the costs of voluntary provision through subsidies, regulators can also encourage voluntary adoption of environmental measures by reducing information costs or the costs of participation in voluntary programs. Both information and education have been shown to affect the adoption of environmentally-friendly farming practices.[25] In addition, Davies and Mazurek attribute the relatively high enrollment rates in the US Environmental Protection Agency's 33/50 Program to the low transaction costs associated with participation.[26] Note that lowering participation costs through a reduction in transaction costs will generally have a very different overall impact than lowering participation costs through a relaxation of the environmental protection measures that participation entails. Although both may increase participation rates, a relaxation of the stringency of the associated protection measures will lead to less environmental protection per participating firm. A reduction in transaction costs will not.

Firms may also choose to undertake voluntary environmental protection in response to negative government inducements, the most common of which is the threat of the imposition of regulation or other mandatory measures (e.g., environmental taxes) to ensure environmental protection.[27] Faced with a threat of regulation or taxation, firms can act to preempt those regulatory actions. For example, the German industries voluntarily agreed to reduce CO_2 emissions in the hope that this would forestall government initiatives to impose a CO_2 energy tax.[28] The French car industry agreement on car waste disposal was a response to a proposed regulatory program on car waste reduction.[29] Even Oregon's memorandum of agreement on the protection and restoration of salmon was designed to prevent the NMFS from listing coho salmon as a threatened or endangered species under the Endangered Species Act.[30]

---

[23] See W. Baumol and W. Oates, *The Theory of Environmental Policy* (Cambridge University Press, 1988).

[24] See A. Atkinson and J. Stiglitz, *Lectures on Public Economics* (McGraw-Hill Book Co., London, 1980).

[25] See Lohr and Park, supra note 22; D. Bosch, et al., "Voluntary versus Mandatory Agricultural Policies to Protect Water Quality: Adoption of Nitrogen Testing in Nebraska" (1995) 17 *Review of Agricultural Economics* 1, 13–24; Ribaudo, et al., supra note 21.

[26] See T. Davies and J. Mazurek, "Industry Incentives for Environmental Improvement: Evaluation of U.S. Federal Initiatives" prepared for Global Environmental Management Initiative, Resources for the Future, Washington, D.C., 1996.

[27] See R. Baggott, "By Voluntary Agreement: The Politics of Instrument Selection" (1986) 64 *Public Administration*, 51–67; Storey et al., supra note 6; Segerson and Miceli, supra note 9; J. Maxwell et al., "Self-Regulation and Social Welfare: The Political Economy of Corporate Environmentalism" (forthcoming) JL & Econ.

[28] See Jochem and Eichhammer, supra note 6; Storey, et al., supra note 6.

[29] See Lévêque and Nadaï, supra note 7; Aggeri and Hatchnel, supra note 7.

[30] Based on voluntary actions promised under the memorandum, the NMFS initially determined that a listing of the coho salmon was not warranted. However, the US District Court for Oregon ordered the NMFS to reconsider its decision without regard to the memorandum or the associated provisions of Oregon's plan for restoration, since neither the memorandum

In some cases the threat of regulation or taxation is explicit, and in other cases it is implicit. A firm may also be granted an exemption to an existing regulation in exchange for voluntarily undertaking alternative measures that ensure comparable environmental protection, as under the US Environmental Protection Agency's Project XL.[31] In such cases, the voluntary program provides a form of regulatory relief. The existence of an underlying regulatory structure is thought by some to be an important component determining the likely success of a voluntary program.[32]

Although regulatory threats may provide an incentive for a firm to adopt voluntary environmental protection measures, they suffer from an important drawback, namely, the potential for free riding. In many cases, a regulation or tax policy may be imposed on an entire industry or sector rather than on a firm-specific basis; yet decisions about voluntary environmental protection are made by individual firms. If a sufficiently large number of firms within the industry undertake voluntary adoption and thereby preempt the regulation, a firm that does not participate will nonetheless enjoy the benefits of avoidance of the regulation. Thus, each individual firm may have an incentive to free ride on the environmental protection measures undertaken by others in the industry. In the remainder of this chapter, we examine this free riding incentive and ask whether the potential for free riding will necessarily undermine the success of a voluntary program based on a regulatory threat.

3 FREE RIDING UNDER REGULATORY THREATS

3.1 An Overview of the Modeling Approach

In the remainder of this chapter, we consider voluntary provision of an environmental good when the industry's motivation is the preemption of regulation. In particular, we consider a scenario in which a regulator has a target level of environmental quality to achieve (for example, a fixed amount of habitat restoration or a fixed level of ambient air or water quality). There is an industry comprised of a number of firms that can supply the environmental good. The regulator gives the industry an opportunity to meet the target, i.e., to supply the given amount of the environmental good, "voluntarily." The explicit threat is that, if the industry fails to achieve the target voluntarily, then the regulator will impose regulatory measures sufficiently stringent to ensure that the target is met. The hypothesis is that, ceteris paribus, it would be potentially more expensive for firms if controls were mandatory, because mandatory controls are often not cost-effective.

---

nor the Oregon Plan were "current enforceable measures." On reconsideration, the NMFS listed the coho as threatened under the Endangered Species Act. See State of Oregon Executive Order EO99-01 < http://www.oregon-plan.org/Eo99-01.htm>.

[31]   See Davies and Mazurek, supra note 26.

[32]   Ibid., Ribaudo, supra note 21; Khanna and Damon, supra note 14.

Methodologically, we draw from two sources. The first is the literature on the economics of voluntary agreements.[33] Most of the theoretical literature explores individual firm behavior, i.e., a firm's decision to participate or not participate in a voluntary agreement.[34] At the individual firm level, our approach is conceptually similar to the approach adopted by Segerson and Miceli.[35] However, when examining individual participation decisions, the models in the literature typically assume that those decisions are independent across firms, i.e., that one firm's payoff from participation is not affected by another firm's participation decision. To examine whether it is possible to form a voluntary agreement with an industry, it is necessary to have a multiple firm model that incorporates the interaction among the firms' payoffs. Although Segerson and Miceli briefly examine the interaction between two firms in a Nash equilibrium, they do not explicitly examine the implications of free riding.[36] Maxwell, Lyon, and Hackett present a model of voluntary abatement with free riding.[37] However, they do not examine the possibility of an equilibrium in which a subset of firms participate and the remaining firms free ride.

The potential for non-participation by some parties has been studied extensively in the economic literature on international environmental agreements, which is the second strand of literature from which we draw methodologically.[38] International environmental agreements (IEAs) differ from the voluntary agreements of interest here in at least two ways. First, with IEAs there is no supra-national regulatory authority that can impose

---

[33]   See Segerson and Li, supra note 2, for an overview of this literature.

[34]   See Gabel and Sinclair-Desgagné, supra note 20; Segerson and Miceli, supra note 9; Maxwell et al., supra note 27; D. Schmelzer, "Voluntary Agreements in Environmental Policy: Negotiating Emission Reductions" in C. Carraro and F. Lévêque (eds), *Voluntary Approaches in Environmental Policy* (Kluwer Academic Publishers, Dordrecht, 1999), pp. 55–74.

[35]   Segerson and Miceli, supra note 9; K. Segerson and T. Miceli, "Voluntary Approaches to Environmental Protection: The Role of Legislative Threats" in C. Carraro and F. Lévêque (eds), *Voluntary Approaches in Environmental Policy* (Kluwer Academic Publishers, Dordrecht, 1999), pp. 105–120. However, we assume that mandatory controls are imposed with certainty if the voluntary approach is unsuccessful. Segerson and Miceli assume an exogeneous probability of regulation. (For a model with an endogenous probability of regulation based on a political influence game, see Maxwell, et al., supra note 27.) In addition, Segerson and Miceli, supra note 9, allow the regulator and firm to bargain over the level that would be required under the voluntary approach. Thus, the level of environmental quality that is realized under the voluntary approach will generally differ from the level that would be imposed under mandatory controls.

[36]   See Segerson and Miceli, supra note 35.

[37]   See Maxwell, et al., supra note 27.

[38]   See S. Barrett, "International Environmental Agreements as Games" in R. Pethig (ed.), *Conflict and Cooperation in Managing Environmental Resources* (Springer-Verlag, Berlin, 1992), pp. 11–36; S. Barrett, "Self-enforcing International Environmental Agreements" (1994) 46 *Oxford Economic Papers* 5, 878–894; S. Barrett, "Heterogeneous International Environmental Agreements" in C. Carraro (ed.), *International Environmental Agreements: Strategic Policy Issues* (Edward Elgar Publishing, Cheltenham, 1997), pp. 9–25; S. Barrett, "Towards a Theory of International Cooperation" in C. Carraro and D. Siniscalco (eds), *New Directions in the Economic Theory of the Environment* (Cambridge University Press, 1997), pp. 239–280; S. Barrett,"A Theory of International Cooperation" (1998), Fondazione Eni Enrico Mattei Working Paper No. 43.98, Milan; C. Carraro and D. Siniscalco, "Strategies for the International Protection of

mandatory controls if the IEA is unsuccessful. In the absence of an agreement, all firms simply receive the payoffs from the non-cooperative outcome. In our context, the alternative to meeting the target voluntarily is the imposition of mandatory controls. Second, IEAs are typically negotiated for global pollutants, which harm all countries. When emissions are reduced by any country, all countries benefit directly. Thus, under an IEA each firm's payoff, for both signatories (participants) and non-signatories (non-participants), increases with the number of signatories. In our context, firms do not directly benefit from pollution reductions. A firm benefits from another firm's reductions (as well as its own reductions) only if that reduction is pivotal in determining whether the target will be met voluntarily. Thus, each firm's payoff increases with the number of firms participating in the voluntary program (i.e., undertaking voluntary provision) if and only if the increase is pivotal in meeting the target. In other words, there is a discontinuous jump in the payoff of the firm at the point where the number of participants is sufficiently high (given the abatement level of each participant) to ensure that the target is met voluntarily.[39]

Despite these differences, the basic notion of an equilibrium level of participation that has been developed in the context of international agreements applies in our context as well. In particular, Barrett has argued that, since international agreements are not binding, in equilibrium an agreement must be self-enforcing.[40] Similarly, in our context since participation in the program is voluntary, it must be self-enforcing. We employ the concept of a self-enforcing agreement to characterize the equilibrium participation in a voluntary program. We present here a general description of the main results of our analysis regarding the role of free riding. These results are derived from a formal mathematical model, which is described in more detail in Segerson and Dawson.[41]

We consider a scenario in which a fixed aggregate target for environmental quality (denoted X) is set by a regulatory authority.[42] The regulator

"the Environment" (1993) 52 *Journal of Public Economics* 3, 309–328; C. Carraro and D. Siniscalco, "Voluntary Agreements in Environmental Policy: A Theoretical Appraisal," in A. Xepapadeas (ed.), *Economic Policy for the Environment and Natural Resources: Techniques for the Management and Control of Pollution* (Edward Elgar, Cheltenham, 1996), pp. 80–94; C. Carraro and D. Siniscalco, "International Environmental Agreements, Incentives and Political Economy" (1998) 42 Eur Econ Rev 3–5, 561–572; E. Dockner and N. Van Long, "International Pollution Control: Cooperative vs. Non-Cooperative Strategies" (1993) 25 J Envtl Econ & Mgmt 13–29; M. Hoel, "International Environ-mental Conventions: The Case of Uniform Reductions of Emissions" (1992) 2 Envtl and Resource Econ 2, 141–159; M. Hoel, "Efficient Climate Policy in the Presence of Free-Riders" (1994) 27 J Envtl Econ & Mgmt 3, 259–274; C. Schmit, "Incentives for International Environmental Cooperation: Theoretic Models and Economic Instruments" Fondazione Eni Enrico Mattei Working Paper No. 56.98, Milan, 1998.

[39] This point is further discussed below.

[40] See references given in note 38.

[41] K. Segerson and N. Dawson, "Voluntary Environmental Agreements with Multiple Firms: The Role of Free Riding" Working Paper, Department of Economics, University of Connecticut, 1999.

[42] For a model with an endogenous determination of environmental quality under the voluntary approach, see Segerson and Miceli, supra note 9; Segerson and Miceli, supra note 35.

provides the firms in the industry with the opportunity to meet the aggregate target, i.e., to supply the given amount of the environmental good, "voluntarily." If the standard is not met, then the regulator will (with certainty) impose mandatory controls on all firms in the industry sufficient to ensure that the standard is met. Thus, the regulator is effectively providing the industry with a chance to avoid mandatory controls by meeting the standard voluntarily. Note that it is possible for the industry to meet the target even if some firms do not participate, i.e., even if some firms do not supply any of the environmental good. A subset of firms in the industry can choose to meet the environmental target collectively without the help of the remaining firms. Thus, it is possible to avoid mandatory controls even though some firms free ride. The question is whether it will be in the interest of a subset of firms to do this, i.e., whether participation by a subset of firms would ever be an equilibrium outcome.

To examine the equilibrium outcome, we consider the case where all firms are identical in the sense of having identical cost structures. In many real-world cases, the firms that contribute to a particular environmental problem will be quite different, and these differences can affect incentives for participation. Nonetheless, considering the case of identical firms serves two purposes. First, it provides a benchmark. If we can first understand participation incentives when all firms are identical, then we can subsequently introduce heterogeneity across firms to determine the role that heterogeneity may play.[43] Second, if an industry is composed of two general types of firms (e.g., "large" firms and "small" firms), it is possible that the group targeted for possible regulation is only one type of firm (e.g., the large firms). Thus, the group of targeted firms may be fairly homogeneous even if the entire group of contributing polluters is not.

With identical firms, it is reasonable to assume that, if mandatory controls are imposed, they will be uniform across all firms, i.e., each firm will be required to supply X/N units of environmental quality, where N is the number of firms. Further, we assume that if the controls were voluntary, firms would have more flexibility, and hence lower costs, than under mandatory controls, both in total and at the margin. Note that these costs could include both the cost of providing the environmental good (e.g., abatement costs or the cost of providing protected habitat) and any associated transaction costs for the firm. The Commission of European Communities cites the potential for greater flexibility and lower costs under a voluntary approach as one of the main advantages of the use of voluntary approaches.[44] If C_m and C_v denote the costs under mandatory and voluntary controls respectively, then the cost advantage under mandatory controls implies that $C_v(x) \leqslant C_m(x)$ for any given level of provision x. Of course,

---

[43] For models of self-enforcing IEAs with heterogeneous countries, see Barrett, "Heterogeneous International Environmental Agreements," supra note 38; M. Botteon and C. Carraro, "Burden Sharing and Coalition Stability in Environmental Negotiations with Asymmetric Countries" in C. Carraro (ed.), *International Environmental Negotiations: Strategic Policy Issues* (Edward Elgar Publishing, Cheltenham, 1997), pp. 26–55.
[44] Commission of the European Communities, supra note 4.

a cost savings is only possible if the mandatory controls that would be imposed are not cost efficient. Historically, regulatory approaches to pollution control have not been cost efficient, since they have relied primarily on technology and design standards as policy tools.[45] However, the recent move toward greater reliance on performance standards and marketable emission permits implies a corresponding reduction in the cost of meeting environmental quality goals through mandatory approaches.[46] Nonetheless, the recent surge in interest in the use of voluntary approaches suggests a belief that these approaches have some advantage over regulation. In the context of our model, that advantage takes the form of the potential cost savings. Without it, there is no reason, ceteris paribus, for firms to prefer a voluntary approach. Finally, we consider the case where the firms within the industry do not directly benefit from improvements in environmental quality. Thus, absent the threat of regulation, they have no incentive to supply environmental quality unilaterally. In some cases, firms may benefit directly either because the pollution or contamination directly affects their production (i.e., it is "fouling their own nests") or because the demand for their product or cost of an input is tied to their environmental performance. In such cases, "corporate environmentalism" may emerge even without any threat of regulation. However, because our interest is in the implications of potential free riding, we limit consideration to cases when firms do not realize any direct benefit from their own provision of environmental quality or that of others in the industry.

3.2 The Equilibrium Amount of Participation

To determine the equilibrium participation rate, we draw on the equilibrium concepts developed by Barret and Carraro and Siniscalco in the literature on self-enforcing or stable international environmental agreements.[47] In particular, we define a self-enforcing equilibrium (hereinafter, simply an equilibrium) as follows:

Definition: An equilibrium outcome is one under which:
(i) all participating firms are behaving optimally, given their decision to participate;

---

[45] See Hahn, supra note 1.
[46] See Burtraw, supra note 4.
[47] See references given in note 38. These papers use a definition of stability under which there is no threat against defecting singletons. An alternative approach assumes that participants will play Nash against defecting coalitions. For models based on this alternative definition of stability, see P. Chander and H. Tulkens, "A Core-Theoretic Solution for the Design of Cooperative Agreements on Transfrontier Pollution" (1995) 2 *International Tax and Public Finance* 2, 279–294; P. Chander and H. Tulkens, "The Core of an Economy with Multilateral Environmental Externalities" (1997) 25 *International Journal of Game Theory* 3, 379–401. For a discussion of the implications of the two alternatives, see H. Tulkens, "Cooperation vs. Free Riding in International Environmental Affairs: Two Approaches" CORE Discussion Paper 9752, Center for Operations Research and Econometrics, Universite Catholique de Louvain, Belgium, 1997.

(ii) all non-participating firms are behaving optimally, given their deci-
      sion not to participate;
(iii) no participating firm has an incentive to become a non-participat-
      ing firm; and
(iv) no non-participating firm has an incentive to become a participat-
      ing firm.

We first consider the provision levels that would be chosen by participating
firms and non-participating firms, assuming that some percentage of firms
choose to participate. Given this behavior, we then examine the number of
firms that would choose to participate in equilibrium. In particular, we ask
whether (or under what conditions) there exists an equilibrium outcome
under which a subset of firms choose to participate.

Assume initially that some firms participate. The group of participating
firms is assumed to minimize the aggregate cost of meeting the target. Of
course, with identical firms, this would imply that each firm supplies the
same fraction of the aggregate target, $X/\alpha N$, where α is the percent of firms
that participate.[48] Note that if all firms do not participate, then the fraction
of the total that each participating firm would be required to supply under
the voluntary approach $(X/\alpha N)$ would exceed the fraction it would be
required to supply under mandatory controls (X/N), because under mandatory controls the aggregate is allocated across all firms rather than only
across the subset of participating firms. Furthermore, given that participants undertake enough abatement to meet the target and hence non-
participants do not benefit from any additional abatement, in equilibrium
non-participants do not supply any of the environmental good.

We turn next to the incentive for a participating or non-participating
firm to switch to the other group. Consider first the incentive of a non-
participating firm. A non-participating firm would choose to become a participating firm if and only if its costs would be lower if it participated.
However, since it incurs zero costs under non-participation, it can never
realize lower costs under participation. Thus, as expected, (iv) always
holds, i.e., a non-participant would never have an incentive to become a
participant.

Consider next the incentives of a participating firm that is considering
defecting to the group of non-participants. The cost of defection depends
upon whether the other participating firms would increase their supply to
make up for the lost supply by this firm, and hence ensure that the target
continues to be met, or instead would simply let the agreement fall apart,
thereby triggering the imposition of mandatory controls. With the former
response, the defecting firm's costs under defection would be zero, and the
participating firm would clearly have an incentive to defect. Under the

---

[48] More generally, if participants had different cost structures, the group would choose to
allocate the total provision such that marginal costs would be equal across firms. Thus, under
the agreement, the target would be met at minimum cost.

latter response, the cost under defection would be $C_m(X/N)$. In this case, the firm would prefer to continue to participate if and only if[49]

$$C_v(X/\alpha N) \le C_m(X/N). \tag{1}$$

We assume that the remaining firms respond rationally, i.e., they choose to pick up the slack left by the defection if and only if it is optimal for them to do so. Given this, it can be shown[50] that, if some firms participate, the industry will be in equilibrium if and only if

$$C_v(X/\alpha N) = C_m(X/N), \tag{2}$$

i.e., if and only if the cost a participating firm incurs with participation equals the cost it would incur under mandatory controls. Furthermore, it can be shown that in this equilibrium, the percent of firms that participate is equal to the ratio of the average costs under the voluntary and mandatory approaches at the control levels that are necessary to meet the aggregate target, given the equilibrium level of participation.

The equilibrium level of participation (α^*) is depicted graphically in Figures 1 and 2. In Figure 1, the horizontal axis denotes the provision amount (x) for each participating firm, and the vertical axis denotes the cost of provision. Under mandatory controls, the amount of provision is X/N, with a corresponding cost of C. A participating firm will be in equilibrium, i.e., will be indifferent between participating and not participating, when

Figure 1

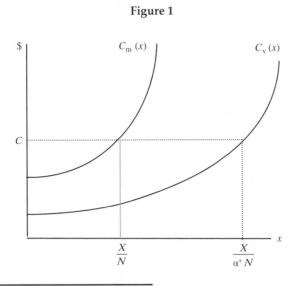

[49]   We assume throughout that if the cost of the voluntary program equals the cost under mandatory controls, the firm would be willing to participate.
[50]   See Segerson and Dawson, supra note 41.

Figure 2

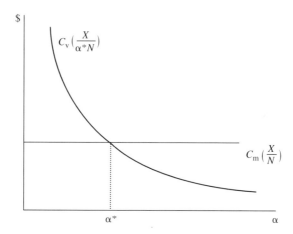

the cost under the two options is the same. This occurs when the extent of participation (α) is such that, at the corresponding level of provision under the voluntary approach ($X/\alpha N$), the vertical distance to the cost function under voluntary controls (C_v) is also equal to C.

Figure 2 depicts the same condition in a different way. In Figure 2, the horizontal axis denotes the extent of participation, and the vertical axis again denotes costs for a participating firm under the two options (participate or defect). At a participation rate where the two costs are the same (α^*), a participating firm will be indifferent between the two options and will hence have no incentive to defect.

Although this description characterizes one possible equilibrium condition, this equilibrium is not necessarily unique. For example, it is also possible to have an equilibrium under which no firms participate. If no firms are participating, then no individual firm has an incentive to participate unilaterally, i.e., to meet the target on its own, unless $C_m(X/N) > C_v(X)$. Thus, a situation in which no firms participate can also be an equilibrium. However because we are interested in whether it is possible for a voluntary approach to be successful despite the potential for free riding, we focus throughout the remainder of the analysis on equilibria under which some firms choose to participate, i.e., equilibria under which the voluntary approach is successful in achieving the given environmental target.

3.3   The Free Rider Problem

The result from the previous section suggests that a participating firm might still be willing to participate voluntarily even though it must supply a larger share of the environmental good under the voluntary approach than it would face under mandatory controls. This willingness stems from the cost advantage of the voluntary approach. If the voluntary approach offers a cost advantage, the firm might be willing to accept a higher provision level in exchange for the increased flexibility or other gain derived from voluntary rather than mandatory provision. Thus, some firms might be willing to tolerate some free riding by other firms if, by doing so, they can avoid regulation. In fact, with a successful voluntary program, free riding is an unavoidable consequence of exploiting the potential cost savings from voluntary approaches. It can be easily shown that, in an equilibrium with participation, there will always be some free riding if there is a cost advantage to the voluntary approach. Conversely, if there is no cost savings from the voluntary approach, then all firms will be indifferent between meeting the goal voluntarily and facing the imposition of mandatory controls. As a result, all firms will be willing to participate and the free rider problem disappears.

The above result also suggests that the severity of the free rider problem will depend on the magnitude of the potential cost savings from the voluntary approach. This can be easily illustrated using a specific example. Suppose, for example, that the cost functions are quadratic under both the voluntary and mandatory approaches, i.e.,

$$C_v = c_v x^2 / 2 \quad \text{and} \quad C_m = c_m x^2 / 2, \tag{3}$$

where $c_v \leqslant c_m$. In this case,

$$\alpha^* = (c_v / c_m)^{1/2} \tag{4}$$

Clearly, as c_v / c_m decreases, i.e., as the voluntary approach becomes relatively less expensive, α^* decreases. Thus, the greater the cost savings (e.g., the more inefficient the regulatory approach is), the smaller is the number of firms that participate in equilibrium. This result is also intuitively clear from Figure 2. With C_m held constant, a downward shift in C_v will reduce α^*.

3.4 Welfare Gains

Because the same level of environmental quality (X) is realized under either the voluntary or the mandatory approach, free riding per se is not necessarily welfare-reducing because it does not reduce the amount of the good supplied. The more important question is whether the voluntary approach allows the target to be met at a lower total cost, and thus whether it reduces the inefficiency of a regulatory approach.

Given that free riding is an unavoidable consequence of the potential for cost savings under the successful voluntary approach, we might expect it to dissipate the potential gains from use of the voluntary approach. However, in general this will not be true. Despite free riding, there is still a gain from use of the voluntary approach, i.e., a total cost savings. This savings is equal to the total cost of mandatory controls to the non-participating firms. In equilibrium, as noted above, participating firms are willing to bear individual costs to meet the aggregate target up to the level that they would have incurred under mandatory controls. Thus, the total cost of meeting the target voluntarily is the cost per firm under mandatory controls times the number of participating firms. The total cost of meeting the target through mandatory controls is this same per firm cost times the total number of firms (those who would have participated in a voluntary program as well as those who would not have). Thus, under the mandatory approach the total cost is higher by the amount of the costs that would have been incurred by the non-participating firms. Given that the same level of environmental quality is achieved under both the voluntary and the mandatory approaches, and having shown that the total cost of achieving that target is lower under the voluntary approach, it follows that the voluntary approach is more efficient than the regulatory approach despite the existence of free riding.

3.5   The Effect of Industry Size

Conventional wisdom suggests that as the number of firms in the industry increases, the free rider problem would worsen and any gain from the use of a voluntary approach would be reduced. In this section we examine the impact of industry size on the equilibrium outcome to determine whether the conventional wisdom holds here. We find that in general it does not. However, it should be kept in mind that we are limiting our attention to cases where the target level of environmental quality does not change in response to an increase in the number of firms. This seems likely when the environmental good that is being supplied is a good such as wildlife habitat where, for example, a fixed number of acres must be set aside for protection. However, when the environmental good is reduction in emissions of air or water pollutants, then an increase in the number of firms may increase the amount of reduction that is necessary in order to maintain a given level of ambient air or water quality. In this case, the regulator may adjust X when N increases. To incorporate this effect, the choice of X would have to be made endogenous, an extension that we leave for future research. Here we consider only cases where X remains unchanged as industry size increases.

When the number of firms in the industry increases, the free rider problem can get better or worse. In other words, as the number of firms in the industry increases, the participation rate (α^*) can increase, decrease, or remain unchanged. In addition, the effect of the increase in industry size depends on the relative magnitudes of the cost elasticities for the mandatory and voluntary approaches.

We illustrate this result using a specific example. Consider again the case of quadratic cost functions, with α^* given by (4). It is clear from (4) that with a simple quadratic cost function the extent of the free rider problem is independent of industry size, i.e., an increase in N has no effect on the participation rate. However, with more general cost functions of the form $C_i(x) = k_i + c_i x^2/2$, where k_i is the fixed cost under approach i,

$$\alpha^* = \{c_v X^2/[c_m X^2 + 2N^2(k_m - k_v)]\}^{\frac{1}{2}} \tag{5}$$

In this case, the effect of an increase in N depends on the relative magnitudes of the fixed costs k_m and k_v. Thus, in general, the effect on the participation rate can be positive, negative, or zero. The intuition for this result is as follows. Ceteris paribus, an increase in N decreases both sides of (2). The relative decreases depend on the relative marginal costs and on α^*, which is equal to the relative average costs. These determine the relative cost elasticities. Thus, which side of (2) decreases by more (and hence whether α^* must increase or decrease to restore equilibrium) depends on the relative cost elasticities. Note that this is in contrast to the result of Maxwell, Lyon, and Hackett, who argue that on the supply side the free rider problem always worsens with an increase in industry size.[51]

As before, the main concern is not with free riding per se but with its implications for the welfare gain that is possible with use of a voluntary approach. As with the effect on participation rates, the welfare gain from use of a voluntary approach can also increase, decrease, or remain unchanged as the industry size increases.

The explanation for this result is as follows. The effect of an increase in N on welfare will be both direct and indirect through α^*. As noted above, the indirect effect depends on the relative cost elasticities. The direct effect depends on how an increase in N affects the total cost of meeting the environmental quality target under mandatory controls. With more firms, each firm has a smaller share of the target to meet and hence a lower cost. However, there are more firms incurring this cost. The net effect of these two effects depends on whether the average cost under the mandatory approach is larger or smaller than the marginal cost, i.e., on whether the cost elasticity under the mandatory approach is greater or less than one. If this elasticity is greater than one at X/N (implying decreasing return to scale at X/N), then when N increases the reduction in the cost per firm (as a result of the reduction in each firm's share of the target) exceeds the increase in costs due to the increase in the number of firms that are subject to controls. As a result, the direct effect of an increase in N is negative. However, if the reverse is true, i.e., if the elasticity is less than one at X/N (implying increasing returns to scale), then the direct effect is positive. With increasing returns to scale, additional cost savings can be realized by concentrating production. The voluntary approach exploits this potential by having the fixed level of environmental quality supplied by a subset of firms (the participating firms) rather than spreading it across all firms (as under the mandatory approach). Conversely, with decreasing returns to scale, the concentration of production in a subset of firms increases total cost, implying that the direct effect of an increase in N is negative. If C_m has constant returns to scale at X/N (i.e., if C_m has global constant returns to scale or X/N happens to be at the point of minimum average cost), then the indirect effect is zero, because the increase in the number of firms incurring the cost of supplying the good exactly offsets the reduction in cost per firm from the reduction in the amount supplied per firm.

---

[51]   See Maxwell, et al., supra note 27.

Again we illustrate the result by means of an example. With quadratic costs and no fixed costs, the indirect effect will be zero (see above). In addition, the cost elasticity for the quadratic cost function is 2, implying decreasing returns to scale. Thus, the direct (and hence total) effect of the increase in N on the gain from using a voluntary approach is negative. While this result is consistent with the conventional wisdom, the explanation is not the conventional one. The smaller welfare gain for a large industry is not due to increased free riding (since here the extent of free riding is independent of industry size) but rather to the existence of decreasing returns to scale.

It is easy to construct examples for which larger industries would generate larger welfare gains. Consider again the quadratic cost function but assume that there is a constant fixed cost of k, i.e., let $C_i(x) = k + c_i x^2 / 2$. The existence of a common fixed cost does not change the equilibrium α, i.e., $\alpha^* = (c_v / c_m)^{1/2}$ as before. Thus, the indirect effect is again zero. The sign of the direct effect, on the other hand, depends on the magnitude of X/N. If $X/N > (2k/c_m)^{1/2}$, then the cost elasticity exceeds one at X/N and the previous result continues to hold. However, if $X/N < (2k/c_m)^{1/2}$, the cost elasticity is less than one, implying increasing returns to scale and a positive direct effect. In this case, the welfare gain from use of a voluntary approach is greater in a large industry than a small industry, despite the presence of free riding.

4 CONCLUSION

Voluntary approaches to environmental protection have been viewed by some as a potentially promising alternative to the use of more traditional regulatory approaches.[52] However, the success of any voluntary approach hinges on the participation by polluting firms. A number of possible incentives for participation exist. For example, market forces stemming from the demand for green products or fear of liability for environmental contamination can create incentives for voluntary environmental protection. However, the strength of market-based incentives can vary considerably across industries and firms. In cases where these market forces are not sufficiently strong, incentives for voluntary adoption of environmental protection measures can be created through government policies designed to promote voluntary adoption. These policies can rely on positive inducements, such as financial subsidies or other forms of cost reduction, or negative inducements, such as threats to impose mandatory controls or environmental taxes. Financial subsidies have well-known drawbacks relating to excessive entry incentives and the distortions that generally arise from the need to fund the subsidy through distortionary taxation. Regulatory threats do not require explicit government outlays, but when applied to an industry or group of firms as a whole, they create the potential for free riding.

---

[52] See, e.g., Commission of the European Communities, *supra* note 4.

The potential for free riding raises the question of whether a voluntary approach based on a regulatory threat for a group of firms can be a successful means of meeting environmental goals. We have addressed this question using a simple model of firm behavior. We use the model to determine whether in equilibrium some firms within an industry may be willing to meet an environmental quality target voluntarily, despite the incentive for individual firms to free ride on the participation decisions of other firms. The equilibrium rate of participation in the voluntary agreement is determined by the point at which the firm's cost under regulation is equal to the cost that a participating firm would incur under the voluntary program, given that the provision of the environmental good by those firms participating in the voluntary program is sufficient to preempt regulation. Although with less than full participation (i.e., with free riding) each participating firm would provide a higher level of the environmental good under the voluntary approach than under regulation, in equilibrium participating firms would be willing to provide this higher level if the cost of providing any given level of environmental quality is lower under the voluntary approach than under mandatory regulation. An equilibrium participation rate is achieved when the increased cost attributable to the provision of a higher level of environmental quality per firm is exactly offset by the reduction in cost attributable to the use of the less expensive (more flexible) approach. Thus, as long as there is a potential cost savings from the voluntary approach (for example, in allowing firms more flexibility), an equilibrium can be achieved with less than full participation, i.e., with free riding.

In addition, in this equilibrium the voluntary approach will be more efficient despite the presence of free riding. Even though in equilibrium each participating firm incurs the same cost under the voluntary approach as under regulation, the total cost of meeting the environmental quality target is still lower under the voluntary approach, because non-participating firms incur zero costs under the voluntary approach but positive costs under regulation. The cost savings realized by the non-participating firms generates a welfare gain from use of the voluntary approach, which is not dissipated by free riding.

Finally, we considered how the equilibrium participation rate and the welfare gain from the voluntary approach depend on industry size, assuming that the regulator does not adjust the aggregate level of provision of the environmental good in response to the industry size. Contrary to what might be expected, it is not universally true that the free rider problem worsens as the industry size increases. Rather, the impact of an increase in industry size on free riders depends on the relative cost elasticities under the voluntary and mandatory approaches. If the cost elasticity is higher under the mandatory approach, the equilibrium participation rate will actually be higher in a large industry than in a small industry.

Similarly, industry size has an ambiguous effect on the welfare gain from the use of a voluntary approach. The effect on the welfare gain depends on two factors: (1) the impact on free riders, which as noted above depends on the relative cost elasticities, and (2) the impact on the total cost of provision, given a level of participation, which depends in turn on the returns to scale under mandatory controls. The latter effect arises because, under mandatory controls with an increase in industry size, each firm is required to supply less, but there are more firms supplying the good. Whether spreading provision of the environmental good across more firms increases or decreases total costs depends on the returns to scale.

The results of the analysis here suggest that the incentive for firms to free ride does not destroy the viability of a voluntary approach. As long as there is some cost savings from the voluntary approach, an equilibrium exists under which some firms will participate and efficiency will be increased. In addition, there is no a priori reason to believe that voluntary approaches will necessarily be more successful for small industries than for large industries. Thus, despite the free rider problem, by providing industries with an opportunity to meet environmental quality targets voluntarily, with an explicit recognition that failure to do so will trigger potentially more expensive mandatory controls, regulators can reduce the aggregate cost of meeting environmental quality goals.

16. Third-Party Inspection as an Alternative to Command-and-Control Regulation

Howard C. Kunreuther, Patrick J. McNulty, and Yong Kang*

1 INTRODUCTION

Over the past decade government agencies have recognized that relying on traditional command-and-control procedures for enforcing its regulations might not be the most cost-effective strategy for it to follow. More specifically, considerable time and effort has been invested by the U.S. Environmental Protection Agency (EPA) in examining how market-based mechanisms can be utilized for promoting industrial safety and reducing the risks from accidents and disasters.

As private chemical firms have increasingly produced socially useful goods and services, small firms have become a national treasure, the source of greatest employment in the chemical industry and the seedbed of much of our innovative technologies. However, some small firms may present significant hazards to employees and the community, as the following recent example illustrates. At 8:15 on Friday evening, 19 February 1999, workers at Concept Sciences, Inc. (CSI) were distilling a batch of aqueous hydroxlamine when it exploded killing five individuals and injuring fourteen. Four of the individuals killed were employees and one was an independent businessman in an adjoining building. The blast damaged 11 buildings, caused an estimated $5.0 million in damages and was heard 15 miles away.[1]

CSI is a small firm located in the Lehigh Valley Industrial Park in Hanover Township, Lehigh County, eastern Pennsylvania. Previously, it had occupied a site in the City of Allentown, manufacturing small quantities of the free base, aqueous hydroxylamine, and this was the first attempt

*Support for this chapter under the U.S. Environmental Protection Agency's Cooperative Agreement C R 826583 with the University of Pennsylvania is gratefully acknowledged.
[1] D.C. Berg and D. Hartzell "Five Found Dead in Aftermath at Chemical Plant: 13 Are Hurt as a Result of Blast Now Being Called Worst Disaster in Lehigh County History" *The Morning Call*, 21 February 1999.

to scale-up the operation using a 1000-gallon glass still. At this writing, we still do not know the details of what happened at CSI. However, on 11 August 1999, six months after the explosion, the Occupational Safety and Health Administration (OSHA) released a 60-page report citing CSI for 20 violations. Some of these were deemed willful and committed with intentional disregard or plain indifference to federal safety standards. Hence OSHA issued a $641,000 fine against CSI.[2]

This example demonstrates that small firms with limited resources can harbor significant and sophisticated technical risks. Several factors might contribute to the causes of accidents in small firms. One reason might relate to the entrepreneurial spirit of the firm. Small firms probably are inclined to be risk-takers because they have more to gain than to lose by taking chances. Automobile drivers with marginal financial resources that operate without liability insurance illustrate the point. One might expect drivers with substantial financial assets to lose more, in case of an accident, and therefore to be much less likely to take such risks.

In addition to the lack of capital resources, small firms frequently lack the technical skills and constraints that are common in the corporate cultures of large companies and are necessary to conduct process safety reviews in a complete and systematic manner. This is not to suggest that small firms do not conduct process safety reviews but that they might be less able or willing to commit their resources necessary to define risk reliably.[3] This is also not to suggest that large firms do not have accidents. We are well aware of the tragedies that have occurred, perhaps most notably the Union Carbide explosion in Bhopal, India in 1984.

One promising option for reducing the likelihood and consequences of chemical accidents is the use of third parties coupled with insurance contracts as economic incentives for encouraging firms to reduce their risks. The passage of Section 112(r) of the Clean Air Act Amendments (CAAA) of 1990 requires the EPA to develop regulations for the prevention and mitigation of major chemical accidental releases, including worst case releases. The principal advantage of these inspections over command-and-control procedures is that there is a voluntary contractual relationship between the firm and the party auditing the facility. Rather than being viewed strictly as an enforcer, the inspector can assist the firm in complying with a set of regulations.[4]

This chapter examines the role that third-party inspections coupled with insurance can play in reducing the losses from chemical accidents. It builds on earlier work undertaken by researchers at the Wharton Risk Management and Decision Processes Center on innovative market-based

---

[2]   G. Tomchick, Jr., U.S. Department of Labor, OSHA Citation Report on Concept Sciences, Inc., Inspection Number 302328760, 8 August 1999.

[3]   Federal regulatory agencies, such as the EPA, OSHA, and the U.S. Chemical Safety and Hazard Investigation Board (CSB), are aware of this concern. For more detail see <http://ww.csb.gov/1999/news/n9903.htm>, Internet Homepage for the U.S. Chemical Safety and Hazard Investigation Board.

[4]   J. Er, et al. "Utilizing Third-Party Inspections for Preventing Major Chemical Accidents" *Risk Analysis* (1998), 145–154.

approaches to environmental policy that was published as a special issue of *Risk Analysis* in 1998.[5]

After characterizing the risk and the role of risk management plans (RMPs) for reducing future losses from chemical accidents in the next section, we turn to why firms do not voluntarily adopt RMPs. The chapter then examines the need for regulations to prevent and minimize the consequences associated with chemical accident releases. We then examine the role of third-party inspections in other contexts such as steam boiler pressure vehicles, underground storage tanks in Massachusetts, and pork producers in the United States.

Building on this experience we evaluate the conditions under which third parties coupled with insurance can be successfully used for reducing the risks of chemical accidents. We then describe a pilot study currently underway in Delaware which is trying to implement a third-party/insurance approach to managing industrial facilities subject to Section 112(r) of the CAAA of 1990. The concluding section summarizes the chapter and suggests directions for future research.

2 THE ROLE OF RISK MANAGEMENT PLANS

It is relatively easy to characterize the risk from chemical accidents but much more difficult to implement programs that will reduce future losses. Consider a chemical plant that has a relatively high probability (p_h) of producing an accident which results in a loss (L), where L is a multidimensional vector reflecting both direct and indirect impacts. Direct impacts include lives lost or injured, damage to physical property, environmental impacts. Indirect impacts include business interruption should the plant be damaged or destroyed, the effect on property values in the community, social and emotional stress to the community, and long-term impacts on the industry.[6]

Often the indirect impacts are more significant than the direct losses as illustrated by the explosion of the Union Carbide plant in Bhopal, India in 1984. This event had a significant impact on the way the chemical industry has been regulating itself and has been regulated by the government in the past 15 years. Similarly the future of nuclear power in the United States was changed radically after the Three Mile Island (TMI) accident in 1978. Since TMI, the Nuclear Regulatory Commission has issued no new permits, though 52 facilities that had already received construction permits were completed. Twelve commercial reactors have been shut down, many before

---

[5] Risk Analysis (April 1998) Special Collection of Papers on "Innovative Market-Based Approaches to Environmental Policy: Implementing the Major Accident Provisions of the Clean Air Act Amendments" pp. 131–204.

[6] A detailed discussion of the direct and indirect impacts of natural disasters appears in Heinz Center for Science, Economics, and the Environment. *The Hidden Costs of Coastal Hazards: Implications for Risk Assessment and Mitigation* (1999). Washington, DC, Island Press. These concepts are relevant for technological disasters such as chemical accidents.

their normal life of 40 years was completed. These shut downs do not include experimental reactors, some of which were also shut down.[7]

A chemical plant has an opportunity to reduce future direct and indirect losses from accidents by implementing an RMP that will reduce the probability of an accident to $p_l < p_h$ at a cost of C. The value of C reflects the expenditures in both time and money in implementing a strategy for reducing the risks of future accidents. There are often organizational costs of implementing such a plan that need to be taken into account by the firm before committing to a particular course of action.

If the chemical plant could undertake these changes voluntarily it would determine whether the expected benefits from implementing such a plan would exceed the costs. Suppose the chemical plant was risk neutral and determined that by implementing an RMP it would lower its annual probability of an accident from p_h to p_l. Then the annual savings from taking this action would be $(p_h - p_l)L$. If the plant used an annual discount rate (r) and expected to be in business for T years, then the expected discounted benefits of undertaking an RMP would be given by:

$$B = \sum_{t=1} (p_h - p_l)L / (1+r)^t. \qquad (1)$$

The decision rule facing the chemical plant is a simple one. If $B > C$ then they should invest in the RMP; otherwise they should not.

3   WHY FIRMS MAY NOT VOLUNTARILY INVEST IN RMPs

There are a number of reasons why firms may not invest the time and money in RMPs even if the benefits implied by equation (1) suggest that it would be profitable for them to do so. Below we discuss several factors that may affect firms' decisions.

3.1   Threshold Models of Choice

For one thing, it may be very difficult for the firm to compute the reduction in probabilities and losses that will occur if they implement such a plan. Instead of undertaking the costs of such an exercise, the plant may estimate that the probability (p_h) of a catastrophic accident under its current operations was below some threshold probability p^* and utilize the following simplified decision rule: if $p_h < p^*$, then do not invest in an RMP. In other

[7] The Nuclear Regulatory Council Information Digest (1998). Private Communication, 3 September 1999, Neil Sheehan, Public Relations Officer, Nuclear Regulatory Commission, PECO Nuclear Power Plant Limerick, PA.

words the chemical plant would not even compute the expected benefits implied by (1) and compare them with the costs of the RMP.

There is considerable empirical evidence that many firms utilize this type of threshold model for making their decisions. The nuclear power industry eliminated a number of fault trees by following such a rule when determining what type of protective measures it should take. If Union Carbide had vertically integrated their process of synthesizing and then simultaneously using methyl isocyanate (MIC) to make the insecticides, Sevin and Temik, it would not have had to store MIC in large quantities. This would have prevented the Bhopal accident from occurring. The cost of this type of batch process is slightly less than a continuous process that does not require storing chemicals. However, the principal reason that chemical companies have not moved in this direction is that they perceive the chances of a chemical accident such as a Bhopal disaster as so small that they do not take it into account when making their decision on the choice of a production process.

3.2 Short Time Horizons

Another reason why firms may not invest in RMPs is that their decisions are guided by short-run considerations. Managers responsible for these decisions may have their performance evaluated on their expenditures during the year and hence would want to make sure the expected benefits over a relatively short time horizon exceed the upfront investment costs, C. If one truncates the time horizon T to a relatively short interval, then the benefits shown in equation (1) will decrease as T becomes smaller.

To illustrate this point consider the case where $L = 6,000,000$, $p_h = 1/100$, and $p_l = 1/200$, so that the expected *annual* benefits from investing in an RMP is

$$(p_h - p_l)L = (1/100 - 1/200)\, 6,000,000 = 30,000. \tag{2}$$

If the annual discount rate were 8 percent and the time horizon T were 20 years, then B from (1) would be approximately \$295,000. If the managers were utilizing a time horizon of $T = 2$ then B would be only \$53,500. There would thus be a wide dollar range for C where the plant would want to invest in an RMP had they utilized a long time horizon but would prefer not to incur these costs if they were more myopic.

3.3 Limited Assets

Small firms may also not want to invest in RMPs because they have limited assets (A) and hence they would declare insolvency should their losses after a catastrophic accident exceed A. Rather than investing some of their limited capital in an RMP, they may prefer to take their chances since the net benefits in any year would be less than if they had enough assets to cover their losses.

Note that if a firm's asset (A) is lower than losses (L), the firm's benefits from risk reduction is $(p_h - p_l)A$, instead of $(p_h - p_l)L$. For example, if the

RMP reduced the probability of an accident from $p=1/100$ to $p=1/200$ and $A<L=\$6,000,000$, then the expected annual savings from an RMP would be $1/100A$. If the costs of the RMP is lower than $(p_h-p_l)L$ but higher than $(p_h-p_l)A$, the firm will not want to have a voluntary inspection.

4   NEED FOR REGULATIONS

Accidents such as in Bhopal raise the public's consciousness regarding the potential consequences. Catastrophic accidents or even near misses may be viewed by individuals as signals that there are problems with a particular technology.[8] If there are emotional concerns, such as fear, dread, and anxiety, which arise from these events, then there will be pressure placed on government agencies to impose rules and regulations to reduce future losses. Furthermore, individuals may not trust the firms to do a good job on their own. Hence the passage of Section 112(r) of the CAAA of 1990 requires that facilities (both public and private) that manufacture, process, use, store, or handle regulated substances must execute RMPs that include an accident release prevention program.[9]

4.1   Inability to Distinguish Low Probabilities

One reason that such regulation may be desirable from a societal point of view is the inability of most individuals to appreciate accident probabilities when the event has a very small chance of occurrence. More specifically, if chemical plants were able to invest C dollars to reduce the annual probability of an accident from p_h to p_l, it is doubtful that these benefits would be appreciated by the affected public. Furthermore many managers in firms evaluating these measures may not compute the impact of the change in probability on expected benefits of an RMP.

There are a number of published studies which show the difficulties people have in interpreting low probabilities when faced with risks that may affect them personally.[10] In a recent study of several hypothetical managerial decisions, Huber, Wider, and Huber find that when subjects are required to search out their own information they rarely even ask for probability information.[11] One group was given a minimal description and the opportunity to ask questions. Only 22 percent of these respondents asked for probability information, and the questions they asked only concerned

---

[8]   P. Slovic, et al., "Modeling the Societal Impact of Fatal Accidents" (1984) 30 *Management Science* 464–474.

[9]   I. Rosenthal et al., "The Role of the Community in the Implementation of the EPA's Rule on Risk Management Programs" (1998) 18 *Risk Analysis* 171–180.

[10]   C. Camerer and H. Kunreuther "Decision Processes for Low Probability Events: Policy Implications"(1998) 8 *Journal of Policy Analysis and Management*, 565–592; W. Magat, et al., "Risk-dollar Tradeoffs, Risk Perceptions, and Consumer Behavior" in W. Viscusi and W. Magat (eds), *Learning About Risk* (Harvard University Press, 1987), pp. 83–97.

[11]   O. Huber, et al., "Active Information Search and Complete Information Presentation in Naturalistic Risky Decision Tasks" (1997) 95 *Acta Psychologica* 15–29.

imprecise probability information. Not a single person asked for precise probability information. Another group of respondents was given precise probability information, and less than one in five of these individuals mentioned the probability in their verbal protocols.

A recent series of experiments supports these findings with respect to individuals' insensitivity to probabilities of a chemical accident even when the differences were ten orders of magnitude.[12] A questionnaire involving the hypothetical ABC Chemical Company was administered to 241 individuals visiting the San Francisco Exploratorium in July 1998. The subjects were told that a fictitious chemical labeled Syntox, the only toxic chemical used at the plant, would be regulated under the Environmental Protection Agency's Clean Air Act Amendments. They were also told that ABC Chemicals had determined that the worst conceivable accident at the plant would occur if its entire inventory of Syntox was accidentally released into the atmosphere in a very short time period. If this did occur, a plume of toxic vapors would form that could cover any home in the community, depending on how the wind blows. This vapor would only affect a few homes in the community.

One-third of the subjects were told that the probability of a discharge of Syntox causing deaths in the community surrounding the plant was one in 100,000. Another one-third were given the same scenario but were told that the probability was one in 1,000,000. The other third was told the probability was one in 10 million. As background for assessing the risks of Syntox, all the subjects were informed that the probability of an individual dying in a car accident is 1 in 6,000 per year and that a regulatory agency has determined that for both car accidents and Syntox discharges these probability estimates are accurate.

Following the scenario, subjects were asked the following four questions regarding the perceived risk of the chemical plant: (1) whether the plant posed a serious health and safety risk to those living in the community, (2) whether the plant could operate in a manner that was safe for the community, (3) how serious is the risk of death posed by the plant, and (4) how close to the plant respondents would be willing to live. Because the responses to these four questions were highly intercorrelated ($\alpha = 0.81$), they were combined into a single scale. The score for each respondent represents his or her overall perception of the risk of the chemical plant. This score was scaled to range between one (lowest risk) to five (highest risk). The means for the three probability conditions were 3.03 for a one in 100,000 probability, 2.93 for a one in 1,000,000 probability and 3.01 for a one in 10 million probability. A statistical analysis revealed that these risk perceptions did not differ significantly from one another.

4.2 Externalities

There is another important reason why regulations may be needed to assure that industrial plants undertake an accidental release prevention program.

---

[12] H. Kunreuther, N. Novemsky and D. Kahneman, "Making Low Probabilities Useful" (in press) *Journal of Risk and Uncertainty*.

Some of the consequences of a chemical accident will impact the residents in the area surrounding the plant, but the industrial plant will not be legally liable for these impacts. Hence they will not include them in their evaluation of an RMP. For example, if there are decreases in property values to homes in the surrounding area or there are disruptions in community life because of the accident, the chemical firm will not be held liable for these costs. The firms will thus underestimate the benefits from an RMP and hence may decide not to take action when it would be in the public interest that the plant do so. Ashford has reported that for every \$1 of direct cost associated with an accident there is \$4 to \$10 individual social costs not borne by the firm.[13]

The same rationale has been used to justify well-enforced building codes on homes in hazard-prone areas.[14] When a building collapses it may create externalities in the form of economic dislocations and other social costs that are beyond the economic loss suffered by the owners. These may not be taken into account when the owners evaluate the importance of adopting a specific mitigation measure. For example, if a building topples off its foundation after an earthquake, it could break a pipeline and cause a major fire that would damage other homes not affected by the earthquake in the first place. In other words, there may be an additional annual expected benefit from mitigation over and above the reduction in losses to the specific structure adopting this loss-reduction measure.[15]

4.3   Challenges to Using Command-and-Control Procedures

The EPA and other regulatory agencies have been searching for other alternatives to their current command-and-control procedures to implement regulatory obligations. In the case of enforcing Section 112(r), there is some urgency for command-and-control alternatives due to the EPA's limited personnel and funds for providing technical guidance and auditing regulated facilities to ensure a high compliance level.

Researchers have argued for alternative approaches to command-and-control because of concerns that administrative agencies responsible for issuing regulations are vulnerable to "capture" by the very industries they are supposed to regulate. More specifically, there is concern that organized groups can utilize the regulation to gain monopoly power. Empirical evidence supporting this claim comes from a study on water pollution regulation where it was shown that weaker standards were applied to industries that have higher profits and better financed trade associations.[16]

---

[13] N. Ashford "The Encouragement of Technological Change for Preventing Accidents: Moving Firms from Secondary Prevention and Mitigation to Primary Prevention" (Center for Technology and Industrial Development, Massachusetts Institute of Technology, April 1993).

[14] L. Cohen and R. Noll, "The Economics of Building Codes to Resist Seismic Structures," (1987) *Public Policy* (Winter) 1–29.

[15] P. Kleindorfer and H. Kunreuther, "The Complementary Roles of Mitigation and Insurance in Managing Catastrophic Risks" (1999) 19 *Risk Analysis* 727–38.

[16] W. Magat, et al., *Rules in the Making* (Resources for the Future Washington, DC, 1986).

Chemical firms, particularly smaller ones, have little incentive to follow regulatory procedures if they estimate the chances of their being inspected by a regulatory agency to be very small or they view the fine (F) to be sufficiently low. Then they are willing to take their chances and incur the fine should they violate the existing rule or regulation and get caught. To see this point, consider the trade-offs that a firm faces when determining whether to adopt a particular regulation for which they incur a cost (C). For simplicity, assume that the firm perceives no benefits from adopting the regulation and that it is myopic in its decision making process so that it considers the consequences to the firm of being inspected only over the next year. Suppose the firm estimates the chances that the regulatory agency will inspect it next year as q, in which case it will incur a fine F (which will include the cost of adopting the regulation). If the firm is risk neutral then it will only decide to incur a cost C today if $C < qF$. Should the firm be so small that its assets A are less than F, then one would replace F with A in the above equation to reflect the maximum the firm could pay before becoming insolvent.

Given that the EPA has limited resources, it is likely that regulated firms will estimate q to be very low. Under the General Duty Clause of the Clean Air Act, there are fines of up to $27,500 per day. Discussions with a number of chemical firms suggests that the General Duty Clause is rarely imposed by the EPA because they do so little monitoring. For example, EPA's Region III has three auditors for over 5,000 facilities in Pennsylvania, Virginia, Maryland, Delaware, West Virginia, and the District of Columbia. Fines under the General Duty Clause could increase now that regulated facilities have had to file an RMP. Failure to do so might be considered egregious behavior and might cause the EPA to be more likely to take action.

5 USE OF THIRD PARTIES TO ENFORCE REGULATIONS

The use of third-party auditors is not a new concept and its popularity recently seems to be accelerating. Some firms, especially high-risk firms, actually seek risk management help from the use of third-party auditors. Social pressure may play a role in acceptance of third parties in the future. If the public views firms who refuse to be inspected as high-risk facilities, the potential loss of public confidence might cause the firm to obtain voluntary inspection in order to keep public attention away from adversely affecting their business.

The practice of using third parties to audit safe and acceptable performance varies from state to state and from technology to technology. Inspecting pressure vessels; qualifying testing laboratories; approving mechanical devices, such as elevators, automobiles, and airplanes; dealing with underground storage tanks; and handling radioactive substances illustrate some of the many instances where third-parties auditors are used. Several examples of the successful use of third parties as an alternative to regulations are briefly described below.

5.1   Underground Storage Tanks in Massachusetts[17]

The Commonwealth of Massachusetts was unable to provide sufficient funding and staffing to oversee all assessments and remedial actions conducted by Potentially Responsible Parties (PRP) at Oil and Hazardous Materials (OHM) sites in the state. This led the state Department of Environmental Protection (DEP) and the environmental community to work two years as a stakeholder advisory committee to reach agreement on all of the key features of the program before launching legislation.

Under Massachusetts state law enacted in 1983, the DEP must ensure permanent cleanup of OHM releases from underground storage tanks by the parties responsible for them. The law is implemented through regulations known as the Massachusetts Contingency Plan (MCP). In 1992, a Licensed Site Professional (LSP) program was passed as part of a comprehensive bill that redesigned the state's waste cleanup program.

The DEP and the LSP board evaluated the program and published a draft report on 30 June 1998. In the first four years of the LSP program 3,146 sites were cleaned up compared to 225 in the previous four years. The program is highly effective but there have been some complaints from facility owners over some of the fees that LSDs charge.

The cleanup of hazardous waste sites in Massachusetts by third-party cleanup professionals seems very successful. From a regulatory, community, and financial perspective it looks sustainable. Part of the success results from the role of the community in the establishment of the criteria for selecting LSPs, the evaluation of their performance by the LSP board, and the LSP competent performance for their clients.

5.2   Auditing Pork Producers in the United States[18]

On 25 November 1998, as part of President Clinton's Clean Water Action Plan, the EPA and the National Pork Producers Council (NPPC) announced a voluntary compliance program to reduce environmental and public health threats to the nation's waterways from runoff of animal waste from pork-producing operations. Under the program, pork producers will have their operations voluntarily assessed for Clean Water Act violations by certified independent inspectors. Producers who promptly disclose and correct any discovered violations from these audits will receive much smaller civil penalties that they might have otherwise been liable for under the law.

The compliance audit program provides an incentive for pork producers to take the initiative to find and correct Clean Water Act violations and prevent discharges to waterways without compromising the ability of the

---

[17] The information on underground storage tanks in Massachusetts came from communication with Allan R. Fierce, Executive Director, Board of Registration of Hazardous Waste Cleanup Professionals of the Commonwealth of Massachusetts.

[18] The information on pork producers came from a private communication with Daniel Uthe, National Pork Producers Council, Iowa, 9 March 1999. More data can be obtained at <http://es.epa.gov/oeca/ore/porkcap/>.

EPA or states to enforce the law. Pork producers who undergo the assessment and promptly report and correct violations will receive certification from the NPPC. The NPPC, a national association representing all state pork producers, plans to assess more than 10,000 pork production facilities. The NPPC developed the assessment program at a cost of $1.5 million, and it will fund the training of independent inspectors and the program's oversight. The EPA has provided a $5 million grant to America's Clean Water Foundation to assist with the assessments. The compliance audit program does not extend to slaughterhouses, pork-processing, packing facilities, or other ancillary operations.

The EPA will consult closely with the states in implementing the compliance audit program. States may elect to administer the program directly in which case the EPA will refer any disclosures to the states for consideration and response.

5.3 Steam Boilers[19]

The Hartford Steam Boiler Inspection and Insurance Company (HSB) initiated boiler inspections coupled with insurance in the 1860s. HSB has always stressed that insurance was secondary to loss prevention, with engineering and inspection services making up a large part of the insurance premium. In an effort to reduce future risks, HSB undertook studies of boiler construction, which eventually led to boilermakers adopting safer designs.

One of the key elements leading to the reduction in the number of boiler accidents is that all of the states in the US require annual inspections of pressure vessels by a representative licensed by the state, county, or municipality in which the facility is located. Inspectors are qualified by either a formal examination or through a certificate of competency issued by the National Board of Boiler and Pressure Vessel Inspectors.

The actual requirements for boiler inspection vary from state to state. For example, in Nebraska, the Boiler Inspection Act requires that all boilers must be inspected at least once every year to determine that the boilers are safe and in satisfactory operating condition, properly constructed, and properly maintained for the purpose for which the boiler is to be used. Unfired pressure vessels must be inspected externally every two years.

6 COUPLING THIRD PARTIES WITH INSURANCE

The previous experience with third parties suggests that it has the potential of being used by the EPA to enforce RMPs required by Section 112(r) of the CAAA of 1990. Without employing third parties, the EPA has to provide technical guidance and audit regulated facilities to ensure a high compliance

---

[19] The information on steam boilers comes primarily from J. Er, "A Third Party Approach to Environmental Regulation and Possible Roles for Insurance Companies" (1996) PhD Dissertation, University of Pennsylvania.

level. The third-party approach transfers a portion of these regulatory costs back to the generators of the externalities because the inspectors would be hired and paid for by the regulated firms.

The need for RMPs in this type of environment becomes clear. A model RMP translates required general performance standards to specific technological standards and codes. With specific requirements, it is easier for third-party inspectors to help clients meet compliance requirements and prove non-negligence if a litigation should arise. The greater ease in assuring compliance under the third-party approach translates to higher compliance rates and thus more cost-effective accident prevention. The EPA is then able to reduce its frequency of audits, resulting in lower enforcement costs.

In this section we discuss how third parties can be used in conjunction with insurance as an alternative to command-and-control procedures. In particular, we show that the combination of these two policy tools can be a powerful force in convincing firms of the advantages of undertaking appropriate steps for making their plants safer. To show the conditions under which third parties can be effective we develop a simple model where there are two types of firms—high and low risk.

6.1   Basic Assumptions

We assume that low risk facilities that have adopted RMPs have a lower chance of an accidental chemical release than high risk firms who have not complied with the regulation. The probability of an accident is p_l for a low-risk firm and p_h for a high risk firm. The losses from an accident are L whether one is a low- or high-risk firm.

Insurance is available through a competitive market with rates based on risk and equal to the expected cost of an accident. Inspections can distinguish low- from high-risk firms. If a firm agrees to be inspected, insurance companies will charge premiums that reflect the result of inspections. If firms refuse to be inspected, they will be presumed to be high-risk and hence will be charged the higher premium.

Firms are assumed to want to maximize their expected profits but required to have insurance. For example, they may be required to have coverage by financial institutions as a condition for their mortgage. Being insured can also help firms gain public confidence that they are operating safely and avoid bankruptcy in case of a catastrophe.

To determine how firms make the decision on whether to be inspected by third-party auditors, we assume that they have short-time horizons and consider only the next two time periods. In the first period, firms' initial assets are A and they have to decide whether to be inspected. If a high-risk firm chooses inspection voluntarily, it has to pay a penalty (F_1) for non-compliance and investment (I_1) to reduce its risk level from p_h to p_l. Third parties will help firms reduce investment costs by providing technical and other kinds of assistance as part of their inspection services. In the second period, insurance companies provide firms with policies with premiums based on risk.

Firms who do not volunteer to be inspected may be audited by a regulatory agency with probability (q). If a high-risk firm is audited, it will incur a

Table 1

	Premium	*Penalty*	*Investment Cost*
If inspected by third parties	p_lL	F_1	I_1
If not inspected by third parties and audited by a regulatory agency	p_hL	F_2	I_2

penalty F_2 and in addition will have to incur an investment cost $(I_2 > I_1)$. Table 1 summarizes firms' payoffs in the second period.

6.2 Assessing Trade-offs

It is clear that low-risk firms will want to be inspected, for they can receive a more favorable premium and don't have to worry about paying the penalty for being high-risk. The more important question is whether high-risk firms will choose inspections voluntarily rather than taking their chances. The benefit that firms can get from inspection is a lower premium $(p_h - p_l)L$. The bigger the magnitude of accident (L) and the bigger the difference between the accident rates for high-risk and low-risk $(p_h - p_l)$, the greater the benefits firms will get from third-party inspections.

What are the trade-offs firms have to make in determining whether or not to voluntarily choose to be inspected? If high-risk firms are audited by a regulatory agency, they have to pay a penalty F_2 and investment costs I_2. The probability of being inspected by government is q. So the expected expenditures are $q(F_2 + I_2)$. But if firms choose inspections by third party auditors, they have to pay a penalty F_1 and investment costs I_1. From Table 1 we see that the trade-off between having a third party inspection or taking ones chances that a government agency will not audit them is given by

$$D = p_hL + q(F_2 + I_2) - [p_lL + F_1 + I_1]. \qquad (3)$$

Whenever $D > 0$ the firm will want to incur a third-party inspection. Regulatory agencies can increase the chance that a firm will want to have a third party inspection by increasing the penalty (F_2) or the probability that they will audit a firm (q).[20]

---

[20] This footnote provides a more formal proof of the trade-offs between a high risk firm deciding to a third-party inspection or taking its chances on being audited by a regulatory agency. If a high-risk firm chooses third-party inspection in the first period, its expected assets at the end of the second period is $U_1 = A - I_1 - F_1 - p_lL$. If the firm does not choose inspection, the expected assets is $U_2 = q(A - p_hL - I_2 - F_2) + (1-q)(A - p_hL)$. $U_1 \geq U_2$ if and only if, $(I_1 - qI_2) + (F_1 - qF_2) \leq \Delta p \cdot L$ where $\Delta p = p_h - p_l$. Or, $F_2 \geq \frac{1}{q}F_1 - \frac{1}{q}[\Delta p \cdot L - (I_1 - qI_2)]$.

Figure 1

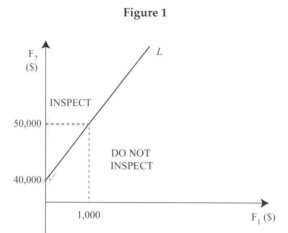

To illustrate consider the following simple example. Let $p_h = 1/100$, $p_1 = 1/200$, $L = \$1,000,000$, $q = 1/10$, $I_1 = I_2 = \$10,000$. Based on (3) then $F_2 > 10F_1 + 40,000$ for $D > 0$ and to motivate firms to choose third party inspections. Figure 1 provides a graphical depiction of the trade-offs between F_1 and F_2 that will lead a firm to want to undertake a third-party inspection for the above example.

The horizontal and vertical axes are the respective penalties charged on high-risk firms that choose third-party inspections or decide to take their chances. Line L are those penalty combinations that make high-risk firms indifferent between being inspected by third-party auditors or not. Any penalty combination above L makes it profitable for firms to be inspected by third parties; those combinations below L lead the firm to take its chances that the regulatory agency will not monitor it. For instance, if $F_1 = \$1,000$, then one sees from Figure 1 that F_2 has to be greater than $50,000$ for firms to want to be inspected voluntarily. If F_2 is less than $\$40,000$, high-risk firms will not choose third-party inspections even if there is no penalty for non-compliance (i.e. $F_1 = 0$).

Next let us consider the case when third parties can help high-risk firms reduce the costs to achieve compliance. Assume that third parties can help firms reduce the costs from $I_1 = \$10,000$ in the previous example to $I_1 = \$8,000$. The lower limit of F_2 for high-risk firms to be inspected is now $10F_1 + 20,000$. The trade-offs between the two fines are now shown in Figure 2. When F_1 be $\$1,000$, F_2 has to be greater than $\$30,000$ for the firm to want to engage in third-party inspections. The penalty, F_2, is $\$20,000$ less than in the previous example because inspection is now used to help high-risk firms reduce their compliance costs over what they would have to pay if a government regulatory agency audited them. Note the slopes of L in both Figures 1 and 2 are bigger than 1 ($1/q$), which means that the penalty

Figure 2

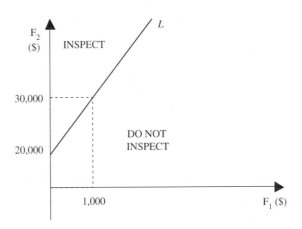

charged by the government on firms not inspected by third-party auditors will always have to be higher than if the firms were inspected.

This analysis suggests that the government fine for not undertaking a third-party inspection needs to be carefully considered as a part of the policy process. If there is a small chance that a firm will be audited by a regulatory agency, then F_2 has to be much larger than if q was relatively high. To the extent that third parties provide other risk management services to firms, then voluntary inspection becomes a more attractive option.

7 IMPLEMENTATION CHALLENGES: THE DELAWARE PILOT EXPERIMENT[21]

During the past year, the Wharton Risk Management and Decision Processes Center has been investigating the possibility of using third parties to ensure compliance with Section 112(r) of the CAAA of 1990. This activity is being undertaken by a task force, consisting of the EPA's Chemical Emergency Preparedness and Prevention Office (CEPPO), EPA Region III, and the State of Delaware's Department of Natural Resources and Environmental Control (DNREC).[22]

---

[21] This section is based on material in P. McNulty, et al., "Evaluating the Use of Third Parties to Measure Process Safety Management in Small Firms" Annual Symposium, Mary Kay O'Connor Process Safety Center, Texas A &M University, 26 October 1999.

[22] The DNREC is the state agency responsible for the implementation of the Extremely Hazardous Substances Risk Management Act.

One of the early suggestions for finding a financial incentive for facilities to voluntarily use third-party auditors was for an insurance company to establish that a facility was in compliance with Section 112(r). If this was the case, then the insurer might conclude the facility had a reasonable risk management program in place and might be a better risk. Consequently, the insurance company might lower its premium, which would provide the financial incentive to the firm to have a third party audit. Because it seemed that small facilities would be reluctant to pay a voluntary inspection fee, the insurer was willing to provide this as a pro bono service with the expectation that it would be financially sustainable to both parties.

7.1 The Rationale for a Pilot Experiment in Delaware

One of the legal challenges the task force faced was determining which criteria it might use to select third-party auditors and what legal responsibility the EPA might have if an accidental release occurred after a satisfactory third-party audit had been conducted. Because of the legal and reputational consequences that such a release could be damaging to the Agency, the EPA was reluctant to establish criteria for third-party auditors in the pilot experiment. As a result, and for purely practical reasons, the task force decided to base the pilot in Delaware. (Under the Delaware Code, the DNREC can use trained and tested representatives.) Furthermore, facilities and communities in Delaware are close to the Wharton School and EPA Region III headquarters and therefore could be visited for evaluation purposes with relatively short commutes from Philadelphia.

The selection of auditors for the pilot was legally and administratively the responsibility of the DNREC. The task force received recommendations from a number of trade and professional organizations of individuals that they thought would be good third-party auditors, and the DNREC selected candidates based upon their industrial audit experience and professional credentials. A total of eight individuals were selected from three different background sources: insurance, professional consultants, and government business assistance agencies. The auditors agreed to participate in the pilot on a pro bono basis. All candidates had auditing experience, primarily in environmental or industrial hygiene.

Stationary sources subject to Section 112(r) range from the simplest (small chlorination processes) to the most complex (large refineries). Training auditors to conduct compliance inspections for all covered facilities was beyond the scope of this pilot project. Training was limited to two business segments: small chlorination processes and facilities using anhydrous ammonia refrigeration systems. These two business segments represent an estimated 50 percent of the stationary sources subject to Section 112(r) in Delaware and are probably similar to the national distribution. DNREC's Accidental Release Prevention Group conducted a two-day training session with the assistance of EPA's Region III Office of Solid Waste and Emergency Response. Following the training session, Wharton developed a questionnaire to allow the auditors to comment on the training. The responses were tabulated by the Risk Management and Decision Processes Center and found to be very favorable.

In Delaware, at this writing, six chlorination process owners or operators and twelve ammonia refrigerated system owners or operators have submitted federal RMPs. Some of these facilities are not eligible to participate in the pilot project because of past compliance history. The DNREC has yet to approach the stationary sources that have agreed to participate and to test the strength of their prevention programs in the spirit of cooperative compliance that has already been established.

In Delaware, the auditors will give the results of the audit to DNREC's Accidental Release Prevention Group (ARP). The results of the inspections will be compared to previous inspections. The ARP will follow-up by visiting the stationary sources to discuss the results of the inspection by the third-party auditors. In some cases, it may be necessary to conduct a partial or full inspection to verify the results.

7.2 Findings from the Third-Party Pilot Experiment

Based on the pilot study, we found that the use of third parties to ensure compliance with Section 112(r) is a sensible way to reduce chemical releases for small firms. In future work, we hope to determine the benefit to the facilities, third-party auditors, enforcement agencies, and the local communities. With the exception of communities that have a large chemical or petrochemical industry presence, we do not expect the general public to take a great interest in chemical safety matters.[23]

Indeed, companies seeking to communicate with their neighbors have resorted to open houses, plant tours, give-aways, and public displays in an effort to stimulate interest with only limited success. Of course, this situation could change quickly should a disaster occur, such as the explosion at Concept Sciences described above.[24] On the other hand, the media, local emergency planning committees, and local entities responsible for responding to emergencies are more likely to be interested in activities that may affect public safety, such as compliance audits.

8 CONCLUSIONS

In this chapter we have focused on the role of third-party inspections coupled with insurance as an alternative to the standard command-and-control

---

[23] P. McNulty, et al., "Communicating Under Section 112(r) of the Clean Air Act" (1998) 18 *Risk Analysis* 191–197; L. Schaller, et al., "Impact of Hazardous Substances Regulations on Small Firms in Delaware and New Jersey" (1998) 18 *Risk Analysis* 181–189.

[24] See supra notes 1–2 and accompanying text. Reporting on the explosion at Concept Sciences, Inc., the local newspaper, The Allentown Morning Call, published 125 articles in the six-month period following the accident.

procedures used by regulatory agencies in the past. The passage of Section 112(r) of the Clean Air Act Amendments of 1990 provides an opportunity for utilizing these market-type mechanisms as a way for firms to show that they have adopted an RMP.

Firms are often reluctant to adopt an RMP because of its cost and the feeling that the chances of severe chemical accidents are so small that it is below their threshold of concern. Small companies have an additional reason not to consider undertaking RMPs: they know that if there is a major accident they will become insolvent and it is not cost-effective for them to invest in preventive measures.

By linking an insurance policy with a third-party inspection, there is an opportunity to convince both large and small firms that it is worthwhile for them to undertake an RMP and voluntarily have an audit. This action will be particularly attractive if the inspector can provide special risk management services in addition to its audit function. If the regulatory agency imposes a large enough fine if it discovers that a non-inspected firm doesn't have an RMP, then this provides an added incentive for firms to volunteer to be audited.

A pilot experiment in Delaware is now underway which will provide data on the success of third-party inspections coupled with insurance. To the extent that firms subject to Section 112(r) are receptive to having audits and insurance premiums reflect the risk of these facilities, then an important step will have been taken to move in the direction of implementing market mechanisms in place of command-and-control procedures. The City of Philadelphia has also expressed serious interest in participating in this program.

At a theoretical level, this chapter should be viewed as a first step in exploring the role of third parties with insurance to deal with the risk management of firms. There are a number of open issues that have to be explored in future research. These include the ability of inspections to determine correctly how safe a firm actually is; the asymmetry of information between firms, insurers, and inspectors; and the ability to estimate the risks of chemical accidents and the costs of preventive actions.

Part IV
A Comparative Case Study: Electricity and Contracts

17. Environmental Voluntary Contracts between Individuals and Industry: An Analysis of Consumer Preferences for Green Electricity

Matthew J. Kotchen, Michael R. Moore, and Christopher F. Clark*

1   INTRODUCTION

Stakeholders in environmental problems increasingly perceive voluntary contracts as a viable form of environmental policy and regulatory reform. These stakeholders include governments, corporations, interest groups, and individuals. Tietenberg identifies many of these voluntary agreements as a disclosure strategy for pollution control.[1] Disclosure strategies are policies that seek to increase the availability of information on pollution as a mechanism to achieve environmental goals. These strategies are based on the premise that increasing the availability of information will mitigate informational market failure, reduce transaction costs, and induce market forces to adjust toward efficient pollution control. Thus, disclosure strategies may serve as substitutes or complements for traditional regulatory approaches (such as emission standards) and incentive-based approaches (such as tradable pollution permits and emission charges).

Several governmental programs in the United States take advantage of disclosure strategies through voluntary contracts. Project XL (or "excellent leadership"), the Common Sense Initiative, and the 33/50 Program provide examples of voluntary contracts between corporations and the Environmental Protection Agency. Habitat Conservation Plans under the Endangered Species Act provide another example of voluntary contracts that may arise between individuals and the federal government.[2] In addition, several

*The authors are grateful to Ruth A. Seleske, Elvana M. Hammoud, and Norm J. Stevens of Detroit Edison for information on the Solar*Currents*® program and constructive comments on the survey instrument. This research was partially funded through Research Agreement No. 98–1516 with Detroit Edison.

[1]   T. Tietenberg, "Disclosure Strategies for Pollution Control" (1998) 11 *Environmental and Resource Economics* 587–602.
[2]   Details on these programs are discussed by other chapters in this volume.

U.S. Department of Agriculture programs (e.g., the Conservation Reserve Program and the Environmental Quality Incentive Program) use voluntary contracts between farm producers and the government to improve environmental quality through changes in production practices. A common feature of these examples is their inclusion of the government as a party to the contract.

Environmental voluntary contracts based on the information disclosure strategy also arise directly between individuals and industry. These contracts may arise implicitly or explicitly. Market transactions between producers and consumers define an implicit contract that is increasingly used to promote "environmentally friendly" or "green" goods and services. Markets for organic produce and certified sustainable forest products are examples. In both cases, producers disclose information about the goods being produced, and consumers are generally willing to pay a price premium for the green production practices.

Individuals and industries may agree to explicit contracts to reduce the supply and demand uncertainty of implicit agreements. Markets for "green" electricity demonstrate the use of explicit contracts. Green electricity is electricity generated from renewable energy sources, including solar, wind, geothermal, and biomass energy. A large part of this market is structured through explicit contracts between electric utility companies agreeing to produce green electricity and customers agreeing to purchase green electricity at a predetermined price premium for a set period of time. The rationale for these contracts is to enable consumers to choose from generation technologies that impose lower social costs of pollution emissions.

This chapter analyzes the explicit contracts between individuals and companies for green electricity. The focus is on the question of why individuals agree to these voluntary contracts. Industry incentives are understood as attempts to market a differentiated product and retain environmentally-minded customers as deregulation of the electric utility industry in the United States opens the door for retail competition.[3] Individual incentives, however, are less well understood despite their importance to voluntary contracts for green electricity. The analysis presented in this chapter combines economic and psychological theories to explain why individuals may decide to engage in voluntary contracts for environmental improvement. These theories are then tested in an empirical study of electricity consumers in southeastern Michigan. The overall objectives are (1) to highlight green electricity as an environmental contract between individuals and industry, (2) to expand the understanding of why individuals are willing to engage in voluntary environmental contracts, and (3) to assess the potential of disclosure strategies through environmental contracts between individuals and industry.

---

[3] Other sources discuss industry incentives for green electricity in detail. See, for example, R. Wiser and S. Pickle, *Selling Green Power in California: Product, Industry, and Market Trends*, Environmental Energy Technologies Division, Ernest Orlando Lawrence Berkeley National Laboratory, University of California, Berkeley, LBNL-41807, 1998.

The chapter is organized in the following manner. Section 2 describes the United States market for green electricity based on voluntary contracts. The section also includes information on the empirical setting for this study: Detroit Edison's SolarCurrents® program. Section 3 develops a conceptual framework to explain individual behavior in environmental voluntary contracts. The framework combines insights from economic theory on the private provision of public goods and psychological theory on pro-environmental behavior. Section 4 describes the survey instrument and data collection for the empirical study of Detroit Edison's SolarCurrents® program. Section 5 reports results for both participants and nonparticipants in the program. These results are discussed in Section 6, along with more general lessons for disclosure strategies through individual–industry environmental contracts.

2   GREEN ELECTRICITY AS AN ENVIRONMENTAL CONTRACT

Green electricity is being offered to households as a supplement to electricity generated by fossil fuels and nuclear power. Production of green electricity displaces the pollution emissions and resource degradation associated with generation from conventional fuels. Participants in programs offering green electricity agree to pay a price premium to meet part or all of their household's electricity demand with green electricity. The number of utility-sponsored green electricity programs in the United States has grown in response to marketing studies that indicate a resounding consumer preference and willingness to pay for electricity generated from renewable energy.[4] Seventy-five electric utilities have established or designated green electricity programs.[5]

The number of green electricity programs is likely to continue growing as the United States deregulates its electricity industry.[6] Recent rulings at the federal and state level have opened the door for retail competition among electricity producers. As a consequence, utilities that were once guaranteed monopoly status will be forced to compete for customers. With the advent of choice for electricity consumers, public utilities will increasingly look to sponsor green electricity programs to help secure environmentally-minded consumers. These utilities will face competition from new entrants offering green electricity in the market.

---

[4]   E. Holt, *Green Pricing Resource Guide* (Ed Holt & Associates, The Regulatory Assistance Project, Gardner, Maine, 1997).
[5]   U.S. Department of Energy, "Summary of Green Pricing Programs" <http://www.eren.doe.gov/greenpower>, 20 June 2000.
[6]   R. Wiser and S. Pickle, *Green Marketing, Renewables, and Free Riders: Increasing Consumer Demand for a Public Good*, Environmental Energy Technologies Division, Ernest Orlando Lawrence Berkeley National Laboratory, University of California, Berkeley, LBNL-40632, 1997.

Many existing green electricity programs operate with contracts between electric utilities and consumers. To participate in these green electricity programs, consumers must agree to purchase green electricity at a pre-determined price premium for a set period of time.[7] Table 1 provides an overview of selected green electricity programs in the United States that operate with explicit contracts. These programs are generally organized as capacity-based or energy-based.[8] Capacity-based programs are presently limited to solar energy programs, which generate electricity either on household rooftops or at centralized facilities. Customers in these programs choose to purchase a fixed block of green electric capacity, with amounts chosen typically below customers' total electricity requirements. Monthly price premiums range from $2.50 to $6.59 per month for 100 watts of capac-ity. Energy-based programs require customers to choose a percentage of their total electricity consumption as green. In several of these programs, customers can choose 100 percent of their electricity as green. Price premi-ums in this type of program range from 0.5 to 5.0 cents per kilowatt-hour.

The empirical setting for this study is Detroit Edison's SolarCurrents® program. Detroit Edison supplies electricity to over two million customers in southeastern Michigan. The SolarCurrents® program commenced opera-tion in August 1996. Solar energy is generated at two centralized facilities in the Detroit metropolitan area with a total capacity of 54.8 kilowatts. Electricity produced at these facilities is fed directly onto the company's regional power grid and displaces an equivalent amount of electricity gen-erated by Detroit Edison's coal, oil, and nuclear power plants. Customers who enroll in the SolarCurrents® program pay an additional average fee of $6.59 per month to lease each 100-watt block of solar electric service. A 100-watt block produces an equivalent of twelve kilowatt-hours of solar electricity per month. Customers sign a two-year contract to enroll in the program.

3 ECONOMIC AND PSYCHOLOGICAL PERSPECTIVES ON CONSUMER PREFERENCES

This section describes and, to a degree, synthesizes economic and psycho-logical perspectives on why individuals may contract for green electricity. The economic perspective focuses on the private provision of a public good, while the psychology perspective focuses on motives for pro-environmental behavior (PEB).

Pollution reduction is a byproduct of green electricity production. For example, solar energy (ignoring the production process for solar panels)

---

[7] Other programs are simply structured as voluntary contributions to help support green electricity. Programs of this type have no designated prices, and consumers make no formal commitments to the program.

[8] See B. Swezey and L. Bird, *Information Brief on Green Power Marketing*, National Renewable Energy Laboratory, NREL/TP-620-26901 (Colorado, 4th edn, 1999).

Table 1 Overview of Contracts in Selected Green Electricity Programs

State	Utility	Program	Technology	Premium	Contract	Type
CA	Sacramento Municipal	Photovoltaic Pioneers	PV	$4/month	10 years	Capacity
CO	Fort Collins Light and Power	Wind Power Pilot Program	Wind	2.5 cents/kWh	3 years	Energy
MI	Detroit Edison	SolarCurrents	PV	$6.59/100 W unit	2 years	Capacity
MI	Traverse City Light and Power	Green Rate	Wind	1.58 cents/kWh	3 years	Energy
MN	Northern States Power	Solar Advantage	PV	$36/month	5 years	Capacity
OR	Portland General Electric	Share the Wind	Wind	1.0 cent/kWh	1 year	Energy
WI	Wisconsin Public Service	SolarWise	PV	$17/month	10 years	Capacity

Notes: PV is photovoltaic. Table adapted from Holt (supra note 4) and Swezey and Bird (supra note 8).

emits no pollutants, while combustion of fossil fuels emits carbon dioxide, sulfur dioxide, nitrogen oxides, and other pollutants. The environmental conditions produced by these emissions—global warming, acid precipitation, and ground-level ozone—satisfy the non-rivalry and non-exclusivity characteristics of pure public goods. Thus, consumption of green electricity supplies an environmental public good through displacement of emissions from conventional electricity. From an economic perspective, voluntary contracts for green electricity are an example of the private provision of a public good.

Beginning with Olsen's *The Logic of Collective Action*, economists have developed theoretical models to examine different conditions for the private provision of public goods.[9] Olsen's analysis employs a rational-choice approach to demonstrate that individual members of a group may have little incentive to contribute to the collective provision of a public good. Rather than contribute, the self-interested individual may choose to free ride: to enjoy the benefits derived from the public good that is provided by others. The irony of the public goods model is that everyone in the group could be made better off if all members contributed.

More recently, this general framework has been extended to predict which individuals in the group will make contributions.[10] This inquiry gives rise to three general predictions. First, voluntary contributions depend on individual "tastes" for the public good, as well as income. Second, individuals sort into two groups: those with relatively high income or a taste for the particular public good, and those with relatively low income or little taste for the public good. The former will choose to contribute, and the latter will choose to free ride. Finally, the fraction of individuals making contributions decreases as group size increases.

While these predictions shape the economic understanding of privately provided public goods, they are rarely demonstrated empirically. Actual contributions to public goods generally exceed contribution levels predicted by rational choice models.[11] This observation underscores the sense that most real-world examples violate strict assumptions of rational egoism. Accordingly, economists are recognizing that a fuller understanding of public goods provision requires consideration of additional motives. For example, studies are now examining the role of various types of altruism in motivating individuals to contribute to public goods.[12] More generally,

---

[9]   M. Olsen, *The Logic of Collective Action* (Harvard University Press, 1965).
[10]   See, e.g., J. Andreoni and M. McGuire, "Identifying the Free Riders: A Simple Algorithm for Determining Who Will Contribute to a Public Good" (1993) 51 *Journal of Public Economics* 447–454; J. Andreoni, "Privately Provided Public Goods in a Large Economy: The Limits of Altruism" (1988) 35 *Journal of Public Economics* 57–73; T. Bergstrom, et al., "On the Private Provision of Public Goods" (1986) 33 *Journal of Public Economics* 25–49.
[11]   See J. Piliavin and H. Charng, "Altruism: A Review of Recent Theory and Research" (1990) 16 *Annual Review of Sociology* 27–65.
[12]   See J. Andreoni, "Impure Altruism and Donations to Public Goods: A Theory of Warm-Glow Giving" (1990) 100 *The Economic Journal* 464–477; J. Palfrey and J. Prisbrey, "Anomalous Behavior in Public Goods Experiments: How Much and Why?" (1997) 87 *American Economic Review* 829–846.

Rose-Ackerman calls for "a richer conception of individual utility functions and a base in cognitive psychology that incorporates the power of ideas and emotions in motivating behavior."[13]

Rose-Ackerman's recommendation begins to describe the approach psychologists use when studying the incidence of PEB. The majority of psychological research on PEB examines the influence of attitudes, beliefs, and values. A large literature establishes attitudes as predictors of behavior and behavioral intentions.[14] Similarly, a body of research explores relationships between underlying value orientations and PEB, whereby value orientations are hypothesized to precede attitudes. Stern, Dietz, and Kalof conclude that motivations for environmental behavior are derived from a combination of egoistic, social altruistic, and biocentric value orientations.[15] Although all three value orientations are found to predict willingness to take political action, only awareness of consequences for oneself (egoism) reliably predicts intended willingness to pay for environmental protection. In a related study, Thompson and Barton find that ecocentric and anthropocentric value orientations independently contribute to explanations of apathy toward the environment, conservation behaviors, and membership in environmental organizations.[16]

Much like economists, psychologists are also beginning to utilize theory from other disciplines with the purpose of developing a more comprehensive explanation of PEB. For example, Guagnano, Stern, and Dietz test the hypothesis that interactions between psychological and socioeconomic variables affect the incidence of PEB.[17] Their model posits that attitudinal and socioeconomic factors act jointly to influence behavior. In an application to recycling, they find that socioeconomic factors affect the strength of attitude-behavior relationships, whereby attitudes are less likely to induce behavior in the presence of strong negative socioeconomic conditions. Alternatively, strong socioeconomic conditions increase the likelihood of attitudes giving rise to particular behaviors.

The application studied here takes advantage of insights from both the economic literature on private provision of public goods and the psychology literature on PEB. In this context, PEB is equivalent to the provision of an environmental public good. Attitudes toward both altruism and the environment are identified as psychological factors that could affect PEB. Combining these psychological factors with socioeconomic characteristics

---

[13] S. Rose-Ackerman, "Altruism, Nonprofits, and Economic Theory" (1996) 24 *Journal of Economic Literature* 701–728.

[14] See, e.g., I. Ajzen, *Attitudes, Personality, and Behavior* (The Dorsey Press, Chicago, 1988); Ajzen and M. Fishbein, *Understanding Attitudes and Predicting Social Behavior* (Prentice Hall, Inc., New York, 1980); T. Heberlein, "Attitudes and Environmental Management" (1989) 45 *Journal of Social Issues* 37–57.

[15] P. Stern, et al., "Value Orientations, Gender and Environmental Concern" (1993) 25 *Environment and Behavior* 322–348.

[16] S. Thompson and M. Barton, "Ecocentric and Anthropocentric Attitudes Toward the Environment" (1994) 14 *Journal of Environmental Psychology* 149–157.

[17] G. Guagnano, et al., "Influences on Attitude-Behavior Relationships: A Natural Experiment with Curbside Recycling" (1995) 27 *Environment and Behavior* 699–718.

enables an economic and psychological investigation of determinants of participation in a green electricity program.

4 SURVEY INSTRUMENT AND DATA COLLECTION

Mail surveys were sent to 281 participants and 619 non-participants in the Solar*Currents*® green electricity program. The 281 participants comprise the complete population of participants in the program. The sample of 619 non-participants was randomly selected from 80,000 Detroit Edison customers who were solicited to join the Solar*Currents*® program.[18] Mailing addresses for participants and non-participants were provided by Detroit Edison. The survey was administered in 1998 using the Dillman Total Design Method.[19] Two participant and 70 non-participant surveys could not be delivered due to incorrect addresses; 263 and 361 surveys were completed and returned for participants and non-participants, respectively. Response rates were 95 percent for participants, 67 percent for non-participants, and 76 percent overall.

Participants and non-participants in the program received different versions of the survey instrument.[20] Versions differed only in one section, where respondents were asked about their personal motivations for enrolling or not enrolling in the program. An additional set of questions for participants focused attention on their environmental reasons for enrollment. Drafts of the surveys were pre-tested in two separate focus groups. The survey instrument was modified to increase clarity based on focus group input.

The final survey instrument consisted of 43 and 37 questions for the participant and non-participant versions, respectively. All respondents completed two scales: a ten-item modified New Ecological Paradigm (NEP) scale[21] and a newly developed, nine-item Altruism scale. A five-point Likert response scale was used for each item in the NEP and Altruism scales. The NEP scale, along with its original predecessor, has been used and examined by social scientists for over two decades.[22] Previous research in the area provides a basis for hypothesis testing and a framework for interpretation.

---

[18] Detroit Edison selected the 80,000 solicited customers from a random sample of households meeting minimum credit history qualifications. Solicitations were based on informational inserts in monthly statements.

[19] D. Dillman, *Mail and Telephone Surveys* (Wiley and Sons, New York, 1978).

[20] Copies of the survey instruments are available upon request from the authors.

[21] R. Dunlap, et al., "Measuring Endorsement of an Ecological Worldview: A Revised NEP Scale" (1992). Paper presented at the 1992 Meeting of the Rural Sociological Society, State College, Pennsylvania.

[22] For the original version, see R. Dunlap and K. Van Liere, "The New Environmental Paradigm: A Proposed Measuring Instrument and Preliminary Results" (1978) 9 *Journal of Environmental Education* 10–19. A recent application is found in P. Stern, et al., "The New Ecological Paradigm Scale in Social-Psychological Context" (1995) 27 *Environment and Behavior* 723–743.

In the context of analyzing contracts for green electricity, the NEP scale provides a method for measuring attitudes toward the environment.

The Altruism scale developed for this research applies the Schwartz norm-activation model to measure altruistic beliefs.[23] According to the Schwartz model, altruistic behavior arises from personal norms if two criteria are met: an individual must be aware that particular actions or inactions have negative consequences for the welfare of others (Awareness of Consequences, or AC) and an individual must ascribe responsibility for those actions and their consequences to himself or herself (Ascription of Responsibility, or AR). The presence of AC and AR in a specific situation enables personal norms to motivate behavior. Without the concurrent presence of AC, AR, and a relevant personal norm, altruistic behavior is unlikely to occur. Our research operationalizes the Schwartz model in the form of a general Altruism scale. The scale contains a total of nine items that test for the presence of individual personal norms, AC, and AR.[24]

In addition to the NEP and Altruism scales, survey questions collected data on the respondents' socioeconomic and demographic characteristics. Variables were formed from these data for the statistical analysis.

5   EMPIRICAL RESULTS

The empirical analysis considers: (1) the factors that affect participation in the SolarCurrents[R] program and (2) participants' motives for enrolling in the program. Several variables are considered as possible determinants of participation, including psychological factors and socioeconomic and demographic characteristics. For attitudinal variables, *NEP* and *ALT* represent summed responses to the NEP and Altruism scales, respectively. *NEP* responses are bounded between a high of 50 and a low of 10. Higher summated responses indicate stronger pro-environmental attitudes. *ALT* responses are bounded between a high of 45 and a low of 9. Similarly, higher summated responses indicate stronger altruistic attitudes according to the Schwartz norm-activation model. Other variables include *AGE*, *ASTHMA* (whether or not any household members have asthma or other respiratory diseases, no = 0, yes = 1), *GENDER* (female = 0, male = 1), *HOUSEHLD* (number of individuals living in the household), *INCOME* (1997 household income before taxes), and *SATISFAC* (level of general satisfaction with Detroit Edison on a five-point scale, from 1 = *very dissatisfied* to 5 = *very satisfied*).

---

[23]   S. Schwartz, "Elicitation of Moral Obligation and Self-Sacrificing Behavior" (1970) 15 *Journal of Personal and Social Psychology* 283–293.
[24]   Specific items included in the scale and reliability results can be found in C. Clark, et al., "Internal and External Influences on Behavior: An Analysis of Participation in a Green Electricity Program" (1998) Working Paper, School of Natural Resources and Environment, University of Michigan.

Table 2 provides a comparison of means between participants and non-participants in the Solar*Currents*® program. Both participants and nonparticipants appear to demonstrate reasonably strong pro-environmental and altruistic attitudes, although summated mean responses for *NEP* and *ALT* are higher for participants. *AGE* and *ASTHMA* appear similar for participants and nonparticipants. The average age of respondents is just above 50 years, and the proportion reporting asthma or other respiratory diseases is above 20 percent. The proportion of respondents that are female is greater for participants, and the number of individuals living in the household is greater for nonparticipants. Finally, participants show greater household income and greater customer satisfaction with Detroit Edison.

Statistical comparisons of means between groups are not presented due to the degree of choice-based sampling. The choice-based sampling occurs at highly disproportionate rates, with all of the participants sampled and only 619 of 80,000 non-participants sampled. Unbiased statistical comparisons of means between participants and nonparticipants require weighting observations based on the degree of disproportionate sampling. The high degree of disproportionate sampling in this case, however, renders all comparisons statistically insignificant. Thus, beyond qualitative comparisons between groups, no further insights follow from statistical comparisons of means.

Table 2 Comparison of Means between Participants and Non-participants in the Green Electricity Program

Variable	Participants	Nonparticipants
NEP	37.84	33.93
	(7.32)	(6.9)
ALT	35.08	31.0
	(4.55)	(5.2)
AGE	52.34	51.3
	(12.93)	(13.53)
ASTHMA (% yes)	0.22	0.24
	(0.42)	(0.43)
GENDER (% male)	0.58	0.70
	(0.49)	(0.46)
HOUSEHLD	2.53	2.94
	(1.29)	(1.48)
INCOME	79,714	66,753
	(46,651)	(42,480)
SATISFAC	4.22	4.01
	(0.89)	(0.91)

Notes: Standard deviations are given in parentheses. The number of observations for each variable ranges from 245 to 264 for participants and from 308 to 351 for nonparticipants. *NEP* = summated scale indexing environmental attitude; *ALT* = summated scale indexing altruisitic attitude; *AGE* = age of respondent; *ASTHMA* = whether any member of household suffers from respiratory ailment (0 = no; 1 = yes); *GENDER* = gender of respondent (0 = female; 1 = male); *HOUSEHLD* = number of people living in household; *INCOME* = household income ($/year); *SATISFAC* = customer satisfaction with the electric utility on a scale ranging from 1 = *very dissatisfied* to 5 = *very satisfied*.

Table 3   Logit Regression Results of Green Electricity Participation Decision

Variable	Coefficient	Standard Error
Constant[a]	−5.517***	1.168
NEP	0.041**	0.018
ALT	0.152***	0.025
AGE	0.009	0.009
ASTHMA	−0.075	0.244
GENDER	−0.360*	0.220
HOUSEHLD	−0.253***	0.085
INCOME	$4.90E-06$***	$2.325E-06$
SATISFAC	0.298***	0.117
N	509	
% correct predictions	71.32	
Log Likelihood	−290.23	
Nagelkerke R^2	0.28	

Notes: *, **, ***, indicate significance at the 0.1, 0.05, and 0.01 levels, respectively. [a]The constant term is corrected for choice-based sampling. The method is discussed on pages 90–91 in Maddala (supra note 25). Variables are defined in the text and the notes to Table 2.

The decision of whether or not to enroll in the Solar*Currents*® program is evaluated with a multivariate, logit regression model. The logit model has the advantage of readily handling choice-based sampling. Maddala shows that the logit model with choice-based sampling still produces consistent coefficients, except for the constant term, which is easily corrected.[25] All attitudinal, socioeconomic, and demographic variables are included in the model (see Table 3). Both attitudinal variables are statistically significant in the expected direction. The positive signs on *NEP* and *ALT* indicate that stronger pro-environmental and altruistic attitudes lead to higher probabilities of participating in the green electricity program. The coefficients for *AGE* and *ASTHMA* are not significantly different from zero, indicating that neither affects the probability of participation. The negative significance of *GENDER* and *HOUSEHLD* indicate that males and larger households are less likely to participate. Finally, respondents with greater *INCOME* are significantly more likely to participate, as are those with greater customer satisfaction (*SATISFAC*). The percentage of correct predictions from the model is approximately 71 percent and the Nagelkerke *R* squared is 0.28.

In general, these results indicate the importance of both economic and psychological perspectives for explaining individuals' participation in a voluntary green electricity program. In particular, the finding that *INCOME*, *NEP*, and *ALT* influence the decision is consistent with predictions from the

---

[25] G. Maddala, *Limited Dependent and Qualitative Variables in Econometrics* (Cambridge University Press, 1983).

Table 4   General Reasons for Green Electricity Participation

Reason	Percent "Yes"	Standard Deviation
My support of SolarCurrents® may help lower the costs of solar energy in the future	76	43
Solar Energy is more environmentally sound than other ways of producing electricity	92	27
I like to encourage development of new technology	65	48
Supporting SolarCurrents® is personally satisfying independently of the program's impacts	30	46
Solar energy helps reduce our reliance on imported oil	68	47

Notes: Percent "Yes" corresponds to the percent of respondents indicating that the reason was a motivating factor in the participation decision. The number of observations included is 262 participants.

economic model of private provision of a public good and the psychological model of PEB.

Motivations for participation are probed further with questions geared only to participants. Initially, participants were asked to indicate which of five general reasons motivated them to enroll in the green electricity program. Table 4 reports the percentage of "yes" responses for each general reason. Over 90 percent of the participants responded "yes" to the reason that solar energy is an environmentally sound way to generate electricity. Another relevant reason is that participants believe their support of the program will reduce the costs of solar energy in the future, as 76 percent responded "yes" to this reason. Over 65 percent also indicated the importance of encouraging new technology and reducing reliance on imported oil. The idea that participants find the program personally satisfying independent of its impact was less relevant, with only 30 percent responding "yes".

Environmental reasons were then investigated in more depth with a ranking question. Participants were asked to rank five environmental reasons, in order of importance, for their participation in the green electricity program. The reasons are designed to reflect: benefits to Michigan residents (MICHRES); specific beliefs about ecosystem health (ECOHLTH); warm-glow satisfaction (WARMGLOW);[26] personal and family health (OURHLTH); and global warming (GLOBWARM). More generally, these

---

[26] Warm-glow is the term economists have given to forms of altruism whereby people gain satisfaction from the actual process of giving rather than from tangible consequences of their giving. See, for example, Andreoni, supra note 12; Palfrey and Prisbrey, supra note 12; D. Kahneman and J. Knetsch, "Valuing Public Goods: The Purchase of Moral Satisfaction" (1992) 22 J Envtl Econ & Mgmt 57–70.

statements are designed to elicit responses that reflect biocentrism, altruism, egoism, altruism/biocentrism, and warm-glow altruism, respectively. Respondents began by completing a 5-point Likert scale for each individual motivation. Then, the relative importance of these items was determined by asking participants to rank these motivations in order of importance.

Table 5 reports mean ranks and percentile distributions of these five specific environmental motivations. Beliefs about ecosystem health have the highest mean rank, followed respectively by beliefs about benefits to southeastern Michigan residents; personal and family health; global warming; and warm-glow altruism.[27] Improving ecosystem health is ranked as the top motivation 39 percent of the time; motivations based on warm-glow

Table 5 Percentage Distributions and Relative Rankings of Environmental Motivations for Green Electricity Participation

Motivation	Mean Rank*	Percentage for Each Rank				
		1	2	3	4	5
Reducing air pollution from electricity production will improve the health of natural ecosystems	2.08	39.4	25.9	23.5	9.6	1.6
Reducing air pollution from electricity production will benefit residents of southeastern Michigan	2.49	20.6	32.0	27.7	17.4	2.4
My health, and the health of my family, may improve because the program will improve air quality	2.85	17.9	22.6	22.6	31.0	6.0
Decreasing carbon dioxide emissions from electricity production will slow the rate of global warming	3.04	19.0	16.3	20.2	31.0	13.5
I take satisfaction in participating in this program, regardless of its environmental effects	4.51	4.0	3.2	6.1	10.9	75.7

Notes: Within a row, percentages may not sum to 100 due to rounding. Mean Rank is calculated based on 1 = most important, 2 = second most important, 3 = third most important, 4 = fourth most important, and 5 = least important. *The Friedman test, applied to mean ranks for each motivation, shows that the rankings are statistically different ($p < 0.05$). The summary ranking of reasons from most to least important is therefore a statistically valid rank ordering.

---

[27] Results related to the warm-glow altruism question should be interpreted with caution. Designing questions to probe this motivation is inherently difficult, as people are not accustomed to thinking in these terms. While the question used here is conceptually correct, respondents may have misinterpreted it to mean the program will actually have no effects. In subsequent research on warm-glow motivations for shade-grown coffee, the question is reworded as "purchase of this coffee gives me moral satisfaction." In that study, the importance of warm glow altruism becomes indistinguishable from egoistic and general altruistic motivations. See M. Kotchen, et al., "Green Products as Impure Public Goods: Shade Grown Coffee and Tropical Forest Conservation" (1999) Working Paper, School of Natural Resources and Environment, University of Michigan.

altruism are ranked as least important 76 percent of the time. The Friedman test, a non-parametric test that compares ranked data for three or more paired groups, is applied to all possible bivariate combinations of the five ranked reasons.[28] Mean rankings for each of the five reasons are shown to be statistically different ($p < 0.05$) for all possible pairings. Thus, the summary ranking of reasons from most to least important is statistically valid.

6 DISCUSSION

This study analyzes the household participation decision in a green electricity program as an example of a voluntary environmental contract between an individual and a corporation. A conceptual framework embedded in economics and psychology is applied to understand the characteristics of households that tend to enroll in such a program. Income, environmental attitudes, and altruistic attitudes exert a positive effect on the probability of participating in the program. These results are consistent with the economic model of private provision of a public good and the psychological model of motives for pro-environmental behavior.

Two results are interesting in the relative rankings of participants' environmental motives for program enrollment. First, altruism toward the environment (biocentricism) is generally more important than either altruism toward regional residents or health-based egoism. This may suggest that the notion in environmental economics of a natural environment's existence value is quantitatively important, at least to a subset of the population.[29] Second, local concerns about benefits for southeastern Michigan residents (ranked second) are more important than global concerns associated with the greenhouse effect (ranked fourth). The greater importance attached to a local environmental issue, as opposed to a global issue, suggests that voluntary environmental contracts may be most successful in addressing market failures associated with local public goods.

As an exchange between two private parties, green electricity is an example of a purely voluntary information disclosure strategy. The supplier of green electricity has a clear incentive to reveal information on production technologies as a means of obtaining a price premium and, in some cases, strategically improving corporate image. A subset of interested consumers demands this information and then makes a program participation decision. As a form of public policy, information disclosure strategies are labeled the "third wave" in pollution control policy, following the first wave of legal regulation and the second wave of market-based instruments.[30]

---

[28] See J. Gibbons, _Nonparametric Statistics: An Introduction_ (Sage Publications, Newbury Park, 1993).

[29] Existence value is roughly defined as individuals' economic value from simply knowing that a certain natural environment exists, independently of their use of that environment. See J. Krutilla, "Conservation Reconsidered" (1967) 57 _American Economic Review_ 777–786.

[30] See Tietenberg, supra note 1.

From the perspective of environmental policy, can private contracts substitute for regulatory policy in the control of pollution emissions? For the case of green electricity, the answer is likely "no" on purely conceptual grounds. The economic benefits from reductions in pollution emissions from fossil-fuel-based electricity production are public goods in most cases. Relying on voluntary actions to privately provide pollution abatement would result in inefficiently low levels of abatement. While individuals do engage in voluntary contracts for green electricity, public goods theory demonstrates that actual participation will be below socially efficient levels. Voluntary environmental contracts should not be expected to function as the exclusive tool of environmental policy.

Nevertheless, voluntary environmental contracts for green electricity can complement existing regulatory policies. They provide an opportunity for individuals to express personal preferences for environmental quality and, thus, are beneficial to consumers. They provide a niche market for both existing electric utilities and new energy supply companies. These niches will be created by the introduction of retail competition on a state-by-state basis. In California, for example, several renewable power suppliers began operating after the electricity market was opened to retail competition in 1998.[31] With retail competition in effect in only a few states, yet seemingly destined to occur in every state, voluntary contracts for green electricity will continue to expand over the next decade.

---

[31] The Center for Resource Solutions, a California-based nonprofit organization, established the *Green-e* program as a voluntary certification and verification program to assure that green power suppliers accurately represent their fuel mix. Suppliers that meet certain program guidelines receive the *Green-e* certification. The *Green-e* program is in effect in California and Pennsylvania.

18. Your Contribution Counts! An Empirical Analysis of the Decision to Support Solar Energy

Felix Oberholzer-Gee

1 INTRODUCTION

Economic theory predicts that individuals do not contribute to the provision of public goods at levels that are desirable from a social point of view.[1] Recent laboratory research shows indeed that contributions in finitely repeated public good games decline from round to round towards the (inefficient) Nash equilibrium level.[2] However, the Nash prediction is not exactly borne out. In environments where income-maximizing subjects should make zero contributions, approximately 25 percent of all subjects make positive gifts even in the last round of public good games.[3] Similarly, several field studies report sizable contributions to public goods over extended periods of time.[4]

There are four leading explanations for the observed willingness to further the group's interests in linear public good environments where the dominant strategy is not to contribute. First, voluntary cooperation may be the result of selfish individuals mimicking cooperative strategies, thereby building up positive reputations and reaping some of the benefits of cooperation.[5] Second, individuals may also contribute to public goods if they have altruistic preferences or, third, if they experience feelings of

---

[1]   R. Cornes and T. Sandler, "Easy Riders, Joint Production, and Public Goods" (1984) 94 *Economic Journal* 580–598.
[2]   J. Ledyard "Public Goods: A Survey of Experimental Research" in A. Roth and J. Kagel (eds), *The Handbook of Experimental Economics* (Princeton University Press, 1995), p. 145.
[3]   See E. Fehr and K. Schmidt, "A Theory of Fairness, Competition, and Cooperation" (1999) 114 *Quarterly Journal of Economics* 3, 769–816.
[4]   See E. Ostrom and J. Walker, "Neither Markets nor States: Linking Transformation Processes in Collective Action Arenas" in D. Mueller (ed.), *Perspectives on Public Choice: A Handbook* (Cambridge University Press, 1997), p. 45.
[5]   D. Kreps, et al., "Rational Cooperation in the Finitely Repeated Prisoner's Dilemma" (1982) 27 *Journal of Economic Theory* 245–252.

"warm-glow" when giving to the group.[6] Fourth, it may be that public good experiments confuse subjects and that positive contributions are simply decision-making errors.

The controlled environment of laboratory studies has enabled experimental economists to design institutions that test the power of these four explanations. The emerging consensus of these studies is that reputation cannot explain the observed behavior because subjects remain anonymous in these experiments. Also, most analysts study last-period behavior where there is no motivation to invest in a good reputation. Similarly, decision-making errors do not appear to be the cause of cooperation. Several studies find that decision-making errors explain cooperative behavior in the early rounds of the game, but they are not important in the final stages.[7] The experimental evidence suggests that feelings of warm-glow are the most powerful explanation for cooperative behavior.[8] In contrast, altruism does not appear to be a major force.[9]

In this chapter, I test the importance of the motivations identified in laboratory studies in a field setting. I study the decision of households to purchase power produced from solar energy that costs six times the price of regular electricity. In the city of Zurich, more than 6,000 households currently participate in such a program. My main interest is to see if the behavior of these households is consistent with the predictions of a model of impure altruism. Impure altruists contribute to public goods both due to altruistic concerns and due to feelings of warm-glow. Although warm-glow is generally recognized as a potential factor that explains voluntary contributions, not much is known about the conditions under which warm-glow feelings arise. For example, is it always the case that public goods of higher value produce more intense feelings of warm-glow? Or is there a purely symbolic aspect to warm-glow that lets individuals enjoy giving even if they themselves do not highly value this particular good? For instance, is it possible that individuals experience feelings of warm-glow when giving to the poor in Africa even though they doubt that help in this form will improve the situation on that continent? A goal of this contribution is to shed some light on questions such as these and to understand better the conditions under which feelings of warm-glow arise. Section 2 of this chapter describes the Zurich solar energy program. In section 3, I report the empirical results and compare them with the predictions of the theory. Conclusions are offered in section 4.

---

[6] J. Andreoni, "Giving with Impure Altruism: Applications to Charity and Ricardian Equivalence" (1989) 97 *Journal of Political Economy* 6, 1447–1458.

[7] See J. Andreoni, "Cooperation in Public-Goods Experiments: Kindness or Confusion?" (1995) 85 *American Economic Review* 4, 891–904.

[8] See e.g., T. Palfrey and J. Prisbrey, "Anomalous Behavior in Public Good Experiments: How Much and Why?" (1997) 87 *American Economic Review* 5, 829–845.

[9] See R. Croson, "Theories of Altruism and Reciprocity: Evidence from Linear Public Good Games" (1998) Mimeo: The Wharton School, University of Pennsylvania.

2 THE SOLAR ENERGY PROGRAM

In late 1996, the Zurich Electric Power Company started to market solar energy in the city of Zurich. The utility gave households the option to order solar energy at an increased price. Regular power produced by hydroelectric or nuclear power plants costs 0.18 Swiss Francs per kilowatt-hour ($0.12). Solar energy, currently priced at Swiss Francs 1.11, is more than six times as expensive as regular power. If households order solar energy, the Zurich Electric Power Company purchases this power from independent producers. These producers tend to be comparatively small. Many of them are private businesses that have a few solar panels on their roofs. The utility reimburses these producers based on their cost. It then "sells" this solar energy without adding a mark-up to the households that have ordered it.

Why do households participate in this program? It seems natural to think of their decision to purchase green power as a contribution to a public good. The main changes brought about by green power—cleaner air, the preservation of natural resources such as coal or oil, and a reduced reliance on nuclear power—are all examples of public goods. Solar energy has two characteristics that make it particularly suitable for a study of contributions to public goods. The first is that issues of quality do not matter. In this respect, solar power is different from other forms of green consumption. If individuals buy apples that are produced in an environmentally responsible manner, they may be motivated by a concern for the environment, or they may believe that it is healthier to eat organic apples. Thus, it is generally not possible to interpret the price difference between regular and organic produce as contributions toward a public good. In contrast, purchases of solar power represent such contributions because power produced by solar energy is identical to regular power. And even if people erroneously believed that the two forms of power were somehow different, they would still contribute to a public good because the households that demand this "superior" form of energy do not necessarily consume it. Solar energy is simply fed into the utility's network and every household—participants and non participants—have a similar chance of receiving this green power.

The second attractive feature of green power is that donations to the public good are difficult to observe, making it harder for individuals to reap reputational gains. Reputation effects are likely to be relevant for many forms of green behavior. For example, people may contribute to a cleaner environment by buying smaller cars, using public transportation, or carrying their used newspapers and bottles to a recycling center. In all these cases, the desire to build up a reputation for being an environmentally conscious person may support these decisions because the resulting behavior is easily observable. This is not the case with solar power. Short of seeing someone's utility bill, no one will notice that a household participates in the program. Thus, individuals who would like to reap reputational gains need to advertise the fact that they consume green power. In my empirical work, I will use the efforts of individuals to make their participation in solar power purchasing programs known as a control for reputation effects.

The Zurich solar energy program has been a remarkable success right from the start. At the beginning, the utility was not even able to supply as much solar power as households ordered. By May 1998, 4,420 households demanded more than 500,000 kilowatt-hours of solar energy. This corresponds approximately to the total energy consumption of 180 households. More than 5 percent of all households in Zurich now participate in the program. The managers of the utility are confident that these numbers will further increase in the future. Private suppliers have started more than ten new installations. These tend to have much larger solar panels than the earlier projects. In addition, other cities in Switzerland and southern Germany have started programs similar to the Zurich initiative.

3   IMPURE ALTRUISM

The participation rates in public good experiments such as the Zurich solar energy program do not come as a surprise to economists and policy analysts who are familiar with the recent experimental literature on the subject. In the laboratory, cooperative behavior is mostly motivated by feelings of warm-glow.[10] Does this conclusion hold for real-life situations like the participation in the solar energy program? Is altruism more important outside the laboratory?

To study how altruism and warm-glow increase voluntary contributions, I conducted a pencil-and-paper survey in May 1998 of the 4,420 households that participate in the Zurich program.[11] Almost 45 percent of these green power consumers, a total of 1,987 individuals, filled in the questionnaire. On average, these individuals spend $57 annually on green power. Solar power covers 12 percent of their total power consumption.

In designing the questionnaire, I hope to separate altruistic concerns and warm-glow effects. Unfortunately, it is hardly possible to ask individuals directly if they support the program for altruistic reasons. There is much evidence that survey respondents have a tendency to overemphasize their own socially desirable behavior.[12] For example, individuals often exaggerate their support for recycling, energy conservation, and voting. The resulting bias, which is well documented in the fields of psychology and personnel testing, is known as social desirability bias.[13] The bias arises because individuals try to present themselves in the best possible light.

---

[10]   See Palfrey and Prisbey, supra note 8.

[11]   This is one of two surveys that I plan to undertake. In the future, I will survey households that do not participate in the program. However, the findings presented here are all conditional upon participation.

[12]   See D. Crowne and D. Marlowe, "A New Scale for Social Desirability Independent of Psychopathology" (1960) 24 *Journal of Consulting Psychology* 4, 349–354; T. Kuran, "Preference Falsification, Policy Continuity and Collective Conservatism" (1987) 97 *Economic Journal* 642–665.

[13]   See D. Paulhus, "Two-Component Models of Socially Desirable Responsible" (1984) 46 *Journal of Personality and Social Psychology* 3, 598–609.

Thus, when asked if altruistic concerns were important for their decision to purchase green power, respondents are likely to overreport the extent to which altruism matters. In order to avoid social desirability bias, I asked questions that get at differences between altruistic concerns and warm-glow effects in a more indirect way.

The idea for the two measures that I use is quite simple: For selfish individuals and for altruists, it only makes sense to contribute to a public good if they believe that their contributions will truly make a difference. In contrast, if individuals are motivated by feelings of warm-glow, they "only" need to believe that purchasing green power is a noble cause. Whether or not their contribution actually improves the quality of the environment is of secondary importance. Technically speaking, the utility function of an impure altruist contains three elements: a private good, the public good, and the size of the gift that the impure altruist makes. Feelings of warm-glow are determined by the size of the gift, not by the resulting level of public goods. Andreoni remarks: "This is meant to capture the fact that an individual's own gift has properties of a private good that are independent of its properties as a public good."[14] Independence implies that a person may experience warm-glow feelings even if the level of public goods is unchanged by his or her gift. The first of my two measures thus attempts to identify whether respondents think they contribute to an important cause. The second measure is related to actual changes that the green power program is expected to bring about.

Prior to designing the questionnaire, I interviewed several participants in the green program. These interviews were unstructured. Their main purpose was to identify reasons that are likely to motivate the purchase of green power. In these interviews, six different reasons for contributing to green power were frequently mentioned. I used these six motivations in the main survey. For each of these reasons, I wanted to know how important they were for individual decisions to buy green power. I offered the following six statements:

1. I wish to support technologies that will strengthen the Swiss economy and create new jobs.
2. I wish to contribute to efforts that no new nuclear power plants be built.
3. I wish to contribute to a cleaner environment.
4. I wish to contribute to efforts to save energy resources for future generations.
5. I wish to contribute to efforts that Switzerland need not import more energy.
6. I wish to contribute to efforts to make solar energy cheaper.

Respondents rated these items on a six-point scale ranging from "1 = not important at all" to "6 = very important." If a person regards one of these

---

[14] See J. Andreoni, "Impure Altruism and Donations to Public Goods: A Theory of Warm Glow Giving" (1990) 100 *Economic Journal* 464–477.

outcomes as important, it is possible that contributing toward that goal may generate feelings of warm-glow.

For a selfish individual or an altruist, the motivation to contribute is different. Selfish contributions are only meaningful if outcomes are changed in a direction that is valued by the person who makes the contribution. That is, selfish contributions make sense if purchasing green power actually improves the quality of the environment. In the case of altruistic concerns, changes in outcomes need to be valued by the individuals the contributor cares about. Take clean air as an example. From an altruist's perspective, purchasing solar power is appropriate if this program actually improves the air quality *and* if his children (whose well-being he cares about) value clean air.

I tested for the existence of selfish or altruistic motivations by asking about the effectiveness of the solar energy program:

Today, Zurich's households order approximately 500,000 kilowatt-hours of solar energy. Imagine that this situation remains unchanged in the future. In your view, what will be the effects of this program given that households will not order more solar energy in the future. The effects on the strength of the Swiss economy and the creation of new jobs are ...

Respondents answered this type of question for all six items mentioned above. They rated the expected effects on a six-point scale from "1 = very small" to "6 = very big."

In addition to warm-glow effects and altruism, I control for the income of respondents. I also include a variable that is designed to capture reputation effects. I asked respondents if they had ever discussed the fact that they purchase solar power. Forty-three percent indicated that they did. It is possible that respondents receive recognition for their green behavior in such discussions. Thus, the regression includes an indicator variable that identifies those who reported such conversations. Table 1 presents five specifications of a model that explains how much respondents contribute to green power. The dependent variable is the amount (in Swiss Francs) that individuals spend on solar energy.

I first test the warm-glow, the altruistic, and the selfish variables separately. Model I includes three warm-glow variables and the controls.[15] The results indicate that individuals contribute more if they see a cleaner environment as a more important goal. The effect is quite sizeable: For every one-point increase on the six-point scale, respondents spend 13.33 Swiss Francs (or approximately $9) more. As can be seen from Model II, the importance of the environmental quality variable does not depend on the actual environmental effects of the green power program. Those who think that these effects are larger do not significantly contribute more. Thus, it appears that individuals are motivated to contribute to a public good even

---

[15] The variables related to technology and jobs, to energy savings and to the price of solar power were never significant. Thus, they are omitted from Table 1.

Table 1 Determinants of Contributions to Solar Power: OLS Regression-Dependent Variable Contributions in CHF

	(I) Coefficient (Std. Err.)	(II) Coefficient (Std. Err.)	(III) Coefficient (Std. Err.)	(IV) Coefficient (Std. Err.)	(V) Coefficient (Std. Err.)
Goal no nuclear power	0.18 (3.18)	—	—	3.33 (7.24)	—
Goal cleaner environment	13.33 (6.18)*	—	—	9.75 (6.57)*	15.96 (6.36)***
Goal import substitution	0.58 (2.21)	—	—	−1.10 (4.66)	—
Effect no nuclear power	—	9.94 (4.16)**	—	19.64 (14.65)	10.83 (3.94)***
Effect cleaner environment	—	1.59 (3.55)	—	−14.49 (30.63)	—
Effect import substitution	—	8.89 (3.31)***	—	14.51 (8.03)*	8.78 (3.05)***
Interaction goal × effect no nuclear power	—	—	1.21 (0.69)	−1.77 (2.61)	—
Interaction goal × effect cleaner environment	—	—	0.17 (0.59)	2.79 (5.25)	—
Interaction goal × effect import substitution	—	—	−0.85 (0.54)	1.08 (1.62)	—
Income (in CHF 1,000)	0.01 (0.00)***	0.01 (0.00)***	0.01 (0.00)***	0.01 (0.00)***	0.01 (0.00)***
Discussion DY 1 = yes	14.04 (6.79)**	15.11 (7.51)**	14.59 (7.59)*	14.38 (7.58)*	14.52 (7.48)**
Constant	−50.83 (35.33)	28.67 (13.58)	22.49 (13.52)	−42.65 (80.56)	−63.07 (39.51)

*** Significant at the 1% level, ** significant at the 5% level, * significant at the 10% level. (I): $N = 1{,}742$, adjusted R-squared $= 0.02$, (II): $N = 1{,}545$, adjusted R-squared $= 0.02$, (III): $N = 1{,}530$, adjusted R-squared $= 0.02$, (IV): $N = 1{,}530$, adjusted R-squared $= 0.02$, (V): $N = 1{,}551$, adjusted R-squared $= 0.03$.

if they do not believe that their contribution actually increases its provision. In other words, warm-glow effects may exist independent of how contributions affect the provision of the public good. The actual outcome (e.g., cleaner air) does not determine the size of contributions, but the view that one contributes to an important cause does.

The reverse holds for the impact of the program on nuclear power and on energy imports. In these cases, the effects of the program matter, while the personal perception of the importance of these goals is not significantly linked to the size of the contributions. Model III tests the interaction effects of the importance of goals and the expected effectiveness of the program. These interaction effects are a proxy for selfish concerns. A selfish individual contributes if the program has the desired effect *and* if this effect is important from the individual's perspective. The results show that individuals do not contribute for purely selfish reasons. Model V presents the preferred specification: Both warm-glow effects and altruistic concerns determine the size of individual contributions. The warm-glow effect related to the environment exerts the greatest influence on the amount that individuals spend on green power.

The results in Table 1 also show that reputation plays a role. The respondents who discussed the program with others spend about 15 Swiss Francs ($10) more on solar energy. The positive coefficient of the income variable indicates that green power is a normal good. Income effects, however, are very small. An increase in monthly income of 1,000 Swiss Francs ($666) increases green-power purchases by less than one cent. This finding is in stark contrast to the pure altruism model which predicts that contributions increase in a 1:1 ratio to income.[16]

One concern with the results in Table 1 is that they give a biased view because the solar energy program is analyzed in isolation. However, even if an altruist cared about the air quality in his hometown, he need not contribute to solar power if there were some other program that allowed him to improve environmental quality more effectively. Similarly, if an individual had some more attractive way to experience feelings of warm-glow, we would erroneously conclude that warm-glow does not influence green behavior. Thus, to corroborate the results in Table 1, I need to control for the relative importance of the green power program. I do this by including a dummy variable that identifies the respondents who would not change their demand for green power in response to a price change. Price elasticities tend to be larger if individuals have easy access to substitutes for the good in question. In contrast, a price inelastic demand indicates that individuals view the good in question as rather unique. I asked respondents how much more solar energy they would demand if the price fell from 1.20 Swiss Francs to 1.11.[17] Thirty-six percent of all respondents indicated that their demand would remain unchanged. The indicator variable "no change in demand" equals one if a respondent gave this answer. I expect a positive coefficient for this variable. (See Table 2.)

The relative attractiveness of the green program exerts a decisive influence. Individuals without close substitutes for the support of green power (those with a completely price inelastic demand) contribute significantly more. As expected, the size of the warm-glow and altruism effects also tends to increase, indicating that omitting the relative attractiveness of green power tends to bias the estimates downward. I conclude this part of my discussion with a sobering comment. Even though I find broad support for a model of impure altruism in which both warm-glow and altruistic

---

[16] See T. Bergstrom, et al., "On the Private Provision of Public Goods" (1986) 29 *Journal of Public Economics* 25–49.

[17] This is the price change that the Zurich Electric Power Company announced in mid-1998. The change took effect in early 1999, after the survey was completed. I also asked respondents how much more green power they would order, hoping that this would enable me to calculate individual price elasticities. Unfortunately, most respondents did not answer this question.

Table 2 Determinants of Contributions to Solar Power: OLS Regression-Dependent Variable Contributions in CHF

	(VI) *Coefficient* *(Std.Err.)*
No change in demand	44.14
DY 1 = yes	(7.87)***
Goal cleaner environment	18.41
	(6.40)***
Effect no nuclear power	11.71
	(3.98)***
Effect import substitution	8.25
	(3.07)***
Income	0.01
(in CHF 1,000)	(0.00)***
Discussion	14.35
DY 1 = yes	(7.54)*
Constant	−99.83
	(40.35)

***Significant at the 1% level, **significant at the 5% level, *significant at the 10% level. (VI): $N = 1,516$, adjusted R-squared $= 0.05$.

concerns matter, the explanatory power of my model is disappointing. The value of the multiple coefficient of determination indicates that it explains a meager 5 percent of the total variation in the size of contributions.

4 CONCLUSIONS

Voluntary contributions to the development of solar power are a significant source of income for those who produce this type of energy. In this chapter, I used the Zurich Solar Energy experiment to analyze the motivations of those who contribute to this public good. The results indicate that participation in the program can be explained by reference to feelings of warm-glow and altruistic effects. The warm-glow part of the motivation to contribute appears to be independent of the value of the public good in the sense that individuals participate in the program even if they do not believe that their use of solar energy will improve the quality of the environment. For these individuals, it is sufficient that they contribute to a cause which they believe to be important.

The Zurich Electric Power Company invested heavily in a campaign to convince its customers that solar energy is an environmentally superior alternative to regular power. The tacit assumption underlying this campaign was that "greenish" customers needed to be convinced of the positive environmental effects of solar power. Our results suggest a complementary

business strategy. If warm-glow significantly influences the level of donations, the environmental effects are but one selling point. It would appear
equally important to make sure that those who contribute feel good about
themselves. For example, a marketing strategy that focuses on the group of
contributors and portrays their personalities and life-styles as particularly
exciting may further increase support for this program. There is probably a
significant downside to warm-glow support as well. Although activities
supported by altruism would seem to be fairly stable over time, decisions
motivated by warm-glow are more prone to trends in fashion and changes
in the zeitgeist. This suggests that electric utilities need to be cautious with
regard to long-term investments in solar power.

INDEX

COMPARATIVE ENVIRONMENTAL LAW AND POLICY SERIES

1. Environmental Contracts and Regulation, Eric W. Orts and Kurt Deketelaere (eds). ISBN 90-411-9821-0

KLUWER LAW INTERNATIONAL – THE HAGUE, LONDON, BOSTON